T0122915

Praise for the previous edition, *Java 8 in Action*, by Raoul-Gabriel Urma, Mario Fusco, and Alan Mycroft.

A great and concise guide to what's new in Java 8, with plenty of examples to get you going in a hurry.

—Jason Lee, Oracle

The best guide to Java 8 that will ever be written!

—William Wheeler, ProData Computer Systems

The new Streams API and lambda examples are especially useful.

—Steve Rogers, CGTck, Inc.

A must-have to get functional with Java 8.

—Mayur S. Patil, MIT Academy of Engineering

Helpful as a concise, practice-oriented guide to the exciting new features of Java 8. Functional interfaces and spliterators, oh my!

—Will Hayworth, Developer, Atlassian

Modern Java in Action

LAMBDAS, STREAMS, FUNCTIONAL AND REACTIVE PROGRAMMING

RAOUL-GABRIEL URMA, MARIO FUSCO, AND ALAN MYCROFT

MANNING

SHELTER ISLAND

For online information and ordering of this and other Manning books, please visit
www.manning.com. The publisher offers discounts on this book when ordered in quantity.
For more information, please contact

> Special Sales Department
> Manning Publications Co.
> 20 Baldwin Road
> PO Box 761
> Shelter Island, NY 11964
> Email: orders@manning.com

Manning Publications Co.
20 Baldwin Road
PO Box 761
Shelter Island, NY 11964

Development editor:	Kevin Harreld
Technical development editor:	Dennis Sellinger
Review editor:	Aleksandar Dragosavljević
Project manager:	Deirdre Hiam
Copy editors:	Heidi Ward and Kathy Simpson
Proofreader:	Carol Shields
Technical proofreader:	Jean-François Morin
Typesetter:	Dennis Dalinnik
Cover designer:	Marija Tudor

ISBN: 9781617293566
Printed in the United States of America
1 2 3 4 5 6 7 8 9 10 – DP – 23 22 21 20 19 18

brief contents

contents

6 *Collecting data with streams   134*

7 *Parallel data processing and performance   172*

preface

Back in 1998 when I was eight years old, I picked up my first book on computing—on JavaScript and HTML. Little did I know that opening that book would transform my life by exposing me to programming languages and the amazing things I could do with them. I was hooked. Every so often, I still find a new programming language feature that revives this excitement because it enables me to write clearer, more concise code in half the time. I hope that the new ideas in Java 8, Java 9, and Java 10, incorporated from functional programming and explored in this book, inspire you in the same way.

So, you may wonder, how did this book—and its second edition—come about?

Well, back in 2011, Brian Goetz (the Java Language Architect at Oracle) was sharing various proposals to add lambda expressions to Java, with the aim of getting the community involved. These rekindled my excitement, and I started to evangelize the ideas, organizing Java 8 workshops at various developer conferences and giving lectures to students at the University of Cambridge.

By April 2013, word had spread, and our publisher at Manning emailed asking whether I was interested in writing a book about lambdas in Java 8. At the time I was a "humble" second-year PhD candidate, and that seemed to be a bad idea because it would interfere with my thesis submission schedule. On the other hand, *carpe diem*. I thought writing a short book shouldn't be too much work, right? (It was only later that I realized I was utterly wrong!) So, I sought advice from my PhD supervisor, Professor Alan Mycroft, who, it turned out, was ready to support me in this adventure (even offering to help in such non-PhD work—I'm forever in his debt). A few days later, we met fellow Java 8 evangelist Mario Fusco, who had vast professional experience and had become well known at major developer conferences for his talks on functional programming.

We quickly realized that by combining our energy and diverse backgrounds we could deliver, not just a short book on Java 8 lambdas, but instead a book that, we hope, the Java community will still be reading in five or ten years. We had a unique opportunity to discuss many topics in depth that will benefit Java programmers and open doors to a new universe of ideas: functional programming.

Now, it's 2018, and we find that the first edition amazingly sold 20,000 copies, Java 9 has just been released, Java 10 is about to be released, and time has dulled the memory of many long nights of editing. So, here it is—the second edition *Modern Java in Action*, covering Java 8, Java 9, and Java 10. We hope you will enjoy it!

RAOUL-GABRIEL URMA
CAMBRIDGE SPARK

acknowledgments

This book would not have been possible without the support of many amazing people:

- Personal friends and people who provided valuable reviews and suggestions on a volunteer basis: Richard Walker, Jan Saganowski, Brian Goetz, Stuart Marks, Cem Redif, Paul Sandoz, Stephen Colebourne, Íñigo Mediavilla, Allahbaksh Asadullah, Tomasz Nurkiewicz, and Michael Müller
- Our Manning Early Access Program (MEAP) readers who posted comments in the Author Online forum
- The reviewers from the development process who provided helpful feedback: Antonio Magnaghi, Brent Stains, Franziska Meyer, Furkan Kamachi, Jason Lee, Jörn Dinkla, Lochana Menikarachchi, Mayur Patil, Nikolaos Kaintantzis, Simone Bordet, Steve Rogers, Will Hayworth, and William Wheeler
- Kevin Harreld, our development editor at Manning, who was very patient in answering all our questions and concerns, provided detailed feedback for each of our draft chapters, and supported us in all possible ways
- Dennis Selinger and Jean-François Morin, who provided a thorough technical proofread of the manuscript shortly before it went to production; and Al Scherer, who provided technical expertise during development

RAOUL-GABRIEL URMA

First and foremost, I'd like to thank my parents for their endless love and support in my life. This little dream of writing a book has now come true! Next, I would like to express my eternal gratitude to Alan Mycroft, my PhD supervisor and coauthor, for his trust and support. I'd also like to thank my coauthor Mario Fusco for sharing this fun journey. Finally, I'd like to thank friends who have provided mentorship, useful advice, and encouragement in my life: Sophia Drossopoulou, Aidan Roche, Alex Buckley, Haadi Jabado, and Jaspar Robertson. You guys rock!

MARIO FUSCO

I'd like to especially thank my wife, Marilena, whose boundless patience allowed me to stay focused on the book, and our daughter, Sofia, because the infinite chaos she can produce allowed me to get creatively distracted from the book. As you'll discover reading the book, Sofia also taught us, like only a two-year-old baby girl can, the difference between internal and external iteration. I'd like to also thank Raoul-Gabriel Urma and Alan Mycroft, with whom I shared the (big) joys and the (small) pains of this writing experience.

ALAN MYCROFT

I'd like to thank my wife, Hilary, and the rest of my family for enduring the many hours that "just a bit more work to do on the book" consumed. I also thank my colleagues and students over the years for teaching me how to teach, Mario and Raoul for being such efficient coauthors, and particularly Raoul for his skill at being so pleasantly demanding when requiring "the next bit of text by Friday."

about this book

Put simply, the new features in Java 8 along with the (less-obvious) changes in Java 9 are the biggest change to Java in the 21 years since Java 1.0 was released. Nothing has been taken away, so all your existing Java code continues to work—but the new features provide powerful new idioms and design patterns to help you write clearer, more concise code. At first you might think (as with all new features), "Why are they changing my language again?" But then, after a bit of practice, comes the revelation that you've just used the features to write shorter, clearer code in half the time you expected—and you realize you could never go back to "old Java" again.

The second edition of this book, *Modern Java in Action: Lambdas, Streams, Functional and Reactive Programming*, is written to get you over that initial hump of "sounds good in principle, but it's all a bit new and unfamiliar" and into coding like a native.

"Perhaps," you might think, "but lambdas, functional programming—aren't those the sort of things that bearded sandal-wearing academics talk about in their ivory towers?" They might be, but Java 8 has incorporated just the right balance of ideas into Java to gain many of their advantages in a way that's comprehensible to ordinary Java programmers. And this book tells the story from the ordinary-programmer viewpoint, with an occasional "how this arose" for perspective.

"Lambdas—that sounds Greek to me!" Yes, it does, but it's a great idea for enabling you to write concise Java programs. Many of you are familiar with event handlers and callbacks, where you register an object containing a method to be used when some event happens. Lambdas make this sort of idea much more widely usable in Java. Put simply, lambdas and their friends, method references, provide the ability to concisely pass code or methods as arguments to be executed in the middle of doing something else. You'll see in this book how this idea occurs more frequently than you might think: from simply parameterizing a sort method with code to do the comparison to expressing complex queries on collections of data using the new Streams API.

"Streams—what are they?" They're a great new Java 8 addition. They behave like collections but have several advantages that enable new styles of programming. First, if you've ever programmed using a database-query language such as SQL, you'll recognize that it enables queries to be written in a few lines that would take many lines in Java. Java 8 streams support this concise database-queries style of programming—but with Java syntax and none of the need to know about databases! Second, streams are designed so that not all their data needs to be in memory (or even computed) at once. Thus, you can process streams that are too big to fit in your computer memory. But Java 8 can optimize operations on streams in a way that Java can't do for collections—for example, it can group together several operations on the same stream so that the data is traversed only once instead of expensively traversing it multiple times. Even better, Java can automatically parallelize stream operations for you (unlike collections).

"And functional-style programming, what's that?" It's another style of programming, just like object-oriented programming, but centered on using functions as values, just as we mentioned previously when discussing lambdas.

What's great about Java 8 is that it incorporates many of the best ideas from functional programming into the familiar Java syntax. The fine design choices enable you to see functional-style programming in Java 8 as an additional set of design patterns and idioms to enable you to write clearer, more concise code in less time. Think of it as having a wider range of weapons in your programming armory.

Oh yes, in addition to these features that lean on big conceptual additions to Java, we also explain the many other useful Java 8 features and updates such as default methods, the new Optional class, CompletableFuture, and the new Date and Time API.

And there are the Java 9 additions: a new module system, support for reactive programming via the Flow API, and various other enhancements.

But hey, this is an overview, and it's time now for us to leave you to read the book.

How this book is organized: a roadmap

Modern Java in Action is divided into six parts: "Fundamentals," "Functional-style data processing with streams," "Effective programming with streams and lambdas," "Everyday Java," "Enhanced Java concurrency," and "Functional programming and future Java evolution." While we strongly recommend that you read the chapters in the first two parts first (and in order because many of the concepts presented build on previous chapters), the remaining four parts can be read reasonably independently. Most chapters include several quizzes to help you work through the material.

The first part of the book provides the fundamentals to help you get started with the new Java ideas introduced in Java 8. By the end of this first part, you'll have a full understanding of what lambda expressions are, and you'll be able to write code that's both concise and flexible enough to easily adapt to changing requirements.

- In chapter 1, we summarize the main changes to Java (lambda expressions, method references, streams, and default methods) and set the scene for the book.
- In chapter 2, you'll learn about behavior parameterization, a software-development pattern that Java 8 relies heavily on and is the motivation for lambda expressions.
- Chapter 3 gives a full explanation, with code examples and quizzes at every step, of the concepts of lambda expressions and method references.

The second part of this book is a deep exploration of the new Streams API, which lets you write powerful code that processes a collection of data in a declarative way. By the end of this second part, you'll have a full understanding of what streams are and how you can use them in your codebase to process a collection of data concisely and efficiently.

- Chapter 4 introduces the concept of a stream and explains how it compares with a collection.
- Chapter 5 investigates in detail the stream operations available to express sophisticated data-processing queries. You'll look at many patterns such as filtering, slicing, finding, matching, mapping, and reducing.
- Chapter 6 covers collectors—a feature of the Streams API that lets you express even more complex data-processing queries.
- In chapter 7, you'll learn about how streams can automatically run in parallel and leverage your multicore architectures. In addition, you'll learn about various pitfalls to avoid when using parallel streams correctly and effectively.

The third part of this book explores various Java 8 and Java 9 topics that will make you more effective at using Java and will enhance your codebase with modern idioms. Because it is oriented toward more-advanced programming ideas we have arranged, nothing later in the book depends on the techniques described here.

- Chapter 8 is a new chapter for the second edition and explores the Collection API Enhancements of Java 8 and Java 9. It covers using collection factories and learning new idiomatic patterns to work with List and Set collections along with idiomatic patterns involving Map.
- Chapter 9 explores how you can improve your existing code using new Java 8 features and a few recipes. In addition, it explores vital software-development techniques such as design patterns, refactoring, testing, and debugging.
- Chapter 10 is also new for the second edition. It explores the idea of basing an API on a domain-specific language (DSL). This is not only a powerful way of designing APIs but one which is both becoming increasingly popular and is already appearing in the Java classes such as `Comparators`, `Stream`, and `Collectors`.

The fourth part of this book explores various new features in Java 8 and Java 9 centered around making it easier and more reliable to code your projects. We start with two APIs introduced in Java 8.

- Chapter 11 covers the `java.util.Optional` class, which allows you to both design better APIs and reduce `null` pointer exceptions.
- Chapter 12 explores the Date and Time API, which greatly improves the previous error-prone APIs for working with dates and time.
- In chapter 13, you'll learn what default methods are, how you can use them to evolve APIs in a compatible way, some practical usage patterns, and rules for using default methods effectively.
- Chapter 14 is new for this second edition and explores the Java Module System—a major enhancement in Java 9 that enables huge systems to be modularized in a documented and enforceable way, rather than being "just a haphazard collection of packages."

The fifth part of this book explores the more advanced ways of structuring concurrent programs in Java—beyond the ideas of easy-to-use parallel processing for streams introduced in chapters 6 and 7. Chapter 15 is new to this second edition and covers the "big-picture" idea of asynchronous APIs—including the ideas of Futures and the Publish-Subscribe protocol behind Reactive Programming and encapsulated in the Java 9 Flow API.

- Chapter 16 explores `CompletableFuture`, which lets you express complex asynchronous computations in a declarative way—paralleling the design of the Streams API.
- Chapter 17 is again new to this second edition and explores the Java 9 Flow API in detail, focusing on practical reactive programming code.

In the sixth and final part of this book, we draw back a little with a tutorial introduction to writing effective functional-style programs in Java, along with a comparison of Java 8 features with those of Scala.

- Chapter 18 gives a full tutorial on functional programming, introduces some of its terminology, and explains how to write functional-style programs in Java.
- Chapter 19 covers more advanced functional programming techniques including higher-order functions, currying persistent data structures, lazy lists, and pattern matching. You can view this chapter as a mix of practical techniques to apply in your codebase as well as academic information that will make you a more knowledgeable programmer.
- Chapter 20 follows by discussing how Java 8 features compare to features in the Scala language—a language that, like Java, is implemented on top of the JVM and that has evolved quickly to threaten some aspects of Java's niche in the programming language ecosystem.

- In chapter 21, we review the journey of learning about Java 8 and the gentle push toward functional-style programming. In addition, we speculate on what future enhancements and great new features may be in Java's pipeline beyond Java 8, Java 9, and the small additions in Java 10.

Finally, there are four appendixes, which cover a number of other topics related to Java 8. Appendix A summarizes minor Java 8 language features that we didn't discuss in the book. Appendix B gives an overview of other main additions to the Java library that you may find useful. Appendix C is a continuation of part 2 and looks at advanced uses of streams. Appendix D explores how the Java compiler implements lambda expressions behind the scenes.

About the code

All source code in listings or in text is in a `fixed-width font like this` to separate it from ordinary text. Code annotations accompany many of the listings, highlighting important concepts.

Source code for all the working examples in the book and instructions to run them are available on a GitHub repository and as a download via the book's website. Both links to the source code may be found at www.manning.com/books/modern-java-in-action.

Book forum

Purchase of *Modern Java in Action* includes free access to a private web forum run by Manning Publications where you can make comments about the book, ask technical questions, and receive help from the authors and from other users. To access the forum, go to https://forums.manning.com/forums/modern-java-in-action. You can also learn more about Manning's forums and the rules of conduct at https://forums.manning.com/forums/about.

Manning's commitment to our readers is to provide a venue where a meaningful dialogue between individual readers and between readers and the authors can take place. It is not a commitment to any specific amount of participation on the part of the authors, whose contribution to the forum remains voluntary (and unpaid). We suggest you try asking the authors some challenging questions lest their interest stray! The forum and the archives of previous discussions will be accessible from the publisher's website as long as the book is in print.

about the authors

RAOUL-GABRIEL URMA is CEO and co-founder of Cambridge Spark, a leading learning community for data scientists and developers in the UK. Raoul was nominated a Java Champion in 2017. He has worked for Google, eBay, Oracle, and Goldman Sachs. Raoul completed a PhD in Computer Science at the University of Cambridge. In addition, he holds a MEng in Computer Science from Imperial College London and graduated with first-class honors, having won several prizes for technical innovation. Raoul has delivered over 100 technical talks at international conferences.

MARIO FUSCO is a senior software engineer at Red Hat working on the core development of Drools, the JBoss rule engine. He has vast experience as a Java developer, having been involved in (and often leading) many enterprise-level projects in several industries ranging from media companies to the financial sector. Among his interests are functional programming and domain-specific languages. By leveraging these two passions, he created the open source library lambdaj with the goal of providing an internal Java DSL for manipulating collections and allowing a bit of functional programming in Java.

ALAN MYCROFT is professor of computing in the Computer Laboratory of Cambridge University, where he has been a faculty member since 1984. He's also a fellow at Robinson College, a co-founder of the European Association for Programming Languages and Systems, and a co-founder and trustee of the Raspberry Pi Foundation. He has degrees in Mathematics (Cambridge) and Computer Science (Edinburgh). He's the author of about 100 research papers and has supervised more than 20 PhD theses. His research centers on programming languages and their semantics, optimization, and implementation. He maintains strong industrial links, having worked at AT&T Laboratories and Intel Research during academic leave, as well as spinning out Codemist Ltd., which built the original ARM C compiler under the Norcroft name.

about the cover illustration

The figure on the cover of *Java in Action* is captioned "Habit of a Mandarin of War in Chinese Tartary in 1700." The Mandarin's habit is ornately decorated, and he is carrying a sword and a bow and quiver on his back. If you look carefully at his belt, you will find a lambda buckle (added by our designer as a wink at one of the topics of this book). The illustration is taken from Thomas Jefferys' *A Collection of the Dresses of Different Nations, Ancient and Modern*, London, published between 1757 and 1772. The title page states that these are hand-colored copperplate engravings, heightened with gum Arabic. Thomas Jefferys (1719–1771) was called "Geographer to King George III." He was an English cartographer who was the leading map supplier of his day. He engraved and printed maps for government and other official bodies and produced a wide range of commercial maps and atlases, especially of North America. His work as a mapmaker sparked an interest in local dress customs of the lands he surveyed and mapped; they are brilliantly displayed in this four-volume collection.

Fascination with faraway lands and travel for pleasure were relatively new phenomena in the eighteenth century, and collections such as this one were popular, introducing both the tourist as well as the armchair traveler to the inhabitants of other countries. The diversity of the drawings in Jefferys' volumes speaks vividly of the uniqueness and individuality of the world's nations centuries ago. Dress codes have changed, and the diversity by region and country, so rich at one time, has faded away. It is now often hard to tell the inhabitant of one continent from another. Perhaps, trying to view it optimistically, we have traded a cultural and visual diversity for a more varied personal life—or a more varied and interesting intellectual and technical life.

At a time when it is hard to tell one computer book from another, Manning celebrates the inventiveness and initiative of the computer business with book covers based on the rich diversity of national costumes three centuries ago, brought back to life by Jefferys' pictures.

Part 1

Fundamentals

This first part of the book provides the fundamentals to help you get started with the new Java ideas introduced in Java 8. By the end of this first part, you'll have a full understanding of what lambda expressions are, and you'll be able to write code that's both concise and flexible enough to easily adapt to changing requirements.

In chapter 1, we summarize the main changes to Java (lambda expressions, method references, streams, and default methods) and set the scene for the book.

In chapter 2, you'll learn about behavior parameterization, a software development pattern that Java 8 relies heavily on and is the motivation for lambda expressions.

Chapter 3 gives a full explanation, with code examples and quizzes at every step, of the concepts of lambda expressions and method references.

Java 8, 9, 10, and 11: what's happening?

This chapter covers

- Why Java keeps changing
- Changing computing background
- Pressures for Java to evolve
- Introducing new core features of Java 8 and 9

Since the release of Java Development Kit (JDK 1.0) in 1996, Java has won a large following of students, project managers, and programmers who are active users. It's an expressive language and continues to be used for projects both large and small. Its evolution (via the addition of new features) from Java 1.1 (1997) to Java 7 (2011) has been well managed. Java 8 was released in March 2014, Java 9 in September 2017, Java 10 in March 2018, and Java 11 planned for September 2018. The question is this: Why should you care about these changes?

1.1 So, what's the big story?

We argue that the changes to Java 8 were in many ways more profound than any other changes to Java in its history (Java 9 adds important, but less-profound, productivity changes, as you'll see later in this chapter, while Java 10 makes much

3

smaller adjustments to type inference). The good news is that the changes enable you to write programs more easily. For example, instead of writing verbose code (to sort a list of apples in `inventory` based on their weight) like

```
Collections.sort(inventory, new Comparator<Apple>() {
    public int compare(Apple a1, Apple a2){
        return a1.getWeight().compareTo(a2.getWeight());
    }
});
```

in Java 8 you can write more concise code that reads a lot closer to the problem statement, like the following:

```
inventory.sort(comparing(Apple::getWeight));
```
          ⊲—| **The first Java 8 code
             of the book!**

It reads "sort inventory comparing apple weight." Don't worry about this code for now. This book will explain what it does and how you can write similar code.

There's also a hardware influence: commodity CPUs have become multicore—the processor in your laptop or desktop machine probably contains four or more CPU cores. But the vast majority of existing Java programs use only one of these cores and leave the other three idle (or spend a small fraction of their processing power running part of the operating system or a virus checker).

Prior to Java 8, experts might tell you that you have to use threads to use these cores. The problem is that working with threads is difficult and error-prone. Java has followed an evolutionary path of continually trying to make concurrency easier and less error-prone. Java 1.0 had threads and locks and even a memory model—the best practice at the time—but these primitives proved too difficult to use reliably in non-specialist project teams. Java 5 added industrial-strength building blocks like thread pools and concurrent collections. Java 7 added the fork/join framework, making parallelism more practical but still difficult. Java 8 gave us a new, simpler way of thinking about parallelism. But you still have to follow some rules, which you'll learn in this book.

As you'll see later in this book, Java 9 adds a further structuring method for concurrency—reactive programming. Although this has more-specialist use, it standardizes a means of exploiting the RxJava and Akka reactive streams toolkits that are becoming popular for highly concurrent systems.

From the previous two desiderata (more concise code and simpler use of multicore processors) springs the whole consistent edifice captured by Java 8. We start by giving you a quick taste of these ideas (hopefully enough to intrigue you, but short enough to summarize them):

- The Streams API
- Techniques for passing code to methods
- Default methods in interfaces

Java 8 provides a new API (called Streams) that supports many parallel operations to process data and resembles the way you might think in database query languages—you express what you want in a higher-level manner, and the implementation (here the Streams library) chooses the best low-level execution mechanism. As a result, it avoids the need for you to write code that uses synchronized, which is not only highly error-prone but also more expensive than you may realize on multicore CPUs.[1]

From a slightly revisionist viewpoint, the addition of Streams in Java 8 can be seen as a direct cause of the two other additions to Java 8: *concise techniques to pass code to methods* (method references, lambdas) and *default methods* in interfaces.

But thinking of passing code to methods as a mere consequence of Streams downplays its range of uses within Java 8. It gives you a new concise way to express *behavior parameterization*. Suppose you want to write two methods that differ in only a few lines of code. You can now simply pass the code of the parts that differ as an argument (this programming technique is shorter, clearer, and less error-prone than the common tendency to use copy and paste). Experts will here note that behavior parameterization could, prior to Java 8, be encoded using anonymous classes—but we'll let the example at the beginning of this chapter, which shows increased code conciseness with Java 8, speak for itself in terms of clarity.

The Java 8 feature of passing code to methods (and being able to return it and incorporate it into data structures) also provides access to a range of additional techniques that are commonly referred to as *functional-style programming*. In a nutshell, such code, called *functions* in the functional programming community, can be passed around and combined in a way to produce powerful programming idioms that you'll see in Java guise throughout this book.

The meat of this chapter begins with a high-level discussion on why languages evolve, continues with sections on the core features of Java 8, and then introduces the ideas of functional-style programming that the new features simplify using and that new computer architectures favor. In essence, section 1.2 discusses the evolution process and the concepts, which Java was previously lacking, to exploit multicore parallelism in an easy way. Section 1.3 explains why passing code to methods in Java 8 is such a powerful new programming idiom, and section 1.4 does the same for Streams—the new Java 8 way of representing sequenced data and indicating whether these can be processed in parallel. Section 1.5 explains how the new Java 8 feature of default methods enables interfaces and their libraries to evolve with less fuss and less recompilation; it also explains the *modules* addition to Java 9, which enables components of large Java systems to be specified more clearly than "just a JAR file of packages." Finally, section 1.6 looks ahead at the ideas of functional-style programming in Java and other languages sharing the JVM. In summary, this chapter introduces ideas that are successively elaborated in the rest of the book. Enjoy the ride!

---

[1] Multicore CPUs have separate caches (fast memory) attached to each processor core. Locking requires these to be synchronized, requiring relatively slow cache-coherency-protocol inter-core communication.

1.2   *Why is Java still changing?*

With the 1960s came the quest for the perfect programming language. Peter Landin, a famous computer scientist of his day, noted in 1966 in a landmark article[2] that there had *already* been 700 programming languages and speculated on what the next 700 would be like—including arguments for functional-style programming similar to that in Java 8.

Many thousands of programming languages later, academics have concluded that programming languages behave like ecosystems: new languages appear, and old languages are supplanted unless they evolve. We all hope for a perfect universal language, but in reality certain languages are better fitted for certain niches. For example, C and C++ remain popular for building operating systems and various other embedded systems because of their small runtime footprint and in spite of their lack of programming safety. This lack of safety can lead to programs crashing unpredictably and exposing security holes for viruses and the like; indeed, type-safe languages such as Java and C# have supplanted C and C++ in various applications when the additional runtime footprint is acceptable.

Prior occupancy of a niche tends to discourage competitors. Changing to a new language and tool chain is often too painful for just a single feature, but newcomers will eventually displace existing languages, unless they evolve fast enough to keep up. (Older readers are often able to quote a range of such languages in which they've previously coded but whose popularity has since waned—Ada, Algol, COBOL, Pascal, Delphi, and SNOBOL, to name but a few.)

You're a Java programmer, and Java has been successful at colonizing (and displacing competitor languages in) a large ecosystem niche of programming tasks for nearly 20 years. Let's examine some reasons for that.

1.2.1   *Java's place in the programming language ecosystem*

Java started well. Right from the start, it was a well-designed object-oriented language with many useful libraries. It also supported small-scale concurrency from day one with its integrated support for threads and locks (and with its early prescient acknowledgment, in the form of a hardware-neutral memory model, that concurrent threads on multicore processors can have unexpected behaviors in addition to those that happen on single-core processors). Also, the decision to compile Java to JVM bytecode (a virtual machine code that soon every browser supported) meant that it became the language of choice for internet applet programs (do you remember applets?). Indeed, there's a danger that the Java Virtual Machine (JVM) and its bytecode will be seen as more important than the Java language itself and that, for certain applications, Java might be replaced by one of its competing languages such as Scala, Groovy, or Kotlin, which also run on the JVM. Various recent updates to the JVM (for example, the new `invokedynamic` bytecode in JDK7) aim to help such competitor languages

---

[2]   P. J. Landin, "The Next 700 Programming Languages," CACM 9(3):157–65, March 1966.

run smoothly on the JVM—and to interoperate with Java. Java has also been successful at colonizing various aspects of embedded computing (everything from smart cards, toasters, and set-top boxes to car-braking systems).

How did Java get into a general programming niche?

Object orientation became fashionable in the 1990s for two reasons: its encapsulation discipline resulted in fewer software engineering issues than those of C; and as a mental model it easily captured the WIMP programming model of Windows 95 and up. This can be summarized as follows: everything is an object; and a mouse click sends an event message to a handler (invokes the `clicked` method in a `Mouse` object). The write-once, run-anywhere model of Java and the ability of early browsers to (safely) execute Java code applets gave it a niche in universities, whose graduates then populated industry. There was initial resistance to the additional run cost of Java over C/C++, but machines got faster, and programmer time became more and more important. Microsoft's C# further validated the Java-style object-oriented model.

But the climate is changing for the programming language ecosystem; programmers are increasingly dealing with so-called *big data* (data sets of terabytes and up) and wishing to exploit multicore computers or computing clusters effectively to process it. And this means using parallel processing—something Java wasn't previously friendly to. You may have come across ideas from other programming niches (for example, Google's map-reduce or the relative ease of data manipulation using database query languages such as SQL) that help you work with large volumes of data and multicore CPUs. Figure 1.1 summarizes the language ecosystem pictorially: think of the landscape as the space of programming problems and the dominant vegetation for a particular bit of ground as the favorite language for that program. Climate change is the idea that new hardware or new programming influences (for example, "Why can't I program in an SQL-like style?") mean that different languages become the language

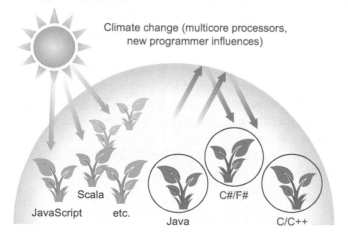

Climate change (multicore processors, new programmer influences)

Scala

JavaScript   etc.

Java

C#/F#

C/C++

Figure 1.1   Programming-language ecosystem and climate change

of choice for new projects, just like increasing regional temperatures mean grapes now thrive in higher latitudes. But there's hysteresis—many an old farmer will keep raising traditional crops. In summary, new languages are appearing and becoming increasingly popular because they've adapted quickly to the climate change.

The main benefit of the Java 8 additions for a programmer is that they provide more programming tools and concepts to solve new or existing programming problems more quickly or, more importantly, in a more concise, more easily maintainable way. Although the concepts are new to Java, they've proved powerful in niche research-like languages. In the following sections, we'll highlight and develop the ideas behind three such programming concepts that have driven the development of the Java 8 features to exploit parallelism and write more concise code in general. We'll introduce them in a slightly different order from the rest of the book to enable a Unix-based analogy and to expose the "need *this* because of *that*" dependencies in Java 8's new parallelism for multicore.

Another climate-change factor for Java

One climate-change factor involves how large systems are designed. Nowadays, it's common for a large system to incorporate large component subsystems from elsewhere, and perhaps these are built on top of other components from other vendors. Worse still, these components and their interfaces also tend to evolve. Java 8 and Java 9 have addressed these aspects by providing default methods and modules to facilitate this design style.

The next three sections examine the three programming concepts that drove the design of Java 8.

1.2.2   Stream processing

The first programming concept is *stream processing*. For introductory purposes, a *stream* is a sequence of data items that are conceptually produced one at a time. A program might read items from an input stream one by one and similarly write items to an output stream. The output stream of one program could well be the input stream of another.

One practical example is in Unix or Linux, where many programs operate by reading data from standard input (*stdin* in Unix and C, System.in in Java), operating on it, and then writing their results to standard output (*stdout* in Unix and C, System.out in Java). First, a little background: Unix cat creates a stream by concatenating two files, tr translates the characters in a stream, sort sorts lines in a stream, and tail -3 gives the last three lines in a stream. The Unix command line allows such programs to be linked together with pipes (|), giving examples such as

```
cat file1 file2  |  tr "[A-Z]"  "[a-z]"  |  sort  |  tail -3
```

which (supposing `file1` and `file2` contain a single word per line) prints the three words from the files that appear latest in dictionary order, after first translating them to lowercase. We say that `sort` takes a *stream* of lines[3] as input and produces another stream of lines as output (the latter being sorted), as illustrated in figure 1.2. Note that in Unix these commands (`cat`, `tr`, `sort`, and `tail`) are executed concurrently, so that `sort` can be processing the first few lines before `cat` or `tr` has finished. A more mechanical analogy is a car-manufacturing assembly line where a stream of cars is queued between processing stations that each take a car, modify it, and pass it on to the next station for further processing; processing at separate stations is typically concurrent even though the assembly line is physically a sequence.

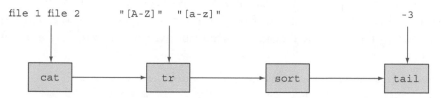

Figure 1.2   Unix commands operating on streams

Java 8 adds a Streams API (note the uppercase *S*) in `java.util.stream` based on this idea; `Stream<T>` is a sequence of items of type `T`. You can think of it as a fancy iterator for now. The Streams API has many methods that can be chained to form a complex pipeline just like Unix commands were chained in the previous example.

The key motivation for this is that you can now program in Java 8 at a higher level of abstraction, structuring your thoughts of turning a stream of this into a stream of that (similar to how you think when writing database queries) rather than one item at a time. Another advantage is that Java 8 can transparently run your pipeline of `Stream` operations on several CPU cores on disjoint parts of the input—this is parallelism *almost for free* instead of hard work using Threads. We cover the Java 8 Streams API in detail in chapters 4–7.

1.2.3   *Passing code to methods with behavior parameterization*

The second programming concept added to Java 8 is the ability to pass a piece of code to an API. This sounds awfully abstract. In the Unix example, you might want to tell the `sort` command to use a custom ordering. Although the `sort` command supports command-line parameters to perform various predefined kinds of sorting such as reverse order, these are limited.

For example, let's say you have a collection of invoice IDs with a format similar to 2013UK0001, 2014US0002, and so on. The first four digits represent the year, the next two letters a country code, and last four digits the ID of a client. You may want to sort

---

[3]   Purists will say a "stream of characters," but it's conceptually simpler to think that `sort` reorders *lines*.

these invoice IDs by year or perhaps using the customer ID or even the country code. What you want is the ability to tell the sort command to take as an argument an ordering defined by the user: a separate piece of code passed to the sort command.

Now, as a direct parallel in Java, you want to tell a sort method to compare using a customized order. You could write a method compareUsingCustomerId to compare two invoice IDs, but, prior to Java 8, you couldn't pass this method to another method! You could create a Comparator object to pass to the sort method as we showed at the start of this chapter, but this is verbose and obfuscates the idea of simply reusing an existing piece of behavior. Java 8 adds the ability to pass methods (your code) as arguments to other methods. Figure 1.3, based on figure 1.2, illustrates this idea. We also refer to this conceptually as *behavior parameterization.* Why is this important? The Streams API is built on the idea of passing code to parameterize the behavior of its operations, just as you passed compareUsingCustomerId to parameterize the behavior of sort.

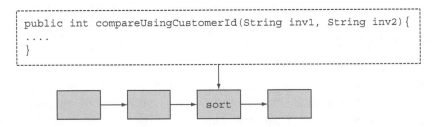

Figure 1.3   Passing method compareUsingCustomerId **as an argument to** sort

We summarize how this works in section 1.3 of this chapter, but leave full details to chapters 2 and 3. Chapters 18 and 19 look at more advanced things you can do using this feature, with techniques from the *functional programming* community.

1.2.4 *Parallelism and shared mutable data*

The third programming concept is rather more implicit and arises from the phrase "parallelism almost for free" in our previous discussion on stream processing. What do you have to give up? You may have to make some small changes in the way you code the behavior passed to stream methods. At first, these changes might feel a little uncomfortable, but once you get used to them, you'll love them. You must provide behavior that *is safe to execute* concurrently on different pieces of the input. Typically this means writing code that doesn't access shared mutable data to do its job. Sometimes these are referred to as pure functions or side-effect-free functions or stateless functions, and we'll discuss these in detail in chapters 18 and 19. The previous parallelism arises only by assuming that multiple copies of your piece of code can work independently. If there's a shared variable or object, which is written to, then things no longer work. What if two processes want to modify the shared variable at the same time? (Section 1.4 gives a more detailed explanation with a diagram.) You'll find more about this style throughout the book.

Java 8 streams exploit parallelism more easily than Java's existing Threads API, so although it's *possible* to use synchronized to break the no-shared-mutable-data rule, it's fighting the system in that it's abusing an abstraction optimized around that rule. Using synchronized across multiple processing cores is often far more expensive than you expect, because synchronization forces code to execute sequentially, which works against the goal of parallelism.

Two of these points (no shared mutable data and the ability to pass methods and functions—code—to other methods) are the cornerstones of what's generally described as the paradigm of *functional programming*, which you'll see in detail in chapters 18 and 19. In contrast, in the *imperative programming* paradigm you typically describe a program in terms of a sequence of statements that mutate state. The no-shared-mutable-data requirement means that a method is perfectly described solely by the way it transforms arguments to results; in other words, it behaves as a mathematical function and has no (visible) side effects.

1.2.5 *Java needs to evolve*

You've seen evolution in Java before. For example, the introduction of generics and using List<String> instead of just List may initially have been irritating. But you're now familiar with this style and the benefits it brings (catching more errors at compile time and making code easier to read, because you now know what something is a list of).

Other changes have made common things easier to express (for example, using a for-each loop instead of exposing the boilerplate use of an Iterator). The main changes in Java 8 reflect a move away from classical object orientation, which often focuses on mutating existing values, and toward the functional-style programming spectrum in which *what* you want to do in broad-brush terms (for example, *create a value* representing all transport routes from A to B for less than a given price) is considered prime and separated from *how* you can achieve this (for example, *scan* a data structure *modifying* certain components). Note that classical object-oriented programming and functional programming, as extremes, might appear to be in conflict. But the idea is to get the best from both programming paradigms, so you have a better chance of having the right tool for the job. We discuss this in detail in sections 1.3 and 1.4.

A takeaway line might be this: languages need to evolve to track changing hardware or programmer expectations (if you need convincing, consider that COBOL was once one of the most important languages commercially). To endure, Java has to evolve by adding new features. This evolution will be pointless unless the new features are used, so in using Java 8 you're protecting your way of life as a Java programmer. On top of that, we have a feeling you'll love using Java 8's new features. Ask anyone who's used Java 8 whether they're willing to go back! Additionally, the new Java 8 features might, in the ecosystem analogy, enable Java to conquer programming-task territory currently occupied by other languages, so Java 8 programmers will be even more in demand.

We now introduce the new concepts in Java 8, one by one, pointing out the chapters that cover these concepts in more detail.

1.3   Functions in Java

The word *function* in programming languages is commonly used as a synonym for *method*, particularly a static method; this is in addition to it being used for *mathematical function*, one without side effects. Fortunately, as you'll see, when Java 8 refers to functions these usages nearly coincide.

Java 8 adds functions as new forms of value. These facilitate the use of streams, covered in section 1.4, which Java 8 provides to exploit parallel programming on multicore processors. We start by showing that functions as values are useful in themselves.

Think about the possible values manipulated by Java programs. First, there are primitive values such as 42 (of type int) and 3.14 (of type double). Second, values can be objects (more strictly, references to objects). The only way to get one of these is by using new, perhaps via a factory method or a library function; object references point to *instances* of a class. Examples include "abc" (of type String), new Integer(1111) (of type Integer), and the result new HashMap<Integer, String>(100) of explicitly calling a constructor for HashMap. Even arrays are objects. What's the problem?

To help answer this, we'll note that the whole point of a programming language is to manipulate values, which, following historical programming-language tradition, are therefore called first-class values (or citizens, in the terminology borrowed from the 1960s civil rights movement in the United States). Other structures in our programming languages, which perhaps help us express the structure of values but which can't be passed around during program execution, are second-class citizens. Values as listed previously are first-class Java citizens, but various other Java concepts, such as methods and classes, exemplify second-class citizens. Methods are fine when used to define classes, which in turn may be instantiated to produce values, but neither are values themselves. Does this matter? Yes, it turns out that being able to pass methods around at runtime, and hence making them first-class citizens, is useful in programming, so the Java 8 designers added the ability to express this directly in Java. Incidentally, you might wonder whether making other second-class citizens such as classes into first-class-citizen values might also be a good idea. Various languages such as Smalltalk and JavaScript have explored this route.

1.3.1   Methods and lambdas as first-class citizens

Experiments in other languages, such as Scala and Groovy, have determined that allowing concepts like methods to be used as first-class values made programming easier by adding to the toolset available to programmers. And once programmers become familiar with a powerful feature, they become reluctant to use languages without it! The designers of Java 8 decided to allow methods to be values—to make it easier for you to program. Moreover, the Java 8 feature of methods as values forms the basis of various other Java 8 features (such as Streams).

The first new Java 8 feature we introduce is that of *method references*. Suppose you want to filter all the hidden files in a directory. You need to start writing a method that, given a File, will tell you whether it's hidden. Fortunately, there's such a method in the File class called isHidden. It can be viewed as a function that takes a File and returns a boolean. But to use it for filtering, you need to wrap it into a FileFilter object that you then pass to the File.listFiles method, as follows:

```
File[] hiddenFiles = new File(".").listFiles(new FileFilter() {
    public boolean accept(File file) {
        return file.isHidden();              ⊲————— Filtering hidden files!
    }
});
```

Yuck! That's horrible. Although it's only three significant lines, it's three opaque lines—we all remember saying "Do I really have to do it this way?" on first encounter. You already have the method isHidden that you could use. Why do you have to wrap it up in a verbose FileFilter class and then instantiate it? Because that's what you had to do prior to Java 8.

Now, you can rewrite that code as follows:

```
File[] hiddenFiles = new File(".").listFiles(File::isHidden);
```

Wow! Isn't that cool? You already have the function isHidden available, so you pass it to the listFiles method using the Java 8 *method reference* :: syntax (meaning "use this method as a value"); note that we've also slipped into using the word *function* for methods. We'll explain later how the mechanics work. One advantage is that your code now reads closer to the problem statement.

Here's a taste of what's coming: methods are no longer second-class values. Analogous to using an *object reference* when you pass an object around (and object references are created by new), in Java 8 when you write File::isHidden, you create a *method reference*, which can similarly be passed around. This concept is discussed in detail in chapter 3. Given that methods contain code (the executable body of a method), using method references enables passing code around as in figure 1.3. Figure 1.4 illustrates the concept. You'll also see a concrete example (selecting apples from an inventory) in the next section.

LAMBDAS: ANONYMOUS FUNCTIONS

As well as allowing (named) methods to be first-class values, Java 8 allows a richer idea of *functions as values*, including *lambdas*[4] (or anonymous functions). For example, you can now write (int x) -> x + 1 to mean "the function that, when called with argument

---

[4] Originally named after the Greek letter λ (lambda). Although the symbol isn't used in Java, its name lives on.

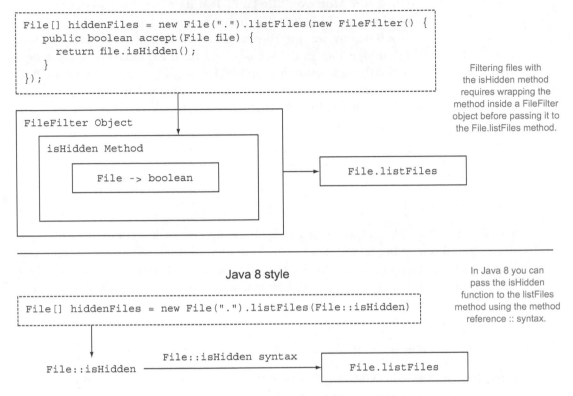

Figure 1.4   **Passing the method reference `File::isHidden` to the method `listFiles`**

x, returns the value x + 1." You might wonder why this is necessary, because you could define a method `add1` inside a class `MyMathsUtils` and then write `MyMathsUtils::add1`! Yes, you could, but the new lambda syntax is more concise for cases where you don't have a convenient method and class available. Chapter 3 explores lambdas in detail. Programs using these concepts are said to be written in functional-programming style; this phrase means "writing programs that pass functions around as first-class values."

1.3.2   *Passing code: an example*

Let's look at an example of how this helps you write programs (discussed in more detail in chapter 2). All the code for the examples is available on a GitHub repository and as a download via the book's website. Both links may be found at www.manning .com/books/modern-java-in-action. Suppose you have a class `Apple` with a method `getColor` and a variable `inventory` holding a list of `Apples`; then you might wish to select all the green apples (here using a `Color` enum type that includes values GREEN and RED) and return them in a list. The word *filter* is commonly used to express this concept. Before Java 8, you might write a method filterGreenApples:

```java
public static List<Apple> filterGreenApples(List<Apple> inventory) {
    List<Apple> result = new ArrayList<>();
    for (Apple apple: inventory){
        if (GREEN.equals(apple.getColor())) {
            result.add(apple);
        }
    }
    return result;
}
```

The result list accumulates the result; it starts as empty, and then green apples are added one by one.

The highlighted text selects only green apples.

But next, somebody would like the list of heavy apples (say over 150 g), and so, with a heavy heart, you'd write the following method to achieve this (perhaps even using copy and paste):

```java
public static List<Apple> filterHeavyApples(List<Apple> inventory) {
    List<Apple> result = new ArrayList<>();
    for (Apple apple: inventory){
        if (apple.getWeight() > 150) {
            result.add(apple);
        }
    }
    return result;
}
```

Here the highlighted text selects only heavy apples.

We all know the dangers of copy and paste for software engineering (updates and bug fixes to one variant but not the other), and hey, these two methods vary only in one line: the highlighted condition inside the if construct. If the difference between the two method calls in the highlighted code had been what weight range was acceptable, then you could have passed lower and upper acceptable weights as arguments to filter—perhaps (150, 1000) to select heavy apples (over 150 g) or (0, 80) to select light apples (under 80 g).

But as we mentioned previously, Java 8 makes it possible to pass the code of the condition as an argument, avoiding code duplication of the filter method. You can now write this:

```java
public static boolean isGreenApple(Apple apple) {
    return GREEN.equals(apple.getColor());
}
public static boolean isHeavyApple(Apple apple) {
    return apple.getWeight() > 150;
}
public interface Predicate<T>{
    boolean test(T t);
}
static List<Apple> filterApples(List<Apple> inventory,
                                Predicate<Apple> p) {
    List<Apple> result = new ArrayList<>();
    for (Apple apple: inventory){
```

Included for clarity (normally imported from java.util.function)

A method is passed as a Predicate parameter named p (see the sidebar "What's a Predicate?").

```
        if (p.test(apple)) {
            result.add(apple);
        }
    }
    return result;
}
```

Does the apple match
the condition
represented by p?

And to use this, you call either

```
filterApples(inventory, Apple::isGreenApple);
```

or

```
filterApples(inventory, Apple::isHeavyApple);
```

We explain how this works in detail in the next two chapters. The key idea to take away for now is that you can pass around a method in Java 8.

> **What's a Predicate?**
>
> The previous code passed a method `Apple::isGreenApple` (which takes an `Apple` for argument and returns a `boolean`) to `filterApples`, which expected a `Predicate <Apple>` parameter. The word *predicate* is often used in mathematics to mean something function-like that takes a value for an argument and returns `true` or `false`. As you'll see later, Java 8 would also allow you to write `Function<Apple, Boolean>`—more familiar to readers who learned about functions but not predicates at school—but using `Predicate<Apple>` is more standard (and slightly more efficient because it avoids boxing a `boolean` into a `Boolean`).

1.3.3   *From passing methods to lambdas*

Passing methods as values is clearly useful, but it's annoying having to write a definition for short methods such as `isHeavyApple` and `isGreenApple` when they're used perhaps only once or twice. But Java 8 has solved this, too. It introduces a new notation (anonymous functions, or lambdas) that enables you to write just

```
filterApples(inventory, (Apple a) -> GREEN.equals(a.getColor()) );
```

or

```
filterApples(inventory, (Apple a) -> a.getWeight() > 150 );
```

or even

```
filterApples(inventory, (Apple a) -> a.getWeight() < 80 ||
                                     RED.equals(a.getColor()) );
```

You don't even need to write a method definition that's used only once; the code is crisper and clearer because you don't need to search to find the code you're passing.

But if such a lambda exceeds a few lines in length (so that its behavior isn't instantly clear), you should instead use a method reference to a method with a descriptive name instead of using an anonymous lambda. Code clarity should be your guide.

The Java 8 designers could almost have stopped here, and perhaps they would have done so before multicore CPUs. Functional-style programming as presented so far turns out to be powerful, as you'll see. Java might then have been rounded off by adding `filter` and a few friends as generic library methods, such as

```
static <T> Collection<T> filter(Collection<T> c, Predicate<T> p);
```

You wouldn't even have to write methods like `filterApples` because, for example, the previous call

```
filterApples(inventory, (Apple a) -> a.getWeight() > 150 );
```

could be written as a call to the library method `filter`:

```
filter(inventory, (Apple a) -> a.getWeight() > 150 );
```

But, for reasons centered on better exploiting parallelism, the designers didn't do this. Java 8 instead contains a new Collection-like API called Stream, containing a comprehensive set of operations similar to the `filter` operation that functional programmers may be familiar with (for example, `map` and `reduce`), along with methods to convert between `Collections` and `Streams`, which we now investigate.

1.4 Streams

Nearly every Java application *makes* and *processes* collections. But working with collections isn't always ideal. For example, let's say you need to filter expensive transactions from a list and then group them by currency. You'd need to write a lot of boilerplate code to implement this data-processing query, as shown here:

Creates the Map where the grouped transaction will be accumulated

```
Map<Currency, List<Transaction>> transactionsByCurrencies =
    new HashMap<>();
for (Transaction transaction : transactions) {
    if(transaction.getPrice() > 1000){
        Currency currency = transaction.getCurrency();
        List<Transaction> transactionsForCurrency =
            transactionsByCurrencies.get(currency);
        if (transactionsForCurrency == null) {
            transactionsForCurrency = new ArrayList<>();
            transactionsByCurrencies.put(currency,
                                         transactionsForCurrency);
        }
        transactionsForCurrency.add(transaction);
    }
}
```

Filters expensive transactions

Iterates the List of transactions

Extracts the transaction's currency

If there isn't an entry in the grouping Map for this currency, create it.

Adds the currently traversed transaction to the List of transactions with the same currency

In addition, it's difficult to understand at a glance what the code does because of the multiple nested control-flow statements.

Using the Streams API, you can solve this problem as follows:

```
import static java.util.stream.Collectors.groupingBy;
Map<Currency, List<Transaction>> transactionsByCurrencies =
    transactions.stream()
                .filter((Transaction t) -> t.getPrice() > 1000)
                .collect(groupingBy(Transaction::getCurrency));
```

Filters expensive transactions

Groups them by currency

Don't worry about this code for now because it may look like a bit of magic. Chapters 4–7 are dedicated to explaining how to make sense of the Streams API. For now, it's worth noticing that the Streams API provides a different way to process data in comparison to the Collections API. Using a collection, you're managing the iteration process yourself. You need to iterate through the elements one by one using a for-each loop processing them in turn. We call this way of iterating over data *external iteration*. In contrast, using the Streams API, you don't need to think in terms of loops. The data processing happens internally inside the library. We call this idea *internal iteration*. We come back to these ideas in chapter 4.

As a second pain point of working with collections, think for a second about how you would process the list of transactions if you had a vast number of them; how can you process this huge list? A single CPU wouldn't be able to process this large amount of data, but you probably have a multicore computer on your desk. Ideally, you'd like to share the work among the different CPU cores available on your machine to reduce the processing time. In theory, if you have eight cores, they should be able to process your data eight times as fast as using one core, because they work in parallel.[5]

Multicore computers

All new desktop and laptop computers are multicore computers. Instead of a single CPU, they have four or eight or more CPUs (usually called Cores5). The problem is that a classic Java program uses just a single one of these cores, and the power of the others is wasted. Similarly, many companies use *computing clusters* (computers connected together with fast networks) to be able to process vast amounts of data efficiently. Java 8 facilitates new programming styles to better exploit such computers.

Google's search engine is an example of a piece of code that's too big to run on a single computer. It reads every page on the internet and creates an index, mapping every word appearing on any internet page back to every URL containing that word. Then, when you do a Google search involving several words, software can quickly use this index to give you a set of web pages containing those words. Try to imagine how you might code this algorithm in Java (even for a smaller index than Google's, you'd need to exploit all the cores in your computer).

---

[5] This naming is unfortunate in some ways. Each of the cores in a multicore chip is a full-fledged CPU. But the phrase multicore CPU has become common, so core is used to refer to the individual CPUs.

1.4.1 *Multithreading is difficult*

The problem is that exploiting parallelism by writing *multithreaded* code (using the Threads API from previous versions of Java) is difficult. You have to think differently: threads can access and update shared variables at the same time. As a result, data could change unexpectedly if not coordinated[6] properly. This model is harder to think about[7] than a step-by-step sequential model. For example, figure 1.5 shows a possible problem with two threads trying to add a number to a shared variable sum if they're not synchronized properly.

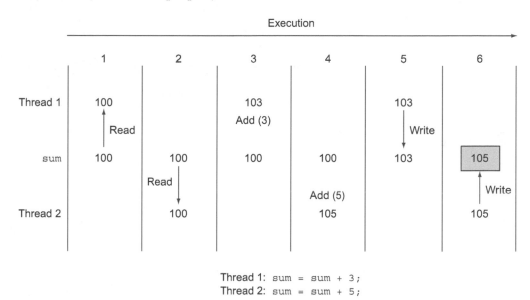

Thread 1: sum = sum + 3;
Thread 2: sum = sum + 5;

Figure 1.5 A possible problem with two threads trying to add to a shared sum variable. The result is 105 instead of an expected result of 108.

Java 8 also addresses both problems (boilerplate and obscurity involving processing collections and difficulty exploiting multicore) with the Streams API (java.util .stream). The first design motivator is that there are many data-processing patterns (similar to filterApples in the previous section or operations familiar from database query languages such as SQL) that occur over and over again and that would benefit from forming part of a library: *filtering* data based on a criterion (for example, heavy apples), *extracting* data (for example, extracting the weight field from each apple in a list), or *grouping* data (for example, grouping a list of numbers into separate lists of even and odd numbers), and so on. The second motivator is that such operations can

---

[6] Traditionally via the keyword synchronized, but many subtle bugs arise from its misplacement. Java 8's Stream-based parallelism encourages a functional programming style where synchronized is rarely used; it focuses on partitioning the data rather than coordinating access to it.

[7] Aha—a source of pressure for the language to evolve!

often be parallelized. For instance, as illustrated in figure 1.6, filtering a list on two CPUs could be done by asking one CPU to process the first half of a list and the second CPU to process the other half of the list. This is called the *forking step* (1). The CPUs then filter their respective half-lists (2). Finally (3), one CPU would join the two results. (This is closely related to how Google searches work so quickly, using many more than two processors.)

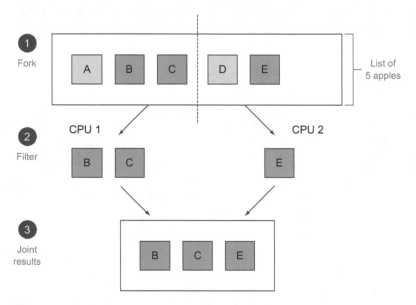

Figure 1.6   Forking `filter` onto two CPUs and joining the result

For now, we'll just say that the new Streams API behaves similarly to Java's existing Collections API: both provide access to sequences of data items. But it's useful for now to keep in mind that Collections is mostly about storing and accessing data, whereas Streams is mostly about describing computations on data. The key point here is that the Streams API allows and encourages the elements within a stream to be processed in parallel. Although it may seem odd at first, often the fastest way to filter a collection (for example, to use `filterApples` in the previous section on a list) is to convert it to a stream, process it in parallel, and then convert it back to a list. Again, we'll just say "parallelism almost for free" and provide a taste of how you can filter heavy apples from a list sequentially or in parallel using streams and a lambda expression.

Here's an example of sequential processing:

```
import static java.util.stream.Collectors.toList;
List<Apple> heavyApples =
    inventory.stream().filter((Apple a) -> a.getWeight() > 150)
                      .collect(toList());
```

And here it is using parallel processing:

```
import static java.util.stream.Collectors.toList;
List<Apple> heavyApples =
    inventory.parallelStream().filter((Apple a) -> a.getWeight() > 150)
                              .collect(toList());
```

> ### Parallelism in Java and no shared mutable state
>
> People have always said parallelism in Java is difficult, and all this stuff about `synchronized` is error-prone. Where's the magic bullet in Java 8?
>
> There are two magic bullets. First, the library handles partitioning—breaking down a big stream into several smaller streams to be processed in parallel for you. Second, this parallelism almost for free from streams, works only if the methods passed to library methods like `filter` don't interact (for example, by having mutable shared objects). But it turns out that this restriction feels natural to a coder (see, by way of example, our `Apple::isGreenApple` example). Although the primary meaning of *functional* in *functional programming* means "using functions as first-class values," it often has a secondary nuance of "no interaction during execution between components."

Chapter 7 explores parallel data processing in Java 8 and its performance in more detail. One of the practical issues the Java 8 developers found in evolving Java with all these new goodies was that of evolving existing interfaces. For example, the method `Collections.sort` belongs to the `List` interface but was never included. Ideally, you'd like to do `list.sort(comparator)` instead of `Collections.sort(list, comparator)`. This may seem trivial but, prior to Java 8 you can update an interface only if you update all the classes that implement it—a logistical nightmare! This issue is resolved in Java 8 by *default methods*.

1.5   *Default methods and Java modules*

As we mentioned earlier, modern systems tend to be built from components—perhaps bought-in from elsewhere. Historically, Java had little support for this, apart from a JAR file containing a set of Java packages with no particular structure. Moreover, evolving interfaces to such packages was hard—changing a Java interface meant changing every class that implements it. Java 8 and 9 have started to address this.

First, Java 9 provides a module system that provide you with syntax to define *modules* containing collections of packages—and keep much better control over visibility and namespaces. Modules enrich a simple JAR-like component with structure, both as user documentation and for machine checking; we explain them in detail in chapter 14. Second, Java 8 added default methods to support *evolvable* interfaces. We cover these in detail in chapter 13. They're important because you'll increasingly encounter them in interfaces, but because relatively few programmers will need to write default methods themselves and because they facilitate program evolution rather than helping write any particular program, we keep the explanation here short and example-based.

In section 1.4, we gave the following example Java 8 code:

```
List<Apple> heavyApples1 =
    inventory.stream().filter((Apple a) -> a.getWeight() > 150)
                    .collect(toList());
List<Apple> heavyApples2 =
    inventory.parallelStream().filter((Apple a) -> a.getWeight() > 150)
                            .collect(toList());
```

But there's a problem here: a List<T> prior to Java 8 doesn't have stream or parallel-Stream methods—and neither does the Collection<T> interface that it implements—because these methods hadn't been conceived of. And without these methods, this code won't compile. The simplest solution, which you might employ for your own interfaces, would have been for the Java 8 designers to add the stream method to the Collection interface and add the implementation in the ArrayList class.

But doing this would have been a nightmare for users. Many alternative collection frameworks implement interfaces from the Collections API. Adding a new method to an interface means all concrete classes must provide an implementation for it. Language designers have no control over existing implementations of Collection, so you have a dilemma: How can you evolve published interfaces without disrupting existing implementations?

The Java 8 solution is to break the last link: an interface can now contain method signatures for which an implementing class doesn't provide an implementation. Then who implements them? The missing method bodies are given as part of the interface (hence default implementations) rather than in the implementing class.

This provides a way for an interface designer to enlarge an interface beyond those methods that were originally planned—without breaking existing code. Java 8 allows the existing default keyword to be used in interface specifications to achieve this.

For example, in Java 8, you can call the sort method directly on a list. This is made possible with the following default method in the Java 8 List interface, which calls the static method Collections.sort:

```
default void sort(Comparator<? super E> c) {
    Collections.sort(this, c);
}
```

This means any concrete classes of List don't have to explicitly implement sort, whereas in previous Java versions such concrete classes would fail to recompile unless they provided an implementation for sort.

But wait a second. A single class can implement multiple interfaces, right? If you have multiple default implementations in several interfaces, does that mean you have a form of multiple inheritance in Java? Yes, to some extent. We show in chapter 13 that there are some rules that prevent issues such as the infamous *diamond inheritance problem* in C++.

1.6 *Other good ideas from functional programming*

The previous sections introduced two core ideas from functional programming that are now part of Java: using methods and lambdas as first-class values, and the idea that calls to functions or methods can be efficiently and safely executed in parallel in the absence of mutable shared state. Both of these ideas are exploited by the new Streams API we described earlier.

Common functional languages (SML, OCaml, Haskell) also provide further constructs to help programmers. One of these is avoiding `null` by explicit use of more descriptive data types. Tony Hoare, one of the giants of computer science, said this in a presentation at QCon London 2009:

> *I call it my billion-dollar mistake. It was the invention of the null reference in 1965. . . . I couldn't resist the temptation to put in a null reference, simply because it was so easy to implement.*

Java 8 introduced the `Optional<T>` class that, if used consistently, can help you avoid null-pointer exceptions. It's a container object that may or may not contain a value. `Optional<T>` includes methods to explicitly deal with the case where a value is absent, and as a result you can avoid null-pointer exceptions. It uses the type system to allow you to indicate when a variable is anticipated to potentially have a missing value. We discuss `Optional<T>` in detail in chapter 11.

A second idea is that of *(structural) pattern matching.*[8] This is used in mathematics. For example:

```
f(0) = 1
f(n) = n*f(n-1) otherwise
```

In Java, you would write an `if-then-else` or a `switch` statement. Other languages have shown that, for more complex data types, pattern matching can express programming ideas more concisely compared to using `if-then-else`. For such data types, you might also use polymorphism and method overriding as an alternative to `if-then-else`, but there's ongoing language-design discussion as to which is more appropriate.[9] We'd say that both are useful tools and that you should have both in your armory. Unfortunately, Java 8 doesn't have full support for pattern matching, although we show how it can be expressed in chapter 19. A Java Enhancement Proposal is also being discussed to support pattern matching in a future version of Java (see http://openjdk.java.net/jeps/305). In the meantime, let's illustrate with an example expressed in the Scala programming language (another Java-like language using the JVM that has inspired some aspects of Java evolution; see chapter 20). Suppose you

---

[8] This phrase has two uses. Here we mean the one familiar from mathematics and functional programming whereby a function is defined by cases, rather than using `if-then-else`. The other meaning concerns phrases like "find all files of the form 'IMG*.JPG' in a given directory" associated with so-called regular expressions.

[9] The Wikipedia article on the "expression problem" (a term coined by Phil Wadler) provides an entry to the discussion.

want to write a program that does basic simplifications on a tree representing an arithmetic expression. Given a data type `Expr` representing such expressions, in Scala you can write the following code to decompose an `Expr` into its parts and then return another `Expr`:

```
def simplifyExpression(expr: Expr): Expr = expr match {          Adds 0
    case BinOp("+", e, Number(0)) => e
    case BinOp("-", e, Number(0)) => e                  Subtracts 0
    case BinOp("*", e, Number(1)) => e
    case BinOp("/", e, Number(1)) => e                  Multiplies by 1
    case _ => expr
}                                                       Divides by 1
                        Can't be simplified with
                        these cases, so leave alone
```

Here Scala's syntax `expr match` corresponds to Java's `switch (expr)`. Don't worry about this code for now—you'll read more on pattern matching in chapter 19. For now, you can think of pattern matching as an extended form of `switch` that can decompose a data type into its components at the same time.

Why should the `switch` statement in Java be limited to primitive values and strings? Functional languages tend to allow `switch` to be used on many more data types, including allowing pattern matching (in the Scala code, this is achieved using a `match` operation). In object-oriented design, the visitor pattern is a common pattern used to walk through a family of classes (such as the different components of a car: wheel, engine, chassis, and so on) and apply an operation to each object visited. One advantage of pattern matching is that a compiler can report common errors such as, "Class `Brakes` is part of the family of classes used to represent components of class `Car`. You forgot to explicitly deal with it."

Chapters 18 and 19 give a full tutorial introduction to functional programming and how to write functional-style programs in Java 8—including the toolkit of functions provided in its library. Chapter 20 follows by discussing how Java 8 features compare to those in Scala—a language that, like Java, is implemented on top of the JVM and that has evolved quickly to threaten some aspects of Java's niche in the programming language ecosystem. This material is positioned toward the end of the book to provide additional insight into why the new Java 8 and Java 9 features were added.

Java 8, 9, 10, and 11 features: Where do you start?

Java 8 and Java 9 both provided significant updates to Java. But as a Java programmer, it's likely to be the Java 8 additions that affect you most on a daily small-scale-coding basis—the idea of passing a method or a lambda is rapidly becoming vital Java knowledge. In contrast, the Java 9 enhancements enrich our ability to define and use larger-scale components, be it structuring a system using modules or importing a reactive-programming toolkit. Finally, Java 10 is a much smaller increment compared to previous upgrades and consists of allowing type inference for local variables, which we discuss briefly in chapter 21, where we also mention the related richer syntax for arguments of lambda expressions due to be introduced in Java 11.

At the time of writing, Java 11 is scheduled to be released in September 2018. Java 11 also brings a new asynchronous HTTP client library (http://openjdk.java.net/jeps/321) that leverages the Java 8 and Java 9 developments (details in chapters 15, 16, and 17) of `CompletableFuture` and reactive programming.

Summary

- Keep in mind the idea of the language ecosystem and the consequent evolve-or-wither pressure on languages. Although Java may be supremely healthy at the moment, we can recall other healthy languages such as COBOL that failed to evolve.

- The core additions to Java 8 provide exciting new concepts and functionality to ease the writing of programs that are both effective and concise.

- Multicore processors aren't fully served by pre-Java-8 programming practice.

- Functions are first-class values; remember how methods can be passed as functional values and how anonymous functions (lambdas) are written.

- The Java 8 concept of streams generalizes many aspects of collections, but the former often enables more readable code and allows elements of a stream to be processed in parallel.

- Large-scale component-based programming, and evolving a system's interfaces, weren't historically well served by Java. You can now specify modules to structure systems in Java 9 and use default methods to allow an interface to be enhanced without changing all the classes that implement it.

- Other interesting ideas from functional programming include dealing with `null` and using pattern matching.

Passing code with behavior parameterization

This chapter covers

- Coping with changing requirements
- Behavior parameterization
- Anonymous classes
- Preview of lambda expressions
- Real-world examples: `Comparator`, `Runnable`, and GUI

A well-known problem in software engineering is that no matter what you do, user requirements will change. For example, imagine an application to help a farmer understand his inventory. The farmer might want a functionality to find all green apples in his inventory. But the next day he might tell you, "Actually, I also want to find all apples heavier than 150 g." Two days later, the farmer comes back and adds, "It would be really nice if I could find all apples that are green *and* heavier than 150 g." How can you cope with these changing requirements? Ideally, you'd like to minimize your engineering effort. In addition, similar new functionalities ought to be straightforward to implement and maintainable in the long term.

Behavior parameterization is a software development pattern that lets you handle frequent requirement changes. In a nutshell, it means taking a block of code and making it available without executing it. This block of code can be called later by other parts of your programs, which means that you can defer the execution of that block of code. For instance, you could pass the block of code as an argument to another method that will execute it later. As a result, the method's behavior is parameterized based on that block of code. For example, if you process a collection, you may want to write a method that

- Can do "something" for every element of a list
- Can do "something else" when you finish processing the list
- Can do "yet something else" if you encounter an error

This is what *behavior parameterization* refers to. Here's an analogy: your roommate knows how to drive to the supermarket and back home. You can tell him to buy a list of things such as bread, cheese, and wine. This is equivalent to calling a method goAndBuy passing a list of products as its argument. But one day you're at the office, and you need him to do something he's never done before—pick up a package from the post office. You need to pass him a list of instructions: go to the post office, use this reference number, talk to the manager, and pick up the parcel. You could pass him the list of instructions by email, and when he receives it, he can follow the instructions. You've now done something a bit more advanced that's equivalent to a method goAndDo, which can execute various new behaviors as arguments.

We'll start this chapter by walking you through an example of how you can evolve your code to be more flexible for changing requirements. Building on this knowledge, we show how to use behavior parameterization for several real-world examples. For example, you may have used the behavior parameterization pattern already, using existing classes and interfaces in the Java API to sort a List, to filter names of files, or to tell a Thread to execute a block of code or even perform GUI event handling. You'll soon realize that this pattern is historically verbose in Java. Lambda expressions in Java 8 onward tackle the problem of verbosity. We'll show in chapter 3 how to construct lambda expressions, where to use them, and how you can make your code more concise by adopting them.

2.1 Coping with changing requirements

Writing code that can cope with changing requirements is difficult. Let's walk through an example that we'll gradually improve, showing some best practices for making your code more flexible. In the context of a farm-inventory application, you have to implement a functionality to filter *green* apples from a list. Sounds easy, right?

2.1.1   *First attempt: filtering green apples*

Assume, as in chapter 1, you have a Color enum available to represent different colors of an apple:

```
enum Color { RED, GREEN }
```

A first solution might be as follows:

```
public static List<Apple> filterGreenApples(List<Apple> inventory) {
    List<Apple> result = new ArrayList<>();                    ◁——    An accumulator
    for(Apple apple: inventory){                                       list for apples
        if( GREEN.equals(apple.getColor()) ) {     ◁——
            result.add(apple);
        }                                                  Selects only green apples
    }
    return result;
}
```

The highlighted line shows the condition required to select green apples. You can assume that you have a Color enum with a set of colors, such as GREEN, available. But now the farmer changes his mind and wants to also filter *red* apples. What can you do? A naïve solution would be to duplicate your method, rename it as filterRedApples, and change the if condition to match red apples. However, this approach doesn't cope well with changes if the farmer wants multiple colors. A good principle is this: when you find yourself writing nearly repeated code, try to abstract instead.

2.1.2   *Second attempt: parameterizing the color*

How do we avoid duplicating most of the code in filterGreenApples to make filter-RedApples? To parameterize the color and be more flexible to such changes, what you could do is add a parameter to your method:

```
public static List<Apple> filterApplesByColor(List<Apple> inventory,
Color color) {
    List<Apple> result = new ArrayList<>();
    for (Apple apple: inventory) {
        if ( apple.getColor().equals(color) ) {
            result.add(apple);
        }
    }
    return result;
}
```

You can now make the farmer happy and invoke your method as follows:

```
List<Apple> greenApples = filterApplesByColor(inventory, GREEN);
List<Apple> redApples = filterApplesByColor(inventory, RED);
...
```

Too easy, right? Let's complicate the example a bit. The farmer comes back to you and says, "It would be really cool to differentiate between light apples and heavy apples. Heavy apples typically have a weight greater than 150 g."

Wearing your software engineering hat, you realize in advance that the farmer may want to vary the weight. So you create the following method to cope with various weights through an additional parameter:

```
public static List<Apple> filterApplesByWeight(List<Apple> inventory,
int weight) {
    List<Apple> result = new ArrayList<>();
    For (Apple apple: inventory){
        if ( apple.getWeight() > weight ) {
            result.add(apple);
        }
    }
    return result;
}
```

This is a good solution, but notice how you have to duplicate most of the implementation for traversing the inventory and applying the filtering criteria on each apple. This is somewhat disappointing because it breaks the DRY (don't repeat yourself) principle of software engineering. What if you want to alter the filter traversing to enhance performance? You now have to modify the implementation of *all* of your methods instead of only a single one. This is expensive from an engineering-effort perspective.

You could combine the color and weight into one method, called filter. But then you'd still need a way to differentiate what attribute you want to filter on. You could add a flag to differentiate between color and weight queries. (But never do this! We'll explain why shortly.)

2.1.3 *Third attempt: filtering with every attribute you can think of*

An ugly attempt to merge all attributes might be as follows:

```
public static List<Apple> filterApples(List<Apple> inventory, Color color,
                                 int weight, boolean flag) {
    List<Apple> result = new ArrayList<>();
    for (Apple apple: inventory) {
        if ( (flag && apple.getColor().equals(color)) ||
             (!flag && apple.getWeight() > weight) ){    ◁── An ugly way to
            result.add(apple);                               select color or
        }                                                    weight
    }
    return result;
}
```

You could use this as follows (but it's ugly):

```
List<Apple> greenApples = filterApples(inventory, GREEN, 0, true);
List<Apple> heavyApples = filterApples(inventory, null, 150, false);
...
```

This solution is extremely bad. First, the client code looks terrible. What do `true` and `false` mean? In addition, this solution doesn't cope well with changing requirements. What if the farmer asks you to filter with different attributes of an apple, for example, its size, its shape, its origin, and so on? Furthermore, what if the farmer asks you for more complicated queries that combine attributes, such as green apples that are also heavy? You'd either have multiple duplicated `filter` methods or one hugely complex method. So far, you've parameterized the `filterApples` method *with values* such as a `String`, an `Integer`, an enum type, or a `boolean`. This can be fine for certain well-defined problems. But in this case, what you need is a better way to tell your `filter-Apples` method the selection criteria for apples. In the next section, we describe how to make use of *behavior parameterization* to attain that flexibility.

2.2   *Behavior parameterization*

You saw in the previous section that you need a better way than adding lots of parameters to cope with changing requirements. Let's step back and find a better level of abstraction. One possible solution is to model your selection criteria: you're working with apples and returning a `boolean` based on some attributes of `Apple`. For example, is it green? Is it heavier than 150 g? We call this a *predicate* (a function that returns a `boolean`). Let's therefore define an interface *to model the selection criteria:*

```
public interface ApplePredicate{
    boolean test (Apple apple);
}
```

You can now declare multiple implementations of `ApplePredicate` to represent different selection criteria, as shown in the following (and illustrated in figure 2.1):

```
public class AppleHeavyWeightPredicate implements ApplePredicate {        ◁──┐
    public boolean test(Apple apple) {                                        │
        return apple.getWeight() > 150;          Selects only heavy apples    │
    }
}
public class AppleGreenColorPredicate implements ApplePredicate {          ◁──┐
    public boolean test(Apple apple) {                                        │
        return GREEN.equals(apple.getColor());   Selects only green apples    │
    }
}
```

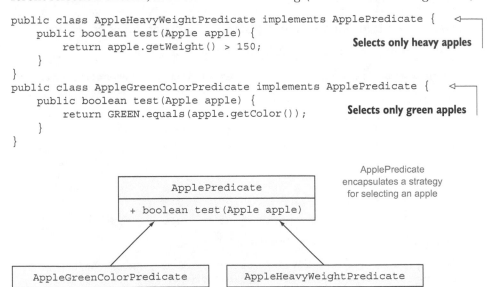

Figure 2.1   **Different strategies for selecting an `Apple`**

You can see these criteria as different behaviors for the filter method. What you just did is related to the strategy design pattern (see http://en.wikipedia.org/wiki/Strategy_pattern), which lets you define a family of algorithms, encapsulate each algorithm (called a strategy), and select an algorithm at run time. In this case the family of algorithms is AplePredicate and the different strategies are AppleHeavyWeightPredicate and AppleGreenColorPredicate.

But how can you make use of the different implementations of ApplePredicate? You need your filterApples method to accept ApplePredicate objects to test a condition on an Apple. This is what *behavior parameterization* means: the ability to tell a method to *take* multiple behaviors (or strategies) as parameters and use them internally to *accomplish* different behaviors.

To achieve this in the running example, you add a parameter to the filterApples method to take an ApplePredicate object. This has a great software engineering benefit: you can now separate the logic of iterating the collection inside the filterApples method with the behavior you want to apply to each element of the collection (in this case a predicate).

2.2.1 Fourth attempt: filtering by abstract criteria

Our modified filter method, which uses an ApplePredicate, looks like this:

```
public static List<Apple> filterApples(List<Apple> inventory,
                                        ApplePredicate p) {
    List<Apple> result = new ArrayList<>();
    for(Apple apple: inventory) {
        if(p.test(apple)) {          ◁──  Predicate p encapsulates
            result.add(apple);             the condition to test on
        }                                  an apple.
    }
    return result;
}
```

PASSING CODE/BEHAVIOR

It's worth pausing for a moment for a small celebration. This code is much more flexible than our first attempt, but at the same time it's easy to read and to use! You can now create different ApplePredicate objects and pass them to the filterApples method. Free flexibility! For example, if the farmer asks you to find all red apples that are heavier than 150 g, all you need to do is create a class that implements the ApplePredicate accordingly. Your code is now flexible enough for any change of requirements involving the attributes of Apple:

```
public class AppleRedAndHeavyPredicate implements ApplePredicate {
        public boolean test(Apple apple){
                return RED.equals(apple.getColor())
                        && apple.getWeight() > 150;
        }
}
List<Apple> redAndHeavyApples =
    filterApples(inventory, new AppleRedAndHeavyPredicate());
```

You've achieved something cool; the behavior of the filterApples method depends on the *code you pass* to it via the AplePredicate object. You've parameterized the behavior of the filterApples method!

Note that in the previous example, the only code that matters is the implementation of the test method, as illustrated in figure 2.2; this is what defines the new behaviors for the filterApples method. Unfortunately, because the filterApples method can only take objects, you have to wrap that code inside an AplePredicate object. What you're doing is similar to passing code inline, because you're passing a boolean expression through an object that implements the test method. You'll see in section 2.3 (and in more detail in chapter 3) that by using lambdas, you can directly pass the expression RED.equals(apple.getColor()) && apple.getWeight() > 150 to the filterApples method without having to define multiple AplePredicate classes. This removes unnecessary verbosity.

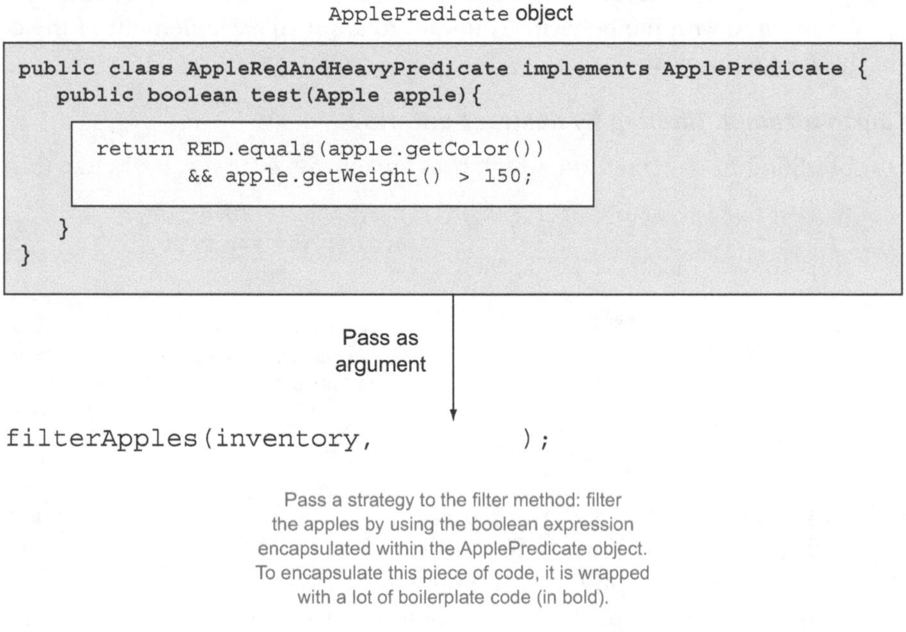

AplePredicate **object**

```
public class AppleRedAndHeavyPredicate implements ApplePredicate {
   public boolean test(Apple apple){

      return RED.equals(apple.getColor())
              && apple.getWeight() > 150;

   }
}
```

Pass as
argument

```
filterApples(inventory,              );
```

Pass a strategy to the filter method: filter
the apples by using the boolean expression
encapsulated within the ApplePredicate object.
To encapsulate this piece of code, it is wrapped
with a lot of boilerplate code (in bold).

Figure 2.2   Parameterizing the behavior of filterApples and passing different filter strategies

MULTIPLE BEHAVIORS, ONE PARAMETER

As we explained earlier, behavior parameterization is great because it enables you to separate the logic of iterating the collection to filter and the behavior to apply on each element of that collection. As a consequence, you can reuse the same method and give it different behaviors to achieve different things, as illustrated in figure 2.3. This is why *behavior parameterization* is a useful concept you should have in your toolset for creating flexible APIs.

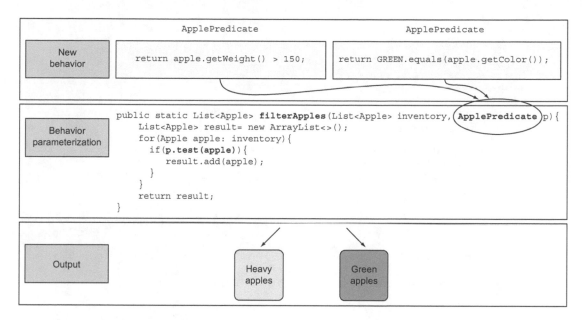

Figure 2.3 Parameterizing the behavior of `filterApples` and passing different filter strategies

To make sure you feel comfortable with the idea of behavior parameterization, try to do quiz 2.1!

Quiz 2.1: Write a flexible `prettyPrintApple` method

Write a `prettyPrintApple` method that takes a `List` of `Apples` and that can be parameterized with multiple ways to generate a `String` output from an `apple` (a bit like multiple customized `toString` methods). For example, you could tell your `prettyPrintApple` method to print only the weight of each apple. In addition, you could tell your `prettyPrintApple` method to print each apple individually and mention whether it's heavy or light. The solution is similar to the filtering examples we've explored so far. To help you get started, we provide a rough skeleton of the `pretty-PrintApple` method:

```
public static void prettyPrintApple(List<Apple> inventory, ???) {
    for(Apple apple: inventory) {
        String output = ???.???(apple);
        System.out.println(output);
    }
}
```

Answer:

First, you need a way to represent a behavior that takes an `Apple` and returns a formatted `String` result. You did something similar when you created an `Apple-Predicate` interface:

(continued)

```
public interface AppleFormatter {
    String accept(Apple a);
}
```

You can now represent multiple formatting behaviors by implementing the Apple-Formatter interface:

```
public class AppleFancyFormatter implements AppleFormatter {
    public String accept(Apple apple) {
        String characteristic = apple.getWeight() > 150 ? "heavy" :
            "light";
        return "A " + characteristic +
            " " + apple.getColor() +" apple";
    }
}
public class AppleSimpleFormatter implements AppleFormatter {
    public String accept(Apple apple) {
        return "An apple of " + apple.getWeight() + "g";
    }
}
```

Finally, you need to tell your prettyPrintApple method to take AppleFormatter objects and use them internally. You can do this by adding a parameter to pretty-PrintApple:

```
public static void prettyPrintApple(List<Apple> inventory,
                                    AppleFormatter formatter) {
  for(Apple apple: inventory) {
    String output = formatter.accept(apple);
    System.out.println(output);
  }
}
```

Bingo! You're now able to pass multiple behaviors to your prettyPrintApple method. You do this by instantiating implementations of AppleFormatter and giving them as arguments to prettyPrintApple:

```
prettyPrintApple(inventory, new AppleFancyFormatter());
```

This will produce an output along the lines of

```
A light green apple
A heavy red apple
…
```

Or try this:

```
prettyPrintApple(inventory, new AppleSimpleFormatter());
```

This will produce an output along the lines of

```
An apple of 80g
An apple of 155g
…
```

You've seen that you can abstract over behavior and make your code adapt to requirement changes, but the process is verbose because you need to declare multiple classes that you instantiate only once. Let's see how to improve that.

2.3 *Tackling verbosity*

We all know that a feature or concept that's cumbersome to use will be avoided. At the moment, when you want to pass new behavior to your `filterApples` method, you're forced to declare several classes that implement the `ApplePredicate` interface and then instantiate several `ApplePredicate` objects that you allocate only once, as shown in the following listing that summarizes what you've seen so far. There's a lot of verbosity involved and it's a time-consuming process!

Listing 2.1 Behavior parameterization: filtering apples with predicates

```
public class AppleHeavyWeightPredicate implements ApplePredicate {      ◄─┐
    public boolean test(Apple apple) {
        return apple.getWeight() > 150;                     Selects heavy apples │
    }
}
public class AppleGreenColorPredicate implements ApplePredicate {        ◄─┐
    public boolean test(Apple apple) {
        return GREEN.equals(apple.getColor());              Selects green apples │
    }
}
public class FilteringApples {
    public static void main(String...args) {
        List<Apple> inventory = Arrays.asList(new Apple(80, GREEN),
                                              new Apple(155, GREEN),
                                              new Apple(120, RED));
        List<Apple> heavyApples =
            filterApples(inventory, new AppleHeavyWeightPredicate());
        List<Apple> greenApples =
            filterApples(inventory, new AppleGreenColorPredicate());   ◄─┐
    }                                                                      Results
    public static List<Apple> filterApples(List<Apple> inventory,         in a List
                                           ApplePredicate p) {            containing
        List<Apple> result = new ArrayList<>();                          two green
        for (Apple apple : inventory) {                                  Apples
            if (p.test(apple)){
                result.add(apple);
            }
        }
        return result;
    }
}
```

Results in a List containing one Apple of 155 g — points to `filterApples(inventory, new AppleHeavyWeightPredicate());`

This is unnecessary overhead. Can you do better? Java has mechanisms called *anonymous classes*, which let you declare and instantiate a class at the same time. They enable you to improve your code one step further by making it a little more concise. But they're not entirely satisfactory. Section 2.3.3 anticipates the next chapter with a short preview of how lambda expressions can make your code more readable.

2.3.1 Anonymous classes

Anonymous classes are like the local classes (a class defined in a block) that you're already familiar with in Java. But anonymous classes don't have a name. They allow you to declare and instantiate a class at the same time. In short, they allow you to create ad hoc implementations.

2.3.2 Fifth attempt: using an anonymous class

The following code shows how to rewrite the filtering example by creating an object that implements `ApplePredicate` using an anonymous class:

```
List<Apple> redApples = filterApples(inventory, new ApplePredicate() {
    public boolean test(Apple apple){
        return RED.equals(apple.getColor());
    }
});
```

Parameterizes the behavior of the method filterApples with an anonymous class.

Anonymous classes are often used in the context of GUI applications to create event-handler objects. We don't want to bring back painful memories of Swing, but the following is a common pattern that you see in practice (here using the JavaFX API, a modern UI platform for Java):

```
button.setOnAction(new EventHandler<ActionEvent>() {
    public void handle(ActionEvent event) {
        System.out.println("Whoooo a click!!");
    }
});
```

But anonymous classes are still not good enough. First, they tend to be bulky because they take a lot of space, as shown in the boldface code here using the same two examples used previously:

```
List<Apple> redApples = filterApples(inventory, new ApplePredicate() {
    public boolean test(Apple a){
        return RED.equals(a.getColor());
    }
});
button.setOnAction(new EventHandler<ActionEvent>() {
    public void handle(ActionEvent event) {
        System.out.println("Whoooo a click!!");
    }
```

Lots of boilerplate code

Second, many programmers find them confusing to use. For example, quiz 2.2 shows a classic Java puzzler that catches most programmers off guard! Try your hand at it.

Quiz 2.2: Anonymous class puzzler

What will the output be when this code is executed: 4, 5, 6, or 42?

```
public class MeaningOfThis {
    public final int value = 4;
    public void doIt() {
        int value = 6;
        Runnable r = new Runnable() {
                public final int value = 5;
                public void run(){
                    int value = 10;
                    System.out.println(this.value);
                }
        };
        r.run();
    }
    public static void main(String...args) {
        MeaningOfThis m = new MeaningOfThis();
        m.doIt();          <-----    What's the output
    }                                of this line?
}
```

Answer:

The answer is 5, because this refers to the enclosing Runnable, not the enclosing class MeaningOfThis.

Verbosity in general is bad; it discourages the use of a language feature because it takes a long time to write and maintain verbose code, and it's not pleasant to read! Good code should be easy to comprehend at a glance. Even though anonymous classes somewhat tackle the verbosity associated with declaring multiple concrete classes for an interface, they're still unsatisfactory. In the context of passing a simple piece of code (for example, a boolean expression representing a selection criterion), you still have to create an object and explicitly implement a method to define a new behavior (for example, the method test for Predicate or the method handle for EventHandler).

Ideally we'd like to encourage programmers to use the behavior parameterization pattern, because as you've just seen, it makes your code more adaptive to requirement changes. In chapter 3, you'll see that the Java 8 language designers solved this problem by introducing lambda expressions, a more concise way to pass code. Enough suspense; here's a short preview of how lambda expressions can help you in your quest for clean code.

2.3.3 *Sixth attempt: using a lambda expression*

The previous code can be rewritten as follows in Java 8 using a lambda expression:

```
List<Apple> result =
  filterApples(inventory, (Apple apple) -> RED.equals(apple.getColor()));
```

You have to admit this code looks a lot cleaner than our previous attempts! It's great because it's starting to look a lot closer to the problem statement. We've now tackled the verbosity issue. Figure 2.4 summarizes our journey so far.

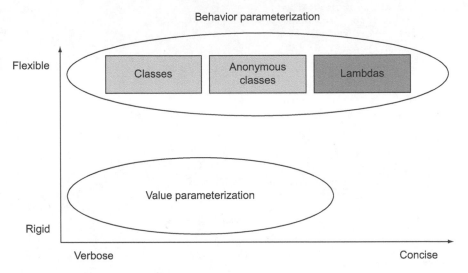

Figure 2.4   Behavior parameterization versus value parameterization

2.3.4   *Seventh attempt: abstracting over List type*

There's one more step that you can do in your journey toward abstraction. At the moment, the `filterApples` method works only for `Apple`. But you can also abstract on the `List` type to go beyond the problem domain you're thinking of, as shown:

```
public interface Predicate<T> {
    boolean test(T t);
}
public static <T> List<T> filter(List<T> list, Predicate<T> p) {
    List<T> result = new ArrayList<>();
    for(T e: list) {
        if(p.test(e)) {
            result.add(e);
        }
    }
    return result;
}
```

Introduces a type parameter T

You can now use the method `filter` with a `List` of bananas, oranges, `Integers`, or `Strings`! Here's an example, using lambda expressions:

```
List<Apple> redApples =
  filter(inventory, (Apple apple) -> RED.equals(apple.getColor()));
List<Integer> evenNumbers =
  filter(numbers, (Integer i) -> i % 2 == 0);
```

Isn't it cool? You've managed to find the sweet spot between flexibility and conciseness, which wasn't possible prior to Java 8!

2.4 *Real-world examples*

You've now seen that behavior parameterization is a useful pattern to easily adapt to changing requirements. This pattern lets you encapsulate a behavior (a piece of code) and parameterize the behavior of methods by passing and using these behaviors you create (for example, different predicates for an Apple). We mentioned earlier that this approach is similar to the strategy design pattern. You may have already used this pattern in practice. Many methods in the Java API can be parameterized with different behaviors. These methods are often used together with anonymous classes. We show four examples, which should solidify the idea of passing code for you: sorting with a Comparator, executing a block of code with Runnable, returning a result from a task using Callable, and GUI event handling.

2.4.1 *Sorting with a Comparator*

Sorting a collection is a recurring programming task. For example, say your farmer wants you to sort the inventory of apples based on their weight. Or perhaps he changes his mind and wants you to sort the apples by color. Sound familiar? Yes, you need a way to represent and use different sorting behaviors to easily adapt to changing requirements.

From Java 8, a List comes with a sort method (you could also use Collections .sort). The behavior of sort can be parameterized using a java.util.Comparator object, which has the following interface:

```
// java.util.Comparator
public interface Comparator<T> {
    int compare(T o1, T o2);
}
```

You can therefore create different behaviors for the sort method by creating an ad hoc implementation of Comparator. For example, you can use it to sort the inventory by increasing weight using an anonymous class:

```
inventory.sort(new Comparator<Apple>() {
public int compare(Apple a1, Apple a2) {
return a1.getWeight().compareTo(a2.getWeight());
}
});
```

If the farmer changes his mind about how to sort apples, you can create an ad hoc Comparator to match the new requirement and pass it to the sort method. The internal details of how to sort are abstracted away. With a lambda expression it would look like this:

```
inventory.sort(
  (Apple a1, Apple a2) -> a1.getWeight().compareTo(a2.getWeight()));
```

Again, don't worry about this new syntax for now; the next chapter covers in detail how to write and use lambda expressions.

2.4.2 *Executing a block of code with Runnable*

Java *threads* allow a block of code to be executed concurrently with the rest of the program. But how can you tell a thread what block of code it should run? Several threads may each run different code. What you need is a way to represent a piece of code to be executed later. Until Java 8, only objects could be passed to the Thread constructor, so the typical clumsy usage pattern was to pass an anonymous class containing a run method that returns void (no result). Such anonymous classes implement the Runnable interface.

In Java, you can use the Runnable interface to represent a block of code to be executed; note that the code returns void (no result):

```
// java.lang.Runnable
public interface Runnable {
    void run();
}
```

You can use this interface to create threads with your choice of behavior, as follows:

```
Thread t = new Thread(new Runnable() {
    public void run() {
        System.out.println("Hello world");
    }
});
```

But since Java 8 you can use a lambda expression, so the call to Thread would look like this:

```
Thread t = new Thread(() -> System.out.println("Hello world"));
```

2.4.3 *Returning a result using Callable*

You may be familiar with the ExecutorService abstraction that was introduced in Java 5. The ExecutorService interface decouples how tasks are submitted and executed. What's useful in comparison to using threads and Runnable is that by using an ExecutorService you can send a task to a pool of threads and have its result stored in a Future. Don't worry if this is unfamiliar, we will revisit this topic in later chapters when we discuss concurrency in more detail. For now, all you need to know is that the Callable interface is used to model a task that returns a result. You can see it as an upgraded Runnable:

```
// java.util.concurrent.Callable
public interface Callable<V> {
    V call();
}
```

You can use it, as follows, by submitting a task to an executor service. Here you return the name of the Thread that is responsible for executing the task:

```
ExecutorService executorService = Executors.newCachedThreadPool();
Future<String> threadName = executorService.submit(new Callable<String>() {
    @Override
    public String call() throws Exception {
        return Thread.currentThread().getName();
    }
});
```

Using a lambda expression, this code simplifies to the following:

```
Future<String> threadName = executorService.submit(
                    () -> Thread.currentThread().getName());
```

2.4.4 GUI event handling

A typical pattern in GUI programming is to perform an action in response to a certain event such as clicking or hovering over text. For example, if the user clicks the Send button, you may wish to display a pop up or perhaps log the action in a file. Again, you need a way to cope with changes; you should be able to perform any response. In JavaFX, you can use an EventHandler to represent a response to an event by passing it to setOnAction:

```
Button button = new Button("Send");
button.setOnAction(new EventHandler<ActionEvent>() {
    public void handle(ActionEvent event) {
        label.setText("Sent!!");
    }
});
```

Here, the behavior of the setOnAction method is parameterized with EventHandler objects. With a lambda expression it would look like the following:

```
button.setOnAction((ActionEvent event) -> label.setText("Sent!!"));
```

Summary

- Behavior parameterization is the ability for a method to *take* multiple different behaviors as parameters and use them internally to *accomplish* different behaviors.
- Behavior parameterization lets you make your code more adaptive to changing requirements and saves on engineering efforts in the future.
- Passing code is a way to give new behaviors as arguments to a method. But it's verbose prior to Java 8. Anonymous classes helped a bit before Java 8 to get rid of the verbosity associated with declaring multiple concrete classes for an interface that are needed only once.
- The Java API contains many methods that can be parameterized with different behaviors, which include sorting, threads, and GUI handling.

Lambda expressions

This chapter covers

- Lambdas in a nutshell
- Where and how to use lambdas
- The execute-around pattern
- Functional interfaces, type inference
- Method references
- Composing lambdas

In the previous chapter, you saw that passing code with behavior parameterization is useful for coping with frequent requirement changes in your code. It lets you define a block of code that represents a behavior and then pass it around. You can decide to run that block of code when a certain event happens (for example, a button click) or at certain points in an algorithm (for example, a predicate such as "only apples heavier than 150 g" in the filtering algorithm or the customized comparison operation in sorting). In general, using this concept you can write code that's more flexible and reusable.

But you saw that using anonymous classes to represent different behaviors is unsatisfying. It's verbose, which doesn't encourage programmers to use behavior parameterization in practice. In this chapter, we'll teach you about a new feature in

Java 8 that tackles this problem: lambda expressions. They let you represent a behavior or pass code in a concise way. For now you can think of lambda expressions as anonymous functions, methods without declared names, but which can also be passed as arguments to a method as you can with an anonymous class.

We'll show how to construct them, where to use them, and how you can make your code more concise by using them. We also explain some new goodies such as type inference and new important interfaces available in the Java 8 API. Finally, we introduce method references, a useful new feature that goes hand in hand with lambda expressions.

This chapter is organized in such a way as to teach you step-by-step how to write more concise and flexible code. At the end of this chapter, we bring together all the concepts taught into a concrete example; we take the sorting example shown in chapter 2 and gradually improve it using lambda expressions and method references to make it more concise and readable. This chapter is important in itself and also because you'll use lambdas extensively throughout the book.

3.1 Lambdas in a nutshell

A *lambda expression* can be understood as a concise representation of an anonymous function that can be passed around. It doesn't have a name, but it has a list of parameters, a body, a return type, and also possibly a list of exceptions that can be thrown. That's one big definition; let's break it down:

- *Anonymous*—We say *anonymous* because it doesn't have an explicit name like a method would normally have; less to write and think about!
- *Function*—We say *function* because a lambda isn't associated with a particular class like a method is. But like a method, a lambda has a list of parameters, a body, a return type, and a possible list of exceptions that can be thrown.
- *Passed around*—A lambda expression can be passed as argument to a method or stored in a variable.
- *Concise*—You don't need to write a lot of boilerplate like you do for anonymous classes.

If you're wondering where the term *lambda* comes from, it originates from a system developed in academia called *lambda calculus*, which is used to describe computations.

Why should you care about lambda expressions? You saw in the previous chapter that passing code is currently tedious and verbose in Java. Well, good news! Lambdas fix this problem; they let you pass code in a concise way. Lambdas technically don't let you do anything that you couldn't do prior to Java 8. But you no longer have to write clumsy code using anonymous classes to benefit from behavior parameterization! Lambda expressions will encourage you to adopt the style of behavior parameterization that we described in the previous chapter. The net result is that your code will be clearer and more flexible. For example, using a lambda expression you can create a custom `Comparator` object in a more concise way.

Before:

```
Comparator<Apple> byWeight = new Comparator<Apple>() {
    public int compare(Apple a1, Apple a2){
        return a1.getWeight().compareTo(a2.getWeight());
    }
};
```

After (with lambda expressions):

```
Comparator<Apple> byWeight =
    (Apple a1, Apple a2) -> a1.getWeight().compareTo(a2.getWeight());
```

You must admit that the code looks clearer! Don't worry if all the parts of the lambda expression don't make sense yet; we'll explain all the pieces soon. For now, note that you're literally passing only the code that's needed to compare two apples using their weight. It looks like you're passing the body of the method compare. You'll learn soon that you can simplify your code even more. We'll explain in the next section exactly where and how you can use lambda expressions.

The lambda we just showed you has three parts, as shown in figure 3.1:

Figure 3.1   A lambda expression is composed of parameters, an arrow, and a body.

- *A list of parameters*—In this case it mirrors the parameters of the compare method of a Comparator—two Apples.
- *An arrow*—The arrow -> separates the list of parameters from the body of the lambda.
- *The body of the lambda*—Compare two Apples using their weights. The expression is considered the lambda's return value.

To illustrate further, the following listing shows five examples of valid lambda expressions in Java 8.

Listing 3.1   Valid lambda expressions in Java 8

```
(String s) -> s.length()        ◁───  Takes one parameter of type String and returns an int.
                                       It has no return statement as return is implied.
(Apple a) -> a.getWeight() > 150    ◁
(int x, int y) -> {                    Takes one parameter of type Apple and returns a
    System.out.println("Result:");     boolean (whether the apple is heavier than 150 g).
    System.out.println(x + y);
}                               ◁───   Takes two parameters of type int and returns no value
                                       (void return). Its body contains two statements.
```

```
() -> 42
(Apple a1, Apple a2) -> a1.getWeight().compareTo(a2.getWeight())
```

Takes two parameters of type Apple and returns an   **Takes no parameter**
int representing the comparison of their weights   **and returns the int 42**

This syntax was chosen by the Java language designers because it was well received in other languages, such as C# and Scala. JavaScript has a similar syntax. The basic syntax of a lambda is either (referred to as an *expression-style* lambda)

```
(parameters) -> expression
```

or (note the curly braces for statements, this lambda is often called a *block-style* lambda)

```
(parameters) -> { statements; }
```

As you can see, lambda expressions follow a simple syntax. Working through quiz 3.1 should let you know if you understand the pattern.

Quiz 3.1: Lambda syntax

Based on the syntax rules just shown, which of the following are not valid lambda expressions?

1. `() -> {}`
2. `() -> "Raoul"`
3. `() -> { return "Mario"; }`
4. `(Integer i) -> return "Alan" + i;`
5. `(String s) -> { "Iron Man"; }`

Answer:

4 and 5 are invalid lambdas; the rest are valid. Details:

1. This lambda has no parameters and returns `void`. It's similar to a method with an empty body: `public void run() { }`. Fun fact: this is usually called the burger lambda. Take a look at it from the side, and you will see it has a burger shape with two buns.
2. This lambda has no parameters and returns a `String` as an expression.
3. This lambda has no parameters and returns a `String` (using an explicit return statement, within a block).
4. `return` is a control-flow statement. To make this lambda valid, curly braces are required as follows: `(Integer i) -> { return "Alan" + i; }`.
5. "Iron Man" is an expression, not a statement. To make this lambda valid, you can remove the curly braces and semicolon as follows: `(String s) -> "Iron Man"`. Or if you prefer, you can use an explicit return statement as follows: `(String s) -> { return "Iron Man"; }`.

Table 3.1 This provides a list of example lambdas with examples of use cases.

Table 3.1   Examples of lambdas

Use case	Examples of lambdas
A boolean expression	`(List<String> list) -> list.isEmpty()`
Creating objects	`() -> new Apple(10)`

Consuming from an object	`(Apple a) -> {`
	`    System.out.println(a.getWeight());`
	`}`

Select/extract from an object	`(String s) -> s.length()`
Combine two values	`(int a, int b) -> a * b`
Compare two objects	`(Apple a1, Apple a2) ->` `a1.getWeight().compareTo(a2.getWeight())`

3.2   Where and how to use lambdas

You may now be wondering where you're allowed to use lambda expressions. In the previous example, you assigned a lambda to a variable of type `Comparator<Apple>`. You could also use another lambda with the `filter` method you implemented in the previous chapter:

```
List<Apple> greenApples =
        filter(inventory, (Apple a) -> GREEN.equals(a.getColor()));
```

Where exactly can you use lambdas? You can use a lambda expression in the context of a functional interface. In the code shown here, you can pass a lambda as second argument to the method `filter` because it expects an object of type `Predicate<T>`, which is a functional interface. Don't worry if this sounds abstract; we'll now explain in detail what this means and what a functional interface is.

3.2.1   Functional interface

Remember the interface `Predicate<T>` you created in chapter 2 so you could parameterize the behavior of the `filter` method? It's a functional interface! Why? Because `Predicate` specifies only one abstract method:

```
public interface Predicate<T> {
    boolean test (T t);
}
```

In a nutshell, a *functional interface* is an interface that specifies exactly one abstract method. You already know several other functional interfaces in the Java API such as `Comparator` and `Runnable`, which we explored in chapter 2:

```
public interface Comparator<T> {          ◁——— java.util.Comparator
    int compare(T o1, T o2);
}
public interface Runnable {               ◁——— java.lang.Runnable
    void run();
}
public interface ActionListener extends EventListener {◁— java.awt.event.ActionListener
    void actionPerformed(ActionEvent e);
}
public interface Callable<V> {            ◁——— java.util.concurrent.Callable
    V call() throws Exception;
}
public interface PrivilegedAction<T> {    ◁——— java.security.PrivilegedAction
    T run();
}
```

NOTE You'll see in chapter 13 that interfaces can now also have *default methods* (a method with a body that provides some default implementation for a method in case it isn't implemented by a class). An interface is still a functional interface if it has many default methods as long as it specifies *only one abstract method*.

To check your understanding, quiz 3.2 should let you know if you grasp the concept of a functional interface.

Quiz 3.2: Functional interface
Which of these interfaces are functional interfaces?

```
public interface Adder {
    int add(int a, int b);
}
public interface SmartAdder extends Adder {
    int add(double a, double b);
}
public interface Nothing {
}
```

Answer:

Only `Adder` is a functional interface.

`SmartAdder` isn't a functional interface because it specifies two abstract methods called `add` (one is inherited from `Adder`).

`Nothing` isn't a functional interface because it declares no abstract method at all.

What can you do with functional interfaces? Lambda expressions let you provide the implementation of the abstract method of a functional interface directly inline and *treat the whole expression as an instance of a functional interface* (more technically speaking, an instance of a *concrete implementation* of the functional interface). You can achieve the same thing with an anonymous inner class, although it's clumsier: you provide an implementation and instantiate it directly inline. The following code is valid because Runnable is a functional interface defining only one abstract method, run:

```
Runnable r1 = () -> System.out.println("Hello World 1");        <--- Uses a lambda
Runnable r2 = new Runnable() {                     <--┐
    public void run() {                               │   Uses an
        System.out.println("Hello World 2");          │   anonymous class
    }
};
public static void process(Runnable r) {
    r.run();
}
process(r1);                        <--┐ Prints "Hello
process(r2);                           │ World 1"
process(() -> System.out.println("Hello World 3"));
```

Uses an anonymous class

Prints "Hello World 2"

Prints "Hello World 3" with a lambda passed directly

3.2.2 *Function descriptor*

The signature of the abstract method of the functional interface describes the signature of the lambda expression. We call this abstract method a *function descriptor*. For example, the Runnable interface can be viewed as the signature of a function that accepts nothing and returns nothing (void) because it has only one abstract method called run, which accepts nothing and returns nothing (void).[1]

We use a special notation throughout this chapter to describe the signatures of lambdas and functional interfaces. The notation () -> void represents a function with an empty list of parameters returning void. This is exactly what the Runnable interface represents. As another example, (Apple, Apple) -> int denotes a function taking two Apples as parameters and returning an int. We will provide more information about function descriptors in section 3.4 and table 3.2 later in the chapter.

You may already be wondering how lambda expressions are type checked. We detail how the compiler checks whether a lambda is valid in a given context in section 3.5. For now, it suffices to understand that a lambda expression can be assigned to a variable or passed to a method expecting a functional interface as argument, provided the lambda expression has the same signature as the abstract method of the functional interface. For instance, in our earlier example, you could pass a lambda directly to the process method as follows:

```
public void process(Runnable r) {
    r.run();
}
process(() -> System.out.println("This is awesome!!"));
```

---

[1] Some languages such as Scala provide explicit type annotations in their type system to describe the type of a function (called function types). Java reuses existing nominal types provided by functional interfaces and maps them into a form of function types behind the scenes.

This code when executed will print "This is awesome!!" The lambda expression `() -> System.out.println("This is awesome!!")` takes no parameters and returns `void`. This is exactly the signature of the `run` method defined in the `Runnable` interface.

> ### Lambdas and void method invocation
>
> Although this may feel weird, the following lambda expression is valid:
>
> ```
> process(() -> System.out.println("This is awesome"));
> ```
>
> After all, `System.out.println` returns `void` so this is clearly not an expression! Why don't we have to enclose the body with curly braces like this?
>
> ```
> process(() -> { System.out.println("This is awesome"); });
> ```
>
> It turns out that there's a special rule for a void method invocation defined in the Java Language Specification. You don't have to enclose a single void method invocation in braces.

You may be wondering, "Why can we pass a lambda only where a functional interface is expected?" The language designers considered alternative approaches such as adding function types (a bit like the special notation we introduced to describe the signature of lambda expressions—we'll revisit this topic in chapters 20 and 21) to Java. But they chose this way because it fits naturally without increasing the complexity of the language. In addition, most Java programmers are already familiar with the idea of an interface with a single abstract method (for example, for event handling). However, the most important reason is that functional interfaces were already extensively used before Java 8. This means that they provide a nice migration path for using lambda expressions. In fact, if you've been using functional interfaces such as `Comparator` and `Runnable` or even your own interfaces that happen to define only a single abstract method, you can now use lambda expressions without changing your APIs. Try quiz 3.3 to test your knowledge of where lambdas can be used.

> ### Quiz 3.3: Where can you use lambdas?
> Which of the following are valid uses of lambda expressions?
>
> 1. ```
>    execute(() -> {});
>    public void execute(Runnable r) {
>      r.run();
>    }
>    ```
>
> 2. ```
>    public Callable<String> fetch() {
>      return () -> "Tricky example ;-)";
>    }
>    ```
>
> 3. ```
>    Predicate<Apple> p = (Apple a) -> a.getWeight();
>    ```

(continued)

Answer:

Only 1 and 2 are valid.

The first example is valid because the lambda `() -> {}` has the signature `() -> void`, which matches the signature of the abstract method `run` defined in `Runnable`. Note that running this code will do nothing because the body of the lambda is empty!

The second example is also valid. Indeed, the return type of the method `fetch` is `Callable<String>`. `Callable<String>` defines a method with the signature `() -> String` when `T` is replaced with `String`. Because the lambda `() -> "Tricky example ;-)"` has the signature `() -> String`, the lambda can be used in this context.

The third example is invalid because the lambda expression `(Apple a) -> a.get-Weight()` has the signature `(Apple) -> Integer`, which is different from the signature of the method `test` defined in `Predicate<Apple>`: `(Apple) -> boolean`.

What about @FunctionalInterface?

If you explore the new Java API, you will notice that functional interfaces are *generally* annotated with `@FunctionalInterface`. (We show an extensive list in section 3.4, where we explore how to use functional interfaces in depth.) This annotation is used to indicate that the interface is intended to be a functional interface and is therefore useful for documentation. In addition, the compiler will return a meaningful error if you define an interface using the `@FunctionalInterface` annotation, and it isn't a functional interface. For example, an error message could be "Multiple non-overriding abstract methods found in interface Foo" to indicate that more than one abstract method is available. Note that the `@FunctionalInterface` annotation isn't mandatory, but it's good practice to use it when an interface is designed for that purpose. You can think of it like the `@Override` notation to indicate that a method is overridden.

3.3 Putting lambdas into practice: the execute-around pattern

Let's look at an example of how lambdas, together with behavior parameterization, can be used in practice to make your code more flexible and concise. A recurrent pattern in resource processing (for example, dealing with files or databases) is to open a resource, do some processing on it, and then close the resource. The setup and cleanup phases are always similar and surround the important code doing the processing. This is called the *execute-around* pattern, as illustrated in figure 3.2. For example, in the following code, the highlighted lines show the boilerplate code required to read one line from a file (note also that you use Java 7's try-with-resources statement, which already simplifies the code, because you don't have to close the resource explicitly):

```
public String processFile() throws IOException {
try (BufferedReader br =
            new BufferedReader(new FileReader("data.txt"))) {
        return br.readLine();
    }
}
```
This is the line that does useful work.

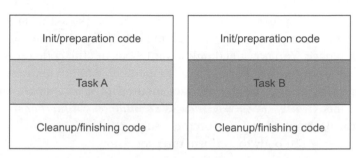

Figure 3.2 Tasks A and B are surrounded by boilerplate code responsible for preparation/cleanup.

3.3.1 Step 1: Remember behavior parameterization

This current code is limited. You can read only the first line of the file. What if you'd like to return the first two lines instead or even the word used most frequently? Ideally, you'd like to reuse the code doing setup and cleanup and tell the `processFile` method to perform different actions on the file. Does this sound familiar? Yes, you need to parameterize the behavior of `processFile`. You need a way to pass behavior to `processFile` so it can execute different behaviors using a `BufferedReader`.

Passing behavior is exactly what lambdas are for. What should the new `process-File` method look like if you want to read two lines at once? You need a lambda that takes a `BufferedReader` and returns a `String`. For example, here's how to print two lines of a `BufferedReader`:

```
String result
    = processFile((BufferedReader br) -> br.readLine() + br.readLine());
```

3.3.2 Step 2: Use a functional interface to pass behaviors

We explained earlier that lambdas can be used only in the context of a functional interface. You need to create one that matches the signature `BufferedReader ->` `String` and that may throw an `IOException`. Let's call this interface `BufferedReader-Processor`:

```
@FunctionalInterface
public interface BufferedReaderProcessor {
    String process(BufferedReader b) throws IOException;
}
```

You can now use this interface as the argument to your new `processFile` method:

```
public String processFile(BufferedReaderProcessor p) throws IOException {
    ...
}
```

3.3.3   *Step 3: Execute a behavior!*

Any lambdas of the form `BufferedReader -> String` can be passed as arguments, because they match the signature of the `process` method defined in the `Buffered-ReaderProcessor` interface. You now need only a way to execute the code represented by the lambda inside the body of `processFile`. Remember, lambda expressions let you provide the implementation of the abstract method of a functional interface directly inline, and they *treat the whole expression as an instance of a functional interface.* You can therefore call the method `process` on the resulting `BufferedReaderProcessor` object inside the `processFile` body to perform the processing:

```
public String processFile(BufferedReaderProcessor p) throws IOException {
    try (BufferedReader br =
                    new BufferedReader(new FileReader("data.txt"))) {
        return p.process(br);          ◁──┐
    }                                       Processes the
}                                           BufferedReader object
```

3.3.4   *Step 4: Pass lambdas*

You can now reuse the `processFile` method and process files in different ways by passing different lambdas.

The following shows processing one line:

```
String oneLine =
    processFile((BufferedReader br) -> br.readLine());
```

The following shows processing two lines:

```
String twoLines =
    processFile((BufferedReader br) -> br.readLine() + br.readLine());
```

Figure 3.3 summarizes the four steps taken to make the `processFile` method more flexible.

We've shown how you can make use of functional interfaces to pass lambdas. But you had to define your own interfaces. In the next section, we explore new interfaces that were added to Java 8 that you can reuse to pass multiple different lambdas.

```
public String processFile() throws IOException {            ①
    try (BufferedReader br =
            new BufferedReader(new FileReader("data.txt"))){
        return br.readLine();
    }
}
```

```
public interface BufferedReaderProcessor {                   ②
    String process(BufferedReader b) throws IOException;
}

public String processFile(BufferedReaderProcessor p) throws
IOException {

    ...

}
```

```
public String processFile(BufferedReaderProcessor p)         ③
throws IOException {
    try (BufferedReader br =
            new BufferedReader(new FileReader("data.txt"))){
        return p.process(br);
    }
}
```

```
String oneLine = processFile((BufferedReader br) ->          ④
                               br.readLine());

String twoLines = processFile((BufferedReader br) ->
                               br.readLine + br.readLine());
```

Figure 3.3 Four-step process to apply the execute-around pattern

3.4   *Using functional interfaces*

As you learned in section 3.2.1, a functional interface specifies exactly one abstract method. Functional interfaces are useful because the signature of the abstract method can describe the signature of a lambda expression. The signature of the abstract method of a functional interface is called a *function descriptor*. In order to use different lambda expressions, you need a set of functional interfaces that can describe common function descriptors. Several functional interfaces are already available in the Java API such as Comparable, Runnable, and Callable, which you saw in section 3.2.

The Java library designers for Java 8 have helped you by introducing several new functional interfaces inside the java.util.function package. We'll describe the interfaces Predicate, Consumer, and Function next. A more complete list is available in table 3.2 at the end of this section.

3.4.1   *Predicate*

The `java.util.function.Predicate<T>` interface defines an abstract method named `test` that accepts an object of generic type `T` and returns a `boolean`. It's exactly the same one that you created earlier, but it's available out of the box! You might want to use this interface when you need to represent a boolean expression that uses an object of type `T`. For example, you can define a lambda that accepts `String` objects, as shown in the following listing.

Listing 3.2   Working with a `Predicate`

```
@FunctionalInterface
public interface Predicate<T> {
    boolean test(T t);
}
public <T> List<T> filter(List<T> list, Predicate<T> p) {
    List<T> results = new ArrayList<>();
    for(T t: list) {
        if(p.test(t)) {
            results.add(t);
        }
    }
    return results;
}
Predicate<String> nonEmptyStringPredicate = (String s) -> !s.isEmpty();
List<String> nonEmpty = filter(listOfStrings, nonEmptyStringPredicate);
```

If you look up the Javadoc specification of the `Predicate` interface, you may notice additional methods such as and and or. Don't worry about them for now. We'll come back to these in section 3.8.

3.4.2   *Consumer*

The `java.util.function.Consumer<T>` interface defines an abstract method named `accept` that takes an object of generic type `T` and returns no result (`void`). You might use this interface when you need to access an object of type `T` and perform some operations on it. For example, you can use it to create a method `forEach`, which takes a list of `Integers` and applies an operation on each element of that list. In the following listing, you'll use this `forEach` method combined with a lambda to print all the elements of the list.

Listing 3.3   Working with a `Consumer`

```
@FunctionalInterface
public interface Consumer<T> {
    void accept(T t);
}
public <T> void forEach(List<T> list, Consumer<T> c) {
    for(T t: list) {
        c.accept(t);
    }
```

```
}
forEach(
        Arrays.asList(1,2,3,4,5),
        (Integer i) -> System.out.println(i)
      );
```

> **The lambda is the implementation of the accept method from Consumer.**

3.4.3 Function

The `java.util.function.Function<T, R>` interface defines an abstract method named `apply` that takes an object of generic type `T` as input and returns an object of generic type `R`. You might use this interface when you need to define a lambda that maps information from an input object to an output (for example, extracting the weight of an apple or mapping a string to its length). In the listing that follows, we show how you can use it to create a method `map` to transform a list of `Strings` into a list of `Integers` containing the length of each `String`.

Listing 3.4 Working with a `Function`

```
@FunctionalInterface
public interface Function<T, R> {
    R apply(T t);
}
public <T, R> List<R> map(List<T> list, Function<T, R> f) {
    List<R> result = new ArrayList<>();
    for(T t: list) {
        result.add(f.apply(t));
    }
    return result;
}
// [7, 2, 6]
List<Integer> l = map(
                    Arrays.asList("lambdas", "in", "action"),
                    (String s) -> s.length()
              );
```

> **Implements the apply method of Function**

PRIMITIVE SPECIALIZATIONS

We described three functional interfaces that are generic: `Predicate<T>`, `Consumer<T>`, and `Function<T, R>`. There are also functional interfaces that are specialized with certain types.

To refresh a little: every Java type is either a reference type (for example, `Byte`, `Integer`, `Object`, `List`) or a primitive type (for example, `int`, `double`, `byte`, `char`). But generic parameters (for example, the `T` in `Consumer<T>`) can be bound only to reference types. This is due to how generics are internally implemented.[2] As a result, in Java there's a mechanism to convert a primitive type into a corresponding reference type. This mechanism is called *boxing*. The opposite approach (converting a

---

[2] Some other languages, such as C#, don't have this restriction. Other languages, such as Scala, have only reference types. We revisit this issue in chapter 20.

reference type into a corresponding primitive type) is called *unboxing*. Java also has an *autoboxing* mechanism to facilitate the task for programmers: boxing and unboxing operations are done automatically. For example, this is why the following code is valid (an int gets boxed to an Integer):

```
List<Integer> list = new ArrayList<>();
for (int i = 300; i < 400; i++){
    list.add(i);
}
```

But this comes with a performance cost. Boxed values are a wrapper around primitive types and are stored on the heap. Therefore, boxed values use more memory and require additional memory lookups to fetch the wrapped primitive value.

Java 8 also added a specialized version of the functional interfaces we described earlier in order to avoid autoboxing operations when the inputs or outputs are primitives. For example, in the following code, using an IntPredicate avoids a boxing operation of the value 1000, whereas using a Predicate<Integer> would box the argument 1000 to an Integer object:

```
public interface IntPredicate {
    boolean test(int t);
}
IntPredicate evenNumbers = (int i) -> i % 2 == 0;        True (no boxing)
evenNumbers.test(1000);                                  ←———┘
Predicate<Integer> oddNumbers = (Integer i) -> i % 2 != 0;
oddNumbers.test(1000);                                   ←———┘ False (boxing)
```

In general, the appropriate primitive type precedes the names of functional interfaces that have a specialization for the input type parameter (for example, DoublePredicate, IntConsumer, LongBinaryOperator, IntFunction, and so on). The Function interface also has variants for the output type parameter: ToIntFunction<T>, IntToDouble-Function, and so on.

Table 3.2 summarizes the most commonly used functional interfaces available in the Java API and their function descriptors, along with their primitive specializations. Keep in mind that these are only a starter kit, and you can always create your own if needed (quiz 3.7 invents TriFunction for this purpose). Creating your own interfaces can also help when a domain-specific name will help with program comprehension and maintenance. Remember, the notation (T, U) -> R shows how to think about a function descriptor. The left side of the arrow is a list representing the types of the arguments, and the right side represents the types of the results. In this case, it represents a function with two arguments of respectively generic type T and U and that has a return type of R.

You've now seen a lot of functional interfaces that can be used to describe the signature of various lambda expressions. To check your understanding so far, try quiz 3.4.

Table 3.2   Common functional interfaces added in Java 8

Functional interface	Function descriptor	Primitive specializations
Predicate<T>	T -> boolean	IntPredicate, LongPredicate, DoublePredicate
Consumer<T>	T -> void	IntConsumer, LongConsumer, DoubleConsumer
Function<T, R>	T -> R	IntFunction<R>, IntToDoubleFunction, IntToLongFunction, LongFunction<R>, LongToDoubleFunction, LongToIntFunction, DoubleFunction<R>, DoubleToIntFunction, DoubleToLongFunction, ToIntFunction<T>, ToDoubleFunction<T>, ToLongFunction<T>
Supplier<T>	() -> T	BooleanSupplier, IntSupplier, LongSupplier, DoubleSupplier
UnaryOperator<T>	T -> T	IntUnaryOperator, LongUnaryOperator, DoubleUnaryOperator
BinaryOperator<T>	(T, T) -> T	IntBinaryOperator, LongBinaryOperator, DoubleBinaryOperator
BiPredicate<T, U>	(T, U) -> boolean	
BiConsumer<T, U>	(T, U) -> void	ObjIntConsumer<T>, ObjLongConsumer<T>, ObjDoubleConsumer<T>
BiFunction<T, U, R>	(T, U) -> R	ToIntBiFunction<T, U>, ToLongBiFunction<T, U>, ToDoubleBiFunction<T, U>

Quiz 3.4: Functional interfaces

What functional interfaces would you use for the following function descriptors (lambda-expression signatures)? You'll find most of the answers in table 3.2. As a further exercise, come up with valid lambda expressions that you can use with these functional interfaces.

1 T -> R
2 (int, int) -> int
3 T -> void

(continued)

   4 `() -> T`
   5 `(T, U) -> R`

Answers:

1 `Function<T, R>` is a good candidate. It's typically used for converting an object of type `T` into an object of type `R` (for example, `Function<Apple, Integer>` to extract the weight of an apple).
2 `IntBinaryOperator` has a single abstract method called `applyAsInt` representing a function descriptor `(int, int) -> int`.
3 `Consumer<T>` has a single abstract method called `accept` representing a function descriptor `T -> void`.
4 `Supplier<T>` has a single abstract method called `get` representing a function descriptor `() -> T`.
5 `BiFunction<T, U, R>` has a single abstract method called `apply` representing a function descriptor `(T, U) -> R`.

To summarize the discussion about functional interfaces and lambdas, table 3.3 provides a summary of use cases, examples of lambdas, and functional interfaces that can be used.

Table 3.3   Examples of lambdas with functional interfaces

Use case	Example of lambda	Matching functional interface
A boolean expression	`(List<String> list) -> list.isEmpty()`	`Predicate<List<String>>`
Creating objects	`() -> new Apple(10)`	`Supplier<Apple>`
Consuming from an object	`(Apple a) -> System.out.println(a.getWeight())`	`Consumer<Apple>`
Select/extract from an object	`(String s) -> s.length()`	`Function<String, Integer>` or `ToIntFunction<String>`
Combine two values	`(int a, int b) -> a * b`	`IntBinaryOperator`
Compare two objects	`(Apple a1, Apple a2) -> a1.getWeight().compareTo(a2.getWeight())`	`Comparator<Apple>` or `BiFunction<Apple, Apple, Integer>` or `ToIntBiFunction<Apple, Apple>`

What about exceptions, lambdas, and functional interfaces?

Note that none of the functional interfaces allow for a checked exception to be thrown. You have two options if you need the body of a lambda expression to throw an exception: define your own functional interface that declares the checked exception, or wrap the lambda body with a `try`/`catch` block.

For example, in section 3.3 we introduced a new functional interface `Buffered-ReaderProcessor` that explicitly declared an `IOException`:

```
@FunctionalInterface
public interface BufferedReaderProcessor {
    String process(BufferedReader b) throws IOException;
}
BufferedReaderProcessor p = (BufferedReader br) -> br.readLine();
```

But you may be using an API that expects a functional interface such as `Function<T, R>` and there's no option to create your own. You'll see in the next chapter that the Streams API makes heavy use of the functional interfaces from table 3.2. In this case, you can explicitly catch the checked exception:

```
Function<BufferedReader, String> f =
  (BufferedReader b) -> {
    try {
      return b.readLine();
    }
    catch(IOException e) {
      throw new RuntimeException(e);
    }
  };
```

You've now seen how to create lambdas and where and how to use them. Next, we'll explain some more advanced details: how lambdas are type checked by the compiler and rules you should be aware of, such as lambdas referencing local variables inside their body and void-compatible lambdas. There's no need to fully understand the next section right away, and you may wish to come back to it later and move on to section 3.6 about method references.

3.5 Type checking, type inference, and restrictions

When we first mentioned lambda expressions, we said that they let you generate an instance of a functional interface. Nonetheless, a lambda expression itself doesn't contain the information about which functional interface it's implementing. In order to have a more formal understanding of lambda expressions, you should know what the type of a lambda is.

3.5.1 Type checking

The type of a lambda is deduced from the context in which the lambda is used. The type expected for the lambda expression inside the context (for example, a method parameter that it's passed to or a local variable that it's assigned to) is called the *target type.* Let's look at an example to see what happens behind the scenes when you use a lambda expression. Figure 3.4 summarizes the type-checking process for the following code:

```
List<Apple> heavierThan150g =
        filter(inventory, (Apple apple) -> apple.getWeight() > 150);
```

The type-checking process is deconstructed as follows:

- First, you look up the declaration of the filter method.
- Second, it expects, as the second formal parameter, an object of type Predicate<Apple> (the target type).
- Third, Predicate<Apple> is a functional interface defining a single abstract method called test.
- Fourth, the test method describes a function descriptor that accepts an Apple and returns a boolean.
- Finally, any argument to the filter method needs to match this requirement.

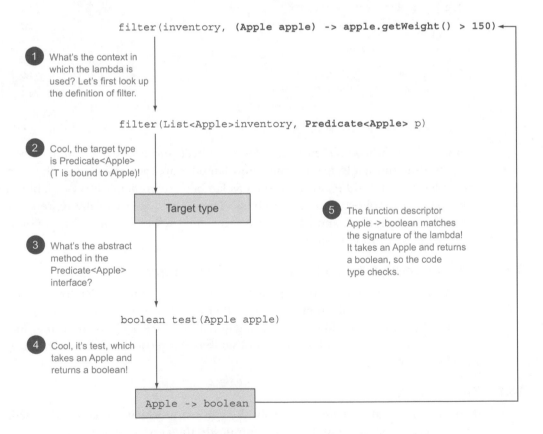

Figure 3.4   Deconstructing the type-checking process of a lambda expression

The code is valid because the lambda expression that we're passing also takes an `Apple` as parameter and returns a `boolean`. Note that if the lambda expression was throwing an exception, then the declared `throws` clause of the abstract method would also have to match.

3.5.2 *Same lambda, different functional interfaces*

Because of the idea of *target typing*, the same lambda expression can be associated with different functional interfaces if they have a compatible abstract method signature. For example, both interfaces `Callable` and `PrivilegedAction` described earlier represent functions that accept nothing and return a generic type `T`. The following two assignments are therefore valid:

```
Callable<Integer> c = () -> 42;
PrivilegedAction<Integer> p = () -> 42;
```

In this case the first assignment has target type `Callable<Integer>` and the second assignment has target type `PrivilegedAction<Integer>`.

In table 3.3 we showed a similar example; the same lambda can be used with multiple different functional interfaces:

```
Comparator<Apple> c1 =
   (Apple a1, Apple a2) -> a1.getWeight().compareTo(a2.getWeight());
ToIntBiFunction<Apple, Apple> c2 =
   (Apple a1, Apple a2) -> a1.getWeight().compareTo(a2.getWeight());
BiFunction<Apple, Apple, Integer> c3 =
   (Apple a1, Apple a2) -> a1.getWeight().compareTo(a2.getWeight());
```

> **Diamond operator**
>
> Those of you who are familiar with Java's evolution will recall that Java 7 had already introduced the idea of types being inferred from context with generic inference using the diamond operator (`<>`) (this idea can be found even earlier with generic methods). A given class-instance expression can appear in two or more different contexts, and the appropriate type argument will be inferred as exemplified here:
>
> ```
> List<String> listOfStrings = new ArrayList<>();
> List<Integer> listOfIntegers = new ArrayList<>();
> ```

> **Special void-compatibility rule**
>
> If a lambda has a statement expression as its body, it's compatible with a function descriptor that returns `void` (provided the parameter list is compatible, too). For example, both of the following lines are legal even though the method `add` of a `List` returns a `boolean` and not `void` as expected in the `Consumer` context (`T -> void`):
>
> ```
> // Predicate has a boolean return
> Predicate<String> p = (String s) -> list.add(s);
> // Consumer has a void return
> Consumer<String> b = (String s) -> list.add(s);
> ```

By now you should have a good understanding of when and where you're allowed to use lambda expressions. They can get their target type from an assignment context, method-invocation context (parameters and return), and a cast context. To check your knowledge, try quiz 3.5.

Quiz 3.5: Type checking—why won't the following code compile?
How could you fix the problem?

```
Object o = () -> { System.out.println("Tricky example"); };
```

Answer:

The context of the lambda expression is `Object` (the target type). But `Object` isn't a functional interface. To fix this you can change the target type to `Runnable`, which represents a function descriptor `() -> void`:

```
Runnable r = () -> { System.out.println("Tricky example"); };
```

You could also fix the problem by casting the lambda expression to `Runnable`, which explicitly provides a target type.

```
Object o = (Runnable) () -> { System.out.println("Tricky example"); };
```

This technique can be useful in the context of overloading with a method taking two different functional interfaces that have the same function descriptor. You can cast the lambda in order to explicitly disambiguate which method signature should be selected.

For example, the call `execute(() -> {})` using the method `execute`, as shown in the following, would be ambiguous, because both `Runnable` and `Action` have the same function descriptor:

```
public void execute(Runnable runnable) {
    runnable.run();
}
public void execute(Action<T> action) {
    action.act();
}
@FunctionalInterface
interface Action {
    void act();
}
```

But, you can explicitly disambiguate the call by using a cast expression: `execute ((Action) () -> {});`

You've seen how the target type can be used to check whether a lambda can be used in a particular context. It can also be used to do something slightly different: infer the types of the parameters of a lambda.

3.5.3 Type inference

You can simplify your code one step further. The Java compiler deduces what functional interface to associate with a lambda expression from its surrounding context (the target type), meaning it can also deduce an appropriate signature for the lambda because the function descriptor is available through the target type. The benefit is that the compiler has access to the types of the parameters of a lambda expression, and they can be omitted in the lambda syntax. The Java compiler infers the types of the parameters of a lambda as shown here:[3]

```
                                                         No explicit type on
                                                         the parameter apple
List<Apple> greenApples =
        filter(inventory, apple -> GREEN.equals(apple.getColor()));    ◁──┘
```

The benefits of code readability are more noticeable with lambda expressions that have several parameters. For example, here's how to create a `Comparator` object:

```
                                                       Without type inference
Comparator<Apple> c =
  (Apple a1, Apple a2) -> a1.getWeight().compareTo(a2.getWeight());   ◁──┘
Comparator<Apple> c =
  (a1, a2) -> a1.getWeight().compareTo(a2.getWeight());   ◁──── With type inference
```

Note that sometimes it's more readable to include the types explicitly, and sometimes it's more readable to exclude them. There's no rule for which way is better; developers must make their own choices about what makes their code more readable.

3.5.4 Using local variables

All the lambda expressions we've shown so far used only their arguments inside their body. But lambda expressions are also allowed to use *free variables* (variables that aren't the parameters and are defined in an outer scope) like anonymous classes can. They're called *capturing lambdas*. For example, the following lambda captures the variable `portNumber`:

```
int portNumber = 1337;
Runnable r = () -> System.out.println(portNumber);
```

Nonetheless, there's a small twist. There are some restrictions on what you can do with these variables. Lambdas are allowed to capture (to reference in their bodies) instance variables and static variables without restrictions. But when local variables are captured, they have to be explicitly declared `final` or be effectively `final`. Lambda expressions can capture local variables that are assigned to only once. (Note: capturing an instance variable can be seen as capturing the final local variable `this`.) For

---

[3] Note that when a lambda has a single parameter whose type is inferred, the parentheses surrounding the parameter name can also be omitted.

example, the following code doesn't compile because the variable `portNumber` is assigned to twice:

```
int portNumber = 1337;
Runnable r = () -> System.out.println(portNumber);     ◁─┐
portNumber = 31337;
```

Error: local variable portNumber is not final or effectively final.

RESTRICTIONS ON LOCAL VARIABLES

You may be asking yourself why local variables have these restrictions. First, there's a key difference in how instance and local variables are implemented behind the scenes. Instance variables are stored on the heap, whereas local variables live on the stack. If a lambda could access the local variable directly and the lambda was used in a thread, then the thread using the lambda could try to access the variable after the thread that allocated the variable had deallocated it. Hence, Java implements access to a free local variable as access to a copy of it, rather than access to the original variable. This makes no difference if the local variable is assigned to only once—hence the restriction.

Second, this restriction also discourages typical imperative programming patterns (which, as we explain in later chapters, prevent easy parallelization) that mutate an outer variable.

Closure

You may have heard of the term *closure* and may be wondering whether lambdas meet the definition of a closure (not to be confused with the Clojure programming language). To put it scientifically, a *closure* is an instance of a function that can reference nonlocal variables of that function with no restrictions. For example, a closure could be passed as argument to another function. It could also *access and modify* variables defined outside its scope. Now, Java 8 lambdas and anonymous classes do something similar to closures: they can be passed as argument to methods and can access variables outside their scope. But they have a restriction: they can't modify the content of local variables of a method in which the lambda is defined. Those variables have to be implicitly final. It helps to think that lambdas close over *values* rather than *variables*. As explained previously, this restriction exists because local variables live on the stack and are implicitly confined to the thread they're in. Allowing capture of mutable local variables opens new thread-unsafe possibilities, which are undesirable (instance variables are fine because they live on the heap, which is shared across threads).

We'll now describe another great feature that was introduced in Java 8 code: *method references*. Think of them as shorthand versions of certain lambdas.

3.6   *Method references*

Method references let you reuse existing method definitions and pass them like lambdas. In some cases they appear more readable and feel more natural than using lambda expressions. Here's our sorting example written with a method reference and a bit of help from the updated Java 8 API (we explore this example in more detail in section 3.7).

Before:

```
inventory.sort((Apple a1, Apple a2)
a1.getWeight().compareTo(a2.getWeight()));
```

After (using a method reference and `java.util.Comparator.comparing`):

```
inventory.sort(comparing(Apple::getWeight));
```
⟵—| **Your first method reference**

Don't worry about the new syntax and how things work. You'll learn that over the next few sections!

3.6.1 In a nutshell

Why should you care about method references? Method references can be seen as shorthand for lambdas calling only a specific method. The basic idea is that if a lambda represents "call this method directly," it's best to refer to the method by name rather than by a description of how to call it. Indeed, a method reference lets you create a lambda expression from an existing method implementation. But by referring to a method name explicitly, your code *can gain better readability*. How does it work? When you need a method reference, the target reference is placed before the delimiter `::` and the name of the method is provided after it. For example, `Apple::getWeight` is a method reference to the method `getWeight` defined in the `Apple` class. (Remember that no brackets are needed after `getWeight` because you're not calling it at the moment, you're merely quoting its name.) This method reference is shorthand for the lambda expression `(Apple apple) -> apple.getWeight()`. Table 3.4 gives a few more examples of possible method references in Java 8.

Table 3.4 Examples of lambdas and method reference equivalents

Lambda	Method reference equivalent
`(Apple apple) -> apple.getWeight()`	`Apple::getWeight`
`() -> Thread.currentThread().dumpStack()`	`Thread.currentThread()::dumpStack`
`(str, i) -> str.substring(i)`	`String::substring`
`(String s) -> System.out.println(s)` `(String s) -> this.isValidName(s)`	`System.out::println` `this::isValidName`

You can think of method references as syntactic sugar for lambdas that refer only to a single method because you write less to express the same thing.

RECIPE FOR CONSTRUCTING METHOD REFERENCES

There are three main kinds of method references:

1 A method reference to a *static method* (for example, the method `parseInt` of `Integer`, written `Integer::parseInt`)
2 A method reference to an instance method of an arbitrary type (for example, the method `length` of a `String`, written `String::length`)
3 A method reference to an *instance method of an existing object or expression* (for example, suppose you have a local variable `expensiveTransaction` that holds an object of type `Transaction`, which supports an instance method `getValue`; you can write `expensiveTransaction::getValue`)

The second and third kinds of method references may be a bit overwhelming at first. The idea with the second kind of method references, such as `String::length`, is that you're referring to a method to an object that will be supplied as one of the parameters of the lambda. For example, the lambda expression `(String s) -> s.toUpperCase()` can be rewritten as `String::toUpperCase`. But the third kind of method reference refers to a situation when you're calling a method in a lambda to an external object that already exists. For example, the lambda expression `() -> expensiveTransaction.getValue()` can be rewritten as `expensiveTransaction::getValue`. This third kind of method reference is particularly useful when you need to pass around a method defined as a private helper. For example, say you defined a helper method `isValidName`:

```
private boolean isValidName(String string) {
    return Character.isUpperCase(string.charAt(0));
}
```

You can now pass this method around in the context of a `Predicate<String>` using a method reference:

```
filter(words, this::isValidName)
```

To help you digest this new knowledge, the shorthand rules to refactor a lambda expression to an equivalent method reference follow simple recipes, shown in figure 3.5.

Note that there are also special forms of method references for constructors, array constructors, and super-calls. Let's apply method references in a concrete example. Say you'd like to sort a `List` of strings, ignoring case differences. The `sort` method on a `List` expects a `Comparator` as parameter. You saw earlier that `Comparator` describes a function descriptor with the signature `(T, T) -> int`. You can define a lambda expression that uses the method `compareToIgnoreCase` in the `String` class as follows (note that `compareToIgnoreCase` is predefined in the `String` class):

```
List<String> str = Arrays.asList("a","b","A","B");
str.sort((s1, s2) -> s1.compareToIgnoreCase(s2));
```

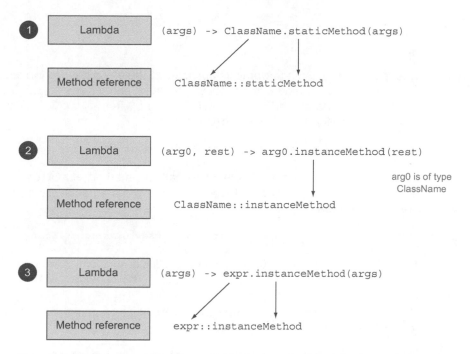

Figure 3.5 Recipes for constructing method references for three different types of lambda expressions

The lambda expression has a signature compatible with the function descriptor of Comparator. Using the recipes described previously, the example can also be written using a method reference; this results in more concise code, as follows:

```
List<String> str = Arrays.asList("a","b","A","B");
str.sort(String::compareToIgnoreCase);
```

Note that the compiler goes through a similar type-checking process as for lambda expressions to figure out whether a method reference is valid with a given functional interface. The signature of the method reference has to match the type of the context.

To check your understanding of method references, do try quiz 3.6!

Quiz 3.6: Method references

What are equivalent method references for the following lambda expressions?

1 ```
   ToIntFunction<String> stringToInt =
                (String s) -> Integer.parseInt(s);
   ```

2  ```
   BiPredicate<List<String>, String> contains =
                (list, element) -> list.contains(element);
   ```

3 ```
   Predicate<String> startsWithNumber =
                (String string) -> this .startsWithNumber(string);
   ```
   ```

(continued)

Answers:

1 This lambda expression forwards its argument to the static method `parseInt` of `Integer`. This method takes a `String` to parse and returns an `int`. As a result, the lambda can be rewritten using recipe ❶ from figure 3.5 (lambda expressions calling a static method) as follows:

```
ToIntFunction<String> stringToInt = Integer::parseInt;
```

2 This lambda uses its first argument to call the method `contains` on it. Because the first argument is of type `List`, you can use recipe ❷ from figure 3.5 as follows:

```
BiPredicate<List<String>, String> contains = List::contains;
```

This is because the target type describes a function descriptor (List<String>, String) -> boolean, and `List::contains` can be unpacked to that function descriptor.

3 This expression-style lambda invokes a private helper method. You can use recipe ❸ from figure 3.5 as follows:

```
Predicate<String> startsWithNumber = this::startsWithNumber
```

We've shown only how to reuse existing method implementations and create method references. But you can do something similar with constructors of a class.

3.6.2 *Constructor references*

You can create a reference to an existing constructor using its name and the keyword `new` as follows: `ClassName::new`. It works similarly to a reference to a static method. For example, suppose there's a zero-argument constructor. This fits the signature `() -> Apple` of `Supplier`; you can do the following:

```
Supplier<Apple> c1 = Apple::new;      ⟵  Constructor reference to the
Apple a1 = c1.get();                        default Apple() constructor
                                      ⟵  Calling Supplier's get method
                                          produces a new Apple.
```

which is equivalent to

```
Supplier<Apple> c1 = () -> new Apple();   ⟵  Lambda expression to create an
Apple a1 = c1.get();                            Apple using the default constructor
                                          ⟵  Calling Supplier's get method
                                              produces a new Apple.
```

If you have a constructor with signature `Apple(Integer weight)`, it fits the signature of the `Function` interface, so you can do this

```
Function<Integer, Apple> c2 = Apple::new;
Apple a2 = c2.apply(110);
```

Constructor reference to Apple (Integer weight)

Calling Function's apply method with a given weight produces an Apple.

which is equivalent to

Lambda expression to create an Apple with a given weight

```
Function<Integer, Apple> c2 = (weight) -> new Apple(weight);
Apple a2 = c2.apply(110);
```

Calling Function's apply method with a given weight produces a new Apple object.

In the following code, each element of a List of Integers is passed to the constructor of Apple using a similar map method we defined earlier, resulting in a List of apples with various weights:

```
List<Integer> weights = Arrays.asList(7, 3, 4, 10);
List<Apple> apples = map(weights, Apple::new);
public List<Apple> map(List<Integer> list, Function<Integer, Apple> f) {
    List<Apple> result = new ArrayList<>();
    for(Integer i: list) {
        result.add(f.apply(i));
    }
    return result;
}
```

Passing a constructor reference to the map method

If you have a two-argument constructor, Apple(Color color, Integer weight), it fits the signature of the BiFunction interface, so you can do this:

```
BiFunction<Color, Integer, Apple> c3 = Apple::new;
Apple a3 = c3.apply(GREEN, 110);
```

Constructor reference to Apple (Color color, Integer weight)

BiFunction's apply method with a given color and weight produces a new Apple object.

which is equivalent to

Lambda expression to create an Apple with a given color and weight

```
BiFunction<String, Integer, Apple> c3 =
    (color, weight) -> new Apple(color, weight);
Apple a3 = c3.apply(GREEN, 110);
```

BiFunction's apply method with a given color and weight produces a new Apple object.

The capability of referring to a constructor without instantiating it enables interesting applications. For example, you can use a Map to associate constructors with a string value. You can then create a method giveMeFruit that, given a String and an Integer, can create different types of fruits with different weights, as follows:

```
static Map<String, Function<Integer, Fruit>> map = new HashMap<>();
static {
    map.put("apple", Apple::new);
```

```
        map.put("orange", Orange::new);
        // etc...
}
public static Fruit giveMeFruit(String fruit, Integer weight){
    return map.get(fruit.toLowerCase())
            .apply(weight);
}
```

Get a Function<Integer, Fruit> from the map

Function's apply method with an Integer weight parameter creates the requested Fruit.

To check your understanding of method and constructor references, try out quiz 3.7.

Quiz 3.7: Constructor references

You saw how to transform zero-, one-, and two-argument constructors into constructor references. What would you need to do in order to use a constructor reference for a three-argument constructor such as `RGB(int, int, int)`?

Answer:

You saw that the syntax for a constructor reference is `ClassName::new`, so in this case it's `RGB::new`. But you need a functional interface that will match the signature of that constructor reference. Because there isn't one in the functional interface starter set, you can create your own:

```
public interface TriFunction<T, U, V, R> {
    R apply(T t, U u, V v);
}
```

And you can now use the constructor reference as follows:

```
TriFunction<Integer, Integer, Integer, RGB> colorFactory = RGB::new;
```

We've gone through a lot of new information: lambdas, functional interfaces, and method references. We'll put it all into practice in the next section.

3.7   *Putting lambdas and method references into practice*

To wrap up this chapter and our discussion on lambdas, we'll continue with our initial problem of sorting a list of `Apples` with different ordering strategies. And we'll show how you can progressively evolve a naïve solution into a concise solution, using all the concepts and features explained so far in the book: behavior parameterization, anonymous classes, lambda expressions, and method references. The final solution we'll work toward is the following (note that all source code is available on the book's website: www.manning.com/books/modern-java-in-action):

```
inventory.sort(comparing(Apple::getWeight));
```

3.7.1   *Step 1: Pass code*

You're lucky; the Java 8 API already provides you with a sort method available on List so you don't have to implement it. The hard part is done! But how can you pass an ordering strategy to the sort method? Well, the sort method has the following signature:

```
void sort(Comparator<? super E> c)
```

It expects a Comparator object as argument to compare two Apples! This is how you can pass different strategies in Java: they have to be wrapped in an object. We say that the *behavior* of sort is *parameterized*: its behavior will be different based on different ordering strategies passed to it.

Your first solution looks like this:

```
public class AppleComparator implements Comparator<Apple> {
        public int compare(Apple a1, Apple a2){
                return a1.getWeight().compareTo(a2.getWeight());
        }
}
inventory.sort(new AppleComparator());
```

3.7.2   *Step 2: Use an anonymous class*

Rather than implementing Comparator for the purpose of instantiating it once, you saw that you could use an *anonymous class* to improve your solution:

```
inventory.sort(new Comparator<Apple>() {
    public int compare(Apple a1, Apple a2){
        return a1.getWeight().compareTo(a2.getWeight());
    }
});
```

3.7.3   *Step 3: Use lambda expressions*

But your current solution is still verbose. Java 8 introduced lambda expressions, which provide a lightweight syntax to achieve the same goal: *passing code.* You saw that a lambda expression can be used where a *functional interface* is expected. As a reminder, a functional interface is an interface defining only one abstract method. The signature of the abstract method (called *function descriptor*) can describe the signature of a lambda expression. In this case, the Comparator represents a function descriptor (T, T) -> int. Because you're using Apples, it represents more specifically (Apple, Apple) -> int. Your new improved solution looks therefore as follows:

```
inventory.sort((Apple a1, Apple a2)
                -> a1.getWeight().compareTo(a2.getWeight())
);
```

We explained that the Java compiler could *infer the types* of the parameters of a lambda expression by using the context in which the lambda appears. You can therefore rewrite your solution as follows:

```
inventory.sort((a1, a2) -> a1.getWeight().compareTo(a2.getWeight()));
```

Can you make your code even more readable? Comparator includes a static helper method called comparing that takes a Function extracting a Comparable key and produces a Comparator object (we explain why interfaces can have static methods in chapter 13). It can be used as follows (note that you now pass a lambda with only one argument; the lambda specifies how to extract the key for comparison from an Apple):

```
Comparator<Apple> c = Comparator.comparing((Apple a) -> a.getWeight());
```

You can now rewrite your solution in a slightly more compact form:

```
import static java.util.Comparator.comparing;
inventory.sort(comparing(apple -> apple.getWeight()));
```

3.7.4 *Step 4: Use method references*

We explained that method references are syntactic sugar for lambda expressions that forwards their arguments. You can use a method reference to make your code slightly less verbose (assuming a static import of java.util.Comparator.comparing):

```
inventory.sort(comparing(Apple::getWeight));
```

Congratulations, this is your final solution! Why is this better than code prior to Java 8? It's not only because it's shorter; it's also obvious what it means. The code reads like the problem statement "sort inventory comparing the weight of the apples."

3.8   *Useful methods to compose lambda expressions*

Several functional interfaces in the Java 8 API contain convenience methods. Specifically, many functional interfaces such as Comparator, Function, and Predicate that are used to pass lambda expressions provide methods that allow composition. What does this mean? In practice it means you can combine several simple lambda expressions to build more complicated ones. For example, you can combine two predicates into a larger predicate that performs an or operation between the two predicates. Moreover, you can also compose functions such that the result of one becomes the input of another function. You may wonder how it's possible that there are additional methods in a functional interface. (After all, this goes against the definition of a functional interface!) The trick is that the methods that we'll introduce are called *default methods* (they're not abstract methods). We explain them in detail in chapter 13. For now, trust us and read chapter 13 later, when you want to find out more about default methods and what you can do with them.

3.8.1 Composing Comparators

You've seen that you can use the static method `Comparator.comparing` to return a `Comparator` based on a `Function` that extracts a key for comparison as follows:

```
Comparator<Apple> c = Comparator.comparing(Apple::getWeight);
```

REVERSED ORDER

What if you wanted to sort the apples by decreasing weight? There's no need to create a different instance of a `Comparator`. The interface includes a default method reversed that reverses the ordering of a given comparator. You can modify the previous example to sort the apples by decreasing weight by reusing the initial `Comparator`:

```
inventory.sort(comparing(Apple::getWeight).reversed());
```
← **Sorts by decreasing weight**

CHAINING COMPARATORS

This is all nice, but what if you find two apples that have the same weight? Which apple should have priority in the sorted list? You may want to provide a second `Comparator` to further refine the comparison. For example, after two apples are compared based on their weight, you may want to sort them by country of origin. The thenComparing method allows you to do that. It takes a function as parameter (like the method comparing) and provides a second `Comparator` if two objects are considered equal using the initial `Comparator`. You can solve the problem elegantly again as follows:

```
inventory.sort(comparing(Apple::getWeight)
        .reversed()
        .thenComparing(Apple::getCountry));
```
Sorts by decreasing weight

← **Sorts further by country when two apples have same weight**

3.8.2 Composing Predicates

The `Predicate` interface includes three methods that let you reuse an existing `Predicate` to create more complicated ones: negate, and, and or. For example, you can use the method negate to return the negation of a `Predicate`, such as an apple that is not red:

```
Predicate<Apple> notRedApple = redApple.negate();
```
← **Produces the negation of the existing Predicate object redApple**

You may want to combine two lambdas to say that an apple is both red and heavy with the and method:

Chains two predicates to produce another Predicate object

```
Predicate<Apple> redAndHeavyApple =
    redApple.and(apple -> apple.getWeight() > 150);
```
←

You can combine the resulting predicate one step further to express apples that are red and heavy (above 150 g) or only green apples:

```
Predicate<Apple> redAndHeavyAppleOrGreen =
    redApple.and(apple -> apple.getWeight() > 150)
            .or(apple -> GREEN.equals(a.getColor()));
```
Chains three predicates to construct a more complex Predicate object

Why is this great? From simpler lambda expressions you can represent more complicated lambda expressions that still read like the problem statement! Note that the precedence of methods and and or in the chain is from left to right—there is no equivalent of bracketing. So a.or(b).and(c) must be read as (a || b) && c. Similarly, a.and(b).or(c) must be read as as (a && b) || c.

3.8.3 *Composing Functions*

Finally, you can also compose lambda expressions represented by the Function interface. The Function interface comes with two default methods for this, andThen and compose, which both return an instance of Function.

The method andThen returns a function that first applies a given function to an input and then applies another function to the result of that application. For example, given a function f that increments a number (x -> x + 1) and another function g that multiples a number by 2, you can combine them to create a function h that first increments a number and then multiplies the result by 2:

```
Function<Integer, Integer> f = x -> x + 1;
Function<Integer, Integer> g = x -> x * 2;
Function<Integer, Integer> h = f.andThen(g);
int result = h.apply(1);
```
In mathematics you'd write g(f(x)) or (g o f)(x).

This returns 4.

You can also use the method compose similarly to first apply the function given as argument to compose and then apply the function to the result. For example, in the previous example using compose, it would mean f(g(x)) instead of g(f(x)) using andThen:

```
Function<Integer, Integer> f = x -> x + 1;
Function<Integer, Integer> g = x -> x * 2;
Function<Integer, Integer> h = f.compose(g);
int result = h.apply(1);
```
In mathematics you'd write f(g(x)) or (f o g)(x).

This returns 3.

Figure 3.6 illustrates the difference between andThen and compose.

This all sounds a bit too abstract. How can you use these in practice? Let's say you have various utility methods that do text transformation on a letter represented as a String:

```
public class Letter{
    public static String addHeader(String text) {
        return "From Raoul, Mario and Alan: " + text;
    }
```

```
    public static String addFooter(String text) {
        return text + " Kind regards";
    }
    public static String checkSpelling(String text) {
        return text.replaceAll("labda", "lambda");
    }
}
```

f.andThen(g)

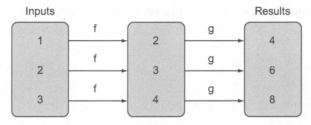

```
Function<Integer, Integer> f = x -> x + 1;
Function<Integer, Integer> g = x -> x * 2;
```

f.compose(g)

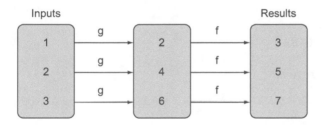

Figure 3.6   Using andThen **versus** compose

You can now create various transformation pipelines by composing the utility methods. For example, creating a pipeline that first adds a header, then checks spelling, and finally adds a footer, as shown in the following (and as illustrated in figure 3.7):

```
Function<String, String> addHeader = Letter::addHeader;
Function<String, String> transformationPipeline
  = addHeader.andThen(Letter::checkSpelling)
          .andThen(Letter::addFooter);
```

Transformation pipeline

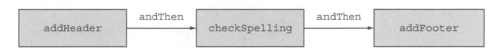

Figure 3.7   A transformation pipeline using andThen

A second pipeline might be only adding a header and footer without checking for spelling:

```
Function<String, String> addHeader = Letter::addHeader;
Function<String, String> transformationPipeline
  = addHeader.andThen(Letter::addFooter);
```

3.9   *Similar ideas from mathematics*

If you feel comfortable with high school mathematics, this section gives another viewpoint of the idea of lambda expressions and passing around functions. Feel free to skip it; nothing else in the book depends on it. But you may enjoy seeing another perspective.

3.9.1   *Integration*

Suppose you have a (mathematical, not Java) function f, perhaps defined by

$$f(x) = x + 10$$

Then, one question that's often asked (at school and in science and engineering degrees) is to find the area beneath the function when drawn on paper (counting the x-axis as the zero line). For example, you write

$$\int_3^7 f(x)\,dx \quad \text{or} \quad \int_3^7 (x+10)\,dx$$

for the area shown in figure 3.8.

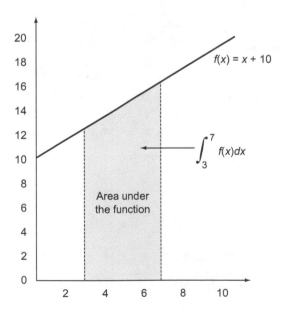

Figure 3.8   **Area under the function**
f (x) = x + 10 for x from 3 to 7

In this example, the function f is a straight line, and so you can easily work out this area by the trapezium method (drawing triangles and rectangles) to discover the solution:

$$1/2 \times ((3 + 10) + (7 + 10)) \times (7 - 3) = 60$$

Now, how might you express this in Java? Your first problem is reconciling the strange notation like the integration symbol or dy/dx with familiar programming language notation.

Indeed, thinking from first principles you need a method, perhaps called integrate, that takes three arguments: one is f, and the others are the limits (3.0 and 7.0 here). Thus, you want to write in Java something that looks like this, where the function f is passed as an argument:

```
integrate(f, 3, 7)
```

Note that you can't write something as simple as

```
integrate(x + 10, 3, 7)
```

for two reasons. First, the scope of x is unclear, and second, this would pass a value of x+10 to integrate instead of passing the function f.

Indeed, the secret role of dx in mathematics is to say "that function taking argument x whose result is x + 10."

3.9.2 Connecting to Java 8 lambdas

As we mentioned earlier, Java 8 uses the notation (double x) -> x + 10 (a lambda expression) for exactly this purpose; hence you can write

```
integrate((double x) -> x + 10, 3, 7)
```

or

```
integrate((double x) -> f(x), 3, 7)
```

or, using a method reference as mentioned earlier,

```
integrate(C::f, 3, 7)
```

if C is a class containing f as a static method. The idea is that you're passing the code for f to the method integrate.

You may now wonder how you'd write the method integrate itself. Continue to suppose that f is a linear function (straight line). You'd probably like to write in a form similar to mathematics:

```
public double integrate((double -> double) f, double a, double b) {      <──┐
    return (f(a) + f(b)) * (b - a) / 2.0
}                                      Incorrect Java code! (You can't write
                                       functions as you do in mathematics.)
```

But because lambda expressions can be used only in a context expecting a functional interface (in this case, DoubleFunction[4]), you have to write it the following way:

```
public double integrate(DoubleFunction<Double> f, double a, double b) {
    return (f.apply(a) + f.apply(b)) * (b - a) / 2.0;
}
```

or using DoubleUnaryOperator, which also avoids boxing the result:

```
public double integrate(DoubleUnaryOperator f, double a, double b) {
    return (f.applyAsDouble(a) + f.applyAsDouble(b)) * (b - a) / 2.0;
}
```

As a side remark, it's a bit of a shame that you have to write f.apply(a) instead of simply writing f(a) as in mathematics, but Java just can't get away from the view that everything is an object instead of the idea of a function being truly independent!

Summary

- A *lambda expression* can be understood as a kind of anonymous function: it doesn't have a name, but it has a list of parameters, a body, a return type, and also possibly a list of exceptions that can be thrown.
- Lambda expressions let you pass code concisely.
- A *functional interface* is an interface that declares exactly one abstract method.
- Lambda expressions can be used only where a functional interface is expected.
- Lambda expressions let you provide the implementation of the abstract method of a functional interface directly inline and *treat the whole expression as an instance of a functional interface.*
- Java 8 comes with a list of common functional interfaces in the java.util .function package, which includes Predicate<T>, Function<T, R>, Supplier<T>, Consumer<T>, and BinaryOperator<T>, described in table 3.2.
- Primitive specializations of common generic functional interfaces such as Predicate<T> and Function<T, R> can be used to avoid boxing operations: IntPredicate, IntToLongFunction, and so on.
- The execute-around pattern (for when you need to execute some given behavior in the middle of boilerplate code that's necessary in a method, for example, resource allocation and cleanup) can be used with lambdas to gain additional flexibility and reusability.
- The type expected for a lambda expression is called the *target* type.
- Method references let you reuse an existing method implementation and pass it around directly.
- Functional interfaces such as Comparator, Predicate, and Function have several default methods that can be used to combine lambda expressions.

---

[4] Using DoubleFunction<Double> is more efficient than using Function<Double,Double> as it avoids boxing the result.

Part 2

Functional-style data processing with streams

The second part of this book is a deep exploration of the new Streams API, which lets you write powerful code that processes a collection of data in a declarative way. By the end of this second part, you'll have a full understanding of what streams are and how you can use them in your codebase to process a collection of data concisely and efficiently.

Chapter 4 introduces the concept of a stream and explains how it compares with a collection.

Chapter 5 investigates in detail the stream operations available to express sophisticated data-processing queries. You'll look at many patterns such as filtering, slicing, finding, matching, mapping, and reducing.

Chapter 6 covers collectors—a feature of the Streams API that lets you express even more complex data-processing queries.

In chapter 7, you'll learn about how streams can automatically run in parallel and leverage your multicore architectures. In addition, you'll learn about various pitfalls to avoid when using parallel streams correctly and effectively.

Introducing streams

4

This chapter covers

- What is a stream?
- Collections versus streams
- Internal versus external iteration
- Intermediate versus terminal operations

What would you do without collections in Java? Nearly every Java application *makes* and *processes* collections. Collections are fundamental to many programming tasks: they let you group and process data. To illustrate collections in action, imagine you are tasked to create a collection of dishes to represent a menu to calculate different queries. For example, you may want to find out the total number of calories for the menu. Or, you may need to filter the menu to select only low-calorie dishes for a special healthy menu. But despite collections being necessary for almost any Java application, manipulating collections is far from perfect:

- Much business logic entails database-like operations such as *grouping* a list of dishes by category (for example, all vegetarian dishes) or *finding* the most expensive dish. How many times do you find yourself re-implementing these operations using iterators? Most databases let you specify such operations declaratively. For example, the following SQL query lets you select (or "filter") the names of dishes that are low in calories: SELECT name FROM dishes WHERE calorie < 400. As you can see, in SQL you don't need to implement *how* to filter using the calorie attribute of a dish (as you would with Java collections, for example, using an iterator and an accumulator). Instead, you write *what* you want as result. This basic idea means that you worry less about how to explicitly implement such queries—it's handled for you! Why can't you do something similar with collections?

- How would you process a large collection of elements? To gain performance you'd need to process it in parallel and use multicore architectures. But writing parallel code is complicated in comparison to working with iterators. In addition, it's no fun to debug!

What could the Java language designers do to save your precious time and make your life as programmers easier? You may have guessed: the answer is *streams*.

4.1   *What are streams?*

Streams are an update to the Java API that let you manipulate collections of data in a declarative way (you express a query rather than code an ad hoc implementation for it). For now you can think of them as fancy iterators over a collection of data. In addition, streams can be processed in parallel *transparently*, without you having to write any multithreaded code! We explain in detail in chapter 7 how streams and parallelization work. To see the benefits of using streams, compare the following code to return the names of dishes that are low in calories, sorted by number of calories—first in Java 7 and then in Java 8 using streams. Don't worry about the Java 8 code too much; we explain it in detail in the next sections!

Before (Java 7):

```
List<Dish> lowCaloricDishes = new ArrayList<>();       Filters the elements
for(Dish dish: menu) {                                 using an accumulator
    if(dish.getCalories() < 400) {          ◄──────
        lowCaloricDishes.add(dish);
    }                                                             Sorts the
}                                                                 dishes with an
Collections.sort(lowCaloricDishes, new Comparator<Dish>() {  ◄──┘ anonymous class
    public int compare(Dish dish1, Dish dish2) {
        return Integer.compare(dish1.getCalories(), dish2.getCalories());
    }
});
List<String> lowCaloricDishesName = new ArrayList<>();     Processes the
for(Dish dish: lowCaloricDishes) {                         sorted list to select
    lowCaloricDishesName.add(dish.getName());       ◄──── the names of dishes
}
```

In this code you use a "garbage variable," lowCaloricDishes. Its only purpose is to act as an intermediate throwaway container. In Java 8, this implementation detail is pushed into the library where it belongs.

After (Java 8):

```
import static java.util.Comparator.comparing;
import static java.util.stream.Collectors.toList;
List<String> lowCaloricDishesName =
                menu.stream()
                    .filter(d -> d.getCalories() < 400)
                    .sorted(comparing(Dish::getCalories))
                    .map(Dish::getName)
                    .collect(toList());
```

Selects dishes that are below 400 calories

Sorts them by calories

Stores all the names in a List

Extracts the names of these dishes

To exploit a multicore architecture and execute this code in parallel, you need only to change stream() to parallelStream():

```
List<String> lowCaloricDishesName =
                menu.parallelStream()
                    .filter(d -> d.getCalories() < 400)
                    .sorted(comparing(Dishes::getCalories))
                    .map(Dish::getName)
                    .collect(toList());
```

You may be wondering what exactly happens when you invoke the method parallel-Stream. How many threads are being used? What are the performance benefits? Should you use this method at all? Chapter 7 covers these questions in detail. For now, you can see that the new approach offers several immediate benefits from a software engineering point of view:

- The code is written in a *declarative way*: you specify *what* you want to achieve (*filter* dishes that are *low* in calories) as opposed to specifying *how* to implement an operation (using control-flow blocks such as loops and if conditions). As you saw in the previous chapter, this approach, together with behavior parameterization, enables you to cope with changing requirements: you could easily create an additional version of your code to filter high-calorie dishes using a lambda expression, without having to copy and paste code. Another way to think about the benefit of this approach is that the threading model is decoupled from the query itself. Because you are providing a recipe for a query, it could be executed sequentially or in parallel. You will learn more about this in chapter 7.
- You chain together several building-block operations to express a complicated data-processing pipeline (you chain the filter by linking sorted, map, and collect operations, as illustrated in figure 4.1) while keeping your code readable and its intent clear. The result of the filter is passed to the sorted method, which is then passed to the map method and then to the collect method.

Because operations such as filter (or sorted, map, and collect) are available as *high-level building blocks* that don't depend on a specific threading model, their internal implementation could be single-threaded or could potentially maximize your multicore

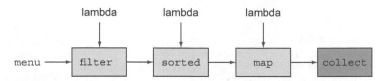

Figure 4.1   Chaining stream operations forming a stream pipeline

architecture transparently! In practice, this means you no longer have to worry about threads and locks to figure out how to parallelize certain data processing tasks: the Streams API does it for you!

The new Streams API is expressive. For example, after reading this chapter and chapters 5 and 6, you'll be able to write code like the following:

```
Map<Dish.Type, List<Dish>> dishesByType =
    menu.stream().collect(groupingBy(Dish::getType));
```

This particular example is explained in detail in chapter 6. It groups dishes by their types inside a `Map`. For example, the `Map` may contain the following result:

```
{FISH=[prawns, salmon],
 OTHER=[french fries, rice, season fruit, pizza],
 MEAT=[pork, beef, chicken]}
```

Now consider how you'd implement this with the typical imperative programming approach using loops. But don't waste too much of your time. Instead, embrace the power of streams in this and the following chapters!

> ### Other libraries: Guava, Apache, and lambdaj
>
> There have been many attempts at providing Java programmers with better libraries to manipulate collections. For example, Guava is a popular library created by Google. It provides additional container classes such as multimaps and multisets. The Apache Commons Collections library provides similar features. Finally, lambdaj, written by Mario Fusco, coauthor of this book, provides many utilities to manipulate collections in a declarative manner, inspired by functional programming.
>
> Now, Java 8 comes with its own official library for manipulating collections in a more declarative style.

To summarize, the Streams API in Java 8 lets you write code that's

- *Declarative*—More concise and readable
- *Composable*—Greater flexibility
- *Parallelizable*—Better performance

For the remainder of this chapter and the next, we'll use the following domain for our examples: a menu that's nothing more than a list of dishes

```
List<Dish> menu = Arrays.asList(
    new Dish("pork", false, 800, Dish.Type.MEAT),
    new Dish("beef", false, 700, Dish.Type.MEAT),
    new Dish("chicken", false, 400, Dish.Type.MEAT),
    new Dish("french fries", true, 530, Dish.Type.OTHER),
    new Dish("rice", true, 350, Dish.Type.OTHER),
    new Dish("season fruit", true, 120, Dish.Type.OTHER),
    new Dish("pizza", true, 550, Dish.Type.OTHER),
    new Dish("prawns", false, 300, Dish.Type.FISH),
    new Dish("salmon", false, 450, Dish.Type.FISH) );
```

where a Dish is an immutable class defined as

```
public class Dish {
    private final String name;
    private final boolean vegetarian;
    private final int calories;
    private final Type type;
    public Dish(String name, boolean vegetarian, int calories, Type type) {
        this.name = name;
        this.vegetarian = vegetarian;
        this.calories = calories;
        this.type = type;
    }
    public String getName() {
        return name;
    }
    public boolean isVegetarian() {
        return vegetarian;
    }
    public int getCalories() {
        return calories;
    }
    public Type getType() {
        return type;
    }
    @Override
    public String toString() {
        return name;
    }
    public enum Type { MEAT, FISH, OTHER }
}
```

We'll now explore how you can use the Streams API in more detail. We'll compare streams to collections and provide some background. In the next chapter, we'll investigate in detail the stream operations available to express sophisticated data processing queries. We'll look at many patterns such as filtering, slicing, finding, matching, mapping, and reducing. There will be many quizzes and exercises to try to solidify your understanding.

Next, we'll discuss how you can create and manipulate numeric streams (for example, to generate a stream of even numbers or Pythagorean triples). Finally, we'll discuss how you can create streams from different sources, such as from a file. We'll also discuss how to generate streams with an infinite number of elements—something you definitely can't do with collections!

4.2   Getting started with streams

We start our discussion of streams with collections, because that's the simplest way to begin working with streams. Collections in Java 8 support a new `stream` method that returns a stream (the interface definition is available in `java.util.stream.Stream`). You'll later see that you can also get streams in various other ways (for example, generating stream elements from a numeric range or from I/O resources).

First, what exactly is a *stream*? A short definition is "a sequence of elements from a source that supports data-processing operations." Let's break down this definition step-by-step:

- *Sequence of elements*—Like a collection, a stream provides an interface to a sequenced set of values of a specific element type. Because collections are data structures, they're mostly about storing and accessing elements with specific time/space complexities (for example, an `ArrayList` versus a `LinkedList`). But streams are about expressing computations such as `filter`, `sorted`, and `map`, which you saw earlier. Collections are about data; streams are about computations. We explain this idea in greater detail in the coming sections.

- *Source*—Streams consume from a data-providing source such as collections, arrays, or I/O resources. Note that generating a stream from an ordered collection preserves the ordering. The elements of a stream coming from a list will have the same order as the list.

- *Data-processing operations*—Streams support database-like operations and common operations from functional programming languages to manipulate data, such as `filter`, `map`, `reduce`, `find`, `match`, `sort`, and so on. Stream operations can be executed either sequentially or in parallel.

In addition, stream operations have two important characteristics:

- *Pipelining*—Many stream operations return a stream themselves, allowing operations to be chained to form a larger pipeline. This enables certain optimizations that we explain in the next chapter, such as *laziness* and *short-circuiting*. A pipeline of operations can be viewed as a database-like query on the data source.

- *Internal iteration*—In contrast to collections, which are iterated explicitly using an iterator, stream operations do the iteration behind the scenes for you. We briefly mentioned this idea in chapter 1 and will return to it later in the next section.

Let's look at a code example to explain all of these ideas:

Gets a stream from menu (the list of dishes)

```
import static java.util.stream.Collectors.toList;
List<String> threeHighCaloricDishNames =
    menu.stream()
        .filter(dish -> dish.getCalories() > 300)
        .map(Dish::getName)
        .limit(3)
        .collect(toList());
System.out.println(threeHighCaloricDishNames);
```

Creates a pipeline of operations: first filter high-calorie dishes

Gets the names of the dishes

Selects only the first three

Stores the results in another List

Gives results [pork, beef, chicken]

In this example, you first get a stream from the list of dishes by calling the `stream` method on `menu`. The *data source* is the list of dishes (the menu) and it provides *a sequence of elements* to the stream. Next, you apply a series of *data-processing operations* on the stream: `filter`, `map`, `limit`, and `collect`. All these operations except `collect` return another stream so they can be connected to form a *pipeline*, which can be viewed as a query on the source. Finally, the `collect` operation starts processing the pipeline to return a result (it's different because it returns something other than a stream—here, a List). No result is produced, and indeed no element from `menu` is even selected, until `collect` is invoked. You can think of it as if the method invocations in the chain are queued up until `collect` is called. Figure 4.2 shows the sequence of stream operations: `filter`, `map`, `limit`, and `collect`, each of which is briefly described here:

- `filter`—Takes a lambda to exclude certain elements from the stream. In this case, you select dishes that have more than 300 calories by passing the lambda `d -> d.getCalories() > 300`.
- `map`—Takes a lambda to transform an element into another one or to extract information. In this case, you extract the name for each dish by passing the method reference `Dish::getName`, which is equivalent to the lambda `d -> d.getName()`.
- `limit`—Truncates a stream to contain no more than a given number of elements.
- `collect`—Converts a stream into another form. In this case you convert the stream into a list. It looks like a bit of magic; we'll describe how `collect` works in more detail in chapter 6. At the moment, you can see `collect` as an operation that takes as an argument various recipes for accumulating the elements of a stream into a summary result. Here, `toList()` describes a recipe for converting a stream into a list.

Notice how the code we described is different than what you'd write if you were to process the list of menu items step-by-step. First, you use a much more declarative style

Menu stream

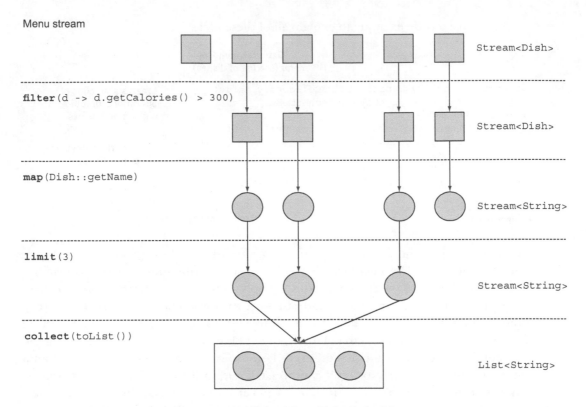

Figure 4.2   Filtering a menu using a stream to find out three high-calorie dish names

to process the data in the menu where you say *what* needs to be done: "Find names of three high-calorie dishes." You don't implement the filtering (`filter`), extracting (`map`), or truncating (`limit`) functionalities; they're available through the Streams library. As a result, the Streams API has more flexibility to decide how to optimize this pipeline. For example, the filtering, extracting, and truncating steps could be merged into a single pass and stop as soon as three dishes are found. We show an example to demonstrate that in the next chapter.

Let's stand back a little and examine the conceptual differences between the Collections API and the new Streams API before we explore in more detail what operations you can perform with a stream.

4.3   *Streams vs. collections*

Both the existing Java notion of collections and the new notion of streams provide interfaces to data structures representing a sequenced set of values of the element type. By *sequenced*, we mean that we commonly step through the values in turn rather than randomly accessing them in any order. What's the difference?

We'll start with a visual metaphor. Consider a movie stored on a DVD. This is a collection (perhaps of bytes or of frames—we don't care which here) because it contains the whole data structure. Now consider watching the same video when it's being *streamed* over the internet. This is now a stream (of bytes or frames). The streaming video player needs to have downloaded only a few frames in advance of where the user is watching, so you can start displaying values from the beginning of the stream before most of the values in the stream have even been computed (consider streaming a live football game). Note particularly that the video player may lack the memory to buffer the whole stream in memory as a collection—and the startup time would be appalling if you had to wait for the final frame to appear before you could start showing the video. You might choose for video-player implementation reasons to *buffer* a part of a stream into a collection, but this is distinct from the conceptual difference.

In coarsest terms, the difference between collections and streams has to do with *when* things are computed. A collection is an in-memory data structure that holds *all* the values the data structure currently has—every element in the collection has to be computed before it can be added to the collection. (You can add things to, and remove them from, the collection, but at each moment in time, every element in the collection is stored in memory; elements have to be computed before becoming part of the collection.)

By contrast, a stream is a conceptually fixed data structure (you can't add or remove elements from it) whose elements are *computed on demand.* This gives rise to significant programming benefits. In chapter 6, we'll show how simple it is to construct a stream containing all the prime numbers (2, 3, 5, 7, 11, . . .) even though there are an infinite number of them. The idea is that a user will extract only the values they require from a stream and these elements are produced—invisibly to the user—only *as* and *when* required. This is a form of a producer-consumer relationship. Another view is that a stream is like a lazily constructed collection: values are computed when they're solicited by a consumer (in management speak this is demand-driven, or even just-in-time, manufacturing).

In contrast, a collection is eagerly constructed (supplier-driven: fill your warehouse before you start selling, like a Christmas novelty that has a limited life). Imagine applying this to the primes example. Attempting to construct a collection of all prime numbers would result in a program loop that forever computes a new prime—adding it to the collection—but could never finish making the collection, so the consumer would never get to see it.

Figure 4.3 illustrates the difference between a stream and a collection, applied to our DVD versus internet streaming example.

Another example is a browser internet search. Suppose you search for a phrase with many matches in Google or in an e-commerce online shop. Instead of waiting for the whole collection of results along with their photographs to be downloaded, you get a stream whose elements are the best 10 or 20 matches, along with a button to click for the next 10 or 20. When you, the consumer, click for the next 10, the supplier computes these on demand, before returning them to your browser for display.

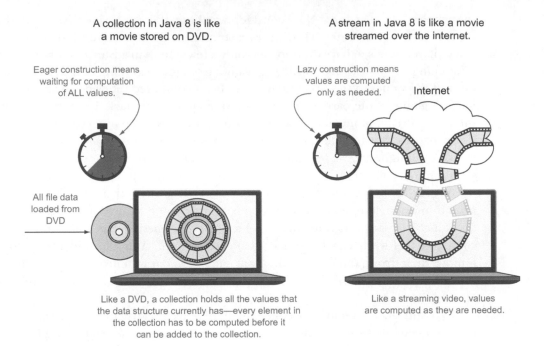

A collection in Java 8 is like a movie stored on DVD.

A stream in Java 8 is like a movie streamed over the internet.

Eager construction means waiting for computation of ALL values.

Lazy construction means values are computed only as needed.

Internet

All file data loaded from DVD

Like a DVD, a collection holds all the values that the data structure currently has—every element in the collection has to be computed before it can be added to the collection.

Like a streaming video, values are computed as they are needed.

Figure 4.3   Streams versus collections

4.3.1   *Traversable only once*

Note that, similarly to iterators, a stream can be traversed only once. After that a stream is said to be consumed. You can get a new stream from the initial data source to traverse it again as you would for an iterator (assuming it's a repeatable source like a collection; if it's an I/O channel, you're out of luck). For example, the following code would throw an exception indicating the stream has been consumed:

```
List<String> title = Arrays.asList("Modern", "Java", "In", "Action");
Stream<String> s = title.stream();
s.forEach(System.out::println);            Prints each word in the title
s.forEach(System.out::println);

                                java.lang.IllegalStateException: stream has
                                already been operated upon or closed
```

Keep in mind that you can consume a stream only once!

> ### Streams and collections philosophically
>
> For readers who like philosophical viewpoints, you can see a stream as a set of values spread out in time. In contrast, a collection is a set of values spread out in space (here, computer memory), which all exist at a single point in time—and which you access using an iterator to access members inside a `for-each` loop.

Another key difference between collections and streams is how they manage the iteration over data.

4.3.2 *External vs. internal iteration*

Using the `Collection` interface requires iteration to be done by the user (for example, using for-each); this is called *external iteration.* The Streams library, by contrast, uses *internal iteration*—it does the iteration for you and takes care of storing the resulting stream value somewhere; you merely provide a function saying what's to be done. The following code listings illustrate this difference.

Listing 4.1 Collections: external iteration with a `for-each` loop

```
List<String> names = new ArrayList<>();
for(Dish dish: menu) {
    names.add(dish.getName());
}
```

Explicitly iterates the list of menu sequentially

Extracts the name and adds it to an accumulator

Note that the for-each hides some of the iteration complexity. The for-each construct is syntactic sugar that translates into something much uglier using an `Iterator` object.

Listing 4.2 Collections: external iteration using an iterator behind the scenes

```
List<String> names = new ArrayList<>();
Iterator<String> iterator = menu.iterator();
while(iterator.hasNext()) {
    Dish dish = iterator.next();
    names.add(dish.getName());
}
```

Iterates explicitly

Listing 4.3 Streams: internal iteration

```
List<String> names = menu.stream()
                     .map(Dish::getName)
                     .collect(toList());
```

Starts executing the pipeline of operations; no iteration

Parameterizes map with the getName method to extract the name of a dish

Let's use an analogy to understand the differences and benefits of internal iteration. Let's say you're talking to your two-year-old daughter, Sofia, and want her to put her toys away:

> You: "Sofia, let's put the toys away. Is there a toy on the ground?"
> Sofia: "Yes, the ball."
> You: "Okay, put the ball in the box. Is there something else?"
> Sofia: "Yes, there's my doll."
> You: "Okay, put the doll in the box. Is there something else?"
> Sofia: "Yes, there's my book."

You: "Okay, put the book in the box. Is there something else?"
Sofia: "No, nothing else."
You: "Fine, we're finished."

This is exactly what you do every day with your Java collections. You iterate a collection *externally*, explicitly pulling out and processing the items one by one. It would be far better if you could tell Sofia, "Put all the toys that are on the floor inside the box." There are two other reasons why an internal iteration is preferable: first, Sofia could choose to take the doll with one hand and the ball with the other at the same time, and second, she could decide to take the objects closest to the box first and then the others. In the same way, using an internal iteration, the processing of items could be transparently done in parallel or in a different order that may be more optimized. These optimizations are difficult if you iterate the collection externally as you're used to doing in Java. This may seem like nit-picking, but it's much of the raison-d'être of Java 8's introduction of streams. The internal iteration in the Streams library can automatically choose a data representation and implementation of parallelism to match your hardware. By contrast, once you've chosen external iteration by writing for-each, then you've committed to self-manage any parallelism. (*Self-managing* in practice means either "one fine day we'll parallelize this" or "starting the long and arduous battle involving tasks and synchronized.") Java 8 needed an interface like Collection but without iterators, ergo Stream! Figure 4.4 illustrates the difference between a stream (internal iteration) and a collection (external iteration).

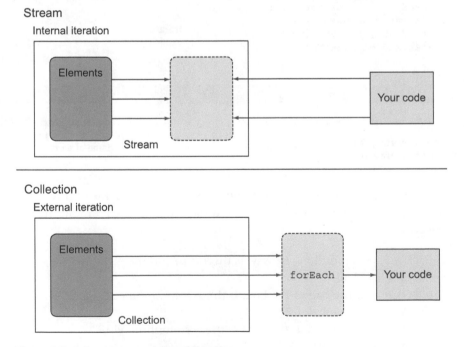

Figure 4.4   Internal versus external iteration

We've described the conceptual differences between collections and streams. Specifically, streams make use of internal iteration, where a library takes care of iterating for you. But this is useful only if you have a list of predefined operations to work with (for example, `filter` or `map`) that hide the iteration. Most of these operations take lambda expressions as arguments so you can parameterize their behavior as we showed in the previous chapter. The Java language designers shipped the Streams API with an extensive list of operations you can use to express complicated data processing queries. We'll briefly look at this list of operations now and explore them in more detail with examples in the next chapter. To check your understanding of external versus internal iteration, try quiz 4.1 below.

Quiz 4.1: External vs. internal iteration

Based on what you learned about external iteration in listing 4.1 and 4.2, which stream operation would you use to refactor the following code?

```
List<String> highCaloricDishes = new ArrayList<>();
Iterator<String> iterator = menu.iterator();
while(iterator.hasNext()) {
    Dish dish = iterator.next();
    if(dish.getCalories() > 300) {
        highCaloricDishes.add(d.getName());
    }
}
```

Answer: You need to use the `filter` pattern

```
List<String> highCaloricDish =
    menu.stream()
        .filter(dish -> dish.getCalories() > 300)
        .collect(toList());
```

Don't worry if you're still unfamiliar with how to precisely write a stream query, you will learn this in more detail in the next chapter.

4.4 Stream operations

The streams interface in `java.util.stream.Stream` defines many operations. They can be classified into two categories. Let's look at our previous example once again:

```
List<String> names = menu.stream()                              ←── Gets a stream from
                         .filter(dish -> dish.getCalories() > 300)     the list of dishes
                         .map(Dish::getName)              ←── Intermediate
                         .limit(3)                            operation
                         .collect(toList());          ←──
```

Intermediate operation

Converts the Stream into a List

Intermediate operation

You can see two groups of operations:

- `filter`, `map`, and `limit` can be connected together to form a pipeline.
- `collect` causes the pipeline to be executed and closes it.

Stream operations that can be connected are called *intermediate operations*, and operations that close a stream are called *terminal operations*. Figure 4.5 highlights these two groups. Why is the distinction important?

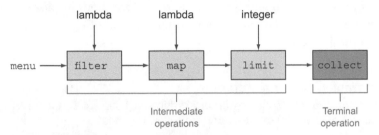

Figure 4.5   Intermediate versus terminal operations

4.4.1   *Intermediate operations*

Intermediate operations such as `filter` or `sorted` return another stream as the return type. This allows the operations to be connected to form a query. What's important is that intermediate operations don't perform any processing until a terminal operation is invoked on the stream pipeline—they're lazy. This is because intermediate operations can usually be merged and processed into a single pass by the terminal operation.

To understand what's happening in the stream pipeline, modify the code so each lambda also prints the current dish it's processing. (Like many demonstration and debugging techniques, this is appalling programming style for production code, but directly explains the order of evaluation when you're learning.)

```
List<String> names =
    menu.stream()
        .filter(dish -> {
                            System.out.println("filtering:" + dish.getName());
                            return dish.getCalories() > 300;
                        })
        .map(dish -> {
                        System.out.println("mapping:" + dish.getName());
                        return dish.getName();
                    })
        .limit(3)
        .collect(toList());
System.out.println(names);
```

Prints the dishes as they're filtered

Prints the dishes as you extract their names

This code, when executed, will print the following:

```
filtering:pork
mapping:pork
```

```
filtering:beef
mapping:beef
filtering:chicken
mapping:chicken
[pork, beef, chicken]
```

By doing this, you can notice that the Streams library performs several optimizations exploiting the lazy nature of streams. First, despite the fact that many dishes have more than 300 calories, only the first three are selected! This is because of the limit operation and a technique called *short-circuiting*, as we'll explain in the next chapter. Second, despite the fact that filter and map are two separate operations, they were merged into the same pass (compiler experts call this technique *loop fusion*).

4.4.2   Terminal operations

Terminal operations produce a result from a stream pipeline. A result is any non-stream value such as a List, an Integer, or even void. For example, in the following pipeline, forEach is a terminal operation that returns void and applies a lambda to each dish in the source. Passing System.out.println to forEach asks it to print every Dish in the stream created from menu:

```
menu.stream().forEach(System.out::println);
```

To check your understanding of intermediate versus terminal operations, try out quiz 4.2.

Quiz 4.2: Intermediate vs. terminal operations
In the stream pipeline that follows, can you identify the intermediate and terminal operations?

```
long count = menu.stream()
                 .filter(dish -> dish.getCalories() > 300)
                 .distinct()
                 .limit(3)
                 .count();
```

Answer:

The last operation in the stream pipeline count returns a long, which is a non-stream value. It's therefore a *terminal operation*. All previous operations, filter, distinct, limit, are connected and return a stream. They are therefore *intermediate operations*.

4.4.3   Working with streams

To summarize, working with streams in general involves three items:

- A *data source* (such as a collection) to perform a query on
- A chain of *intermediate operations* that form a stream pipeline
- A *terminal operation* that executes the stream pipeline and produces a result

The idea behind a stream pipeline is similar to the builder pattern (see http://en .wikipedia.org/wiki/Builder_pattern). In the builder pattern, there's a chain of calls to set up a configuration (for streams this is a chain of intermediate operations), followed by a call to a build method (for streams this is a terminal operation).

For convenience, tables 4.1 and 4.2 summarize the intermediate and terminal stream operations you've seen in the code examples so far. Note that this is an incomplete list of operations provided by the Streams API; you'll see several more in the next chapter!

Table 4.1 Intermediate operations

Operation	Type	Return type	Argument of the operation	Function descriptor
filter	Intermediate	Stream\<T\>	Predicate\<T\>	T -> boolean
map	Intermediate	Stream\<R\>	Function\<T, R\>	T -> R
limit	Intermediate	Stream\<T\>		
sorted	Intermediate	Stream\<T\>	Comparator\<T\>	(T, T) -> int
distinct	Intermediate	Stream\<T\>		

Table 4.2 Terminal operations

Operation	Type	Return type	Purpose
forEach	Terminal	void	Consumes each element from a stream and applies a lambda to each of them.
count	Terminal	long	Returns the number of elements in a stream.
collect	Terminal	(generic)	Reduces the stream to create a collection such as a List, a Map, or even an Integer. See chapter 6 for more detail.

4.5   Road map

In the next chapter, we'll detail the available stream operations with use cases so you can see what kinds of queries you can express with them. We look at many patterns such as filtering, slicing, finding, matching, mapping, and reducing, which can be used to express sophisticated data-processing queries.

Chapter 6 then explores collectors in detail. In this chapter we have only made use of the collect() terminal operation on streams (see table 4.2) in the stylized form of collect(toList()), which creates a List whose elements are the same as those of the stream it's applied to.

Summary

- A stream is a sequence of elements from a source that supports data-processing operations.
- Streams make use of internal iteration: the iteration is abstracted away through operations such as `filter`, `map`, and `sorted`.
- There are two types of stream operations: intermediate and terminal operations.
- Intermediate operations such as `filter` and `map` return a stream and can be chained together. They're used to set up a pipeline of operations but don't produce any result.
- Terminal operations such as `forEach` and `count` return a non-stream value and process a stream pipeline to return a result.
- The elements of a stream are computed on demand ("lazily").

Working with streams 5

In the previous chapter, you saw that streams let you move from *external iteration* to *internal iteration*. Instead of writing code, as follows, where you explicitly manage the iteration over a collection of data (external iteration),

```
List<Dish> vegetarianDishes = new ArrayList<>();
for(Dish d: menu) {
    if(d.isVegetarian()){
        vegetarianDishes.add(d);
    }
}
```

you can use the Streams API (internal iteration), which supports the `filter` and `collect` operations, to manage the iteration over the collection of data for you. All you need to do is pass the filtering behavior as argument to the `filter` method:

```
import static java.util.stream.Collectors.toList;
List<Dish> vegetarianDishes =
    menu.stream()
        .filter(Dish::isVegetarian)
        .collect(toList());
```

This different way of working with data is useful because you let the Streams API manage how to process the data. As a consequence, the Streams API can work out several optimizations behind the scenes. In addition, using internal iteration, the Streams API can decide to run your code in parallel. Using external iteration, this isn't possible because you're committed to a single-threaded step-by-step sequential iteration.

In this chapter, you'll have an extensive look at the various operations supported by the Streams API. You will learn about operations available in Java 8 and also new additions in Java 9. These operations will let you express complex data-processing queries such as filtering, slicing, mapping, finding, matching, and reducing. Next, we'll explore special cases of streams: numeric streams, streams built from multiple sources such as files and arrays, and finally infinite streams.

5.1 Filtering

In this section, we'll look at the ways to select elements of a stream: filtering with a predicate and filtering only unique elements.

5.1.1 Filtering with a predicate

The `Stream` interface supports a `filter` method (which you should be familiar with by now). This operation takes as argument a *predicate* (a function returning a `boolean`) and returns a stream including all elements that match the predicate. For example, you can create a vegetarian menu by filtering all vegetarian dishes as illustrated in figure 5.1 and the code that follows it:

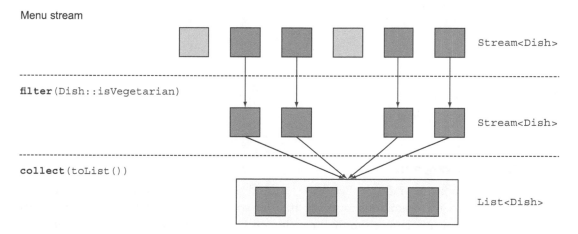

Figure 5.1 Filtering a stream with a predicate

```
List<Dish> vegetarianMenu = menu.stream()
                          .filter(Dish::isVegetarian)
                          .collect(toList());
```

> Use a method reference to check if a dish is vegetarian friendly.

5.1.2 *Filtering unique elements*

Streams also support a method called `distinct` that returns a stream with unique elements (according to the implementation of the `hashcode` and `equals` methods of the objects produced by the stream). For example, the following code filters all even numbers from a list and then eliminates duplicates (using the `equals` method for the comparison). Figure 5.2 shows this visually.

```
List<Integer> numbers = Arrays.asList(1, 2, 1, 3, 3, 2, 4);
numbers.stream()
       .filter(i -> i % 2 == 0)
       .distinct()
       .forEach(System.out::println);
```

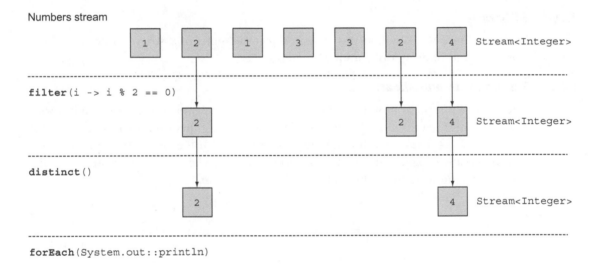

Numbers stream

filter(i -> i % 2 == 0)

distinct()

forEach(System.out::println)

```
System.out.println(2);
System.out.println(4);
```

void

Figure 5.2   Filtering unique elements in a stream

5.2   *Slicing a stream*

In this section, we'll discuss how to select and skip elements in a stream in different ways. There are operations available that let you efficiently select or drop elements using a predicate, ignore the first few elements of a stream, or truncate a stream to a given size.

5.2.1 *Slicing using a predicate*

Java 9 added two new methods that are useful for efficiently selecting elements in a stream: takeWhile and dropWhile.

USING TAKEWHILE

Let's say you have the following special list of dishes:

```
List<Dish> specialMenu = Arrays.asList(
    new Dish("seasonal fruit", true, 120, Dish.Type.OTHER),
    new Dish("prawns", false, 300, Dish.Type.FISH),
    new Dish("rice", true, 350, Dish.Type.OTHER),
    new Dish("chicken", false, 400, Dish.Type.MEAT),
    new Dish("french fries", true, 530, Dish.Type.OTHER));
```

How would you select the dishes that have fewer than 320 calories? Instinctively, you know already from the previous section that the operation filter can be used as follows:

```
List<Dish> filteredMenu
    = specialMenu.stream()
                .filter(dish -> dish.getCalories() < 320)      Lists seasonal
                .collect(toList());                       ◁─┘  fruit, prawns
```

But, you'll notice that the initial list was already sorted on the number of calories! The downside of using the filter operation here is that you need to iterate through the whole stream and the predicate is applied to each element. Instead, you could stop once you found a dish that is greater than (or equal to) 320 calories. With a small list this may not seem like a huge benefit, but it can become useful if you work with potentially large stream of elements. But how do you specify this? The takeWhile operation is here to rescue you! It lets you slice any stream (even an infinite stream as you will learn later) using a predicate. But thankfully, it stops once it has found an element that fails to match. Here's how you can use it:

```
List<Dish> slicedMenu1
    = specialMenu.stream()
                .takeWhile(dish -> dish.getCalories() < 320)     Lists seasonal
                .collect(toList());                       ◁─┘    fruit, prawns
```

USING DROPWHILE

How about getting the other elements though? How about finding the elements that have greater than 320 calories? You can use the dropWhile operation for this:

```
List<Dish> slicedMenu2
    = specialMenu.stream()
                .dropWhile(dish -> dish.getCalories() < 320)     Lists rice, chicken,
                .collect(toList());                       ◁─┘    french fries
```

The dropWhile operation is the complement of takeWhile. It throws away the elements at the start where the predicate is false. Once the predicate evaluates to true it stops and returns all the remaining elements, and it even works if there are an infinite number of remaining elements!

5.2.2 *Truncating a stream*

Streams support the limit(n) method, which returns another stream that's no longer than a given size. The requested size is passed as argument to limit. If the stream is ordered, the first elements are returned up to a maximum of n. For example, you can create a List by selecting the first three dishes that have more than 300 calories as follows:

```
List<Dish> dishes = specialMenu
                    .stream()
                    .filter(dish -> dish.getCalories() > 300)
                    .limit(3)
                    .collect(toList());
```

Lists rice, chicken, french fries

Figure 5.3 illustrates a combination of filter and limit. You can see that only the first three elements that match the predicate are selected, and the result is immediately returned.

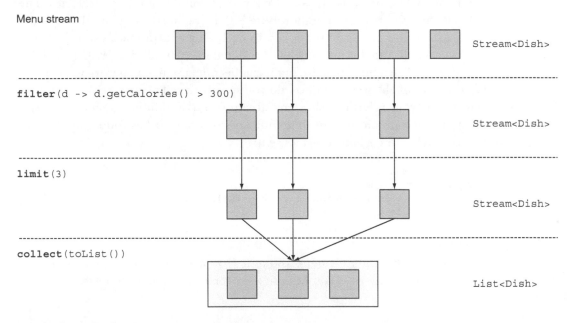

Figure 5.3   Truncating a stream

Note that `limit` also works on unordered streams (for example, if the source is a `Set`). In this case you shouldn't assume any order on the result produced by `limit`.

5.2.3 *Skipping elements*

Streams support the `skip(n)` method to return a stream that discards the first n elements. If the stream has fewer than n elements, an empty stream is returned. Note that `limit(n)` and `skip(n)` are complementary! For example, the following code skips the first two dishes that have more than 300 calories and returns the rest. Figure 5.4 illustrates this query.

```
List<Dish> dishes = menu.stream()
                        .filter(d -> d.getCalories() > 300)
                        .skip(2)
                        .collect(toList());
```

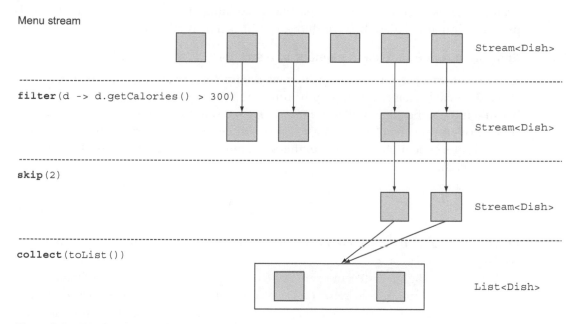

Figure 5.4 Skipping elements in a stream

Put what you've learned in this section into practice with quiz 5.1 before we move to mapping operations.

Quiz 5.1: Filtering

How would you use streams to filter the first two meat dishes?

Answer:

You can solve this problem by composing the methods `filter` and `limit` together and using `collect(toList())` to convert the stream into a list as follows:

```
List<Dish> dishes =
    menu.stream()
        .filter(dish -> dish.getType() == Dish.Type.MEAT)
        .limit(2)
        .collect(toList());
```

5.3   *Mapping*

A common data processing idiom is to select information from certain objects. For example, in SQL you can select a particular column from a table. The Streams API provides similar facilities through the map and flatMap methods.

5.3.1   *Applying a function to each element of a stream*

Streams support the map method, which takes a function as argument. The function is applied to each element, mapping it into a new element (the word *mapping* is used because it has a meaning similar to *transforming* but with the nuance of "creating a new version of" rather than "modifying"). For example, in the following code you pass a method reference Dish::getName to the map method to *extract* the names of the dishes in the stream:

```
List<String> dishNames = menu.stream()
                             .map(Dish::getName)
                             .collect(toList());
```

Because the method getName returns a string, the stream outputted by the map method is of type Stream<String>.

Let's take a slightly different example to solidify your understanding of map. Given a list of words, you'd like to return a list of the number of characters for each word. How would you do it? You'd need to apply a function to each element of the list. This sounds like a job for the map method! The function to apply should take a word and return its length. You can solve this problem, as follows, by passing a method reference String::length to map:

```
List<String> words = Arrays.asList("Modern", "Java", "In", "Action");
List<Integer> wordLengths = words.stream()
                                 .map(String::length)
                                 .collect(toList());
```

Let's return to the example where you extracted the name of each dish. What if you wanted to find out the length of the name of each dish? You could do this by chaining another map as follows:

```
List<Integer> dishNameLengths = menu.stream()
                                    .map(Dish::getName)
                                    .map(String::length)
                                    .collect(toList());
```

5.3.2 *Flattening streams*

You saw how to return the length for each word in a list using the map method. Let's extend this idea a bit further: How could you return a list of all the *unique characters* for a list of words? For example, given the list of words ["Hello," "World"] you'd like to return the list ["H," "e," "l," "o," "W," "r," "d"].

You might think that this is easy, that you can map each word into a list of characters and then call distinct to filter duplicate characters. A first go could be like the following:

```
words.stream()
    .map(word -> word.split(""))
    .distinct()
    .collect(toList());
```

The problem with this approach is that the lambda passed to the map method returns a String[] (an array of String) for each word. The stream returned by the map method is of type Stream<String[]>. What you want is Stream<String> to represent a stream of characters. Figure 5.5 illustrates the problem.

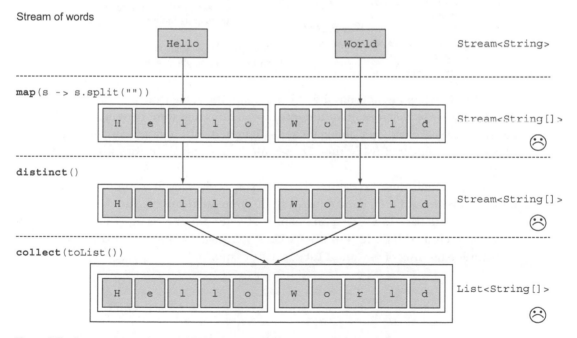

Figure 5.5 Incorrect use of map to find unique characters from a list of words

Luckily there's a solution to this problem using the method `flatMap`! Let's see step-by-step how to solve it.

ATTEMPT USING MAP AND ARRAYS.STREAM

First, you need a stream of characters instead of a stream of arrays. There's a method called `Arrays.stream()` that takes an array and produces a stream:

```
String[] arrayOfWords = {"Goodbye", "World"};
Stream<String> streamOfwords = Arrays.stream(arrayOfWords);
```

Use it in the previous pipeline to see what happens:

```
words.stream()
     .map(word -> word.split(""))      ← Converts each word into an
     .map(Arrays::stream)      ←          array of its individual letters
     .distinct()               Makes each array into
     .collect(toList());       a separate stream
```

The current solution still doesn't work! This is because you now end up with a list of streams (more precisely, `List<Stream<String>>`). Indeed, you first convert each word into an array of its individual letters and then make each array into a separate stream.

USING FLATMAP

You can fix this problem by using `flatMap` as follows:

```
List<String> uniqueCharacters =
  words.stream()
       .map(word -> word.split(""))      Converts each word into an
       .flatMap(Arrays::stream)   ←      array of its individual letters
       .distinct()               Flattens each generated
       .collect(toList());       stream into a single stream
```

Using the `flatMap` method has the effect of mapping each array not with a stream but *with the contents of that stream.* All the separate streams that were generated when using `map(Arrays::stream)` get amalgamated—flattened into a single stream. Figure 5.6 illustrates the effect of using the `flatMap` method. Compare it with what `map` does in figure 5.5.

In a nutshell, the `flatMap` method lets you replace each value of a stream with another stream and then concatenates all the generated streams into a single stream.

We'll come back to `flatMap` in chapter 11 when we discuss more advanced Java 8 patterns such as using the new library class `Optional` for `null` checking. To solidify your understanding of `map` and `flatMap`, try out quiz 5.2.

Stream of words

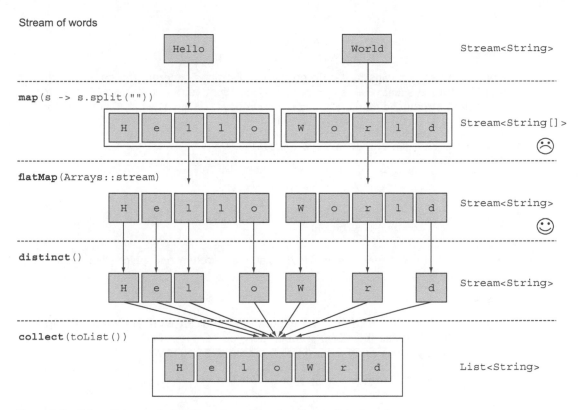

Figure 5.6 Using `flatMap` to find the unique characters from a list of words

Quiz 5.2: Mapping

1. Given a list of numbers, how would you return a list of the square of each number? For example, given [1, 2, 3, 4, 5] you should return [1, 4, 9, 16, 25].

Answer:

You can solve this problem by using `map` with a lambda that takes a number and returns the square of the number:

```
List<Integer> numbers = Arrays.asList(1, 2, 3, 4, 5);
List<Integer> squares =
    numbers.stream()
           .map(n -> n * n)
           .collect(toList());
```

2. Given two lists of numbers, how would you return all pairs of numbers? For example, given a list [1, 2, 3] and a list [3, 4] you should return [(1, 3), (1, 4), (2, 3), (2, 4), (3, 3), (3, 4)]. For simplicity, you can represent a pair as an array with two elements.

(continued)

Answer:

You could use two `map`s to iterate on the two lists and generate the pairs. But this would return a `Stream<Stream<Integer[]>>`. What you need to do is flatten the generated streams to result in a `Stream<Integer[]>`. This is what `flatMap` is for:

```
List<Integer> numbers1 = Arrays.asList(1, 2, 3);
List<Integer> numbers2 = Arrays.asList(3, 4);
List<int[]> pairs =
    numbers1.stream()
            .flatMap(i -> numbers2.stream()
                                  .map(j -> new int[]{i, j})
                   )
            .collect(toList());
```

3. How would you extend the previous example to return only pairs whose sum is divisible by 3?

Answer:

You saw earlier that `filter` can be used with a predicate to filter elements from a stream. Because after the `flatMap` operation you have a stream of `int[]` that represent a pair, you only need a predicate to check if the sum is divisible by 3:

```
List<Integer> numbers1 = Arrays.asList(1, 2, 3);
List<Integer> numbers2 = Arrays.asList(3, 4);
List<int[]> pairs =
    numbers1.stream()
            .flatMap(i ->
                        numbers2.stream()
                                .filter(j -> (i + j) % 3 == 0)
                                .map(j -> new int[]{i, j})
                    )
            .collect(toList());
```

The result is [(2, 4), (3, 3)].

5.4   Finding and matching

Another common data processing idiom is finding whether some elements in a set of data match a given property. The Streams API provides such facilities through the `allMatch`, `anyMatch`, `noneMatch`, `findFirst`, and `findAny` methods of a stream.

5.4.1   Checking to see if a predicate matches at least one element

The `anyMatch` method can be used to answer the question "Is there an element in the stream matching the given predicate?" For example, you can use it to find out whether the menu has a vegetarian option:

```
if(menu.stream().anyMatch(Dish::isVegetarian)) {
    System.out.println("The menu is (somewhat) vegetarian friendly!!");
}
```

The anyMatch method returns a boolean and is therefore a terminal operation.

5.4.2 Checking to see if a predicate matches all elements

The allMatch method works similarly to anyMatch but will check to see if all the elements of the stream match the given predicate. For example, you can use it to find out whether the menu is healthy (all dishes are below 1000 calories):

```
boolean isHealthy = menu.stream()
                        .allMatch(dish -> dish.getCalories() < 1000);
```

NONEMATCH

The opposite of allMatch is noneMatch. It ensures that no elements in the stream match the given predicate. For example, you could rewrite the previous example as follows using noneMatch:

```
boolean isHealthy = menu.stream()
                        .noneMatch(d -> d.getCalories() >= 1000);
```

These three operations—anyMatch, allMatch, and noneMatch—make use of what we call *short-circuiting*, a stream version of the familiar Java short-circuiting && and || operators.

> ### Short-circuiting evaluation
>
> Some operations don't need to process the whole stream to produce a result. For example, say you need to evaluate a large boolean expression chained with and operators. You need only find out that one expression is false to deduce that the whole expression will return false, no matter how long the expression is; there's no need to evaluate the entire expression. This is what *short-circuiting* refers to.
>
> In relation to streams, certain operations such as allMatch, noneMatch, findFirst, and findAny don't need to process the whole stream to produce a result. As soon as an element is found, a result can be produced. Similarly, limit is also a short-circuiting operation. The operation only needs to create a stream of a given size without processing all the elements in the stream. Such operations are useful (for example, when you need to deal with streams of infinite size, because they can turn an infinite stream into a stream of finite size). We'll show examples of infinite streams in section 5.7.

5.4.3 Finding an element

The findAny method returns an arbitrary element of the current stream. It can be used in conjunction with other stream operations. For example, you may wish to find a dish that's vegetarian. You can combine the `filter` method and `findAny` to express this query:

```
Optional<Dish> dish =
  menu.stream()
      .filter(Dish::isVegetarian)
      .findAny();
```

The stream pipeline will be optimized behind the scenes to perform a single pass and finish as soon as a result is found by using short-circuiting. But wait a minute; what's this `Optional` thing in the code?

OPTIONAL IN A NUTSHELL

The `Optional<T>` class (`java.util.Optional`) is a container class to represent the existence or absence of a value. In the previous code, it's possible that `findAny` doesn't find any element. Instead of returning `null`, which is well known for being error-prone, the Java 8 library designers introduced `Optional<T>`. We won't go into the details of `Optional` here, because we'll show in detail in chapter 11 how your code can benefit from using `Optional` to avoid bugs related to `null` checking. But for now, it's good to know that there are a few methods available in `Optional` that force you to explicitly check for the presence of a value or deal with the absence of a value:

- `isPresent()` returns `true` if `Optional` contains a value, `false` otherwise.
- `ifPresent(Consumer<T> block)` executes the given block if a value is present. We introduced the `Consumer` functional interface in chapter 3; it lets you pass a lambda that takes an argument of type `T` and returns void.
- `T get()` returns the value if present; otherwise it throws a `NoSuchElement-Exception`.
- `T orElse(T other)` returns the value if present; otherwise it returns a default value.

For example, in the previous code you'd need to explicitly check for the presence of a dish in the `Optional` object to access its name:

```
menu.stream()
    .filter(Dish::isVegetarian)              Returns an
    .findAny()                               Optional<Dish>.     If a value is contained,
    .ifPresent(dish -> System.out.println(dish.getName()));   it's printed; otherwise
                                                              nothing happens.
```

5.4.4 *Finding the first element*

Some streams have an *encounter order* that specifies the order in which items logically appear in the stream (for example, a stream generated from a `List` or from a sorted sequence of data). For such streams you may wish to find the first element. There's the `findFirst` method for this, which works similarly to `findAny` (for example, the code that follows, given a list of numbers, finds the first square that's divisible by 3):

```
List<Integer> someNumbers = Arrays.asList(1, 2, 3, 4, 5);
Optional<Integer> firstSquareDivisibleByThree =
  someNumbers.stream()
             .map(n -> n * n)
             .filter(n -> n % 3 == 0)
             .findFirst(); // 9
```

> **When to use findFirst and findAny**
>
> You may wonder why we have both findFirst and findAny. The answer is parallel-ism. Finding the first element is more constraining in parallel. If you don't care about which element is returned, use findAny because it's less constraining when using parallel streams.

5.5 *Reducing*

The terminal operations you've seen either return a boolean (allMatch and so on), void (forEach), or an Optional object (findAny and so on). You've also been using collect to combine all elements in a stream into a List.

In this section, you'll see how you can combine elements of a stream to express more complicated queries such as "Calculate the sum of all calories in the menu," or "What is the highest calorie dish in the menu?" using the reduce operation. Such queries combine all the elements in the stream repeatedly to produce a single value such as an Integer. These queries can be classified as *reduction operations* (a stream is reduced to a value). In functional programming-language jargon, this is referred to as a *fold* because you can view this operation as repeatedly folding a long piece of paper (your stream) until it forms a small square, which is the result of the fold operation.

5.5.1 *Summing the elements*

Before we investigate how to use the reduce method, it helps to first see how you'd sum the elements of a list of numbers using a for-each loop:

```
int sum = 0;
for (int x : numbers) {
    sum += x;
}
```

Each element of numbers is combined iteratively with the addition operator to form a result. You *reduce* the list of numbers into one number by repeatedly using addition. There are two parameters in this code:

- The initial value of the sum variable, in this case 0
- The operation to combine all the elements of the list, in this case +

Wouldn't it be great if you could also multiply all the numbers without having to repeatedly copy and paste this code? This is where the reduce operation, which abstracts over this pattern of repeated application, can help. You can sum all the elements of a stream as follows:

```
int sum = numbers.stream().reduce(0, (a, b) -> a + b);
```

reduce takes two arguments:

- An initial value, here 0.
- A BinaryOperator<T> to combine two elements and produce a new value; here you use the lambda (a, b) -> a + b.

You could just as easily multiply all the elements by passing a different lambda, (a, b) -> a * b, to the reduce operation:

```
int product = numbers.stream().reduce(1, (a, b) -> a * b);
```

Figure 5.7 illustrates how the reduce operation works on a stream: the lambda combines each element repeatedly until the stream containing the integers 4, 5, 3, 9, are reduced to a single value.

Numbers stream

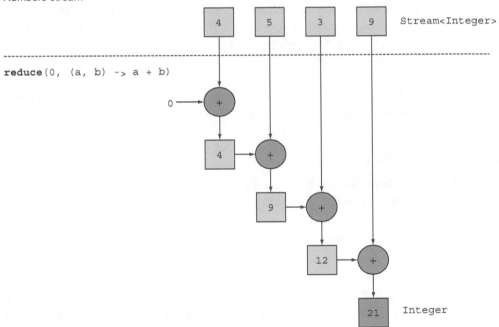

Figure 5.7 Using reduce to sum the numbers in a stream

Let's take an in-depth look into how the reduce operation happens to sum a stream of numbers. First, 0 is used as the first parameter of the lambda (a), and 4 is consumed from the stream and used as the second parameter (b). 0 + 4 produces 4, and it becomes the new accumulated value. Then the lambda is called again with the accumulated value and the next element of the stream, 5, which produces the new accumulated value, 9. Moving forward, the lambda is called again with the accumulated value and the next element, 3, which produces 12. Finally, the lambda is called with 12 and the last element of the stream, 9, which produces the final value, 21.

You can make this code more concise by using a method reference. From Java 8 the Integer class now comes with a static sum method to add two numbers, which is what you want instead of repeatedly writing out the same code as lambda:

```
int sum = numbers.stream().reduce(0, Integer::sum);
```

No initial value

There's also an overloaded variant of reduce that doesn't take an initial value, but it returns an Optional object:

```
Optional<Integer> sum = numbers.stream().reduce((a, b) -> (a + b));
```

Why does it return an Optional<Integer>? Consider the case when the stream contains no elements. The reduce operation can't return a sum because it doesn't have an initial value. This is why the result is wrapped in an Optional object to indicate that the sum may be absent. Now see what else you can do with reduce.

5.5.2 Maximum and minimum

It turns out that reduction is all you need to compute maxima and minima as well! Let's see how you can apply what you just learned about reduce to calculate the maximum or minimum element in a stream. As you saw, reduce takes two parameters:

- An initial value
- A lambda to combine two stream elements and produce a new value

The lambda is applied step-by-step to each element of the stream with the addition operator, as shown in figure 5.7. You need a lambda that, given two elements, returns the maximum of them. The reduce operation will use the new value with the next element of the stream to produce a new maximum until the whole stream is consumed! You can use reduce as follows to calculate the maximum in a stream; this is illustrated in figure 5.8.

```
Optional<Integer> max = numbers.stream().reduce(Integer::max);
```

To calculate the minimum, you need to pass Integer.min to the reduce operation instead of Integer.max:

```
Optional<Integer> min = numbers.stream().reduce(Integer::min);
```

You could have equally well used the lambda (x, y) -> x < y ? x : y instead of Integer::min, but the latter is definitely easier to read!

Numbers stream

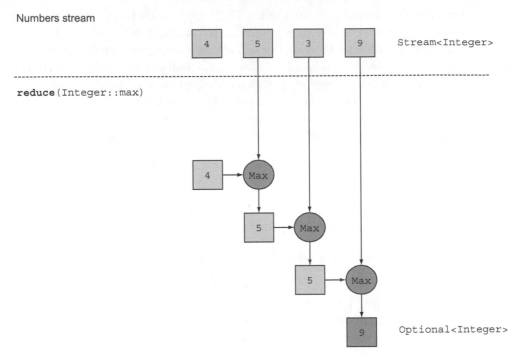

Figure 5.8   **A `reduce` operation—calculating the maximum**

To test your understanding of the reduce operation, try quiz 5.3.

Quiz 5.3: Reducing

How would you count the number of dishes in a stream using the `map` and `reduce` methods?

Answer:

You can solve this problem by mapping each element of a stream into the number 1 and then summing them using `reduce`! This is equivalent to counting, in order, the number of elements in the stream:

```
int count = menu.stream()
                .map(d -> 1)
                .reduce(0, (a, b) -> a + b);
```

A chain of `map` and `reduce` is commonly known as the map-reduce pattern, made famous by Google's use of it for web searching because it can be easily parallelized. Note that in chapter 4 you saw the built-in method `count` to count the number of elements in the stream:

```
long count = menu.stream().count();
```

Benefit of the reduce method and parallelism

The benefit of using `reduce` compared to the step-by-step iteration summation that you wrote earlier is that the iteration is abstracted using internal iteration, which enables the internal implementation to choose to perform the `reduce` operation in parallel. The iterative summation example involves shared updates to a `sum` variable, which doesn't parallelize gracefully. If you add in the needed synchronization, you'll likely discover that thread contention robs you of all the performance that parallelism was supposed to give you! Parallelizing this computation requires a different approach: partition the input, sum the partitions, and combine the sums. But now the code is starting to look very different. You'll see what this looks like in chapter 7 using the fork/join framework. But for now it's important to realize that the mutable-accumulator pattern is a dead end for parallelization. You need a new pattern, and this is what `reduce` provides you. You'll also see in chapter 7 that to sum all the elements in parallel using streams, there's almost no modification to your code: `stream()` becomes `parallelStream()`:

```
int sum = numbers.parallelStream().reduce(0, Integer::sum);
```

But there's a price to pay to execute this code in parallel, as we'll explain later: the lambda passed to `reduce` can't change state (for example, instance variables), and the operation needs to be associative and commutative so it can be executed in any order.

You have seen reduction examples that produced an `Integer`: the sum of a stream, the maximum of a stream, or the number of elements in a stream. You'll see, in section 5.6, that additional built-in methods such as `sum` and `max` are available to help you write slightly more concise code for common reduction patterns. We'll investigate a more complex form of reductions using the `collect` method in the next chapter. For example, instead of reducing a stream into an `Integer`, you can also reduce it into a `Map` if you want to group dishes by types.

Stream operations: stateless vs. stateful

You've seen a lot of stream operations. An initial presentation can make them seem a panacea. Everything works smoothly, and you get parallelism for free when you use `parallelStream` instead of `stream` to get a stream from a collection.

Certainly for many applications this is the case, as you've seen in the previous examples. You can turn a list of dishes into a stream, `filter` to select various dishes of a certain type, then `map` down the resulting stream to add on the number of calories, and then `reduce` to produce the total number of calories of the menu. You can even do such stream calculations in parallel. But these operations have different characteristics. There are issues about what internal state they need to operate.

Operations like `map` and `filter` take *each* element from the input stream and produce *zero or one* result in the output stream. These operations are in general *stateless*: they don't have an internal state (assuming the user-supplied lambda or method reference has no internal mutable state).

(continued)

But operations like `reduce`, `sum`, and `max` need to have internal state to accumulate the result. In this case the internal state is small. In our example it consisted of an `int` or `double`. The internal state is of *bounded size* no matter how many elements are in the stream being processed.

By contrast, some operations such as `sorted` or `distinct` seem at first to behave like `filter` or `map`—all take a stream and produce another stream (an intermediate operation)—but there's a crucial difference. Both sorting and removing duplicates from a stream require knowing the previous history to do their job. For example, sorting requires *all the elements to be buffered* before a single item can be added to the output stream; the storage requirement of the operation is *unbounded*. This can be problematic if the data stream is large or infinite. (What should reversing the stream of all prime numbers do? It should return the largest prime number, which mathematics tells us doesn't exist.) We call these operations *stateful operations*.

You've now seen a lot of stream operations that you can use to express sophisticated data processing queries! Table 5.1 summarizes the operations seen so far. You get to practice them in the next section through an exercise.

Table 5.1   Intermediate and terminal operations

Operation	Type	Return type	Type/functional interface used	Function descriptor
`filter`	Intermediate	`Stream<T>`	`Predicate<T>`	`T -> boolean`
`distinct`	Intermediate (stateful-unbounded)	`Stream<T>`		
`takeWhile`	Intermediate	`Stream<T>`	`Predicate<T>`	`T -> boolean`
`dropWhile`	Intermediate	`Stream<T>`	`Predicate<T>`	`T -> boolean`
`skip`	Intermediate (stateful-bounded)	`Stream<T>`	`long`	
`limit`	Intermediate (stateful-bounded)	`Stream<T>`	`long`	
`map`	Intermediate	`Stream<R>`	`Function<T, R>`	`T -> R`
`flatMap`	Intermediate	`Stream<R>`	`Function<T, Stream<R>>`	`T -> Stream<R>`
`sorted`	Intermediate (stateful-unbounded)	`Stream<T>`	`Comparator<T>`	`(T, T) -> int`
`anyMatch`	Terminal	`boolean`	`Predicate<T>`	`T -> boolean`
`noneMatch`	Terminal	`boolean`	`Predicate<T>`	`T -> boolean`

Table 5.1   Intermediate and terminal operations *(continued)*

Operation	Type	Return type	Type/functional interface used	Function descriptor
allMatch	Terminal	boolean	Predicate<T>	T -> boolean
findAny	Terminal	Optional<T>		
findFirst	Terminal	Optional<T>		
forEach	Terminal	void	Consumer<T>	T -> void
collect	Terminal	R	Collector<T, A, R>	
reduce	Terminal (stateful-bounded)	Optional<T>	BinaryOperator<T>	(T, T) -> T
count	Terminal	long		

5.6   Putting it all into practice

In this section, you get to practice what you've learned about streams so far. We now explore a different domain: traders executing transactions. You're asked by your manager to find answers to eight queries. Can you do it? We give the solutions in section 5.6.2, but you should try them yourself first to get some practice:

1 Find all transactions in the year 2011 and sort them by value (small to high).
2 What are all the unique cities where the traders work?
3 Find all traders from Cambridge and sort them by name.
4 Return a string of all traders' names sorted alphabetically.
5 Are any traders based in Milan?
6 Print the values of all transactions from the traders living in Cambridge.
7 What's the highest value of all the transactions?
8 Find the transaction with the smallest value.

5.6.1   The domain: Traders and Transactions

Here's the domain you'll be working with, a list of Traders and Transactions:

```
Trader raoul = new Trader("Raoul", "Cambridge");
Trader mario = new Trader("Mario","Milan");
Trader alan = new Trader("Alan","Cambridge");
Trader brian = new Trader("Brian","Cambridge");
List<Transaction> transactions = Arrays.asList(
    new Transaction(brian, 2011, 300),
    new Transaction(raoul, 2012, 1000),
    new Transaction(raoul, 2011, 400),
    new Transaction(mario, 2012, 710),
    new Transaction(mario, 2012, 700),
    new Transaction(alan, 2012, 950)
);
```

Trader and Transaction are classes defined as follows:

```java
public class Trader{
    private final String name;
    private final String city;
    public Trader(String n, String c){
        this.name = n;
        this.city = c;
    }
    public String getName(){
        return this.name;
    }
    public String getCity(){
        return this.city;
    }
    public String toString(){
        return "Trader:"+this.name + " in " + this.city;
    }
}
public class Transaction{
    private final Trader trader;
    private final int year;
    private final int value;
    public Transaction(Trader trader, int year, int value){
        this.trader = trader;
        this.year = year;
        this.value = value;
    }
    public Trader getTrader(){
        return this.trader;
    }
    public int getYear(){
        return this.year;
    }
    public int getValue(){
        return this.value;
    }
    public String toString(){
        return "{" + this.trader + ", " +
                "year: "+this.year+", " +
                "value:" + this.value +"}";
    }
}
```

5.6.2   *Solutions*

We now provide the solutions in the following code listings, so you can verify your understanding of what you've learned so far. Well done!

Listing 5.1   **Finds all transactions in 2011 and sort by value (small to high)**

```java
List<Transaction> tr2011 =
    transactions.stream()
            .filter(transaction -> transaction.getYear() == 2011)
```

Passes a predicate to filter to select transactions in year 2011

Collects all the elements of the resulting Stream into a List

```
.sorted(comparing(Transaction::getValue))
.collect(toList());
```

Sorts them by using the value of the transaction

Listing 5.2   What are all the unique cities where the traders work?

Extracts the city from each trader associated with the transaction

```
List<String> cities =
    transactions.stream()
              .map(transaction -> transaction.getTrader().getCity())
              .distinct()
              .collect(toList());
```

Selects only unique cities

You haven't seen this yet, but you could also drop `distinct()` and use `toSet()` instead, which would convert the stream into a set. You'll learn more about it in chapter 6.

```
Set<String> cities =
    transactions.stream()
              .map(transaction -> transaction.getTrader().getCity())
              .collect(toSet());
```

Listing 5.3   Finds all traders from Cambridge and sort them by name

```
List<Trader> traders =
    transactions.stream()
              .map(Transaction::getTrader)
              .filter(trader -> trader.getCity().equals("Cambridge"))
              .distinct()
              .sorted(comparing(Trader::getName))
              .collect(toList());
```

Extracts all traders from the transactions

Selects only the traders from Cambridge

Removes any duplicates

Sorts the resulting stream of traders by their names

Listing 5.4   Returns a string of all traders' names sorted alphabetically

Extracts all the names of the traders as a Stream of Strings

```
String traderStr =
    transactions.stream()
              .map(transaction -> transaction.getTrader().getName())
              .distinct()
              .sorted()
              .reduce("", (n1, n2) -> n1 + n2);
```

Removes duplicate names

Sorts the names alphabetically

Combines the names one by one to form a String that concatenates all the names

Note that this solution is inefficient (all Strings are repeatedly concatenated, which creates a new `String` object at each iteration). In the next chapter, you'll see a more efficient solution that uses `joining()` as follows (which internally makes use of a `StringBuilder`):

```
String traderStr =
    transactions.stream()
```

```
            .map(transaction -> transaction.getTrader().getName())
            .distinct()
            .sorted()
            .collect(joining());
```

Listing 5.5   Are any traders based in Milan?

```
boolean milanBased =
    transactions.stream()
                .anyMatch(transaction -> transaction.getTrader()
                                                     .getCity()
                                                     .equals("Milan"));
```

**Pass a predicate to anyMatch to
check if there's a trader from Milan.**

Listing 5.6   Prints all transactions' values from the traders living in Cambridge

**Selects the transactions where
the traders live in Cambridge**

```
transactions.stream()
            .filter(t -> "Cambridge".equals(t.getTrader().getCity()))
            .map(Transaction::getValue)
            .forEach(System.out::println);
```

**Prints
each value**

**Extracts the values
of these trades**

Listing 5.7   What's the highest value of all the transactions?

```
Optional<Integer> highestValue =
    transactions.stream()
                .map(Transaction::getValue)
                .reduce(Integer::max);
```

**Extracts the value of
each transaction**

**Calculates the max of
the resulting stream**

Listing 5.8   Finds the transaction with the smallest value

**Finds the smallest transaction by
repeatedly comparing the values
of each transaction**

```
Optional<Transaction> smallestTransaction =
  transactions.stream()
              .reduce((t1, t2) ->
                      t1.getValue() < t2.getValue() ? t1 : t2);
```

You can do better. A stream supports the methods min and max that take a Comparator
as argument to specify which key to compare with when calculating the minimum
or maximum:

```
Optional<Transaction> smallestTransaction =
  transactions.stream()
              .min(comparing(Transaction::getValue));
```

5.7 Numeric streams

You saw earlier that you could use the reduce method to calculate the sum of the elements of a stream. For example, you can calculate the number of calories in the menu as follows:

```
int calories = menu.stream()
                   .map(Dish::getCalories)
                   .reduce(0, Integer::sum);
```

The problem with this code is that there's an insidious boxing cost. Behind the scenes each Integer needs to be unboxed to a primitive before performing the summation. In addition, wouldn't it be nicer if you could call a sum method directly as follows?

```
int calories = menu.stream()
                   .map(Dish::getCalories)
                   .sum();
```

But this isn't possible. The problem is that the method map generates a Stream<T>. Even though the elements of the stream are of type Integer, the streams interface doesn't define a sum method. Why not? Say you had only a Stream<Dish> like the menu; it wouldn't make any sense to be able to sum dishes. But don't worry; the Streams API also supplies *primitive stream specializations* that support specialized methods to work with streams of numbers.

5.7.1 Primitive stream specializations

Java 8 introduces three primitive specialized stream interfaces to tackle this issue, Int-Stream, DoubleStream, and LongStream, which respectively specialize the elements of a stream to be int, long, and double—and thereby avoid hidden boxing costs. Each of these interfaces brings new methods to perform common numeric reductions, such as sum to calculate the sum of a numeric stream and max to find the maximum element. In addition, they have methods to convert back to a stream of objects when necessary. The thing to remember is that the additional complexity of these specializations isn't inherent to streams. It reflects the complexity of boxing—the (efficiency-based) difference between int and Integer and so on.

MAPPING TO A NUMERIC STREAM

The most common methods you'll use to convert a stream to a specialized version are mapToInt, mapToDouble, and mapToLong. These methods work exactly like the method map that you saw earlier but return a specialized stream instead of a Stream<T>. For example, you can use mapToInt as follows to calculate the sum of calories in the menu:

```
int calories = menu.stream()                          ←—┐ Returns a Stream<Dish>
                   .mapToInt(Dish::getCalories)   ←——┘
                   .sum();                              │ Returns an IntStream
```

Here, the method mapToInt extracts all the calories from each dish (represented as an Integer) and returns an IntStream as the result (rather than a Stream<Integer>).

You can then call the sum method defined on the `IntStream` interface to calculate the sum of calories! Note that if the stream were empty, sum would return 0 by default. `IntStream` also supports other convenience methods such as max, min, and average.

CONVERTING BACK TO A STREAM OF OBJECTS

Similarly, once you have a numeric stream, you may be interested in converting it back to a nonspecialized stream. For example, the operations of an `IntStream` are restricted to produce primitive integers: the map operation of an `IntStream` takes a lambda that takes an int and produces an int (an `IntUnaryOperator`). But you may want to produce a different value such as a `Dish`. For this you need to access the operations defined in the `Streams` interface that are more general. To convert from a primitive stream to a general stream (each int will be boxed to an `Integer`) you can use the method boxed, as follows:

```
IntStream intStream = menu.stream().mapToInt(Dish::getCalories);   ← Converts a Stream to a numeric stream
Stream<Integer> stream = intStream.boxed();   ← Converts the numeric stream to a Stream
```

You'll learn in the next section that boxed is particularly useful when you deal with numeric ranges that need to be boxed into a general stream.

DEFAULT VALUES: OPTIONALINT

The sum example was convenient because it has a default value: 0. But if you want to calculate the maximum element in an `IntStream`, you'll need something different because 0 is a wrong result. How can you differentiate that the stream has no element and that the real maximum is 0? Earlier we introduced the `Optional` class, which is a container that indicates the presence or absence of a value. `Optional` can be parameterized with reference types such as `Integer`, `String`, and so on. There's a primitive specialized version of `Optional` as well for the three primitive stream specializations: `OptionalInt`, `OptionalDouble`, and `OptionalLong`.

For example, you can find the maximal element of an `IntStream` by calling the max method, which returns an `OptionalInt`:

```
OptionalInt maxCalories = menu.stream()
                              .mapToInt(Dish::getCalories)
                              .max();
```

You can now process the `OptionalInt` explicitly to define a default value if there's no maximum:

```
int max = maxCalories.orElse(1);   ← Provides an explicit default maximum if there's no value
```

5.7.2 Numeric ranges

A common use case when dealing with numbers is working with ranges of numeric values. For example, suppose you'd like to generate all numbers between 1 and 100. Java 8 introduces two static methods available on IntStream and LongStream to help generate such ranges: range and rangeClosed. Both methods take the starting value of the range as the first parameter and the end value of the range as the second parameter. But range is exclusive, whereas rangeClosed is inclusive. Let's look at an example:

Represents the range 1 to 100 ⟶

```
IntStream evenNumbers = IntStream.rangeClosed(1, 100)
                                 .filter(n -> n % 2 == 0);
System.out.println(evenNumbers.count());
```

Represents stream of even numbers from 1 to 100

Represents 50 even numbers from 1 to 100

Here you use the rangeClosed method to generate a range of all numbers from 1 to 100. It produces a stream so you can chain the filter method to select only even numbers. At this stage no computation has been done. Finally, you call count on the resulting stream. Because count is a terminal operation, it will process the stream and return the result 50, which is the number of even numbers from 1 to 100, inclusive. Note that by comparison, if you were using IntStream.range(1, 100) instead, the result would be 49 even numbers because range is exclusive.

5.7.3 Putting numerical streams into practice: Pythagorean triples

Now we'll look at a more difficult example so you can solidify what you've learned about numeric streams and all the stream operations you've learned so far. Your mission, if you choose to accept it, is to create a stream of Pythagorean triples.

PYTHAGOREAN TRIPLE

What's a Pythagorean triple? We have to go back a few years in the past. In one of your exciting math classes, you learned that the famous Greek mathematician Pythagoras discovered that certain triples of numbers (a, b, c) satisfy the formula a * a + b * b = c * c where a, b, and c are integers. For example, (3, 4, 5) is a valid Pythagorean triple because 3 * 3 + 4 * 4 = 5 * 5 or 9 + 16 = 25. There are an infinite number of such triples. For example, (5, 12, 13), (6, 8, 10), and (7, 24, 25) are all valid Pythagorean triples. Such triples are useful because they describe the three side lengths of a right-angled triangle, as illustrated in figure 5.9.

REPRESENTING A TRIPLE

Where do you start? The first step is to define a triple. Instead of (more properly) defining a new class to represent a triple, you can use an array of int with three elements. For example, new int[]{3, 4, 5} to represent the tuple (3, 4, 5). You can now access each individual component of the tuple using array indexing.

FILTERING GOOD COMBINATIONS

Let's assume someone provides you with the first two numbers of the triple: a and b. How do you know whether that will form a good combination? You need to test whether

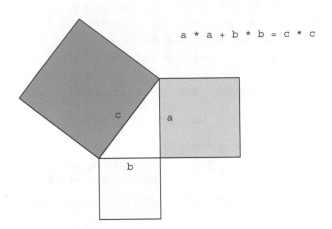

Figure 5.9   The Pythagorean theorem

the square root of a * a + b * b is a whole number. This is expressed in Java as `Math`
`.sqrt(a*a + b*b) % 1 == 0`. (Given a floating-point number, x, in Java its fractional part is
obtained using `x % 1.0`, and whole numbers like 5.0 have zero fractional part.) Our code
uses this idea in a `filter` operation (you'll see how to use this later to form valid code):

```
filter(b -> Math.sqrt(a*a + b*b) % 1 == 0)
```

Assuming that surrounding code has given a value for a, and assuming `stream` provides possible values for b, `filter` will select only those values for b that can form a
Pythagorean triple with a.

GENERATING TUPLES
Following the `filter`, you know that both a and b can form a correct combination.
You now need to create a triple. You can use the `map` operation to transform each ele-
ment into a Pythagorean triple as follows:

```
stream.filter(b -> Math.sqrt(a*a + b*b) % 1 == 0)
      .map(b -> new int[]{a, b, (int) Math.sqrt(a * a + b * b)});
```

GENERATING B VALUES
You're getting closer! You now need to generate values for b. You saw that `Stream`
`.rangeClosed` allows you to generate a stream of numbers in a given interval. You can
use it to provide numeric values for b, here 1 to 100:

```
IntStream.rangeClosed(1, 100)
        .filter(b -> Math.sqrt(a*a + b*b) % 1 == 0)
        .boxed()
        .map(b -> new int[]{a, b, (int) Math.sqrt(a * a + b * b)});
```

Note that you call boxed after the filter to generate a Stream<Integer> from the IntStream returned by rangeClosed. This is because map returns an array of int for each element of the stream. The map method from an IntStream expects only another int to be returned for each element of the stream, which isn't what you want! You can rewrite this using the method mapToObj of an IntStream, which returns an object-valued stream:

```
IntStream.rangeClosed(1, 100)
         .filter(b -> Math.sqrt(a*a + b*b) % 1 == 0)
         .mapToObj(b -> new int[]{a, b, (int) Math.sqrt(a * a + b * b)});
```

GENERATING A VALUES

There's one crucial component that we assumed was given: the value for a. You now have a stream that produces Pythagorean triples provided the value a is known. How can you fix this? Just like with b, you need to generate numeric values for a! The final solution is as follows:

```
Stream<int[]> pythagoreanTriples =
    IntStream.rangeClosed(1, 100).boxed()
            .flatMap(a ->
                IntStream.rangeClosed(a, 100)
                        .filter(b -> Math.sqrt(a*a + b*b) % 1 == 0)
                        .mapToObj(b ->
                            new int[]{a, b, (int)Math.sqrt(a * a + b * b)})
                );
```

Okay, what's the flatMap about? First, you create a numeric range from 1 to 100 to generate values for a. For each given value of a you're creating a stream of triples. Mapping a value of a to a stream of triples would result in a stream of streams! The flatMap method does the mapping and also flattens all the generated streams of triples into a single stream. As a result, you produce a stream of triples. Note also that you change the range of b to be a to 100. There's no need to start the range at the value 1 because this would create duplicate triples (for example, (3, 4, 5) and (4, 3, 5)).

RUNNING THE CODE

You can now run your solution and select explicitly how many triples you'd like to return from the generated stream using the limit operation that you saw earlier:

```
pythagoreanTriples.limit(5)
                  .forEach(t ->
                      System.out.println(t[0] + ", " + t[1] + ", " + t[2]));
```

This will print

```
3, 4, 5
5, 12, 13
6, 8, 10
7, 24, 25
8, 15, 17
```

CAN YOU DO BETTER?

The current solution isn't optimal because you calculate the square root twice. One possible way to make your code more compact is to generate all triples of the form (a*a, b*b, a*a+b*b) and then filter the ones that match your criteria:

```
Stream<double[]> pythagoreanTriples2 =
  IntStream.rangeClosed(1, 100).boxed()
          .flatMap(a ->
              IntStream.rangeClosed(a, 100)                    Produces triples
                  .mapToObj(
                      b -> new double[]{a, b, Math.sqrt(a*a + b*b)})   <──┘
                  .filter(t -> t[2] % 1 == 0));
```

The third element of the tuple must be a whole number.

5.8   *Building streams*

Hopefully, by now you're convinced that streams are powerful and useful to express data-processing queries. You were able to get a stream from a collection using the stream method. In addition, we showed you how to create numerical streams from a range of numbers. But you can create streams in many more ways! This section shows how you can create a stream from a sequence of values, from an array, from a file, and even from a generative function to create infinite streams!

5.8.1   *Streams from values*

You can create a stream with explicit values by using the static method Stream.of, which can take any number of parameters. For example, in the following code you create a stream of strings directly using Stream.of. You then convert the strings to uppercase before printing them one by one:

```
Stream<String> stream = Stream.of("Modern ", "Java ", "In ", "Action");
stream.map(String::toUpperCase).forEach(System.out::println);
```

You can get an empty stream using the empty method as follows:

```
Stream<String> emptyStream = Stream.empty();
```

5.8.2   *Stream from nullable*

In Java 9, a new method was added that lets you create a stream from a nullable object. After playing with streams, you may have encountered a situation where you extracted an object that may be null and then needs to be converted into a stream (or an empty stream for null). For example, the method System.getProperty returns null if there is no property with the given key. To use it together with a stream, you'd need to explicitly check for null as follows:

```
String homeValue = System.getProperty("home");
Stream<String> homeValueStream
    = homeValue == null ? Stream.empty() : Stream.of(value);
```

Using `Stream.ofNullable` you can rewrite this code more simply:

```
Stream<String> homeValueStream
    = Stream.ofNullable(System.getProperty("home"));
```

This pattern can be particularly handy in conjunction with `flatMap` and a stream of values that may include nullable objects:

```
Stream<String> values =
    Stream.of("config", "home", "user")
          .flatMap(key -> Stream.ofNullable(System.getProperty(key)));
```

5.8.3 Streams from arrays

You can create a stream from an array using the static method `Arrays.stream`, which takes an array as parameter. For example, you can convert an array of primitive `int`s into an `IntStream` and then sum the `IntStream` to produce an `int`, as follows:

```
int[] numbers = {2, 3, 5, 7, 11, 13};
int sum = Arrays.stream(numbers).sum();          ←— The sum is 41.
```

5.8.4 Streams from files

Java's NIO API (non-blocking I/O), which is used for I/O operations such as processing a file, has been updated to take advantage of the Streams API. Many static methods in `java.nio.file.Files` return a stream. For example, a useful method is `Files.lines`, which returns a stream of lines as strings from a given file. Using what you've learned so far, you could use this method to find out the number of unique words in a file as follows:

```
long uniqueWords = 0;                                    Streams are AutoCloseable so
try(Stream<String> lines =                               there's no need for try-finally
        Files.lines(Paths.get("data.txt"), Charset.defaultCharset())){  ←—
uniqueWords = lines.flatMap(line -> Arrays.stream(line.split(" ")))  ←—
                   .distinct()                   ←—       Removes       Generates
                   .count();    ←—                        duplicates    a stream
}                                     Counts the number                 of words
catch(IOException e){                 of unique words
                        ←—
}                              Deals with the exception if one
                               occurs when opening the file
```

You use `Files.lines` to return a stream where each element is a line in the given file. This call is surrounded by a `try/catch` block because the source of the stream is an I/O resource. In fact, the call `Files.lines` will open an I/O resource, which needs to be closed to avoid a leak. In the past, you'd need an explicit `finally` block to do this. Conveniently, the `Stream` interface implements the interface `AutoCloseable`. This means that the management of the resource is handled for you within the `try` block. Once you have a stream of lines, you can then split each line into words by calling the `split` method on `line`. Notice how you use `flatMap` to produce one flattened stream of words instead of multiple streams of words for each line. Finally, you count each distinct word in the stream by chaining the methods `distinct` and `count`.

5.8.5   *Streams from functions: creating infinite streams!*

The Streams API provides two static methods to generate a stream from a function: `Stream.iterate` and `Stream.generate`. These two operations let you create what we call an *infinite stream*, a stream that doesn't have a fixed size like when you create a stream from a fixed collection. Streams produced by `iterate` and `generate` create values on demand given a function and can therefore calculate values forever! It's generally sensible to use `limit(n)` on such streams to avoid printing an infinite number of values.

ITERATE

Let's look at a simple example of how to use `iterate` before we explain it:

```
Stream.iterate(0, n -> n + 2)
      .limit(10)
      .forEach(System.out::println);
```

The `iterate` method takes an initial value, here 0, and a lambda (of type `UnaryOperator<T>`) to apply successively on each new value produced. Here you return the previous element added with 2 using the lambda `n -> n + 2`. As a result, the `iterate` method produces a stream of all even numbers: the first element of the stream is the initial value 0. Then it adds 2 to produce the new value 2; it adds 2 again to produce the new value 4 and so on. This `iterate` operation is fundamentally sequential because the result depends on the previous application. Note that this operation produces an *infinite stream*—the stream doesn't have an end because values are computed on demand and can be computed forever. We say the stream is *unbounded*. As we discussed earlier, this is a key difference between a stream and a collection. You're using the `limit` method to explicitly limit the size of the stream. Here you select only the first 10 even numbers. You then call the `forEach` terminal operation to consume the stream and print each element individually.

In general, you should use `iterate` when you need to produce a sequence of successive values (for example, a date followed by its next date: January 31, February 1, and so on). To see a more difficult example of how you can apply `iterate`, try out quiz 5.4.

Quiz 5.4: Fibonacci tuples series

The Fibonacci series is famous as a classic programming exercise. The numbers in the following sequence are part of the Fibonacci series: 0, 1, 1, 2, 3, 5, 8, 13, 21, 34, 55. . . . The first two numbers of the series are 0 and 1, and each subsequent number is the sum of the previous two.

The series of Fibonacci tuples is similar; you have a sequence of a number and its successor in the series: (0, 1), (1, 1), (1, 2), (2, 3), (3, 5), (5, 8), (8, 13), (13, 21). . . .

Your task is to generate the first 20 elements of the series of Fibonacci tuples using the iterate method!

Let us help you get started. The first problem is that the iterate method takes a UnaryOperator<T> as argument, and you need a stream of tuples such as (0, 1). You can, again rather sloppily, use an array of two elements to represent a tuple. For example, new int[]{0, 1} represents the first element of the Fibonacci series (0, 1). This will be the initial value of the iterate method:

```
Stream.iterate(new int[]{0, 1}, ???)
    .limit(20)
    .forEach(t -> System.out.println("(" + t[0] + "," + t[1] +")"));
```

In this quiz, you need to figure out the highlighted ??? in the code. Remember that iterate will apply the given lambda successively.

Answer:

```
Stream.iterate(new int[]{0, 1},
            t -> new int[]{t[1], t[0]+t[1]})
    .limit(20)
    .forEach(t -> System.out.println("(" + t[0] + "," + t[1] +")"));
```

How does it work? iterate needs a lambda to specify the successor element. In the case of the tuple (3, 5) the successor is (5, 3+5) = (5, 8). The next one is (8, 5+8). Can you see the pattern? Given a tuple, the successor is (t[1], t[0] + t[1]). This is what the following lambda specifies: t -> new int[]{t[1],t[0] + t[1]}. By running this code you'll get the series (0, 1), (1, 1), (1, 2), (2, 3), (3, 5), (5, 8), (8, 13), (13, 21). . . . Note that if you wanted to print the normal Fibonacci series, you could use a map to extract only the first element of each tuple:

```
Stream.iterate(new int[]{0, 1},
            t -> new int[]{t[1],t[0] + t[1]})
    .limit(10)
    .map(t -> t[0])
    .forEach(System.out::println);
```

This code will produce the Fibonacci series: 0, 1, 1, 2, 3, 5, 8, 13, 21, 34 . . .

In Java 9, the iterate method was enhanced with support for a predicate. For example, you can generate numbers starting at 0 but stop the iteration once the number is greater than 100:

```
IntStream.iterate(0, n -> n < 100, n -> n + 4)
        .forEach(System.out::println);
```

The `iterate` method takes a predicate as its second argument that tells you when to continue iterating up until. Note that you may think that you can use the `filter` operation to achieve the same result:

```
IntStream.iterate(0, n -> n + 4)
         .filter(n -> n < 100)
         .forEach(System.out::println);
```

Unfortunately that isn't the case. In fact, this code wouldn't terminate! The reason is that there's no way to know in the filter that the numbers continue to increase, so it keeps on filtering them infinitely! You could solve the problem by using `takeWhile`, which would short-circuit the stream:

```
IntStream.iterate(0, n -> n + 4)
         .takeWhile(n -> n < 100)
         .forEach(System.out::println);
```

But, you have to admit that `iterate` with a predicate is a bit more concise!

GENERATE

Similarly to the method `iterate`, the method `generate` lets you produce an infinite stream of values computed on demand. But `generate` doesn't apply successively a function on each new produced value. It takes a lambda of type `Supplier<T>` to provide new values. Let's look at an example of how to use it:

```
Stream.generate(Math::random)
      .limit(5)
      .forEach(System.out::println);
```

This code will generate a stream of five random double numbers from 0 to 1. For example, one run gives the following:

```
0.9410810294106129
0.6586270755634592
0.9592859117266873
0.13743396659487006
0.3942776037651241
```

The static method `Math.random` is used as a generator for new values. Again you limit the size of the stream explicitly using the `limit` method; otherwise the stream would be unbounded!

You may be wondering whether there's anything else useful you can do using the method `generate`. The supplier we used (a method reference to `Math.random`) was stateless: it wasn't recording any values somewhere that can be used in later computations. But a supplier doesn't have to be stateless. You can create a supplier that stores state that it can modify and use when generating the next value of the stream. As an example, we'll show how you can also create the Fibonacci series from quiz 5.4 using `generate` so that you can compare it with the approach using the `iterate` method!

But it's important to note that a supplier that's stateful isn't safe to use in parallel code. The stateful `IntSupplier` for Fibonacci is shown at the end of this chapter for completeness but should generally be avoided! We discuss the problem of operations with side effects and parallel streams further in chapter 7.

We'll use an `IntStream` in our example to illustrate code that's designed to avoid boxing operations. The `generate` method on `IntStream` takes an `IntSupplier` instead of a `Supplier<T>`. For example, here's how to generate an infinite stream of ones:

```
IntStream ones = IntStream.generate(() -> 1);
```

You saw in chapter 3 that lambdas let you create an instance of a functional interface by providing the implementation of the method directly inline. You can also pass an explicit object, as follows, by implementing the `getAsInt` method defined in the `IntSupplier` interface (although this seems gratuitously long-winded, please bear with us):

```
IntStream twos = IntStream.generate(new IntSupplier(){
        public int getAsInt(){
            return 2;
        }
    });
```

The `generate` method will use the given supplier and repeatedly call the `getAsInt` method, which always returns 2. But the difference between the anonymous class used here and a lambda is that the anonymous class can define state via fields, which the `getAsInt` method can modify. This is an example of a side effect. All lambdas you've seen so far were side-effect free; they didn't change any state.

To come back to our Fibonacci tasks, what you need to do now is create an `Int-Supplier` that maintains in its state the previous value in the series, so `getAsInt` can use it to calculate the next element. In addition, it can update the state of the `IntSupplier` for the next time it's called. The following code shows how to create an `IntSupplier` that will return the next Fibonacci element when it's called:

```
IntSupplier fib = new IntSupplier(){
    private int previous = 0;
    private int current = 1;
    public int getAsInt(){
        int oldPrevious = this.previous;
        int nextValue = this.previous + this.current;
        this.previous = this.current;
        this.current = nextValue;
        return oldPrevious;
    }
};
IntStream.generate(fib).limit(10).forEach(System.out::println);
```

The code creates an instance of `IntSupplier`. This object has a *mutable* state: it tracks the previous Fibonacci element and the current Fibonacci element in two instance variables. The `getAsInt` method changes the state of the object when it's called so that it produces new values on each call. In comparison, our approach using `iterate` was purely *immutable*; you didn't modify existing state but were creating new tuples at each iteration. You'll learn in chapter 7 that you should always prefer an *immutable approach* in order to process a stream in parallel and expect a correct result.

Note that because you're dealing with a stream of infinite size, you have to limit its size explicitly using the operation `limit`; otherwise, the terminal operation (in this case `forEach`) will compute forever. Similarly, you can't sort or reduce an infinite stream because all elements need to be processed, but this would take forever because the stream contains an infinite number of elements!

5.9   Overview

It's been a long but rewarding chapter! You can now process collections more effectively. Indeed, streams let you express sophisticated data processing queries concisely. In addition, streams can be parallelized transparently.

Summary

- The Streams API lets you express complex data processing queries. Common stream operations are summarized in table 5.1.
- You can filter and slice a stream using the `filter`, `distinct`, `takeWhile` (Java 9), `dropWhile` (Java 9), `skip`, and `limit` methods.
- The methods `takeWhile` and `dropWhile` are more efficient than a filter when you know that the source is sorted.
- You can extract or transform elements of a stream using the `map` and `flatMap` methods.
- You can find elements in a stream using the `findFirst` and `findAny` methods. You can match a given predicate in a stream using the `allMatch`, `noneMatch`, and `anyMatch` methods.
- These methods make use of short-circuiting: a computation stops as soon as a result is found; there's no need to process the whole stream.
- You can combine all elements of a stream iteratively to produce a result using the `reduce` method, for example, to calculate the sum or find the maximum of a stream.
- Some operations such as `filter` and `map` are stateless: they don't store any state. Some operations such as `reduce` store state to calculate a value. Some operations such as `sorted` and `distinct` also store state because they need to buffer all the elements of a stream before returning a new stream. Such operations are called *stateful operations*.

- There are three primitive specializations of streams: `IntStream`, `DoubleStream`, and `LongStream`. Their operations are also specialized accordingly.
- Streams can be created not only from a collection but also from values, arrays, files, and specific methods such as `iterate` and `generate`.
- An infinite stream has an infinite number of elements (for example all possible strings). This is possible because the elements of a stream are only produced *on demand*. You can get a finite stream from an infinite stream using methods such as `limit`.

Collecting data with streams

You learned in the previous chapter that streams help you process collections with database-like operations. You can view Java 8 streams as fancy lazy iterators of sets of data. They support two types of operations: intermediate operations such as `filter` or `map` and terminal operations such as `count`, `findFirst`, `forEach`, and `reduce`. Intermediate operations can be chained to convert a stream into another stream. These operations don't consume from a stream; their purpose is to set up a pipeline of streams. By contrast, terminal operations *do* consume from a stream—to produce a final result (for example, returning the largest element in a stream). They can often shorten computations by optimizing the pipeline of a stream.

We already used the `collect` terminal operation on streams in chapters 4 and 5, but we employed it there mainly to combine all the elements of a stream into a

List. In this chapter, you'll discover that `collect` is a reduction operation, like `reduce`, that takes as an argument various recipes for accumulating the elements of a stream into a summary result. These recipes are defined by a new `Collector` interface, so it's important to distinguish `Collection`, `Collector`, and `collect`!

Here are some example queries of what you'll be able to do using `collect` and collectors:

- Group a list of transactions by currency to obtain the sum of the values of all transactions with that currency (returning a `Map<Currency, Integer>`)
- Partition a list of transactions into two groups: expensive and not expensive (returning a `Map<Boolean, List<Transaction>>`)
- Create multilevel groupings, such as grouping transactions by cities and then further categorizing by whether they're expensive or not (returning a `Map<String, Map<Boolean, List<Transaction>>>`)

Excited? Great. Let's start by exploring an example that benefits from collectors. Imagine a scenario where you have a `List` of `Transactions`, and you want to group them based on their nominal currency. Prior to Java 8, even a simple use case like this is cumbersome to implement, as shown in the following listing.

Listing 6.1 Grouping transactions by currency in imperative style

Iterates the List of Transactions

Creates the Map where the grouped transaction will be accumulated

```
Map<Currency, List<Transaction>> transactionsByCurrencies =
                                        new HashMap<>();
for (Transaction transaction : transactions) {
    Currency currency = transaction.getCurrency();
    List<Transaction> transactionsForCurrency =
                        transactionsByCurrencies.get(currency);
    if (transactionsForCurrency == null) {
        transactionsForCurrency = new ArrayList<>();
        transactionsByCurrencies
                    .put(currency, transactionsForCurrency);
    }
    transactionsForCurrency.add(transaction);
}
```

Extracts the Transaction's currency

Adds the currently traversed Transaction to the List of Transactions with the same currency

If there's no entry in the grouping Map for this currency, creates it

---

If you're an experienced Java developer, you'll probably feel comfortable writing something like this, but you have to admit that it's a lot of code for such a simple task. Even worse, this is probably harder to read than to write! The purpose of the code isn't immediately evident at first glance, even though it can be expressed in a straightforward manner in plain English: "Group a list of transactions by their currency." As you'll learn in this chapter, you can achieve exactly the same result with a single statement by using a more general `Collector` parameter to the `collect` method on stream rather than the `toList` special case used in the previous chapter:

```
Map<Currency, List<Transaction>> transactionsByCurrencies =
        transactions.stream().collect(groupingBy(Transaction::getCurrency));
```

The comparison is quite embarrassing, isn't it?

6.1   *Collectors in a nutshell*

The previous example clearly shows one of the main advantages of functional-style programming over an imperative approach: you have to formulate the result you want to obtain the "what" and not the steps performed to obtain it, the "how." In the previous example, the argument passed to the `collect` method is an implementation of the `Collector` interface, which is a recipe for how to build a summary of the elements in the stream. In the previous chapter, the `toList` recipe said, "Make a list of each element in turn." In this example, the `groupingBy` recipe says, "Make a `Map` whose keys are (currency) buckets and whose values are a list of elements in those buckets."

The difference between the imperative and functional versions of this example is even more pronounced if you perform multilevel groupings: in that case the imperative code quickly becomes harder to read, maintain, and modify due to the number of deeply nested loops and conditions required. In comparison, the functional-style version, as you'll discover in section 6.3, can be easily enhanced with an additional collector.

6.1.1   *Collectors as advanced reductions*

This last observation brings up another typical benefit of a well-designed functional API: its higher degree of composability and reusability. Collectors are extremely useful, because they provide a concise yet flexible way to define the criteria that `collect` uses to produce the resulting collection. More specifically, invoking the `collect` method on a stream triggers a reduction operation (parameterized by a `Collector`) on the elements of the stream itself. This *reduction operation*, illustrated in figure 6.1, does for you internally what you had to code imperatively in listing 6.1. It traverses each element of the stream and lets the `Collector` process them.

Typically, the `Collector` applies a transforming function to the element. Quite often this is the identity transformation, which has no effect (for example, as in `toList`). The function then accumulates the result in a data structure that forms the final output of this process. For instance, in our transaction-grouping example shown previously, the transformation function extracts the currency from each transaction, and subsequently the transaction itself is accumulated in the resulting `Map`, using the currency as key.

The implementation of the methods of the `Collector` interface defines how to perform a reduction operation on a stream, such as the one in our currency example. We'll investigate how to create customized collectors in sections 6.5 and 6.6. But the `Collectors` utility class provides lots of static factory methods to conveniently create

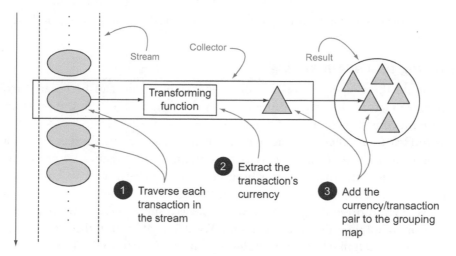

Figure 6.1 The reduction process grouping the transactions by currency

an instance of the most common collectors that are ready to use. The most straightforward and frequently used collector is the `toList` static method, which gathers all the elements of a stream into a `List`:

```
List<Transaction> transactions =
    transactionStream.collect(Collectors.toList());
```

6.1.2 *Predefined collectors*

In the rest of this chapter, we'll mainly explore the features of the predefined collectors, those that can be created from the factory methods (such as `groupingBy`) provided by the `Collectors` class. These offer three main functionalities:

- Reducing and summarizing stream elements to a single value
- Grouping elements
- Partitioning elements

We start with collectors that allow you to reduce and summarize. These are handy in a variety of use cases, such as finding the total amount of the transacted values in the list of transactions in the previous example.

You'll then see how to group the elements of a stream, generalizing the previous example to multiple levels of grouping or combining different collectors to apply further reduction operations on each of the resulting subgroups. We'll also describe *partitioning* as a special case of grouping, using a predicate (a one-argument function returning a boolean) as a grouping function.

At the end of section 6.4 you'll find a table summarizing all the predefined collectors explored in this chapter. Finally, in section 6.5 you'll learn more about the `Collector` interface before you explore (in section 6.6) how you can create your own custom collectors to be used in the cases not covered by the factory methods of the `Collectors` class.

6.2   *Reducing and summarizing*

To illustrate the range of possible collector instances that can be created from the `Collectors` factory class, we'll reuse the domain we introduced in the previous chapter: a menu consisting of a list of delicious dishes!

As you learned, collectors (the parameters to the `stream` method `collect`) are typically used in cases where it's necessary to reorganize the stream's items into a collection. But more generally, they can be used every time you want to combine all the items in the stream into a single result. This result can be of any type, as complex as a multilevel map representing a tree or as simple as a single integer, perhaps representing the sum of all the calories in the menu. We'll look at both of these result types: single integers in section 6.2.2 and multilevel grouping in section 6.3.1.

As a first simple example, let's count the number of dishes in the menu, using the collector returned by the `counting` factory method:

```
long howManyDishes = menu.stream().collect(Collectors.counting());
```

You can write this far more directly as

```
long howManyDishes = menu.stream().count();
```

but the `counting` collector can be useful when used in combination with other collectors, as we'll demonstrate later.

In the rest of this chapter, we'll assume that you've imported all the static factory methods of the `Collectors` class with

```
import static java.util.stream.Collectors.*;
```

so you can write `counting()` instead of `Collectors.counting()` and so on.

Let's continue exploring simple predefined collectors by looking at how you can find the maximum and minimum values in a stream.

6.2.1   *Finding maximum and minimum in a stream of values*

Suppose you want to find the highest-calorie dish in the menu. You can use two collectors, `Collectors.maxBy` and `Collectors.minBy`, to calculate the maximum or minimum value in a stream. These two collectors take a `Comparator` as argument to compare the elements in the stream. Here you create a `Comparator` comparing dishes based on their calorie content and pass it to `Collectors.maxBy`:

```
Comparator<Dish> dishCaloriesComparator =
    Comparator.comparingInt(Dish::getCalories);
Optional<Dish> mostCalorieDish =
    menu.stream()
        .collect(maxBy(dishCaloriesComparator));
```

You may wonder what the `Optional<Dish>` is about. To answer this we have to ask the question, "What if menu were empty?" There's no dish to return! Java 8 introduces `Optional`, which is a container that may or may not contain a value. Here it perfectly represents the idea that there may or may not be a dish returned. We briefly mentioned it in chapter 5 when you encountered the method `findAny`. Don't worry about it for now; we devote chapter 11 to the study of `Optional<T>` and its operations.

Another common reduction operation that returns a single value is to sum the values of a numeric field of the objects in a stream. Alternatively, you may want to average the values. Such operations are called *summarization* operations. Let's see how you can express them using collectors.

6.2.2 Summarization

The `Collectors` class provides a specific factory method for summing: `Collectors.summingInt`. It accepts a function that maps an object into the `int` that has to be summed and returns a collector that, when passed to the usual `collect` method, performs the requested summarization. For instance, you can find the total number of calories in your menu list with

```
int totalCalories = menu.stream().collect(summingInt(Dish::getCalories));
```

Here the collection process proceeds as illustrated in figure 6.2. While traversing the stream each dish is mapped into its number of calories, and that number is added to an accumulator starting from an initial value (in this case the value is `0`).

The `Collectors.summingLong` and `Collectors.summingDouble` methods behave exactly the same way and can be used where the field to be summed is respectively a `long` or a `double`.

But there's more to summarization than mere summing. A `Collectors.averagingInt`, together with its `averagingLong` and `averagingDouble` counterparts, is also available to calculate the average of the same set of numeric values:

```
double avgCalories =
    menu.stream().collect(averagingInt(Dish::getCalories));
```

So far, you've seen how to use collectors to count the elements in a stream, find the maximum and minimum values of a numeric property of those elements, and calculate their sum and average. Quite often, though, you may want to retrieve two or more of these results, and possibly you'd like to do it in a single operation. In this case, you can use the collector returned by the `summarizingInt` factory method. For example, you can count the elements in the menu and obtain the sum, average, maximum, and minimum of the calories contained in each dish with a single summarizing operation:

```
IntSummaryStatistics menuStatistics =
        menu.stream().collect(summarizingInt(Dish::getCalories));
```

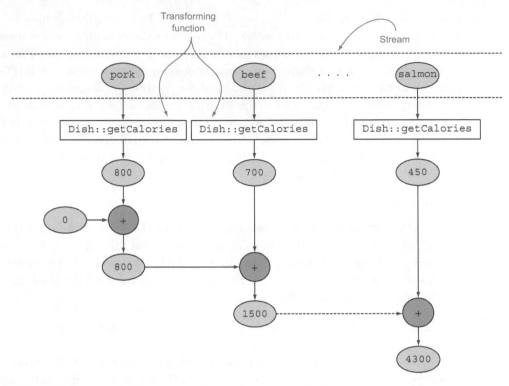

Figure 6.2 The aggregation process of the `summingInt` collector

This collector gathers all that information in a class called `IntSummaryStatistics` that provides convenient getter methods to access the results. Printing the menu-Statistic object produces the following output:

```
IntSummaryStatistics{count=9, sum=4300, min=120,
                     average=477.777778, max=800}
```

As usual, there are corresponding `summarizingLong` and `summarizingDouble` factory methods with associated types `LongSummaryStatistics` and `DoubleSummary-Statistics`. These are used when the property to be collected is a primitive-type `long` or a `double`.

6.2.3 *Joining Strings*

The collector returned by the `joining` factory method concatenates into a single string, all strings resulting from invoking the `toString` method on each object in the stream. This means you can concatenate the names of all the dishes in the menu as follows:

```
String shortMenu = menu.stream().map(Dish::getName).collect(joining());
```

Note that `joining` internally makes use of a `StringBuilder` to append the generated strings into one. Also note that if the `Dish` class had a `toString` method returning the dish's name, you'd obtain the same result without needing to map over the original stream with a function extracting the name from each dish:

```
String shortMenu = menu.stream().collect(joining());
```

Both produce the string

```
porkbeefchickenfrench friesriceseason fruitpizzaprawnssalmon
```

which is hard to read. Fortunately, the `joining` factory method is overloaded, with one of its overloaded variants taking a string used to delimit two consecutive elements, so you can obtain a comma-separated list of the dishes' names with

```
String shortMenu = menu.stream().map(Dish::getName).collect(joining(", "));
```

which, as expected, will generate

```
pork, beef, chicken, french fries, rice, season fruit, pizza, prawns, salmon
```

Until now, we've explored various collectors that reduce a stream to a single value. In the next section, we'll demonstrate how all the reduction processes of this form are special cases of the more general reduction collector provided by the `Collectors` `.reducing` factory method.

6.2.4 *Generalized summarization with reduction*

All the collectors we've discussed so far are, in reality, only convenient specializations of a reduction process that can be defined using the `reducing` factory method. The `Collectors.reducing` factory method is a generalization of all of them. The special cases discussed earlier are arguably provided only for programmer convenience. (But remember that programmer convenience and readability are of prime importance!) For instance, it's *possible* to calculate the total calories in your menu with a collector created from the `reducing` method as follows:

```
int totalCalories = menu.stream().collect(reducing(
                                0, Dish::getCalories, (i, j) -> i + j));
```

It takes three arguments:

- The first argument is the starting value of the reduction operation and will also be the value returned in the case of a stream with no elements, so clearly `0` is the appropriate value in the case of a numeric sum.
- The second argument is the same function you used in section 6.2.2 to transform a dish into an `int` representing its calorie content.
- The third argument is a `BinaryOperator` that aggregates two items into a single value of the same type. Here, it sums two `int`s.

Similarly, you could find the highest-calorie dish using the one-argument version of reducing as follows:

```
Optional<Dish> mostCalorieDish =
    menu.stream().collect(reducing(
        (d1, d2) -> d1.getCalories() > d2.getCalories() ? d1 : d2));
```

You can think of the collector created with the one-argument reducing factory method as a particular case of the three-argument method, which uses the first item in the stream as a starting point and an *identity function* (a function that returns its input argument as is) as a transformation function. This also implies that the one-argument reducing collector won't have any starting point when passed to the collect method of an empty stream and, as we explained in section 6.2.1, for this reason it returns an Optional<Dish> object.

Collect vs. reduce

We've discussed reductions a lot in the previous chapter and this one. You may wonder what the differences between the collect and reduce methods of the stream interface are, because often you can obtain the same results using either method. For instance, you can achieve what is done by the toList Collector using the reduce method as follows:

```
Stream<Integer> stream = Arrays.asList(1, 2, 3, 4, 5, 6).stream();
List<Integer> numbers = stream.reduce(
                            new ArrayList<Integer>(),
                            (List<Integer> l, Integer e) -> {
                                    l.add(e);
                                    return l; },
                            (List<Integer> l1, List<Integer> l2) -> {
                                    l1.addAll(l2);
                                    return l1; });
```

This solution has two problems: a semantic one and a practical one. The semantic problem lies in the fact that the reduce method is meant to combine two values and produce a new one; it's an immutable reduction. In contrast, the collect method is designed to mutate a container to accumulate the result it's supposed to produce. This means that the previous snippet of code is misusing the reduce method, because it's mutating in place the List used as accumulator. As you'll see in more detail in the next chapter, using the reduce method with the wrong semantic is also the cause of a practical problem: this reduction process can't work in parallel, because the concurrent modification of the same data structure operated by multiple threads can corrupt the List itself. In this case, if you want thread safety, you'll need to allocate a new List every time, which would impair performance by object allocation. This is the main reason why the collect method is useful for expressing reduction working on a mutable container but crucially in a parallel-friendly way, as you'll learn later in the chapter.

COLLECTION FRAMEWORK FLEXIBILITY: DOING THE SAME OPERATION IN DIFFERENT WAYS

You can further simplify the previous sum example using the `reducing` collector by using a reference to the `sum` method of the `Integer` class instead of the lambda expression you used to encode the same operation. This results in the following:

```
int totalCalories = menu.stream().collect(reducing(0,       ←——— Initial value
                            Dish::getCalories,        ←—
          Aggregating  |——→  Integer::sum));              Transformation
          function     |                                  function
```

Logically, this reduction operation proceeds as shown in figure 6.3, where an accumulator—initialized with a starting value—is iteratively combined using an aggregating function, with the result of the application of the transforming function on each element of the stream.

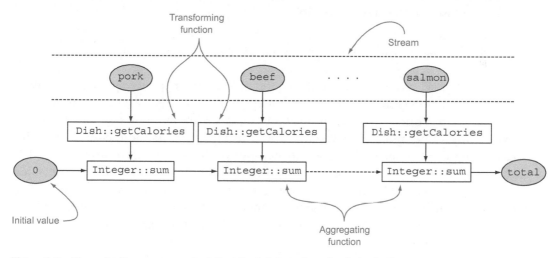

Figure 6.3 The reduction process calculating the total number of calories in the menu

The `counting` collector we mentioned at the beginning of section 6.2 is, in reality, similarly implemented using the three-argument `reducing` factory method. It transforms each element in the stream into an object of type `Long` with value `1` and then sums all these ones. It is implemented as follows:

```
public static <T> Collector<T, ?, Long> counting() {
    return reducing(0L, e -> 1L, Long::sum);
}
```

> ### Use of the generic ? wildcard
>
> In the code snippet just shown, you probably noticed the ? wildcard, used as the second generic type in the signature of the collector returned by the `counting` factory method. You should already be familiar with this notation, especially if you use the Java Collection Framework quite frequently. But here it means only that the type of the collector's accumulator is unknown, or equivalently the accumulator itself can be of any type. We used it here to exactly report the signature of the method as originally defined in the `Collectors` class, but in the rest of the chapter, we avoid any wildcard notation to keep the discussion as simple as possible.

We already observed in chapter 5 that there's another way to perform the same operation without using a collector—by mapping the stream of dishes into the number of calories of each dish and then reducing this resulting stream with the same method reference used in the previous version:

```
int totalCalories =
    menu.stream().map(Dish::getCalories).reduce(Integer::sum).get();
```

Note that, like any one-argument `reduce` operation on a stream, the invocation `reduce(Integer::sum)` doesn't return an int but an `Optional<Integer>` to manage the case of a reduction operation over an empty stream in a null-safe way. Here you extract the value inside the `Optional` object using its `get` method. Note that in this case using the `get` method is safe only because you're sure that the stream of dishes isn't empty. In general, as you'll learn in chapter 10, it's safer to unwrap the value eventually contained in an `Optional` using a method that also allows you to provide a default, such as `orElse` or `orElseGet`. Finally, and even more concisely, you can achieve the same result by mapping the stream to an `IntStream` and then invoking the `sum` method on it:

```
int totalCalories = menu.stream().mapToInt(Dish::getCalories).sum();
```

CHOOSING THE BEST SOLUTION FOR YOUR SITUATION

Once again, this demonstrates how functional programming in general (and the new API based on functional-style principles added to the Collections framework in Java 8 in particular) often provides multiple ways to perform the same operation. This example also shows that collectors are somewhat more complex to use than the methods directly available on the Streams interface, but in exchange they offer higher levels of abstraction and generalization and are more reusable and customizable.

Our suggestion is to explore the largest number of solutions possible to the problem at hand, but always choose the most specialized one that's general enough to solve it. This is often the best decision for both readability and performance reasons. For instance, to calculate the total calories in our menu, we'd prefer the last solution (using `IntStream`) because it's the most concise and likely also the most readable one.

At the same time, it's also the one that performs best, because IntStream lets us avoid all the *auto-unboxing* operations, or implicit conversions from Integer to int, that are useless in this case.

Next, test your understanding of how reducing can be used as a generalization of other collectors by working through the exercise in quiz 6.1.

Quiz 6.1: Joining strings with reducing

Which of the following statements using the reducing collector are valid replacements for this joining collector (as used in section 6.2.3)?

```
String shortMenu = menu.stream().map(Dish::getName).collect(joining());
```

1 String shortMenu = menu.stream().map(Dish::getName)
                          .collect(reducing((s1, s2) -> s1 + s2)).get();

2 String shortMenu = menu.stream()
      .collect(reducing((d1, d2) -> d1.getName() + d2.getName())
).get();

3 String shortMenu = menu.stream()
              .collect(reducing("", Dish::getName, (s1, s2) -> s1 + s2));

Answer:

Statements 1 and 3 are valid, whereas 2 doesn't compile.

1 This converts each dish in its name, as done by the original statement using the joining collector, and then reduces the resulting stream of strings using a String as accumulator and appending to it the names of the dishes one by one.

2 This doesn't compile because the one argument that reducing accepts is a BinaryOperator<T> that's a BiFunction<T,T,T>. This means that it wants a function taking two arguments and returns a value of the same type, but the lambda expression used there has two dishes as arguments but returns a string.

3 This starts the reduction process with an empty string as the accumulator, and when traversing the stream of dishes, it converts each dish to its name and appends this name to the accumulator. Note that, as we mentioned, reducing doesn't need the three arguments to return an Optional because in the case of an empty stream it can return a more meaningful value, which is the empty string used as the initial accumulator value.

Note that even though statements 1 and 3 are valid replacements for the joining collector, they've been used here to demonstrate how the reducing one can be seen, at least conceptually, as a generalization of all other collectors discussed in this chapter. Nevertheless, for all practical purposes we always suggest using the joining collector for both readability and performance reasons.

6.3   *Grouping*

A common database operation is to group items in a set, based on one or more properties. As you saw in the earlier transactions-currency-grouping example, this operation can be cumbersome, verbose, and error-prone when implemented with an
imperative style. But it can be easily translated in a single, readable statement by
rewriting it in a more functional style as encouraged by Java 8. As a second example of
how this feature works, suppose you want to classify the dishes in the menu according
to their type, putting the ones containing meat in a group, the ones with fish in
another group, and all others in a third group. You can easily perform this task using
a collector returned by the `Collectors.groupingBy` factory method, as follows:

```
Map<Dish.Type, List<Dish>> dishesByType =
                    menu.stream().collect(groupingBy(Dish::getType));
```

This will result in the following `Map`:

```
{FISH=[prawns, salmon], OTHER=[french fries, rice, season fruit, pizza],
 MEAT=[pork, beef, chicken]}
```

Here, you pass to the `groupingBy` method a `Function` (expressed in the form of a
method reference) extracting the corresponding `Dish.Type` for each `Dish` in the
stream. We call this `Function` a *classification* function specifically because it's used to
classify the elements of the stream into different groups. The result of this grouping
operation, shown in figure 6.4, is a `Map` having as map key the value returned by the classification function and as corresponding map value a list of all the items in the stream
having that classified value. In the menu-classification example, a key is the type of
dish, and its value is a list containing all the dishes of that type.

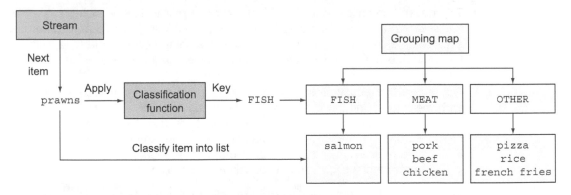

Figure 6.4   Classification of an item in the stream during the grouping process

But it isn't always possible to use a method reference as a classification function, because
you may wish to classify using something more complex than a simple property accessor.
For instance, you could decide to classify as "diet" all dishes with 400 calories or fewer,

set to "normal" the dishes having between 400 and 700 calories, and set to "fat" the ones with more than 700 calories. Because the author of the `Dish` class unhelpfully didn't provide such an operation as a method, you can't use a method reference in this case, but you can express this logic in a lambda expression:

```
public enum CaloricLevel { DIET, NORMAL, FAT }
Map<CaloricLevel, List<Dish>> dishesByCaloricLevel = menu.stream().collect(
        groupingBy(dish -> {
                if (dish.getCalories() <= 400) return CaloricLevel.DIET;
                else if (dish.getCalories() <= 700) return CaloricLevel.NORMAL;
                else return CaloricLevel.FAT;
        } ));
```

Now you've seen how to group the dishes in the menu, both by their type and by calories, but it could be also quite common that you may need to further manipulate the results of the original grouping, and in the next section we'll show how you achieve this.

6.3.1   *Manipulating grouped elements*

Frequently after performing a grouping operation you may need to manipulate the elements in each resulting group. Suppose, for example, that you want to filter only the caloric dishes, let's say the ones with more than 500 calories. You may argue that in this case you could apply this filtering predicate before the grouping like the following:

```
Map<Dish.Type, List<Dish>> caloricDishesByType =
                    menu.stream().filter(dish -> dish.getCalories() > 500)
                              .collect(groupingBy(Dish::getType));
```

This solution works but has a possibly relevant drawback. If you try to use it on the dishes in our menu, you will obtain a `Map` like the following:

```
{OTHER=[french fries, pizza], MEAT=[pork, beef]}
```

Do you see the problem there? Because there is no dish of type FISH satisfying our filtering predicate, that key totally disappeared from the resulting map. To workaround this problem the `Collectors` class overloads the `groupingBy` factory method, with one variant also taking a second argument of type `Collector` along with the usual classification function. In this way, it's possible to move the filtering predicate inside this second `Collector`, as follows:

```
Map<Dish.Type, List<Dish>> caloricDishesByType =
        menu.stream()
            .collect(groupingBy(Dish::getType,
                        filtering(dish -> dish.getCalories() > 500, toList())));
```

The `filtering` method is another static factory method of the `Collectors` class accepting a `Predicate` to filter the elements in each group and a further `Collector` that is used to regroup the filtered elements. In this way, the resulting Map will also keep an entry for the FISH type even if it maps an empty List:

```
{OTHER=[french fries, pizza], MEAT=[pork, beef], FISH=[]}
```

Another even more common way in which it could be useful to manipulate the grouped elements is transforming them through a mapping function. To this purpose, similarly to what you have seen for the filtering Collector, the Collectors class provides another Collector through the mapping method that accepts a mapping function and another Collector used to gather the elements resulting from the application of that function to each of them. By using it you can, for instance, convert each Dish in the groups into their respective names in this way:

```
Map<Dish.Type, List<String>> dishNamesByType =
    menu.stream()
        .collect(groupingBy(Dish::getType,
                    mapping(Dish::getName, toList())));
```

Note that in this case each group in the resulting Map is a List of Strings rather than one of Dishes as it was in the former examples. You could also use a third Collector in combination with the groupingBy to perform a flatMap transformation instead of a plain map. To demonstrate how this works let's suppose that we have a Map associating to each Dish a list of tags as it follows:

```
Map<String, List<String>> dishTags = new HashMap<>();
dishTags.put("pork", asList("greasy", "salty"));
dishTags.put("beef", asList("salty", "roasted"));
dishTags.put("chicken", asList("fried", "crisp"));
dishTags.put("french fries", asList("greasy", "fried"));
dishTags.put("rice", asList("light", "natural"));
dishTags.put("season fruit", asList("fresh", "natural"));
dishTags.put("pizza", asList("tasty", "salty"));
dishTags.put("prawns", asList("tasty", "roasted"));
dishTags.put("salmon", asList("delicious", "fresh"));
```

In case you are required to extract these tags for each group of type of dishes you can easily achieve this using the flatMapping Collector:

```
Map<Dish.Type, Set<String>> dishNamesByType =
    menu.stream()
        .collect(groupingBy(Dish::getType,
                    flatMapping(dish -> dishTags.get( dish.getName() ).stream(),
                        toSet())));
```

Here for each Dish we are obtaining a List of tags. So analogously to what we have already seen in the former chapter, we need to perform a flatMap in order to flatten the resulting two-level list into a single one. Also note that this time we collected the result of the flatMapping operations executed in each group into a Set instead of using a List as we did before, in order to avoid repetitions of same tags associated to more than one `Dish` in the same type. The `Map` resulting from this operation is then the following:

```
{MEAT=[salty, greasy, roasted, fried, crisp], FISH=[roasted, tasty, fresh,
    delicious], OTHER=[salty, greasy, natural, light, tasty, fresh, fried]}
```

Until this point we only used a single criterion to group the dishes in the menu, for instance by their type or by calories, but what if you want to use more than one criterion at the same time? Grouping is powerful because it composes effectively. Let's see how to do this.

6.3.2 Multilevel grouping

The two arguments `Collectors.groupingBy` factory method that we used in a former section to manipulate the elements in the groups resulting from the grouping operation can be used also to perform a two-level grouping. To achieve this you can pass to it a second inner `groupingBy` to the outer `groupingBy`, defining a second-level criterion to classify the stream's items, as shown in the next listing.

Listing 6.2 Multilevel grouping

```
Map<Dish.Type, Map<CaloricLevel, List<Dish>>> dishesByTypeCaloricLevel =
menu.stream().collect(
        groupingBy(Dish::getType,                ⟵──┤ First-level
          groupingBy(dish -> {                         classification function
                if (dish.getCalories() <= 400) return CaloricLevel.DIET;
                else if (dish.getCalories() <= 700) return CaloricLevel.NORMAL;
                else return CaloricLevel.FAT;
          } )
        )
);
```

Second-level classification function

The result of this two-level grouping is a two-level `Map` like the following:

```
{MEAT={DIET=[chicken], NORMAL=[beef], FAT=[pork]},
 FISH={DIET=[prawns], NORMAL=[salmon]},
 OTHER={DIET=[rice, seasonal fruit], NORMAL=[french fries, pizza]}}
```

Here the outer `Map` has as keys the values generated by the first-level classification function: fish, meat, other. The values of this `Map` are in turn other `Map`s, having as keys the values generated by the second-level classification function: normal, diet, or fat. Finally, the second-level `Map`s have as values the `List` of the elements in the stream returning the corresponding first- and second-level key values when applied respectively to the first and second classification functions: salmon, pizza, and so on. This multilevel grouping operation can be extended to any number of levels, and an *n*-level grouping has as a result an *n*-level `Map`, modeling an *n*-level tree structure.

Figure 6.5 shows how this structure is also equivalent to an *n*-dimensional table, highlighting the classification purpose of the grouping operation.

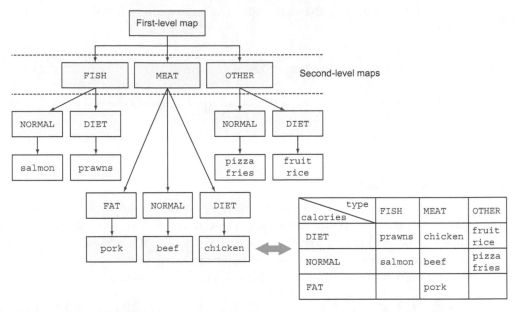

Figure 6.5   Equivalence between *n*-level nested map and *n*-dimensional classification table

In general, it helps to think that groupingBy works in terms of "buckets." The first groupingBy creates a bucket for each key. You then collect the elements in each bucket with the downstream collector and so on to achieve *n*-level groupings!

6.3.3   *Collecting data in subgroups*

In the previous section, you saw that it's possible to pass a second groupingBy collector to the outer one to achieve a multilevel grouping. But more generally, the second collector passed to the first groupingBy can be any type of collector, not just another groupingBy. For instance, it's possible to count the number of Dishes in the menu for each type, by passing the counting collector as a second argument to the groupingBy collector:

```
Map<Dish.Type, Long> typesCount = menu.stream().collect(
                    groupingBy(Dish::getType, counting()));
```

The result is the following Map:

```
{MEAT=3, FISH=2, OTHER=4}
```

Also note that the regular one-argument groupingBy(f), where f is the classification function is, in reality, shorthand for groupingBy(f, toList()).

To give another example, you could rework the collector you already used to find the highest-calorie dish in the menu to achieve a similar result, but now classified by the *type* of dish:

```
Map<Dish.Type, Optional<Dish>> mostCaloricByType =
    menu.stream()
        .collect(groupingBy(Dish::getType,
                            maxBy(comparingInt(Dish::getCalories)))));
```

The result of this grouping is then clearly a Map, having as keys the available types of Dishes and as values the Optional<Dish>, wrapping the corresponding highest-calorie Dish for a given type:

```
{FISH=Optional[salmon], OTHER=Optional[pizza], MEAT=Optional[pork]}
```

> **NOTE** The values in this Map are Optionals because this is the resulting type of the collector generated by the maxBy factory method, but in reality if there's no Dish in the menu for a given type, that type won't have an Optional.empty() as value; it won't be present at all as a key in the Map. The groupingBy collector lazily adds a new key in the grouping Map only the first time it finds an element in the stream, producing that key when applying on it the grouping criteria being used. This means that in this case, the Optional wrapper isn't useful, because it's not modeling a value that could be possibly absent but is there incidentally, only because this is the type returned by the reducing collector.

ADAPTING THE COLLECTOR RESULT TO A DIFFERENT TYPE

Because the Optionals wrapping all the values in the Map resulting from the last grouping operation aren't useful in this case, you may want to get rid of them. To achieve this, or more generally, to adapt the result returned by a collector to a different type, you could use the collector returned by the Collectors.collectingAndThen factory method, as shown in the following listing.

Listing 6.3   Finding the highest-calorie dish in each subgroup

```
Map<Dish.Type, Dish> mostCaloricByType =
    menu.stream()
        .collect(groupingBy(Dish::getType,            ←──┘ Classification function
                            collectingAndThen(
                                maxBy(comparingInt(Dish::getCalories)),   ←──┘ Wrapped collector
                                Optional::get)));
```

Transformation function └──▷

This factory method takes two arguments—the collector to be adapted and a transformation function—and returns another collector. This additional collector acts as a wrapper for the old one and maps the value it returns using the transformation function as the last step of the collect operation. In this case, the wrapped collector is the one created with maxBy, and the transformation function, Optional::get, extracts the value contained in the Optional returned. As we've said, here this is safe because the reducing collector will never return an Optional.empty(). The result is the following Map:

```
{FISH=salmon, OTHER=pizza, MEAT=pork}
```

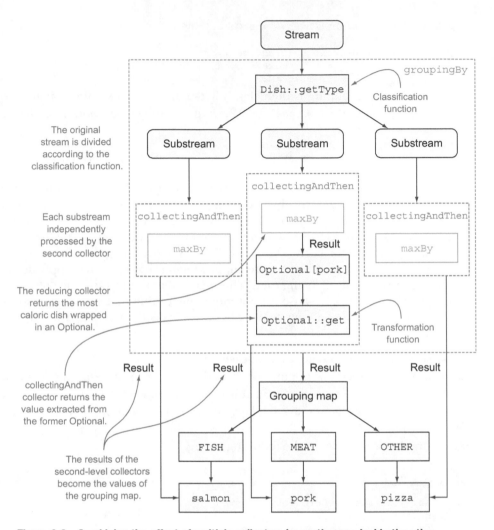

Figure 6.6   Combining the effect of multiple collectors by nesting one inside the other

It's quite common to use multiple nested collectors, and at first the way they interact may not always be obvious. Figure 6.6 helps you visualize how they work together. From the outermost layer and moving inward, note the following:

- The collectors are represented by the dashed lines, so groupingBy is the outermost one and groups the menu stream into three substreams according to the different dishes' types.
- The groupingBy collector wraps the collectingAndThen collector, so each substream resulting from the grouping operation is further reduced by this second collector.
- The collectingAndThen collector wraps in turn a third collector, the maxBy one.

- The reduction operation on the substreams is then performed by the reducing collector, but the `collectingAndThen` collector containing it applies the `Optional::get` transformation function to its result.
- The three transformed values, being the highest-calorie `Dishes` for a given type (resulting from the execution of this process on each of the three substreams), will be the values associated with the respective classification keys, the types of `Dishes`, in theMap returned by the `groupingBy` collector.

OTHER EXAMPLES OF COLLECTORS USED IN CONJUNCTION WITH GROUPINGBY

More generally, the collector passed as second argument to the `groupingBy` factory method will be used to perform a further reduction operation on all the elements in the stream classified into the same group. For example, you could also reuse the collector created to sum the calories of all the dishes in the menu to obtain a similar result, but this time for each group of `Dishes`:

```
Map<Dish.Type, Integer> totalCaloriesByType =
            menu.stream().collect(groupingBy(Dish::getType,
                    summingInt(Dish::getCalories)));
```

Yet another collector, commonly used in conjunction with `groupingBy`, is one generated by the `mapping` method. This method takes two arguments: a function transforming the elements in a stream and a further collector accumulating the objects resulting from this transformation. Its purpose is to adapt a collector accepting elements of a given type to one working on objects of a different type, by applying a mapping function to each input element before accumulating them. To see a practical example of using this collector, suppose you want to know which `CaloricLevels` are available in the menu for each type of `Dish`. You could achieve this result combining a `groupingBy` and a `mapping` collector, as follows:

```
Map<Dish.Type, Set<CaloricLevel>> caloricLevelsByType =
menu.stream().collect(
    groupingBy(Dish::getType, mapping(dish -> {
            if (dish.getCalories() <= 400) return CaloricLevel.DIET;
            else if (dish.getCalories() <= 700) return CaloricLevel.NORMAL;
            else return CaloricLevel.FAT; },
    toSet() )));
```

Here the transformation function passed to the mapping method maps a `Dish` into its `CaloricLevel`, as you've seen before. The resulting stream of `CaloricLevels` is then passed to a `toSet` collector, analogous to the `toList` one, but accumulating the elements of a stream into a `Set` instead of into a `List`, to keep only the distinct values. As in earlier examples, this mapping collector will then be used to collect the elements in each substream generated by the grouping function, allowing you to obtain as a result the following `Map`:

```
{OTHER=[DIET, NORMAL], MEAT=[DIET, NORMAL, FAT], FISH=[DIET, NORMAL]}
```

From this you can easily figure out your choices. If you're in the mood for fish and you're on a diet, you could easily find a dish; likewise, if you're hungry and want something with lots of calories, you could satisfy your robust appetite by choosing something from the meat section of the menu. Note that in the previous example, there are no guarantees about what type of `Set` is returned. But by using `toCollection`, you can have more control. For example, you can ask for a `HashSet` by passing a constructor reference to it:

```
Map<Dish.Type, Set<CaloricLevel>> caloricLevelsByType =
menu.stream().collect(
    groupingBy(Dish::getType, mapping(dish -> {
            if (dish.getCalories() <= 400) return CaloricLevel.DIET;
            else if (dish.getCalories() <= 700) return CaloricLevel.NORMAL;
            else return CaloricLevel.FAT; },
    toCollection(HashSet::new) )));
```

6.4   *Partitioning*

Partitioning is a special case of grouping: having a predicate called a *partitioning function* as a classification function. The fact that the partitioning function returns a boolean means the resulting grouping `Map` will have a `Boolean` as a key type, and therefore, there can be at most two different groups—one for `true` and one for `false`. For instance, if you're vegetarian or have invited a vegetarian friend to have dinner with you, you may be interested in partitioning the menu into vegetarian and nonvegetarian dishes:

Partitioning function

```
Map<Boolean, List<Dish>> partitionedMenu =
            menu.stream().collect(partitioningBy(Dish::isVegetarian));   ◁─┘
```

This will return the following `Map`:

```
{false=[pork, beef, chicken, prawns, salmon],
 true=[french fries, rice, season fruit, pizza]}
```

So you could retrieve all the vegetarian dishes by getting from this `Map` the value indexed with the key `true`:

```
List<Dish> vegetarianDishes = partitionedMenu.get(true);
```

Note that you could achieve the same result by filtering the stream created from the menu `List` with the same predicate used for partitioning and then collecting the result in an additional `List`:

```
List<Dish> vegetarianDishes =
            menu.stream().filter(Dish::isVegetarian).collect(toList());
```

6.4.1 *Advantages of partitioning*

Partitioning has the advantage of keeping both lists of the stream elements, for which the application of the partitioning function returns `true` or `false`. In the previous example, you can obtain the `List` of the nonvegetarian `Dishes` by accessing the value of the key `false` in the `partitionedMenu` Map, using two separate filtering operations: one with the predicate and one with its negation. Also, as you already saw for grouping, the `partitioningBy` factory method has an overloaded version to which you can pass a second collector, as shown here:

```
Map<Boolean, Map<Dish.Type, List<Dish>>> vegetarianDishesByType =
menu.stream().collect(
        partitioningBy(Dish::isVegetarian,          ◁——— Partitioning function
                groupingBy(Dish::getType)));        ◁——— Second collector
```

This will produce a two-level `Map`:

```
{false={FISH=[prawns, salmon], MEAT=[pork, beef, chicken]},
 true={OTHER=[french fries, rice, season fruit, pizza]}}
```

Here the grouping of the dishes by their type is applied individually to both of the substreams of vegetarian and nonvegetarian dishes resulting from the partitioning, producing a two-level `Map` that's similar to the one you obtained when you performed the two-level grouping in section 6.3.1. As another example, you can reuse your earlier code to find the most caloric dish among both vegetarian and nonvegetarian dishes:

```
Map<Boolean, Dish> mostCaloricPartitionedByVegetarian =
menu.stream().collect(
    partitioningBy(Dish::isVegetarian,
        collectingAndThen(maxBy(comparingInt(Dish::getCalories)),
                        Optional::get)));
```

That will produce the following result:

```
{false=pork, true=pizza}
```

We started this section by saying that you can think of partitioning as a special case of grouping. It's worth also noting that the `Map` implementation returned by `partitioningBy` is more compact and efficient as it only needs to contain two keys: true and false. In fact, the internal implementation is a specialized `Map` with two fields. The analogies between the `groupingBy` and `partitioningBy` collectors don't end here; as you'll see in the next quiz, you can also perform multilevel partitioning in a way similar to what you did for grouping in section 6.3.1.

To give one last example of how you can use the `partitioningBy` collector, we'll put aside the menu data model and look at something a bit more complex but also more interesting: partitioning numbers into prime and nonprime.

Quiz 6.2: Using partitioningBy

As you've seen, like the `groupingBy` collector, the `partitioningBy` collector can be used in combination with other collectors. In particular it could be used with a second `partitioningBy` collector to achieve a multilevel partitioning. What will be the result of the following multilevel partitionings?

```
1  menu.stream().collect(partitioningBy(Dish::isVegetarian,
                           partitioningBy(d -> d.getCalories() > 500)));


2  menu.stream().collect(partitioningBy(Dish::isVegetarian,
                           partitioningBy(Dish::getType)));


3  menu.stream().collect(partitioningBy(Dish::isVegetarian,
                           counting()));
```

Answer:

1 This is a valid multilevel partitioning, producing the following two-level `Map`:

```
{ false={false=[chicken, prawns, salmon], true=[pork, beef]},
   true={false=[rice, season fruit], true=[french fries, pizza]}}
```

2 This won't compile because `partitioningBy` requires a predicate, a function returning a boolean. And the method reference `Dish::getType` can't be used as a predicate.

3 This counts the number of items in each partition, resulting in the following `Map`:

```
{false=5, true=4}
```

6.4.2   *Partitioning numbers into prime and nonprime*

Suppose you want to write a method accepting as argument an `int` n and partitioning the first n natural numbers into prime and nonprime. But first, it will be useful to develop a predicate that tests to see if a given candidate number is prime or not:

```
public boolean isPrime(int candidate) {
    return IntStream.range(2, candidate)
                    .noneMatch(i -> candidate % i == 0);
}
```

Generates a range of natural numbers starting from and including 2, up to but excluding candidate

Returns true if the candidate isn't divisible for any of the numbers in the stream

A simple optimization is to test only for factors less than or equal to the square root of the candidate:

```
public boolean isPrime(int candidate) {
    int candidateRoot = (int) Math.sqrt((double) candidate);
    return IntStream.rangeClosed(2, candidateRoot)
                    .noneMatch(i -> candidate % i == 0);
}
```

Now the biggest part of the job is done. To partition the first *n* numbers into prime and nonprime, it's enough to create a stream containing those *n* numbers, and reduce it with a `partitioningBy` collector using as predicate the `isPrime` method you just developed:

```
public Map<Boolean, List<Integer>> partitionPrimes(int n) {
    return IntStream.rangeClosed(2, n).boxed()
                    .collect(
                        partitioningBy(candidate -> isPrime(candidate)));
}
```

We've now covered all the collectors that can be created using the static factory methods of the `Collectors` class, showing practical examples of how they work. Table 6.1 brings them all together with the type they return when applied to a `Stream<T>`, and a practical example of their use on a `Stream<Dish>` named `menuStream`.

Table 6.1 The main static factory methods of the `Collectors` class

Factory method	Returned type	Used to
`toList`	`List<T>`	Gather all the stream's items in a `List`.
Example use: `List<Dish> dishes = menuStream.collect(toList());`		
`toSet`	`Set<T>`	Gather all the stream's items in a `Set`, eliminating duplicates.
Example use: `Set<Dish> dishes = menuStream.collect(toSet());`		
`toCollection`	`Collection<T>`	Gather all the stream's items in the collection created by the provided supplier.
Example use: `Collection<Dish> dishes = menuStream.collect(toCollection(), ArrayList::new);`		
`counting`	`Long`	Count the number of items in the stream.
Example use: `long howManyDishes = menuStream.collect(counting());`		
`summingInt`	`Integer`	Sum the values of an Integer property of the items in the stream.
Example use: `int totalCalories = menuStream.collect(summingInt(Dish::getCalories));`		
`averagingInt`	`Double`	Calculate the average value of an `Integer` property of the items in the stream.
Example use: `double avgCalories = menuStream.collect(averagingInt(Dish::getCalories));`		
`summarizingInt`	`IntSummaryStatistics`	Collect statistics regarding an `Integer` property of the items in the stream, such as the maximum, minimum, total, and average.
Example use: `IntSummaryStatistics menuStatistics = menuStream.collect(summarizingInt(Dish::getCalories));`		

Table 6.1 The main static factory methods of the `Collectors` class *(continued)*

Factory method	Returned type	Used to
`joining`	`String`	Concatenate the strings resulting from the invocation of the `toString` method on each item of the stream.
Example use: `String shortMenu =` `        menuStream.map(Dish::getName).collect(joining(", "));`		
`maxBy`	`Optional<T>`	An `Optional` wrapping the maximal element in this stream according to the given comparator or `Optional.empty()` if the stream is empty.
Example use: `Optional<Dish> fattest =` `        menuStream.collect(maxBy(comparingInt(Dish::getCalories)));`		
`minBy`	`Optional<T>`	An `Optional` wrapping the minimal element in this stream according to the given comparator or `Optional.empty()` if the stream is empty.
Example use: `Optional<Dish> lightest =` `        menuStream.collect(minBy(comparingInt(Dish::getCalories)));`		
`reducing`	The type produced by the reduction operation	Reduce the stream to a single value starting from an initial value used as accumulator and iteratively combining it with each item of the stream using a `BinaryOperator`.
Example use: `int totalCalories =` `        menuStream.collect(reducing(0, Dish::getCalories, Integer::sum));`		
`collectingAndThen`	The type returned by the transforming function	Wrap another collector and apply a transformation function to its result.
Example use: `int howManyDishes =` `        menuStream.collect(collectingAndThen(toList(), List::size));`		
`groupingBy`	`Map<K, List<T>>`	Group the items in the stream based on the value of one of their properties and use those values as keys in the resulting `Map`.
Example use: `Map<Dish.Type,List<Dish>> dishesByType =` `        menuStream.collect(groupingBy(Dish::getType));`		
`partitioningBy`	`Map<Boolean, List<T>>`	Partition the items in the stream based on the result of the application of a predicate to each of them.
Example use: `Map<Boolean,List<Dish>> vegetarianDishes =` `        menuStream.collect(partitioningBy(Dish::isVegetarian));`		

As we mentioned at the beginning of the chapter, all these collectors implement the `Collector` interface, so in the remaining part of the chapter we investigate this interface in more detail. We investigate the methods in that interface and then explore how you can implement your own collectors.

6.5 *The Collector interface*

The `Collector` interface consists of a set of methods that provide a blueprint for how to implement specific reduction operations (collectors). You've seen many collectors that implement the `Collector` interface, such as `toList` or `groupingBy`. This also implies that you're free to create customized reduction operations by providing your own implementation of the `Collector` interface. In section 6.6 we'll show how you can implement the `Collector` interface to create a collector to partition a stream of numbers into prime and nonprime more efficiently than what you've seen so far.

To get started with the `Collector` interface, we focus on one of the first collectors you encountered at the beginning of this chapter: the `toList` factory method, which gathers all the elements of a stream in a `List`. We said that you'll frequently use this collector in your day-to-day job, but it's also one that, at least conceptually, is straightforward to develop. Investigating in more detail how this collector is implemented is a good way to understand how the `Collector` interface is defined and how the functions returned by its methods are internally used by the `collect` method.

Let's start by taking a look at the definition of the `Collector` interface in the next listing, which shows the interface signature together with the five methods it declares.

> **Listing 6.4 The `Collector` interface**

```
public interface Collector<T, A, R> {
    Supplier<A> supplier();
    BiConsumer<A, T> accumulator();
    Function<A, R> finisher();
    BinaryOperator<A> combiner();
    Set<Characteristics> characteristics();
}
```

In this listing, the following definitions apply:

- `T` is the generic type of the items in the stream to be collected.
- `A` is the type of the accumulator, the object on which the partial result will be accumulated during the collection process.
- `R` is the type of the object (typically, but not always, the collection) resulting from the collect operation.

For instance, you could implement a `ToListCollector<T>` class that gathers all the elements of a `Stream<T>` into a `List<T>` having the following signature

```
public class ToListCollector<T> implements Collector<T, List<T>, List<T>>
```

where, as we'll clarify shortly, the object used for the accumulation process will also be the final result of the collection process.

6.5.1   *Making sense of the methods declared by Collector interface*

We can now analyze the five methods declared by the Collector interface one by one. When we do so, you'll notice that each of the first four methods returns a function that will be invoked by the collect method, whereas the fifth one, characteristics, provides a set of characteristics that's a list of hints used by the collect method itself to know which optimizations (for example, parallelization) it's allowed to employ while performing the reduction operation.

MAKING A NEW RESULT CONTAINER: THE SUPPLIER METHOD

The supplier method has to return a Supplier of an empty accumulator—a parameterless function that when invoked creates an instance of an empty accumulator used during the collection process. Clearly, for a collector returning the accumulator itself as result, like our ToListCollector, this empty accumulator will also represent the result of the collection process when performed on an empty stream. In our ToListCollector the supplier will then return an empty List, as follows:

```
public Supplier<List<T>> supplier() {
    return () -> new ArrayList<T>();
}
```

Note that you could also pass a constructor reference:

```
public Supplier<List<T>> supplier() {
    return ArrayList::new;
}
```

ADDING AN ELEMENT TO A RESULT CONTAINER: THE ACCUMULATOR METHOD

The accumulator method returns the function that performs the reduction operation. When traversing the nth element in the stream, this function is applied with two arguments, the accumulator being the result of the reduction (after having collected the first $n-1$ items of the stream) and the nth element itself. The function returns void because the accumulator is modified in place, meaning that its internal state is changed by the function application to reflect the effect of the traversed element. For ToListCollector, this function merely has to add the current item to the list containing the already traversed ones:

```
public BiConsumer<List<T>, T> accumulator() {
    return (list, item) -> list.add(item);
}
```

You could instead use a method reference, which is more concise:

```
public BiConsumer<List<T>, T> accumulator() {
    return List::add;
}
```

APPLYING THE FINAL TRANSFORMATION TO THE RESULT CONTAINER: THE FINISHER METHOD

The finisher method has to return a function that's invoked at the end of the accumulation process, after having completely traversed the stream, in order to transform the accumulator object into the final result of the whole collection operation. Often, as in the case of the `ToListCollector`, the accumulator object already coincides with the final expected result. As a consequence, there's no need to perform a transformation, so the `finisher` method has to return the `identity` function:

```
public Function<List<T>, List<T>> finisher() {
    return Function.identity();
}
```

These first three methods are enough to execute a sequential reduction of the stream that, at least from a logical point of view, could proceed as in figure 6.7. The implementation details are a bit more difficult in practice due to both the lazy nature of the stream, which could require a pipeline of other intermediate operations to execute before the `collect` operation, and the possibility, in theory, of performing the reduction in parallel.

MERGING TWO RESULT CONTAINERS: THE COMBINER METHOD

The `combiner` method, the last of the four methods that return a function used by the reduction operation, defines how the accumulators resulting from the reduction of different subparts of the stream are combined when the subparts are processed in parallel. In the `toList` case, the implementation of this method is simple; add the list

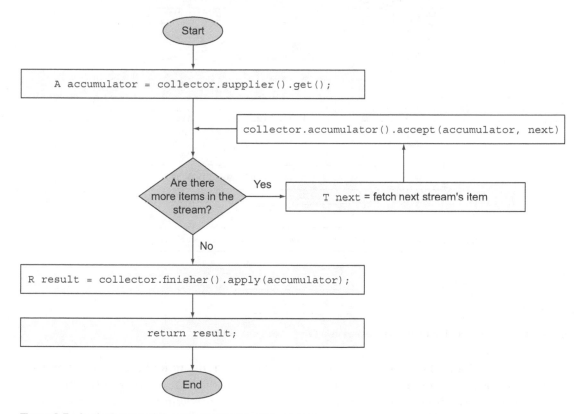

Figure 6.7 Logical steps of the sequential reduction process

containing the items gathered from the second subpart of the stream to the end of the list obtained when traversing the first subpart:

```
public BinaryOperator<List<T>> combiner() {
    return (list1, list2) -> {
        list1.addAll(list2);
        return list1; }
}
```

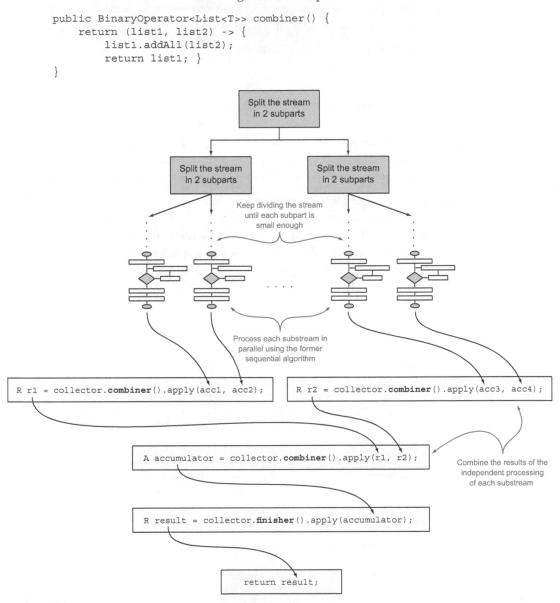

Figure 6.8   Parallelizing the reduction process using the `combiner` method

The addition of this fourth method allows a parallel reduction of the stream. This uses the fork/join framework introduced in Java 7 and the `Spliterator` abstraction that you'll learn about in the next chapter. It follows a process similar to the one shown in figure 6.8 and described in detail here.

- The original *stream* is recursively split in substreams until a condition defining whether a stream needs to be further divided becomes false (parallel computing is often slower than sequential computing when the units of work being distributed are too small, and it's pointless to generate many more parallel tasks than you have processing cores).
- At this point, all *substreams* can be processed in parallel, each of them using the sequential reduction algorithm shown in figure 6.7.
- Finally, all the partial results are combined pairwise using the function returned by the combiner method of the collector. This is done by combining results corresponding to substreams associated with each split of the original stream.

THE CHARACTERISTICS METHOD

The last method, characteristics, returns an immutable set of Characteristics, defining the behavior of the collector—in particular providing hints about whether the stream can be reduced in parallel and which optimizations are valid when doing so. Characteristics is an enumeration containing three items:

- UNORDERED—The result of the reduction isn't affected by the order in which the items in the stream are traversed and accumulated.
- CONCURRENT—The accumulator function can be called concurrently from multiple threads, and then this collector can perform a parallel reduction of the stream. If the collector isn't also flagged as UNORDERED, it can perform a parallel reduction only when it's applied to an unordered data source.
- IDENTITY_FINISH—This indicates the function returned by the finisher method is the identity one, and its application can be omitted. In this case, the accumulator object is directly used as the final result of the reduction process. This also implies that it's safe to do an unchecked cast from the accumulator A to the result R.

The ToListCollector developed so far is IDENTITY_FINISH, because the List used to accumulate the elements in the stream is already the expected final result and doesn't need any further transformation, but it isn't UNORDERED because if you apply it to an ordered stream you want this ordering to be preserved in the resulting List. Finally, it's CONCURRENT, but following what we just said, the stream will be processed in parallel only if its underlying data source is unordered.

6.5.2 *Putting them all together*

The five methods analyzed in the preceding subsection are everything you need to develop your own ToListCollector so you can implement it by putting all of them together, as the next listing shows.

> **Listing 6.5 The ToListCollector**

```
import java.util.*;
import java.util.function.*;
```

```
import java.util.stream.Collector;
import static java.util.stream.Collector.Characteristics.*;
public class ToListCollector<T> implements Collector<T, List<T>, List<T>> {
    @Override
    public Supplier<List<T>> supplier() {          Creates the collection
        return ArrayList::new;                     operation starting point
    }
    @Override
    public BiConsumer<List<T>, T> accumulator() {  Accumulates the traversed
        return List::add;                          item, modifying the
    }                                              accumulator in place
    @Override
    public Function<List<T>, List<T>> finisher() {
        return Function.identity();                Identifies function
    }
    @Override
    public BinaryOperator<List<T>> combiner() {    Modifies the first accumulator,
        return (list1, list2) -> {                 combining it with the content
            list1.addAll(list2);                   of the second one
            return list1;
        };                                         Returns the modified
    }                                              first accumulator
    @Override
    public Set<Characteristics> characteristics() {
        return Collections.unmodifiableSet(EnumSet.of(   Flags the collector as
            IDENTITY_FINISH, CONCURRENT));               IDENTITY_FINISH and
    }                                                    CONCURRENT
}
```

Note that this implementation isn't identical to the one returned by the `Collectors`
`.toList` method, but it differs only in some minor optimizations. These optimizations
are mostly related to the fact that the collector provided by the Java API uses the
`Collections.emptyList()` singleton when it has to return an empty list. This means
that it could be safely used in place of the original Java as an example to gather a list of
all the `Dishes` of a menu stream:

```
List<Dish> dishes = menuStream.collect(new ToListCollector<Dish>());
```

The remaining difference from this and the standard formulation

```
List<Dish> dishes = menuStream.collect(toList());
```

is that `toList` is a factory, whereas you have to use `new` to instantiate your `ToList-`
`Collector`.

PERFORMING A CUSTOM COLLECT WITHOUT CREATING A COLLECTOR IMPLEMENTATION

In the case of an `IDENTITY_FINISH` collection operation, there's a further possibility of
obtaining the same result without developing a completely new implementation of
the `Collector` interface. Streams has an overloaded `collect` method accepting the
three other functions—supplier, accumulator, and combiner—having exactly the same

semantics as the ones returned by the corresponding methods of the Collector interface. For instance, it's possible to collect in a List all the items in a stream of dishes, as follows:

```
List<Dish> dishes = menuStream.collect(          Supplier
                      ArrayList::new,         ◁─┘
                      List::add,              ◁─────── Accumulator
                      List::addAll);          ◁─┐
                                                  Combiner
```

We believe that this second form, even if more compact and concise than the former one, is rather less readable. Also, developing an implementation of your custom collector in a proper class promotes its reuse and helps avoid code duplication. It's also worth noting that you're not allowed to pass any Characteristics to this second collect method, so it always behaves as an IDENTITY_FINISH and CONCURRENT but not UNORDERED collector.

In the next section, you'll take your new knowledge of implementing collectors to the next level. You'll develop your own custom collector for a more complex but hopefully more specific and compelling use case.

6.6 *Developing your own collector for better performance*

In section 6.4, where we discussed partitioning, you created a collector using one of the many convenient factory methods provided by the Collectors class, which divides the first *n* natural numbers into primes and nonprimes, as shown in the following listing.

Listing 6.6 Partitioning the first *n* natural numbers into primes and nonprimes

```
public Map<Boolean, List<Integer>> partitionPrimes(int n) {
return IntStream.rangeClosed(2, n).boxed()
               .collect(partitioningBy(candidate -> isPrime(candidate)));
}
```

There you achieved an improvement over the original isPrime method by limiting the number of divisors to be tested against the candidate prime to those not bigger than the candidate's square root:

```
public boolean isPrime(int candidate) {
    int candidateRoot = (int) Math.sqrt((double) candidate);
    return IntStream.rangeClosed(2, candidateRoot)
               .noneMatch(i -> candidate % i == 0);
}
```

Is there a way to obtain even better performances? The answer is yes, but for this you'll have to develop a custom collector.

6.6.1   *Divide only by prime numbers*

One possible optimization is to test only if the candidate number is divisible by prime numbers. It's pointless to test it against a divisor that's not itself prime! You can limit the test to only the prime numbers found before the current candidate. The problem with the predefined collectors you've used so far, and the reason you have to develop a custom one, is that during the collecting process you don't have access to the partial result. This means that when testing whether a given candidate number is prime or not, you don't have access to the list of the other prime numbers found so far.

Suppose you had this list; you could pass it to the isPrime method and rewrite it as follows:

```
public static boolean isPrime(List<Integer> primes, int candidate) {
    return primes.stream().noneMatch(i -> candidate % i == 0);
}
```

Also, you should implement the same optimization you used before and test only with primes smaller than the square root of the candidate number. You need a way to stop testing whether the candidate is divisible by a prime as soon as the next prime is greater than the candidate's root. You can easily do this by using the Stream's take-While method:

```
public static boolean isPrime(List<Integer> primes, int candidate){
    int candidateRoot = (int) Math.sqrt((double) candidate);
    return primes.stream()
                 .takeWhile(i -> i <= candidateRoot)
                 .noneMatch(i -> candidate % i == 0);
}
```

Quiz 6.3: Simulating takeWhile in Java 8

The takeWhile method was introduced in Java 9, so unfortunately you cannot use this solution if you are still using Java 8. How could you work around this limitation and achieve something similar in Java 8?

Answer:

You could implement your own takeWhile method, which, given a sorted list and a predicate, returns the longest prefix of this list whose elements satisfy the predicate:

```
public static <A> List<A> takeWhile(List<A> list, Predicate<A> p) {
    int i = 0;
    for (A item : list) {
            if (!p.test(item)) {              ◁── Checks if the current item in
                    return list.subList(0, i);    the list satisfies the Predicate
            }                           ◁── If it doesn't, returns the
            i++;                            sublist prefix until the
    }                                       item before the tested one
    return list;    ◁── All the items in the list
}                       satisfy the Predicate, so
                        returns the list itself
```

> Using this method, you can rewrite the `isPrime` method and once again testing only the candidate prime against only the primes that aren't greater than its square root:
>
> ```
> public static boolean isPrime(List<Integer> primes, int candidate){
>     int candidateRoot = (int) Math.sqrt((double) candidate);
>     return takeWhile(primes, i -> i <= candidateRoot)
>                 .stream()
>                 .noneMatch(p -> candidate % p == 0);
> }
> ```
>
> Note that, unlike the one provided by the Streams API, this implementation of `take-While` is eager. When possible, always prefer the Java 9 Stream's lazy version of `takeWhile` so it can be merged with the `noneMatch` operation.

With this new `isPrime` method in hand, you're now ready to implement your own custom collector. First, you need to declare a new class that implements the `Collector` interface. Then, you need to develop the five methods required by the `Collector` interface.

STEP 1: DEFINING THE COLLECTOR CLASS SIGNATURE

Let's start with the class signature, remembering that the `Collector` interface is defined as

```
public interface Collector<T, A, R>
```

where `T`, `A`, and `R` are respectively the type of the elements in the stream, the type of the object used to accumulate partial results, and the type of the final result of the `collect` operation. In this case, you want to collect streams of `Integers` while both the accumulator and the result types are `Map<Boolean, List<Integer>>` (the same `Map` you obtained as a result of the former partitioning operation in listing 6.6), having as keys `true` and `false` and as values respectively the `Lists` of prime and nonprime numbers:

```
public class PrimeNumbersCollector
            implements Collector<Integer,                      ← The type of the elements in the stream
                        Map<Boolean, List<Integer>>,           ← The type of the accumulator
                        Map<Boolean, List<Integer>>>
```
The type of the result of the collect operation →

STEP 2: IMPLEMENTING THE REDUCTION PROCESS

Next, you need to implement the five methods declared in the `Collector` interface. The supplier method has to return a function that when invoked creates the accumulator:

```
public Supplier<Map<Boolean, List<Integer>>> supplier() {
    return () -> new HashMap<Boolean, List<Integer>>() {{
        put(true, new ArrayList<Integer>());
```

```
                put(false, new ArrayList<Integer>());
        }};
}
```

Here you're not only creating the Map that you'll use as the accumulator, but you're also initializing it with two empty lists under the true and false keys. This is where you'll add respectively the prime and nonprime numbers during the collection process. The most important method of your collector is the accumulator method, because it contains the logic defining how the elements of the stream have to be collected. In this case, it's also the key to implementing the optimization we described previously. At any given iteration you can now access the partial result of the collection process, which is the accumulator containing the prime numbers found so far:

```
public BiConsumer<Map<Boolean, List<Integer>>, Integer> accumulator() {
    return (Map<Boolean, List<Integer>> acc, Integer candidate) -> {
        acc.get( isPrime(acc.get(true), candidate) )      ◁────┐   Gets the list of prime
            .add(candidate);                          ◁───┐         or nonprime numbers
    };                                  Adds the candidate to │         depending on the
}                                       the appropriate list │         result of isPrime
```

In this method, you invoke the isPrime method, passing to it (together with the number for which you want to test whether it's prime or not) the list of the prime numbers found so far. (These are the values indexed by the true key in the accumulating Map.) The result of this invocation is then used as the key to get the list of either the prime or nonprime numbers, so you can add the new candidate to the right list.

STEP 3: MAKING THE COLLECTOR WORK IN PARALLEL (IF POSSIBLE)

The next method has to combine two partial accumulators in the case of a parallel collection process, so in this case it has to merge the two Maps by adding all the numbers in the prime and nonprime lists of the second Map to the corresponding lists in the first Map:

```
public BinaryOperator<Map<Boolean, List<Integer>>> combiner() {
    return (Map<Boolean, List<Integer>> map1,
            Map<Boolean, List<Integer>> map2) -> {
                map1.get(true).addAll(map2.get(true));
                map1.get(false).addAll(map2.get(false));
                return map1;
    };
}
```

Note that in reality this collector can't be used in parallel, because the algorithm is inherently sequential. This means the combiner method won't ever be invoked, and you could leave its implementation empty (or better, throw an UnsupportedOperation-Exception). We decided to implement it anyway only for completeness.

STEP 4: THE FINISHER METHOD AND THE COLLECTOR'S CHARACTERISTIC METHOD

The implementation of the last two methods is quite straightforward. As we said, the accumulator coincides with the collector's result so it won't need any further transformation, and the finisher method returns the identity function:

```
public Function<Map<Boolean, List<Integer>>,
                Map<Boolean, List<Integer>>> finisher() {
        return Function.identity();
}
```

As for the characteristic method, we already said that it's neither CONCURRENT nor UNORDERED but is IDENTITY_FINISH:

```
public Set<Characteristics> characteristics() {
    return Collections.unmodifiableSet(EnumSet.of(IDENTITY_FINISH));
}
```

The following listing shows the final implementation of PrimeNumbersCollector.

Listing 6.7 The PrimeNumbersCollector

```
public class PrimeNumbersCollector
    implements Collector<Integer,
            Map<Boolean, List<Integer>>,
            Map<Boolean, List<Integer>>> {
    @Override
    public Supplier<Map<Boolean, List<Integer>>> supplier() {       ←── Starts the
        return () -> new HashMap<Boolean, List<Integer>>() {{           collection
            put(true, new ArrayList<Integer>());                        process with a
            put(false, new ArrayList<Integer>());                       Map containing
        }};                                                             two empty Lists
    }
    @Override
    public BiConsumer<Map<Boolean, List<Integer>>, Integer> accumulator() {
        return (Map<Boolean, List<Integer>> acc, Integer candidate) -> {
            acc.get( isPrime( acc.get(true),
                candidate) )
                .add(candidate);
        };
    }
    @Override
    public BinaryOperator<Map<Boolean, List<Integer>>> combiner() {
        return (Map<Boolean, List<Integer>> map1,
                Map<Boolean, List<Integer>> map2) -> {
                    map1.get(true).addAll(map2.get(true));
                    map1.get(false).addAll(map2.get(false));
                    return map1;
        };
    }
    @Override
    public Function<Map<Boolean, List<Integer>>,
                Map<Boolean, List<Integer>>> finisher() {
                    return Function.identity();
```

Passes to the isPrime method the list of already found primes

Gets from the Map the list of prime or nonprime numbers, according to what the isPrime method returned, and adds to it the current candidate

Merges the second Map into the first one

No transformation necessary at the end of the collection process, so terminate it with the identity function

```
        }
        @Override
        public Set<Characteristics> characteristics() {
            return Collections.unmodifiableSet(EnumSet.of(IDENTITY_FINISH));   ◁─┐
        }                                                                        │
}                                                                                │
```

> **This collector is IDENTITY_FINISH but neither UNORDERED nor CONCURRENT because it relies on the fact that prime numbers are discovered in sequence.**

You can now use this new custom collector in place of the former one created with the partitioningBy factory method in section 6.4 and obtain exactly the same result:

```
public Map<Boolean, List<Integer>>
                        partitionPrimesWithCustomCollector(int n) {
        return IntStream.rangeClosed(2, n).boxed()
                        .collect(new PrimeNumbersCollector());
}
```

6.6.2   *Comparing collectors' performances*

The collector created with the partitioningBy factory method and the custom one you just developed are functionally identical, but did you achieve your goal of improving the performance of the partitioningBy collector with your custom one? Let's write a quick harness to check this:

```
public class CollectorHarness {
    public static void main(String[] args) {
        long fastest = Long.MAX_VALUE;
        for (int i = 0; i < 10; i++) {                    ◁── Runs the test 10 times
            long start = System.nanoTime();
            partitionPrimes(1_000_000);                   ◁── Partitions the first million natural numbers into primes and nonprimes
            long duration = (System.nanoTime() - start) / 1_000_000;   ◁── The duration in milliseconds
            if (duration < fastest) fastest = duration;   ◁── Checks if this execution is the fastest one
        }
        System.out.println(
            "Fastest execution done in " + fastest + " msecs");
    }
}
```

Note that a more scientific benchmarking approach would be to use a framework such as Java Microbenchmark Harness (JMH), but we didn't want to add the complexity of using such a framework here and, for this use case, the results provided by this small benchmarking class are accurate enough. This class partitions the first million natural numbers into primes and nonprimes, invoking the method using the collector created with the partitioningBy factory method 10 times and registering the fastest execution. Running it on an Intel i5 2.4 GHz, it prints the following result:

```
Fastest execution done in 4716 msecs
```

Now replace `partitionPrimes` with `partitionPrimesWithCustomCollector` in the harness, in order to test the performances of the custom collector you developed. Now the program prints

```
Fastest execution done in 3201 msecs
```

Not bad! This means you didn't waste your time developing this custom collector for two reasons: First, you learned how to implement your own collector when you need it. And second, you achieved a performance improvement of around 32%.

Finally, it's important to note that, as you did for the `ToListCollector` in listing 6.5, it's possible to obtain the same result by passing the three functions implementing the core logic of `PrimeNumbersCollector` to the overloaded version of the `collect` method, taking them as arguments:

```
public Map<Boolean, List<Integer>> partitionPrimesWithCustomCollector
            (int n) {
    IntStream.rangeClosed(2, n).boxed()                                Supplier
        .collect(
                () -> new HashMap<Boolean, List<Integer>>() {{     ⟵
                    put(true, new ArrayList<Integer>());
                    put(false, new ArrayList<Integer>());
                }},
            (acc, candidate) -> {                                    ⟵ Accumulator
              acc.get( isPrime(acc.get(true), candidate) )
                .add(candidate);
            },
              (map1, map2) -> {                                     ⟵ Combiner
              map1.get(true).addAll(map2.get(true));
              map1.get(false).addAll(map2.get(false));
            });
}
```

As you can see, in this way you can avoid creating a completely new class that implements the `Collector` interface; the resulting code is more compact, even if it's also probably less readable and certainly less reusable.

Summary

- `collect` is a terminal operation that takes as argument various recipes (called collectors) for accumulating the elements of a stream into a summary result.
- Predefined collectors include reducing and summarizing stream elements into a single value, such as calculating the minimum, maximum, or average. Those collectors are summarized in table 6.1.
- Predefined collectors let you group elements of a stream with `groupingBy` and partition elements of a stream with `partitioningBy`.
- Collectors compose effectively to create multilevel groupings, partitions, and reductions.
- You can develop your own collectors by implementing the methods defined in the `Collector` interface.

Parallel data processing and 7 performance

This chapter covers

- Processing data in parallel with parallel streams
- Performance analysis of parallel streams
- The fork/join framework
- Splitting a stream of data using a `Spliterator`

In the last three chapters, you've seen how the new Streams interface lets you manipulate collections of data in a declarative way. We also explained that the shift from external to internal iteration enables the native Java library to gain control over processing the elements of a stream. This approach relieves Java developers from explicitly implementing optimizations necessary to speed up the processing of collections of data. By far the most important benefit is the possibility of executing a pipeline of operations on these collections that automatically makes use of the multiple cores on your computer.

For instance, before Java 7, processing a collection of data in parallel was extremely cumbersome. First, you needed to explicitly split the data structure containing your data into subparts. Second, you needed to assign each of these subparts to a different thread. Third, you needed to synchronize them opportunely to avoid unwanted race conditions, wait for the completion of all threads, and finally

172

combine the partial results. Java 7 introduced a framework called *fork/join* to perform these operations more consistently and in a less error-prone way. We'll explore this framework in section 7.2.

In this chapter, you'll discover how the Streams interface gives you the opportunity to execute operations in parallel on a collection of data without much effort. It lets you declaratively turn a sequential stream into a parallel one. Moreover, you'll see how Java can make this magic happen or, more practically, how parallel streams work under the hood by employing the fork/join framework introduced in Java 7. You'll also discover that it's important to know how parallel streams work internally, because if you ignore this aspect, you could obtain unexpected (and likely wrong) results by misusing them.

In particular, we'll demonstrate that the way a parallel stream gets divided into chunks, before processing the different chunks in parallel, can in some cases be the origin of these incorrect and apparently unexplainable results. For this reason, you'll learn how to take control of this splitting process by implementing and using your own Spliterator.

7.1 Parallel streams

In chapter 4, we briefly mentioned that the Streams interface allows you to process its elements in parallel in a convenient way: it's possible to turn a collection into a parallel stream by invoking the method parallelStream on the collection source. A *parallel* stream is a stream that splits its elements into multiple chunks, processing each chunk with a different thread. Thus, you can automatically partition the workload of a given operation on all the cores of your multicore processor and keep all of them equally busy. Let's experiment with this idea by using a simple example.

Let's suppose you need to write a method accepting a number *n* as argument and returning the sum of the numbers from one to *n*. A straightforward (perhaps naïve) approach is to generate an infinite stream of numbers, limiting it to the passed numbers, and then reduce the resulting stream with a BinaryOperator that sums two numbers, as follows:

```
public long sequentialSum(long n) {
    return Stream.iterate(1L, i -> i + 1)        Generates the infinite
                                                 stream of natural numbers
            .limit(n)                            Limits it to the
                                                 first n numbers
            .reduce(0L, Long::sum);              Reduces the stream by
}                                                summing all the numbers
```

In more traditional Java terms, this code is equivalent to its iterative counterpart:

```
public long iterativeSum(long n) {
    long result = 0;
    for (long i = 1L; i <= n; i++) {
        result += i;
    }
    return result;
}
```

This operation seems to be a good candidate to use parallelization, especially for large values of *n*. But where do you start? Do you synchronize on the result variable? How many threads do you use? Who does the generation of numbers? Who adds them up?

Don't worry about all of this. It's a much simpler problem to solve if you adopt parallel streams!

7.1.1 *Turning a sequential stream into a parallel one*

You can make the former functional reduction process (summing) run in parallel by turning the stream into a parallel one; call the method `parallel` on the sequential stream:

```
public long parallelSum(long n) {
    return Stream.iterate(1L, i -> i + 1)
                 .limit(n)
                 .parallel()                    Turns the stream
                 .reduce(0L, Long::sum);        into a parallel one
}
```

In the previous code, the reduction process used to sum all the numbers in the stream works in a way that's similar to what's described in section 5.4.1. The difference is that the stream is now internally divided into multiple chunks. As a result, the reduction operation can work on the various chunks independently and in parallel, as shown in figure 7.1. Finally, the same reduction operation combines the values resulting from

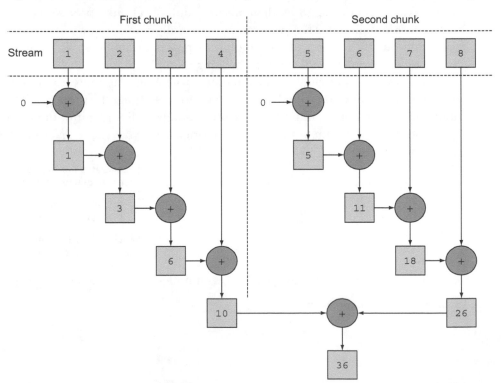

Figure 7.1   A parallel reduction operation

the partial reductions of each substream, producing the result of the reduction process on the whole initial stream.

Note that, in reality, calling the method parallel on a sequential stream doesn't imply any concrete transformation on the stream itself. Internally, a boolean flag is set to signal that you want to run in parallel all the operations that follow the invocation to parallel. Similarly, you can turn a parallel stream into a sequential one by invoking the method sequential on it. Note that you might think that by combining these two methods you could achieve finer-grained control over which operations you want to perform in parallel and which ones sequentially while traversing the stream. For example, you could do something like the following:

```
stream.parallel()
      .filter(...)
      .sequential()
      .map(...)
      .parallel()
      .reduce();
```

But the last call to parallel or sequential wins and affects the pipeline globally. In this example, the pipeline will be executed in parallel because that's the last call in the pipeline.

Configuring the thread pool used by parallel streams

Looking at the stream's parallel method, you may wonder where the threads used by the parallel stream come from, how many there are, and how you can customize the process.

Parallel streams internally use the default ForkJoinPool (you'll learn more about the fork/join framework in section 7.2), which by default has as many threads as you have processors, as returned by Runtime.getRuntime().available-Processors().

But you can change the size of this pool using the system property java.util.concurrent.ForkJoinPool.common.parallelism, as in the following example:

```
System.setProperty("java.util.concurrent.ForkJoinPool.common.parallelism",
    "12");
```

This is a global setting, so it will affect all the parallel streams in your code. Conversely, it currently isn't possible to specify this value for a single parallel stream. In general, having the size of the ForkJoinPool equal to the number of processors on your machine is a meaningful default, and we strongly suggest that you not modify it unless you have a good reason for doing so.

Returning to the number-summing exercise, we said that you can expect a significant performance improvement in its parallel version when running it on a multicore processor. You now have three methods executing exactly the same operation in three different ways (iterative style, sequential reduction, and parallel reduction), so let's see which is the fastest one!

7.1.2　*Measuring stream performance*

We claimed that the parallelized summing method should perform better than the sequential and the iterative methods. Nevertheless, in software engineering, guessing is never a good idea! When optimizing performance, you should always follow three golden rules: measure, measure, measure. To this purpose we will implement a microbenchmark using a library called Java Microbenchmark Harness (JMH). This is a toolkit that helps to create, in a simple, annotation-based way, reliable microbenchmarks for Java programs and for any other language targeting the Java Virtual Machine (JVM). In fact, developing correct and meaningful benchmarks for programs running on the JVM is not an easy task, because there are many factors to consider like the warm-up time required by HotSpot to optimize the bytecode and the overhead introduced by the garbage collector. If you're using Maven as your build tool, then to start using JMH in your project you add a couple of dependencies to your pom.xml file (which defines the Maven build process).

```
<dependency>
  <groupId>org.openjdk.jmh</groupId>
  <artifactId>jmh-core</artifactId>
  <version>1.17.4</version>
</dependency>
<dependency>
  <groupId>org.openjdk.jmh</groupId>
  <artifactId>jmh-generator-annprocess</artifactId>
  <version>1.17.4</version>
</dependency>
```

The first library is the core JMH implementation while the second contains an annotation processor that helps to generate a Java Archive (JAR) file through which you can conveniently run your benchmark once you have also added the following plugin to your Maven configuration:

```
<build>
    <plugin>
      <groupId>org.apache.maven.plugins</groupId>
      <artifactId>maven-shade-plugin</artifactId>
      <executions>
        <execution>
          <phase>package</phase>
          <goals><goal>shade</goal></goals>
          <configuration>
            <finalName>benchmarks</finalName>
            <transformers>
              <transformer implementation="org.apache.maven.plugins.shade.
                                  resource.ManifestResourceTransformer">
                <mainClass>org.openjdk.jmh.Main</mainClass>
              </transformer>
```

```
          </transformers>
        </configuration>
      </execution>
    </executions>
  </plugin>
 </plugins>
</build>
```

Having done this, you can benchmark the `sequentialSum` method introduced at the beginning of this section in this simple way, as shown in the next listing.

Listing 7.1 Measuring performance of a function summing the first *n* numbers

```
@BenchmarkMode(Mode.AverageTime)              ← Measures the average time taken
@OutputTimeUnit(TimeUnit.MILLISECONDS)           to the benchmarked method
@Fork(2, jvmArgs={"-Xms4G", "-Xmx4G"})        ← Prints benchmark results using
public class ParallelStreamBenchmark {           milliseconds as time unit
    private static final long N= 10_000_000L;
                                              Executes the benchmark
    @Benchmark                                2 times to increase the
    public long sequentialSum() {             reliability of results, with
        return Stream.iterate(1L, i -> i + 1).limit(N)    4Gb of heap space
                        .reduce( 0L, Long::sum);
    }

    @TearDown(Level.Invocation)               ← Tries to run the garbage
    public void tearDown() {                     collector after each iteration
        System.gc();                             of the benchmark
    }
}
```

The method to be benchmarked → `@Benchmark`

When you compile this class, the Maven plugin configured before generates a second JAR file named benchmarks.jar that you can run as follows:

```
java -jar ./target/benchmarks.jar ParallelStreamBenchmark
```

We configured the benchmark to use an oversized heap to avoid any influence of the garbage collector as much as possible, and for the same reason, we tried to enforce the garbage collector to run after each iteration of our benchmark. Despite all these precautions, it has to be noted that the results should be taken with a grain of salt. Many factors will influence the execution time, such as how many cores your machine supports! You can try this on your own machine by running the code available on the book's repository.

When you launch the former, command JMH to execute 20 warm-up iterations of the benchmarked method to allow HotSpot to optimize the code, and then 20 more iterations that are used to calculate the final result. These 20+20 iterations are the default behavior of JMH, but you can change both values either through other JMH specific annotations or, even more conveniently, by adding them to the command line using the -w and -i flags. Executing it on a computer equipped with an Intel i7-4600U 2.1 GHz quad-core, it prints the following result:

```
Benchmark                                 Mode  Cnt    Score    Error  Units
ParallelStreamBenchmark.sequentialSum     avgt   40  121.843 ±  3.062  ms/op
```

You should expect that the iterative version using a traditional for loop runs much faster because it works at a much lower level and, more important, doesn't need to perform any boxing or unboxing of the primitive values. We can check this intuition by adding a second method to the benchmarking class of listing 7.1 and also annotate it with @Benchmark:

```
@Benchmark
public long iterativeSum() {
    long result = 0;
    for (long i = 1L; i <= N; i++) {
        result += i;
    }
    return result;
}
```

Running this second benchmark (possibly having commented out the first one to avoid running it again) on our testing machine, we obtained the following result:

```
Benchmark                               Mode  Cnt   Score    Error  Units
ParallelStreamBenchmark.iterativeSum    avgt   40   3.278 ±  0.192  ms/op
```

This confirmed our expectations: the iterative version is almost 40 times faster than the one using the sequential stream for the reasons we anticipated. Now let's do the same with the version using the parallel stream, also adding that method to our benchmarking class. We obtained the following outcome:

```
Benchmark                              Mode  Cnt    Score     Error  Units
ParallelStreamBenchmark.parallelSum    avgt   40  604.059 ± 55.288  ms/op
```

This is quite disappointing: the parallel version of the summing method isn't taking any advantage of our quad-core CPU and is around five times slower than the sequential one. How can you explain this unexpected result? Two issues are mixed together:

- iterate generates boxed objects, which have to be unboxed to numbers before they can be added.
- iterate is difficult to divide into independent chunks to execute in parallel.

The second issue is particularly interesting because you need to keep a mental model that some stream operations are more parallelizable than others. Specifically, the iterate operation is hard to split into chunks that can be executed independently, because the input of one function application always depends on the result of the previous application, as illustrated in figure 7.2.

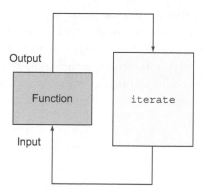

Figure 7.2 `iterate` is inherently sequential.

This means that in this specific case the reduction process isn't proceeding as depicted in figure 7.1: the whole list of numbers isn't available at the beginning of the reduction process, making it impossible to efficiently partition the stream in chunks to be processed in parallel. By flagging the stream as parallel, you're adding the overhead of allocating each sum operation on a different thread to the sequential processing.

This demonstrates how parallel programming can be tricky and sometimes counterintuitive. When misused (for example, using an operation that's not parallel-friendly, like `iterate`) it can worsen the overall performance of your programs, so it's mandatory to understand what happens behind the scenes when you invoke that apparently magic `parallel` method.

USING MORE SPECIALIZED METHODS

So how can you use your multicore processors and use the stream to perform a parallel sum in an effective way? We discussed a method called `LongStream.rangeClosed` in chapter 5. This method has two benefits compared to `iterate`:

- `LongStream.rangeClosed` works on primitive `long` numbers directly so there's no boxing and unboxing overhead.
- `LongStream.rangeClosed` produces ranges of numbers, which can be easily split into independent chunks. For example, the range 1–20 can be split into 1–5, 6–10, 11–15, and 16–20.

Let's first see how it performs on a sequential stream by adding the following method to our benchmarking class to check if the overhead associated with unboxing is relevant:

```
@Benchmark
public long rangedSum() {
    return LongStream.rangeClosed(1, N)
                      .reduce(0L, Long::sum);
}
```

This time the output is

Benchmark	Mode	Cnt	Score		Error	Units
ParallelStreamBenchmark.rangedSum	avgt	40	5.315	±	0.285	ms/op

The numeric stream is much faster than the earlier sequential version, generated with the iterate factory method, because the numeric stream avoids all the overhead caused by all the unnecessary autoboxing and auto-unboxing operations performed by the nonspecialized stream. This is evidence that choosing the right data structures is often more important than parallelizing the algorithm that uses them. But what happens if you try to use a parallel stream in this new version that follows?

```
@Benchmark
public long parallelRangedSum() {
    return LongStream.rangeClosed(1, N)
                     .parallel()
                     .reduce(0L, Long::sum);
}
```

Now, adding this method to our benchmarking class we obtained

```
Benchmark                                       Mode  Cnt  Score    Error   Units
ParallelStreamBenchmark.parallelRangedSum       avgt   40  2.677 ±  0.214   ms/op
```

Finally, we got a parallel reduction that's faster than its sequential counterpart, because this time the reduction operation can be executed as shown in figure 7.1. This also demonstrates that using the right data structure *and* then making it work in parallel guarantees the best performance. Note that this latest version is also around 20% faster than the original iterative one, demonstrating that, when used correctly, the functional-programming style allows us to use the parallelism of modern multi-core CPUs in a simpler and more straightforward way than its imperative counterpart.

Nevertheless, keep in mind that parallelization doesn't come for free. The parallelization process itself requires you to recursively partition the stream, assign the reduction operation of each substream to a different thread, and then combine the results of these operations in a single value. But moving data between multiple cores is also more expensive than you might expect, so it's important that work to be done in parallel on another core takes longer than the time required to transfer the data from one core to another. In general, there are many cases where it isn't possible or convenient to use parallelization. But before you use a parallel stream to make your code faster, you have to be sure that you're using it correctly; it's not helpful to produce a result in less time if the result will be wrong. Let's look at a common pitfall.

7.1.3   *Using parallel streams correctly*

The main cause of errors generated by misuse of parallel streams is the use of algorithms that mutate some shared state. Here's a way to implement the sum of the first n natural numbers by mutating a shared accumulator:

```
public long sideEffectSum(long n) {
    Accumulator accumulator = new Accumulator();
    LongStream.rangeClosed(1, n).forEach(accumulator::add);
    return accumulator.total;
}
```

```
public class Accumulator {
    public long total = 0;
    public void add(long value) { total += value; }
}
```

It's quite common to write this sort of code, especially for developers who are familiar with imperative programming paradigms. This code closely resembles what you're used to doing when iterating imperatively a list of numbers: you initialize an accumulator and traverse the elements in the list one by one, adding them on the accumulator.

What's wrong with this code? Unfortunately, it's irretrievably broken because it's fundamentally sequential. You have a data race on every access of total. And if you try to fix that with synchronization, you'll lose all your parallelism. To understand this, let's try to turn the stream into a parallel one:

```
public long sideEffectParallelSum(long n) {
    Accumulator accumulator = new Accumulator();
    LongStream.rangeClosed(1, n).parallel().forEach(accumulator::add);
    return accumulator.total;
}
```

Try to run this last method with the harness of listing 7.1, also printing the result of each execution:

```
System.out.println("SideEffect parallel sum done in: " +
    measurePerf(ParallelStreams::sideEffectParallelSum, 10_000_000L) + "
    msecs" );
```

You could obtain something like the following:

```
Result: 5959989000692
Result: 7425264100768
Result: 6827235020033
Result: 7192970417739
Result: 6714157975331
Result: 7497810541907
Result: 6435348440385
Result: 6999349840672
Result: 7435914379978
Result: 7715125932481
SideEffect parallel sum done in: 49 msecs
```

This time the performance of your method isn't important. The only relevant thing is that each execution returns a different result, all distant from the correct value of 50000005000000. This is caused by the fact that multiple threads are concurrently accessing the accumulator and, in particular, executing total += value, which, despite its appearance, isn't an atomic operation. The origin of the problem is that the method invoked inside the forEach block has the side effect of changing the mutable state of an object shared among multiple threads. It's mandatory to avoid these kinds of situations if you want to use parallel streams without incurring similar bad surprises.

Now you know that a shared mutable state doesn't play well with parallel streams and with parallel computations in general. We'll come back to this idea of avoiding mutation in chapters 18 and 19 when discussing functional programming in more detail. For now, keep in mind that avoiding a shared mutable state ensures that your parallel stream will produce the right result. Next, we'll look at some practical advice you can use to figure out when it's appropriate to use parallel streams to gain performance.

7.1.4 *Using parallel streams effectively*

In general, it's impossible (and pointless) to try to give any quantitative hint on when to use a parallel stream, because any specific criterion such as "only when the stream contains more than a thousand elements" could be correct for a specific operation running on a specific machine, but completely wrong in a marginally different context. Nonetheless, it's at least possible to provide some qualitative advice that could be useful when deciding whether it makes sense to use a parallel stream in a certain situation:

- If in doubt, measure. Turning a sequential stream into a parallel one is trivial but not always the right thing to do. As we already demonstrated in this section, a parallel stream isn't always faster than the corresponding sequential version. Moreover, parallel streams can sometimes work in a counterintuitive way, so the first and most important suggestion when choosing between sequential and parallel streams is to always check their performance with an appropriate benchmark.

- Watch out for boxing. Automatic boxing and unboxing operations can dramatically hurt performance. Java 8 includes primitive streams (IntStream, Long-Stream, and DoubleStream) to avoid such operations, so use them when possible.

- Some operations naturally perform worse on a parallel stream than on a sequential stream. In particular, operations such as limit and findFirst that rely on the order of the elements are expensive in a parallel stream. For example, findAny will perform better than findFirst because it isn't constrained to operate in the encounter order. You can always turn an ordered stream into an unordered stream by invoking the method unordered on it. For instance, if you need *N* elements of your stream and you're not necessarily interested in the *first* *N* ones, calling limit on an unordered parallel stream may execute more efficiently than on a stream with an encounter order (for example, when the source is a List).

- Consider the total computational cost of the pipeline of operations performed by the stream. With *N* being the number of elements to be processed and *Q* the approximate cost of processing one of these elements through the stream pipeline, the product of *N**Q gives a rough qualitative estimation of this cost. A higher value for *Q* implies a better chance of good performance when using a parallel stream.

- For a small amount of data, choosing a parallel stream is almost never a winning decision. The advantages of processing in parallel only a few elements aren't enough to compensate for the additional cost introduced by the parallelization process.
- Take into account how well the data structure underlying the stream decomposes. For instance, an `ArrayList` can be split much more efficiently than a `LinkedList`, because the first can be evenly divided without traversing it, as it's necessary to do with the second. Also, the primitive streams created with the range factory method can be decomposed quickly. Finally, as you'll learn in section 7.3, you can get full control of this decomposition process by implementing your own `Spliterator`.
- The characteristics of a stream, and how the intermediate operations through the pipeline modify them, can change the performance of the decomposition process. For example, a `SIZED` stream can be divided into two equal parts, and then each part can be processed in parallel more effectively, but a filter operation can throw away an unpredictable number of elements, making the size of the stream itself unknown.
- Consider whether a terminal operation has a cheap or expensive merge step (for example, the `combiner` method in a `Collector`). If this is expensive, then the cost caused by the combination of the partial results generated by each substream can outweigh the performance benefits of a parallel stream.

Table 7.1 gives a summary of the parallel-friendliness of certain stream sources in terms of their decomposability.

Table 7.1 Stream sources and decomposability

Source	Decomposability
`ArrayList`	Excellent
`LinkedList`	Poor
`IntStream.range`	Excellent
`Stream.iterate`	Poor
`HashSet`	Good
`TreeSet`	Good

Finally, we need to emphasize that the infrastructure used behind the scenes by parallel streams to execute operations in parallel is the fork/join framework introduced in Java 7. The parallel summing example proved that it's vital to have a good understanding of the parallel stream internals in order to use them correctly, so we'll investigate in detail the fork/join framework in the next section.

7.2   *The fork/join framework*

The fork/join framework was designed to recursively split a parallelizable task into smaller tasks and then combine the results of each subtask to produce the overall result. It's an implementation of the ExecutorService interface, which distributes those subtasks to worker threads in a thread pool, called ForkJoinPool. Let's start by exploring how to define a task and subtasks.

7.2.1   *Working with RecursiveTask*

To submit tasks to this pool, you have to create a subclass of RecursiveTask<R>, where R is the type of the result produced by the parallelized task (and each of its subtasks) or of RecursiveAction if the task returns no result (it could be updating other nonlocal structures, though). To define RecursiveTasks you need only implement its single abstract method, compute:

```
protected abstract R compute();
```

This method defines both the logic of splitting the task at hand into subtasks and the algorithm to produce the result of a single subtask when it's no longer possible or convenient to further divide it. For this reason an implementation of this method often resembles the following pseudocode:

```
if (task is small enough or no longer divisible) {
    compute task sequentially
} else {
    split task in two subtasks
    call this method recursively possibly further splitting each subtask
    wait for the completion of all subtasks
    combine the results of each subtask
}
```

In general, there are no precise criteria for deciding whether a given task should be further divided or not, but there are various heuristics that you can follow to help you with this decision. We clarify them in more detail in section 7.2.2. The recursive task-splitting process is visually synthesized by figure 7.3.

As you might have noticed, this is nothing more than the parallel version of the well-known divide-and-conquer algorithm. To demonstrate a practical example of how to use the fork/join framework and to build on our previous examples, let's try to calculate the sum of a range of numbers (here represented by an array of numbers long[]) using this framework. As explained, you need to first provide an implementation for the RecursiveTask class, as shown by the ForkJoinSumCalculator in listing 7.2.

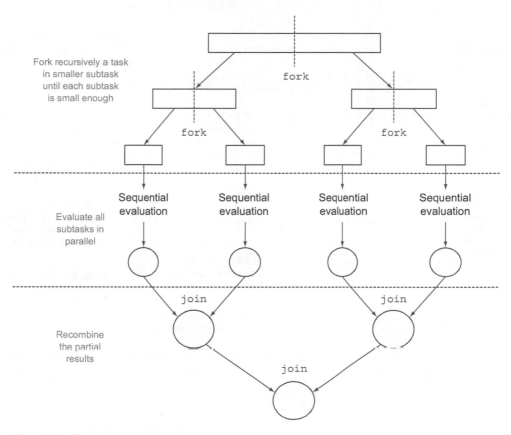

Figure 7.3 The fork/join process

Listing 7.2 Executing a parallel sum using the fork/join framework

The initial and final positions of the subarray processed by this subtask

Extends RecursiveTask to create a task usable with the fork/join framework

```
public class ForkJoinSumCalculator
            extends java.util.concurrent.RecursiveTask<Long> {
    private final long[] numbers;
    private final int start;
    private final int end;
    public static final long THRESHOLD = 10_000;
    public ForkJoinSumCalculator(long[] numbers) {
        this(numbers, 0, numbers.length);
    }
    private ForkJoinSumCalculator(long[] numbers, int start, int end) {
        this.numbers = numbers;
        this.start = start;
        this.end = end;
    }
    @Override
    protected Long compute() {
```

The array of numbers to be summed

The size threshold for splitting into subtasks

Public constructor to create the main task

Private constructor to create subtasks of the main task

Override the abstract method of RecursiveTask

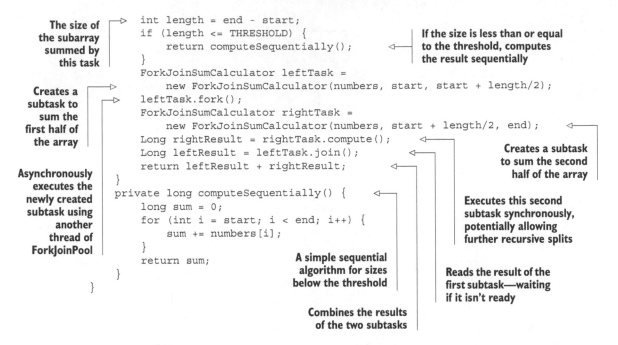

The size of the subarray summed by this task
```
int length = end - start;
if (length <= THRESHOLD) {
    return computeSequentially();
}
```
If the size is less than or equal to the threshold, computes the result sequentially

Creates a subtask to sum the first half of the array
```
ForkJoinSumCalculator leftTask =
    new ForkJoinSumCalculator(numbers, start, start + length/2);
leftTask.fork();
ForkJoinSumCalculator rightTask =
    new ForkJoinSumCalculator(numbers, start + length/2, end);
```
Creates a subtask to sum the second half of the array

```
    Long rightResult = rightTask.compute();
    Long leftResult = leftTask.join();
    return leftResult + rightResult;
}
```

Asynchronously executes the newly created subtask using another thread of ForkJoinPool

Executes this second subtask synchronously, potentially allowing further recursive splits

```
private long computeSequentially() {
    long sum = 0;
    for (int i = start; i < end; i++) {
        sum += numbers[i];
    }
    return sum;
}
}
```

A simple sequential algorithm for sizes below the threshold

Reads the result of the first subtask—waiting if it isn't ready

Combines the results of the two subtasks

Writing a method performing a parallel sum of the first *n* natural numbers is now straightforward. You need to pass the desired array of numbers to the constructor of ForkJoinSumCalculator:

```
public static long forkJoinSum(long n) {
    long[] numbers = LongStream.rangeClosed(1, n).toArray();
    ForkJoinTask<Long> task = new ForkJoinSumCalculator(numbers);
    return new ForkJoinPool().invoke(task);
}
```

Here, you generate an array containing the first *n* natural numbers using a Long-Stream. Then you create a ForkJoinTask (the superclass of RecursiveTask), passing this array to the public constructor of the ForkJoinSumCalculator shown in listing 7.2. Finally, you create a new ForkJoinPool and pass that task to its invoke method. The value returned by this last method is the result of the task defined by the ForkJoin-SumCalculator class when executed inside the ForkJoinPool.

Note that in a real-world application, it doesn't make sense to use more than one ForkJoinPool. For this reason, what you typically should do is instantiate it only once and keep this instance in a static field, making it a singleton, so it could be conveniently reused by any part of your software. Here, to create it you're using its default no-argument constructor, meaning that you want to allow the pool to use all the processors available to the JVM. More precisely, this constructor will use the value returned by Runtime.availableProcessors to determine the number of threads used by the pool. Note that the availableProcessors method, despite its name, in reality returns the number of available cores, including any virtual ones due to hyperthreading.

RUNNING THE FORKJOINSUMCALCULATOR

When you pass the `ForkJoinSumCalculator` task to the `ForkJoinPool`, this task is executed by a thread of the pool that in turn calls the `compute` method of the task. This method checks to see if the task is small enough to be performed sequentially; otherwise, it splits the array of numbers to be summed into two halves and assigns them to two new `ForkJoinSumCalculators` that are scheduled to be executed by the `ForkJoinPool`. As a result, this process can be recursively repeated, allowing the original task to be divided into smaller tasks, until the condition used to check if it's no longer convenient or no longer possible to further split it is met (in this case, if the number of items to be summed is less than or equal to 10,000). At this point, the result of each subtask is computed sequentially, and the (implicit) binary tree of tasks created by the forking process is traversed back toward its root. The result of the task is then computed, combining the partial results of each subtask. This process is shown in figure 7.4.

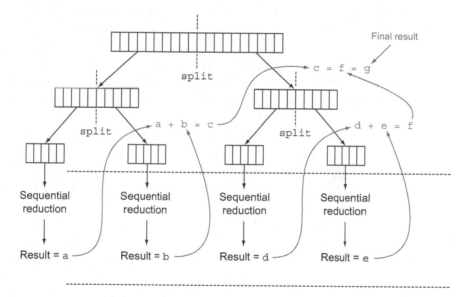

Figure 7.4 The fork/join algorithm

Once again you can check the performance of the summing method explicitly using the fork/join framework with the harness developed at the beginning of this chapter:

```
System.out.println("ForkJoin sum done in: " + measureSumPerf(
        ForkJoinSumCalculator::forkJoinSum, 10_000_000) + " msecs" );
```

In this case it produces the following output:

```
ForkJoin sum done in: 41 msecs
```

Here, the performance is worse than the version using the parallel stream, but only because you're obliged to put the whole stream of numbers into a `long[]` before being allowed to use it in the `ForkJoinSumCalculator` task.

7.2.2   Best practices for using the fork/join framework

Even though the fork/join framework is relatively easy to use, unfortunately it's also easy to misuse. Here are a few best practices to use it effectively:

- Invoking the `join` method on a task blocks the caller until the result produced by that task is ready. For this reason, it's necessary to call it after the computation of both subtasks has been started. Otherwise, you'll end up with a slower and more complex version of your original sequential algorithm because every subtask will have to wait for the other one to complete before starting.

- The `invoke` method of a `ForkJoinPool` shouldn't be used from within a `RecursiveTask`. Instead, you should always call the methods `compute` or `fork` directly; only sequential code should use `invoke` to begin parallel computation.

- Calling the `fork` method on a subtask is the way to schedule it on the `ForkJoinPool`. It might seem natural to invoke it on both the left and right subtasks, but this is less efficient than directly calling `compute` on one of them. Doing this allows you to reuse the same thread for one of the two subtasks and avoid the overhead caused by the unnecessary allocation of a further task on the pool.

- Debugging a parallel computation using the fork/join framework can be tricky. In particular, it's ordinarily quite common to browse a stack trace in your favorite IDE to discover the cause of a problem, but this can't work with a fork/join computation because the call to `compute` occurs in a different thread than the conceptual caller, which is the code that called `fork`.

- As you've discovered with parallel streams, you should never take for granted that a computation using the fork/join framework on a multicore processor is faster than the sequential counterpart. We already said that a task should be decomposable into several independent subtasks in order to be parallelizable with a relevant performance gain. All of these subtasks should take longer to execute than forking a new task; one idiom is to put I/O into one subtask and computation into another, thereby overlapping computation with I/O. More-over, you should consider other things when comparing the performance of the sequential and parallel versions of the same algorithm. Like any other Java code, the fork/join framework needs to be "warmed up," or executed, a few times before being optimized by the JIT compiler. This is why it's always important to run the program multiple times before to measure its perfor-mance, as we did in our harness. Also be aware that optimizations built into the compiler could unfairly give an advantage to the sequential version (for example, by performing dead code analysis—removing a computation that's never used).

The fork/join splitting strategy deserves one last note: you must choose the criteria used to decide if a given subtask should be further split or is small enough to be evaluated sequentially. We'll give some hints about this in the next section.

7.2.3 Work stealing

In our `ForkJoinSumCalculator` example we decided to stop creating more subtasks when the array of numbers to be summed contained at most 10,000 items. This is an arbitrary choice, but in most cases it's difficult to find a good heuristic, other than trying to optimize it by making several attempts with different inputs. In our test case, we started with an array of 10 million items, meaning that the `ForkJoinSumCalculator` will fork at least 1,000 subtasks. This might seem like a waste of resources because we ran it on a machine that has only four cores. In this specific case, that's probably true because all tasks are CPU bound and are expected to take a similar amount of time.

But forking a quite large number of fine-grained tasks is in general a winning choice. This is because ideally you want to partition the workload of a parallelized task in such a way that each subtask takes exactly the same amount of time, keeping all the cores of your CPU equally busy. Unfortunately, especially in cases closer to real-world scenarios than the straightforward example we presented here, the time taken by each subtask can dramatically vary either due to the use of an inefficient partition strategy or because of unpredictable causes like slow access to the disk or the need to coordinate the execution with external services.

The fork/join framework works around this problem with a technique called *work stealing*. In practice, this means that the tasks are more or less evenly divided on all the threads in the `ForkJoinPool`. Each of these threads holds a doubly linked queue of the tasks assigned to it, and as soon as it completes a task it pulls another one from the head of the queue and starts executing it. For the reasons we listed previously, one thread might complete all the tasks assigned to it much faster than the others, which means its queue will become empty while the other threads are still pretty busy. In this case, instead of becoming idle, the thread randomly chooses a queue of a different thread and "steals" a task, taking it from the tail of the queue. This process continues until all the tasks are executed, and then all the queues become empty. That's why having many smaller tasks, instead of only a few bigger ones, can help in better balancing the workload among the worker threads.

More generally, this work-stealing algorithm is used to redistribute and balance the tasks among the worker threads in the pool. Figure 7.5 shows how this process occurs. When a task in the queue of a worker is divided into two subtasks, one of the two subtasks is stolen by another idle worker. As described previously, this process can continue recursively until the condition used to define that a given subtask should be executed sequentially becomes true.

It should now be clear how a stream can use the fork/join framework to process its items in parallel, but there's still one missing ingredient. In this section, we analyzed an example where you explicitly developed the logic to split an array of numbers into

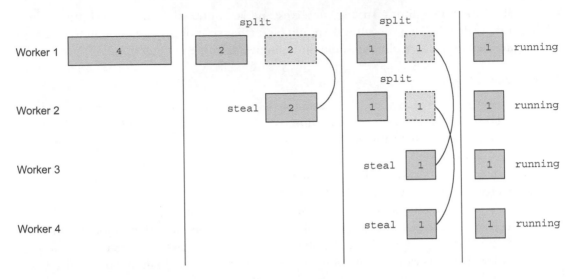

Figure 7.5   The work-stealing algorithm used by the fork/join framework

multiple tasks. Nevertheless, you didn't have to do anything similar when you used the parallel streams at the beginning of this chapter, and this means that there must be an automatic mechanism splitting the stream for you. This new automatic mechanism is called the Spliterator, and we'll explore it in the next section.

7.3   *Spliterator*

The Spliterator is another new interface added to Java 8; its name stands for "splitable iterator." Like Iterators, Spliterators are used to traverse the elements of a source, but they're also designed to do this in parallel. Although you may not have to develop your own Spliterator in practice, understanding how to do so will give you a wider understanding about how parallel streams work. Java 8 already provides a default Spliterator implementation for all the data structures included in its Collections Framework. The Collection interface now provides a default method spliterator() (you will learn more about default methods in chapter 13) which returns a Spliterator object. The Spliterator interface defines several methods, as shown in the following listing.

Listing 7.3   The Spliterator interface

```java
public interface Spliterator<T> {
    boolean tryAdvance(Consumer<? super T> action);
    Spliterator<T> trySplit();
    long estimateSize();
    int characteristics();
}
```

As usual, T is the type of the elements traversed by the Spliterator. The tryAdvance method behaves in a way similar to a normal Iterator in the sense that it's used to sequentially consume the elements of the Spliterator one by one, returning true if there are still other elements to be traversed. But the trySplit method is more specific to the Spliterator interface because it's used to partition off some of its elements to a second Spliterator (the one returned by the method), allowing the two to be processed in parallel. A Spliterator may also provide an estimation of the number of the elements remaining to be traversed via its estimateSize method, because even an inaccurate but quick-to-compute value can be useful to split the structure more or less evenly.

It's important to understand how this splitting process is performed internally in order to take control of it when required. Therefore, we'll analyze it in more detail in the next section.

7.3.1 The splitting process

The algorithm that splits a stream into multiple parts is a recursive process and proceeds as shown in figure 7.6. In the first step, trySplit is invoked on the first Spliterator and generates a second one. Then in step two, it's called again on these two Spliterators, which results in a total of four. The framework keeps invoking the method trySplit on a Spliterator until it returns null to signal that the data

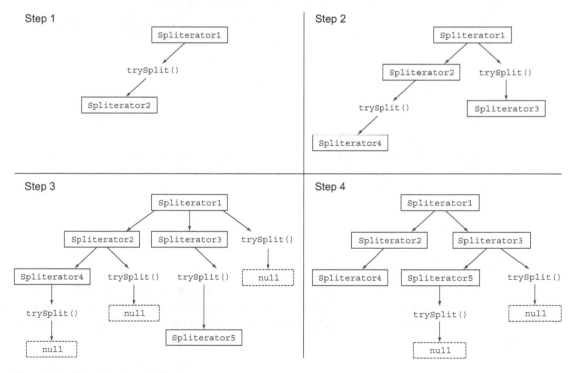

Figure 7.6 The recursive splitting process

structure that it's processing is no longer divisible, as shown in step 3. Finally, this recursive splitting process terminates in step 4 when all `Spliterators` have returned `null` to a `trySplit` invocation.

This splitting process can also be influenced by the characteristics of the `Spliterator` itself, which are declared via the `characteristics` method.

THE SPLITERATOR CHARACTERISTICS

The last abstract method declared by the `Spliterator` interface is `characteristics`, which returns an `int` encoding the set of characteristics of the `Spliterator` itself. The `Spliterator` clients can use these characteristics to better control and optimize its usage. Table 7.2 summarizes them. (Unfortunately, although these conceptually overlap with characteristics of a collector, they're coded differently.) The characteristics are int constants defined in the `Spliterator` interface.

Table 7.2 `Spliterator`'s characteristics

Characteristic	Meaning
ORDERED	Elements have a defined order (for example, a `List`), so the `Spliterator` enforces this order when traversing and partitioning them.
DISTINCT	For each pair of traversed elements x and y, `x.equals(y)` returns `false`.
SORTED	The traversed elements follow a predefined sort order.
SIZED	This `Spliterator` has been created from a source with a known size (for example, a `Set`), so the value returned by `estimatedSize()` is precise.
NON-NULL	It's guaranteed that the traversed elements won't be `null`.
IMMUTABLE	The source of this `Spliterator` can't be modified. This implies that no elements can be added, removed, or modified during their traversal.
CONCURRENT	The source of this `Spliterator` may be safely, concurrently modified by other threads without any synchronization.
SUBSIZED	Both this `Spliterator` and all further `Spliterators` resulting from its split are SIZED.

Now that you've seen what the `Spliterator` interface is and which methods it defines, you can try to develop your own implementation of a `Spliterator`.

7.3.2 *Implementing your own Spliterator*

Let's look at a practical example of where you might need to implement your own `Spliterator`. We'll develop a simple method that counts the number of words in a `String`. An iterative version of this method could be written as shown in the following listing.

Listing 7.4   An iterative word counter method

```
public int countWordsIteratively(String s) {
    int counter = 0;
    boolean lastSpace = true;
    for (char c : s.toCharArray()) {          ◁─┐  Traverses all the characters
        if (Character.isWhitespace(c)) {             in the String one by one
            lastSpace = true;
        } else {
            if (lastSpace) counter++;         ◁─┐  Increases the word counter when
            lastSpace = false;                       the last character is a space and
        }                                            the currently traversed one isn't
    }
    return counter;
}
```

Let's put this method to work on the first sentence of Dante's *Inferno* (see http://en .wikipedia.org/wiki/Inferno_(Dante).):

```
final String SENTENCE =
            " Nel   mezzo del cammin  di nostra  vita " +
            "mi  ritrovai in una  selva oscura" +
            " ché la  dritta via era   smarrita ";
System.out.println("Found " + countWordsIteratively(SENTENCE) + " words");
```

Note that we added some additional random spaces in the sentence to demonstrate that the iterative implementation is working correctly even in the presence of multiple spaces between two words. As expected, this code prints out the following:

```
Found 19 words
```

Ideally you'd like to achieve the same result in a more functional style because this way you'll be able, as shown previously, to parallelize this process using a parallel stream without having to explicitly deal with threads and their synchronization.

REWRITING THE WORDCOUNTER IN FUNCTIONAL STYLE

First, you need to convert the String into a stream. Unfortunately, there are primitive streams only for int, long, and double, so you'll have to use a Stream<Character>:

```
Stream<Character> stream = IntStream.range(0, SENTENCE.length())
                                    .mapToObj(SENTENCE::charAt);
```

You can calculate the number of words by performing a reduction on this stream. While reducing the stream, you'll have to carry a state consisting of two variables: an int counting the number of words found so far and a boolean to remember if the last-encountered Character was a space or not. Because Java doesn't have tuples (a construct to represent an ordered list of heterogeneous elements without the need of a wrapper object), you'll have to create a new class, WordCounter, which will encapsulate this state as shown in the following listing.

Listing 7.5   A class to count words while traversing a stream of `Characters`

```java
class WordCounter {
    private final int counter;
    private final boolean lastSpace;
    public WordCounter(int counter, boolean lastSpace) {
        this.counter = counter;
        this.lastSpace = lastSpace;
    }
    public WordCounter accumulate(Character c) {
        if (Character.isWhitespace(c)) {
            return lastSpace ?
                    this :
                    new WordCounter(counter, true);
        } else {
            return lastSpace ?
                    new WordCounter(counter+1, false) :
                    this;
        }
    }
    public WordCounter combine(WordCounter wordCounter) {
        return new WordCounter(counter + wordCounter.counter,
                            wordCounter.lastSpace);
    }
    public int getCounter() {
        return counter;
    }
}
```

- **Accumulate method traverses Characters one by one as done by the iterative algorithm**
- **Increases the word counter when the last character is a space and the currently traversed one isn't**
- **Combines two WordCounters by summing their counters**
- **Uses only the sum of the counters so you don't care about lastSpace**

In this listing, the `accumulate` method defines how to change the state of the `Word-Counter`, or, more precisely, with which state to create a new `WordCounter` because it's an immutable class. This is important to understand. We are accumulating state with an immutable class specifically so that the process can be parallelized in the next step. The method `accumulate` is called whenever a new `Character` of the stream is traversed. In particular, as you did in the `countWordsIteratively` method in listing 7.4, the counter is incremented when a new nonspace is met, and the last character encountered is a space. Figure 7.7 shows the state transitions of the `WordCounter` when a new `Character` is traversed by the `accumulate` method.

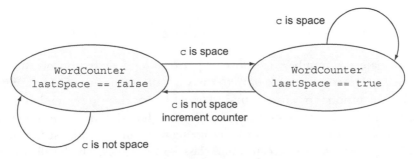

Figure 7.7   The state transitions of the `WordCounter` when a new `Character` c is traversed

The second method, `combine`, is invoked to aggregate the partial results of two Word-Counters operating on two different subparts of the stream of `Characters`, so it combines two `WordCounters` by summing their internal counters.

Now that you've encoded the logic of how to accumulate characters on a WordCounter and how to combine them in the `WordCounter` itself, writing a method that will reduce the stream of `Characters` is straightforward:

```
private int countWords(Stream<Character> stream) {
    WordCounter wordCounter = stream.reduce(new WordCounter(0, true),
                                        WordCounter::accumulate,
                                        WordCounter::combine);
    return wordCounter.getCounter();
}
```

Now you can try this method with the stream created from the `String` containing the first sentence of Dante's *Inferno*:

```
Stream<Character> stream = IntStream.range(0, SENTENCE.length())
                                    .mapToObj(SENTENCE::charAt);
System.out.println("Found " + countWords(stream) + " words");
```

You can check that its output corresponds with the one generated by the iterative version:

```
Found 19 words
```

So far, so good, but we said that one of the main reasons for implementing the Word-Counter in functional terms was to be able to easily parallelize this operation, so let's see how this works.

MAKING THE WORDCOUNTER WORK IN PARALLEL

You could try to speed up the word-counting operation using a parallel stream, as follows:

```
System.out.println("Found " + countWords(stream.parallel()) + " words");
```

Unfortunately, this time the output is

```
Found 25 words
```

Evidently something has gone wrong, but what? The problem isn't hard to discover. Because the original `String` is split at arbitrary positions, sometimes a word is divided in two and then counted twice. In general, this demonstrates that going from a sequential stream to a parallel one can lead to a wrong result if this result may be affected by the position where the stream is split.

How can you fix this issue? The solution consists of ensuring that the `String` isn't split at a random position but only at the end of a word. To do this, you'll have to implement a `Spliterator` of `Character` that splits a `String` only between two words (as shown in the following listing) and then creates the parallel stream from it.

Listing 7.6   The `WordCounterSpliterator`

```
class WordCounterSpliterator implements Spliterator<Character> {
    private final String string;
    private int currentChar = 0;
    public WordCounterSpliterator(String string) {
        this.string = string;                              ◄─── Consumes the
    }                                                           current character
    @Override
    public boolean tryAdvance(Consumer<? super Character> action) {
        action.accept(string.charAt(currentChar++));       ◄───┘
        return currentChar < string.length();      ◄─── Returns true if there
    }                                                   are further characters
    @Override                                           to be consumed
    public Spliterator<Character> trySplit() {
        int currentSize = string.length() - currentChar;
        if (currentSize < 10) {                       Returns null to signal that
            return null;                       ◄───   the String to be parsed
        }                                             is small enough to be
        for (int splitPos = currentSize / 2 + currentChar;   processed sequentially
                 splitPos < string.length(); splitPos++) {
            if (Character.isWhitespace(string.charAt(splitPos))) {
                Spliterator<Character> spliterator =
                    new WordCounterSpliterator(string.substring(currentChar,
                                                                splitPos));
                currentChar = splitPos;          ◄─── Sets the start position
                return spliterator;              ◄─── of the current Word-
            }                                         CounterSpliterator to
        }                                             the split position
        return null;
    }
    @Override                                  Found a space and created
    public long estimateSize() {               the new Spliterator, so
        return string.length() - currentChar;  exit the loop
    }
    @Override
    public int characteristics() {
        return ORDERED + SIZED + SUBSIZED + NON-NULL + IMMUTABLE;
    }
}
```

Annotations (left margin):
- **Sets the candidate split position to be half of the String to be parsed**
- **Advances the split position until the next space**
- **Creates a new WordCounter-Spliterator parsing the String from the start to the split position**

This `Spliterator` is created from the `String` to be parsed and iterates over its `Character`s by holding the index of the one currently being traversed. Let's quickly revisit the methods of the `WordCounterSpliterator` implementing the `Spliterator` interface:

- The `tryAdvance` method feeds the `Consumer` with the `Character` in the `String` at the current index position and increments this position. The `Consumer` passed as its argument is an internal Java class forwarding the consumed `Character` to the set of functions that have to be applied to it while traversing the stream, which in this case is only a reducing function, namely, the `accumulate` method of the `WordCounter` class. The `tryAdvance` method returns `true` if the new cursor position is less than the total `String` length and there are further `Characters` to be iterated.

- The `trySplit` method is the most important one in a `Spliterator`, because it's the one defining the logic used to split the data structure to be iterated. As you did in the `compute` method of the `RecursiveTask` implemented in listing 7.1, the first thing you have to do here is set a limit under which you don't want to perform further splits. Here, you use a low limit of 10 `Characters` only to make sure that your program will perform some splits with the relatively short `String` you're parsing. But in real-world applications you'll have to use a higher limit, as you did in the fork/join example, to avoid creating too many tasks. If the number of remaining `Characters` to be traversed is under this limit, you return `null` to signal that no further split is necessary. Conversely, if you need to perform a split, you set the candidate split position to the half of the `String` chunk remaining to be parsed. But you don't use this split position directly because you want to avoid splitting in the middle of a word, so you move forward until you find a blank `Character`. Once you find an opportune split position, you create a new `Spliterator` that will traverse the substring chunk going from the current position to the split one; you set the current position of `this` to the split one, because the part before it will be managed by the new `Spliterator`, and then you return it.

- The `estimatedSize` of elements still to be traversed is the difference between the total length of the `String` parsed by this `Spliterator` and the position currently iterated.

- Finally, the `characteristics` method signals to the framework that this `Spliterator` is `ORDERED` (the order is the sequence of `Characters` in the `String`), `SIZED` (the value returned by the `estimatedSize` method is exact), `SUBSIZED` (the other `Spliterators` created by the `trySplit` method also have an exact size), `NON-NULL` (there can be no `null` `Characters` in the `String`), and `IMMUTABLE` (no further `Characters` can be added while parsing the `String` because the `String` itself is an immutable class).

PUTTING THE WORDCOUNTERSPLITERATOR TO WORK

You can now use a parallel stream with this new `WordCounterSpliterator` as follows:

```
Spliterator<Character> spliterator = new WordCounterSpliterator(SENTENCE);
Stream<Character> stream = StreamSupport.stream(spliterator, true);
```

The second boolean argument passed to the `StreamSupport.stream` factory method means that you want to create a parallel stream. Passing this parallel stream to the `countWords` method

```
System.out.println("Found " + countWords(stream) + " words");
```

produces the correct output, as expected:

```
Found 19 words
```

You've seen how a `Spliterator` can let you to gain control over the policy used to split a data structure. One last notable feature of `Spliterators` is the possibility of binding the source of the elements to be traversed at the point of first traversal, first split, or first query for estimated size, rather than at the time of its creation. When this happens, it's called a *late-binding* `Spliterator`. We've dedicated appendix C to showing how you can develop a utility class capable of performing multiple operations on the same stream in parallel using this feature.

Summary

- Internal iteration allows you to process a stream in parallel without the need to explicitly use and coordinate different threads in your code.
- Even if processing a stream in parallel is so easy, there's no guarantee that doing so will make your programs run faster under all circumstances. Behavior and performance of parallel software can sometimes be counterintuitive, and for this reason it's always necessary to measure them and be sure that you're not slowing your programs down.
- Parallel execution of an operation on a set of data, as done by a parallel stream, can provide a performance boost, especially when the number of elements to be processed is huge or the processing of each single element is particularly time consuming.
- From a performance point of view, using the right data structure, for instance, employing primitive streams instead of nonspecialized ones whenever possible, is almost always more important than trying to parallelize some operations.
- The fork/join framework lets you recursively split a parallelizable task into smaller tasks, execute them on different threads, and then combine the results of each subtask in order to produce the overall result.
- `Spliterators` define how a parallel stream can split the data it traverses.

Part 3

Effective programming with streams and lambdas

The third part of this book explores various Java 8 and Java 9 topics that will make you more effective at using Java and enhance your codebase with modern idioms. Because it's oriented toward more advanced programming ideas, nothing later in the book depends on the techniques described here.

Chapter 8 is a new chapter for the second edition and explores the Collection API enhancements of Java 8 and Java 9 and covers using collection factories and learning new idiomatic patterns to work with List and Set collections along with idiomatic patterns involving Map.

Chapter 9 explores how you can improve your existing code using new Java 8 features and a few recipes. In addition, it explores vital software development techniques such as design patterns, refactoring, testing, and debugging.

Chapter 10 is again new for the second edition. It explores the idea of basing an API on a domain-specific language (DSL). This is not only a powerful way of designing APIs but also one that is both becoming increasingly popular and already visible in Java, such as in the `Comparator`, `Stream`, and `Collector` interfaces.

Collection API enhancements

This chapter covers

- Using collection factories
- Learning new idiomatic patterns to use with `List` and `Set`
- Learning idiomatic patterns to work with `Map`

Your life as a Java developer would be rather lonely without the Collection API. Collections are used in every Java applications. In previous chapters, you saw how useful the combination of Collections with the Streams API is for expressing data processing queries. Nonetheless, the Collection API had various deficiencies, which made it verbose and error-prone to use at times.

In this chapter, you will learn about new additions to the Collection API in Java 8 and Java 9 that will make your life easier. First, you learn about the collections factories in Java 9—new additions that simplify the process of creating small lists, sets, and maps. Next, you learn how to apply idiomatic removal and replacement patterns in lists and sets thanks to Java 8 enhancements. Finally, you learn about new convenience operations that are available to work with maps.

Chapter 9 explores a wider range of techniques for refactoring old-style Java code.

8.1   *Collection factories*

Java 9 introduced a few convenient ways to create small collection objects. First, we'll review why programmers needed a better way to do things; then we'll show you how to use the new factory methods.

How would you create a small list of elements in Java? You might want to group the names of your friends who are going on a holiday, for example. Here's one way:

```
List<String> friends = new ArrayList<>();
friends.add("Raphael");
friends.add("Olivia");
friends.add("Thibaut");
```

But that's quite a few lines to write for storing three strings! A more convenient way to write this code is to use the `Arrays.asList()` factory method:

```
List<String> friends
    = Arrays.asList("Raphael", "Olivia", "Thibaut");
```

You get a fixed-sized list that you can update, but not add elements to or remove elements from. Attempting to add elements, for example, results in an `Unsupported-ModificationException`, but updating by using the method `set` is allowed:

```
List<String> friends = Arrays.asList("Raphael", "Olivia");
friends.set(0, "Richard");
friends.add("Thibaut");          ⟵  throws an
                                     UnsupportedOperationException
```

This behavior seems slightly surprising because the underlying list is backed by a mutable array of fixed size.

How about a `Set`? Unfortunately, there's no `Arrays.asSet()` factory method, so you need another trick. You can use the `HashSet` constructor, which accepts a `List`:

```
Set<String> friends "
    = new HashSet<>(Arrays.asList("Raphael", "Olivia", Thibaut"));
```

Alternatively you could use the Streams API:

```
Set<String> friends
    = Stream.of("Raphael", "Olivia", "Thibaut")
            .collect(Collectors.toSet());
```

Both solutions, however, are far from elegant and involve unnecessary object allocations behind the scenes. Also note that you get a mutable `Set` as a result.

How about `Map`? There's no elegant way of creating small maps, but don't worry; Java 9 added factory methods to make your life simpler when you need to create small lists, sets, and maps.

We begin the tour of new ways of creating collections in Java by showing you what's new with `Lists`.

> **Collection literals**
>
> Some languages, including Python and Groovy, support collection literals, which let you create collections by using special syntax, such as [42, 1, 5] to create a list of three numbers. Java doesn't provide syntactic support because language changes come with a high maintenance cost and restrict future use of a possible syntax. Instead, Java 9 adds support by enhancing the Collection API.

8.1.1 List factory

You can create a list simply by calling the factory method `List.of`:

```
List<String> friends = List.of("Raphael", "Olivia", "Thibaut");
System.out.println(friends);    ◁──────┐
                                         │  [Raphael, Olivia, Thibaut]
```

You'll notice something strange, however. Try to add an element to your list of friends:

```
List<String> friends = List.of("Raphael", "Olivia", "Thibaut");
friends.add("Chih-Chun");
```

Running this code results in a `java.lang.UnsupportedOperationException`. In fact, the list that's produced is immutable. Replacing an item with the `set()` method throws a similar exception. You won't be able to modify it by using the `set` method either. This restriction is a good thing, however, as it protects you from unwanted mutations of the collections. Nothing is stopping you from having elements that are mutable themselves. If you need a mutable list, you can still instantiate one manually. Finally, note that to prevent unexpected bugs and enable a more-compact internal representation, null elements are disallowed.

> **Overloading vs. varargs**
>
> If you further inspect the `List` interface, you notice several overloaded variants of `List.of`:
>
> ```
> static <E> List<E> of(E e1, E e2, E e3, E e4)
> static <E> List<E> of(E e1, E e2, E e3, E e4, E e5)
> ```
>
> You may wonder why the Java API didn't have one method that uses varargs to accept an arbitrary number of elements in the following style:
>
> ```
> static <E> List<E> of(E... elements)
> ```
>
> Under the hood, the varargs version allocates an extra array, which is wrapped up inside a list. You pay the cost for allocating an array, initializing it, and having it garbage-collected later. By providing a fixed number of elements (up to ten) through an API, you don't pay this cost. Note that you can still create `List.of` using more than ten elements, but in that case the varargs signature is invoked. You also see this pattern appearing with `Set.of` and `Map.of`.

You may wonder whether you should use the Streams API instead of the new collection factory methods to create such lists. After all, you saw in previous chapters that you can use the `Collectors.toList()` collector to transform a stream into a list. Unless you need to set up some form of data processing and transformation of the data, we recommend that you use the factory methods; they're simpler to use, and the implementation of the factory methods is simpler and more adequate.

Now that you've learned about a new factory method for `List`, in the next section, you will work with `Set`s.

8.1.2 *Set factory*

As with `List.of`, you can create an immutable `Set` out of a list of elements:

```
Set<String> friends = Set.of("Raphael", "Olivia", "Thibaut");        [Raphael, Olivia,
System.out.println(friends);                                    ◁┘   Thibaut]
```

If you try to create a `Set` by providing a duplicated element, you receive an `Illegal-ArgumentException`. This exception reflects the contract that sets enforce uniqueness of the elements they contain:

```
Set<String> friends = Set.of("Raphael", "Olivia", "Olivia");    ◁─────┐

                                           java.lang.IllegalArgumentException:
                                                    duplicate element: Olivia
```

Another popular data structure in Java is `Map`. In the next section, you learn about new ways of creating `Map`s.

8.1.3 *Map factories*

Creating a map is a bit more complicated than creating lists and sets because you have to include both the key and the value. You have two ways to initialize an immutable map in Java 9. You can use the factory method `Map.of`, which alternates between keys and values:

```
Map<String, Integer> ageOfFriends                                    {Olivia=25,
    = Map.of("Raphael", 30, "Olivia", 25, "Thibaut", 26);            Raphael=30,
System.out.println(ageOfFriends);                              ◁┘    Thibaut=26}
```

This method is convenient if you want to create a small map of up to ten keys and values. To go beyond this, use the alternative factory method called `Map.ofEntries`, which takes `Map.Entry<K, V>` objects but is implemented with varargs. This method requires additional object allocations to wrap up a key and a value:

```
import static java.util.Map.entry;
Map<String, Integer> ageOfFriends
        = Map.ofEntries(entry("Raphael", 30),
                        entry("Olivia", 25),             {Olivia=25,
                        entry("Thibaut", 26));           Raphael=30,
System.out.println(ageOfFriends);              ◁┘        Thibaut=26}
```

Map.entry is a new factory method to create Map.Entry objects.

> ### Quiz 8.1
> What do you think is the output of the following snippet?
>
> ```
> List<String> actors = List.of("Keanu", "Jessica")
> actors.set(0, "Brad");
> System.out.println(actors)
> ```
>
> **Answer:**
>
> An UnsupportedOperationException is thrown. The collection produced by List.of
> is immutable.

So far, you've seen that the new Java 9 factory methods allow you to create collections more simply. But in practice, you have to process the collections. In the next section, you learn about a few new enhancements to List and Set that implement common processing patterns out of the box.

8.2 Working with List and Set

Java 8 introduced a couple of methods into the List and Set interfaces:

- removeIf removes element matching a predicate. It's available on all classes that implement List or Set (and is inherited from the Collection interface).
- replaceAll is available on List and replaces elements using a (UnaryOperator) function.
- sort is also available on the List interface and sorts the list itself.

All these methods mutate the collections on which they're invoked. In other words, they change the collection itself, unlike stream operations, which produce a new (copied) result. Why would such methods be added? Modifying collections can be error-prone and verbose. So Java 8 added removeIf and replaceAll to help.

8.2.1 removeIf

Consider the following code, which tries to remove transactions that have a reference code starting with a digit:

```
for (Transaction transaction : transactions) {
    if(Character.isDigit(transaction.getReferenceCode().charAt(0))) {
        transactions.remove(transaction);
    }
}
```

Can you see the problem? Unfortunately, this code may result in a Concurrent-ModificationException. Why? Under the hood, the for-each loop uses an Iterator object, so the code executed is as follows:

```
for (Iterator<Transaction> iterator = transactions.iterator();
     iterator.hasNext(); ) {
  Transaction transaction = iterator.next();
  if(Character.isDigit(transaction.getReferenceCode().charAt(0))) {
    transactions.remove(transaction);
  }
}
```

Problem we are iterating and modifying the collection through two separate objects

Notice that two separate objects manage the collection:

- The Iterator object, which is querying the source by using next() and has-Next()
- The Collection object itself, which is removing the element by calling remove()

As a result, the state of the iterator is no longer synced with the state of the collection, and vice versa. To solve this problem, you have to use the Iterator object explicitly and call its remove() method:

```
for (Iterator<Transaction> iterator = transactions.iterator();
     iterator.hasNext(); ) {
  Transaction transaction = iterator.next();
  if(Character.isDigit(transaction.getReferenceCode().charAt(0))) {
    iterator.remove();
  }
}
```

This code has become fairly verbose to write. This code pattern is now directly expressible with the Java 8 removeIf method, which is not only simpler but also protects you from these bugs. It takes a predicate indicating which elements to remove:

```
transactions.removeIf(transaction ->
    Character.isDigit(transaction.getReferenceCode().charAt(0)));
```

Sometimes, though, instead of removing an element, you want to replace it. For this purpose, Java 8 added replaceAll.

8.2.2   *replaceAll*

The replaceAll method on the List interface lets you replace each element in a list with a new one. Using the Streams API, you could solve this problem as follows:

```
referenceCodes.stream()                                        [a12, C14, b13]
            .map(code -> Character.toUpperCase(code.charAt(0)) +
    code.substring(1))
            .collect(Collectors.toList())                      outputs A12,
            .forEach(System.out::println);                     C14, B13
```

This code results in a new collection of strings, however. You want a way to update the existing collection. You can use a ListIterator object as follows (supporting a set() method to replace an element):

```
for (ListIterator<String> iterator = referenceCodes.listIterator();
    iterator.hasNext(); ) {
  String code = iterator.next();
  iterator.set(Character.toUpperCase(code.charAt(0)) + code.substring(1));
}
```

As you can see, this code is fairly verbose. In addition, as we explained earlier, using `Iterator` objects in conjunction with collection objects can be error-prone by mixing iteration and modification of the collection. In Java 8, you can simply write

```
referenceCodes.replaceAll(code -> Character.toUpperCase(code.charAt(0)) +
    code.substring(1));
```

You've learned what's new with `List` and `Set`, but don't forget about `Map`. New additions to the `Map` interface are covered in the next section.

8.3 Working with Map

Java 8 introduced several default methods supported by the `Map` interface. (Default methods are covered in detail in chapter 13, but here you can think of them as being preimplemented methods in an interface.) The purpose of these new operations is to help you write more concise code by using a readily available idiomatic pattern instead of implementing it yourself. We look at these operations in the following sections, starting with the shiny new `forEach`.

8.3.1 forEach

Iterating over the keys and values of a `Map` has traditionally been awkward. In fact, you needed to use an iterator of a `Map.Entry<K, V>` over the entry set of a `Map`:

```
for(Map.Entry<String, Integer> entry: ageOfFriends.entrySet()) {
  String friend = entry.getKey();
  Integer age = entry.getValue();
  System.out.println(friend + " is " + age + " years old");
}
```

Since Java 8, the `Map` interface has supported the `forEach` method, which accepts a `BiConsumer`, taking the key and value as arguments. Using `forEach` makes your code more concise:

```
ageOfFriends.forEach((friend, age) -> System.out.println(friend + " is " +
    age + " years old"));
```

A concern related to iterating over date is sorting it. Java 8 introduced a couple of convenient ways to compare entries in a `Map`.

8.3.2   Sorting

Two new utilities let you sort the entries of a map by values or keys:

- Entry.comparingByValue
- Entry.comparingByKey

The code

```
Map<String, String> favouriteMovies
        = Map.ofEntries(entry("Raphael", "Star Wars"),
        entry("Cristina", "Matrix"),
        entry("Olivia",
        "James Bond"));

favouriteMovies
    .entrySet()
    .stream()
    .sorted(Entry.comparingByKey())
    .forEachOrdered(System.out::println);
```

Processes the elements of the stream in alphabetic order based on the person's name

outputs, in order:

```
Cristina=Matrix
Olivia=James Bond
Raphael=Star Wars
```

HashMap and Performance

The internal structure of a HashMap was updated in Java 8 to improve performance. Entries of a map typically are stored in buckets accessed by the generated hashcode of the key. But if many keys return the same hashcode, performance deteriorates because buckets are implemented as LinkedLists with O(n) retrieval. Nowadays, when the buckets become too big, they're replaced dynamically with sorted trees, which have O(log(n)) retrieval and improve the lookup of colliding elements. Note that this use of sorted trees is possible only when the keys are Comparable (such as String or Number classes).

Another common pattern is how to act when the key you're looking up in the Map isn't present. The new getOrDefault method can help.

8.3.3   getOrDefault

When the key you're looking up isn't present, you receive a null reference that you have to check against to prevent a NullPointerException. A common design style is to provide a default value instead. Now you can encode this idea more simply by using the getOrDefault method. This method takes the key as the first argument and a default value (to be used when the key is absent from the Map) as the second argument:

```
Map<String, String> favouriteMovies
        = Map.ofEntries(entry("Raphael", "Star Wars"),
        entry("Olivia", "James Bond"));
```

```
System.out.println(favouriteMovies.getOrDefault("Olivia", "Matrix"));
System.out.println(favouriteMovies.getOrDefault("Thibaut", "Matrix"));
```

Outputs Matrix   **Outputs James Bond**

Note that if the key existed in the Map but was accidentally associated with a null value, getOrDefault can still return null. Also note that the expression you pass as a fallback is always evaluated, whether the key exists or not.

Java 8 also included a few more advanced patterns to deal with the presence and absence of values for a given key. You will learn about these new methods in the next section.

8.3.4 Compute patterns

Sometimes, you want to perform an operation conditionally and store its result, depending on whether a key is present or absent in a Map. You may want to cache the result of an expensive operation given a key, for example. If the key is present, there's no need to recalculate the result. Three new operations can help:

- computeIfAbsent—If there's no specified value for the given key (it's absent or its value is null), calculate a new value by using the key and add it to the Map.
- computeIfPresent—If the specified key is present, calculate a new value for it and add it to the Map.
- compute—This operation calculates a new value for a given key and stores it in the Map.

One use of computeIfAbsent is for caching information. Suppose that you parse each line of a set of files and calculate their SHA-256 representation. If you've processed the data previously, there's no need to recalculate it.

Now suppose that you implement a cache by using a Map, and you use an instance of MessageDigest to calculate SHA-256 hashes:

```
Map<String, byte[]> dataToHash = new HashMap<>();
MessageDigest messageDigest = MessageDigest.getInstance("SHA-256");
```

Then you can iterate through the data and cache the results:

```
lines.forEach(line ->
    dataToHash.computeIfAbsent(line,
                        this::calculateDigest));
```

line is the key to look up in the map.

The operation to execute if the key is absent

```
private byte[] calculateDigest(String key) {
    return messageDigest.digest(key.getBytes(StandardCharsets.UTF_8));
}
```

The helper that will calculate a hash for the given key

This pattern is also useful for conveniently dealing with maps that store multiple values. If you need to add an element to a Map<K, List<V>>, you need to ensure that the entry has been initialized. This pattern is a verbose one to put in place. Suppose that you want to build up a list of movies for your friend Raphael:

```
String friend = "Raphael";
List<String> movies = friendsToMovies.get(friend);         Check that the list
if(movies == null) {                                        was initialized.
    movies = new ArrayList<>();
    friendsToMovies.put(friend, movies);
}                                                Add the movie.
movies.add("Star Wars");
                                                 {Raphael:
System.out.println(friendsToMovies);             [Star Wars]}
```

How can you use `computeIfAbsent` instead? It returns the calculated value after adding it to the `Map` if the key wasn't found; otherwise, it returns the existing value. You can use it as follows:

```
friendsToMovies.computeIfAbsent("Raphael", name -> new ArrayList<>())
               .add("Star Wars");
                                              {Raphael: [Star Wars]}
```

The `computeIfPresent` method calculates a new value if the current value associated with the key is present in the `Map` and non-null. Note a subtlety: if the function that produces the value returns null, the current mapping is removed from the `Map`. If you need to remove a mapping, however, an overloaded version of the `remove` method is better suited to the task. You learn about this method in the next section.

8.3.5   *Remove patterns*

You already know about the `remove` method that lets you remove a `Map` entry for a given key. Since Java 8, an overloaded version removes an entry only if the key is associated with a specific value. Previously, this code is how you'd implement this behavior (we have nothing against Tom Cruise, but *Jack Reacher 2* received poor reviews):

```
String key = "Raphael";
String value = "Jack Reacher 2";
if (favouriteMovies.containsKey(key) &&
    Objects.equals(favouriteMovies.get(key), value)) {
    favouriteMovies.remove(key);
    return true;
}
else {
    return false;
}
```

Here is how you can do the same thing now, which you have to admit is much more to the point:

```
favouriteMovies.remove(key, value);
```

In the next section, you learn about ways of replacing elements in and removing elements from a Map.

8.3.6 *Replacement patterns*

Map has two new methods that let you replace the entries inside a Map:

- replaceAll—Replaces each entry's value with the result of applying a BiFunction. This method works similarly to replaceAll on a List, which you saw earlier.
- Replace—Lets you replace a value in the Map if a key is present. An additional overload replaces the value only if it the key is mapped to a certain value.

You could format all the values in a Map as follows:

```
Map<String, String> favouriteMovies = new HashMap<>();
favouriteMovies.put("Raphael", "Star Wars");
favouriteMovies.put("Olivia", "james bond");
favouriteMovies.replaceAll((friend, movie) -> movie.toUpperCase());
System.out.println(favouriteMovies);
```

We have to use a mutable map since we will be using replaceAll

{Olivia=JAMES BOND, Raphael=STAR WARS}

The replace patterns you've learned work with a single Map. But what if you have to combine and replace values from two Maps? You can use a new merge method for that task.

8.3.7 *Merge*

Suppose that you'd like to merge two intermediate Maps, perhaps two separate Maps for two groups of contacts. You can use putAll as follows:

```
Map<String, String> family = Map.ofEntries(
    entry("Teo", "Star Wars"), entry("Cristina", "James Bond"));
Map<String, String> friends = Map.ofEntries(
    entry("Raphael", "Star Wars"));
Map<String, String> everyone = new HashMap<>(family);
everyone.putAll(friends);
System.out.println(everyone);
```

Copies all the entries from friends into everyone

{Cristina=James Bond, Raphael= Star Wars, Teo=Star Wars}

This code works as expected as long as you don't have duplicate keys. If you require more flexibility in how values are combined, you can use the new merge method. This method takes a BiFunction to merge values that have a duplicate key. Suppose that Cristina is in both the family and friends maps but with different associated movies:

```
Map<String, String> family = Map.ofEntries(
    entry("Teo", "Star Wars"), entry("Cristina", "James Bond"));
Map<String, String> friends = Map.ofEntries(
    entry("Raphael", "Star Wars"), entry("Cristina", "Matrix"));
```

Then you could use the `merge` method in combination with `forEach` to provide a way to deal with the conflict. The following code concatenates the string names of the two movies:

```
Map<String, String> everyone = new HashMap<>(family);
friends.forEach((k, v) ->
    everyone.merge(k, v, (movie1, movie2) -> movie1 + " & " + movie2));
System.out.println(everyone);
```

> **Given a duplicate key, concatenates the two values**

> **Outputs {Raphael=Star Wars, Cristina= James Bond & Matrix, Teo=Star Wars}**

Note that the `merge` method has a fairly complex way to deal with nulls, as specified in the Javadoc:

> *If the specified key is not already associated with a value or is associated with null, [merge] associates it with the given non-null value. Otherwise, [merge] replaces the associated value with the [result] of the given remapping function, or removes [it] if the result is null.*

You can also use `merge` to implement initialization checks. Suppose that you have a `Map` for recording how many times a movie is watched. You need to check that the key representing the movie is in the map before you can increment its value:

```
Map<String, Long> moviesToCount = new HashMap<>();
String movieName = "JamesBond";
long count = moviesToCount.get(movieName);
if(count == null) {
    moviesToCount.put(movieName, 1);
}
else {
    moviesToCount.put(moviename, count + 1);
}
```

This code can be rewritten as

```
moviesToCount.merge(movieName, 1L, (key, count) -> count + 1L);
```

The second argument to merge in this case is `1L`. The Javadoc specifies that this argument is "the non-null value to be merged with the existing value associated with the key or, if no existing value or a null value is associated with the key, to be associated with the key." Because the value returned for that key is `null`, the value 1 is provided the first time around. The next time around, because the value for the key was initialized to the value of 1, the `BiFunction` is applied to increment the count.

You've learned about the additions to the `Map` interface. New enhancements were added to a cousin: `ConcurrentHashMap` which you will learn about next.

8.4   Improved ConcurrentHashMap

The `ConcurrentHashMap` class was introduced to provide a more modern `HashMap`, which is also concurrency friendly. `ConcurrentHashMap` allows concurrent `add` and `update` operations that lock only certain parts of the internal data structure. Thus, read and write operations have improved performance compared with the synchronized `Hashtable` alternative. (Note that the standard `HashMap` is unsynchronized.)

8.4.1   Reduce and Search

`ConcurrentHashMap` supports three new kinds of operations, reminiscent of what you saw with streams:

- `forEach`—Performs a given action for each (key, value)
- `reduce`—Combines all (key, value) given a reduction function into a result
- `search`—Applies a function on each (key, value) until the function produces a non-null result

Each kind of operation supports four forms, accepting functions with keys, values, `Map.Entry`, and (key, value) arguments:

- Operates with keys and values (`forEach`, `reduce`, `search`)
- Operates with keys (`forEachKey`, `reduceKeys`, `searchKeys`)

- Operates with values (forEachValue, reduceValues, searchValues)
- Operates with Map.Entry objects (forEachEntry, reduceEntries, search-Entries)

Note that these operations don't lock the state of the ConcurrentHashMap; they operate on the elements as they go along. The functions supplied to these operations shouldn't depend on any ordering or on any other objects or values that may change while computation is in progress.

In addition, you need to specify a parallelism threshold for all these operations. The operations execute sequentially if the current size of the map is less than the given threshold. A value of 1 enables maximal parallelism using the common thread pool. A threshold value of Long.MAX_VALUE runs the operation on a single thread. You generally should stick to these values unless your software architecture has advanced resource-use optimization.

In this example, you use the reduceValues method to find the maximum value in the map:

A ConcurrentHashMap, presumed to be updated to contain several keys and values

```
ConcurrentHashMap<String, Long> map = new ConcurrentHashMap<>();        ⟵─┘
long parallelismThreshold = 1;
Optional<Integer> maxValue =
    Optional.ofNullable(map.reduceValues(parallelismThreshold, Long::max));
```

Note the primitive specializations for int, long, and double for each reduce operation (reduceValuesToInt, reduceKeysToLong, and so on), which are more efficient, as they prevent boxing.

8.4.2 *Counting*

The ConcurrentHashMap class provides a new method called mappingCount, which returns the number of mappings in the map as a long. You should use it for new code in preference to the size method, which returns an int. Doing so future proofs your code for use when the number of mappings no longer fits in an int.

8.4.3 *Set views*

The ConcurrentHashMap class provides a new method called keySet that returns a view of the ConcurrentHashMap as a Set. (Changes in the map are reflected in the Set, and vice versa.) You can also create a Set backed by a ConcurrentHashMap by using the new static method newKeySet.

Summary

- Java 9 supports collection factories, which let you create small immutable lists, sets, and maps by using List.of, Set.of, Map.of, and Map.ofEntries.
- The objects returned by these collection factories are immutable, which means that you can't change their state after creation.

- The `List` interface supports the default methods `removeIf`, `replaceAll`, and sort.
- The `Set` interface supports the default method `removeIf`.
- The `Map` interface includes several new default methods for common patterns and reduces the scope for bugs.
- `ConcurrentHashMap` supports the new default methods inherited from `Map` but provides thread-safe implementations for them.

Refactoring, testing, and debugging

This chapter covers

- Refactoring code to use lambda expressions
- Appreciating the impact of lambda expressions on object-oriented design patterns
- Testing lambda expressions
- Debugging code that uses lambda expressions and the Streams API

In the first eight chapters of this book, you saw the expressive power of lambdas and the Streams API. You were mainly creating new code that used these features. If you have to start a new Java project, you can use lambdas and streams immediately.

Unfortunately, you don't always get to start a new project from scratch. Most of the time you have to deal with an existing code base written in an older version of Java.

This chapter presents several recipes that show you how to refactor existing code to use lambda expressions to gain readability and flexibility. In addition, we discuss how several object-oriented design patterns (including strategy, template method, observer, chain of responsibility, and factory) can be made more concise

216

thanks to lambda expressions. Finally, we explore how you can test and debug code that uses lambda expressions and the Streams API.

In chapter 10, we explore a more wide-ranging way of refactoring code to make the application logic more readable: creating a domain-specific language.

9.1   Refactoring for improved readability and flexibility

From the start of this book, we've argued that lambda expressions let you write more concise and flexible code. The code is more concise because lambda expressions let you represent a piece of behavior in a more compact form compared with using anonymous classes. We also showed you in chapter 3 that method references let you write even more concise code when all you want to do is pass an existing method as an argument to another method.

Your code is more flexible because lambda expressions encourage the style of behavior parameterization that we introduced in chapter 2. Your code can use and execute multiple behaviors passed as arguments to cope with requirement changes.

In this section, we bring everything together and show you simple steps for refactoring code to gain readability and flexibility, using the features you learned in previous chapters: lambdas, method references, and streams.

9.1.1   Improving code readability

What does it mean to improve the readability of code? Defining good readability can be subjective. The general view is that the term means "how easily this code can be understood by another human." Improving code readability ensures that your code is understandable and maintainable by people other than you. You can take a few steps to make sure that your code is understandable to other people, such as making sure that your code is well documented and follows coding standards.

Using features introduced in Java 8 can also improve code readability compared with previous versions. You can reduce the verbosity of your code, making it easier to understand. Also, you can better show the intent of your code by using method references and the Streams API.

In this chapter, we describe three simple refactorings that use lambdas, method references, and streams, which you can apply to your code to improve its readability:

- Refactoring anonymous classes to lambda expressions
- Refactoring lambda expressions to method references
- Refactoring imperative-style data processing to streams

9.1.2   From anonymous classes to lambda expressions

The first simple refactoring you should consider is converting uses of anonymous classes implementing one single abstract method to lambda expressions. Why? We hope that in earlier chapters, we convinced you that anonymous classes are verbose and error-prone. By adopting lambda expressions, you produce code that's more succinct and readable. As shown in chapter 3, here's an anonymous class for creating a `Runnable` object and its lambda-expression counterpart:

```
Runnable r1 = new Runnable() {          ◄┐  Before, using an
    public void run(){                       anonymous class
        System.out.println("Hello");
    }
};
Runnable r2 = () -> System.out.println("Hello");    ◄┐  After, using a
                                                         lambda expression
```

But converting anonymous classes to lambda expressions can be a difficult process in certain situations.[1] First, the meanings of `this` and `super` are different for anonymous classes and lambda expressions. Inside an anonymous class, `this` refers to the anonymous class itself, but inside a lambda, it refers to the enclosing class. Second, anonymous classes are allowed to shadow variables from the enclosing class. Lambda expressions can't (they'll cause a compile error), as shown in the following code:

```
int a = 10;
Runnable r1 = () -> {
    int a = 2;                    ◄┘  Compile error
    System.out.println(a);
};
Runnable r2 = new Runnable(){
    public void run(){
        int a = 2;                ◄┘  Everything
        System.out.println(a);         is fine!
    }
};
```

Finally, converting an anonymous class to a lambda expression can make the resulting code ambiguous in the context of overloading. Indeed, the type of anonymous class is explicit at instantiation, but the type of the lambda depends on its context. Here's an example of how this situation can be problematic. Suppose that you've declared a functional interface with the same signature as `Runnable`, here called `Task` (as might occur when you need more-meaningful interface names in your domain model):

```
interface Task {
    public void execute();
}
public static void doSomething(Runnable r){ r.run(); }
public static void doSomething(Task a){ r.execute(); }
```

Now you can pass an anonymous class implementing `Task` without a problem:

```
doSomething(new Task() {
    public void execute() {
        System.out.println("Danger danger!!");
    }
});
```

---

[1] This excellent paper describes the process in more detail: http://dig.cs.illinois.edu/papers/lambdaRefactoring.pdf.

But converting this anonymous class to a lambda expression results in an ambiguous method call, because both `Runnable` and `Task` are valid target types:

```
doSomething(() -> System.out.println("Danger danger!!"));
```

**Problem; both doSomething(Runnable)
and doSomething(Task) match.**

You can solve the ambiguity by providing an explicit cast (`Task`):

```
doSomething((Task)() -> System.out.println("Danger danger!!"));
```

Don't be turned off by these issues, though; there's good news! Most integrated development environments (IDEs)—such as NetBeans, Eclipse, and IntelliJ—support this refactoring and automatically ensure that these gotchas don't arise.

9.1.3 *From lambda expressions to method references*

Lambda expressions are great for short code that needs to be passed around. But consider using method references whenever possible to improve code readability. A method name states the intent of your code more clearly. In chapter 6, for example, we showed you the following code to group dishes by caloric levels:

```
Map<CaloricLevel, List<Dish>> dishesByCaloricLevel =
    menu.stream()
        .collect(
            groupingBy(dish -> {
                if (dish.getCalories() <= 400) return CaloricLevel.DIET;
                else if (dish.getCalories() <= 700) return CaloricLevel.NORMAL;
                else return CaloricLevel.FAT;
            }));
```

You can extract the lambda expression into a separate method and pass it as an argument to groupingBy. The code becomes more concise, and its intent is more explicit:

```
Map<CaloricLevel, List<Dish>> dishesByCaloricLevel =
    menu.stream().collect(groupingBy(Dish::getCaloricLevel));
```

**The lambda expression is
extracted into a method.**

You need to add the method getCaloricLevel inside the Dish class itself for this code to work:

```
public class Dish{
    ...
    public CaloricLevel getCaloricLevel() {
        if (this.getCalories() <= 400) return CaloricLevel.DIET;
        else if (this.getCalories() <= 700) return CaloricLevel.NORMAL;
        else return CaloricLevel.FAT;
    }
}
```

In addition, consider using helper static methods such as `comparing` and `maxBy` whenever possible. These methods were designed for use with method references! Indeed, this code states much more clearly its intent than its counterpart using a lambda expression, as we showed you in chapter 3:

You need to think about the implementation of comparison.

```
inventory.sort(
    (Apple a1, Apple a2) -> a1.getWeight().compareTo(a2.getWeight()));
inventory.sort(comparing(Apple::getWeight));
```

Reads like the problem statement

Moreover, for many common reduction operations such as *sum, maximum,* there are built-in helper methods that can be combined with method references. We showed you, for example, that by using the `Collectors` API, you can find the maximum or sum in a clearer way than by using a combination of a lambda expression and a lower-level `reduce` operation. Instead of writing

```
int totalCalories =
    menu.stream().map(Dish::getCalories)
                 .reduce(0, (c1, c2) -> c1 + c2);
```

try using alternative built-in collectors, which state the problem statement more clearly. Here, we use the collector `summingInt` (names go a long way in documenting your code):

```
int totalCalories = menu.stream().collect(summingInt(Dish::getCalories));
```

9.1.4   *From imperative data processing to Streams*

Ideally, you should try to convert all code that processes a collection with typical data processing patterns with an iterator to use the Streams API instead. Why? The Streams API expresses more clearly the intent of a data processing pipeline. In addition, streams can be optimized behind the scenes, making use of short-circuiting and laziness as well as leveraging your multicore architecture, as we explained in chapter 7.

The following imperative code expresses two patterns (filtering and extracting) that are mangled together, forcing the programmer to carefully figure out the whole implementation before figuring out what the code does. In addition, an implementation that executes in parallel would be a lot more difficult to write. See chapter 7 (particularly section 7.2) to get an idea of the work involved:

```
List<String> dishNames = new ArrayList<>();
for(Dish dish: menu) {
    if(dish.getCalories() > 300){
        dishNames.add(dish.getName());
    }
}
```

The alternative, which uses the Streams API, reads more like the problem statement, and it can be easily parallelized:

```
menu.parallelStream()
    .filter(d -> d.getCalories() > 300)
    .map(Dish::getName)
    .collect(toList());
```

Unfortunately, converting imperative code to the Streams API can be a difficult task, because you need to think about control-flow statements such as break, continue, and return and then infer the right stream operations to use. The good news is that some tools can help you with this task as well. The good news is that some tools (e.g., Lambda-Ficator, https://ieeexplore.ieee.org/document/6606699) can help you with this task as well.

9.1.5 *Improving code flexibility*

We argued in chapters 2 and 3 that lambda expressions encourage the style of behavior parameterization. You can represent multiple behaviors with different lambdas that you can then pass around to execute. This style lets you cope with requirement changes (creating multiple ways of filtering with a Predicate or comparing with a Comparator, for example). In the next section, we look at a couple of patterns that you can apply to your code base to benefit immediately from lambda expressions.

ADOPTING FUNCTIONAL INTERFACES

First, you can't use lambda expressions without functional interfaces; therefore, you should start introducing them in your code base. But in which situations should you introduce them? In this chapter, we discuss two common code patterns that can be refactored to leverage lambda expressions: conditional deferred execution and execute around. Also, in the next section, we show you how various object-oriented design patterns—such as the strategy and template-method design patterns—can be rewritten more concisely with lambda expressions.

CONDITIONAL DEFERRED EXECUTION

It's common to see control-flow statements mangled inside business-logic code. Typical scenarios include security checks and logging. Consider the following code, which uses the built-in Java Logger class:

```
if (logger.isLoggable(Log.FINER)) {
    logger.finer("Problem: " + generateDiagnostic());
}
```

What's wrong with it? A couple of things:

- The state of the logger (what level it supports) is exposed in the client code through the method isLoggable.
- Why should you have to query the state of the logger object every time before you log a message? It clutters your code.

A better alternative is to use the `log` method, which checks internally to see whether the logger object is set to the right level before logging the message:

```
logger.log(Level.FINER, "Problem: " + generateDiagnostic());
```

This approach is better because your code isn't cluttered with `if` checks, and the state of the logger is no longer exposed. Unfortunately, this code still has an issue: the logging message is always evaluated, even if the logger isn't enabled for the message level passed as an argument.

Lambda expressions can help. What you need is a way to defer the construction of the message so that it can be generated only under a given condition (here, when the logger level is set to `FINER`). It turns out that the Java 8 API designers knew about this problem and introduced an overloaded alternative to `log` that takes a `Supplier` as an argument. This alternative `log` method has the following signature:

```
public void log(Level level, Supplier<String> msgSupplier)
```

Now you can call it as follows:

```
logger.log(Level.FINER, () -> "Problem: " + generateDiagnostic());
```

The `log` method internally executes the lambda passed as an argument only if the logger is of the right level. The internal implementation of the `log` method is along these lines:

```
public void log(Level level, Supplier<String> msgSupplier) {
    if(logger.isLoggable(level)){
        log(level, msgSupplier.get());      ⟵┐ Executing
    }                                         │ the lambda
}
```

What's the takeaway from the story? If you see yourself querying the state of an object (such as the state of the logger) many times in client code, only to call some method on this object with arguments (such as to log a message), consider introducing a new method that calls that method, passed as a lambda or method reference, only after internally checking the state of the object. Your code will be more readable (less cluttered) and better encapsulated, without exposing the state of the object in client code.

EXECUTE AROUND

In chapter 3, we discussed another pattern that you can adopt: execute around. If you find yourself surrounding different code with the same preparation and cleanup phases, you can often pull that code into a lambda. The benefit is that you can reuse the logic dealing with the preparation and cleanup phases, thus reducing code duplication.

Here's the code that you saw in chapter 3. It reuses the same logic to open and close a file but can be parameterized with different lambdas to process the file:

```
String oneLine =
    processFile((BufferedReader b) -> b.readLine());        ⟵—— Pass a lambda.
String twoLines =
    processFile((BufferedReader b) -> b.readLine() + b.readLine());  ⟵┐ Pass a
public static String processFile(BufferedReaderProcessor p) throws      │ different
    IOException {                                                       │ lambda.
    try(BufferedReader br = new BufferedReader(new
    FileReader("ModernJavaInAction/chap9/data.txt"))) {
        return p.process(br);                               ⟵—— Execute the Buffered-
    }                                                            ReaderProcessor passed
}                                                                as an argument.
public interface BufferedReaderProcessor {                  ⟵
    String process(BufferedReader b) throws IOException;    A functional interface
}                                                           for a lambda, which can
                                                            throw an IOException
```

This code was made possible by introducing the functional interface `BufferedReader-Processor`, which lets you pass different lambdas to work with a `BufferedReader` object.

In this section, you've seen how to apply various recipes to improve the readability and flexibility of your code. In the next section, you see how lambda expressions can remove boilerplate code associated with common object-oriented design patterns.

9.2 Refactoring object-oriented design patterns with lambdas

New language features often make existing code patterns or idioms less popular. The introduction of the `for-each` loop in Java 5, for example, has replaced many uses of explicit iterators because it's less error-prone and more concise. The introduction of the diamond operator `<>` in Java 7 reduced the use of explicit generics at instance creation (and slowly pushed Java programmers to embrace type inference).

A specific class of patterns is called design patterns.[2] *Design patterns* are reusable blueprints, if you will, for common problems in designing software. They are rather like how construction engineers have a set of reusable solutions to construct bridges for specific scenarios (suspension bridge, arch bridge, and so on). The *visitor design pattern*, for example, is a common solution for separating an algorithm from a structure on which it needs to operate. The *singleton pattern* is a common solution to restrict the instantiation of a class to one object.

Lambda expressions provide yet another new tool in the programmer's toolbox. They can provide alternative solutions to the problems that the design patterns are tackling, but often with less work and in a simpler way. Many existing object-oriented design patterns can be made redundant or written in a more concise way with lambda expressions.

---

[2] See *Design Patterns: Elements of Reusable Object-Oriented Software*, by Erich Gamma, Richard Helm, Ralph Johnson, and John Vlissides; ISBN 978-0201633610, ISBN 0-201-63361-2

In this section, we explore five design patterns:

- Strategy
- Template method
- Observer
- Chain of responsibility
- Factory

We show you how lambda expressions can provide an alternative way to solve the problem that each design pattern is intended to solve.

9.2.1   Strategy

The strategy pattern is a common solution for representing a family of algorithms and letting you choose among them at runtime. You saw this pattern briefly in chapter 2 when we showed you how to filter an inventory with different predicates (such as heavy apples or green apples). You can apply this pattern to a multitude of scenarios, such as validating an input with different criteria, using different ways of parsing, or formatting an input.

The strategy pattern consists of three parts, as illustrated in figure 9.1:

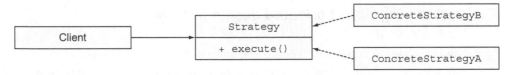

Figure 9.1   The strategy design pattern

- An interface to represent some algorithm (the interface `Strategy`)
- One or more concrete implementations of that interface to represent multiple algorithms (the concrete classes `ConcreteStrategyA`, `ConcreteStrategyB`)
- One or more clients that use the strategy objects

Suppose that you'd like to validate whether a text input is properly formatted for different criteria (consists of only lowercase letters or is numeric, for example). You start by defining an interface to validate the text (represented as a `String`):

```
public interface ValidationStrategy {
    boolean execute(String s);
}
```

Second, you define one or more implementation(s) of that interface:

```
public class IsAllLowerCase implements ValidationStrategy {
    public boolean execute(String s){
        return s.matches("[a-z]+");
    }
}
```

```
public class IsNumeric implements ValidationStrategy {
    public boolean execute(String s){
        return s.matches("\\d+");
    }
}
```

Then you can use these different validation strategies in your program:

```
public class Validator {
    private final ValidationStrategy strategy;
    public Validator(ValidationStrategy v) {
        this.strategy = v;
    }
    public boolean validate(String s) {
        return strategy.execute(s);
    }
}
Validator numericValidator = new Validator(new IsNumeric());      Returns false
boolean b1 = numericValidator.validate("aaaa");              ◁──┘
Validator lowerCaseValidator = new Validator(new IsAllLowerCase ());
boolean b2 = lowerCaseValidator.validate("bbbb");              ◁──┐ Returns true
```

USING LAMBDA EXPRESSIONS

By now, you should recognize that `ValidationStrategy` is a functional interface. In addition, it has the same function descriptor as `Predicate<String>`. As a result, instead of declaring new classes to implement different strategies, you can pass more concise lambda expressions directly:

```
Validator numericValidator =
    new Validator((String s) -> s.matches("[a-z]+"));       ◁──┐
boolean b1 = numericValidator.validate("aaaa");                 │ Passing a
Validator lowerCaseValidator =                                  │ lambda
    new Validator((String s) -> s.matches("\\d+"));         ◁──┘ directly
boolean b2 = lowerCaseValidator.validate("bbbb");
```

As you can see, lambda expressions remove the boilerplate code that's inherent to the strategy design pattern. If you think about it, lambda expressions encapsulate a piece of code (or strategy), which is what the strategy design pattern was created for, so we recommend that you use lambda expressions instead for similar problems.

9.2.2 *Template method*

The template method design pattern is a common solution when you need to represent the outline of an algorithm and have the additional flexibility to change certain parts of it. Okay, this pattern sounds a bit abstract. In other words, the template method pattern is useful when you find yourself saying "I'd love to use this algorithm, but I need to change a few lines so it does what I want."

Here's an example of how this pattern works. Suppose that you need to write a simple online banking application. Users typically enter a customer ID; the application fetches the customer's details from the bank's database and does something to make the customer happy. Different online banking applications for different banking branches may have different ways of making a customer happy (such as adding a bonus to his account or sending him less paperwork). You can write the following abstract class to represent the online banking application:

```
abstract class OnlineBanking {
    public void processCustomer(int id){
        Customer c = Database.getCustomerWithId(id);
        makeCustomerHappy(c);
    }
    abstract void makeCustomerHappy(Customer c);
}
```

The processCustomer method provides a sketch for the online banking algorithm: Fetch the customer given its ID and make the customer happy. Now different branches can provide different implementations of the makeCustomerHappy method by sub-classing the OnlineBanking class.

USING LAMBDA EXPRESSIONS

You can tackle the same problem (creating an outline of an algorithm and letting implementers plug in some parts) by using your favorite lambdas. The components of the algorithms you want to plug in can be represented by lambda expressions or method references.

Here, we introduce a second argument to the processCustomer method of type Consumer<Customer> because it matches the signature of the method makeCustomer-Happy defined earlier:

```
public void processCustomer(int id, Consumer<Customer> makeCustomerHappy) {
    Customer c = Database.getCustomerWithId(id);
    makeCustomerHappy.accept(c);
}
```

Now you can plug in different behaviors directly without subclassing the Online-Banking class by passing lambda expressions:

```
new OnlineBankingLambda().processCustomer(1337, (Customer c) ->
    System.out.println("Hello " + c.getName());
```

This example shows how lambda expressions can help you remove the boilerplate inherent to design patterns.

9.2.3   *Observer*

The observer design pattern is a common solution when an object (called the *subject*) needs to automatically notify a list of other objects (called *observers*) when some event happens (such as a state change). You typically come across this pattern when working with GUI applications. You register a set of observers on a GUI component such as a button. If the button is clicked, the observers are notified and can execute a specific action. But the observer pattern isn't limited to GUIs. The observer design pattern is also suitable in a situation in which several traders (observers) want to react to the change of price of a stock (subject). Figure 9.2 illustrates the UML diagram of the observer pattern.

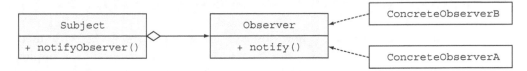

Figure 9.2 The observer design pattern

Now write some code to see how useful the observer pattern is in practice. You'll design and implement a customized notification system for an application such as Twitter. The concept is simple: several newspaper agencies (*The New York Times*, *The Guardian*, and *Le Monde*) are subscribed to a feed of news tweets and may want to receive a notification if a tweet contains a particular keyword.

First, you need an `Observer` interface that groups the observers. It has one method, called `notify`, that will be called by the subject (`Feed`) when a new tweet is available:

```java
interface Observer {
    void notify(String tweet);
}
```

Now you can declare different observers (here, the three newspapers) that produce a different action for each different keyword contained in a tweet:

```java
class NYTimes implements Observer {
    public void notify(String tweet) {
        if(tweet != null && tweet.contains("money")){
            System.out.println("Breaking news in NY! " + tweet);
        }
    }
}
class Guardian implements Observer {
    public void notify(String tweet) {
        if(tweet != null && tweet.contains("queen")){
            System.out.println("Yet more news from London... " + tweet);
        }
    }
}
class LeMonde implements Observer {
    public void notify(String tweet) {
        if(tweet != null && tweet.contains("wine")){
            System.out.println("Today cheese, wine and news! " + tweet);
        }
    }
}
```

You're still missing the crucial part: the subject. Define an interface for the subject:

```
interface Subject {
    void registerObserver(Observer o);
    void notifyObservers(String tweet);
}
```

The subject can register a new observer using the `registerObserver` method and notify his observers of a tweet with the `notifyObservers` method. Now implement the Feed class:

```
class Feed implements Subject {
    private final List<Observer> observers = new ArrayList<>();
    public void registerObserver(Observer o) {
        this.observers.add(o);
    }
    public void notifyObservers(String tweet) {
        observers.forEach(o -> o.notify(tweet));
    }
}
```

This implementation is straightforward: the feed keeps an internal list of observers that it can notify when a tweet arrives. You can create a demo application to wire up the subject and observers:

```
Feed f = new Feed();
f.registerObserver(new NYTimes());
f.registerObserver(new Guardian());
f.registerObserver(new LeMonde());
f.notifyObservers("The queen said her favourite book is Modern Java in Action!");
```

Unsurprisingly, *The Guardian* picks up this tweet.

USING LAMBDA EXPRESSIONS

You may be wondering how to use lambda expressions with the observer design pattern. Notice that the various classes that implement the `Observer` interface all provide implementation for a single method: `notify`. They're wrapping a piece of behavior to execute when a tweet arrives. Lambda expressions are designed specifically to remove that boilerplate. Instead of instantiating three observer objects explicitly, you can pass a lambda expression directly to represent the behavior to execute:

```
f.registerObserver((String tweet) -> {
        if(tweet != null && tweet.contains("money")){
            System.out.println("Breaking news in NY! " + tweet);
        }
});
f.registerObserver((String tweet) -> {
        if(tweet != null && tweet.contains("queen")){
            System.out.println("Yet more news from London... " + tweet);
        }
});
```

Should you use lambda expressions all the time? The answer is no. In the example we described, lambda expressions work great because the behavior to execute is simple, so they're helpful for removing boilerplate code. But the observers may be more complex; they could have state, define several methods, and the like. In those situations, you should stick with classes.

9.2.4 *Chain of responsibility*

The chain of responsibility pattern is a common solution to create a chain of processing objects (such as a chain of operations). One processing object may do some work and pass the result to another object, which also does some work and passes it on to yet another processing object, and so on.

Generally, this pattern is implemented by defining an abstract class representing a processing object that defines a field to keep track of a successor. When it finishes its work, the processing object hands over its work to its successor. The code looks like this:

```
public abstract class ProcessingObject<T> {
    protected ProcessingObject<T> successor;
    public void setSuccessor(ProcessingObject<T> successor){
        this.successor = successor;
    }
    public T handle(T input) {
        T r = handleWork(input);
        if(successor != null){
            return successor.handle(r);
        }
        return r;
    }
    abstract protected T handleWork(T input);
}
```

Figure 9.3 illustrates the chain of responsibility pattern in UML.

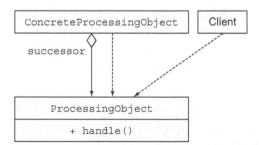

Figure 9.3   The chain of responsibility design pattern

Here, you may recognize the template method design pattern, which we discussed in section 9.2.2. The `handle` method provides an outline for dealing with a piece of work. You can create different kinds of processing objects by subclassing the `Processing-Object` class and by providing an implementation for the `handleWork` method.

Here's an example of how to use this pattern. You can create two processing objects doing some text processing:

```
public class HeaderTextProcessing extends ProcessingObject<String> {
    public String handleWork(String text) {
        return "From Raoul, Mario and Alan: " + text;
    }
}
public class SpellCheckerProcessing extends ProcessingObject<String> {
    public String handleWork(String text) {
        return text.replaceAll("labda", "lambda");      ⟵  Oops—we forgot the
    }                                                          'm' in "lambda"!
}
```

Now you can connect two processing objects to construct a chain of operations:

```
ProcessingObject<String> p1 = new HeaderTextProcessing();        Chaining two
ProcessingObject<String> p2 = new SpellCheckerProcessing();      processing
p1.setSuccessor(p2);                                         ⟵  objects
String result = p1.handle("Aren't labdas really sexy?!!");
System.out.println(result);       ⟵
```
                                      Prints "From Raoul, Mario and Alan:
                                      Aren't lambdas really sexy?!!"

USING LAMBDA EXPRESSIONS

Wait a minute—this pattern looks like chaining (that is, composing) functions. We discussed composing lambda expressions in chapter 3. You can represent the processing objects as an instance of Function<String, String>, or (more precisely) a UnaryOperator<String>. To chain them, compose these functions by using the andThen method:

```
                                                              The first
                                                              processing
UnaryOperator<String> headerProcessing =                      object
    (String text) -> "From Raoul, Mario and Alan: " + text;  ⟵
UnaryOperator<String> spellCheckerProcessing =                The second
    (String text) -> text.replaceAll("labda", "lambda");   ⟵ processing object
Function<String, String> pipeline =
    headerProcessing.andThen(spellCheckerProcessing);       ⟵
String result = pipeline.apply("Aren't labdas really sexy?!!");
```
                                      Compose the two functions,
                                      resulting in a chain of operations.

9.2.5 *Factory*

The factory design pattern lets you create objects without exposing the instantiation logic to the client. Suppose that you're working for a bank that needs a way of creating different financial products: loans, bonds, stocks, and so on.

Typically, you'd create a Factory class with a method that's responsible for the creation of different objects, as shown here:

```
public class ProductFactory {
    public static Product createProduct(String name) {
        switch(name){
```

```
            case "loan": return new Loan();
            case "stock": return new Stock();
            case "bond": return new Bond();
            default: throw new RuntimeException("No such product " + name);
        }
    }
}
```

Here, `Loan`, `Stock`, and `Bond` are subtypes of `Product`. The `createProduct` method could have additional logic to configure each created product. But the benefit is that you can create these objects without exposing the constructor and the configuration to the client, which makes the creation of products simpler for the client, as follows:

```
Product p = ProductFactory.createProduct("loan");
```

USING LAMBDA EXPRESSIONS

You saw in chapter 3 that you can refer to constructors the way that you refer to methods: by using method references. Here's how to refer to the `Loan` constructor:

```
Supplier<Product> loanSupplier = Loan::new;
Loan loan = loanSupplier.get();
```

Using this technique, you could rewrite the preceding code by creating a `Map` that maps a product name to its constructor:

```
final static Map<String, Supplier<Product>> map = new HashMap<>();
static {
    map.put("loan", Loan::new);
    map.put("stock", Stock::new);
    map.put("bond", Bond::new);
}
```

You can use this `Map` to instantiate different products, as you did with the factory design pattern:

```
public static Product createProduct(String name){
    Supplier<Product> p = map.get(name);
    if(p != null) return p.get();
    throw new IllegalArgumentException("No such product " + name);
}
```

This technique is a neat way to use this Java 8 feature to achieve the same intent as the factory pattern. But this technique doesn't scale well if the factory method `create-Product` needs to take multiple arguments to pass to the product constructors. You'd have to provide a functional interface other than a simple `Supplier`.

Suppose that you want to refer to constructors for products that take three arguments (two `Integers` and a `String`); you need to create a special functional interface

`TriFunction` to support such constructors. As a result, the signature of the `Map` becomes more complex:

```
public interface TriFunction<T, U, V, R> {
    R apply(T t, U u, V v);
}
Map<String, TriFunction<Integer, Integer, String, Product>> map
    = new HashMap<>();
```

You've seen how to write and refactor code by using lambda expressions. In the next section, you see how to ensure that your new code is correct.

9.3   *Testing lambdas*

You've sprinkled your code with lambda expressions, and it looks nice and concise. But in most developer jobs, you're paid not for writing nice code, but for writing code that's correct.

Generally, good software engineering practice involves using unit testing to ensure that your program behaves as intended. You write test cases, which assert that small individual parts of your source code are producing the expected results. Consider a simple `Point` class for a graphical application:

```
public class Point {
    private final int x;
    private final int y;
    private Point(int x, int y) {
        this.x = x;
        this.y = y;
    }
    public int getX() { return x; }
    public int getY() { return y; }
    public Point moveRightBy(int x) {
        return new Point(this.x + x, this.y);
    }
}
```

The following unit test checks whether the method `moveRightBy` behaves as expected:

```
@Test
public void testMoveRightBy() throws Exception {
    Point p1 = new Point(5, 5);
    Point p2 = p1.moveRightBy(10);
    assertEquals(15, p2.getX());
    assertEquals(5, p2.getY());
}
```

9.3.1   *Testing the behavior of a visible lambda*

This code works nicely because the `moveRightBy` method is public and, therefore, can be tested inside the test case. But lambdas don't have names (they're anonymous functions, after all), and testing them in your code is tricky because you can't refer to them by name.

Sometimes, you have access to a lambda via a field so that you can reuse it, and you'd like to test the logic encapsulated in that lambda. What can you do? You could test the lambda as you do when calling methods. Suppose that you add a static field compareByXAndThenY in the Point class that gives you access to a Comparator object generated from method references:

```
public class Point {
    public final static Comparator<Point> compareByXAndThenY =
        comparing(Point::getX).thenComparing(Point::getY);
    ...
}
```

Remember that lambda expressions generate an instance of a functional interface. As a result, you can test the behavior of that instance. Here, you can call the compare method on the Comparator object compareByXAndThenY with different arguments to test whether its behavior is as intended:

```
@Test
public void testComparingTwoPoints() throws Exception {
    Point p1 = new Point(10, 15);
    Point p2 = new Point(10, 20);
    int result = Point.compareByXAndThenY.compare(p1 , p2);
    assertTrue(result < 0);
}
```

9.3.2 *Focusing on the behavior of the method using a lambda*

But the purpose of lambdas is to encapsulate a one-off piece of behavior to be used by another method. In that case, you shouldn't make lambda expressions available publicly; they're only implementation details. Instead, we argue that you should test the behavior of the method that uses a lambda expression. Consider the moveAllPoints-RightBy method shown here:

```
public static List<Point> moveAllPointsRightBy(List<Point> points, int x) {
    return points.stream()
                 .map(p -> new Point(p.getX() + x, p.getY()))
                 .collect(toList());
}
```

There's no point (pun intended) in testing the lambda p -> new Point(p.getX() + x, p.getY()); it's only an implementation detail for the moveAllPointsRightBy method. Instead, you should focus on testing the behavior of the moveAllPointsRightBy method:

```
@Test
public void testMoveAllPointsRightBy() throws Exception {
    List<Point> points =
        Arrays.asList(new Point(5, 5), new Point(10, 5));
    List<Point> expectedPoints =
        Arrays.asList(new Point(15, 5), new Point(20, 5));
```

```
        List<Point> newPoints = Point.moveAllPointsRightBy(points, 10);
        assertEquals(expectedPoints, newPoints);
}
```

Note that in the unit test, it's important for the Point class to implement the equals method appropriately; otherwise, it relies on the default implementation from Object.

9.3.3 *Pulling complex lambdas into separate methods*

Perhaps you come across a really complicated lambda expression that contains a lot of logic (such as a technical pricing algorithm with corner cases). What do you do, because you can't refer to the lambda expression inside your test? One strategy is to convert the lambda expression to a method reference (which involves declaring a new regular method), as we explained in section 9.1.3. Then you can test the behavior of the new method as you would that of any regular method.

9.3.4 *Testing high-order functions*

Methods that take a function as an argument or return another function (so-called higher-order functions, explained in chapter 19) are a little harder to deal with. One thing you can do if a method takes a lambda as an argument is test its behavior with different lambdas. You can test the filter method that you created in chapter 2 with different predicates:

```
@Test
public void testFilter() throws Exception {
    List<Integer> numbers = Arrays.asList(1, 2, 3, 4);
    List<Integer> even = filter(numbers, i -> i % 2 == 0);
    List<Integer> smallerThanThree = filter(numbers, i -> i < 3);
    assertEquals(Arrays.asList(2, 4), even);
    assertEquals(Arrays.asList(1, 2), smallerThanThree);
}
```

What if the method that needs to be tested returns another function? You can test the behavior of that function by treating it as an instance of a functional interface, as we showed you earlier with a Comparator.

Unfortunately, not everything works the first time, and your tests may report some errors related to your use of lambda expressions. So, in the next section we turn to debugging.

9.4   *Debugging*

A developer's arsenal has two main old-school weapons for debugging problematic code:

- Examining the stack trace
- Logging

Lambda expressions and streams can bring new challenges to your typical debugging routine. We explore both in this section.

9.4.1 *Examining the stack trace*

When your program has stopped (because an exception was thrown, for example), the first thing you need to know is where the program stopped and how it got there. Stack frames are useful for this purpose. Each time your program performs a method call, information about the call is generated, including the location of the call in your program, the arguments of the call, and the local variables of the method being called. This information is stored on a stack frame.

When your program fails, you get a *stack trace*, which is a summary of how your program got to that failure, stack frame by stack frame. In other words, you get a valuable list of method calls up to when the failure appeared. This list helps you understand how the problem occurred.

USING LAMBDA EXPRESSIONS

Unfortunately, due to the fact that lambda expressions don't have names, stack traces can be slightly puzzling. Consider the following simple code, which is made to fail on purpose:

```
import java.util.*;
public class Debugging{
    public static void main(String[] args) {
        List<Point> points = Arrays.asList(new Point(12, 2), null);
        points.stream().map(p -> p.getX()).forEach(System.out::println);
    }
}
```

Running this code produces a stack trace along the lines of the following (depending on your javac version; you may not have the same stack trace):

```
Exception in thread "main" java.lang.NullPointerException        What does $0 in
    at Debugging.lambda$main$0(Debugging.java:6)          ◀──┘   this line mean?
    at Debugging$$Lambda$5/284720968.apply(Unknown Source)
    at java.util.stream.ReferencePipeline$3$1.accept(ReferencePipeline
    .java:193)
    at java.util.Spliterators$ArraySpliterator.forEachRemaining(Spliterators
    .java:948)
...
```

Yuck! What's going on? The program fails, of course, because the second element of the list of points is `null`. You try to process a `null` reference. Because the error occurs in a stream pipeline, the whole sequence of method calls that make a stream pipeline work is exposed to you. But notice that the stack trace produces the following cryptic lines:

```
at Debugging.lambda$main$0(Debugging.java:6)
    at Debugging$$Lambda$5/284720968.apply(Unknown Source)
```

These lines mean that the error occurred inside a lambda expression. Unfortunately, because lambda expressions don't have names, the compiler has to make up a name to refer to them. In this case, the name is lambda$main$0, which isn't intuitive and can be problematic if you have large classes containing several lambda expressions.

Even if you use method references, it's still possible that the stack won't show you the name of the method you used. Changing the preceding lambda p -> p.getX() to the method reference Point::getX also results in a problematic stack trace:

```
points.stream().map(Point::getX).forEach(System.out::println);
Exception in thread "main" java.lang.NullPointerException
    at Debugging$$Lambda$5/284720968.apply(Unknown Source)
    at java.util.stream.ReferencePipeline$3$1.accept(ReferencePipeline
     .java:193)
...
```

What does this line mean?

Note that if a method reference refers to a method declared in the same class where it's used, it appears in the stack trace. In the following example:

```
import java.util.*;
public class Debugging{
    public static void main(String[] args) {
        List<Integer> numbers = Arrays.asList(1, 2, 3);
        numbers.stream().map(Debugging::divideByZero).forEach(System
     .out::println);
    }
    public static int divideByZero(int n){
        return n / 0;
    }
}
```

The divideByZero method is reported correctly in the stack trace:

```
Exception in thread "main" java.lang.ArithmeticException: / by zero
    at Debugging.divideByZero(Debugging.java:10)
    at Debugging$$Lambda$1/999966131.apply(Unknown Source)
    at java.util.stream.ReferencePipeline$3$1.accept(ReferencePipeline
     .java:193)
...
```

divideByZero appears in the stack trace.

In general, keep in mind that stack traces involving lambda expressions may be more difficult to understand. This area is one in which the compiler can be improved in a future version of Java.

9.4.2 Logging information

Suppose that you're trying to debug a pipeline of operations in a stream. What can you do? You could use forEach to print or log the result of a stream as follows:

```
List<Integer> numbers = Arrays.asList(2, 3, 4, 5);
numbers.stream()
        .map(x -> x + 17)
        .filter(x -> x % 2 == 0)
        .limit(3)
        .forEach(System.out::println);
```

This code produces the following output:

```
20
22
```

Unfortunately, after you call forEach, the whole stream is consumed. It would be useful to understand what each operation (map, filter, limit) produces in the pipeline of a stream.

The stream operation peek can help. The purpose of peek is to execute an action on each element of a stream as it's consumed. It doesn't consume the whole stream the way forEach does, however; it forwards the element on which it performed an action to the next operation in the pipeline. Figure 9.4 illustrates the peek operation.

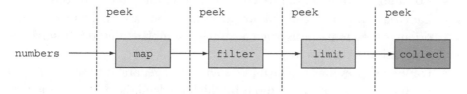

Figure 9.4   Examining values flowing in a stream pipeline with peek

In the following code, you use peek to print the intermediate values before and after each operation in the stream pipeline:

```
List<Integer> result =
  numbers.stream()
         .peek(x -> System.out.println("from stream: " + x))
         .map(x -> x + 17)
         .peek(x -> System.out.println("after map: " + x))
         .filter(x -> x % 2 == 0)
         .peek(x -> System.out.println("after filter: " + x))
         .limit(3)
         .peek(x -> System.out.println("after limit: " + x))
         .collect(toList());
```

Print the current element consumed from the source.

Print the result of the map operation.

Print the number selected after the filter operation.

Print the number selected after the limit operation.

This code produces useful output at each step of the pipeline:

```
from stream: 2
after map: 19
from stream: 3
after map: 20
after filter: 20
after limit: 20
from stream: 4
after map: 21
from stream: 5
```

```
after map: 22
after filter: 22
after limit: 22
```

Summary

- Lambda expressions can make your code more readable and flexible.
- Consider converting anonymous classes to lambda expressions, but be wary of subtle semantic differences such as the meaning of the keyword `this` and shadowing of variables.
- Method references can make your code more readable compared with lambda expressions.
- Consider converting iterative collection processing to use the Streams API.
- Lambda expressions can remove boilerplate code associated with several object-oriented design patterns, such as strategy, template method, observer, chain of responsibility, and factory.
- Lambda expressions can be unit-tested, but in general, you should focus on testing the behavior of the methods in which the lambda expressions appear.
- Consider extracting complex lambda expressions into regular methods.
- Lambda expressions can make stack traces less readable.
- The `peek` method of a stream is useful for logging intermediate values as they flow past certain points of a stream pipeline.

Domain-specific languages using lambdas

10

This chapter covers

- What domain-specific languages (DSLs) and their forms arc

- The pros and cons of adding a DSL to your API

- The alternatives available on the JVM to a plain Java-based DSL

- Learning from the DSLs present in modern Java interfaces and classes

- Patterns and techniques to implement effective Java-based DSLs

- How commonly used Java libraries and tools use these patterns

Developers often forget that a programming language is first of all a language. The main purpose of any language is to convey a message in the clearest, most understandable way. Perhaps the most important characteristic of well-written software is clear communication of its intentions—or, as famous computer scientist Harold Abelson stated, "Programs must be written for people to read and only incidentally for machines to execute."

Readability and understandability are even more important in the parts of the software that are intended to model the core business of your application. Writing code that can be shared and understood by both the development team and the domain experts is helpful for productivity. Domain experts can be involved in the software development process and verify the correctness of the software from a business point of view. As a result, bugs and misunderstandings can be caught early on.

To achieve this result, it's common to express the application's business logic through a domain-specific language (DSL). A *DSL* is a small, usually non-general-purpose programming language explicitly tailored for a specific domain. The DSL uses the terminology characteristic of that domain. You may be familiar with Maven and Ant, for example. You can see them as DSLs for expressing build processes. You're also familiar with HTML, which is a language tailored to define the structure of a web page. Historically, due to its rigidity and excessive verbosity, Java has never been popular for implementing a compact DSL that's also suitable to be read by non-technical people. Now that Java supports lambda expressions, however, you have new tools in your toolbox! In fact, you learned in chapter 3 that lambda expressions help reduce code verbosity and improve the signal/noise ratio of your programs.

Think about a database implemented in Java. Deep down in the database, there's likely to be lots of elaborate code determining where on disk to store a given record, constructing indexes for tables, and dealing with concurrent transactions. This database is likely to be programmed by relatively expert programmers. Suppose that now you want to program a query similar to those we explored in chapters 4 and 5: "Find all menu entries on a given menu that have fewer than 400 calories."

Historically, such expert programmers might have quickly written low-level code in this style and thought that the task was easy:

```
while (block != null) {
    read(block, buffer)
    for (every record in buffer) {
        if (record.calorie < 400) {
            System.out.println (record.name);
        }
    }
    block = buffer.next();
}
```

This solution has two main problems: it's hard for a less-experienced programmer to create (it may need subtle details of locking, I/O, or disc allocation), and more important, it deals in system-level concepts, not application-level concepts.

A new-joining user-facing programmer might say, "Why can't you provide me an SQL interface so I can write SELECT name FROM menu WHERE calorie < 400, where menu holds the restaurant menu expressed as an SQL table? Now I can program far more effectively than all this system-level nonsense!" It's hard to argue with this statement! In essence the programmer has asked for a DSL to interact with the database instead of writing pure Java code. Technically, this type of DSL is called *external* because it expects the database to have an API that can parse and evaluate SQL expressions written in text. You learn more about the distinction between external and internal DSL later in this chapter.

But if you think back to chapters 4 and 5, you notice that this code could also be written more concisely in Java using the `Stream` API , such as the following:

```
menu.stream()
    .filter(d -> d.getCalories() < 400)
    .map(Dish::getName)
    .forEach(System.out::println)
```

This use of chaining methods, which is so characteristic of the `Stream` API, is often called *fluent style* in that it's easy to understand quickly, in contrast to complex control flow in Java loops.

This style effectively captures a DSL. In this case, this DSL isn't external, but internal. In an *internal* DSL, the application-level primitives are exposed as Java methods to use on one or more class types that represent the database, in contrast to the non-Java syntax for primitives in an external DSL, such as SELECT FROM in the SQL discussion above.

In essence, designing a DSL consists of deciding what operations the application-level programmer needs to manipulate (carefully avoiding any unnecessary pollution caused by system-level concepts) and providing these operations to the programmer.

For an internal DSL, this process means exposing appropriate classes and methods so that code can be written fluently. An external DSL takes more effort; you must not only design the DSL syntax, but also implement a parser and evaluator for the DSL. If you get the design right, however, perhaps lower-skilled programmers can write code quickly and effectively (thus making the money that keeps your company in business) without having to program directly within your beautiful (but hard for non-experts to understand) system-level code!

In this chapter, you learn what a DSL is through several examples and use cases; you learn when you should consider implementing one and what the benefits are. Then you explore some of the small DSLs that were introduced in the Java 8 API. You also learn how you could employ the same patterns to create your own DSLs. Finally, you investigate how some widely used Java libraries and frameworks have adopted these techniques to offer their functionalities through a set of DSLs, making their APIs more accessible and easy to use.

10.1 *A specific language for your domain*

A DSL is a custom-built language designed to solve a problem for a specific business domain. You may be developing a software application for accounting, for example. Your business domain includes concepts such as bank statements and operations such as reconciling. You could create a custom DSL to express problems in that domain. In

Java, you need to come up with a set of classes and methods to represent that domain. In a way, you can see the DSL as an API created to interface with a specific business domain.

A DSL isn't a general-purpose programming language; it restricts the operations and vocabulary available to a specific domain, which means that you have less to worry about and can invest more attention in solving the business problem at hand. Your DSL should allow its users to deal only with the complexities of that domain. Other lower-level implementation details should be hidden – just like making lower-level implementation-detail methods of a class private. This results in a user-friendly DSL.

What isn't a DSL? A DSL isn't plain English. It's also not a language that lets domain experts implement low-level business logic. Two reasons should drive you toward the development of a DSL:

- *Communication is king.* Your code should clearly communicate its intentions and be understandable even by a non-programmer. This way, this person can contribute to validating whether the code matches the business requirements.
- *Code is written once but read many times.* Readability is vital for maintainability. In other words, you should always code in a way that your colleagues thank you for rather than hate you for!

A well-designed DSL offers many benefits. Nonetheless, developing and using a bespoke DSL has pros and cons. In section 10.1.1, we explore the pros and cons in more detail so that you can decide when a DSL is appropriate (or not) for a particular scenario.

10.1.1 *Pros and cons of DSLs*

DSLs, like other technologies and solutions in software development, aren't silver bullets. Using a DSL to work with your domain can be both an asset and a liability. A DSL can be an asset because it raises the level of abstraction with which you can clarify the business intention of the code and makes the code more readable. But it can also be a liability because the implementation of the DSL is code in its own right that needs to be tested and maintained. For this reason, it's useful to investigate the benefits and costs of DSLs so that you can evaluate whether adding one to your project will result in a positive return of investment.

DSLs offer the following benefits:

- *Conciseness*—An API that conveniently encapsulates the business logic allows you to avoid repetition, resulting in code that's less verbose.
- *Readability*—Using words that belong to the vocabulary of the domain makes the code understandable even by domain non-experts. Consequently, code and domain knowledge can be shared across a wider range of members of the organization.
- *Maintainability*—Code written against a well-designed DSL is easier to maintain and modify. Maintainability is especially important for business-related code, which is the part of the application that may change most frequently.

- *Higher level of abstraction*—The operations available in a DSL work at the same level of abstraction as the domain, thus hiding the details that aren't strictly related to the domain's problems.
- *Focus*—Having a language designed for the sole purpose of expressing the rules of the business domain helps programmers stay focused on that specific part of the code. The result is increased productivity.
- *Separation of concerns*—Expressing the business logic in a dedicated language makes it easier to keep the business-related code isolated from the infrastructural part of the application. The result is code that's easier to maintain.

Conversely, introducing a DSL into your code base can have a few disadvantages:

- *Difficulty of DSL design*—It's hard to capture domain knowledge in a concise limited language.
- *Development cost*—Adding a DSL to your code base is a long-term investment with a high up-front cost, which could delay your project in its early stages. In addition, the maintenance of the DSL and its evolution add further engineering overhead.
- *Additional indirection layer*—A DSL wraps your domain model in an additional layer that has to be as thin as possible to avoid incurring performance problems.
- *Another language to learn*—Nowadays, developers are used to employing multiple languages. Adding a DSL to your project, however, implicitly implies that you and your team have one more language to learn. Worse, if you decide to have multiple DSLs covering different areas of your business domain, combining them in a seamless way could be hard, because DSLs tend to evolve independently.
- *Hosting-language limitations*—Some general-purpose programming languages (Java is one of them) are known for being verbose and having rigid syntax. These languages make it difficult to design a user-friendly DSL. In fact, DSLs developed on top of a verbose programming language are constrained by the cumbersome syntax and may not be nice to read. The introduction of lambda expression in Java 8 offers a powerful new tool to mitigate this problem.

Given these lists of positive and negative arguments, deciding whether to develop a DSL for your project isn't easy. Moreover, you have alternatives to Java for implementing your own DSL. Before investigating which patterns and strategies you could employ to develop a readable easy-to-use DSL in Java 8 and beyond, we quickly explore these alternatives and describe the circumstances under which they could be appropriate solutions.

10.1.2   *Different DSL solutions available on the JVM*

In this section, you learn the categories of DSLs. You also learn that you have many choices besides Java for implementing DSLs. In later sections, we focus on how to implement DSLs by using Java features.

The most common way to categorize DSLs, introduced by Martin Fowler, is to distinguish between internal and external DSLs. Internal DSLs (also known as embedded DSLs) are implemented on top of the existing hosting language (which could be plain Java code), whereas external DSLs are called stand-alone because they're developed from scratch with a syntax that's independent of the hosting language.

Moreover, the JVM gives you a third possibility that falls between an internal and an external DSL: another general-purpose programming language that also runs on the JVM but is more flexible and expressive than Java, such as Scala or Groovy. We refer to this third alternative as a polyglot DSL.

In the following sections, we look at these three types of DSLs in order.

INTERNAL DSL

Because this book is about Java, when we speak about an internal DSL, we clearly mean a DSL written in Java. Historically, Java hasn't been considered to be a DSL-friendly language because its cumbersome, inflexible syntax makes it difficult to produce an easy-to-read, concise, expressive DSL. This issue has been largely mitigated by the introduction of lambda expressions. As you saw in chapter 3, lambdas are useful for using behavior parameterization in a concise manner. In fact, using lambdas extensively results in a DSL with a more acceptable signal/noise ratio by reducing the verbosity that you get with anonymous inner classes. To demonstrate the signal/noise ratio, try to print a list of `Strings` with Java 7 syntax, but use Java 8's new `forEach` method:

```
List<String> numbers = Arrays.asList("one", "two", "three");
numbers.forEach( new Consumer<String>() {
    @Override
    public void accept( String s ) {
        System.out.println(s);
    }
} );
```

In this snippet, the part that is bold is carrying the signal of the code. All the remaining code is syntactic noise that provides no additional benefit and (even better) is no longer necessary in Java 8. The anonymous inner class can be replaced by the lambda expression

```
numbers.forEach(s -> System.out.println(s));
```

or even more concisely by a method reference:

```
numbers.forEach(System.out::println);
```

You may be happy to build your DSL with Java when you expect users to be somewhat technically minded. If the Java syntax isn't an issue, choosing to develop your DSL in plain Java has many advantages:

- The effort of learning the patterns and techniques necessary to implement a good Java DSL is modest compared with the effort required to learn a new programming language and the tools normally used to develop an external DSL.
- Your DSL is written in plain Java, so it's compiled with the rest of your code. There's no additional building cost caused by the integration of a second language compiler or of the tool employed to generate the external DSL.
- Your development team won't need to get familiar with a different language or with a potentially unfamiliar and complex external tool.
- The users of your DSL will have all the features normally provided by your favorite Java IDE, such as autocompletion and refactoring facilities. Modern IDEs are improving their support for other popular JVM languages, but still don't have support comparable to what they offer Java developers.
- If you need to implement more than one DSL to cover various parts of your domain or multiple domains, you won't have any problem composing them if they're written in plain Java.

Another possibility is combining DSLs that use the same Java bytecode by combining JVM-based programming languages. We call these DSLs polyglot and describe them in the next section.

POLYGLOT DSL

Nowadays, probably more than 100 languages run on the JVM. Some of these languages, such as Scala and Groovy, are quite popular, and it isn't difficult to find developers who are skilled in them. Other languages, including JRuby and Jython, are ports of other well-known programming languages to the JVM. Finally, other emerging languages, such as Kotlin and Ceylon, are gaining traction mostly because they claim to have features comparable with those of Scala, but with lower intrinsic complexity and a gentle learning curve. All these languages are younger than Java and have been designed with less-constrained, less-verbose syntax. This characteristic is important because it helps implement a DSL that has less inherent verbosity due to the programming language in which it's embedded.

Scala in particular has several features, such as currying and implicit conversion, that are convenient in developing a DSL. You get an overview of Scala and how it compares to Java in chapter 20. For now, we want to give you a feeling for what you can do with these features by giving you a small example.

Suppose that you want to build a utility function that repeats the execution of another function, f, a given number of times. As a first attempt, you could end up with the following recursive implementation in Scala. (Don't worry about the syntax; the overall idea is what's important.)

```
def times(i: Int, f: => Unit): Unit = {
  f
  if (i > 1) times(i - 1, f)
}
```

**Execute the
f function.**

**If the counter i is positive,
decrement it and recursively
invoke the times function.**

Note that in Scala, invoking this function with large values of i won't cause a stack over-flow, as would happen in Java, because Scala has the tail call optimization, which means that the recursive invocation to the `times` function won't be added to the stack. You learn more about this topic in chapters 18 and 19. You can use this function to execute another function repeatedly (one that prints "Hello World" three times) as follows:

```
times(3, println("Hello World"))
```

If you curry the `times` function, or put its arguments in two groups (we cover currying in detail in chapter 19),

```
def times(i: Int)(f: => Unit): Unit = {
  f
  if (i > 1 times(i - 1)(f)
}
```

you can achieve the same result by passing the function to be executed multiple times in curly braces:

```
times(3) {
  println("Hello World")
}
```

Finally, in Scala you can define an implicit conversion from an `Int` to an anonymous class by having only one function that in turn has as argument the function to be repeated. Again, don't worry about the syntax and details. The objective of this example is to give you an idea of what's possible beyond Java.

```
implicit def intToTimes(i: Int) = new {
  def times(f: => Unit): Unit = {
    def times(i: Int, f: => Unit): Unit = {
      f
      if (i > 1) times(i - 1, f)
    }
    times(i, f)
  }
}
```

**Defines an implicit conversion from
an Int to an anonymous class**

**The class has only a times
function accepting another
function f as argument.**

**A second times function takes
two arguments and is defined
in the scope of the first one.**

**Invokes the inner
times function**

In this way the user of your small Scala-embedded DSL can execute a function that prints "Hello World" three times as follows:

```
3 times {
  println("Hello World")
}
```

As you can see, the result has no syntactic noise, and it's easily understandable even by a non-developer. Here, the number 3 is automatically converted by the compiler in an instance of a class that stores the number in its i field. Then the times function is invoked with dotless notation, taking as an argument the function to be repeated.

Obtaining a similar result in Java is impossible, so the advantages of using a more DSL-friendly language are obvious. This choice also has some clear inconveniences, however:

- You have to learn a new programming language or have somebody on your team who's already skilled in it. Because developing a nice DSL in these languages generally requires the use of relatively advanced features, superficial knowledge of the new language normally isn't enough.
- You need to complicate your build process a bit by integrating multiple compilers to build the source written with two or more languages.
- Finally, although the majority of languages running on the JVM claim to be 100 percent Java-compatible, making them interoperate with Java often requires awkward tricks and compromises. Also, this interoperation sometimes causes a performance loss. Scala and Java collections aren't compatible, for example, so when a Scala collection has to be passed to a Java function or vice versa, the original collection has to be converted to one that belongs to the native API of the target language.

EXTERNAL DSL

The third option for adding a DSL to your project is implementing an external one. In this case, you have to design a new language from the ground up, with its own syntax and semantics. You also need to set up a separate infrastructure to parse the new language, analyze the output of the parser, and generate the code to execute your external DSL. This is a lot of work! The skills required to perform these tasks are neither common nor easy to acquire. If you do want to go down this road, ANTLR is a parser generator that's commonly used to help and that goes hand in hand with Java.

Moreover, even designing a coherent programming language from scratch isn't a trivial task. Another common problem is that it's easy for an external DSL to grow out of control and to cover areas and purposes for which it wasn't designed.

The biggest advantage in developing an external DSL is the practically unlimited degree of flexibility that it provides. It's possible for you to design a language that perfectly fits the needs and peculiarities of your domain. If you do a good job, the result is an extremely readable language specifically tailored to describe and solve the problems of your business. The other positive outcome is the clear separation between the infrastructural code developed in Java and the business code written with the external DSL. This separation is a double-edged sword, however, because it also creates an artificial layer between the DSL and the host language.

In the remainder of this chapter, you learn about patterns and techniques that can help you develop effective modern-Java-based internal DSLs. You start by exploring how these ideas have been used in the design of the native Java API, especially the API additions in Java 8 and beyond.

10.2   Small DSLs in modern Java APIs

The first APIs to take advantage of the new functional capabilities of Java are the native Java APIs themselves. Before Java 8, the native Java API already had a few interfaces with a single abstract method, but as you saw in section 10.1, their use required the implementation of an anonymous inner class with a bulky syntax. The addition of lambdas and (maybe even more important from a DSL point of view) method references changed the rules of the game, making functional interfaces a cornerstone of Java API design.

The `Comparator` interface in Java 8 has been updated with new methods. You learn in chapter 13 that an interface can include both static method and default methods. For now, the `Comparator` interface serves as a good example of how lambdas improve the reusability and composability of methods in native Java API.

Suppose that you have a list of objects representing people (`Persons`), and you want to sort these objects based on the people's ages. Before lambdas, you had to implement the `Comparator` interface by using an inner class:

```
Collections.sort(persons, new Comparator<Person>() {
    public int compare(Person p1, Person p2) {
        return p1.getAge() - p2.getAge();
    }
});
```

As you've seen in many other examples in this book, now you can replace the inner class with a more compact lambda expression:

```
Collections.sort(people, (p1, p2) -> p1.getAge() - p2.getAge());
```

This technique greatly increases the signal/noise ratio of your code. Java, however, also has a set of static utility methods that let you create `Comparator` objects in a more readable manner. These static methods are included in the `Comparator` interface. By statically importing the `Comparator.comparing` method, you can rewrite the preceding sorting example as follows:

```
Collections.sort(persons, comparing(p -> p.getAge()));
```

Even better, you can replace the lambda with a method reference:

```
Collections.sort(persons, comparing(Person::getAge));
```

The benefit of this approach can be pushed even further. If you want to sort the people by age, but in reverse order, you can exploit the instance method `reverse` (also added in Java 8):

```
Collections.sort(persons, comparing(Person::getAge).reverse());
```

Moreover, if you want the people of the same age to be sorted alphabetically, you can compose that Comparator with one that performs the comparison on the names:

```
Collections.sort(persons, comparing(Person::getAge)
                  .thenComparing(Person::getName));
```

Finally, you could use the new sort method added on the List interface to tidy things further:

```
persons.sort(comparing(Person::getAge)
          .thenComparing(Person::getName));
```

This small API is a minimal DSL for the domain of collection sorting. Despite its limited scope, this DSL already shows you how a well-designed use of lambdas and method reference can improve the readability, reusability, and composability of your code.

In the next section, we explore a richer and more widely used Java 8 class in which the readability improvement is even more evident: the Stream API.

10.2.1 *The Stream API seen as a DSL to manipulate collections*

The Stream interface is a great example of a small internal DSL introduced into the native Java API. In fact, a Stream can be seen as a compact but powerful DSL that filters, sorts, transforms, groups, and manipulates the items of a collection. Suppose that you're required to read a log file and collect the first 40 lines, starting with the word "ERROR" in a List<String>. You could perform this task in an imperative style, as shown in the following listing.

Listing 10.1 Reading the error lines in a log file in imperative style

```
List<String> errors = new ArrayList<>();
int errorCount = 0;
BufferedReader bufferedReader
    = new BufferedReader(new FileReader(fileName));
String line = bufferedReader.readLine();
while (errorCount < 40 && line != null) {
    if (line.startsWith("ERROR")) {
        errors.add(line);
            errorCount++;
    }
    line = bufferedReader.readLine();
}
```

Here, we omitted the error-handling part of the code for brevity. Despite this fact, the code is excessively verbose, and its intention isn't immediately evident. The other aspect that harms both readability and maintainability is the lack of a clear separation of concerns. In fact, the code with the same responsibility is scattered across multiple statements. The code used to read the file line by line, for example, is located in three places:

- Where the `FileReader` is created
- The second condition of the `while` loop, which checks whether the file has terminated
- The end of the `while` loop itself that reads the next line in the file

Similarly, the code that limits the number of lines collected in the list to the first 40 results is scattered across three statements:

- The one initializing the variable `errorCount`
- The first condition of the `while` loop
- The statement incrementing the counter when a line starting with `"ERROR"` is found in the log

Achieving the same result in a more functional style through the `Stream` interface is much easier and results in far more compact code, as shown in listing 10.2.

Listing 10.2   Reading the error lines in a log file in functional style

Opens the file and creates a Stream of Strings where each String corresponds to a line in the file.

```
List<String> errors = Files.lines(Paths.get(fileName))
                           .filter(line -> line.startsWith("ERROR"))
                           .limit(40)
                           .collect(toList());
```

Limits the result to the first 40 lines.

Filters the line starting with "ERROR".

Collects the resulting Strings in a List.

`Files.lines` is a static utility method that returns a `Stream<String>` where each `String` represents a line in the file to be parsed. That part of the code is the only part that has to read the file line by line. In the same way, the statement `limit(40)` is enough to limit the number of collected error lines to the first 40. Can you imagine something more obviously readable?

The fluent style of the `Stream` API is another interesting aspect that's typical of a well-designed DSL. All intermediate operations are lazy and return another `Stream` allowing a sequence of operations to be pipelined. The terminal operation is eager and triggers the computation of the result of the whole pipeline.

It's time to investigate the APIs of another small DSL designed to be used in conjunction with the `collect` method of the `Stream` interface: the `Collectors` API.

10.2.2 *Collectors as a DSL to aggregate data*

You saw that the `Stream` interface can be viewed as a DSL that manipulates lists of data. Similarly, the `Collector` interface can be viewed as a DSL that performs aggregation on data. In chapter 6, we explored the `Collector` interface and explained how to use it to collect, to group, and to partition the items in a `Stream`. We also investigated the static factory methods provided by the Collectors class to conveniently create different flavors of Collector objects and combine them. It's time to review how these methods are designed from a DSL point of view. In particular, as the methods in the Comparator interface can be combined to support multifield sorting, Collectors can be combined to achieve multilevel grouping. You can group a list of cars, for example, first by their brand and then by their color as follows:

```
Map<String, Map<Color, List<Car>>> carsByBrandAndColor =
        cars.stream().collect(groupingBy(Car::getBrand,
                                    groupingBy(Car::getColor)));
```

What do you notice here compared with what you did to concatenate two Comparators? You defined the multifield Comparator by composing two Comparators in a fluent way,

```
Comparator<Person> comparator =
        comparing(Person::getAge).thenComparing(Person::getName);
```

whereas the Collectors API allows you to create a multilevel Collector by nesting the Collectors:

```
Collector<? super Car, ?, Map<Brand, Map<Color, List<Car>>>>
    carGroupingCollector =
        groupingBy(Car::getBrand, groupingBy(Car::getColor));
```

Normally, the fluent style is considered to be more readable than the nesting style, especially when the composition involves three or more components. Is this difference in style a curiosity? In fact, it reflects a deliberate design choice caused by the fact that the innermost Collector has to be evaluated first, but logically, it's the last grouping to be performed. In this case, nesting the Collector creations with several static methods instead of fluently concatenating them allows the innermost grouping to be evaluated first but makes it appear to be the last one in the code.

It would be easier (except for the use of generics in the definitions) to implement a GroupingBuilder that delegates to the groupingBy factory method but allows multiple grouping operations to be composed fluently. This next listing shows how.

> **Listing 10.3   A fluent grouping collectors builder**

```
import static java.util.stream.Collectors.groupingBy;

public class GroupingBuilder<T, D, K> {
    private final Collector<? super T, ?, Map<K, D>> collector;

    private GroupingBuilder(Collector<? super T, ?, Map<K, D>> collector) {
        this.collector = collector;
    }

    public Collector<? super T, ?, Map<K, D>> get() {
        return collector;
    }
```

```
    public <J> GroupingBuilder<T, Map<K, D>, J>
                        after(Function<? super T, ? extends J> classifier) {
        return new GroupingBuilder<>(groupingBy(classifier, collector));
    }

    public static <T, D, K> GroupingBuilder<T, List<T>, K>
                    groupOn(Function<? super T, ? extends K> classifier) {
        return new GroupingBuilder<>(groupingBy(classifier));
    }
}
```

What's the problem with this fluent builder? Trying to use it makes the problem evident:

```
Collector<? super Car, ?, Map<Brand, Map<Color, List<Car>>>>
    carGroupingCollector =
        groupOn(Car::getColor).after(Car::getBrand).get()
```

As you can see, the use of this utility class is counterintuitive because the grouping functions have to be written in reverse order relative to the corresponding nested grouping level. If you try to refactor this fluent builder to fix the ordering issue, you realize that unfortunately, the Java type system won't allow you to do this.

By looking more closely at the native Java API and the reasons behind its design decisions, you've started to learn a few patterns and useful tricks for implementing readable DSLs. In the next section, you continue to investigate techniques for developing effective DSLs.

10.3   *Patterns and techniques to create DSLs in Java*

A DSL provides a friendly, readable API to work with a particular domain model. For that reason, we start this section by defining a simple domain model; then we discuss the patterns that can be used to create a DSL on top of it.

The sample domain model is made of three things. The first thing is plain Java beans modeling a stock quoted on a given market:

```
public class Stock {

    private String symbol;
    private String market;

    public String getSymbol() {
        return symbol;
    }
    public void setSymbol(String symbol) {
        this.symbol = symbol;
    }

    public String getMarket() {
        return market;
    }
    public void setMarket(String market) {
        this.market = market;
    }
}
```

The second thing is a trade to buy or sell a given quantity of a stock at a given price:

```java
public class Trade {

    public enum Type { BUY, SELL }
    private Type type;

    private Stock stock;
    private int quantity;
    private double price;

    public Type getType() {
        return type;
    }
    public void setType(Type type) {
        this.type = type;
    }

    public int getQuantity() {
        return quantity;
    }
    public void setQuantity(int quantity) {
        this.quantity = quantity;
    }

    public double getPrice() {
        return price;
    }
    public void setPrice(double price) {
        this.price = price;
    }

    public Stock getStock() {
        return stock;
    }
    public void setStock(Stock stock) {
        this.stock = stock;
    }

    public double getValue() {
        return quantity * price;
    }
}
```

The final thing is an order placed by a customer to settle one or more trades:

```java
public class Order {

    private String customer;
    private List<Trade> trades = new ArrayList<>();

    public void addTrade(Trade trade) {
        trades.add(trade);
    }
```

```
    public String getCustomer() {
        return customer;
    }
    public void setCustomer(String customer) {
        this.customer = customer;
    }

    public double getValue() {
        return trades.stream().mapToDouble(Trade::getValue).sum();
    }
}
```

This domain model is straightforward. It's cumbersome to create objects representing orders, for example. Try to define a simple order that contains two trades for your customer BigBank, as shown in listing 10.4.

> **Listing 10.4   Creating a stock trading order by using the domain object's API directly**

```
Order order = new Order();
order.setCustomer("BigBank");

Trade trade1 = new Trade();
trade1.setType(Trade.Type.BUY);

Stock stock1 = new Stock();
stock1.setSymbol("IBM");
stock1.setMarket("NYSE");

trade1.setStock(stock1);
trade1.setPrice(125.00);
trade1.setQuantity(80);
order.addTrade(trade1);

Trade trade2 = new Trade();
trade2.setType(Trade.Type.BUY);

Stock stock2 = new Stock();
stock2.setSymbol("GOOGLE");
stock2.setMarket("NASDAQ");

trade2.setStock(stock2);
trade2.setPrice(375.00);
trade2.setQuantity(50);
order.addTrade(trade2);
```

The verbosity of this code is hardly acceptable; you can't expect a non-developer domain expert to understand and validate it at first glance. What you need is a DSL that reflects the domain model and allows it to be manipulated in a more immediate, intuitive way. You can employ various approaches to achieve this result. In the rest of this section, you learn the pros and cons of these approaches.

10.3.1 Method chaining

The first style of DSL to explore is one of the most common. It allows you to define a trading order with a single chain of method invocations. The following listing shows an example of this type of DSL.

Listing 10.5 Creating a stock trading order with method chaining

```
Order order = forCustomer( "BigBank" )
                 .buy( 80 )
                 .stock( "IBM" )
                     .on( "NYSE" )
                 .at( 125.00 )
                 .sell( 50 )
                 .stock( "GOOGLE" )
                     .on( "NASDAQ" )
                 .at( 375.00 )
              .end();
```

This code looks like a big improvement, doesn't it? It's very likely that your domain expert will understand this code effortlessly. But how can you implement a DSL to achieve this result? You need a few builders that create the objects of this domain through a fluent API. The top-level builder creates and wraps an order, making it possible to add one or more trades to it, as shown in the next listing.

Listing 10.6 An order builder providing a method-chaining DSL

```
public class MethodChainingOrderBuilder {

    public final Order order = new Order();          ←─ The order
                                                        wrapped by
                                                        this builder

    private MethodChainingOrderBuilder(String customer) {    A static factory
        order.setCustomer(customer);                         method to create a
    }                                                        builder of an order
                                                             placed by a given
                                                             customer

    public static MethodChainingOrderBuilder forCustomer(String customer) {
        return new MethodChainingOrderBuilder(customer);      ←─
    }

                                                              Creates a
    public TradeBuilder buy(int quantity) {                   TradeBuilder
        return new TradeBuilder(this, Trade.Type.BUY, quantity);  ←─ to build a
    }                                                         trade to buy
                                                              a stock

    public TradeBuilder sell(int quantity) {
        return new TradeBuilder(this, Trade.Type.SELL, quantity);
    }

    public MethodChainingOrderBuilder addTrade(Trade trade) {
        order.addTrade(trade);
        return this;                  ←─ Returns the order builder itself,
    }                                    allowing you to fluently create
                                         and add further trades
```

Creates a TradeBuilder to build a trade to sell a stock

Adds a trade to the order

```
    public Order end() {
        return order;
    }
}
```

◀—┐ **Terminates the building of
     the order and returns it**

The buy() and sell() methods of the order builder create and return another builder
that builds a trade and adds it to the order itself:

```
public class TradeBuilder {
    private final MethodChainingOrderBuilder builder;
    public final Trade trade = new Trade();

    private TradeBuilder(MethodChainingOrderBuilder builder,
                         Trade.Type type, int quantity) {
        this.builder = builder;
        trade.setType( type );
        trade.setQuantity( quantity );
    }

    public StockBuilder stock(String symbol) {
        return new StockBuilder(builder, trade, symbol);
    }
}
```

The only public method of the TradeBuilder is used to create a further builder,
which then builds an instance of the Stock class:

```
public class StockBuilder {
    private final MethodChainingOrderBuilder builder;
    private final Trade trade;
    private final Stock stock = new Stock();

    private StockBuilder(MethodChainingOrderBuilder builder,
                         Trade trade, String symbol) {
        this.builder = builder;
        this.trade = trade;
        stock.setSymbol(symbol);
    }

    public TradeBuilderWithStock on(String market) {
        stock.setMarket(market);
        trade.setStock(stock);
        return new TradeBuilderWithStock(builder, trade);
    }
}
```

The StockBuilder has a single method, on(), that specifies the market for the stock,
adds the stock to the trade, and returns one last builder:

```
public class TradeBuilderWithStock {
    private final MethodChainingOrderBuilder builder;
    private final Trade trade;
```

```
    public TradeBuilderWithStock(MethodChainingOrderBuilder builder,
                                 Trade trade) {
        this.builder = builder;
        this.trade = trade;
    }

    public MethodChainingOrderBuilder at(double price) {
        trade.setPrice(price);
        return builder.addTrade(trade);
    }
}
```

This one public method of `TradeBuilderWithStock` sets the unit price of the traded stock and returns the original order builder. As you've seen, this method allows you to fluently add other trades to the order until the end method of the `MethodChaining-OrderBuilder` is called. The choice of having multiple builder classes—and in particular, two different trade builders—is made to force the user of this DSL to call the methods of its fluent API in a predetermined sequence, ensuring that a trade has been configured correctly before the user starts creating the next one. The other advantage of this approach is that the parameters used to set an order up are scoped inside the builder. This approach minimizes the use of static methods and allows the names of the methods to act as named arguments, thus further improving the readability of this style of DSL. Finally, the fluent DSL resulting from this technique has the least syntactic noise possible.

Unfortunately, the main issue in method chaining is the verbosity required to implement the builders. A lot of glue code is necessary to mix the top-level builders with the lower-level ones. Another evident disadvantage is the fact that you have no way to enforce the indentation convention that you used to underline the nesting hierarchy of the objects in your domain.

In the next section, you investigate a second DSL pattern that has quite different characteristics.

10.3.2 Using nested functions

The *nested function* DSL pattern takes its name from the fact that it populates the domain model by using functions that are nested within other functions. The following listing illustrates the DSL style resulting from this approach.

Listing 10.7 Creating a stock-trading order with nested functions

```
Order order = order("BigBank",
                buy(80,
                    stock("IBM", on("NYSE")),
                    at(125.00)),
                sell(50,
                    stock("GOOGLE", on("NASDAQ")),
                    at(375.00))
                );
```

The code required to implement this DSL style is far more compact than what you learned in section 10.3.1.

The NestedFunctionOrderBuilder in the following listing shows that it's possible to provide an API with this DSL style to your users. (In this listing, we implicitly assume that all its static methods are imported.)

Listing 10.8   An order builder providing a nested-function DSL

```
public class NestedFunctionOrderBuilder {

    public static Order order(String customer, Trade... trades) {          Creates an
        Order order = new Order();                                         order for a
        order.setCustomer(customer);                                       given customer
        Stream.of(trades).forEach(order::addTrade);        Adds all trades
        return order;                                      to the order
    }

    public static Trade buy(int quantity, Stock stock, double price) {
        return buildTrade(quantity, stock, price, Trade.Type.BUY);
    }

    public static Trade sell(int quantity, Stock stock, double price) {
        return buildTrade(quantity, stock, price, Trade.Type.SELL);
    }

    private static Trade buildTrade(int quantity, Stock stock, double price,
                                    Trade.Type buy) {
        Trade trade = new Trade();
        trade.setQuantity(quantity);
        trade.setType(buy);
        trade.setStock(stock);
        trade.setPrice(price);
        return trade;                           A dummy method to
    }                                           define the unit price
                                                of the traded stock
    public static double at(double price) {
        return price;
    }

    public static Stock stock(String symbol, String market) {
        Stock stock = new Stock();
        stock.setSymbol(symbol);
        stock.setMarket(market);                A dummy method to
        return stock;                           define the market
    }                                           where the stock is
                                                traded
    public static String on(String market) {
        return market;
    }
}
```

Creates a trade to buy a stock → `public static Trade buy(...)`

Creates a trade to sell a stock → `public static Trade sell(...)`

Creates the traded stock → `Stock stock = new Stock();`

The other advantage of this technique compared with method chaining is that the hierarchy structure of your domain objects (an order contains one or more trades, and each trade refers to a single stock in the example) is visible by the way in which the different functions are nested.

Unfortunately, this pattern also has some issues. You may have noticed that the resulting DSL requires a lot of parentheses. Moreover, the list of arguments that have to be passed to the static methods is rigidly predetermined. If the objects of your domain have some optional fields, you need to implement different overloaded versions of those methods, which allows you to omit the missing parameters. Finally, the meanings of the different arguments are defined by their positions rather than their names. You can mitigate this last problem by introducing a few dummy methods, as you did with the `at()` and `on()` methods in your `NestedFunctionOrderBuilder`, the only purpose of which is to clarify the role of an argument.

The two DSL patterns we've shown you so far don't require the use of lambda expressions. In the next section, we illustrate a third technique that leverages the functional capabilities introduced by Java 8.

10.3.3 *Function sequencing with lambda expressions*

The next DSL pattern employs a sequence of functions defined with lambda expressions. Implementing a DSL in this style on top of your usual stock-trading domain model allows you to define an order, as shown in listing 10.9.

Listing 10.9 Creating a stock-trading order with function sequencing

```
Order order = order( o -> {
    o.forCustomer( "BigBank" );
    o.buy( t -> {
        t.quantity( 80 );
        t.price( 125.00 );
        t.stock( s -> {
            s.symbol( "IBM" );
            s.market( "NYSE" );
        } );
    });
    o.sell( t -> {
        t.quantity( 50 );
        t.price( 375.00 );
        t.stock( s -> {
            s.symbol( "GOOGLE" );
            s.market( "NASDAQ" );
        } );
    });
} );
```

To implement this approach, you need to develop several builders that accept lambda expressions and to populate the domain model by executing them. These builders keep the intermediate state of the objects to be created the way you did in the DSL implementation by using method chaining. As you did in the method-chaining pattern, you have a top-level builder to create the order, but this time, the builder takes

Consumer objects as parameters so that the user of the DSL can use lambda expressions to implement them. The next listing shows the code required to implement this approach.

Listing 10.10   An order builder providing a function-sequencing DSL

```
public class LambdaOrderBuilder {

    private Order order = new Order();          ◁──┐ The order wrapped
                                                    by this builder

    public static Order order(Consumer<LambdaOrderBuilder> consumer) {
        LambdaOrderBuilder builder = new LambdaOrderBuilder();
        consumer.accept(builder);            ◁──── Executes the lambda expression
        return builder.order;                ◁──   passed to the order builder
    }
                                             Returns the order populated
    public void forCustomer(String customer) {    by executing the Consumer
        order.setCustomer(customer);              of the OrderBuilder
    }

    public void buy(Consumer<TradeBuilder> consumer) {    │ Consumes a TradeBuilder
        trade(consumer, Trade.Type.BUY);           ◁──│ to create a trade to
    }                                                   │ buy a stock

    public void sell(Consumer<TradeBuilder> consumer) {   │ Consumes a TradeBuilder
        trade(consumer, Trade.Type.SELL);          ◁──│ to create a trade to
    }                                                   │ sell a stock

    private void trade(Consumer<TradeBuilder> consumer, Trade.Type type) {
        TradeBuilder builder = new TradeBuilder();
        builder.trade.setType(type);
        consumer.accept(builder);          ◁──── Executes the lambda
        order.addTrade(builder.trade);     ◁──   expression passed to
    }                                             the TradeBuilder
}
```

Sets the customer who placed the order — (points to `order.setCustomer(customer);`)

Adds to the order the trade populated by executing the Consumer of the TradeBuilder — (points to `order.addTrade(builder.trade);`)

The `buy()` and `sell()` methods of the order builder accept two lambda expressions that are `Consumer<TradeBuilder>`. When executed, these methods populate a buying or selling trade, as follows:

```
public class TradeBuilder {
    private Trade trade = new Trade();

    public void quantity(int quantity) {
        trade.setQuantity( quantity );
    }

    public void price(double price) {
        trade.setPrice( price );
    }

    public void stock(Consumer<StockBuilder> consumer) {
        StockBuilder builder = new StockBuilder();
```

```
        consumer.accept(builder);
        trade.setStock(builder.stock);
    }
}
```

Finally, the `TradeBuilder` accepts the `Consumer` of a third builder that's intended to define the traded stock:

```
public class StockBuilder {
    private Stock stock = new Stock();

    public void symbol(String symbol) {
        stock.setSymbol( symbol );
    }

    public void market(String market) {
        stock.setMarket( market );
    }
}
```

This pattern has the merit of combining two positive characteristics of the two previous DSL styles. Like the method-chaining pattern it allows to define the trading order in a fluent way. In addition, similarly to the nested-function style, it preserves the hierarchy structure of our domain objects in the nesting level of the different lambda expressions.

Unfortunately, this approach requires a lot of setup code, and using the DSL itself is affected by the noise of the Java 8 lambda-expression syntax.

Choosing among these three DSL styles is mainly a matter of taste. It also requires some experience to find the best fit for the domain model for which you want to create a domain language. Moreover, it's possible to combine two or more of these styles in a single DSL, as you see in the next section.

10.3.4 *Putting it all together*

As you've seen so far, all three DSL patterns have pros and cons, but nothing prevents you from using them together within a single DSL. You could end up developing a DSL through which you could define your stock-trading order as shown in the following listing.

> **Listing 10.11 Creating a stock-trading order by using multiple DSL patterns**

```
Order order =
        forCustomer( "BigBank",                  ←——————  Nested function to
                  buy( t -> t.quantity( 80 )  ←——┐        specify attributes of
                            .stock( "IBM" )       │        the top-level order
 Method chaining in   ┌——→   .on( "NYSE" )        │
   the body of the           .at( 125.00 )),      │
 lambda expression    sell( t -> t.quantity( 50 )         Lambda expression to
 that populates the              .stock( "GOOGLE" )        create a single trade
      trade object               .on( "NASDAQ" )
                                 .at( 125.00 )) );
```

In this example, the nested-function pattern is combined with the lambda approach. Each trade is created by a `Consumer` of a `TradeBuilder` that's implemented by a lambda expression, as shown in the next listing.

Listing 10.12   An order builder providing a DSL that mixes multiple styles

```java
public class MixedBuilder {

    public static Order forCustomer(String customer,
                                    TradeBuilder... builders) {
        Order order = new Order();
        order.setCustomer(customer);
        Stream.of(builders).forEach(b -> order.addTrade(b.trade));
        return order;
    }

    public static TradeBuilder buy(Consumer<TradeBuilder> consumer) {
        return buildTrade(consumer, Trade.Type.BUY);
    }

    public static TradeBuilder sell(Consumer<TradeBuilder> consumer) {
        return buildTrade(consumer, Trade.Type.SELL);
    }

    private static TradeBuilder buildTrade(Consumer<TradeBuilder> consumer,
                                           Trade.Type buy) {
        TradeBuilder builder = new TradeBuilder();
        builder.trade.setType(buy);
        consumer.accept(builder);
        return builder;
    }
}
```

Finally, the helper class `TradeBuilder` and the `StockBuilder` that it uses internally (implementation shown immediately after this paragraph) provide a fluent API implementing the method-chaining pattern. After you make this choice, you can write the body of the lambda expression through which the trade will be populated in the most compact way possible:

```java
public class TradeBuilder {
    private Trade trade = new Trade();

    public TradeBuilder quantity(int quantity) {
        trade.setQuantity(quantity);
        return this;
    }

    public TradeBuilder at(double price) {
        trade.setPrice(price);
        return this;
    }
```

```
    public StockBuilder stock(String symbol) {
        return new StockBuilder(this, trade, symbol);
    }
}

public class StockBuilder {
    private final TradeBuilder builder;
    private final Trade trade;
    private final Stock stock = new Stock();

    private StockBuilder(TradeBuilder builder, Trade trade, String symbol){
        this.builder = builder;
        this.trade = trade;
        stock.setSymbol(symbol);
    }

    public TradeBuilder on(String market) {
        stock.setMarket(market);
        trade.setStock(stock);
        return builder;
    }
}
```

Listing 10.12 is an example of how the three DSL patterns discussed in this chapter can be combined to achieve a readable DSL. Doing so allows you to take advantage of the pros of the various DSL styles, but this technique has a minor drawback: the resulting DSL appears to be less uniform than one that uses a single technique, so users of this DSL probably will need more time to learn it.

So far, you've used lambda expressions, but, as the `Comparator` and `Stream` APIs show, using method references can further improve the readability of many DSLs. We demonstrate this fact in the next section through a practical example of using method references in the stock-trading domain model.

10.3.5 *Using method references in a DSL*

In this section, you try to add another simple feature to your stock-trading domain model. This feature calculates the final value of an order after adding zero or more of the following taxes to the order's net value, as shown in the next listing.

Listing 10.13   The taxes that can be applied to the order's net value

```
public class Tax {
    public static double regional(double value) {
        return value * 1.1;
    }

    public static double general(double value) {
        return value * 1.3;
    }
```

```
    public static double surcharge(double value) {
        return value * 1.05;
    }
}
```

The simplest way to implement such a tax calculator is to use a static method that accepts the order plus one Boolean flag for each tax that could be applied (listing 10.14).

Listing 10.14 Applying taxes to the order's net value with a set of Boolean flags

```
public static double calculate(Order order, boolean useRegional,
                               boolean useGeneral, boolean useSurcharge) {
    double value = order.getValue();
    if (useRegional) value = Tax.regional(value);
    if (useGeneral) value = Tax.general(value);
    if (useSurcharge) value = Tax.surcharge(value);
    return value;
}
```

This way, it's possible to calculate the final value of an order after applying the regional tax and the surcharge, but not the general tax, as follows:

```
double value = calculate(order, true, false, true);
```

The readability problem of this implementation is evident: it's difficult to remember the right sequence of Boolean variables and to understand which taxes have been applied and which haven't. The canonical way to fix this issue is to implement a Tax-Calculator that provides a minimal DSL to fluently set the Boolean flags one by one, as shown the next listing.

Listing 10.15 A tax calculator that fluently defines the taxes to be applied

```
public class TaxCalculator {
    private boolean useRegional;
    private boolean useGeneral;
    private boolean useSurcharge;

    public TaxCalculator withTaxRegional() {
        useRegional = true;
        return this;
    }

    public TaxCalculator withTaxGeneral() {
        useGeneral= true;
        return this;
    }

    public TaxCalculator withTaxSurcharge() {
        useSurcharge = true;
        return this;
    }
```

```
    public double calculate(Order order) {
        return calculate(order, useRegional, useGeneral, useSurcharge);
    }
}
```

Using this `TaxCalculator` makes clear that you want to apply the regional tax and the surcharge to the net value of the order:

```
double value = new TaxCalculator().withTaxRegional()
                                  .withTaxSurcharge()
                                  .calculate(order);
```

The main issue with this solution is its verbosity. It doesn't scale because you need a Boolean field and a method for each tax in your domain. By using the functional capabilities of Java, you can achieve the same result in terms of readability in a far more compact and flexible way. To see how, refactor your `TaxCalculator` as shown in this next listing.

> **Listing 10.16 A tax calculator that fluently combines the tax functions to be applied**

```
public class TaxCalculator {
    public DoubleUnaryOperator taxFunction = d -> d;      ◁── The function calculating all the taxes to be applied to the order's value

    public TaxCalculator with(DoubleUnaryOperator f) {
        taxFunction = taxFunction.andThen(f);             ◁── Obtains the new tax-calculating function, composing the current one with the one passed as argument
        return this;
    }

    public double calculate(Order order) {
        return taxFunction.applyAsDouble(order.getValue());   ◁──
    }
}
```

Returns this, allowing further tax functions to be concatenated fluently

Calculates the final order's value by applying the tax-calculating function to the order's net value

With this solution, you need only one field: the function that, when applied to the order's net value, adds in one shot all the taxes configured through the `TaxCalculator` class. The starting value of this function is the identity function. At this point, no tax has been added yet, so the order's final value is the same as the net value. When a new tax is added through the `with()` method, this tax is composed with the current tax-calculating function, thus encompassing all the added taxes in a single function. Finally, when an order is passed to the `calculate()` method, the tax-calculating function resulting from the composition of the various configured taxes is applied to the order's net value. This refactored `TaxCalculator` can be used as follows:

```
double value = new TaxCalculator().with(Tax::regional)
                                  .with(Tax::surcharge)
                                  .calculate(order);
```

This solution uses method references, is easy to read, and gives succinct code. It's also flexible in that if and when a new tax function is added to the `Tax` class, you can use it immediately with your functional `TaxCalculator` without modification.

Now that we've discussed the various techniques that can be used to implement a DSL in Java 8 and beyond, it's interesting to investigate how these strategies have been used in widely adopted Java tools and frameworks.

10.4   *Real World Java 8 DSL*

In section 10.3, you learned three useful patterns for developing DSLs in Java, together with their pros and cons. Table 10.1 summarizes what we've discussed so far.

Table 10.1   DSLs patterns with their pros and cons

Pattern name	Pros	Cons
Method chaining	▪ Method names that act as keyword arguments ▪ Works well with optional parameters ▪ Possible to enforce the DSL user to call methods in a pre-determined order ▪ Minimal or no use of static methods ▪ Lowest possible syntactic noise	▪ Verbose implementation ▪ Glue code to bind the builders ▪ Hierarchy of domain objects defined only by indentation convention
Nested functions	▪ Lower implementation verbosity ▪ Domain objects hierarchy echoed by function nesting	▪ Heavy use of static methods ▪ Arguments defined by position rather than name ▪ Method overloading required for optional parameters
Function sequencing with lambdas	▪ Works well with optional parameters ▪ Minimal or no use of static methods ▪ Hierarchy of domain objects echoed by lambdas nesting ▪ No glue code for builders	▪ Verbose implementation ▪ More syntactic noise from lambda expressions in the DSL

It's time to consolidate what you've learned so far by analyzing how these patterns are employed in three well-known Java libraries: an SQL mapping tool, a behavior-driven development framework, and a tool that implements Enterprise Integration Patterns.

10.4.1 *jOOQ*

SQL is one of the most common and widely used DSLs. For this reason, it shouldn't be surprising that there's a Java library providing a nice DSL to write and execute SQL queries. jOOQ is an internal DSL that implements SQL as a type-safe embedded language directly in Java. A source-code generator reverse-engineers the database schema, which allows the Java compiler to type-check complex SQL statements. The product of this reverse-engineering process generates information with which you can navigate your database schema. As a simple example, the following SQL query

```
SELECT * FROM BOOK
WHERE BOOK.PUBLISHED_IN = 2016
ORDER BY BOOK.TITLE
```

can be written using the jOOQ DSL like this:

```
create.selectFrom(BOOK)
      .where(BOOK.PUBLISHED_IN.eq(2016))
      .orderBy(BOOK.TITLE)
```

Another nice feature of the jOOQ DSL is the possibility of using it in combination with the `Stream` API. This feature allows you to manipulate in memory, with a single fluent statement, the data resulting from the execution of the SQL query, as shown in the next listing.

Listing 10.17 Selecting books from a database by using the jOOQ DSL

Starts manipulating data fetched from database with Stream API

Creates the connection to the SQL database

```
Class.forName("org.h2.Driver");
try (Connection c =
        getConnection("jdbc:h2:~/sql-goodies-with-mapping", "sa", "")) {
    DSL.using(c)
       .select(BOOK.AUTHOR, BOOK.TITLE)
       .where(BOOK.PUBLISHED_IN.eq(2016))
    .orderBy(BOOK.TITLE)
    .fetch()
    .stream()
    .collect(groupingBy(
        r -> r.getValue(BOOK.AUTHOR),
        LinkedHashMap::new,
        mapping(r -> r.getValue(BOOK.TITLE), toList())))
        .forEach((author, titles) ->
    System.out.println(author + " is author of " + titles));
}
```

Starts the jOOQ SQL statement, using the just-created database connection

Defines the SQL statement through the jOOQ DSL

Groups the books by author

Fetches the data from the database; jOOQ statement ends here

Prints the authors' names together with the books they wrote

It's evident that the main DSL pattern chosen to implement the jOOQ DSL is method-chaining. In fact, various characteristics of this pattern (allowing optional parameters and requiring certain methods to be called only in a predetermined sequence) are essential to mimic the syntax of a well-formed SQL query. These features, together with its lower syntactic noise, make the method-chaining pattern a good fit for jOOQ's needs.

10.4.2 Cucumber

Behavior-driven development (BDD) is an extension of test-driven development that uses a simple domain-specific scripting language made of structured statements that describe various business scenarios. Cucumber, like other BDD frameworks, translates these statements into executable test cases. As a result, the scripts resulting from the application of this development technique can be used both as runnable tests and as acceptance criteria for a given business feature. BDD also focuses the development effort on the delivery of prioritized, verifiable business value and bridges the gap between domain experts and programmers by making them share a business vocabulary.

These abstract concepts can be clarified by a practical example that uses Cucumber, a BDD tool that enables developers to write business scenarios in plain English. Use Cucumber's scripting language as follows to define a simple business scenario:

```
Feature: Buy stock
  Scenario: Buy 10 IBM stocks
    Given the price of a "IBM" stock is 125$
    When I buy 10 "IBM"
    Then the order value should be 1250$
```

Cucumber uses notation that's divided into three parts: the definition of prerequisites (Given), the actual calls to the domain objects under test, and (When) the assertions checking the outcome of the test case (Then).

The script that defines the test scenario is written with an external DSL that has a limited number of keywords and lets you write sentences in a free format. These sentences are matched through regular expressions that capture the variables of the test case and pass them as arguments to the methods that implement the test itself. Using the stock-trading domain model from the beginning of section 10.3, it's possible to develop a Cucumber test case that checks whether the value of a stock-trading order is calculated correctly, as shown in the next listing.

Listing 10.18 Implementing a test scenario by using Cucumber annotations

```
public class BuyStocksSteps {
    private Map<String, Integer> stockUnitPrices = new HashMap<>();
    private Order order = new Order();

    @Given("^the price of a \"(.*?)\" stock is (\\d+)\\$$")       ← Defines the unit
    public void setUnitPrice(String stockName, int unitPrice) {      price of a stock as
        stockUnitValues.put(stockName, unitPrice);                   a prerequisite of
    }                                                                 this scenario
                                                       Stores
                                                       the stock
                                                       unit price
    @When("^I buy (\\d+) \"(.*?)\"$")                              ← Defines the
    public void buyStocks(int quantity, String stockName) {          actions to be
        Trade trade = new Trade();          ←                        taken on the
        trade.setType(Trade.Type.BUY);                Populates the  domain model
                                                      domain model   under test
        Stock stock = new Stock();                    accordingly
        stock.setSymbol(stockName);

        trade.setStock(stock);
        trade.setPrice(stockUnitPrices.get(stockName));
        trade.setQuantity(quantity);
        order.addTrade(trade);
    }
```

Checks the test assertions →
```
@Then("^the order value should be (\\d+)\\$$")
public void checkOrderValue(int expectedValue) {
    assertEquals(expectedValue, order.getValue());
}
```
← **Defines the expected scenario outcome**
```
}
```

The introduction of lambda expressions in Java 8 allowed Cucumber to develop an alternative syntax that eliminated annotations by using two-argument methods: the regular expression previously contained in the annotation value and the lambda implementing the test method. When you use this second type of notation, you can rewrite the test scenario like this:

```
public class BuyStocksSteps implements cucumber.api.java8.En {
    private Map<String, Integer> stockUnitPrices = new HashMap<>();
    private Order order = new Order();
    public BuyStocksSteps() {
        Given("^the price of a \"(.*?)\" stock is (\\d+)\\$$",
            (String stockName, int unitPrice) -> {
                stockUnitValues.put(stockName, unitPrice);
        });
        // ... When and Then lambdas omitted for brevity
    }
}
```

This alternative syntax has the obvious advantage of being compact. In particular, replacing the test methods with anonymous lambdas eliminates the burden of finding meaningful method names (which rarely adds anything to readability in a test scenario).

Cucumber's DSL is extremely simple, but it demonstrates how to effectively combine an external DSL with an internal one and (once again) shows that lambdas allow you to write more compact, readable code.

10.4.3 Spring Integration

Spring Integration extends the dependency-injection-based Spring programming model to support the well-known Enterprise Integration Patterns.[1] Spring Integration's primary goals are to provide a simple model to implement complex enterprise integration solutions and to promote the adoption of an asynchronous, message-driven architecture.

Spring Integration enables lightweight remoting, messaging, and scheduling within Spring-based applications. These features are also available through a rich, fluent DSL that's more than syntactic sugar built on top of traditional Spring XML configuration files.

---

[1] For more details see the book: "Enterprise Integration Patterns: Designing, Building, and Deploying Messaging Solutions" (Addison-Wesley) Gregor Hohpe and Bobby Woolf, 2004.

Spring Integration implements all the most common patterns necessary for message-based applications, such as channels, endpoints, pollers, and channel interceptors. Endpoints are expressed as verbs in the DSL to improve readability, and integration processes are constructed by composing these endpoints into one or more message flows. The next listing shows how Spring Integration works with a simple but complete example.

> **Listing 10.19   Configuring a Spring Integration flow by using the Spring Integration DSL**

```
@Configuration
@EnableIntegration
public class MyConfiguration {

    @Bean
    public MessageSource<?> integerMessageSource() {
        MethodInvokingMessageSource source =
                new MethodInvokingMessageSource();
        source.setObject(new AtomicInteger());
        source.setMethodName("getAndIncrement");
        return source;
    }

    @Bean
    public DirectChannel inputChannel() {
        return new DirectChannel();
    }

    @Bean
    public IntegrationFlow myFlow() {
        return IntegrationFlows
                    .from(this.integerMessageSource(),
                        c -> c.poller(Pollers.fixedRate(10)))
                    .channel(this.inputChannel())
                    .filter((Integer p) -> p % 2 == 0)
                    .transform(Object::toString)
                    .channel(MessageChannels.queue("queueChannel"))
                    .get();
    }
}
```

Annotations:
- **Creates a new MessageSource that at each invocation increments an AtomicInteger**
- **The channel conveying the data arriving from the MessageSource**
- **Starts creating the IntegrationFlow through a builder following the method-chaining pattern**
- **Uses the formerly defined MessageSource as the source for this IntegrationFlow**
- **Polls the MessageSource to dequeue the data it conveys**
- **Filters only the even numbers**
- **Terminates the building of the IntegrationFlow and returns it**
- **Sets channel queueChannel as output for this IntegrationFlow**
- **Converts the Integers retrieved from the MessageSource into Strings**

Here, the method `myFlow()` builds an `IntegrationFlow` by using the Spring Integration DSL. It uses the fluent builder provided by the `IntegrationFlows` class, which implements the method-chaining pattern. In this case, the resulting flow polls a `MessageSource` at a fixed rate, providing a sequence of `Integers`; filters the even ones and converts them to `Strings`, and finally sends the result to an output channel in a style that's similar to the native Java 8 `Stream` API. This API allows a message to be sent to any component within the flow if you know its `inputChannel` name. If the flow starts with a direct channel, not a `MessageSource`, it's possible to define the `IntegrationFlow` with a lambda expression as follows:

```
@Bean
public IntegrationFlow myFlow() {
    return flow -> flow.filter((Integer p) -> p % 2 == 0)
                       .transform(Object::toString)
                       .handle(System.out::println);
}
```

As you see, the most widely used pattern in Spring Integration DSL is method chaining. This pattern fits well with the main purpose of the `IntegrationFlow` builder: creating a flow of message-passing and data transformations. As shown in this last example, however, it also uses function sequencing with lambda expressions for the top-level object to be built (and in some cases also for inner, more-complex method arguments).

Summary

- The main purpose of a DSL is to fill the gap between developers and domain experts. It's rare for the person who writes the code that implements the business logic of an application to also have deep knowledge in the business field in which the program will be used. Writing this business logic in a language that non-developers can understand doesn't turn domain experts into programmers, but it does allow them to read and validate the logic.

- The two main categories of DSLs are *internal* (implemented in the same language used to develop the application in which the DSL will be used) and *external* (using a different language designed ad hoc). Internal DSLs require less development effort but have a syntax constrained by the hosting language. External DSLs offer a higher degree of flexibility but are harder to implement.

- It's possible to develop a polyglot DSL by using another programming language already available on the JVM, such as Scala or Groovy. These languages are often more flexible and concise than Java. Integrating them with Java requires a more-complex building process, however, and their interoperability with Java can be far from seamless.

- Due to its verbosity and rigid syntax, Java isn't the ideal programming language to use to develop internal DSLs, but the introduction of lambda expressions and method references in Java 8 hugely improved this situation.

- Modern Java already provides small DSLs in its native API. These DSLs, like the ones in the `Stream` and `Collectors` classes, are useful and convenient, particularly for sorting, filtering, transforming, and grouping collections of data.

- The three main patterns used to implement DSLs in Java are method chaining, nested functions, and function sequencing. Each pattern has pros and cons, but you can combine all three patterns in a single DSL to take advantage of all three techniques.

- Many Java frameworks and libraries allow their features to be used through a DSL. This chapter looked at three of them: jOOQ, an SQL mapping tool; Cucumber, a BDD framework; and Spring Integration, a Spring extension that implements Enterprise Integration Patterns.

Part 4

Everyday Java

The fourth part of this book explores various new features in Java 8 and Java 9 centered around making it easier and more reliable to code your projects. We start with two APIs introduced in Java 8.

Chapter 11 covers the java.util.Optional class, which allows you to both design better APIs and reduce null pointer exceptions.

Chapter 12 explores the Date and Time API, which greatly improves the previous error-prone APIs for working with dates and time.

Then we explain Java 8 and Java 9 enhancements for writing big systems and enabling them to evolve.

In chapter 13, you'll learn what default methods are, how you can use them to evolve APIs in a compatible way, some practical usage patterns, and rules for using default methods effectively.

Chapter 14 is new for this second edition and explores the Java Module System—a major enhancement in Java 9 that enables huge systems to be modularized in a documented and enforceable way, rather than being "only a haphazard collection of packages."

Using Optional as
a better alternative to null

This chapter covers

- What's wrong with `null` references and why you should avoid them
- From `null` to `Optional`: rewriting your domain model in a null-safe way
- Putting optionals to work: removing null checks from your code
- Different ways to read the value possibly contained in an optional
- Rethinking programming given potentially missing values

Raise your hand if you ever got a `NullPointerException` during your life as a Java developer. Keep it up if this `Exception` is the one you encounter most frequently. Unfortunately, we can't see you at this moment, but we believe that there's a high probability that your hand is raised now. We also guess that you may be thinking something like "Yes, I agree. `NullPointerExceptions` are a pain for any Java developer, novice, or expert. But there's not much we can do about them, because this is the price we pay to use such a convenient, and maybe unavoidable, construct as null references." This feeling is common in the (imperative) programming world; nevertheless, it may not be the whole truth and is more likely a bias with solid historical roots.

British computer scientist Tony Hoare introduced null references back in 1965 while designing ALGOL W, one of the first typed programming languages with heap-allocated records, later saying that he did so "simply because it was so easy to implement." Despite his goal "to ensure that all use of references could be absolutely safe, with checking performed automatically by the compiler," he decided to make an exception for null references because he thought that they were the most convenient way to model *the absence of a value*. After many years, he regretted this decision, calling it "my billion-dollar mistake." We've all seen the effect. We examine a field of an object, perhaps to determine whether its value is one of two expected forms, only to find that we're examining not an object but a null pointer that promptly raises that annoying NullPointerException.

In reality, Hoare's statement could underestimate the costs incurred by millions of developers fixing bugs caused by null references in the past 50 years. Indeed, the vast majority of the languages[1] created in recent decades, including Java, have been built with the same design decision, maybe for reasons of compatibility with older languages or (more probably), as Hoare states, "simply because it was so easy to implement." We start by showing you a simple example of the problems with null.

11.1 How do you model the absence of a value?

Imagine that you have the following nested object structure for a person who owns a car and has car insurance in the following listing.

Listing 11.1   The Person/Car/Insurance data model

```
public class Person {
    private Car car;
    public Car getCar() { return car; }
}
public class Car {
    private Insurance insurance;
    public Insurance getInsurance() { return insurance; }
}
public class Insurance {
    private String name;
    public String getName() { return name; }
}
```

---

[1] Notable exceptions include most typed functional languages, such as Haskell and ML. These languages include *algebraic data types* that allow data types to be expressed succinctly, including explicit specification of whether special values such as null are to be included on a type-by-type basis.

What's problematic with the following code?

```
public String getCarInsuranceName(Person person) {
    return person.getCar().getInsurance().getName();
}
```

This code looks pretty reasonable, but many people don't own a car, so what's the result of calling the method getCar? A common unfortunate practice is to return the null reference to indicate the absence of a value (here, to indicate the absence of a car). As a consequence, the call to getInsurance returns the insurance of a null reference, which results in a NullPointerException at runtime and stops your program from running further. But that's not all. What if person was null? What if the method getInsurance returned null too?

11.1.1 Reducing NullPointerExceptions with defensive checking

What can you do to avoid running into an unexpected NullPointerException? Typically, you can add null checks where necessary (and sometimes, in an excess of defensive programming, even where not necessary) and often with different styles. A first attempt to write a method preventing a NullPointerException is shown in the following listing.

Listing 11.2   Null-safe attempt 1: deep doubts

```
public String getCarInsuranceName(Person person) {
    if (person != null) {                              ◁────┐   Each null check
        Car car = person.getCar();                          │   increases the
        if (car != null) {                          ◁───────┤   nesting level of the
            Insurance insurance = car.getInsurance();        │   remaining part of
            if (insurance != null) {                 ◁───────┘   the invocation chain.
                return insurance.getName();
            }
        }
    }
    return "Unknown";
}
```

This method performs a null check every time it dereferences a variable, returning the string "Unknown" if any of the variables traversed in this dereferencing chain is a null value. The only exception to this rule is that you're not checking to see whether the name of the insurance company is null because (like any other company) you *know* it must have a name. Note that you can avoid this last check only because of your knowledge of the business domain, but that fact isn't reflected in the Java classes modeling your data.

We labeled the method in listing 11.2 "deep doubts" because it shows a recurring pattern: every time you doubt that a variable could be null, you're obliged to add a further nested if block, increasing the indentation level of the code. This technique clearly scales poorly and compromises readability, so maybe you'd like to attempt another solution. Try to avoid this problem by doing something different as shown in the next listing.

Listing 11.3 Null-safe attempt 2: too many exits

```
public String getCarInsuranceName(Person person) {
    if (person == null) {                           ◄─────┐
        return "Unknown";
    }
    Car car = person.getCar();                             │   Each null check
    if (car == null) {                              ◄──────┤   adds a further
        return "Unknown";                                  │   exit point.
    }
    Insurance insurance = car.getInsurance();
    if (insurance == null) {                        ◄──────┘
        return "Unknown";
    }
    return insurance.getName();
}
```

In this second attempt, you try to avoid the deeply nested `if` blocks, adopting a different strategy: every time you meet a `null` variable, you return the string `"Unknown"`. Nevertheless, this solution is also far from ideal; now the method has four distinct exit points, making it hard to maintain. Even worse, the default value to be returned in case of a `null`, the string `"Unknown"`, is repeated in three places—and (we hope) not misspelled! (You may want to extract the repeated string into a constant to prevent this problem, of course.)

Furthermore, the process is error-prone. What if you forget to check whether one property could be `null`? We argue in this chapter that using `null` to represent the absence of a value is the wrong approach. What you need is a better way to model the absence and presence of a value.

11.1.2 Problems with null

To recap our discussion so far, the use of `null` references in Java causes both theoretical and practical problems:

- *It's a source of error.* `NullPointerException` is by far the most common exception in Java.
- *It bloats your code.* It worsens readability by making it necessary to fill your code with `null` checks that are often deeply nested.
- *It's meaningless.* It doesn't have any semantic meaning, and in particular, it represents the wrong way to model the absence of a value in a statically typed language.
- *It breaks Java philosophy.* Java always hides pointers from developers except in one case: the `null` pointer.
- *It creates a hole in the type system.* `null` carries no type or other information, so it can be assigned to any reference type. This situation is a problem because when

null is propagated to another part of the system, you have no idea what that null was initially supposed to be.

To provide some context for other solutions, in the next section we briefly look at what other programming languages have to offer.

11.1.3 *What are the alternatives to null in other languages?*

In recent years, languages such as Groovy worked around this problem by introducing a *safe navigation operator*, represented by ?., to safely navigate potentially null values. To understand how this process works, consider the following Groovy code, which retrieves the name of the insurance company used by a given person to insure a car:

```
def carInsuranceName = person?.car?.insurance?.name
```

What this statement does should be clear. A person may not have a car, and you tend to model this possibility by assigning a null to the car reference of the Person object. Similarly, a car may not be insured. The Groovy safe navigation operator allows you to safely navigate these potentially null references without throwing a NullPointer-Exception by propagating the null reference through the invocations chain, return-ing a null in the event that any value in the chain is a null.

A similar feature was proposed and then discarded for Java 7. Somehow, though, we don't seem to miss a safe navigation operator in Java. The first temptation of all Java developers when confronted with a NullPointerException is to fix it quickly by adding an if statement, checking that a value isn't null before invoking a method on it. If you solve this problem in this way, without wondering whether it's correct for your algorithm or your data model to present a null value in that specific situation, you're not fixing a bug but hiding it, making its discovery and remedy far more diffi-cult for whoever will be called to work on it next time (likely you in the next week or month). You're sweeping the dirt under the carpet. Groovy's null-safe dereferencing operator is only a bigger and more powerful broom for making this mistake without worrying too much about its consequences.

Other functional languages, such as Haskell and Scala, take a different view. Has-kell includes a Maybe type, which essentially encapsulates an optional value. A value of type Maybe can contain a value of a given type or nothing. Haskell no concept of a null reference. Scala has a similar construct called Option[T] to encapsulate the pres-ence or absence of a value of type T, which we discuss in chapter 20. Then you have to explicitly check whether a value is present or not using operations available on the Option type, which enforces the idea of "null checking." You can no longer forget to check for null—because checking is enforced by the type system.

Okay, we've diverged a bit, and all this sounds fairly abstract. You may wonder about Java 8. Java 8 takes inspiration from this idea of an optional value by introduc-ing a new class called java.util.Optional<T>! In this chapter, we show the advan-tages of using this class to model potentially absent values instead of assigning a null reference to them. We also clarify how this migration from nulls to Optionals requires you to rethink the way you deal with optional values in your domain model. Finally, we explore the features of this new `Optional` class and provide a few practical examples showing how to use it effectively. Ultimately, you learn how to design better APIs in which users can tell whether to expect an optional value by reading the signature of a method.

11.2   *Introducing the Optional class*

Java 8 introduces a new class called `java.util.Optional<T>` that's inspired by Haskell and Scala. The class encapsulates an optional value. If you know that a person may not have a car, for example, the `car` variable inside the `Person` class shouldn't be declared type `Car` and assigned to a `null` reference when the person doesn't own a car; instead, it should be type `Optional<Car>`, as illustrated in figure 11.1.

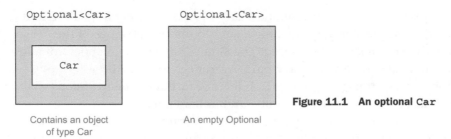

Figure 11.1   An optional `Car`

When a value is present, the `Optional` class wraps it. Conversely, the absence of a value is modeled with an empty optional returned by the method `Optional.empty`. This static factory method returns a special singleton instance of the `Optional` class. You may wonder about the difference between a `null` reference and `Optional.empty()`. Semantically, they could be seen as the same thing, but in practice, the difference is huge. Trying to dereference a `null` invariably causes a `NullPointerException`, whereas `Optional.empty()` is a valid, workable object of type `Optional` that can be invoked in useful ways. You'll soon see how.

An important, practical semantic difference in using `Optional`s instead of `null`s is that in the first case, declaring a variable of type `Optional<Car>` instead of `Car` clearly signals that a missing value is permitted there. Conversely, always using the type `Car` and possibly assigning a `null` reference to a variable of that type implies that you don't have any help, other than your knowledge of the business model, in understanding whether the `null` belongs to the valid domain of that given variable.

With this act in mind, you can rework the original model from listing 11.1, using the `Optional` class as shown in the following listing.

> **Listing 11.4   Redefining the `Person/Car/Insurance` data model by using `Optional`**

```
public class Person {
    private Optional<Car> car;
```
A person may not own a car, so you declare this field Optional.

```
        public Optional<Car> getCar() { return car; }
}
public class Car {
    private Optional<Insurance> insurance;
    public Optional<Insurance> getInsurance() { return insurance; }
}
public class Insurance {
    private String name;
    public String getName() { return name; }
}
```

A car may not be insured, so you declare this field Optional.

An insurance company must have a name.

Note how the use of the Optional class enriches the semantics of your model. The fact that a person references an Optional<Car>, and a car references an Optional <Insurance>, makes it explicit in the domain that a person *may* or *may not* own a car, and that car *may* or *may not* be insured.

At the same time, the fact that the name of the insurance company is declared of type String instead of Optional<String> makes it evident that an insurance company must have a name. This way, you know for certain whether you'll get a NullPointer-Exception when dereferencing the name of an insurance company; you don't have to add a null check, because doing so will hide the problem instead of fixing it. An insurance company must have a name, so if you find one without a name, you'll have to work out what's wrong in your data instead of adding a piece of code to cover up this circumstance. Consistently using Optional values creates a clear distinction between a missing value that's planned for and a value that's absent only because of a bug in your algorithm or a problem in your data. It's important to note that the intention of the Optional class isn't to replace every single null reference. Instead, its purpose is to help you design more-comprehensible APIs so that by reading the signature of a method, you can tell whether to expect an optional value. You're forced to actively unwrap an optional to deal with the absence of a value.

11.3 Patterns for adopting Optionals

So far, so good; you've learned how to employ optionals in types to clarify your domain model, and you've seen the advantages of this process over representing missing values with null references. How can you use optionals now? More specifically, how can you use a value wrapped in an optional?

11.3.1 Creating Optional objects

The first step before working with Optional is learning how to create optional objects! You can create them in several ways.

EMPTY OPTIONAL

As mentioned earlier, you can get hold of an empty optional object by using the static factory method Optional.empty:

```
Optional<Car> optCar = Optional.empty();
```

OPTIONAL FROM A NON-NULL VALUE

You can also create an optional from a non-null value with the static factory method `Optional.of`:

```
Optional<Car> optCar = Optional.of(car);
```

If `car` were `null`, a `NullPointerException` would be thrown immediately (rather than getting a latent error when you try to access properties of the car).

OPTIONAL FROM NULL

Finally, by using the static factory method `Optional.ofNullable`, you can create an `Optional` object that may hold a `null` value:

```
Optional<Car> optCar = Optional.ofNullable(car);
```

If `car` were `null`, the resulting `Optional` object would be empty.

You might imagine that we'll continue by investigating how to get a value out of an optional. A `get` method does precisely this, and we talk more about it later. But `get` raises an exception when the optional is empty, so using it in an ill-disciplined manner effectively re-creates all the maintenance problems caused by using `null`. Instead, we start by looking at ways of using optional values that avoid explicit tests, inspired by similar operations on streams.

11.3.2 *Extracting and transforming values from Optionals with map*

A common pattern is to extract information from an object. You may want to extract the name from an insurance company, for example. You need to check whether insurance is `null` before extracting the name as follows:

```
String name = null;
if(insurance != null){
    name = insurance.getName();
}
```

`Optional` supports a `map` method for this pattern, which works as follows (from here on, we use the model presented in listing 11.4):

```
Optional<Insurance> optInsurance = Optional.ofNullable(insurance);
Optional<String> name = optInsurance.map(Insurance::getName);
```

This method is conceptually similar to the `map` method of Stream you saw in chapters 4 and 5. The `map` operation applies the provided function to each element of a stream. You could also think of an `Optional` object as being a particular collection of data, containing at most a single element. If the `Optional` contains a value, the function passed as argument to `map` transforms that value. If the `Optional` is empty, nothing happens. Figure 11.2 illustrates this similarity, showing what happens when you pass a function that transforms a square into a triangle to the `map` methods of both a stream of square and an optional of square.

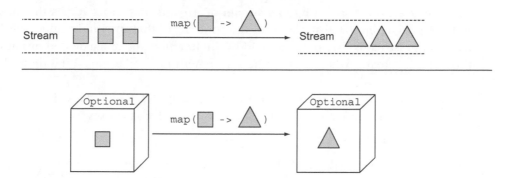

Figure 11.2   Comparing the map methods of Streams and Optionals

This idea looks useful, but how can you use it to rewrite the code in listing 11.1,

```
public String getCarInsuranceName(Person person) {
    return person.getCar().getInsurance().getName();
}
```

which chains several method calls, in a safe way?

The answer is to use another method supported by Optional called flatMap.

11.3.3 Chaining Optional objects with flatMap

Because you've learned how to use map, your first reaction may be to use map to rewrite the code as follows:

```
Optional<Person> optPerson = Optional.of(person);
Optional<String> name =
    optPerson.map(Person::getCar)
             .map(Car::getInsurance)
             .map(Insurance::getName);
```

Unfortunately, this code doesn't compile. Why? The variable optPerson is of type Optional<Person>, so it's perfectly fine to call the map method. But getCar returns an object of type Optional<Car> (as presented in listing 11.4), which means that the result of the map operation is an object of type Optional<Optional<Car>>. As a result, the call to getInsurance is invalid because the outermost optional contains as its value another optional, which of course doesn't support the get-Insurance method. Figure 11.3 illustrates the nested optional structure you'd get.

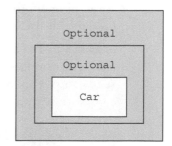

Figure 11.3   A two-level optional

How can you solve this problem? Again, you can look at a pattern you've used previously with streams: the flatMap method. With streams, the flatMap method takes a function as an argument and returns another stream. This function is applied to each element of a stream, resulting in a stream of streams. But flatMap has the effect of replacing each generated stream with the contents of that stream. In other words, all the separate streams that are generated by the function get amalgamated or flattened into a single stream. What you want here is something similar, but you want to flatten a two-level optional into one.

As figure 11.2 does for the map method, figure 11.4 illustrates the similarities between the flatMap methods of the Stream and Optional classes.

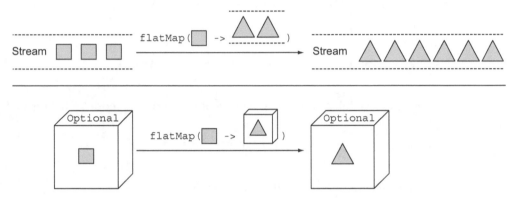

Figure 11.4   Comparing the flatMap methods of Stream and Optional

Here, the function passed to the stream's flatMap method transforms each square into another stream containing two triangles. Then the result of a simple map is a stream containing three other streams, each with two triangles, but the flatMap method flattens this two-level stream into a single stream containing six triangles in total. In the same way, the function passed to the optional's flatMap method transforms the square contained in the original optional into an optional containing a triangle. If this function were passed to the map method, the result would be an optional containing another optional that in turn contains a triangle, but the flatMap method flattens this two-level optional into a single optional containing a triangle.

FINDING A CAR'S INSURANCE COMPANY NAME WITH OPTIONALS

Now that you know the theory of the map and flatMap methods of Optional, you're ready to put them into practice. The ugly attempts made in listings 11.2 and 11.3 can be rewritten by using the optional-based data model of listing 11.4 as follows.

Listing 11.5   Finding a car's insurance company name with Optionals

```
public String getCarInsuranceName(Optional<Person> person) {
    return person.flatMap(Person::getCar)
            .flatMap(Car::getInsurance)
            .map(Insurance::getName)
            .orElse("Unknown");
}
```

A default value if the resulting Optional is empty

Comparing listing 11.5 with the two former attempts shows the advantages of using optionals when dealing with potentially missing values. This time, you can obtain what you want with an easily comprehensible statement instead of increasing the code complexity with conditional branches.

In implementation terms, first note that you modify the signature of the getCar-InsuranceName method from listings 11.2 and 11.3. We explicitly said that there could be a case in which a nonexistent Person is passed to this method, such as when that Person is retrieved from a database via an identifier, and you want to model the possibility that no Person exists in your data for the given identifier. You model this additional requirement by changing the type of the method's argument from Person to Optional<Person>.

Once again, this approach allows you to make explicit through the type system something that otherwise would remain implicit in your knowledge of the domain model: the first purpose of a language, even a programming language, is communication. Declaring a method to take an optional as an argument or to return an optional as a result documents to your colleagues—and all future users of your method—that it can take an empty value or give an empty value as a result.

PERSON/CAR/INSURANCE DEREFERENCING CHAIN USING OPTIONALS
Starting with this Optional<Person>, the Car from the Person, the Insurance from the Car, and the String containing the insurance company name from the Insurance are dereferenced with a combination of the map and flatMap methods introduced earlier in this chapter. Figure 11.5 illustrates this pipeline of operations.

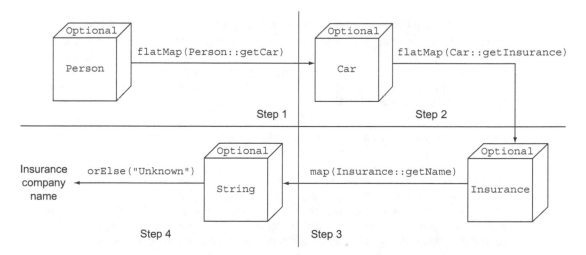

Figure 11.5 The Person/Car/Insurance dereferencing chain using optionals

Here, you begin with the optional that wraps the Person and invokes flat-Map(Person::getCar) on it. As we said, you can logically think of this invocation as something that happens in two steps. In step 1, a Function is applied to the Person inside the optional to transform it. In this case, the Function is expressed with a method reference invoking the method getCar on that Person. Because that method returns an Optional<Car>, the Person inside the optional is transformed into an instance of that type, resulting in a two-level optional that's flattened as part of the flatMap operation. From a theoretical point of view, you can think of this flattening operation as the operation that combines two nested optionals, resulting in an empty optional if at least one of them is empty. What happens in reality is that if you invoke flatMap on an empty optional, nothing is changed, and the empty optional is returned as is. Conversely, if the optional wraps a Person, the Function passed to the flatMap method is applied to that Person. Because the value produced by that Function application is already an optional, the flatMap method can return it as is.

The second step is similar to the first one, transforming the Optional<Car> into an Optional<Insurance>. Step 3 turns the Optional<Insurance> into an Optional <String>: because the Insurance.getName() method returns a String. In this case, a flatMap isn't necessary.

At this point the resulting optional will be empty if any of the methods in this invocation chain returns an empty optional or otherwise contains the desired insurance company name. How do you read that value? After all, you'll end up getting an Optional<String> that may or may not contain the name of the insurance company. In listing 11.5, we used another method called orElse, which provides a default value in case the optional is empty. Many methods provide default actions or unwrap an optional. In the next section, we look at those methods in detail.

Using optionals in a domain model and why they're not serializable

In listing 11.4, we showed how to use Optionals in your domain model to mark with a specific type the values that are allowed to be missing or remain undefined. The designers of the Optional class, however, developed it based on different assumptions and with a different use case in mind. In particular, Java language architect Brian Goetz clearly stated that the purpose of Optional is to support the optional-return idiom only.

Because the Optional class wasn't intended for use as a field type, it doesn't implement the Serializable interface. For this reason, using Optionals in your domain model could break applications with tools or frameworks that require a serializable model to work. Nevertheless, we believe that we've showed you why using Optionals as a proper type in your domain is a good idea, especially when you have to traverse a graph of objects that potentially aren't present. Alternatively, if you need to have a serializable domain model, we suggest that you at least provide a method allowing access to any possibly missing value as an optional, as in the following example:

```
public class Person {
    private Car car;
    public Optional<Car> getCarAsOptional() {
        return Optional.ofNullable(car);
    }
}
```

11.3.4 *Manipulating a stream of optionals*

The `Optional`'s `stream()` method, introduced in Java 9, allows you to convert an `Optional` with a value to a `Stream` containing only that value or an empty `Optional` to an equally empty `Stream`. This technique can be particularly convenient in a common case: when you have a `Stream` of `Optional` and need to transform it into another `Stream` containing only the values present in the nonempty `Optional` of the original `Stream`. In this section, we demonstrate with another practical example why you could find yourself having to deal with a `Stream` of `Optional` and how to perform this operation.

The example in listing 11.6 uses the `Person/Car/Insurance` domain model defined in listing 11.4, Suppose that you're required to implement a method that's passed with a `List<Person>` and that should return a `Set<String>` containing all the distinct names of the insurance companies used by the people in that list who own a car.

Listing 11.6   Finding distinct insurance company names used by a list of `persons`

Convert the list of persons into a
Stream of Optional<Car> with the
cars eventually owned by them.

FlatMap each Optional<Car>
into the corresponding
Optional<Insurance>.

```
public Set<String> getCarInsuranceNames(List<Person> persons) {
    return persons.stream()
                  .map(Person::getCar)
                  .map(optCar -> optCar.flatMap(Car::getInsurance))
                  .map(optIns -> optIns.map(Insurance::getName))
                  .flatMap(Optional::stream)
                  .collect(toSet());
}
```

Collect the result Strings
into a Set to obtain only
the distinct values.

Transform the
Stream<Optional<String>>
into a Stream<String> containing
only the present names.

Map each
Optional<Insurance> into
the Optional<String>
containing the
corresponding name.

Often, manipulating the elements of a `Stream` results in a long chain of transformations, filters, and other operations, but this case has an additional complication because each element is also wrapped into an `Optional`. Remember that you modeled the fact that a person may not have a car by making its `getCar()` method return an `Optional<Car>` instead of a simple `Car`. So, after the first `map` transformation, you obtain a `Stream<Optional<Car>>`. At this point, the two subsequent `maps` allow you to transform each `Optional<Car>` into an `Optional<Insurance>` and then each of them into an `Optional<String>` as you did in listing 11.5 for a single element instead of a `Stream`.

At the end of these three transformations, you obtain a `Stream<Optional<String>>` in which some of these `Optionals` may be empty because a person doesn't own a car or because the car isn't insured. The use of `Optionals` allows you to perform these operations in a completely null-safe way even in case of missing values, but now you have the problem of getting rid of the empty `Optionals` and unwrapping the values contained in the remaining ones before collecting the results into a `Set`. You could have obtained this result with a `filter` followed by a `map`, of course, as follows:

```
Stream<Optional<String>> stream = ...
Set<String> result = stream.filter(Optional::isPresent)
                           .map(Optional::get)
                           .collect(toSet());
```

As anticipated in listing 11.6, however, it's possible to achieve the same result in a single operation instead of two by using the `stream()` method of the `Optional` class. Indeed, this method transforms each `Optional` into a `Stream` with zero or one elements, depending on whether the transformed `Optional` is empty. For this reason, a reference to that method can be seen as a function from a single element of the `Stream` to another `Stream` and then passed to the `flatMap` method invoked on the original `Stream`. As you've already learned, in this way each element is converted to a `Stream` and then the two-level `Stream` of `Streams` is flattened into a single-level one. This trick allows you to unwrap the `Optionals` containing a value and skip the empty ones in only one step.

11.3.5 *Default actions and unwrapping an Optional*

In section 11.3.3, you decided to read an `Optional` value using the `orElse` method, which allows you to also provide a default value that will be returned in the case of an empty optional. The `Optional` class provides several instance methods to read the value contained by an `Optional` instance:

- `get()` is the simplest but also the least safe of these methods. It returns the wrapped value if one is present and throws a `NoSuchElementException` otherwise. For this reason, using this method is almost always a bad idea unless you're sure that the optional contains a value. In addition, this method isn't much of an improvement on nested `null` checks.

- `orElse(T other)` is the method used in listing 11.5, and as we noted there, it allows you to provide a default value when the optional doesn't contain a value.

- `orElseGet(Supplier<? extends T> other)` is the lazy counterpart of the `orElse` method, because the supplier is invoked only if the optional contains no value. You should use this method when the default value is time-consuming to create (to gain efficiency) or you want the supplier to be invoked only if the optional is empty (when using `orElseGet` is vital).

- `or(Supplier<? extends Optional<? extends T>> supplier)` is similar to the former `orElseGet` method, but it doesn't unwrap the value inside the `Optional`, if present. In practice, this method (introduced with Java 9) doesn't perform any action and returns the `Optional` as it is when it contains a value, but lazily provides a different `Optional` when the original one is empty.

- `orElseThrow(Supplier<? extends X> exceptionSupplier)` is similar to the `get` method in that it throws an exception when the `optional` is empty, but it allows you to choose the type of exception that you want to throw.
- `ifPresent(Consumer<? super T> consumer)` lets you execute the action given as argument if a value is present; otherwise, no action is taken.

Java 9 introduced an additional instance method:

- `ifPresentOrElse(Consumer<? super T> action, Runnable emptyAction)`. This differs from `ifPresent` by taking a `Runnable` that gives an empty-based action to be executed when the `Optional` is empty.

11.3.6 *Combining two Optionals*

Now suppose that you have a method that, given a `Person` and a `Car`, queries some external services and implements some complex business logic to find the insurance company that offers the cheapest policy for that combination:

```
public Insurance findCheapestInsurance(Person person, Car car) {
    // queries services provided by the different insurance companies
    // compare all those data
    return cheapestCompany;
}
```

Also suppose that you want to develop a null-safe version of this method, taking two optionals as arguments and returning an `Optional<Insurance>` that will be empty if at least one of the values passed in to it is also empty. The `Optional` class also provides an `isPresent` method that returns `true` if the optional contains a value, so your first attempt could be to implement this method as follows:

```
public Optional<Insurance> nullSafeFindCheapestInsurance(
                           Optional<Person> person, Optional<Car> car) {
    if (person.isPresent() && car.isPresent()) {
        return Optional.of(findCheapestInsurance(person.get(), car.get()));
    } else {
        return Optional.empty();
    }
}
```

This method has the advantage of making clear in its signature that both the `Person` and the `Car` values passed to it could be missing and that for this reason, it couldn't return any value. Unfortunately, its implementation resembles too closely the `null` checks that you'd write if the method took as arguments a `Person` and a `Car`, both of which could be `null`. Is there a better, more idiomatic way to implement this method by using the features of the `Optional` class? Take a few minutes to go through quiz 11.1, and try to find an elegant solution.

The analogies between the `Optional` class and the `Stream` interface aren't limited to the `map` and `flatMap` methods. A third method, `filter`, behaves in a similar fashion on both classes, and we explore it next.

Quiz 11.1: Combining two optionals without unwrapping them

Using a combination of the `map` and `flatMap` methods you learned in this section, rewrite the implementation of the former `nullSafeFindCheapestInsurance()` method in a single statement.

Answer:

You can implement that method in a single statement and without using any conditional constructs like the ternary operator as follows:

```
public Optional<Insurance> nullSafeFindCheapestInsurance(
                              Optional<Person> person, Optional<Car> car) {
    return person.flatMap(p -> car.map(c -> findCheapestInsurance(p, c)));
}
```

Here, you invoke a `flatMap` on the first optional, so if this optional is empty, the lambda expression passed to it won't be executed, and this invocation will return an empty optional. Conversely, if the person is present, `flatMap` uses it as the input to a `Function` returning an `Optional<Insurance>` as required by the `flatMap` method. The body of this function invokes a `map` on the second optional, so if it doesn't contain any `Car`, the `Function` returns an empty optional, and so does the whole `null-SafeFindCheapestInsurance` method. Finally, if both the `Person` and the `Car` are present, the lambda expression passed as an argument to the `map` method can safely invoke the original `findCheapestInsurance` method with them.

11.3.7 *Rejecting certain values with filter*

Often, you need to call a method on an object to check some property. You may need to check whether the insurance's name is equal to `CambridgeInsurance`, for example. To do so in a safe way, first check whether the reference that points to an `Insurance` object is `null` and then call the `getName` method, as follows:

```
Insurance insurance = ...;
if(insurance != null && "CambridgeInsurance".equals(insurance.getName())){
  System.out.println("ok");
}
```

You can rewrite this pattern by using the `filter` method on an `Optional` object, as follows:

```
Optional<Insurance> optInsurance = ...;
optInsurance.filter(insurance ->
                    "CambridgeInsurance".equals(insurance.getName()))
          .ifPresent(x -> System.out.println("ok"));
```

The `filter` method takes a predicate as an argument. If a value is present in the `Optional` object, and that value matches the predicate, the `filter` method returns that value; otherwise, it returns an empty `Optional` object. If you remember that you can think of an optional as being a stream containing at most a single element, the behavior of this method should be clear. If the optional is already empty, it doesn't have any effect; otherwise, it applies the predicate to the value contained in the optional. If this application returns `true`, the optional returns unchanged; otherwise, the value is filtered away, leaving the optional empty. You can test your understanding of how the `filter` method works by working through quiz 11.2.

Quiz 11.2: Filtering an optional

Supposing that the `Person` class of your `Person/Car/Insurance` model also has a method `getAge` to access the age of the person, modify the `getCarInsuranceName` method in listing 11.5 by using the signature

```
public String getCarInsuranceName(Optional<Person> person, int minAge)
```

so that the insurance company name is returned *only* if the person has an age greater than or equal to the `minAge` argument.

Answer:

You can filter the `Optional<Person>`, to remove any contained person whose age fails to be at least the `minAge` argument, by encoding this condition in a predicate passed to the `filter` method as follows:

```
public String getCarInsuranceName(Optional<Person> person, int minAge) {
    return person.filter(p -> p.getAge() >= minAge)
                 .flatMap(Person::getCar)
                 .flatMap(Car::getInsurance)
                 .map(Insurance::getName)
                 .orElse("Unknown");
}
```

In the next section, we investigate the remaining features of the `Optional` class and provide more practical examples of various techniques you could use to reimplement the code you write to manage missing values.

Table 11.1 summarizes the methods of the `Optional` class.

Table 11.1 The methods of the `Optional` class

Method	Description
empty	Returns an empty `Optional` instance
filter	If the value is present and matches the given predicate, returns this `Optional`; otherwise, returns the empty one
flatMap	If a value is present, returns the `Optional` resulting from the application of the provided mapping function to it; otherwise, returns the empty `Optional`
get	Returns the value wrapped by this `Optional` if present; otherwise, throws a `NoSuchElementException`

Table **11.1**   **The methods of the** `Optional` **class** *(continued)*

Method	Description
ifPresent	If a value is present, invokes the specified consumer with the value; otherwise, does nothing
ifPresentOrElse	If a value is present, performs an action with the value as input; otherwise, performs a different action with no input
isPresent	Returns `true` if a value is present; otherwise, returns `false`
map	If a value is present, applies the provided mapping function to it
of	Returns an `Optional` wrapping the given value or throws a `NullPointerException` if this value is `null`
ofNullable	Returns an `Optional` wrapping the given value or the empty `Optional` if this value is `null`
or	If the value is present, returns the same `Optional`; otherwise, returns another `Optional` produced by the supplying function
orElse	Returns the value if present; otherwise, returns the given default value
orElseGet	Returns the value if present; otherwise, returns the one provided by the given `Supplier`
orElseThrow	Returns the value if present; otherwise, throws the exception created by the given `Supplier`
stream	If a value is present, returns a `Stream` containing only it; otherwise, returns an empty `Stream`

11.4   *Practical examples of using Optional*

As you've learned, effective use of the new `Optional` class implies a complete rethink of how you deal with potentially missing values. This rethink involves not only the code you write, but also (and possibly even more important) how you interact with native Java APIs.

Indeed, we believe that many of those APIs would have been written differently if the `Optional` class had been available when they were developed. For backward-compatibility reasons, old Java APIs can't be changed to make proper use of optionals, but all is not lost. You can fix, or at least work around, this issue by adding to your code small utility methods that allow you to benefit from the power of optionals. You see how to do this with a couple of practical examples.

11.4.1   *Wrapping a potentially null value in an Optional*

An existing Java API almost always returns a `null` to signal that the required value is absent or that the computation to obtain it failed for some reason. The `get` method of a `Map` returns `null` as its value if it contains no mapping for the requested key, for example. But for the reasons we listed earlier, in most cases like this one, you prefer for these methods to return an optional. You can't modify the signature of these methods, but you can easily wrap the value they return with an optional. Continuing with the Map example, and supposing that you have a Map<String, Object>, accessing the value indexed by key with

```
Object value = map.get("key");
```

returns null if there's no value in the map associated with the String "key". You can improve such code by wrapping in an optional the value returned by the map. You can either add an ugly if-then-else that adds to code complexity, or you can use the method Optional.ofNullable that we discussed earlier:

```
Optional<Object> value = Optional.ofNullable(map.get("key"));
```

You can use this method every time you want to safely transform a value that could be null into an optional.

11.4.2 Exceptions vs. Optional

Throwing an exception is another common alternative in the Java API to returning a null when a value can't be provided. A typical example is the conversion of String into an int provided by the Integer.parseInt(String) static method. In this case, if the String doesn't contain a parseable integer, this method throws a NumberFormat-Exception. Once again, the net effect is that the code signals an invalid argument if a String doesn't represent an integer, the only difference being that this time, you have to check it with a try/catch block instead of using an if condition to control whether a value isn't null.

You could also model the invalid value caused by nonconvertible Strings with an empty optional, so you prefer that parseInt returns an optional. You can't change the original Java method, but nothing prevents you from implementing a tiny utility method, wrapping it, and returning an optional as desired, as shown in the following listing.

Listing 11.7   Converting a String to an Integer returning an optional

```
public static Optional<Integer> stringToInt(String s) {
    try {
        return Optional.of(Integer.parseInt(s));      ◁——  If the String can
    } catch (NumberFormatException e) {                     be converted to an
        return Optional.empty();   ◁——  Otherwise,          Integer, return an
    }                                    return an           optional containing it.
}                                        empty optional.
```

Our suggestion is to collect several similar methods in a utility class, which you can call OptionalUtility. From then on, you'll always be allowed to convert a String to an Optional<Integer> by using this OptionalUtility.stringToInt method. You can forget that you encapsulated the ugly try/catch logic in it.

11.4.3 *Primitive optionals and why you shouldn't use them*

Note that like streams, optionals also have primitive counterparts—OptionalInt, OptionalLong, and OptionalDouble—so the method in listing 11.7 could have returned OptionalInt instead of Optional<Integer>. In chapter 5, we encouraged the use of primitive streams (especially when they could contain a huge number of elements) for performance reasons, but because an Optional can have at most a single value, that justification doesn't apply here.

We discourage using primitive optionals because they lack the map, flatMap, and filter methods, which (as you saw in section 11.2) are the most useful methods of the Optional class. Moreover, as happens for streams, an optional can't be composed with its primitive counterpart, so if the method of listing 11.7 returned OptionalInt, you couldn't pass it as a method reference to the flatMap method of another optional.

11.4.4 *Putting it all together*

In this section, we demonstrate how the methods of the Optional class that we've presented so far can be used together in a more compelling use case. Suppose that you have some Properties that are passed as configuration arguments to your program. For the purpose of this example and to test the code you'll develop, create some sample Properties as follows:

```
Properties props = new Properties();
props.setProperty("a", "5");
props.setProperty("b", "true");
props.setProperty("c", "-3");
```

Also suppose that your program needs to read a value from these Properties and interpret it as a duration in seconds. Because a duration has to be a positive (>0) number, you'll want a method with the signature

```
public int readDuration(Properties props, String name)
```

so that when the value of a given property is a String representing a positive integer, the method returns that integer, but it returns zero in all other cases. To clarify this requirement, formalize it with a few JUnit assertions:

```
assertEquals(5, readDuration(param, "a"));
assertEquals(0, readDuration(param, "b"));
assertEquals(0, readDuration(param, "c"));
assertEquals(0, readDuration(param, "d"));
```

These assertions reflect the original requirement: the readDuration method returns 5 for the property "a" because the value of this property is a String that's convertible in a positive number, and the method returns 0 for "b" because it isn't a number, returns 0 for "c" because it's a number but is negative, and returns 0 for "d" because a property with that name doesn't exist. Try to implement the method that satisfies this requirement in imperative style, as shown in the next listing.

Listing 11.8   Reading duration from a property imperatively

```
public int readDuration(Properties props, String name) {        Make sure that a
    String value = props.getProperty(name);                     property exists with
    if (value != null) {                                        the required name.
        try {
            int i = Integer.parseInt(value);                    Try to convert the String
            if (i > 0) {                                        property to a number.
                return i;
            }                                                   Check whether the resulting
        } catch (NumberFormatException nfe) { }                 number is positive.
    }
    return 0;              Return 0 if any of
}                         the conditions fails.
```

As you might expect, the resulting implementation is convoluted and not readable, presenting multiple nested conditions coded as both `if` statements and a `try/catch` block. Take a few minutes to figure out in quiz 11.3 how you can achieve the same result by using what you've learned in this chapter.

Quiz 11.3: Reading duration from a property by using an Optional

Using the features of the `Optional` class and the utility method of listing 11.7, try to reimplement the imperative method of listing 11.8 with a single fluent statement.

Answer:

Because the value returned by the `Properties.getProperty(String)` method is a `null` when the required property doesn't exist, it's convenient to turn this value into an optional with the `ofNullable` factory method. Then you can convert the `Optional<String>` to an `Optional<Integer>`, passing to its `flatMap` method a reference to the `OptionalUtility.stringToInt` method developed in listing 11.7. Finally, you can easily filter away the negative number. In this way, if any of these operations returns an empty optional, the method returns the 0 that's passed as the default value to the `orElse` method; otherwise, it returns the positive integer contained in the optional. This description is implemented as follows:

```
public int readDuration(Properties props, String name) {
    return Optional.ofNullable(props.getProperty(name))
                   .flatMap(OptionalUtility::stringToInt)
                   .filter(i -> i > 0)
                   .orElse(0);
}
```

Note the common style in using optionals and streams; both are reminiscent of a database query in which several operations are chained together.

Summary

- null references were historically introduced in programming languages to signal the absence of a value.
- Java 8 introduced the class java.util.Optional<T> to model the presence or absence of a value.
- You can create Optional objects with the static factory methods Optional.empty, Optional.of, and Optional.ofNullable.
- The Optional class supports many methods—such as map, flatMap, and filter—that are conceptually similar to the methods of a stream.
- Using Optional forces you to actively unwrap an optional to deal with the absence of a value; as a result, you protect your code against unintended null pointer exceptions.
- Using Optional can help you design better APIs in which, by reading the signature of a method, users can tell whether to expect an optional value.

New Date and Time API

This chapter covers

- Why we needed a new date and time library, introduced in Java 8
- Representing date and time for both humans and machines
- Defining an amount of time
- Manipulating, formatting, and parsing dates
- Dealing with different time zones and calendars

The Java API includes many useful components to help you build complex applications. Unfortunately, the Java API isn't always perfect. We believe that the majority of experienced Java developers will agree that date and time support before Java 8 was far from ideal. Don't worry, though; Java 8 introduces a brand-new Date and Time API to tackle this issue.

In Java 1.0, the only support for date and time was the `java.util.Date` class. Despite its name, this class doesn't represent a date, but a point in time with millisecond precision. Even worse, the usability of this class is harmed by some nebulous design decisions such as the choice of its offsets: the years start from 1900, whereas the months start at index 0. If you wanted to represent the release date of Java 9, which is 21 September 2017, you'd have to create an instance of `Date` as follows:

```
Date date = new Date(117, 8, 21);
```

Printing this date produces, for the authors:

```
Thu Sep 21 00:00:00 CET 2017
```

Not very intuitive, is it? Moreover, even the `String` returned by the `toString` method of the `Date` class could be quite misleading. It also includes the JVM's default time zone, CET, which is Central Europe Time in our case. Indeed, the `Date` class itself merely inserts the JVM default time zone!

The problems and limitations of the `Date` class were immediately clear when Java 1.0 came out, but it was also clear that the problems couldn't be fixed without breaking its backward compatibility. As a consequence, in Java 1.1 many methods of the `Date` class were deprecated, and the class was replaced by the alternative `java.util.Calendar` class. Unfortunately, `Calendar` has similar problems and design flaws that lead to error-prone code. Months also start at index 0. (At least `Calendar` got rid of the 1900 offset for the year.) Worse, the presence of *both* the `Date` and `Calendar` classes increases confusion among developers. (Which one should you use?) In addition, features such as `DateFormat`, used to format and parse dates or time in a language-independent manner, work only with the `Date` class.

The `DateFormat` comes with its own set of problems. It isn't thread-safe, for example, which means that if two threads try to parse a date by using the same formatter at the same time, you may receive unpredictable results.

Finally, both `Date` and `Calendar` are mutable classes. What does it mean to mutate the 21st of September 2017 to the 25th of October? This design choice can lead you into a maintenance nightmare, as you'll learn in more detail in chapter 18, which is about functional programming.

The consequence is that all these flaws and inconsistencies have encouraged the use of third-party date and time libraries, such as Joda-Time. For these reasons, Oracle decided to provide high-quality date and time support in the native Java API. As a result, Java 8 integrates many of the Joda-Time features in the `java.time` package.

In this chapter, we explore the features introduced by the new Date and Time API. We start with basic use cases such as creating dates and times that are suitable to be used by both humans and machines. Then we gradually explore more-advanced applications of the new Date and Time API, such as manipulating, parsing, and printing date-time objects, and working with different time zones and alternative calendars.

12.1 *LocalDate, LocalTime, LocalDateTime, Instant, Duration, and Period*

We start by exploring how to create simple dates and intervals. The `java.time` package includes many new classes to help you: `LocalDate`, `LocalTime`, `LocalDateTime`, `Instant`, `Duration`, and `Period`.

12.1.1 *Working with LocalDate and LocalTime*

The class LocalDate probably is the first one you'll come across when you start using the new Date and Time API. An instance of this class is an immutable object representing a plain date without the time of day. In particular, it doesn't carry any information about the time zone.

You can create a LocalDate instance by using the of static factory method. A LocalDate instance provides many methods to read its most commonly used values (year, month, day of the week, and so on), as shown in the following listing.

Listing 12.1   Creating a LocalDate and reading its values

```
LocalDate date = LocalDate.of(2017, 9, 21);     ⟵── 2017-09-21
int year = date.getYear();                      ⟵──────── 2017
Month month = date.getMonth();                  ⟵──────── SEPTEMBER
int day = date.getDayOfMonth();                 ⟵──── 21
DayOfWeek dow = date.getDayOfWeek();            ⟵──── THURSDAY
int len = date.lengthOfMonth();                 ⟵──── 30 (days in September)
boolean leap = date.isLeapYear();               ⟵──── false (not a leap year)
```

It's also possible to obtain the current date from the system clock by using the now factory method:

```
LocalDate today = LocalDate.now();
```

All the other date-time classes that we investigate in the remaining part of this chapter provide a similar factory method. You can also access the same information by passing a TemporalField to the get method. The TemporalField is an interface defining how to access the value of a specific field of a temporal object. The ChronoField enumeration implements this interface, so you can conveniently use an element of that enumeration with the get method, as shown in the next listing.

Listing 12.2   Reading LocalDate values by using a TemporalField

```
int year = date.get(ChronoField.YEAR);
int month = date.get(ChronoField.MONTH_OF_YEAR);
int day = date.get(ChronoField.DAY_OF_MONTH);
```

You could use the built-in getYear(), getMonthValue(), and getDayOfMonth() methods in a more-readable form to access the information as follows:

```
int year = date.getYear();
int month = date.getMonthValue();
int day = date.getDayOfMonth();
```

Similarly, the time of day, such as 13:45:20, is represented by the LocalTime class. You can create instances of LocalTime by using two overloaded static factory methods named of. The first one accepts an hour and a minute, and the second one also accepts a second. Like the LocalDate class, the LocalTime class provides some getter methods to access its values, as shown in the following listing.

Listing 12.3   Creating a LocalTime and reading its values

```
LocalTime time = LocalTime.of(13, 45, 20);    ◁──── 13:45:20
int hour = time.getHour();        ◁──── 13
int minute = time.getMinute();        ◁──── 45
int second = time.getSecond();    ◁──── 20
```

You can create both LocalDate and LocalTime by parsing a String representing them. To achieve this task, use their parse static methods:

```
LocalDate date = LocalDate.parse("2017-09-21");
LocalTime time = LocalTime.parse("13:45:20");
```

It's possible to pass a DateTimeFormatter to the parse method. An instance of this class specifies how to format a date and/or a time object. It's intended to be a replacement for the old java.util.DateFormat that we mentioned earlier. We show in more detail how you can use a DateTimeFormatter in section 12.2.2. Also note that both these parse methods throw a DateTimeParseException, which extends Runtime-Exception in case the String argument can't be parsed as a valid LocalDate or LocalTime.

12.1.2 *Combining a date and a time*

The composite class called LocalDateTime pairs a LocalDate and a LocalTime. It represents both a date and a time without a time zone and can be created directly or by combining a date and time, as shown in the following listing.

Listing 12.4   Creating a LocalDateTime directly or by combining a date and a time

```
// 2017-09-21T13:45:20
LocalDateTime dt1 = LocalDateTime.of(2017, Month.SEPTEMBER, 21, 13, 45, 20);
LocalDateTime dt2 = LocalDateTime.of(date, time);
LocalDateTime dt3 = date.atTime(13, 45, 20);
LocalDateTime dt4 = date.atTime(time);
LocalDateTime dt5 = time.atDate(date);
```

Note that it's possible to create a LocalDateTime by passing a time to a LocalDate or a date to a LocalTime, using their atTime or atDate methods, respectively. You can also extract the LocalDate or LocalTime component from a LocalDateTime by using the toLocalDate and toLocalTime methods:

```
LocalDate date1 = dt1.toLocalDate();    ◁──── 2017-09-21
LocalTime time1 = dt1.toLocalTime();    ◁──── 13:45:20
```

12.1.3 Instant: a date and time for machines

As humans, we're used to thinking of dates and time in terms of weeks, days, hours, and minutes. Nonetheless, this representation isn't easy for a computer to deal with. From a machine point of view, the most natural format to model time is a single large number representing a point on a continuous timeline. This approach is used by the new java.time.Instant class, which represents the number of seconds passed since the Unix epoch time, set by convention to midnight of January 1, 1970 UTC.

You can create an instance of this class by passing the number of seconds to its ofEpochSecond static factory method. In addition, the Instant class supports nanosecond precision. A supplementary overloaded version of the ofEpochSecond static factory method accepts a second argument that's a nanosecond adjustment to the passed number of seconds. This overloaded version adjusts the nanosecond argument, ensuring that the stored nanosecond fraction is between 0 and 999,999,999. As a result, the following invocations of the ofEpochSecond factory method return exactly the same Instant:

```
Instant.ofEpochSecond(3);
Instant.ofEpochSecond(3, 0);
Instant.ofEpochSecond(2, 1_000_000_000);
Instant.ofEpochSecond(4, -1_000_000_000);
```

One billion nanoseconds (1 second) after 2 seconds

One billion nanoseconds (1 second) before 4 seconds

As you've already seen for LocalDate and the other human-readable date-time classes, the Instant class supports another static factory method named now, which allows you to capture a timestamp of the current moment. It's important to reinforce that an Instant is intended for use only by a machine. It consists of a number of seconds and nanoseconds. As a consequence, it doesn't provide any ability to handle units of time that are meaningful to humans. A statement like

```
int day = Instant.now().get(ChronoField.DAY_OF_MONTH);
```

throws an exception like this:

```
java.time.temporal.UnsupportedTemporalTypeException: Unsupported field:
    DayOfMonth
```

But you can work with Instants by using the Duration and Period classes, which we look at next.

12.1.4 Defining a Duration or a Period

All the classes you've seen so far implement the Temporal interface, which defines how to read and manipulate the values of an object modeling a generic point in time. We've shown you a few ways to create different Temporal instances. The next natural step is creating a duration between two temporal objects. The between static factory method of the `Duration` class serves exactly this purpose. You can create a duration between two `LocalTimes`, two `LocalDateTimes`, or two `Instants` as follows:

```
Duration d1 = Duration.between(time1, time2);
Duration d1 = Duration.between(dateTime1, dateTime2);
Duration d2 = Duration.between(instant1, instant2);
```

Because `LocalDateTime` and `Instant` are made for different purposes, one to be used by humans and the other by machines, you're not allowed to mix them. If you try to create a duration between them, you'll only obtain a `DateTimeException`. Moreover, because the `Duration` class is used to represent an amount of time measured in seconds and eventually nanoseconds, you can't pass a `LocalDate` to the `between` method.

When you need to model an amount of time in terms of years, months, and days, you can use the `Period` class. You can find out the difference between two `LocalDates` with the `between` factory method of that class:

```
Period tenDays = Period.between(LocalDate.of(2017, 9, 11),
                                LocalDate.of(2017, 9, 21));
```

Finally, the `Duration` and `Period` classes have other convenient factory methods to create instances of them directly, without defining them as the difference between two temporal objects, as shown in the following listing.

> **Listing 12.5   Creating `Durations` and `Periods`**

```
Duration threeMinutes = Duration.ofMinutes(3);
Duration threeMinutes = Duration.of(3, ChronoUnit.MINUTES);
Period tenDays = Period.ofDays(10);
Period threeWeeks = Period.ofWeeks(3);
Period twoYearsSixMonthsOneDay = Period.of(2, 6, 1);
```

The `Duration` and `Period` classes share many similar methods, which table 12.1 lists.

Table 12.1   The common methods of date-time classes representing an interval

Method	Static	Description
between	Yes	Creates an interval between two points in time
from	Yes	Creates an interval from a temporal unit
of	Yes	Creates an instance of this interval from its constituent parts
parse	Yes	Creates an instance of this interval from a `String`
addTo	No	Creates a copy of this interval, adding to it the specified temporal object
get	No	Reads part of the state of this interval
isNegative	No	Checks whether this interval is negative, excluding zero
isZero	No	Checks whether this interval is zero-length

Table 12.1 The common methods of date-time classes representing an interval *(continued)*

Method	Static	Description
minus	No	Creates a copy of this interval with an amount of time subtracted
multipliedBy	No	Creates a copy of this interval multiplied by the given scalar
negated	No	Creates a copy of this interval with the length negated
plus	No	Creates a copy of this interval with an amount of time added
subtractFrom	No	Subtracts this interval from the specified temporal object

All the classes we've investigated so far are immutable, which is a great design choice to allow a more functional programming style, ensure thread safety, and preserve the consistency of the domain model. Nevertheless, the new Date and Time API offers some handy methods for creating modified versions of those objects. You may want to add three days to an existing LocalDate instance, for example, and we explore how to do this in the next section. In addition, we explore how to create a date-time formatter from a given pattern, such as dd/MM/yyyy, or even programmatically, as well as how to use this formatter for both parsing and printing a date.

12.2 Manipulating, parsing, and formatting dates

The most immediate and easiest way to create a modified version of an existing LocalDate is to change one of its attributes, using one of its withAttribute methods. Note that all the methods return a new object with the modified attribute, as shown in listing 12.6; they don't mutate the existing object!

Listing 12.6   Manipulating the attributes of a LocalDate in an absolute way

```
LocalDate date1 = LocalDate.of(2017, 9, 21);       ⟵── 2017-09-21
LocalDate date2 = date1.withYear(2011);            ⟵──── 2011-09-21
LocalDate date3 = date2.withDayOfMonth(25);             ⟵──── 2011-09-25
LocalDate date4 = date3.with(ChronoField.MONTH_OF_YEAR, 2);   ⟵── 2011-02-25
```

You can do the same thing with the more generic with method, taking a Temporal-Field as the first argument, as in the last statement of listing 12.6. This last with method is the dual of the get method used in listing 12.2. Both of these methods are declared in the Temporal interface implemented by all the classes, such as LocalDate, LocalTime, LocalDateTime, and Instant, of the Date and Time API. More precisely, the get and with methods let you respectively read and modify[1] fields of a Temporal object. They throw an UnsupportedTemporalTypeException if the requested field

---

[1] Remember that such 'with' methods don't modify the existing Temporal object but create a copy with the specific field updated. This process is called a *functional update* (see chapter 19).

isn't supported by the specific `Temporal`, such as a `ChronoField.MONTH_OF_YEAR` on an `Instant` or a `ChronoField.NANO_OF_SECOND` on a `LocalDate`.

It's even possible to manipulate a `LocalDate` in a declarative manner. You can add or subtract a given amount of time, for example, as shown in listing 12.7.

Listing 12.7 Manipulating the attributes of a `LocalDate` in a relative way

```
LocalDate date1 = LocalDate.of(2017, 9, 21);          ◁─── 2017-09-21
LocalDate date2 = date1.plusWeeks(1);                 ◁─── 2017-09-28
LocalDate date3 = date2.minusYears(6);                ◁─── 2011-09-28
LocalDate date4 = date3.plus(6, ChronoUnit.MONTHS);   ◁─── 2012-03-28
```

Similarly to what we've explained about the `with` and `get` methods, the generic `plus` method used in the last statement of listing 12.7, together with the analogous `minus` method, is declared in the `Temporal` interface. These methods allow you to move a `Temporal` back or forward a given amount of time, defined by a number plus a `TemporalUnit`, where the `ChronoUnit` enumeration offers a convenient implementation of the `TemporalUnit` interface.

As you may have anticipated, all the date-time classes representing a point in time such as `LocalDate`, `LocalTime`, `LocalDateTime`, and `Instant` have many methods in common. Table 12.2 summarizes these methods.

Table 12.2 The common methods of date-time classes representing a point in time

Method	Static	Description
from	Yes	Creates an instance of this class from the passed temporal object
now	Yes	Creates a temporal object from the system clock
of	Yes	Creates an instance of this temporal object from its constituent parts
parse	Yes	Creates an instance of this temporal object from a `String`
atOffset	No	Combines this temporal object with a zone offset
atZone	No	Combines this temporal object with a time zone
format	No	Converts this temporal object to a `String` by using the specified formatter (not available for `Instant`)
get	No	Reads part of the state of this temporal object
minus	No	Creates a copy of this temporal object with an amount of time subtracted
plus	No	Creates a copy of this temporal object with an amount of time added
with	No	Creates a copy of this temporal object with part of the state changed

Check what you've learned up to now about manipulating dates with quiz 12.1.

> ### Quiz 12.1: Manipulating a `LocalDate`
> What will the value of the date variable be after the following manipulations?
>
> ```
> LocalDate date = LocalDate.of(2014, 3, 18);
> date = date.with(ChronoField.MONTH_OF_YEAR, 9);
> date = date.plusYears(2).minusDays(10);
> date.withYear(2011);
> ```
>
> #### Answer:
>
> ```
> 2016-09-08
> ```
>
> As you've seen, you can manipulate the date both in an absolute way and in a relative way. You can also concatenate more manipulations in a single statement, because every change creates a new `LocalDate` object, and the subsequent invocation manipulates the object created by the former one. Finally, the last statement in this code snippet has no observable effect because as usual, it creates a new `LocalDate` instance, but we're not assigning this new value to any variable.

12.2.1 Working with TemporalAdjusters

All the date manipulations you've seen so far are relatively straightforward. Sometimes, though, you need to perform advanced operations, such as adjusting a date to the next Sunday, the next working day, or the last day of the month. In such cases, you can pass to an overloaded version of the `with` method a `TemporalAdjuster` that provides a more customizable way to define the manipulation needed to operate on a specific date. The Date and Time API already provides many predefined `Temporal-Adjusters` for the most common use cases. You can access them by using the static factory methods contained in the `TemporalAdjusters` class, as shown in listing 12.8.

Listing 12.8   Using the predefined `TemporalAdjusters`

```
import static java.time.temporal.TemporalAdjusters.*;
LocalDate date1 = LocalDate.of(2014, 3, 18);                      ⟵——— 2014-03-18
LocalDate date2 = date1.with(nextOrSame(DayOfWeek.SUNDAY));       ⟵——— 2014-03-23
LocalDate date3 = date2.with(lastDayOfMonth());                   ⟵——— 2014-03-31
```

Table 12.3 lists the `TemporalAdjusters` that you can create with these factory methods.

Table 12.3   The factory methods of the `TemporalAdjusters` class

Method	Description
`dayOfWeekInMonth`	Creates a new date in the same month with the ordinal day of week. (Negative numbers count backward from the end of the month.)
`firstDayOfMonth`	Creates a new date set to the first day of the current month.

Table 12.3   The factory methods of the `TemporalAdjusters` class *(continued)*

Method	Description
`firstDayOfNextMonth`	Creates a new date set to the first day of the next month.
`firstDayOfNextYear`	Creates a new date set to the first day of the next year.
`firstDayOfYear`	Creates a new date set to the first day of the current year.
`firstInMonth`	Creates a new date in the same month with the first matching day of the week.
`lastDayOfMonth`	Creates a new date set to the last day of the current month.
`lastDayOfNextMonth`	Creates a new date set to the last day of the next month.
`lastDayOfNextYear`	Creates a new date set to the last day of the next year.
`lastDayOfYear`	Creates a new date set to the last day of the current year.
`lastInMonth`	Creates a new date in the same month with the last matching day of the week.
`next` `previous`	Creates a new date set to the first occurrence of the specified day of week after/before the date being adjusted.
`nextOrSame` `previousOrSame`	Creates a new date set to the first occurrence of the specified day of week after/before the date being adjusted unless it's already on that day, in which case the same object is returned.

As you can see, `TemporalAdjusters` allow you to perform more-complex date manipulations that still read like the problem statement. Moreover, it's relatively simple to create your own custom `TemporalAdjuster` implementation if you can't find a predefined `TemporalAdjuster` that fits your needs. In fact, the `TemporalAdjuster` interface declares only a single method (which makes it a functional interface), defined as shown in the following listing.

Listing 12.9   The `TemporalAdjuster` interface

```
@FunctionalInterface
public interface TemporalAdjuster {
    Temporal adjustInto(Temporal temporal);
}
```

This example means that an implementation of the `TemporalAdjuster` interface defines how to convert a `Temporal` object to another `Temporal`. You can think of a `TemporalAdjuster` as being like a `UnaryOperator<Temporal>`. Take a few minutes to practice what you've learned so far and implement your own `TemporalAdjuster` in quiz 12.2.

Quiz 12.2: Implementing a custom `TemporalAdjuster`

Develop a class named `NextWorkingDay`, implementing the `TemporalAdjuster` interface that moves a date forward by one day but skips Saturdays and Sundays. Using

```
date = date.with(new NextWorkingDay());
```

should move the date to the next day, if this day is between Monday and Friday, but to the next Monday if it's a Saturday or a Sunday.

Answer:

You can implement the `NextWorkingDay` adjuster as follows:

```
public class NextWorkingDay implements TemporalAdjuster {
    @Override
    public Temporal adjustInto(Temporal temporal) {                    Read the
        DayOfWeek dow =                                                current day.
                DayOfWeek.of(temporal.get(ChronoField.DAY_OF_WEEK));
        int dayToAdd = 1;
        if (dow == DayOfWeek.FRIDAY) dayToAdd = 3;                     But add
        else if (dow == DayOfWeek.SATURDAY) dayToAdd = 2;             three days
        return temporal.plus(dayToAdd, ChronoUnit.DAYS);             if today is
    }                                                                 a Friday.
}
```

Normally add one day. | *Return the modified date adding the right number of days.* | *Add two days if today is a Saturday.*

This `TemporalAdjuster` normally moves a date forward one day, except when today is a Friday or Saturday, in which case it advances the dates by three or two days, respectively. Note that because a `TemporalAdjuster` is a functional interface, you could pass the behavior of this adjuster in a lambda expression:

```
date = date.with(temporal -> {
    DayOfWeek dow =
            DayOfWeek.of(temporal.get(ChronoField.DAY_OF_WEEK));
    int dayToAdd = 1;
    if (dow == DayOfWeek.FRIDAY) dayToAdd = 3;
    else if (dow == DayOfWeek.SATURDAY) dayToAdd = 2;
    return temporal.plus(dayToAdd, ChronoUnit.DAYS);
});
```

You're likely to want to apply this manipulation to a date in several points of your code, and for this reason, we suggest encapsulating its logic in a proper class, as we did here. Do the same for all the manipulations you use frequently. You'll end up with a small library of adjusters that you and your team can easily reuse in your codebase.

If you want to define the `TemporalAdjuster` with a lambda expression, it's preferable to do so by using the `ofDateAdjuster` static factory of the `TemporalAdjusters` class, which accepts a `UnaryOperator<LocalDate>` as follows:

(continued)

```
TemporalAdjuster nextWorkingDay = TemporalAdjusters.ofDateAdjuster(
    temporal -> {
        DayOfWeek dow =
                DayOfWeek.of(temporal.get(ChronoField.DAY_OF_WEEK));
        int dayToAdd = 1;
        if (dow == DayOfWeek.FRIDAY) dayToAdd = 3;
        else if (dow == DayOfWeek.SATURDAY) dayToAdd = 2;
        return temporal.plus(dayToAdd, ChronoUnit.DAYS);
    });
date = date.with(nextWorkingDay);
```

Another common operation that you may want to perform on your date and time objects is printing them in different formats specific to your business domain. Similarly, you may want to convert Strings representing dates in those formats to actual date objects. In the next section, we demonstrate the mechanisms provided by the new Date and Time API to accomplish these tasks.

12.2.2   *Printing and parsing date-time objects*

Formatting and parsing are other relevant features for working with dates and times. The new java.time.format package is devoted to these purposes. The most important class of this package is DateTimeFormatter. The easiest way to create a formatter is through its static factory methods and constants. The constants such as BASIC_ISO_DATE and ISO_LOCAL_DATE are predefined instances of the DateTimeFormatter class. You can use all DateTimeFormatters to create a String representing a given date or time in a specific format. Here, for example, we produce a String by using two different formatters:

```
LocalDate date = LocalDate.of(2014, 3, 18);
String s1 = date.format(DateTimeFormatter.BASIC_ISO_DATE);    ⟵── 20140318
String s2 = date.format(DateTimeFormatter.ISO_LOCAL_DATE);    ⟵── 2014-03-18
```

You can also parse a String representing a date or a time in that format to re-create the date object itself. You can achieve this task by using the parse factory method provided by all the classes of the Date and Time API representing a point in time or an interval:

```
LocalDate date1 = LocalDate.parse("20140318",
                              DateTimeFormatter.BASIC_ISO_DATE);
LocalDate date2 = LocalDate.parse("2014-03-18",
                              DateTimeFormatter.ISO_LOCAL_DATE);
```

In comparison with the old java.util.DateFormat class, all the DateTimeFormatter instances are thread-safe. Therefore, you can create singleton formatters like the ones defined by the DateTimeFormatter constants and share them among multiple threads.

The next listing shows how the `DateTimeFormatter` class also supports a static factory method that lets you create a formatter from a specific pattern.

Listing 12.10 Creating a `DateTimeFormatter` from a pattern

```
DateTimeFormatter formatter = DateTimeFormatter.ofPattern("dd/MM/yyyy");
LocalDate date1 = LocalDate.of(2014, 3, 18);
String formattedDate = date1.format(formatter);
LocalDate date2 = LocalDate.parse(formattedDate, formatter);
```

Here, the `LocalDate`'s format method produces a `String` representing the date with the requested pattern. Next, the static parse method re-creates the same date by parsing the generated `String`, using the same formatter. The `ofPattern` method also has an overloaded version that allows you to create a formatter for a given `Locale`, as shown in the following listing.

Listing 12.11 Creating a localized `DateTimeFormatter`

```
DateTimeFormatter italianFormatter =
            DateTimeFormatter.ofPattern("d. MMMM yyyy", Locale.ITALIAN);
LocalDate date1 = LocalDate.of(2014, 3, 18);
String formattedDate = date.format(italianFormatter); // 18. marzo 2014
LocalDate date2 = LocalDate.parse(formattedDate, italianFormatter);
```

Finally, in case you need even more control, the `DateTimeFormatterBuilder` class lets you define complex formatters step by step by using meaningful methods. In addition, it provides you the ability to have case-insensitive parsing, lenient parsing (allowing the parser to use heuristics to interpret inputs that don't precisely match the specified format), padding, and optional sections of the formatter. You can programmatically build the same `italianFormatter` we used in listing 12.11 through the `DateTime-FormatterBuilder`, for example, as shown in the following listing.

Listing 12.12 Building a `DateTimeFormatter`

```
DateTimeFormatter italianFormatter = new DateTimeFormatterBuilder()
        .appendText(ChronoField.DAY_OF_MONTH)
        .appendLiteral(". ")
        .appendText(ChronoField.MONTH_OF_YEAR)
        .appendLiteral(" ")
        .appendText(ChronoField.YEAR)
        .parseCaseInsensitive()
        .toFormatter(Locale.ITALIAN);
```

So far, you've learned how to create, manipulate, format, and parse both points in time and intervals, but you haven't seen how to deal with subtleties involving dates and time. You may need to deal with different time zones or alternative calendar systems. In the next sections, we explore these topics by using the new Date and Time API.

12.3   *Working with different time zones and calendars*

None of the classes you've seen so far contain any information about time zones. Dealing with time zones is another important issue that's been vastly simplified by the new Date and Time API. The new `java.time.ZoneId` class is the replacement for the old `java.util.TimeZone` class. It aims to better shield you from the complexities related to time zones, such as dealing with Daylight Saving Time (DST). Like the other classes of the Date and Time API, it's immutable.

12.3.1   *Using time zones*

A *time zone* is a set of rules corresponding to a region in which the standard time is the same. About 40 time zones are held in instances of the `ZoneRules` class. You can call `getRules()` on a `ZoneId` to obtain the rules for that time zone. A specific `ZoneId` is identified by a region ID, as in this example:

```
ZoneId romeZone = ZoneId.of("Europe/Rome");
```

All the region IDs are in the format `"{area}/{city}"`, and the set of available locations is the one supplied by the Internet Assigned Numbers Authority (IANA) Time Zone Database (see https://www.iana.org/time-zones). You can also convert an old `TimeZone` object to a `ZoneId` by using the new method `toZoneId`:

```
ZoneId zoneId = TimeZone.getDefault().toZoneId();
```

When you have a `ZoneId` object, you can combine it with a `LocalDate`, a `LocalDate-Time`, or an `Instant` to transform it into `ZonedDateTime` instances, which represent points in time relative to the specified time zone, as shown in the following listing.

> **Listing 12.13   Applying a time zone to a point in time**
>
> ```
> LocalDate date = LocalDate.of(2014, Month.MARCH, 18);
> ZonedDateTime zdt1 = date.atStartOfDay(romeZone);
> LocalDateTime dateTime = LocalDateTime.of(2014, Month.MARCH, 18, 13, 45);
> ZonedDateTime zdt2 = dateTime.atZone(romeZone);
> Instant instant = Instant.now();
> ZonedDateTime zdt3 = instant.atZone(romeZone);
> ```

Figure 12.1 illustrates the components of a `ZonedDateTime` to help you understand the differences among `LocalDate`, `LocalTime`, `LocalDateTime`, and `ZoneId`.

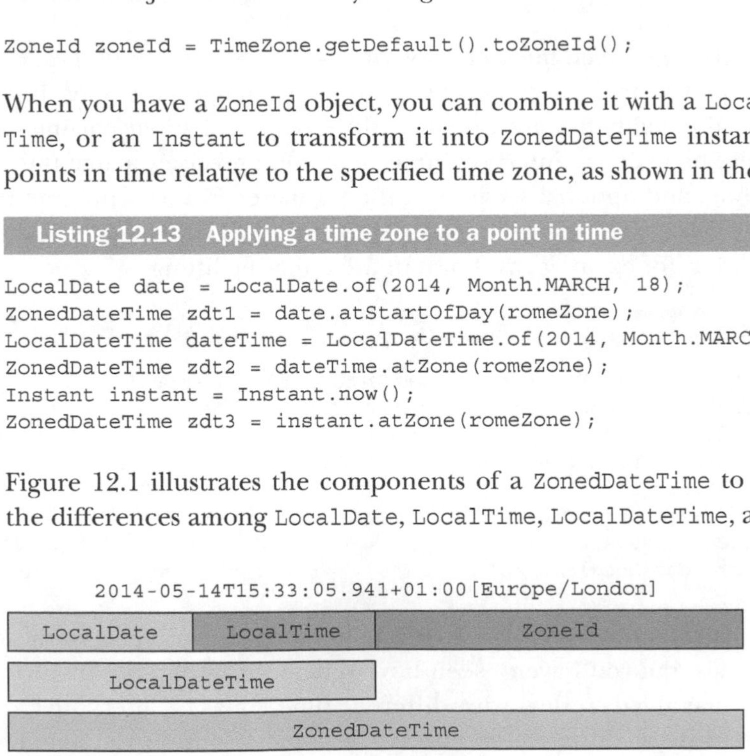

Figure 12.1   Making sense of a `ZonedDateTime`

You can also convert a `LocalDateTime` to an `Instant` by using a `ZoneId`:

```
LocalDateTime dateTime = LocalDateTime.of(2014, Month.MARCH, 18, 13, 45);
Instant instantFromDateTime = dateTime.toInstant(romeZone);
```

Or you can do it the other way around:

```
Instant instant = Instant.now();
LocalDateTime timeFromInstant = LocalDateTime.ofInstant(instant, romeZone);
```

Note that working with `Instant` is quite useful because you often have to work with legacy code that deals with the `Date` class. There, two methods were added to help interoperate between the deprecated API and the new Date and Time API: `toInstant()` and the static method `fromInstant()`.

12.3.2 *Fixed offset from UTC/Greenwich*

Another common way to express a time zone is to use a fixed offset from UTC/Greenwich. You can use this notation to say, "New York is five hours behind London," for example. In cases like this one, you can use the `ZoneOffset` class, a subclass of `ZoneId` that represents the difference between a time and the zero meridian of Greenwich, London, as follows:

```
ZoneOffset newYorkOffset = ZoneOffset.of("-05:00");
```

The -05:00 offset indeed corresponds to U.S. Eastern Standard Time. Be aware, however, that a `ZoneOffset` defined this way doesn't have any Daylight Saving Time management, and for this reason, it isn't suggested in the majority of cases. Because a `ZoneOffset` is also a `ZoneId`, you can use it as shown in listing 12.13 earlier in this chapter. You can also create an `OffsetDateTime`, which represents a date-time with an offset from UTC/Greenwich in the ISO-8601 calendar system:

```
LocalDateTime dateTime = LocalDateTime.of(2014, Month.MARCH, 18, 13, 45);
OffsetDateTime dateTimeInNewYork = OffsetDateTime.of(date, newYorkOffset);
```

Another advanced feature supported by the new Date and Time API is support for non-ISO calendaring systems.

12.3.3 *Using alternative calendar systems*

The ISO-8601 calendar system is the de facto world civil calendar system. But four additional calendar systems are provided in Java 8. Each of these calendar systems has a dedicated date class: `ThaiBuddhistDate`, `MinguoDate`, `JapaneseDate`, and `Hijrah-Date`. All these classes, together with `LocalDate`, implement the `ChronoLocalDate` interface, which is intended to model a date in an arbitrary chronology. You can create an instance of one of these classes out of a `LocalDate`. More generally, you can create any other `Temporal` instance by using their from static factory methods as follows:

```
LocalDate date = LocalDate.of(2014, Month.MARCH, 18);
JapaneseDate japaneseDate = JapaneseDate.from(date);
```

Alternatively, you can explicitly create a calendar system for a specific `Locale` and create an instance of a date for that `Locale`. In the new Date and Time API, the `Chronology` interface models a calendar system, and you can obtain an instance of it by using its `ofLocale` static factory method:

```
Chronology japaneseChronology = Chronology.ofLocale(Locale.JAPAN);
ChronoLocalDate now = japaneseChronology.dateNow();
```

The designers of the Date and Time API advise using `LocalDate` instead of `Chrono-LocalDate` for most cases, because a developer could make assumptions in his code that unfortunately aren't true in a multicalendar system. Such assumptions might include believing that the value of a day or month will never be higher than 31, that a year contains 12 months, or even that a year has a fixed number of months. For these reasons, we recommend using `LocalDate` throughout your application, including all storage, manipulation, and interpretation of business rules, whereas you should employ `ChronoLocalDate` only when you need to localize the input or output of your program.

ISLAMIC CALENDAR

Of the new calendars added to Java 8, the `HijrahDate` (Islamic calendar) seems to be the most complex because it can have variants. The Hijrah calendar system is based on lunar months. There are a variety of methods to determine a new month, such as a new moon that could be visible anywhere in the world or that must be visible first in Saudi Arabia. The `withVariant` method is used to choose the desired variant. Java 8 includes the Umm Al-Qura variant for `HijrahDate` as standard.

The following code illustrates an example of displaying the start and end dates of Ramadan for the current Islamic year in ISO date:

> **Get the current Hijrah date; then change it to have the first day of Ramadan, which is the ninth month.**

```
HijrahDate ramadanDate =
    HijrahDate.now().with(ChronoField.DAY_OF_MONTH, 1)
              .with(ChronoField.MONTH_OF_YEAR, 9);    ⟵
System.out.println("Ramadan starts on " +
                IsoChronology.INSTANCE.date(ramadanDate) +    ⟵
                " and ends on " +
                IsoChronology.INSTANCE.date(
                    ramadanDate.with(
                        TemporalAdjusters.lastDayOfMonth()))));
```

Ramadan 1438 started on 2017-05-26 and ended on 2017-06-24.

> **IsoChronology.INSTANCE is a static instance of the IsoChronology class.**

Summary

- The old `java.util.Date` class and all other classes used to model dates and times in Java before Java 8 have many inconsistencies and design flaws, including mutability and some poorly chosen offsets, defaults, and naming.
- All the date-time objects of the new Date and Time API are immutable.
- This new API provides two different time representations to manage the different needs of humans and machines when operating on it.
- You can manipulate date and time objects in both an absolute and relative manner, and the result of these manipulations is always a new instance, leaving the original one unchanged.
- `TemporalAdjusters` allow you to manipulate a date in a more complex way than changing one of its values, and you can define and use your own custom date transformations.
- You can define a formatter to print and parse date-time objects in a specific format. These formatters can be created from a pattern or programmatically, and they're all thread-safe.
- You can represent a time zone, relative to a specific region/location and as a fixed offset from UTC/Greenwich, and apply it to a date-time object to localize it.
- You can use calendar systems different from the ISO-8601 standard system.

Default methods

Traditionally, a Java interface groups related methods together into a contract. Any (nonabstract) class that implements an interface *must* provide an implementation for each method defined by the interface or inherit the implementation from a superclass. But this requirement causes a problem when library designers need to update an interface to add a new method. Indeed, existing concrete classes (which may not be under the interface designers' control) need to be modified to reflect the new interface contract. This situation is particularly problematic because the Java 8 API introduces many new methods on existing interfaces, such as the sort method on the List interface that you used in previous chapters. Imagine all the angry maintainers of alternative collection frameworks such as Guava and Apache Commons who now need to modify all the classes implementing the List interface to provide an implementation for the sort method too!

But don't worry. Java 8 introduced a new mechanism to tackle this problem. It may sound surprising, but since Java 8 interfaces can declare methods with implementation code in two ways. First, Java 8 allowed *static methods* inside interfaces. Second, Java 8 introduced a new feature called *default methods* that allows you to provide a default implementation for methods in an interface. In other words, interfaces can now provide concrete implementation for methods. As a result, existing classes implementing an interface automatically inherit the default implementations if they don't provide one explicitly, which allows you to evolve interfaces nonintrusively. You've been using several default methods all along. Two examples you've seen are sort in the List interface and stream in the Collection interface.

The sort method in the List interface, which you saw in chapter 1, is new to Java 8 and is defined as follows:

```
default void sort(Comparator<? super E> c){
    Collections.sort(this, c);
}
```

Note the new default modifier before the return type. This modifier is how you can tell that a method is a default method. Here, the sort method calls the Collections .sort method to perform the sorting. Thanks to this new method, you can sort a list by calling the method directly:

```
List<Integer> numbers = Arrays.asList(3, 5, 1, 2, 6);      sort is a default method
numbers.sort(Comparator.naturalOrder());              ⟵——  in the List interface.
```

Something else is new in this code. Notice that you call the Comparator.naturalOrder method. This new static method in the Comparator interface returns a Comparator object to sort the elements in natural order (the standard alphanumerical sort). The stream method in Collection you saw in chapter 4 looks like this:

```
default Stream<E> stream() {
    return StreamSupport.stream(spliterator(), false);
}
```

Here, the stream method, which you used extensively in previous chapters to process collections, calls the StreamSupport.stream method to return a stream. Notice how the body of the stream method is calling the method spliterator, which is also a default method of the Collection interface.

Wow! Are interfaces like abstract classes now? Yes and no; there are fundamental differences, which we explain in this chapter. More important, why should you care about default methods? The main users of default methods are library designers. As we explain later, default methods were introduced to evolve libraries such as the Java API in a compatible way, as illustrated in figure 13.1.

In a nutshell, adding a method to an interface is the source of many problems; existing classes implementing the interface need to be changed to provide an implementation for the method. If you're in control of the interface and all its implementations, the

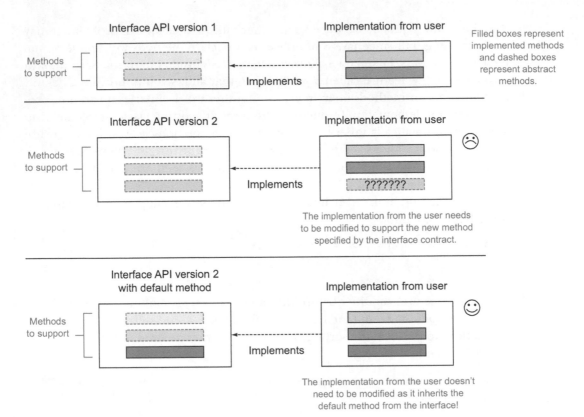

Figure 13.1 Adding a method to an interface

situation isn't too bad. But this is often not the case—and it provides the motivation for default methods, which let classes inherit a default implementation from an interface automatically.

   If you're a library designer, this chapter is important because default methods provide a means of evolving interfaces without modifying existing implementations. Also, as we explain later in the chapter, default methods can help structure your programs by providing a flexible mechanism for multiple inheritance of behavior; a class can inherit default methods from several interfaces. Therefore, you may still be interested in finding out about default methods even if you're not a library designer.

Static methods and interfaces

A common pattern in Java is to define both an interface and a utility companion class defining many static methods for working with instances of the interface. Collections is a companion class to deal with Collection objects, for example. Now that static methods can exist inside interfaces, such utility classes in your code can go away, and their static methods can be moved inside an interface. These companion classes remain in the Java API to preserve backward compatibility.

The chapter is structured as follows. First, we walk you through a use case of evolving an API and the problems that can arise. Then we explain what default methods are and discuss how you can use them to tackle the problems in the use case. Next, we show how you can create your own default methods to achieve a form of multiple inheritance in Java. We conclude with some more technical information about how the Java compiler resolves possible ambiguities when a class inherits several default methods with the same signature.

13.1 Evolving APIs

To understand why it's difficult to evolve an API when it's been published, suppose for the purpose of this section that you're the designer of a popular Java drawing library. Your library contains a `Resizable` interface that defines many methods that a simple resizable shape must support: `setHeight`, `setWidth`, `getHeight`, `getWidth`, and `set-AbsoluteSize`. In addition, you provide several out-of-the-box implementations for it, such as `Square` and `Rectangle`. Because your library is so popular, you have some users who have created their own interesting implementations, such as `Ellipse`, using your `Resizable` interface.

A few months after releasing your API, you realize that `Resizable` is missing some features. It would be nice, for example, if the interface had a `setRelativeSize` method that takes as argument a growth factor to resize a shape. You might add the `setRelativeSize` method to `Resizable` and update your implementations of `Square` and `Rectangle`. But not so fast! What about all your users who created their own implementations of the `Resizable` interface? Unfortunately, you don't have access to and can't change their classes that implement `Resizable`. This problem is the same one that Java library designers face when they need to evolve the Java API. In the next section, we look in detail at an example that shows the consequences of modifying an interface that's already been published.

13.1.1 API version 1

The first version of your `Resizable` interface has the following methods:

```
public interface Resizable extends Drawable{
    int getWidth();
    int getHeight();
    void setWidth(int width);
    void setHeight(int height);
    void setAbsoluteSize(int width, int height);
}
```

USER IMPLEMENTATION

One of your most loyal users decides to create his own implementation of `Resizable` called `Ellipse`:

```
public class Ellipse implements Resizable {
    ...
}
```

He's created a game that processes different types of Resizable shapes (including his own Ellipse):

```
public class Game{                                              A list of shapes
    public static void main(String…args){                    that are resizable
        List<Resizable> resizableShapes =
            Arrays.asList(new Square(), new Rectangle(), new Ellipse());
        Utils.paint(resizableShapes);
    }
}
public class Utils{
    public static void paint(List<Resizable> l){
        l.forEach(r -> {
                        r.setAbsoluteSize(42, 42);      Calling the setAbsoluteSize
                        r.draw();                       method on each shape
                    });
    }
}
```

13.1.2 *API version 2*

After your library has been in use for a few months, you receive many requests to update your implementations of Resizable: Square, Rectangle, and so on to support the setRelativeSize method. You come up with version 2 of your API, as shown here and illustrated in figure 13.2:

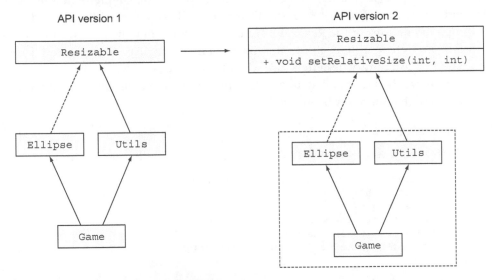

Figure 13.2 Evolving an API by adding a method to Resizable. Recompiling the application produces errors because it depends on the Resizable interface.

```
public interface Resizable {
    int getWidth();
    int getHeight();
    void setWidth(int width);
```

```
    void setHeight(int height);
    void setAbsoluteSize(int width, int height);
    void setRelativeSize(int wFactor, int hFactor);    ◁─┐  Adding a new method
}                                                            for API version 2
```

PROBLEMS FOR YOUR USERS

This update of Resizable creates problems. First, the interface now demands an implementation of setRelativeSize, but the Ellipse implementation that your user created doesn't implement the method setRelativeSize. Adding a new method to an interface is *binary compatible*, which means that existing class file implementations still run without the implementation of the new method if no attempt is made to recompile them. In this case, the game will still run (unless it's recompiled) despite the addition of the setRelativeSize method to the Resizable interface. Nonetheless, the user could modify the method Utils.paint in his game to use the setRelativeSize method because the paint method expects a list of Resizable objects as an argument. If an Ellipse object is passed, an error is thrown at runtime because the setRelativeSize method isn't implemented:

```
Exception in thread "main" java.lang.AbstractMethodError:
    lambdasinaction.chap9.Ellipse.setRelativeSize(II)V
```

Second, if the user tries to rebuild his entire application (including Ellipse), he'll get the following compile error:

```
lambdasinaction/chap9/Ellipse.java:6: error: Ellipse is not abstract and does
    not override abstract method setRelativeSize(int,int) in Resizable
```

Consequently, updating a published API creates backward incompatibilities, which is why evolving existing APIs, such as the official Java Collections API, causes problems for users of the APIs. You have alternatives to evolving an API, but they're poor choices. You could create a separate version of your API and maintain both the old and the new versions, for example, but this option is inconvenient for several reasons. First, it's more complex for you to maintain as a library designer. Second, your users may have to use both versions of your API in the same code base, which affects memory space and loading time because more class files are required for their projects.

In this case, default methods come to the rescue. They let library designers evolve APIs without breaking existing code because classes that implement an updated interface automatically inherit a default implementation.

Different types of compatibilities: binary, source, and behavioral

There are three main kinds of compatibility when introducing a change to a Java program: binary, source, and behavioral compatibilities (see https://blogs.oracle.com/darcy/entry/kinds_of_compatibility). You saw that adding a method to an interface is binary compatible but results in a compiler error if the class implementing the interface is recompiled. It's good to know the different kinds of compatibilities, so in this sidebar, we examine them in detail.

(continued)

Binary compatibility means that existing binaries running without errors continue to link (which involves verification, preparation, and resolution) without error after introducing a change. Adding a method to an interface is binary compatible, for example, because if it's not called, existing methods of the interface can still run without problems.

In its simplest form, *source compatibility* means that an existing program will still compile after introducing a change. Adding a method to an interface isn't source compatible; existing implementations won't recompile because they need to implement the new method.

Finally, *behavioral compatibility* means running a program after a change with the same input results in the same behavior. Adding a method to an interface is behavioral compatible because the method is never called in the program (or gets overridden by an implementation).

13.2   *Default methods in a nutshell*

You've seen how adding methods to a published API disrupts existing implementations. *Default methods* are new in Java 8 to evolve APIs in a compatible way. Now an interface can contain method signatures for which an implementing class doesn't provide an implementation. Who implements them? The missing method bodies are given as part of the interface (hence, default implementations) rather than in the implementing class.

How do you recognize a default method? Simple: it starts with a `default` modifier and contains a body like a method declared in a class. In the context of a collection library, you could define an interface `Sized` with one abstract method `size` and a default method `isEmpty`, as follows:

```
public interface Sized {
    int size();
    default boolean isEmpty() {        ◁────── A default method
        return size() == 0;
    }
}
```

Now any class that implements the `Sized` interface automatically inherits the implementation of `isEmpty`. Consequently, adding a method to an interface with a default implementation isn't a source incompatibility.

Now go back to the initial example of the Java drawing library and your game. Concretely, to evolve your library in a compatible way (which means that the users of your library don't have to modify all their classes that implement `Resizable`), use a default method and provide a default implementation for `setRelativeSize`, as follows:

```
default void setRelativeSize(int wFactor, int hFactor){
    setAbsoluteSize(getWidth() / wFactor, getHeight() / hFactor);
}
```

Because interfaces can now have methods with implementation, does that mean multiple inheritance has arrived in Java? What happens if an implementing class also defines the same method signature or default methods can be overridden? Don't worry about these issues for now; a few rules and mechanisms are available to help you deal with these issues. We explore them in detail in section 13.4.

You may have guessed that default methods are used extensively in the Java 8 API. You saw in the introduction of this chapter that the stream method in the Collection interface that we used extensively in previous chapters is a default method. The sort method in the List interface is also a default method. Many of the functional interfaces we presented in chapter 3—such as Predicate, Function, and Comparator—also introduced new default methods, such as Predicate.and and Function.andThen. (Remember that a functional interface contains only one abstract method; default methods are nonabstract methods.)

Abstract classes vs. interfaces in Java 8

What's the difference between an abstract class and an interface? Both can contain abstract methods and methods with a body.

First, a class can extend only *from one* abstract class, but a class can implement *multiple* interfaces.

Second, an abstract class can enforce a common state through instance variables (fields). An interface can't have instance variables.

To put your knowledge of default methods to use, have a go at quiz 13.1.

Quiz 13.1: removeIf

For this quiz, pretend that you're one of the masters of the Java language and API. You've received many requests for a removeIf method to use on ArrayList, TreeSet, LinkedList, and all other collections. The removeIf method should remove all elements from a collection that match a given predicate. Your task in this quiz is to figure out the best way to enhance the Collections API with this new method.

Answer:

What's the most disruptive way to enhance the Collections API? You could copy and paste the implementation of removeIf in each concrete class of the Collections API, but that solution would be a crime to the Java community. What else can you do? Well, all the Collection classes implement an interface called java.util. Collection. Great; can you add a method there? Yes. You've learned that default

(continued)

methods allow you to add implementations inside an interface in a source-compatible way. All classes that implement `Collection` (including classes from your users that aren't part of the `Collections` API) can use the implementation of `removeIf`. The code solution for `removeIf` is as follows (which is roughly the implementation in the official Java 8 Collections API). This solution is a default method inside the `Collection` interface:

```
default boolean removeIf(Predicate<? super E> filter) {
    boolean removed = false;
    Iterator<E> each = iterator();
    while(each.hasNext()) {
        if(filter.test(each.next())) {
            each.remove();
            removed = true;
        }
    }
    return removed;
}
```

13.3   *Usage patterns for default methods*

You've seen that default methods can be useful for evolving a library in a compatible way. Can you do anything else with them? You can create your own interfaces that have default methods too. You may want to do this for two use cases that we explore in the following sections: optional methods and multiple inheritance of behavior.

13.3.1   *Optional methods*

You're likely to have come across classes that implement an interface but leave empty some method implementations. Take the `Iterator` interface, for example, which defines `hasNext` and `next` but also the `remove` method. Before Java 8, `remove` was often ignored because users decided not to use that capability. As a result, many classes that implement `Iterator` have an empty implementation for `remove`, which results in unnecessary boilerplate code.

With default methods, you can provide a default implementation for such methods, so concrete classes don't need to explicitly provide an empty implementation. The `Iterator` interface in Java 8 provides a default implementation for `remove` as follows:

```
interface Iterator<T> {
    boolean hasNext();
    T next();
    default void remove() {
        throw new UnsupportedOperationException();
    }
}
```

Consequently, you can reduce boilerplate code. Any class that implements the `Iterator` interface no longer needs to declare an empty `remove` method to ignore it because now it has a default implementation.

13.3.2 *Multiple inheritance of behavior*

Default methods enable something elegant that wasn't possible before: *multiple inheritance of behavior*, which is the ability of a class to reuse code from multiple places (figure 13.3).

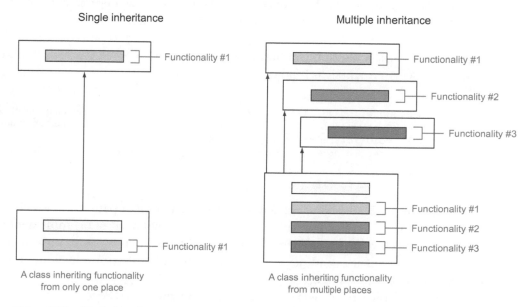

Figure 13.3 **Single inheritance versus multiple inheritance**

Remember that classes in Java can inherit from only one other class, but classes have always been allowed to implement multiple interfaces. To confirm, here's how the class `ArrayList` is defined in the Java API:

```
public class ArrayList<E> extends AbstractList<E>       ⟵┤ Inherits from
     implements List<E>, RandomAccess, Cloneable,           one class
              Serializable {                    ⟵┐ Implements
}                                                 four interfaces
```

MULTIPLE INHERITANCE OF TYPES

Here, `ArrayList` is extending one class and directly implementing four interfaces. As a result, an `ArrayList` is a direct *subtype* of seven types: `AbstractList`, `List`, `RandomAccess`, `Cloneable`, `Serializable`, `Iterable`, and `Collection`. In a sense, you already have multiple inheritance of types.

Because interface methods can have implementations in Java 8, classes can inherit behavior (implementation code) from multiple interfaces. In the next section, we explore an example to show how you can use this capability to your benefit. Keeping interfaces minimal and orthogonal lets you achieve great reuse and composition of behavior inside your code base.

MINIMAL INTERFACES WITH ORTHOGONAL FUNCTIONALITIES

Suppose that you need to define several shapes with different characteristics for the game you're creating. Some shapes should be resizable but not rotatable; some should be rotatable and movable but not resizable. How can you achieve great code reuse?

You can start by defining a stand-alone Rotatable interface with two abstract methods: setRotationAngle and getRotationAngle. The interface also declares a default rotateBy method that you can implement by using the setRotationAngle and getRotationAngle methods as follows:

```
public interface Rotatable {
    void setRotationAngle(int angleInDegrees);
    int getRotationAngle();
    default void rotateBy(int angleInDegrees){
        setRotationAngle((getRotationAngle () + angleInDegrees) % 360);
    }
}
```

A default implementation for the method rotateBy

This technique is somewhat related to the template design pattern, in which a skeleton algorithm is defined in terms of other methods that need to be implemented.

Now any class that implements Rotatable will need to provide an implementation for setRotationAngle and getRotationAngle but will inherit the default implementation of rotateBy for free.

Similarly, you can define two interfaces that you saw earlier: Moveable and Resizable. Both interfaces contain default implementations. Here's the code for Moveable:

```
public interface Moveable {
    int getX();
    int getY();
    void setX(int x);
    void setY(int y);
    default void moveHorizontally(int distance){
        setX(getX() + distance);
    }
    default void moveVertically(int distance){
        setY(getY() + distance);
    }
}
```

And here's the code for Resizable:

```
public interface Resizable {
    int getWidth();
    int getHeight();
    void setWidth(int width);
```

```
    void setHeight(int height);
    void setAbsoluteSize(int width, int height);
    default void setRelativeSize(int wFactor, int hFactor){
        setAbsoluteSize(getWidth() / wFactor, getHeight() / hFactor);
    }
}
```

COMPOSING INTERFACES

You can create different concrete classes for your game by composing these interfaces. Monsters, for example, can be moveable, rotatable, and resizable:

```
public class Monster implements Rotatable, Moveable, Resizable {
...                ◁
}                          Needs to provide implementations for all
                           abstract methods but not the default methods
```

The `Monster` class automatically inherits the default methods from the `Rotatable`, `Moveable`, and `Resizable` interfaces. In this case, `Monster` inherits the implementations of `rotateBy`, `moveHorizontally`, `moveVertically`, and `setRelativeSize`.

   Now you can call the different methods directly:

```
                                        Constructor internally sets the
                                        coordinates, height, width,
                                        and default angle.
Monster m = new Monster();   ◁
m.rotateBy(180);                                  ◁
m.moveVertically(10);  ◁                   Calling rotateBy
                           Calling moveVertically    from Rotatable
                           from Moveable
```

Suppose that now you need to declare another class that's moveable and rotatable but not resizable, such as the sun. You don't need to copy and paste code; you can reuse the default implementations from the `Moveable` and `Rotatable` interfaces, as shown here.

```
public class Sun implements Moveable, Rotatable {
...                ◁
}                          Needs to provide implementations for all
                           abstract methods but not the default methods
```

Figure 13.4 illustrates the UML diagram of this scenario.

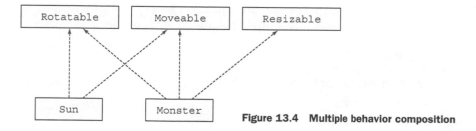

Figure 13.4 Multiple behavior composition

Here's another advantage of defining simple interfaces with default implementations like the ones for your game. Suppose that you need to modify the implementation of moveVertically to make it more efficient. You can change its implementation directly in the Moveable interface, and all classes implementing it automatically inherit the code (provided that they didn't implement the method themselves)!

Inheritance considered harmful

Inheritance shouldn't be your answer to everything when it comes to reusing code. For Inheriting from a class that has 100 methods and fields to reuse one method is a bad idea, for example, because it adds unnecessary complexity. You'd be better off using *delegation*: create a method that calls directly the method of the class you need via a member variable. For this reason, you'll sometimes find classes that are declared "final" intentionally: they can't be inherited from to prevent this kind of anti-pattern or have their core behavior messed with. Note that sometimes, final classes have a place. String is final, for example, because you don't want anybody to be able to interfere with such core functionality.

The same idea applies to interfaces with default methods. By keeping your interface minimal, you can achieve greater composition because you can select only the implementations you need.

You've seen that default methods are useful for many usage patterns. But here's some food for thought: What if a class implements two interfaces that have the same default method signature? Which method is the class allowed to use? We explore this problem in the next section.

13.4   *Resolution rules*

As you know, in Java a class can extend only one parent class but implement multiple interfaces. With the introduction of default methods in Java 8, there's the possibility of a class inheriting more than one method with the same signature. Which version of the method should be used? Such conflicts probably are quite rare in practice, but when they do occur, there must be rules that specify how to deal with the conflict. This section explains how the Java compiler resolves such potential conflicts. We aim to answer questions such as "In the code that follows, which hello method is C calling?" Note that the examples that follow are intended to explore problematic scenarios; such scenarios won't necessarily happen frequently in practice:

```
public interface A {
    default void hello() {
        System.out.println("Hello from A");
    }
}
public interface B extends A {
    default void hello() {
        System.out.println("Hello from B");
    }
}
```

```
public class C implements B, A {
    public static void main(String... args) {
        new C().hello();        ←┐
    }                             │  What gets
}                                 │  printed?
```

In addition, you may have heard of the diamond problem in C++ in which a class can inherit two methods with the same signature. Which one gets chosen? Java 8 provides resolution rules to solve this issue too. Read on!

13.4.1 *Three resolution rules to know*

You have three rules to follow when a class inherits a method with the same signature from multiple places (such as another class or interface):

1. Classes always win. A method declaration in the class or a superclass takes priority over any default method declaration.

2. Otherwise, subinterfaces win: the method with the same signature in the most specific default-providing interface is selected. (If B extends A, B is more specific than A.)

3. Finally, if the choice is still ambiguous, the class inheriting from multiple interfaces has to explicitly select which default method implementation to use by overriding it and calling the desired method explicitly.

We promise that these are the only rules you need to know! In the next section, we look at some examples.

13.4.2 *Most specific default-providing interface wins*

Here, you revisit the example from the beginning of this section in which C implements both B and A, which define a default method called hello. In addition, B extends A. Figure 13.5 provides a UML diagram for the scenario.

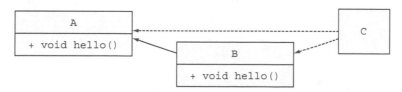

Figure 13.5 The most specific default-providing interface wins.

Which declaration of the hello method will the compiler use? Rule 2 says that the method with the most specific default-providing interface is selected. Because B is more specific than A, the hello from B is selected. Consequently, the program prints "Hello from B".

Now consider what would happen if C were inheriting from D as follows (illustrated in figure 13.6):

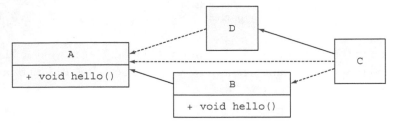

Figure 13.6   Inheriting from a class and implementing two interfaces

```
public class D implements A{ }
public class C extends D implements B, A {
    public static void main(String... args) {
        new C().hello();
    }
}
```

What gets printed?

Rule 1 says that a method declaration in the class takes priority. But D doesn't override hello; it implements interface A. Consequently, it has a default method from interface A. Rule 2 says that if there are no methods in the class or superclass, the method with the most specific default-providing interface is selected. The compiler, therefore, has a choice between the hello method from interface A and the hello method from interface B. Because B is more specific, the program prints "Hello from B" again.

To check your understanding of the resolution rules, try quiz 13.2.

Quiz 13.2: Remember the resolution rules

For this quiz, reuse the preceding example, except that D explicitly overrides the hello method from A. What do you think will get printed?

```
public class D implements A{
    void hello(){
        System.out.println("Hello from D");
    }
}
public class C extends D implements B, A {
    public static void main(String... args) {
        new C().hello();
    }
}
```

Answer:

The program prints "Hello from D" because a method declaration from a superclass has priority, as stated by rule 1.

Note that if D were declared as follows,

```
public abstract class D implements A {
    public abstract void hello();
}
```

C would be forced to implement the method `hello` itself, even though default implementations exist elsewhere in the hierarchy.

13.4.3 Conflicts and explicit disambiguation

The examples you've seen so far could be resolved by the first two resolution rules. Now suppose that B doesn't extend A anymore (illustrated in figure 13.7):

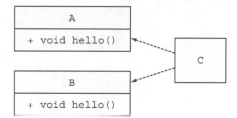

Figure 13.7 Implomonting two interfaces

```
public interface A {
    default void hello() {
        System.out.println("Hello from A");
    }
}
public interface B {
    default void hello() {
        System.out.println("Hello from B");
    }
}
public class C implements B, A { }
```

Rule 2 doesn't help you now because there's no more-specific interface to select. Both `hello` methods from A and B could be valid options. Thus, the Java compiler produces a compile error because it doesn't know which method is more suitable: `"Error: class C inherits unrelated defaults for hello() from types B and A."`

RESOLVING THE CONFLICT

There aren't many solutions to resolve the conflict between the two possible valid methods; you have to explicitly decide which method declaration you want C to use. To do so, you can override the `hello` method in class C and then, in its body, explicitly call the method you want to use. Java 8 introduces the new syntax `X.super.m(…)` where X is the superinterface whose method m you want to call. If you want C to use the default method from B, for example, the code looks like this:

```
public class C implements B, A {
    void hello(){
        B.super.hello();            ←─┐  Explicitly choosing to call
    }                                    the method from interface B
}
```

Have a go at quiz 13.3 to investigate a related tricky case.

> ## Quiz 13.3: Almost the same signature
> For this quiz, assume that interfaces A and B are declared as follows:
>
> ```
> public interface A{
>     default Number getNumber(){
>         return 10;
>     }
> }
> public interface B{
>     default Integer getNumber(){
>         return 42;
>     }
> }
> ```
>
> Also assume that class C is declared as follows:
>
> ```
> public class C implements B, A {
>     public static void main(String... args) {
>         System.out.println(new C().getNumber());
>     }
> }
> ```
>
> What will the program print?
>
> **Answer:**
>
> C can't distinguish which method of A or B is more specific. For this reason, class C won't compile.

13.4.4 *Diamond problem*

Finally, consider a scenario that sends shivers through the C++ community:

```
public interface A{
    default void hello(){
        System.out.println("Hello from A");
    }
}
public interface B extends A { }
public interface C extends A { }
public class D implements B, C {
    public static void main(String... args) {        What gets
        new D().hello();                    ←─┐       printed?
    }
}
```

Figure 13.8 illustrates the UML diagram for this scenario. The problem is called a *diamond problem* because the diagram resembles a diamond. What default method declaration does D inherit: the one from B or the one from C? You have only one method declaration to choose. Only A declares a default method. Because the interface is a superinterface of D, the code prints "Hello from A".

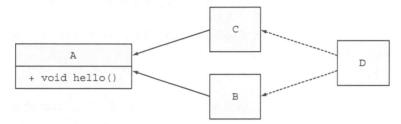

Figure 13.8   The diamond problem

Now what happens if B also has a default `hello` method with the same signature? Rule 2 says that you select the most specific default-providing interface. Because B is more specific than A, the default method declaration from B is selected. If both B and C declare a `hello` method with the same signature, you have a conflict and need to solve it explicitly, as we showed earlier.

As a side note, you may wonder what happens if you add an abstract `hello` method (one that's not default) in interface C as follows (still no methods in A and B):

```
public interface C extends A {
    void hello();
}
```

The new abstract `hello` method in C takes priority over the default `hello` method from interface A because C is more specific. Therefore, class D needs to provide an explicit implementation for `hello`; otherwise, the program won't compile.

C++ diamond problem

The diamond problem is more complicated in C++. First, C++ allows multiple inheritance of classes. By default, if a class D inherits from classes B and C, and classes B and C both inherit from A, class D has access to a copy of a B object and a copy of a C object. As a result, uses of methods from A have to be explicitly qualified: Are they coming from B or C? In addition, classes have state, so modifying member variables from B isn't reflected in the copy of the C object.

You've seen that the default method's resolution mechanism is simple if a class inherits from several methods with the same signature. Follow three rules systematically to solve all possible conflicts:

1 First, an explicit method declaration in the class or a superclass takes priority over any default method declaration.
2 Otherwise, the method with the same signature in the most specific default-providing interface is selected.
3 Finally, if there's still a conflict, you have to explicitly override the default methods and choose which one your class should use.

Summary

- Interfaces in Java 8 can have implementation code through default methods and static methods.
- Default methods start with a `default` keyword and contain a body, as class methods do.
- Adding an abstract method to a published interface is a source incompatibility.
- Default methods help library designers evolve APIs in a backward-compatible way.
- Default methods can be used for creating optional methods and multiple inheritance of behavior.
- Resolution rules exist to resolve conflicts when a class inherits from several default methods with the same signature.
- A method declaration in the class or a superclass takes priority over any default method declaration. Otherwise, the method with the same signature in the most specific default-providing interface is selected.
- When two methods are equally specific, a class must explicitly override this method, such as to select which one to call.

The Java Module System

This chapter covers

- The evolutionary forces causing Java to adopt a module system
- The main structure: module declarations and requires and exports directives
- Automatic modules for legacy Java Archives (JARs)
- Modularization and the JDK library
- Modules and Maven builds
- A brief summary of module directives beyond simple `requires` and `exports`

The main and most-discussed new feature introduced with Java 9 is its module system. This feature was developed within project Jigsaw, and its development took almost a decade. This timeline is a good measure of both the importance of this addition and the difficulties that the Java development team met while implementing it. This chapter provides background on why you should care as a developer what a module system is, as well as an overview of what the new Java Module System is intended for and how you can benefit from it.

Note that the Java Module System is a complex topic that merits a whole book. We recommend *The Java Module System* by Nicolai Parlog (Manning Publications, https://www.manning.com/books/the-java-module-system) for a comprehensive resource. In this chapter, we deliberately keep to the broad-brush picture so that you understand the main motivation and get a rapid overview of how to work with Java modules.

14.1   *The driving force: reasoning about software*

Before you delve into the details of the Java Module System, it's useful to understand some motivation and background to appreciate the goals set out by the Java language designers. What does modularity mean? What problem is the module system looking to address? This book has spent quite a lot of time discussing new language features that help us write code that reads closer to the problem statement and, as a result, is easier to understand and maintain. This concern is a low-level one, however. Ultimately, at a high level (software-architectural level), you want to work with a software project that's easy to reason about because this makes you more productive when you introduce changes in your code base. In the following sections, we highlight two design principles that help produce software that's easier to reason about: *separation of concerns* and *information hiding*.

14.1.1   *Separation of concerns*

Separation of concerns (SoC) is a principle that promotes decomposing a computer program into distinct features. Suppose that you need to develop an accounting application that parses expenses in different formats, analyzes them, and provides summary reports to your customer. By applying SoC, you split parsing, analysis, and reporting into separate parts called *modules*—cohesive groups of code that have little overlap. In other words, a module groups classes, allowing you to express visibility relationships between classes in your application.

You might say, "Ah, but Java packages already group classes." You're right, but Java 9 modules give you finer-grained control of which classes can see which other classes and allow this control to be checked at compile time. In essence, Java packages don't support modularity.

The SoC principle is useful at an architectural point of view (such as model versus view versus controller) and in a low-level approach (such as separating the business logic from the recovery mechanism). The benefits are

- Allowing work on individual parts in isolation, which helps team collaboration
- Facilitating reuse of separate parts
- Easier maintenance of the overall system

14.1.2   *Information hiding*

Information hiding is a principle that encourages hiding implementation details. Why is this principle important? In the context of building software, requirements can change frequently. By hiding implementation details, you can reduce the chances that a local change will require cascading changes in other parts of your program. In other words, it's a useful principle for managing and protecting your code. You often hear the term *encapsulation* used to indicate that a specific piece of code is so well isolated from the other parts of the application that changing its internal implementation won't negatively affect them. In Java, you can get a compiler to check that *components within a class* are well encapsulated by using the `private` keyword appropriately. But until Java 9, there was no language structure to allow the compiler to check that *classes and packages were available only* for the intended purposes.

14.1.3 *Java software*

These two principles are fundamental in any well-designed software. How do they fit with Java language features? Java is an object-oriented language, and you work with classes and interfaces. You make your code *modular* by grouping packages, classes, and interfaces that address a specific concern. In practice, reasoning about raw code is a bit abstract. As a result, tools such as UML diagrams (or, more simply, boxes and arrows) help you reason about your software by visually representing dependencies among parts of your code. Figure 14.1 shows a UML diagram for an application managing a user profile that has been decomposed into three specific concerns.

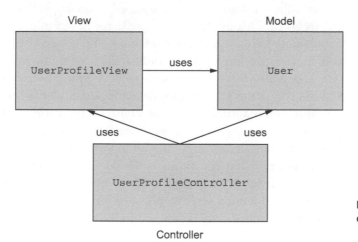

Figure 14.1   Three separate concerns with dependencies

What about information hiding? In Java, you're familiar with using visibility modifiers to control access to methods, fields, and classes: public, protected, package-level, and private. As we clarify in the next section, however, their granularity isn't fine enough in many cases, and you could be obliged to declare a method public even if you didn't intend to make it accessible for end users. This concern wasn't a huge one in the early days of Java, when applications and dependency chains were relatively small. Now that many Java applications are large, the problem is more important. Indeed, if you see a `public` field or method in a class, you probably feel entitled to use it (don't you?), even though the designer may regard it as being only for private use among a few of his own classes!

Now that you understand the benefits of modularization, you may wonder how supporting it causes changes in Java. We explain in the next section.

14.2 *Why the Java Module System was designed*

In this section, you learn why a new module system was designed for the Java language and compiler. First, we cover the limitations of modularity before Java 9. Next, we provide background about the JDK library and explain why modularizing it was important.

14.2.1 *Modularity limitations*

Unfortunately, the built-in support in Java to help produce modular software projects was somewhat limited before Java 9. Java has had three levels at which code was grouped: classes, packages, and JARs. For classes, Java has always had support for access modifiers and encapsulation. There was little encapsulation at the package and JAR levels, however.

LIMITED VISIBILITY CONTROL

As discussed in the previous section, Java provides access modifiers to support information hiding. These modifiers are public, protected, package-level, and private visibility. But what about controlling visibility *between* packages? Most applications have several packages defined to group various classes, but packages have limited support for visibility control. If you want classes and interfaces from one package to be visible to another package, you have to declare them as public. As a consequence, these classes and interfaces are accessible to everyone else as well. A typical occurrence of this problem is when you see companion packages with names that include the string `"impl"` to provide default implementations. In this case, because the code inside that package was defined as public, you have no way to prevent users from using these internal implementations. As a result, it becomes difficult to evolve your code without making breaking changes, because what you thought was for internal use only was used by a programmer temporarily to get something working and then frozen into the system. Worse, this situation is bad from a security point of view because you potentially increase the attack surface as more code is exposed to the risk of tampering.

CLASS PATH

Earlier in this chapter, we discussed the benefits of software written in a way that makes it simple to maintain and understand—in other words, easier to reason about. We also talked about separation of concerns and modeling dependencies between modules. Unfortunately, Java historically falls short in supporting these ideas when it comes to bundling and running an application. In fact, you have to ship all your compiled classes into one single flat JAR, which is made accessible from the class path.[1] Then the JVM can dynamically locate and load classes from the class path as needed.

---

[1]   This spelling is used in Java documentation, but `classpath` is often used for arguments to programs.

Unfortunately, the combination of the class path and JARs has several downsides.

First, the class path has no notion of versioning for the same class. You can't, for example, specify that the class JSONParser from a parsing library should belong to version 1.0 or version 2.0, so you can't predict what will happen if the same library with two different versions is available on the class path. This situation is common in large applications, as you may have different versions of the same libraries used by different components of your application.

Second, the class path doesn't support explicit dependencies; all the classes inside different JARs are merged into one bag of classes on the class path. In other words, the class path doesn't let you declare explicitly that one JAR depends on a set of classes contained inside another JAR. This situation makes it difficult to reason about the class path and to ask questions such as:

- Is anything missing?
- Are there any conflicts?

Build tools such as Maven and Gradle can help you solve this problem. Before Java 9, however, neither Java nor the JVM had any support for explicit dependencies. The issues combined are often referred to as JAR Hell or Class Path Hell. The direct consequence of these problems is that it's common to have to keep adding and removing class files on the class path in a trial-and-error cycle, in the hope that the JVM will execute your application without throwing runtime exceptions such as `ClassNotFound-Exception`. Ideally, you'd like such problems to be discovered early in the development process. Using the Java 9 module system consistently enables all such errors to be detected at compile time.

Encapsulation and Class Path Hell aren't problems only for your software architecture, however. What about the JDK itself?

14.2.2 *Monolithic JDK*

The *Java Development Kit* (JDK) is a collection of tools that lets you work with and run Java programs. Perhaps the most important tools you're familiar with are `javac` to compile Java programs and `java` to load and run a Java application, along with the JDK library, which provides runtime support including input/output, collections, and streams. The first version was released in 1996. It's important to understand that like any software, the JDK has grown and increased considerably in size. Many technologies were added and later deprecated. CORBA is a good example. It doesn't matter whether you're using CORBA in your application or not; its classes are shipped with the JDK. This situation becomes problematic especially in applications that run on mobile or in the cloud and typically don't need all the parts available in the JDK library.

How can you get away from this problem as a whole ecosystem? Java 8 introduced the notion of *compact profiles* as a step forward. Three profiles were introduced to have different memory footprints, depending on which parts of the JDK library you're interested in. Compact profiles, however, provided only a short-term fix. Many internal APIs in the JDK aren't meant for public use. Unfortunately, due to the poor encapsulation provided by the Java language, those APIs are commonly used. The class sun.misc.Unsafe, for example, is used by several libraries (including Spring, Netty, and Mockito) but was never intended to be made available outside the JDK internals. As a result, it's extremely difficult to evolve these APIs without introducing incompatible changes.

All these problems provided the motivation for designing a Java Module System that also can be used to modularize the JDK itself. In a nutshell, new structuring constructs were required to allow you to choose what parts of the JDK you need and how to reason about the class path, and to provide stronger encapsulation to evolve the platform.

14.2.3 *Comparison with OSGi*

This section compares Java 9 modules with OSGi. If you haven't heard of OSGi, we suggest that you skip this section.

Before the introduction of modules based on project Jigsaw into Java 9, Java already had a powerful module system, named OSGi, even if it wasn't formally part of the Java platform. The Open Service Gateway initiative (OSGi) started in 2000 and, until the arrival of Java 9, represented the de-facto standard for implementing a modular application on the JVM.

In reality, OSGi and the new Java 9 Module System aren't mutually exclusive; they can coexist in the same application. In fact, their features overlap only partially. OSGi has a much wider scope and provides many capabilities that aren't available in Jigsaw.

OSGi modules are called *bundles* and run inside a specific OSGi framework. Several certified OSGi framework implementations exist, but the two with the widest adoption are Apache Felix and Equinox (which is also used to run the Eclipse IDE). When running inside an OSGi framework, a single bundle can be remotely installed, started, stopped, updated, and uninstalled without a reboot. In other words, OSGi defines a clear life cycle for bundles made by the states listed in table 14.1.

Table 14.1   Bundle states in OSGi

Bundle state	Description
INSTALLED	The bundle has been successfully installed.
RESOLVED	All Java classes that the bundle needs are available.
STARTING	The bundle is being started, and the BundleActivator.start method has been called, but the start method hasn't yet returned.
ACTIVE	The bundle has been successfully activated and is running.
STOPPING	The bundle is being stopped. The BundleActivator.stop method has been called, but the stop method hasn't yet returned.
UNINSTALLED	The bundle has been uninstalled. It can't move into another state.

The possibility of hot-swapping different subparts of your application without the need to restart it probably is the main advantage of OSGi over Jigsaw. Each bundle is defined through a text file describing which external packages are required by the bundle to work and which internal packages are publicly exported by the bundle and then made available to other bundles.

Another interesting characteristic of OSGi is that it allows different versions of the same bundle to be installed in the framework at the same time. The Java 9 Module System doesn't support version control because Jigsaw still uses one single class loader per application, whereas OSGi loads each bundle in its own class loader.

14.3 Java modules: the big picture

Java 9 provides a new unit of Java program structure: the *module*. A module is introduced with a new keyword[2] module, followed by its name and its body. Such a *module descriptor*[3] lives in a special file: module-info.java, which is compiled to module-info.class. The body of a module descriptor consists of clauses, of which the two most important are requires and exports. The former clause specifies what other modules your modules need to run, and exports specifies everything that your module wants to be visible for other modules to use. You learn about these clauses in more detail in later sections.

A module descriptor describes and encapsulates one or more packages (and typically lives in the same folder as these packages), but in simple use cases, it exports (makes visible) only one of these packages.

The core structure of a Java module descriptor is shown in figure 14.2.

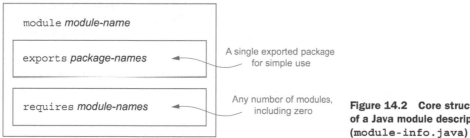

Figure 14.2 Core structure of a Java module descriptor (module-info.java)

It is helpful to think of the exports and requires parts of a module as being respectively like the lugs (or tabs) and holes of a jigsaw puzzle (which is perhaps where the working name Project Jigsaw originated). Figure 14.3 shows an example with several modules.

---

[2] Technically, Java 9 module-forming identifiers—such as module, requires, and export—are *restricted keywords*. You can still use them as identifiers elsewhere in your program (for backward compatibility), but they're interpreted as keywords in a context where modules are allowed.

[3] Legally, the textual form is called a *module declaration*, and the binary form in module-info.class is referred to as a *module descriptor*.

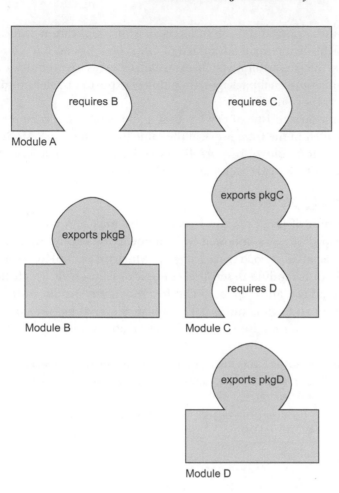

Figure 14.3   Jigsaw-puzzle-style example of a Java system built from four modules (A, B, C, D). Module A requires modules B and C to be present, and thereby gets access to the packages pkgB and pkgC (exported by modules B and C, respectively). Module C may similarly use package pkgD, which it has required from module C, but Module B can't use pkgD.

When you use tools such as Maven, much of the detail of module descriptions is handled by an IDE and is hidden from the user.

Having said that, in the next section we explore these concepts in more detail based on examples.

14.4 Developing an application with the Java Module System

In this section, you get an overview of the Java 9 Module System by building a simple modular application from the ground up. You learn how to structure, package, and launch a small modular application. This section doesn't explain each topic in detail but shows you the big picture, so you can delve independently in more depth if needed.

14.4.1 Setting up an application

To get started with the Java Module System, you need an example project to write code for. Perhaps you're traveling a lot, grocery shopping, or going out for coffee with your friends, and you have to deal with a lot of receipts. Nobody ever enjoyed managing expenses. To help yourself out, you write an application that can manage your expenses. The application needs to conduct several tasks:

- Read a list of expenses from a file or a URL;
- Parse the string representations of these expenses;
- Calculate statistics;
- Display a useful summary;
- Provide a main start-up and close-down coordinator for these tasks.

You need to define different classes and interfaces to model the concepts in this application. First, a `Reader` interface lets you read serialized expenses from a source. You'll have different implementations, such as `HttpReader` or `FileReader`, depending on the source. You also need a `Parser` interface to deserialize the JSON objects into a domain object `Expense` that you can manipulate in your Java application. Finally, you need a class `SummaryCalculator` to be responsible for calculating statistics, given a list of `Expense` objects, and to return `SummaryStatistics` objects.

Now that you have a project, how do you modularize it by using the Java Module System? It's clear that the project involves several concerns, which you want to separate:

- Reading data from different sources (`Reader`, `HttpReader`, `FileReader`)
- Parsing the data from different formats (`Parser`, `JSONParser`, `ExpenseJSON-Parser`)
- Representing domain objects (`Expense`)
- Calculating and returning statistics (`SummaryCalculator`, `SummaryStatistics`)
- Coordinating the different concerns (`ExpensesApplication`)

Here, we'll take a fine-grained approach for pedagogic reasons. You can group each concern into a separate module, as follows (and we discuss the module-naming scheme in more detail later):

- expenses.readers
- expenses.readers.http
- expenses.readers.file
- expenses.parsers
- expenses.parsers.json
- expenses.model
- expenses.statistics
- expenses.application

For this simple application, you adopt a fine-grained decomposition to exemplify the different parts of the module system. In practice, taking such a fine-grained approach for a simple project would result in a high up-front cost for the arguably limited benefit of properly encapsulating small parts of the project. As the project grows and more internal implementations are added, however, the encapsulation and reasoning benefits become more apparent. You could imagine the preceding list as being a list of packages, depending on your application boundaries. A module groups a series of packages. Perhaps each module has implementation-specific packages that you don't want to expose to other modules. The `expenses.statistics` module, for example, may contain several packages for different implementations of experimental statistical methods. Later, you can decide which of these packages to release to users.

14.4.2   *Fine-grained and coarse-grained modularization*

When you're modularizing a system, you can choose the granularity. In the most fine-grained scheme, every package has its own module (as in the previous section); in the most coarse-grained scheme, a single module contains all the packages in your system. As noted in the previous section, the first schema increases the design cost for limited gains, and the second one loses all benefits of modularization. The best choice is a pragmatic decomposition of the system into modules along with a regular review process to ensure that an evolving software project remains sufficiently modularized that you can continue to reason about it and modify it.

In short, modularization is the enemy of software rust.

14.4.3   *Java Module System basics*

Let's begin with a basic modular application, which has only one module to support the main application. The project directory structure is as follows, with each level nested in a directory:

```
|- expenses.application
  |- module-info.java
  |- com
    |- example
      |- expenses
        |- application
          |- ExpensesApplication.java
```

You've noticed this mysterious `module-info.java` that was part of the project structure. This file is a module descriptor, as we explained earlier in the chapter, and it must be located at the root of the module's source-code file hierarchy to let you specify the dependencies of your module and what you want to expose. For your expenses application, the top-level `module-info.java` file contains a module description that has a name but is otherwise empty because it neither depends on any other module nor exposes its functionality to other modules. You'll learn about more-sophisticated features later, starting with section 14.5. The content of `module-info.java` is as follows:

```
module expenses.application {

}
```

How do you run a modular application? Take a look at some commands to understand the low-level parts. This code is automated by your IDE and build system but seeing what's happening is useful. When you're in the module source directory of your project, run the following commands:

```
javac module-info.java
    com/example/expenses/application/ExpensesApplication.java -d target

jar cvfe expenses-application.jar
    com.example.expenses.application.ExpensesApplication -C target
```

These commands produce output similar to the following, which shows which folders and class files are incorporated into the generated JAR (expenses-application.jar):

```
added manifest
added module-info: module-info.class
adding: com/(in = 0) (out= 0)(stored 0%)
adding: com/example/(in = 0) (out= 0)(stored 0%)
adding: com/example/expenses/(in = 0) (out= 0)(stored 0%)
adding: com/example/expenses/application/(in = 0) (out= 0)(stored 0%)
adding: com/example/expenses/application/ExpensesApplication.class(in = 456)
    (out= 306)(deflated 32%)
```

Finally, you run the generated JAR as a modular application:

```
java --module-path expenses-application.jar \
    --module expenses/com.example.expenses.application.ExpensesApplication
```

You should be familiar with the first two steps, which represent a standard way to package a Java application into a JAR. The only new part is that the file module-info.java becomes part of the compilation step.

The java program, which runs Java .class files, has two new options:

- --module-path—This option specifies what modules are available to load. This option differs from the --classpath argument, which makes class files available.
- --module—This option specifies the main module and class to run.

A module's declaration doesn't include a version string. Addressing the version-selection problem wasn't a specific design point for the Java 9 Module System, so versioning isn't supported. The justification was that this problem is one for build tools and container applications to address.

14.5 Working with several modules

Now that you know how to set up a basic application with one module, you're ready to do something a bit more realistic with multiple modules. You want your expense application to read expenses from a source. To this end, introduce a new module expenses.readers that encapsulates these responsibilities. The interaction between the two modules expenses.application and expenses.readers is specified by the Java 9 exports and requires clauses.

14.5.1 *The exports clause*

Here's how we might declare the module expenses.readers. (Don't worry about the syntax and concepts yet; we cover these topics later.)

```
module expenses.readers {

    exports com.example.expenses.readers;
    exports com.example.expenses.readers.file;
    exports com.example.expenses.readers.http;
}
```

These are package names, not module names.

There's one new thing: the exports clause, which makes the public types in specific packages available for use by other modules. By default, everything is encapsulated within a module. The module system takes a whitelist approach that helps you get strong encapsulation, as you need to explicitly decide what to make available for another module to use. (This approach prevents you from accidentally exporting some internal features that a hacker can exploit to compromise your systems several years later.)

The directory structure of the two-module version of your project now looks like this:

```
|- expenses.application
  |- module-info.java
  |- com
    |- example
      |- expenses
        |- application
          |- ExpensesApplication.java

|- expenses.readers
  |- module-info.java
  |- com
    |- example
      |- expenses
        |- readers
          |- Reader.java
        |- file
          |- FileReader.java
        |- http
          |- HttpReader.java
```

14.5.2 *The requires clause*

Alternatively, you could have written module-info.java as follows:

```
module expenses.readers {
    requires java.base;

    exports com.example.expenses.readers;
    exports com.example.expenses.readers.file;
    exports com.example.expenses.readers.http;
}
```

This is a module name, not a package name.

This is a package name, not a module name.

The new element is the `requires` clause, which lets you specify what the module depends on. By default, all modules depend on a platform module called `java.base` that includes the Java main packages such as `net`, `io`, and `util`. This module is always required by default, so you don't need to say so explicitly. (This is similar to how saying `"class Foo { ... }"` in Java is equivalent to saying `"class Foo extends Object { ... }"`).

It becomes useful when you need to import modules other than `java.base`.

The combination of the `requires` and `exports` clauses makes access control of classes more sophisticated in Java 9. Table 14.2 summarizes the differences in visibility with the different access modifiers before and after Java 9.

Table 14.2   Java 9 provides finer control over class visibility

Class visibility	Before Java 9	After Java 9
All classes public to everyone	✓✓	✓✓ (combination of exports and requires clauses)
Limited number of classes public	✗✗	✓✓ (combination of exports and requires clauses)
Public inside one module only	✗✗	✓ (no exports clause)
Protected	✓✓	✓✓
Package	✓✓	✓✓
Private	✓✓	✓✓

14.5.3 Naming

At this stage, it's useful to comment on the naming convention for modules. We went for a short approach (for example, `expenses.application`) so as not to confuse the ideas of modules and packages. (A module can export multiple packages.) The recommended convention is different, however.

Oracle recommends you name modules following the same reverse internet domain-name convention (for example, com.iteratrlearning.training) used for packages. Further, a module's name should correspond to its principal exported API package, which should also follow that convention. If a module doesn't have that package, or if for other reasons it requires a name that doesn't correspond to one of its exported packages, it should start with the reversed form of an internet domain associated with its author.

Now that you've learned how to set up a project with multiple modules, how do you package and run it? We cover this topic in the next section.

14.6 Compiling and packaging

Now that you're comfortable with setting a project and declaring a module, you're ready to see how you can use build tools like Maven to compile your project. This section assumes that you're familiar with Maven, which is one of the most common build tools in the Java ecosystem. Another popular building tool is Gradle, which we encourage you to explore if you haven't heard of it.

First, you need to introduce a `pom.xml` file for each module. In fact, each module can be compiled independently so that it behaves as a project on its own. You also need to add a `pom.xml` for the parent of all the modules to coordinate the build for the whole project. The overall structure now looks as follows:

```
|- pom.xml
|- expenses.application
  |- pom.xml
  |- src
    |- main
      |- java
        |- module-info.java
        |- com
          |- example
            |- expenses
              |- application
                |- ExpensesApplication.java
|- expenses.readers
  |- pom.xml
  |- src
    |- main
      |- java
        |- module-info.java
        |- com
          |- example
            |- expenses
              |- readers
                |- Reader.java
              |- file
                |- FileReader.java
              |- http
                |- HttpReader.java
```

Notice the three new `pom.xml` files and the Maven directory project structure. The module descriptor (`module-info.java`) needs to be located in the `src/main/java` directory. Maven will set up `javac` to use the appropriate module source path.

The `pom.xml` for the `expenses.readers` project looks like this:

```
<?xml version="1.0" encoding="UTF-8"?>
<project xmlns="http://maven.apache.org/POM/4.0.0"
         xmlns:xsi="http://www.w3.org/2001/XMLSchema-instance"
         xsi:schemaLocation="http://maven.apache.org/POM/4.0.0
    http://maven.apache.org/xsd/maven-4.0.0.xsd">
    <modelVersion>4.0.0</modelVersion>

    <groupId>com.example</groupId>
    <artifactId>expenses.readers</artifactId>
    <version>1.0</version>
    <packaging>jar</packaging>
```

```
    <parent>
        <groupId>com.example</groupId>
        <artifactId>expenses</artifactId>
        <version>1.0</version>
    </parent>
</project>
```

The important thing to note is that this code explicitly mentions the parent module to help in the build process. The parent is the artifact with the ID expenses. You need to define the parent in pom.xml, as you see shortly.

Next, you need to specify the pom.xml for the expenses.application module. This file is similar to the preceding one, but you have to add a dependency to the expenses.readers project, because ExpensesApplication requires the classes and interfaces that it contains to compile:

```
<?xml version="1.0" encoding="UTF-8"?>
<project xmlns="http://maven.apache.org/POM/4.0.0"
        xmlns:xsi="http://www.w3.org/2001/XMLSchema-instance"
        xsi:schemaLocation="http://maven.apache.org/POM/4.0.0
    http://maven.apache.org/xsd/maven-4.0.0.xsd">
    <modelVersion>4.0.0</modelVersion>

    <groupId>com.example</groupId>
    <artifactId>expenses.application</artifactId>
    <version>1.0</version>
    <packaging>jar</packaging>

    <parent>
        <groupId>com.example</groupId>
        <artifactId>expenses</artifactId>
        <version>1.0</version>
    </parent>

    <dependencies>
        <dependency>
                <groupId>com.example</groupId>
                <artifactId>expenses.readers</artifactId>
                <version>1.0</version>
        </dependency>
    </dependencies>

</project>
```

Now that two modules, expenses.application and expenses.readers, have their own pom.xml, you can set up the global pom.xml to guide the build process. Maven supports projects that have multiple Maven modules with the special XML element <module>, which refers to the children's artifact IDs. Here's the complete definition, which refers to the two child modules expenses.application and expenses.readers:

```
<?xml version="1.0" encoding="UTF-8"?>
<project xmlns="http://maven.apache.org/POM/4.0.0"
        xmlns:xsi="http://www.w3.org/2001/XMLSchema-instance"
```

```
        xsi:schemaLocation="http://maven.apache.org/POM/4.0.0
   http://maven.apache.org/xsd/maven-4.0.0.xsd">
   <modelVersion>4.0.0</modelVersion>

   <groupId>com.example</groupId>
   <artifactId>expenses</artifactId>
   <packaging>pom</packaging>
   <version>1.0</version>

   <modules>
   <module>expenses.application</module>
       <module>expenses.readers</module>
   </modules>

   <build>
       <pluginManagement>
           <plugins>
           <plugin>
                   <groupId>org.apache.maven.plugins</groupId>
               <artifactId>maven-compiler-plugin</artifactId>
                   <version>3.7.0</version>
               <configuration>
                       <source>9</source>
                       <target>9</target>
               </configuration>
           </plugin>
           </plugins>
       </pluginManagement>
   </build>
</project>
```

Congratulations! Now you can run the command `mvn clean package` to generate the JARs for the modules in your project. This command generates

```
./expenses.application/target/expenses.application-1.0.jar
./expenses.readers/target/expenses.readers-1.0.jar
```

You can run your module application by including these two JARs on the module path as follows:

```
java --module-path \
 ./expenses.application/target/expenses.application-1.0.jar:\
 ./expenses.readers/target/expenses.readers-1.0.jar \
   --module \
 expenses.application/com.example.expenses.application.ExpensesApplication
```

So far, you've learned about modules you created, and you've seen how to use `requires` to reference `java.base`. Real-world software, however, depends on external modules and libraries. How does that process work, and what if legacy libraries haven't been updated with an explicit `module-info.java`? In the next section, we answer these questions by introducing automatic modules.

14.7   *Automatic modules*

You may decide that the implementation of your `HttpReader` is low-level; instead, you'd like to use a specialized library such as the `httpclient` from the Apache project. How do you incorporate that library into your project? You've learned about the `requires` clause, so try to add it in the `module-info.java` for the `expenses.readers` project. Run `mvn clean package` again to see what happens. Unfortunately, the result is bad news:

```
[ERROR] module not found: httpclient
```

You get this error because you also need to update your `pom.xml` to state the dependency. The maven compiler plugin puts all dependencies on the module path when you're building a project that has a `module-info.java` so that the appropriate JARs are downloaded and recognized in your project, as follows:

```
<dependencies>
    <dependency>
        <groupId>org.apache.httpcomponents</groupId>
        <artifactId>httpclient</artifactId>
        <version>4.5.3</version>
    </dependency>
</dependencies>
```

Now running `mvn clean package` builds the project correctly. Notice something interesting, though: the library `httpclient` isn't a Java module. It's an external library that you want to use as a module, but it hasn't yet been modularized. Java turns the appropriate JAR into a so-called automatic module. Any JAR on the module path without a `module-info` file becomes an automatic module. Automatic modules implicitly export all their packages. A name for this automatic module is invented automatically, derived from the JAR name. You have a few ways to derive the name, but the easiest way is to use the `jar` tool with the `--describe-module` argument:

```
jar --file=./expenses.readers/target/dependency/httpclient-4.5.3.jar \
    --describe-module
httpclient@4.5.3 automatic
```

In this case, the name is `httpclient`.

The final step is running the application and adding the `httpclient` JAR to the module path:

```
java --module-path \
 ./expenses.application/target/expenses.application-1.0.jar:\
 ./expenses.readers/target/expenses.readers-1.0.jar \
 ./expenses.readers/target/dependency/httpclient-4.5.3.jar \
   --module \
 expenses.application/com.example.expenses.application.ExpensesApplication
```

NOTE There's a project (https://github.com/moditect/moditect) to provide better support for the Java 9 Module System within Maven, such as to generate `module-info` files automatically.

14.8 Module declaration and clauses

The Java Module System is a large beast. As we mentioned earlier, we recommend that you read a dedicated book on the topic if you'd like to go further. Nonetheless, this section gives you a brief overview of other keywords available in the module declaration language to give you an idea of what's possible.

As you learned in the earlier sections, you declare a module by using the `module` directive. Here, it has the name `com.iteratrlearning.application`:

```
module com.iteratrlearning.application {

}
```

What can go inside the module declaration? You've learned about the `requires` and `exports` clauses, but there are other clauses, including `requires-transitive`, `exports-to`, `open`, `opens`, `uses`, and `provides`. We look at these clauses in turn in the following sections.

14.8.1 requires

The `requires` clause lets you specify that your module depends on another module at both compile time and runtime. The module `com.iteratrlearning.application`, for example, depends on the module `com.iteratrlearning.ui`:

```
module com.iteratrlearning.application {
    requires com.iteratrlearning.ui;
}
```

The result is that only public types that were exported by `com.iteratrlearning.ui` are available for `com.iteratrlearning.application` to use.

14.8.2 exports

The `exports` clause makes the public types in specific packages available for use by other modules. By default, no package is exported. You gain strong encapsulation by making explicit what packages should be exported. In the following example, the packages `com.iteratrlearning.ui.panels` and `com.iteratrlearning.ui.widgets` are exported. (Note that exports takes a *package name* as an argument and that requires takes a *module name*, despite the similar naming schemes.)

```
module com.iteratrlearning.ui {
    requires com.iteratrlearning.core;
    exports com.iteratrlearning.ui.panels;
    exports com.iteratrlearning.ui.widgets;
}
```

14.8.3 *requires transitive*

You can specify that a module can use the public types required by another module. You can modify the `requires` clause, for example, to `requires-transitive` inside the declaration of the module `com.iteratrlearning.ui`:

```
module com.iteratrlearning.ui {
    requires transitive com.iteratrlearning.core;

    exports com.iteratrlearning.ui.panels;
    exports com.iteratrlearning.ui.widgets;
}

module com.iteratrlearning.application {
    requires com.iteratrlearning.ui;
}
```

The result is that the module `com.iteratrlearning.application` has access to the public types exported by `com.iteratrlearning.core`. Transitivity is useful when the module required (here, `com.iteratrlearning.ui`) returns types from another module required by this module (`com.iteratrlearning.core`). It would be annoying to re-declare `requires com.iteratrlearning.core` inside the module `com.iteratrlearning.application`. This problem is solved by `transitive`. Now any module that depends on `com.iteratrlearning.ui` automatically reads the `com.iteratrlearning.core` module.

14.8.4 *exports to*

You have a further level of visibility control, in that you can restrict the allowed users of a particular export by using the `exports to` construct. As you saw in section 14.8.2, you can restrict the allowed users of `com.iteratrlearning.ui.widgets` to `com.iteratrlearning.ui.widgetuser` by adjusting the module declaration like so:

```
module com.iteratrlearning.ui {
    requires com.iteratrlearning.core;

    exports com.iteratrlearning.ui.panels;
    exports com.iteratrlearning.ui.widgets to
     com.iteratrlearning.ui.widgetuser;
}
```

14.8.5 *open and opens*

Using the `open` qualifier on module declaration gives other modules reflective access to all its packages. The `open` qualifier has no effect on module visibility except for allowing reflective access, as in this example:

```
open module com.iteratrlearning.ui {

}
```

Before Java 9, you could inspect the private state of objects by using reflection. In other words, nothing was truly encapsulated. Object-relational mapping (ORM) tools such as Hibernate often use this capability to access and modify state directly. In Java 9, reflection is no longer allowed by default. The open clause in the preceding code serves to allow that behavior when it's needed.

Instead of opening a whole module to reflection, you can use an opens clause within a module declaration to open its packages individually, as required. You can also use the to qualifier in the opens-to variant to limit the modules allowed to perform reflective access, analogous to how exports-to limits the modules allowed to require an exported package.

14.8.6 *uses and provides*

If you're familiar with services and ServiceLoader, the Java Module System allows you to specify a module as a service provider using the provides clause and a service consumer using the uses clause. This topic is advanced, however, and beyond the scope of this chapter. If you're interested in combining modules and service loaders, we recommend that you read a comprehensive resource such as *The Java Module System*, by Nicolai Parlog (Manning Publications), mentioned earlier in this chapter.

14.9   *A bigger example and where to learn more*

You can get a flavor of the module system from the following example, taken from Oracle's Java documentation. This example shows a module declaration using most of the features discussed in this chapter. The example isn't meant to frighten you (the vast majority of module statements are simple exports and requires), but it gives you a look at some richer features:

```
module com.example.foo {
    requires com.example.foo.http;
    requires java.logging;

    requires transitive com.example.foo.network;

    exports com.example.foo.bar;
    exports com.example.foo.internal to com.example.foo.probe;

    opens com.example.foo.quux;
    opens com.example.foo.internal to com.example.foo.network,
                                      com.example.foo.probe;

    uses com.example.foo.spi.Intf;
    provides com.example.foo.spi.Intf with com.example.foo.Impl;
}
```

This chapter discussed the need for the new Java Module System and provided a gentle introduction to its main features. We didn't cover many features, including service loaders, additional module descriptor clauses, and tools for working with modules such as jdeps and jlink. If you're a Java EE developer, it's important to keep in mind when migrating your applications to Java 9 that several packages relevant to EE aren't loaded by default in the modularized Java 9 Virtual Machine. The JAXB API classes, for example, are now considered to be Java EE APIs and are no longer available in the default class path in Java SE 9. You need to explicitly add modules of interest by using the `--add-modules` command-line switch to keep compatibility. To add `java.xml.bind`, for example, you need to specify `--add-modules java.xml.bind`.

As we noted earlier, doing the Java Module System justice would require a whole book, not a single chapter. To explore the details in greater depth, we suggest a book such as *The Java Module System*, by Nicolai Parlog (Manning Publications), mentioned earlier in this chapter.

Summary

- Separation of concerns and information hiding are two important principles to help construct software that you can reason about.
- Before Java 9, you made code modular by introducing packages, classes, and interfaces that have a specific concern, but these elements weren't rich enough for effective encapsulation.
- The Class Path Hell problem makes it hard to reason about the dependencies of an application.
- Before Java 9, the JDK was monolithic, resulting in high maintenance costs and restricted evolution.
- Java 9 introduced a new module system in which a `module-info.java` file names a module and specifies its dependencies (`requires`) and public API (`exports`).
- The `requires` clause lets you specify dependencies on other modules.
- The `exports` clause makes the public types of specific packages in a module available for use by other modules.
- The prefered naming convention for a module follows the reverse internet domain-name convention.
- Any JAR on the module path without a `module-info` file becomes an automatic module.
- Automatic modules implicitly export all their packages.
- Maven supports applications structured with the Java 9 Module System.

Part 5

Enhanced Java concurrency

The fifth part of this book explores the more advanced ways of structuring concurrent programs in Java—beyond the ideas of easy-to-use parallel processing for streams introduced in chapters 6 and 7. Again, nothing in the rest of the book depends on this part, so do feel free to skip this part if you don't (yet) need to explore these ideas.

Chapter 15 is new to this second edition and covers the "big-picture" idea of asynchronous APIs, including the ideas of Futures and the publish-subscribe protocol behind reactive programming and encapsulated in the Java 9 Flow API.

Chapter 16 explores CompletableFuture, which lets you express complex asynchronous computations in a declarative way—paralleling the design of the Streams API.

Chapter 17 is also new to this second edition and explores the Java 9 Flow API in detail, focusing on practical reactive programming code.

Concepts behind CompletableFuture and reactive programming

This chapter covers

- Threads, Futures, and the evolutionary forces causing Java to support richer concurrency APIs
- Asynchronous APIs
- The boxes-and-channels view of concurrent computing
- CompletableFuture combinators to connect boxes dynamically
- The publish-subscribe protocol that forms the basis of the Java 9 Flow API for reactive programming
- Reactive programming and reactive systems

In recent years, two trends are obliging developers to rethink the way software is written. The first trend is related to the hardware on which applications run, and the second trend concerns how applications are structured (particularly how they interact). We discussed the effect of the hardware trend in chapter 7. We noted that since the advent of multicore processors, the most effective way to speed your applications is to write software that can fully exploit multicore processors. You saw that you can split large tasks and make each subtask run in parallel with the others. You also learned how the fork/join framework (available since Java 7) and parallel streams (new in Java 8) allow you to accomplish this task in a simpler, more effective way than working directly with threads.

The second trend reflects the increasing availability and use by applications of Internet services. The adoption of microservices architecture, for example, has grown over the past few years. Instead of being one monolithic application, your application is subdivided into smaller services. The coordination of these smaller services requires increased network communication. Similarly, many more internet services are accessible through public APIs, made available by known providers such as Google (localization information), Facebook (social information), and Twitter (news). Nowadays, it's relatively rare to develop a website or a network application that works in total isolation. It's far more likely that your next web application will be a mashup, using content from multiple sources and aggregating it to ease your users' lives.

You may want to build a website that collects and summarizes social-media sentiment on a given topic to your French users. To do so, you could use the Facebook or Twitter API to find trending comments about that topic in many languages and rank the most relevant ones with your internal algorithms. Then you might use Google Translate to translate the comments into French or use Google Maps to geolocate their authors, aggregate all this information, and display it on your website.

If any of these external network services are slow to respond, of course, you'll want to provide partial results to your users, perhaps showing your text results alongside a generic map with a question mark in it instead of showing a blank screen until the map server responds or times out. Figure 15.1 illustrates how this style of *mashup* application interacts with remote services.

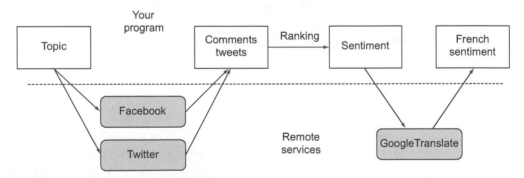

Figure 15.1   A typical mashup application

To implement applications like this, you have to contact multiple web services across the Internet. But you don't want to block your computations and waste billions of precious clock cycles of your CPU waiting for an answer from these services. You shouldn't have to wait for data from Facebook before processing the data coming from Twitter, for example.

This situation represents the other side of the multitask-programming coin. The fork/join framework and parallel streams, discussed in chapter 7, are valuable tools for parallelism; they divide a task into multiple subtasks and perform those subtasks in parallel on different cores, CPUs, or even machines.

Conversely, when you're dealing with concurrency instead of parallelism, or when your main goal is to perform several loosely related tasks on the same CPUs, keeping their cores as busy as possible to maximize the throughput of your application, you want to avoid blocking a thread and wasting its computational resources while waiting (potentially for quite a while) for a result from a remote service or from interrogating a database.

Java offers two main tool sets for such circumstances. First, as you'll see in chapters 16 and 17, the `Future` interface, and particularly its Java 8 `CompletableFuture` implementation, often provide simple and effective solutions (chapter 16). More recently, Java 9 added the idea of reactive programming, built around the idea of the so-called publish-subscribe protocol via the `Flow` API, which offers more sophisticated programming approaches (chapter 17).

Figure 15.2 illustrates the difference between concurrency and parallelism. Concurrency is a programming property (overlapped execution) that can occur even for a single-core machine, whereas parallelism is a property of execution hardware (simultaneous execution).

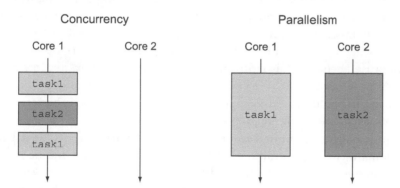

Figure 15.2   Concurrency versus parallelism

The rest of this chapter explains the fundamental ideas underpinning Java's new CompletableFuture and Flow APIs.

We start by explaining the Java evolution of concurrency, including Threads, and higher-level abstractions, including Thread Pools and Futures (section 15.1). We note that chapter 7 dealt with mainly using parallelism in looplike programs. Section 15.2 explores how you can better exploit concurrency for method calls. Section 15.3 gives you a diagrammatic way to see parts of programs as boxes that communicate over

> ### Guidance for the reader
>
> This chapter contains little real-life Java code. We suggest that readers who want to see only code skip to chapters 16 and 17. On the other hand, as we've all discovered, code that implements unfamiliar ideas can be hard to understand. Therefore, we use simple functions and include diagrams to explain the big-picture ideas, such as the publish-subscribe protocol behind the Flow API capturing reactive programming.

channels. Section 15.4 and section 15.5 look at the CompletableFuture and reactive-programming principles in Java 8 and 9. Finally, section 15.6 explains the difference between a reactive system and reactive programming.

We exemplify most of the concepts with a running example showing how to calculate expressions such as f(x)+g(x) and then return, or print, the result by using various Java concurrency features—assuming that f(x) and g(x) are long-running computations.

15.1   Evolving Java support for expressing concurrency

Java has evolved considerably in its support for concurrent programming, largely reflecting the changes in hardware, software systems, and programming concepts over the past 20 years. Summarizing this evolution can help you understand the reason for the new additions and their roles in programming and system design.

Initially, Java had locks (via synchronized classes and methods), Runnables and Threads. In 2004, Java 5 introduced the java.util.concurrent package, which supported more expressive concurrency, particularly the ExecutorService[1] interface (which decoupled task submission from thread execution), as well as Callable<T> and Future<T>, which produced higher-level and result-returning variants of Runnable and Thread and used generics (also introduced in Java 5). ExecutorServices can execute both Runnables and Callables. These features facilitated parallel programming on the multicore CPUs that started to appear the following year. To be honest, nobody enjoyed working with threads directly!

Later versions of Java continued to enhance concurrency support, as it became increasingly demanded by programmers who needed to program multicore CPUs effectively. As you saw in chapter 7, Java 7 added java.util.concurrent.Recursive-Task to support fork/join implementation of divide-and-conquer algorithms, and Java 8 added support for Streams and their parallel processing (building on the newly added support for lambdas).

Java further enriched its concurrency features by providing support for *composing* Futures (via the Java 8 CompletableFuture implementation of Future, section 15.4 and chapter 16), and Java 9, provided explicit support for distributed asynchronous programming. These APIs give you a mental model and toolkit for building the sort of mashup application mentioned in the introduction to this chapter. There the

---

[1] The ExecutorService interface extends the Executor interface with the submit method to run a Callable; the Executor interface merely has an execute method for Runnables.

application worked by contacting various web services and combining their information in real time for a user or to expose it as a further web service. This process is called *reactive programming*, and Java 9 provides support for it via the *publish-subscribe protocol* (specified by the `java.util.concurrent.Flow` interface; see section 15.5 and chapter 17). A key concept of `CompletableFuture` and `java.util.concurrent.Flow` is to provide programming structures that enable independent tasks to execute concurrently wherever possible and in a way that easily exploits as much as possible of the parallelism provided by multicore or multiple machines.

15.1.1 *Threads and higher-level abstractions*

Many of us learned about threads and processes from a course on operating systems. A single-CPU computer can support multiple users because its operating system allocates a process to each user. The operating system gives these processes separate virtual address spaces so that two users feel like they're the only users of the computer. The operating system furthers this illusion by waking periodically to share the CPU among the processes. A process can request that the operating system allocate it one or more *threads*—processes that share an address space as their owning process and therefore can run tasks concurrently and cooperatively.

In a multicore setting, perhaps a single-user laptop running only one user process, a program can never fully exploit the computing power of the laptop unless it uses threads. Each core can be used for one or more processes or threads, but if your program doesn't use threads, it's effectively using only one of the processor cores.

Indeed, if you have a four-core CPU and can arrange for each core to continually do useful work, your program theoretically runs up to four times faster. (Overheads reduce this result somewhere, of course.) Given an array of numbers of size 1,000,000 storing the number of correct questions answered by students in an example, compare the program

```
long sum = 0;
for (int i = 0; i < 1_000_000; i++) {
    sum += stats[i];
}
```

running on a single thread, which worked fine in single-core days, with a version that creates four threads, with the first thread executing

```
long sum0 = 0;
for (int i = 0; i < 250_000; i++) {
    sum0 += stats[i];
}
```

and to the fourth thread executing

```
long sum3 = 0;
for (int i = 750_000; i < 1_000_000; i++) {
    sum3 += stats[i];
}
```

These four threads are complemented by the main program starting them in turn (`.start()` in Java), waiting for them to complete (`.join()`), and then computing

```
sum = sum0 + … + sum3;
```

The trouble is that doing this for each loop is tedious and error-prone. Also, what can you do for code that isn't a loop?

Chapter 7 showed how Java Streams can achieve this parallelism with little programmer effort by using internal iteration instead of external iteration (explicit loops):

```
sum = Arrays.stream(stats).parallel().sum();
```

The takeaway idea is that parallel Stream iteration is a higher-level concept than explicit use of threads. In other words, this use of Streams *abstracts* a given use pattern of threads. This abstraction into Streams is analogous to a design pattern, but with the benefit that much of the complexity is implemented inside the library rather than being boilerplate code. Chapter 7 also explained how to use `java.util.concurrent.RecursiveTask` support in Java 7 for the fork/join abstraction of threads to parallelize divide-and-conquer algorithms, providing a higher-level way to sum the array efficiently on a multicore machine.

Before looking at additional abstractions for threads, we visit the (Java 5) idea of `ExecutorServices` and the thread pools on which these further abstractions are built.

15.1.2 *Executors and thread pools*

Java 5 provided the Executor framework and the idea of thread pools as a higher-level idea capturing the power of threads, which allow Java programmers to decouple task submission from task execution.

PROBLEMS WITH THREADS

Java threads access operating-system threads directly. The problem is that operating-system threads are expensive to create and to destroy (involving interaction with page tables), and moreover, only a limited number exist. Exceeding the number of operating-system threads is likely to cause a Java application to crash mysteriously, so be careful not to leave threads running while continuing to create new ones.

The number of operating system (and Java) threads will significantly exceed the number of hardware threads[2], so all the hardware threads can be usefully occupied executing code even when some operating-system threads are blocked or sleeping. As an example, the 2016 Intel Core i7-6900K server processor has eight cores, each with two symmetric multiprocessing (SMP) hardware threads, leading to 16 hardware threads, and a server may contain several of these processors, consisting of perhaps 64 hardware threads. By contrast, a laptop may have only one or two hardware threads, so portable programs must avoid making assumptions about how many hardware threads

---

[2] We'd use the word *core* here, but CPUs like the Intel i7-6900K have multiple hardware threads per core, so the CPU can execute useful instructions even for short delays such as a cache miss.

are available. Contrarily, the optimum number of Java threads for a given program depends on the number of hardware cores available!

THREAD POOLS AND WHY THEY'RE BETTER

The Java ExecutorService provides an interface where you can submit tasks and obtain their results later. The expected implementation uses a pool of threads, which can be created by one of the factory methods, such as the newFixedThreadPool method:

```
ExecutorService newFixedThreadPool(int nThreads)
```

This method creates an ExecutorService containing nThreads (often called *worker threads*) and stores them in a thread pool, from which unused threads are taken to run submitted tasks on a first-come, first-served basis. These threads are returned to the pool when their tasks terminate. One great outcome is that it's cheap to submit thousands of tasks to a thread pool while keeping the number of tasks to a hardware-appropriate number. Several configurations are possible, including the size of the queue, rejection policy, and priority for different tasks.

Note the wording: The programmer provides a *task* (a Runnable or a Callable), which is executed by a *thread*.

THREAD POOLS AND WHY THEY'RE WORSE

Thread pools are better than explicit thread manipulation in almost all ways, but you need to be aware of two "gotchas:"

- A thread pool with *k* threads can execute only *k* tasks concurrently. Any further task submissions are held in a queue and not allocated a thread until one of the existing tasks completes. This situation is generally good, in that it allows you to submit many tasks without accidentally creating an excessive number of threads, but you have to be wary of tasks that sleep or wait for I/O or network connections. In the context of blocking I/O, these tasks occupy worker threads but do no useful work while they're waiting. Try taking four hardware threads and a thread pool of size 5 and submitting 20 tasks to it (figure 15.3). You might expect that the tasks would run in parallel until all 20 have completed. But suppose that three of the first-submitted tasks sleep or wait for I/O. Then only two threads are available for the remaining 15 tasks, so you're getting only half the throughput you expected (and would have if you created the thread pool with eight threads instead). It's even possible to cause deadlock in a thread pool if earlier task submissions or already running tasks, need to wait for later task submissions, which is a typical use-pattern for Futures.

  The takeaway is to try to avoid submitting tasks that can block (sleep or wait for events) to thread pools, but you can't always do so in existing systems.

- Java typically waits for all threads to complete before allowing a return from main to avoid killing a thread executing vital code. Therefore, it's important in practice and as part of good hygiene to shut down every thread pool before exiting the program (because worker threads for this pool will have been created but

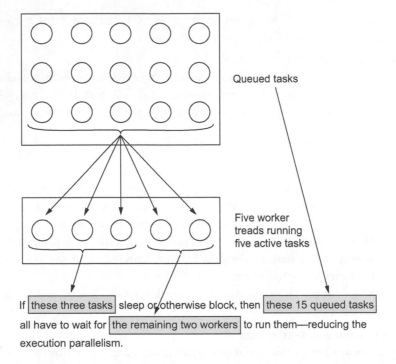

Queued tasks

Five worker
treads running
five active tasks

If these three tasks sleep or otherwise block, then these 15 queued tasks all have to wait for the remaining two workers to run them—reducing the execution parallelism.

Figure 15.3   Sleeping tasks reduce the throughput of thread pools.

not terminated, as they're waiting for another task submission). In practice, it's common to have a long-running `ExecutorService` that manages an always-running Internet service.

Java does provide the `Thread.setDaemon` method to control this behavior, which we discuss in the next section.

15.1.3   *Other abstractions of threads: non-nested with method calls*

To explain why the forms of concurrency used in this chapter differ from those used in chapter 7 (parallel Stream processing and the fork/join framework), we'll note that the forms used in chapter 7 have one special property: whenever any task (or thread) is started within a method call, the same method call waits for it to complete before returning. In other words, thread creation and the matching `join()` happen in a way that nests properly within the call-return nesting of method calls. This idea, called *strict fork/join*, is depicted in figure 15.4.

It's relatively innocuous to have a more relaxed form of fork/join in which a spawned task escapes from an internal method call but is joined in an outer call, so that the interface provided to users still appears to be a normal call,[3] as shown in figure 15.5.

---

[3] Compare "Thinking Functionally" (chapter 18) in which we discuss having a side-effect-free interface to a method that internally uses side-effects!

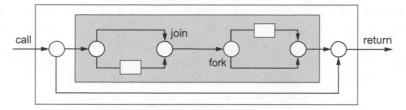

Figure 15.4   Strict fork/join. Arrows denote threads, circles represent forks and joins, and rectangles represent method calls and returns.

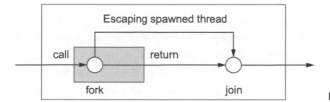

Figure 15.5   Relaxed fork/join

In this chapter, we focus on richer forms of concurrency in which threads created (or tasks spawned) by a user's method call may outlive the call, as shown in figure 15.6.

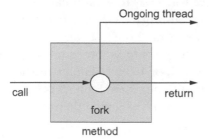

Figure 15.6   An asynchronous method

This type of method is often called an asynchronous method, particularly when the ongoing spawned task continues to do work that's helpful to the method caller. We explore Java 8 and 9 techniques for benefiting from such methods later in this chapter, starting in section 15.2, but first, check the dangers:

- The ongoing thread runs concurrently with the code following the method call and therefore requires careful programming to avoid data races.
- What happens if the Java main() method returns before the ongoing thread has terminated? There are two answers, both rather unsatisfactory:
  - Wait for all such outstanding threads before exiting the application.
  - Kill all outstanding threads and then exit.

The former solution risks a seeming application crash by never terminating due to a forgotten thread; the latter risks interrupting a sequence of I/O operations writing to disk, thereby leaving an external data in an inconsistent state. To avoid both of these problems, ensure that your program keeps track of all threads it creates and joins them all before exiting (including shutting down any thread pools).

Java threads can be labeled as *daemon*[4] or nondaemon, using the setDaemon() method call. Daemon threads are killed on exit (and therefore are useful for services that don't leave the disk in an inconsistent state), whereas returning from main continues to wait for all threads that aren't daemons to terminate before exiting the program.

15.1.4 *What do you want from threads?*

What you want is to be able to structure your program so that whenever it can benefit from parallelism, enough tasks are available to occupy all the hardware threads, which means structuring your program to have many smaller tasks (but not too small because of the cost of task switching). You saw how to do this for loops and divide-conquer algorithms in chapter 7, using parallel stream processing and fork/join, but in the rest of this chapter (and in chapters 16 and 17), you see how to do it for method calls without writing swaths of boilerplate thread-manipulation code.

15.2 *Synchronous and asynchronous APIs*

Chapter 7 showed you that Java 8 Streams give you a way to exploit parallel hardware. This exploitation happens in two stages. First, you replace external iteration (explicit for loops) with internal iteration (using Stream methods). Then you can use the parallel() method on Streams to allow the elements to be processed in parallel by the Java runtime library instead of rewriting every loop to use complex thread-creation operations. An additional advantage is that the runtime system is much better informed about the number of available threads when the loop is executed than is the programmer, who can only guess.

Situations other than loop-based computations can also benefit from parallelism. An important Java development that forms the background of this chapter and chapters 16 and 17 is asynchronous APIs.

Let's take for a running example the problem of summing the results of calls to methods f and g with signatures:

```
int f(int x);
int g(int x);
```

For emphasis, we'll refer to these signatures as a *synchronous API*, as they return their results when they physically return, in a sense that will soon become clear. You might

---

[4] Etymologically, *daemon* and *demon* arise from the same Greek word, but *daemon* captures the idea of a helpful spirit, whereas *demon* captures the idea of an evil spirit. UNIX coined the word *daemon* for computing purposes, using it for system services such as sshd, a process or thread that listens for incoming ssh connections.

invoke this API with a code fragment that calls them both and prints the sum of their results:

```
int y = f(x);
int z = g(x);
System.out.println(y + z);
```

Now suppose that methods f and g execute for a long time. (These methods could implement a mathematical optimization task, such as gradient descent, but in chapters 16 and 17, we consider more-practical cases in which they make Internet queries.) In general, the Java compiler can do nothing to optimize this code because f and g may interact in ways that aren't clear to the compiler. But if you know that f and g don't interact, or you don't care, you want to execute f and g in separate CPU cores, which makes the total execution time only the maximum of that of the calls to f and g instead of the sum. All you need to do is run the calls to f and g in separate threads. This idea is a great one, but it complicates[5] the simple code from before:

```
class ThreadExample {

    public static void main(String[] args) throws InterruptedException {
        int x = 1337;
        Result result = new Result();

        Thread t1 = new Thread(() -> { result.left = f(x); } );
        Thread t2 = new Thread(() -> { result.right = g(x); });
        t1.start();
        t2.start();
        t1.join();
        t2.join();
        System.out.println(result.left + result.right);
    }

    private static class Result {
        private int left;
        private int right;
    }
}
```

You can simplify this code somewhat by using the Future API interface instead of Runnable. Assuming that you previously set up a thread pool as an ExecutorService (such as executorService), you can write

```
public class ExecutorServiceExample {
    public static void main(String[] args)
        throws ExecutionException, InterruptedException {

        int x = 1337;
```

---

[5] Some of the complexity here has to do with transferring results back from the thread. Only final outer-object variables can be used in lambdas or inner classes, but the real problem is all the explicit thread manipulation.

```
ExecutorService executorService = Executors.newFixedThreadPool(2);
Future<Integer> y = executorService.submit(() -> f(x));
Future<Integer> z = executorService.submit(() -> g(x));
System.out.println(y.get() + z.get());

executorService.shutdown();
    }
}
```

but this code is still polluted by the boilerplate code involving explicit calls to `submit`.

You need a better way of expressing this idea, analogous to how internal iteration on Streams avoided the need to use thread-creation syntax to parallelize external iteration.

The answer involves changing the API to an *asynchronous API*.[6] Instead of allowing a method to return its result at the same time that it physically returns to the caller (synchronously), you allow it to return physically before producing its result, as shown in figure 15.6. Thus, the call to f and the code following this call (here, the call to g) can execute in parallel. You can achieve this parallelism by using two techniques, both of which change the signatures of f *and* g.

The first technique uses Java Futures in a better way. Futures appeared in Java 5 and were enriched into `CompletableFuture` in Java 8 to make them composable; we explain this concept in section 15.4 and explore the Java API in detail with a worked Java code example in chapter 16. The second technique is a reactive-programming style that uses the Java 9 `java.util.concurrent.Flow` interfaces, based on the publish-subscribe protocol explained in section 15.5 and exemplified with practical code in chapter 17.

How do these alternatives affect the signatures of f and g?

15.2.1 *Future-style API*

In this alternative, change the signature of f and g to

```
Future<Integer> f(int x);
Future<Integer> g(int x);
```

and change the calls to

```
Future<Integer> y = f(x);
Future<Integer> z = g(x);
System.out.println(y.get() + z.get());
```

The idea is that method f returns a Future, which contains a task that continues to evaluate its original body, but the return from f happens as quickly as possible after the call. Method g similarly returns a future, and the third code line uses `get()` to wait for both Futures to complete and sums their results.

---

[6] Synchronous APIs are also known as *blocking APIs,* as the physical return is delayed until the result is ready (clearest when considering a call to an I/O operation), whereas asynchronous APIs can naturally implement nonblocking I/O (where the API call merely initiates the I/O operation without waiting for the result, provided that the library at hand, such as Netty, supports nonblocking I/O operations).

In this case, you could have left the API and call of g unchanged without reducing parallelism—only introducing Futures for f. You have two reasons not to do so in bigger programs:

- Other uses of g may require a Future-style version, so you prefer a uniform API style.
- To enable parallel hardware to execute your programs as fast as possible, it's useful to have more and smaller tasks (within reason).

15.2.2 Reactive-style API

In the second alternative, the core idea is to use callback-style programming by changing the signature of f and g to

```
void f(int x, IntConsumer dealWithResult);
```

This alternative may seem to be surprising at first. How can f work if it doesn't return a value? The answer is that you instead pass a *callback*[7] (a lambda) to f as an additional argument, and the body of f spawns a task that calls this lambda with the result when it's ready instead of returning a value with `return`. Again, f returns immediately after spawning the task to evaluate the body, which results in the following style of code:

```
public class CallbackStyleExample {
    public static void main(String[] args) {

        int x = 1337;
        Result result = new Result();

        f(x, (int y) -> {
            result.left = y;
            System.out.println((result.left + result.right));
        } );

        g(x, (int z) -> {
            result.right = z;
            System.out.println((result.left + result.right));
        });

    }
}
```

Ah, but this isn't the same! Before this code prints the correct result (the sum of the calls to f and g), it prints the fastest value to complete (and occasionally instead prints

---

[7] Some authors use the term *callback* to mean any lambda or method reference passed as an argument to a method, such as the argument to `Stream.filter` or `Stream.map`. We use it only for those lambda and method references that can be called *after* the method has returned.

the sum twice, as there's no locking here, and both operands to + could be updated before either of the `println` calls is executed). There are two answers:

- You could recover the original behavior by invoking `println` after testing with if-then-else that both callbacks have been called, perhaps by counting them with appropriate locking.
- This reactive-style API is intended to react to a sequence of events, not to single results, for which `Futures` are more appropriate.

Note that this reactive style of programming allows methods `f` and `g` to invoke their callback `dealWithResult` multiple times. The original versions of `f` and `g` were obliged to use a `return` that can be performed only once. Similarly, a `Future` can be completed only once, and its result is available to `get()`. In a sense, the reactive-style asynchronous API naturally enables a sequence (which we will later liken to a stream) of values, whereas the `Future`-style API corresponds to a one-shot conceptual framework.

In section 15.5, we refine this core-idea example to model a spreadsheet call containing a formula such as =C1+C2.

You may argue that both alternatives make the code more complex. To some extent, this argument is correct; you shouldn't thoughtlessly use either API for every method. But APIs keep code simpler (and use higher-level constructs) than explicit thread manipulation does. Also, careful use of these APIs for method calls that (a) cause long-running computations (perhaps longer than several milliseconds) or (b) wait for a network or for input from a human can significantly improve the efficiency of your application. In case (a), these techniques make your program faster without the explicit ubiquitous use of threads polluting your program. In case (b), there's the additional benefit that the underlying system can use threads effectively without clogging up. We turn to the latter point in the next section.

15.2.3   *Sleeping (and other blocking operations) considered harmful*

When you're interacting with a human or an application that needs to restrict the rate at which things happen, one natural way to program is to use the `sleep()` method. A sleeping thread still occupies system resources, however. This situation doesn't matter if you have only a few threads, but it matters if you have many threads, most of which are sleeping. (See the discussion in section 15.2.1 and figure 15.3.)

The lesson to remember is that tasks sleeping in a thread pool consume resources by blocking other tasks from starting to run. (They can't stop tasks already allocated to a thread, as the operating system schedules these tasks.)

It's not only sleeping that can clog the available threads in a thread pool, of course. Any blocking operation can do the same thing. Blocking operations fall into two classes: waiting for another task to do something, such as invoking `get()` on a Future; and waiting for external interactions such as reads from networks, database servers, or human interface devices such as keyboards.

What can you do? One rather totalitarian answer is never to block within a task or at least to do so with a small number of exceptions in your code. (See section 15.2.4 for a reality check.) The better alternative is to break your task into two parts—before and after—and ask Java to schedule the after part only when it won't block.

Compare code A, shown as a single task

```
work1();
Thread.sleep(10000);          ◄─────  Sleep for 10 seconds.
work2();
```

with code B:

```
public class ScheduledExecutorServiceExample {
    public static void main(String[] args) {
        ScheduledExecutorService scheduledExecutorService
            = Executors.newScheduledThreadPool(1);

        work1();
        scheduledExecutorService.schedule(
ScheduledExecutorServiceExample::work2, 10, TimeUnit.SECONDS);   ◄─────┐

        scheduledExecutorService.shutdown();              Schedule a separate task
    }                                                      for work2() 10 seconds
                                                           after work1() finishes.
    public static void work1(){
        System.out.println("Hello from Work1!");
    }

    public static void work2(){
        System.out.println("Hello from Work2!");
    }
}
```

Think of both tasks being executed within a thread pool.

Consider how code A executes. First, it's queued to execute in the thread pool, and later, it starts executing. Halfway through, however, it blocks in the call to sleep, occupying a worker thread for 10 whole seconds doing nothing. Then it executes work2() before terminating and releasing the worker thread. Code B, by comparison, executes work1() and then terminates—but only after having queued a task to do work2() 10 seconds later.

Code B is better, but why? Code A and code B do the same thing. The difference is that code A occupies a precious thread while it sleeps, whereas code B queues another task to execute (with a few bytes of memory and no requirement for a thread) instead of sleeping.

This effect is something that you should always bear in mind when creating tasks. Tasks occupy valuable resources when they start executing, so you should aim to keep them running until they complete and release their resources. Instead of blocking, a task should terminate after submitting a follow-up task to complete the work it intended to do.

Whenever possible, this guideline applies to I/O, too. Instead of doing a classical blocking read, a task should issue a nonblocking "start a read" method call and terminate after asking the runtime library to schedule a follow-up task when the read is complete.

This design pattern may seem to lead to lots of hard-to-read code. But the Java CompletableFuture interface (section 15.4 and chapter 16) abstracts this style of code within the runtime library, using combinators instead of explicit uses of blocking get() operations on Futures, as we discussed earlier.

As a final remark, we'll note that code A and code B would be equally effective if threads were unlimited and cheap. But they aren't, so code B is the way to go whenever you have more than a few tasks that might sleep or otherwise block.

15.2.4 *Reality check*

If you're designing a new system, designing it with many small, concurrent tasks so that all possible blocking operations are implemented with asynchronous calls is probably the way to go if you want to exploit parallel hardware. But reality needs to intrude into this "everything asynchronous" design principle. (Remember, "the best is the enemy of the good.") Java has had nonblocking IO primitives (java.nio) since Java 1.4 in 2002, and they're relatively complicated and not well known. Pragmatically, we suggest that you try to identify situations that would benefit from Java's enhanced concurrency APIs, and use them without worrying about making every API asynchronous.

You may also find it useful to look at newer libraries such as Netty (https://netty.io/), which provides a uniform blocking/nonblocking API for network servers.

15.2.5 *How do exceptions work with asynchronous APIs?*

In both Future-based and reactive-style asynchronous APIs, the conceptual body of the called method executes in a separate thread, and the caller's execution is likely to have exited the scope of any exception handler placed around the call. It's clear that unusual behavior that would have triggered an exception needs to perform an alternative action. But what might this action be? In the CompletableFuture implementation of Futures, the API includes provision for exposing exceptions at the time of the get() method and also provides methods such as exceptionally() to recover from exceptions, which we discuss in chapter 16.

For reactive-style asynchronous APIs, you have to modify the interface by introducing an additional callback, which is called instead of an exception being raised, as the existing callback is called instead of a return being executed. To do this, include multiple callbacks in the reactive API, as in this example:

```
void f(int x, Consumer<Integer> dealWithResult,
             Consumer<Throwable> dealWithException);
```

Then the body of f might perform

```
dealWithException(e);
```

If there are multiple callbacks, instead of supplying them separately, you can equivalently wrap them as methods in a single object. The Java 9 `Flow` API, for example, wraps these multiple callbacks within a single object (of class `Subscriber<T>` containing four methods interpreted as callbacks). Here are three of them:

```
void    onComplete()
void    onError(Throwable throwable)
void    onNext(T item)
```

Separate callbacks indicate when a value is available (`onNext`), when an exception arose while trying to make a value available (`onError`), and when an `onComplete` callback enables the program to indicate that no further values (or exceptions) will be produced. For the preceding example, the API for `f` would now be

```
void f(int x, Subscriber<Integer> s);
```

and the body of `f` would now indicate an exception, represented as `Throwable t`, by performing

```
s.onError(t);
```

Compare this API containing multiple callbacks with reading numbers from a file or keyboard device. If you think of such a device as being a producer rather than a passive data structure, it produces a sequence of "Here's a number" or "Here's a malformed item instead of a number" items, and finally a "There are no more characters left (end-of-file)" notification.

It's common to refer to these calls as messages, or *events*. You might say, for example, that the file reader produced the number events 3, 7, and 42, followed by a malformed-number event, followed by the number event 2 and then by the end-of-file event.

When seeing these events as part of an API, it's important to note that the API signifies nothing about the relative ordering of these events (often called the *channel protocol*). In practice, the accompanying documentation specifies the protocol by using phases such as "After an `onComplete` event, no more events will be produced."

15.3 *The box-and-channel model*

Often, the best way to design and think about concurrent systems is pictorially. We call this technique the *box-and-channel model*. Consider a simple situation involving integers, generalizing the earlier example of calculating `f(x) + g(x)`. Now you want to call method or function `p` with argument `x`, pass its result to functions `q1` and `q2`, call method or function `r` with the results of these two calls, and then print the result. (To avoid clutter in this explanation, we're not going to distinguish between a method `m` of class `C` and its associated function `C::m`.) Pictorially, this task is simple, as shown in figure 15.7.

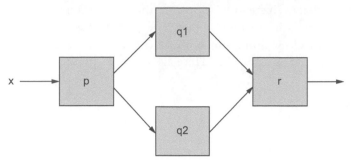

Figure 15.7   A simple box-and-channel diagram

Look at two ways of coding figure 15.7 in Java to see the problems they cause. The first way is

```
int t = p(x);
System.out.println( r(q1(t), q2(t)) );
```

This code appears to be clear, but Java runs the calls to q1 and q2 in turn, which is what you want to avoid when trying to exploit hardware parallelism.

Another way is to use Futures to evaluate f and g in parallel:

```
int t = p(x);
Future<Integer> a1 = executorService.submit(() -> q1(t));
Future<Integer> a2 = executorService.submit(() -> q2(t));
System.out.println( r(a1.get(),a2.get()));
```

Note: We didn't wrap p and r in Futures in this example because of the shape of the box-and-channel diagram. p has to be done before everything else and r after everything else. This would no longer be the case if we changed the example to mimic

```
System.out.println( r(q1(t), q2(t)) + s(x) );
```

in which we'd need to wrap all five functions (p, q1, q2, r, and s) in Futures to maximize concurrency.

This solution works well if the total amount of concurrency in the system is small. But what if the system becomes large, with many separate box-and-channel diagrams, and with some of the boxes themselves internally using their own boxes and channels? In this situation, many tasks might be waiting (with a call to get()) for a Future to complete, and as discussed in section 15.1.2, the result may be underexploitation of hardware parallelism or even deadlock. Moreover, it tends to be hard to understand such large-scale system structure well enough to work out how many tasks are liable to be waiting for a get(). The solution that Java 8 adopts (CompletableFuture; see section 15.4 for details) is to use *combinators*. You've already seen that you can use methods such as compose() and andThen() on two Functions to get another Function (see chapter 3). Assuming that add1 adds 1 to an Integer and that dble doubles an Integer, for example, you can write

```
Function<Integer, Integer> myfun = add1.andThen(dble);
```

to create a `Function` that doubles its argument and adds 2 to the result. But box-and-channel diagrams can be also coded directly and nicely with combinators. Figure 15.7 could be captured succinctly with Java `Functions p, q1, q2` and `BiFunction r` as

```
p.thenBoth(q1,q2).thenCombine(r)
```

Unfortunately, neither `thenBoth` nor `thenCombine` is part of the Java `Function` and `BiFunction` classes in exactly this form.

In the next section, you see how similar ideas of combinators work for `Completable-Future` and prevent tasks from ever to have to wait using `get()`.

Before leaving this section, we want to emphasize the fact that the box-and-channel model can be used to structure thoughts and code. In an important sense, it raises the level of abstraction for constructing a larger system. You draw boxes (or use combinators in programs) to express the computation you want, which is later executed, perhaps more efficiently than you might have obtained by hand-coding the computation. This use of combinators works not only for mathematical functions, but also for Futures and reactive streams of data. In section 15.5, we generalize these box-and-channel diagrams into marble diagrams in which multiple marbles (representing messages) are shown on every channel. The box-and-channel model also helps you change perspective from directly programming concurrency to allowing combinators to do the work internally. Similarly, Java 8 Streams change perspective from the coder having to iterate over a data structure to combinators on Streams doing the work internally.

15.4 *CompletableFuture and combinators for concurrency*

One problem with the `Future` interface is that it's an interface, encouraging you to think of and structure your concurrent coding tasks as Futures. Historically, however, Futures have provided few actions beyond `FutureTask` implementations: creating a future with a given computation, running it, waiting for it to terminate, and so on. Later versions of Java provided more structured support (such as `RecursiveTask`, discussed in chapter 7).

What Java 8 brings to the party is the ability to compose Futures, using the `CompletableFuture` implementation of the `Future` interface. So why call it `CompletableFuture` rather than, say, `ComposableFuture`? Well, an ordinary Future is typically created with a `Callable`, which is run, and the result is obtained with a `get()`. But a `CompletableFuture` allows you to create a Future without giving it any code to run, and a `complete()` method allows some other thread to complete it later with a value (hence the name) so that `get()` can access that value. To sum `f(x)` and `g(x)` concurrently, you can write

```
public class CFComplete {

    public static void main(String[] args)
        throws ExecutionException, InterruptedException {
```

```
        ExecutorService executorService = Executors.newFixedThreadPool(10);
        int x = 1337;

        CompletableFuture<Integer> a = new CompletableFuture<>();
        executorService.submit(() -> a.complete(f(x)));
        int b = g(x);
        System.out.println(a.get() + b);

        executorService.shutdown();
    }
}
```

or you can write

```
public class CFComplete {

    public static void main(String[] args)
        throws ExecutionException, InterruptedException {
        ExecutorService executorService = Executors.newFixedThreadPool(10);
        int x = 1337;

        CompletableFuture<Integer> a = new CompletableFuture<>();
        executorService.submit(() -> b.complete(g(x)));
        int a = f(x);
        System.out.println(a + b.get());

        executorService.shutdown();
    }
}
```

Note that both these code versions can waste processing resources (recall section 15.2.3) by having a thread blocked waiting for a get—the former if f(x) takes longer, and the latter if g(x) takes longer. Using Java 8's CompletableFuture enables you to avoid this situation; but first a quiz.

Quiz 15.1:

Before reading further, think how you might write tasks to exploit threads perfectly in this case: two active threads while both f(x) and g(x) are executing, and one thread starting from when the first one completes up to the return statement.

The answer is that you'd use one task to execute f(x), a second task to execute g(x), and a third task (a new one or one of the existing ones) to calculate the sum, and somehow, the third task can't start before the first two finish. How do you solve this problem in Java?

The solution is to use the idea of composition on Futures.

First, refresh your memory about composing operations, which you've seen twice before in this book. Composing operations is a powerful program-structuring idea used in many other languages, but it took off in Java only with the addition of lambdas in Java 8. One instance of this idea of composition is composing operations on streams, as in this example:

```
myStream.map(…).filter(…).sum()
```

Another instance of this idea is using methods such as compose() and andThen() on two Functions to get another Function (see section 15.5).

This gives you a new and better way to add the results of your two computations by using the thenCombine method from CompletableFuture<T>. Don't worry too much about the details at the moment; we discuss this topic more comprehensively in chapter 16. The method thenCombine has the following signature (slightly simplified to prevent the clutter associated with generics and wildcards):

```
CompletableFuture<V> thenCombine(CompletableFuture<U> other,
                                 BiFunction<T, U, V> fn)
```

The method takes two CompletableFuture values (with result types T and U) and creates a new one (with result type V). When the first two complete, it takes both their results, applies fn to both results, and completes the resulting future without blocking. The preceding code could now be rewritten in the following form:

```
public class CFCombine {

    public static void main(String[] args) throws ExecutionException,
      InterruptedException {

        ExecutorService executorService = Executors.newFixedThreadPool(10);
        int x = 1337;

        CompletableFuture<Integer> a = new CompletableFuture<>();
        CompletableFuture<Integer> b = new CompletableFuture<>();
        CompletableFuture<Integer> c = a.thenCombine(b, (y, z)-> y + z);
        executorService.submit(() -> a.complete(f(x)));
        executorService.submit(() -> b.complete(g(x)));


        System.out.println(c.get());
        executorService.shutdown();
    }
}
```

The thenCombine line is critical: without knowing anything about computations in the Futures a and b, it creates a computation that's scheduled to run in the thread pool only when both of the first two computations have completed. The third computation, c, adds their results and (most important) isn't considered to be eligible to execute on a thread until the other two computations have completed (rather than starting to execute early and then blocking). Therefore, no actual wait operation is performed, which was troublesome in the earlier two versions of this code. In those versions, if the computation in the Future happens to finish second, two threads in the thread pool are still active, even though you need only one! Figure 15.8 shows this situation diagrammatically. In both earlier versions, calculating y+z happens on the same fixed thread that calculates f(x) or g(x)—with a potential wait in between. By contrast, using thenCombine schedules the summing computation only after both f(x) and g(x) have completed.

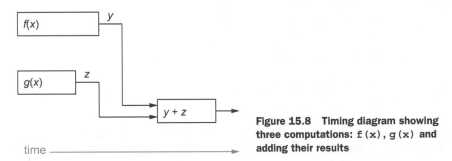

Figure 15.8   Timing diagram showing three computations: f(x), g(x) and adding their results

To be clear, for many pieces of code, you don't need to worry about a few threads being blocked waiting for a get(), so pre-Java 8 Futures remain sensible programming options. In some situations, however, you want to have a large number of Futures (such as for dealing with multiple queries to services). In these cases, using Completable-Future and its combinators to avoid blocking calls to get() and possible loss of parallelism or deadlock is often the best solution.

15.5 *Publish-subscribe and reactive programming*

The mental model for a Future and CompletableFuture is that of a computation that executes independently and concurrently. The result of the Future is available with get() after the computation completes. Thus, Futures are *one-shot*, executing code that runs to completion only once.

By contrast, the mental model for reactive programming is a Future-like object that, over time, yields multiple results. Consider two examples, starting with a thermometer object. You expect this object to yield a result repeatedly, giving you a temperature value every few seconds. Another example is an object representing the listener component of a web server; this object waits until an HTTP request appears over the network and similarly yields with the data from the request. Then other code can process the result: a temperature or data from an HTTP request. Then the thermometer and listener objects go back to sensing temperatures or listening before potentially yielding further results.

Note two points here. The core point is that these examples are like Futures but differ in that they can complete (or yield) multiple times instead of being one-shot. Another point is that in the second example, earlier results may be as important as ones seen later, whereas for a thermometer, most users are interested only in the most-recent temperature. But why is this type of a programming called *reactive?* The answer is that another part of the program may want to *react* to a low temperature report (such as by turning on a heater).

You may think that the preceding idea is only a Stream. If your program fits naturally into the Stream model, a Stream may be the best implementation. In general, though, the reactive-programming paradigm is more expressive. A given Java Stream can be consumed by only one terminal operation. As we mention in section 15.3, the Stream paradigm makes it hard to express Stream-like operations that can split a sequence of values between two processing pipelines (think fork) or process and combine items from two separate streams (think join). Streams have linear processing pipelines.

Java 9 models reactive programming with interfaces available inside `java.util` `.concurrent.Flow` and encodes what's known as the publish-subscribe model (or protocol, often shortened to pub-sub). You learn about the Java 9 Flow API in more detail in chapter 17, but we provide a short overview here. There are three main concepts:

- A *publisher* to which a *subscriber* can subscribe.
- The connection is known as a *subscription.*
- *Messages* (also known an *events*) are transmitted via the connection.

Figure 15.9 shows the idea pictorially, with subscriptions as channels and publishers and subscribers as ports on boxes. Multiple components can subscribe to a single publisher, a component can publish multiple separate streams, and a component can subscribe to multiple publishers. In this next section, we show you how this idea works step by step, using the nomenclature of the Java 9 Flow interface.

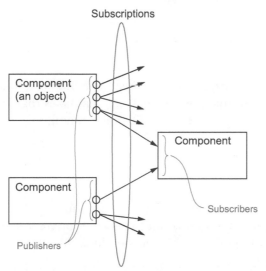

Figure 15.9 The publish-subscribe model

15.5.1 Example use for summing two flows

A simple but characteristic example of publish-subscribe combines events from two sources of information and publishes them for others to see. This process may sound obscure at first, but it's what a cell containing a formula in a spreadsheet does conceptually. Model a spreadsheet cell C3, which contains the formula `"=C1+C2"`. Whenever cell C1 or C2 is updated (by a human or because the cell contains a further formula), C3 is updated to reflect the change. The following code assumes that the only operation available is adding the values of cells.

First, model the concept of a cell that holds a value:

```
private class SimpleCell {
    private int value = 0;
    private String name;

    public SimpleCell(String name) {
        this.name = name;
    }
}
```

At the moment, the code is simple, and you can initialize a few cells, as follows:

```
SimpleCell c2 = new SimpleCell("C2");
SimpleCell c1 = new SimpleCell("C1");
```

How do you specify that when the value of c1 or c2 changes, c3 sums the two values? You need a way for c1 and c2 to subscribe c3 to their events. To do so, introduce the interface `Publisher<T>`, which at its core looks like this:

```
interface Publisher<T> {
    void subscribe(Subscriber<? super T> subscriber);
}
```

This interface takes a subscriber as an argument that it can communicate with. The `Subscriber<T>` interface includes a simple method, `onNext`, that takes that information as an argument and then is free to provide a specific implementation:

```
interface Subscriber<T> {
    void onNext(T t);
}
```

How do you bring these two concepts together? You may realize that a `Cell` is in fact both a `Publisher` (can subscribe cells to its events) and a `Subscriber` (reacts to events from other cells). The implementation of the `Cell` class now looks like this:

```
private class SimpleCell implements Publisher<Integer>, Subscriber<Integer> {
    private int value = 0;
    private String name;
    private List<Subscriber> subscribers = new ArrayList<>();
```

```
    public SimpleCell(String name) {
        this.name = name;
    }

    @Override
    public void subscribe(Subscriber<? super Integer> subscriber) {
        subscribers.add(subscriber);
    }

    private void notifyAllSubscribers() {
        subscribers.forEach(subscriber -> subscriber.onNext(this.value));
    }

    @Override
    public void onNext(Integer newValue) {
        this.value = newValue;
        System.out.println(this.name + ":" + this.value);
        notifyAllSubscribers();
    }
}
```

Reacts to a new value from a cell it is subscribed to by updating its value

Notifies all subscribers about the updated value

This method notifies all the subscribers with a new value.

Prints the value in the console but could be rendering the updated cell as part of an UI

Try a simple example:

```
Simplecell c3 = new SimpleCell("C3");
SimpleCell c2 = new SimpleCell("C2");
SimpleCell c1 = new SimpleCell("C1");

c1.subscribe(c3);

c1.onNext(10); // Update value of C1 to 10
c2.onNext(20); // update value of C2 to 20
```

This code outputs the following result because C3 is directly subscribed to C1:

```
C1:10
C3:10
C2:20
```

How do you implement the behavior of "C3=C1+C2" ? You need to introduce a separate class that's capable of storing two sides of an arithmetic operation (left and right):

```
    public class ArithmeticCell extends SimpleCell {

        private int left;
        private int right;

        public ArithmeticCell(String name) {
            super(name);
        }

        public void setLeft(int left) {
            this.left = left;
            onNext(left + this.right);
        }
```

Update the cell value and notify any subscribers.

```
        public void setRight(int right) {
            this.right = right;
            onNext(right + this.left);
        }
    }
```
Update the cell value and notify any subscribers.

Now you can try a more-realistic example:

```
ArithmeticCell c3 = new ArithmeticCell("C3");
SimpleCell c2 = new SimpleCell("C2");
SimpleCell c1 = new SimpleCell("C1");


c1.subscribe(c3::setLeft);
c2.subscribe(c3::setRight);


c1.onNext(10); // Update value of C1 to 10
c2.onNext(20); // update value of C2 to 20
c1.onNext(15); // update value of C1 to 15
```

The output is

```
C1:10
C3:10
C2:20
C3:30
C1:15
C3:35
```

By inspecting the output, you see that when C1 was updated to 15, C3 immediately reacted and updated its value as well. What's neat about the publisher-subscriber interaction is the fact that you can set up a graph of publishers and subscribers. You could create another cell C5 that depends on C3 and C4 by expressing "C5=C3+C4", for example:

```
ArithmeticCell c5 = new ArithmeticCell("C5");
ArithmeticCell c3 = new ArithmeticCell("C3");
SimpleCell c4 = new SimpleCell("C4");
SimpleCell c2 = new SimpleCell("C2");
SimpleCell c1 = new SimpleCell("C1");


c1.subscribe(c3::setLeft);
c2.subscribe(c3::setRight);


c3.subscribe(c5::setLeft);
c4.subscribe(c5::setRight);
```

Then you can perform various updates in your spreadsheet:

```
c1.onNext(10); // Update value of C1 to 10
c2.onNext(20); // update value of C2 to 20
c1.onNext(15); // update value of C1 to 15
c4.onNext(1); // update value of C4 to 1
c4.onNext(3); // update value of C4 to 3
```

These actions result in the following output:

```
C1:10
C3:10
C5:10
C2:20
C3:30
C5:30
C1:15
C3:35
C5:35
C4:1
C5:36
C4:3
C5:38
```

In the end, the value of C5 is 38 because C1 is 15, C2 is 20, and C4 is 3.

Nomenclature

Because data flows from publisher (producer) to subscriber (consumer), developers often use words such as *upstream* and *downstream*. In the preceding code examples, the data newValue received by the upstream onNext() methods is passed via the call to notifyAllSubscribers() to the downstream onNext() call.

That's the core idea of publish-subscribe. We've left out a few things, however, some of which are straightforward embellishments, and one of which (backpressure) is so vital that we discuss it separately in the next section.

First, we'll discuss the straightforward things. As we remark in section 15.2, practical programming of flows may want to signal things other than an onNext event, so subscribers (listeners) need to define onError and onComplete methods so that the publisher can indicate exceptions and terminations of data flow. (Perhaps the example of a thermometer has been replaced and will never produce more values via onNext.) The methods onError and onComplete are supported in the actual Subscriber interface in the Java 9 Flow API. These methods are among the reasons why this protocol is more powerful than the traditional Observer pattern.

Two simple but vital ideas that significantly complicate the Flow interfaces are pressure and backpressure. These ideas can appear to be unimportant, but they're vital for thread utilization. Suppose that your thermometer, which previously reported a temperature every few seconds, was upgraded to a better one that reports a temperature every millisecond. Could your program react to these events sufficiently quickly, or might some buffer overflow and cause a crash? (Recall the problems giving thread pools large numbers of tasks if more than a few tasks might block.) Similarly, suppose that you subscribe to a publisher that furnishes all the SMS messages onto your phone. The subscription might work well on my newish phone with only a few SMS messages, but what happens in a few years when there are thousands of messages, all potentially sent via calls to onNext in less than a second? This situation is often known as *pressure*.

Now think of a vertical pipe containing messages written on balls. You also need a form of backpressure, such as a mechanism that restricts the number of balls being added to the column. Backpressure is implemented in the Java 9 Flow API by a request() method (in a new interface called Subscription) that invites the publisher to send the next item(s), instead of items being sent at an unlimited rate (the pull model instead of the push model). We turn this topic in the next section.

15.5.2 *Backpressure*

You've seen how to pass a Subscriber object (containing onNext, onError, and OnComplete methods) to a Publisher, which the publisher calls when appropriate. This object passes information from Publisher to Subscriber. You want to limit the rate at which this information is sent via backpressure (flow control), which requires you to send information from Subscriber to Publisher. The problem is that the Publisher may have multiple Subscribers, and you want backpressure to affect only the point-to-point connection involved. In the Java 9 Flow API, the Subscriber interface includes a fourth method

```
void onSubscribe(Subscription subscription);
```

that's called as the first event sent on the channel established between Publisher and Subscriber. The Subscription object contains methods that enable the Subscriber to communicate with the Publisher, as follows:

```
interface Subscription {
    void    cancel();
    void    request(long n);
}
```

Note the usual "this seems backward" effect with callbacks. The Publisher creates the Subscription object and passes it to the Subscriber, which can call its methods to pass information from the Subscriber back to the Publisher.

15.5.3 *A simple form of real backpressure*

To enable a publish-subscribe connection to deal with events one at a time, you need to make the following changes:

- Arrange for the Subscriber to store the Subscription object passed by OnSubscribe locally, perhaps as a field subscription.
- Make the last action of onSubscribe, onNext, and (perhaps) onError be a call to channel.request(1) to request the next event (only one event, which stops the Subscriber from being overwhelmed).
- Change the Publisher so that notifyAllSubscribers (in this example) sends an onNext or onError event along only the channels that made a request.

(Typically, the `Publisher` creates a new `Subscription` object to associate with each `Subscriber` so that multiple `Subscribers` can each process data at their own rate.)

Although this process seems to be simple, implementing backpressure requires thinking about a range of implementation trade-offs:

- Do you send events to multiple `Subscribers` at the speed of the slowest, or do you have a separate queue of as-yet-unsent data for each `Subscriber`?
- What happens when these queues grow excessively?
- Do you drop events if the `Subscriber` isn't ready for them?

The choice depends on the semantics of the data being sent. Losing one temperature report from a sequence may not matter, but losing a credit in your bank account certainly does!

You often hear this concept referred to as reactive pull-based backpressure. The concept is called *reactive pull*-based because it provides a way for the `Subscriber` to pull (request) more information from the `Publisher` via events (reactive). The result is a backpressure mechanism.

15.6 Reactive systems vs. reactive programming

Increasingly in the programming and academic communities, you may hear about reactive systems and reactive programming, and it's important to realize that these terms express quite different ideas.

A *reactive system* is a program whose architecture allows it to react to changes in its runtime environments. Properties that reactive systems should have are formalized in the Reactive Manifesto (http://www.reactivemanifesto.org) (see chapter 17). Three of these properties can be summarized as responsive, resilient, and elastic.

Responsive means that a reactive system can respond to inputs in real time rather delaying a simple query because the system is processing a big job for someone else. *Resilient* means that a system generally doesn't fail because one component fails; a broken network link shouldn't affect queries that don't involve that link, and queries to an unresponsive component can be rerouted to an alternative component. *Elastic* means that a system can adjust to changes in its workload and continue to execute efficiently. As you might dynamically reallocate staff in a bar between serving food and serving drinks so that wait times in both lines are similar, you might adjust the number of worker threads associated with various software services so that no worker is idle while ensuring that each queue continues to be processed.

Clearly, you can achieve these properties in many ways, but one main approach is to use *reactive programming* style, provided in Java by interfaces associated with `java.util.concurrent.Flow`. The design of these interfaces reflects the fourth and final property of the Reactive Manifesto: being message-driven. *Message-driven* systems have internal APIs based on the box-and-channel model, with components waiting for inputs that are processed, with the results sent as messages to other components to enable the system to be responsive.

15.7 Road map

Chapter 16 explores the `CompletableFuture` API with a real Java example, and chapter 17 explores the Java 9 Flow (publish-subscribe) API.

Summary

- Support for concurrency in Java has evolved and continues to evolve. Thread pools are generally helpful but can cause problems when you have many tasks that can block.
- Making methods asynchronous (returning before all their work is done) allows additional parallelism, complementary to that used to optimize loops.
- You can use the box-and-channel model to visualize asynchronous systems.
- The Java 8 `CompletableFuture` class and the Java 9 Flow API can both represent box-and-channel diagrams.
- The `CompletableFuture` class expresses one-shot asynchronous computations. Combinators can be used to compose asynchronous computations without the risk of blocking that's inherent in traditional uses of Futures.
- The Flow API is based on the publish-subscribe protocol, including backpressure, and forms the basis for reactive programming in Java.
- Reactive programming can be used to implement a reactive system.

CompletableFuture: composable asynchronous programming

16

This chapter covers

- Creating an asynchronous computation and retrieving its result
- Increasing throughput by using nonblocking operations
- Designing and implementing an asynchronous API
- Consuming asynchronously a synchronous API
- Pipelining and merging two or more asynchronous operations
- Reacting to the completion of an asynchronous operation

Chapter 15 explored the modern concurrency context: that multiple processing resources (CPU cores and the like) are available, and you want your programs to exploit as many of these resources as possible in a high-level manner (rather than litter your programs with ill-structured, unmaintainable operations on threads). We noted that parallel streams and fork/join parallelism provide higher-level constructs for expressing parallelism in programs iterating over collections and in programs involving divide-and-conquer, but that method invocations provide additional opportunities for executing code in parallel. Java 8 and 9 introduce two specific APIs for this purpose: CompletableFuture and the reactive-programming paradigm. This chapter explains, through practical code examples, how the Java 8 CompletableFuture implementation of the Future interface gives you additional weapons in your programming armory. It also discusses additions introduced in Java 9.

16.1 Simple use of Futures

The Future interface was introduced in Java 5 to model a result made available at some point in the future. A query to a remote service won't be available immediately when the caller makes the request, for example. The Future interface models an asynchronous computation and provides a reference to its result that becomes available when the computation itself is completed. Triggering a potentially time-consuming action inside a Future allows the caller Thread to continue doing useful work instead of waiting for the operation's result. You can think of this process as being like taking a bag of clothes to your favorite dry cleaner. The cleaner gives you a receipt to tell you when your clothes will be cleaned (a Future); in the meantime, you can do some other activities. Another advantage of Future is that it's friendlier to work with than lower-level Threads. To work with a Future, you typically have to wrap the time-consuming operation inside a Callable object and submit it to an ExecutorService. The following listing shows an example written before Java 8.

Listing 16.1   Executing a long-lasting operation asynchronously in a Future

Submit a Callable to the ExecutorService.

Create an ExecutorService allowing you to submit tasks to a thread pool.

```
ExecutorService executor = Executors.newCachedThreadPool();
Future<Double> future = executor.submit(new Callable<Double>() {
    public Double call() {
        return doSomeLongComputation();
    }});
doSomethingElse();
try {
    Double result = future.get(1, TimeUnit.SECONDS);
} catch (ExecutionException ee) {
    // the computation threw an exception
} catch (InterruptedException ie) {
    // the current thread was interrupted while waiting
} catch (TimeoutException te) {
    // the timeout expired before the Future completion
}
```

Do something else while the asynchronous operation is progressing.

Retrieve the result of the asynchronous operation, blocking if it isn't available yet but waiting for 1 second at most before timing out.

Execute a long operation asynchronously in a separate thread.

As depicted in figure 16.1, this style of programming allows your thread to perform some other tasks while the long-lasting operation is executed concurrently in a separate thread provided by the ExecutorService. Then, when you can't do any other meaningful work without having the result of that asynchronous operation, you can retrieve it from the Future by invoking its get method. This method immediately returns the result of the operation if it's already completed or blocks your thread, waiting for its result to be available.

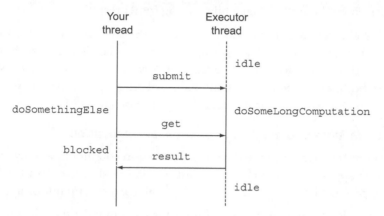

Figure 16.1   Using a Future to execute a long operation asynchronously

Note the problem with this scenario. What if the long operation never returns? To handle this possibility, it's almost always a good idea to use the two-argument version of get, which takes a timeout specifying the maximum time (along with its time unit) that your thread is willing to wait for the Future's result (as in listing 16.1). The zero-argument version of get would instead wait indefinitely.

16.1.1 *Understanding Futures and their limitations*

This first small example shows that the Future interface provides methods for checking whether the asynchronous computation is complete (by using the isDone method), waiting for its completion, and retrieving its result. But these features aren't enough to let you write concise concurrent code. It's difficult, for example, to express dependencies among results of a Future. Declaratively, it's easy to specify, "When the result of the long computation is available, please send its result to another long computation, and when that's done, combine its result with the result from another query." Implementing this specification with the operations available in a Future is a different story, which is why it would be useful to have more declarative features in the implementation, such as these:

- Combining two asynchronous computations both when they're independent and when the second depends on the result of the first
- Waiting for the completion of all tasks performed by a set of Futures
- Waiting for the completion of only the quickest task in a set of Futures (possibly because the Futures are trying to calculate the same value in different ways) and retrieving its result

- Programmatically completing a `Future` (that is, by providing the result of the asynchronous operation manually)
- Reacting to a `Future` completion (that is, being notified when the completion happens and then being able to perform a further action with the result of the `Future` instead of being blocked while waiting for its result)

In the rest of this chapter, you learn how the `CompletableFuture` class (which implements the `Future` interface) makes all these things possible in a declarative way by means of Java 8's new features. The designs of `Stream` and `CompletableFuture` follow similar patterns, because both use lambda expressions and pipelining. For this reason, you could say that `CompletableFuture` is to a plain `Future` what `Stream` is to a `Collection`.

16.1.2 *Using CompletableFutures to build an asynchronous application*

To explore the `CompletableFuture` features, in this section you incrementally develop a best-price-finder application that contacts multiple online shops to find the lowest price for a given product or service. Along the way, you learn several important skills:

- How to provide an asynchronous API for your customers (useful if you're the owner of one of the online shops).
- How to make your code nonblocking when you're a consumer of a synchronous API. You discover how to pipeline two subsequent asynchronous operations, merging them into a single asynchronous computation. This situation arises, for example, when the online shop returns a discount code along with the original price of the item you wanted to buy. You have to contact a second remote discount service to find out the percentage discount associated with this discount code before calculating the actual price of that item.
- How to reactively process events representing the completion of an asynchronous operation and how doing so allows the best-price-finder application to constantly update the best-buy quote for the item you want to buy as each shop returns its price, instead of waiting for all the shops to return their respective quotes. This skill also averts the scenario in which the user sees a blank screen forever if one of the shops' servers is down.

> **Synchronous vs. asynchronous API**
>
> The phrase *synchronous API* is another way of talking about a traditional call to a method: you call it, the caller waits while the method computes, the method returns, and the caller continues with the returned value. Even if the caller and callee were executed on different threads, the caller would still wait for the callee to complete. This situation gives rise to the phrase *blocking call*.
>
> By contrast, in an *asynchronous API* the method returns immediately (or at least before its computation is complete), delegating its remaining computation to a thread, which runs asynchronously to the caller—hence, the phrase *nonblocking call*. The remaining computation gives its value to the caller by calling a callback method,

or the caller invokes a further "wait until the computation is complete" method. This style of computation is common in I/O systems programming: you initiate a disc access, which happens asynchronously while you do more computation, and when you have nothing more useful to do, you wait until the disc blocks are loaded into memory. Note that blocking and nonblocking are often used for specific implementations of I/O by the operating system. However, these terms tend to be used interchangeably with asynchronous and synchronous even in non-I/O contexts.

16.2 Implementing an asynchronous API

To start implementing the best-price-finder application, define the API that each shop should provide. First, a shop declares a method that returns the price of a product, given its name:

```
public class Shop {
    public double getPrice(String product) {
        // to be implemented
    }
}
```

The internal implementation of this method would query the shop's database, but probably also perform other time-consuming tasks, such as contacting other external services (such as the shop's suppliers or manufacturer-related promotional discounts). To fake such a long-running method execution, in the rest of this chapter you use a `delay` method, which introduces an artificial delay of 1 second, as defined in the following listing.

Listing 16.2   A method to simulate a 1-second delay

```
public static void delay() {
    try {
        Thread.sleep(1000L);
    } catch (InterruptedException e) {
        throw new RuntimeException(e);
    }
}
```

For the purposes of this chapter, you can model the `getPrice` method by calling `delay` and then returning a randomly calculated value for the price, as shown in the next listing. The code for returning a randomly calculated price may look like a bit of a hack; it randomizes the price based on the product name by using the result of `charAt` as a number.

Listing 16.3   Introducing a simulated delay in the `getPrice` method

```
public double getPrice(String product) {
    return calculatePrice(product);
}
```

```
private double calculatePrice(String product) {
    delay();
    return random.nextDouble() * product.charAt(0) + product.charAt(1);
}
```

This code implies that when the consumer of this API (in this case, the best-price-finder application) invokes this method, it remains blocked and then is idle for 1 second while waiting for its synchronous completion. This situation is unacceptable, especially considering that the best-price-finder application has to repeat this operation for all the shops in its network. In the subsequent sections of this chapter, you discover how to resolve this problem by consuming this synchronous API in an asynchronous way. But for the purposes of learning how to design an asynchronous API, you continue in this section to pretend to be on the other side of the barricade. You're a wise shop owner who realizes how painful this synchronous API is for its users, and you want to rewrite it as an asynchronous API to make your customers' lives easier.

16.2.1 *Converting a synchronous method into an asynchronous one*

To achieve this goal, you first have to turn the getPrice method into a getPriceAsync method and change its return value, as follows:

```
public Future<Double> getPriceAsync(String product) { ... }
```

As we mentioned in the introduction of this chapter, the java.util.concurrent.Future interface was introduced in Java 5 to represent the result of an asynchronous computation. (That is, the caller thread is allowed to proceed without blocking.) A Future is a handle for a value that isn't available yet but that can be retrieved by invoking its get method after its computation finally terminates. As a result, the getPriceAsync method can return immediately, giving the caller thread a chance to perform other useful computations in the meantime. The Java 8 CompletableFuture class gives you various possibilities to implement this method easily, as shown in the following listing.

Listing 16.4   Implementing the getPriceAsync method

Execute the computation asynchronously in a different Thread.

Create the CompletableFuture that will contain the result of the computation.

```
public Future<Double> getPriceAsync(String product) {
    CompletableFuture<Double> futurePrice = new CompletableFuture<>();   ⟵
    new Thread( () -> {
                double price = calculatePrice(product);
                futurePrice.complete(price);   ⟵
    }).start();
    return futurePrice;   ⟵
}
```

Set the value returned by the long computation on the Future when it becomes available.

Return the Future without waiting for the computation of the result it contains to be completed.

Here, you create an instance of CompletableFuture, representing an asynchronous computation and containing a result when it becomes available. Then you fork a different Thread that will perform the actual price calculation and return the Future instance without waiting for that long-lasting calculation to terminate. When the price of the requested product is finally available, you can complete the CompletableFuture, using its complete method to set the value. This feature also explains the name of this Java 8 implementation of Future. A client of this API can invoke it, as shown in the next listing.

Listing 16.5 Using an asynchronous API

```
Shop shop = new Shop("BestShop");                        Query the shop to retrieve
long start = System.nanoTime();                          the price of a product.
Future<Double> futurePrice = shop.getPriceAsync("my favorite product");
long invocationTime = ((System.nanoTime() - start) / 1_000_000);
System.out.println("Invocation returned after " + invocationTime
                                                 + " msecs");
// Do some more tasks, like querying other shops
doSomethingElse();
// while the price of the product is being calculated
try {                                                    Read the price from the
    double price = futurePrice.get();                    Future or block until it
    System.out.printf("Price is %.2f%n", price);         becomes available.
} catch (Exception e) {
    throw new RuntimeException(e);
}
long retrievalTime = ((System.nanoTime() - start) / 1_000_000);
System.out.println("Price returned after " + retrievalTime + " msecs");
```

As you can see, the client asks the shop to get the price of a certain product. Because the shop provides an asynchronous API, this invocation almost immediately returns the Future, through which the client can retrieve the product's price later. Then the client can perform other tasks, such as querying other shops, instead of remaining blocked, waiting for the first shop to produce the requested result. Later, when the client can do no other meaningful jobs without having the product price, it can invoke get on the Future. By doing so, the client unwraps the value contained in the Future (if the asynchronous task is finished) or remains blocked until that value is available. The output produced by the code in listing 16.5 could be something like this:

```
Invocation returned after 43 msecs
Price is 123.26
Price returned after 1045 msecs
```

You can see that the invocation of the getPriceAsync method returns far sooner than when the price calculation eventually finishes. In section 16.4, you learn that it's also possible for the client to avoid any risk of being blocked. Instead, the client can be notified when the Future is complete and can execute a callback code, defined through a lambda expression or a method reference, only when the result of the computation is available. For now, we'll address another problem: how to manage an error during the execution of the asynchronous task.

16.2.2 Dealing with errors

The code you've developed so far works correctly if everything goes smoothly. But what happens if the price calculation generates an error? Unfortunately, in this case you get a particularly negative outcome: the exception raised to signal the error remains confined in the thread, which is trying to calculate the product price, and ultimately kills the thread. As a consequence, the client remains blocked forever, waiting for the result of the get method to arrive.

The client can prevent this problem by using an overloaded version of the get method that also accepts a timeout. It's good practice to use a timeout to prevent similar situations elsewhere in your code. This way, the client at least avoids waiting indefinitely, but when the timeout expires, it's notified with a TimeoutException. As a consequence, the client won't have a chance to discover what caused that failure inside the thread that was trying to calculate the product price. To make the client aware of the reason why the shop wasn't able to provide the price of the requested product, you have to propagate the Exception that caused the problem inside the CompletableFuture through its completeExceptionally method. Applying this idea to listing 16.4 produces the code shown in the following listing.

> **Listing 16.6 Propagating an error inside the CompletableFuture**

```
public Future<Double> getPriceAsync(String product) {
    CompletableFuture<Double> futurePrice = new CompletableFuture<>();
    new Thread( () -> {
                    try {
                        double price = calculatePrice(product);
                        futurePrice.complete(price);
                    } catch (Exception ex) {
                        futurePrice.completeExceptionally(ex);
                    }
    }).start();
    return futurePrice;
}
```

If the price calculation completed normally, complete the Future with the price. → (`futurePrice.complete(price);`)

Otherwise, complete the Future exceptionally with the Exception that caused the failure. ← (`futurePrice.completeExceptionally(ex);`)

Now the client will be notified with an ExecutionException (which takes an Exception parameter containing the cause—the original Exception thrown by the price calculation method). If that method throws a RuntimeException saying that product isn't available, for example, the client gets an ExecutionException like the following:

```
Exception in thread "main" java.lang.RuntimeException:
    java.util.concurrent.ExecutionException: java.lang.RuntimeException:
        product not available
    at java89inaction.chap16.AsyncShopClient.main(AsyncShopClient.java:16)
Caused by: java.util.concurrent.ExecutionException: java.lang.RuntimeException:
    product not available
    at java.base/java.util.concurrent.CompletableFuture.reportGet
      (CompletableFuture.java:395)
    at java.base/java.util.concurrent.CompletableFuture.get
      (CompletableFuture.java:1999)
```

```
    at java89inaction.chap16.AsyncShopClient.main(AsyncShopClient.java:14)
Caused by: java.lang.RuntimeException: product not available
    at java89inaction.chap16.AsyncShop.calculatePrice(AsyncShop.java:38)
    at java89inaction.chap16.AsyncShop.lambda$0(AsyncShop.java:33)
    at java.base/java.util.concurrent.CompletableFuture$AsyncSupply.run
      (CompletableFuture.java:1700)
    at java.base/java.util.concurrent.CompletableFuture$AsyncSupply.exec
      (CompletableFuture.java:1692)
    at java.base/java.util.concurrent.ForkJoinTask.doExec(ForkJoinTask.java:283)
    at java.base/java.util.concurrent.ForkJoinPool.runWorker
      (ForkJoinPool.java:1603)
    at java.base/java.util.concurrent.ForkJoinWorkerThread.run
      (ForkJoinWorkerThread.java:175)
```

CREATING A COMPLETABLEFUTURE WITH THE SUPPLYASYNC FACTORY METHOD

Up to now, you've created CompletableFutures and completed them programmatically when it seemed convenient to do so, but the CompletableFuture class comes with lots of handy factory methods that can make this process far easier and less verbose. The supplyAsync method, for example, lets you rewrite the getPriceAsync method in listing 16.4 with a single statement, as shown in the next listing.

> Listing 16.7 Creating a `CompletableFuture` with the `supplyAsync` factory method

```
public Future<Double> getPriceAsync(String product) {
    return CompletableFuture.supplyAsync(() -> calculatePrice(product));
}
```

The supplyAsync method accepts a Supplier as argument and returns a CompletableFuture that will be asynchronously completed with the value obtained by invoking that Supplier. This Supplier is run by one of the Executors in the ForkJoinPool, but you can specify a different Executor by passing it as a second argument to the overloaded version of this method. More generally, you can pass an Executor to all other CompletableFuture factory methods. You use this capability in section 16.3.4, where we demonstrate that using an Executor that fits the characteristics of your application can have a positive effect on its performance.

Also note that the CompletableFuture returned by the getPriceAsync method in listing 16.7 is equivalent to the one you created and completed manually in listing 16.6, meaning that it provides the same error management you carefully added.

For the rest of this chapter, we'll suppose that you have no control of the API implemented by the Shop class and that it provides only synchronous blocking methods. This situation typically happens when you want to consume an HTTP API provided by some service. You see how it's still possible to query multiple shops asynchronously, thus avoiding becoming blocked on a single request and thereby increasing the performance and the throughput of your best-price-finder application.

16.3 *Making your code nonblocking*

You've been asked to develop a best-price-finder application, and all the shops you have to query provide only the same synchronous API implemented as shown at the beginning of section 16.2. In other words, you have a list of shops, like this one:

```
List<Shop> shops = List.of(new Shop("BestPrice"),
                           new Shop("LetsSaveBig"),
                           new Shop("MyFavoriteShop"),
                           new Shop("BuyItAll"));
```

You have to implement a method with the following signature, which, given the name of a product, returns a list of strings. Each string contains the name of a shop and the price of the requested product in that shop, as follows:

```
public List<String> findPrices(String product);
```

Your first idea probably will be to use the Stream features you learned in chapters 4, 5, and 6. You may be tempted to write something like this next listing. (Yes, it's good if you're already thinking that this first solution is bad!)

Listing 16.8 **A findPrices implementation sequentially querying all the shops**

```
public List<String> findPrices(String product) {
    return shops.stream()
        .map(shop -> String.format("%s price is %.2f",
                                   shop.getName(), shop.getPrice(product)))
        .collect(toList());
}
```

This solution is straightforward. Now try to put the method findPrices to work with the only product you want madly these days: the myPhone27S. In addition, record how long the method takes to run, as shown in the following listing. This information lets you compare the method's performance with that of the improved method you develop later.

Listing 16.9 **Checking findPrices correctness and performance**

```
long start = System.nanoTime();
System.out.println(findPrices("myPhone27S"));
long duration = (System.nanoTime() - start) / 1_000_000;
System.out.println("Done in " + duration + " msecs");
```

The code in listing 16.9 produces output like this:

```
[BestPrice price is 123.26, LetsSaveBig price is 169.47, MyFavoriteShop price
     is 214.13, BuyItAll price is 184.74]
Done in 4032 msecs
```

As you may have expected, the time that the findPrices method takes to run is a few milliseconds longer than 4 seconds, because the four shops are queried sequentially and blocking one after the other, and each shop takes 1 second to calculate the price of the requested product. How can you improve on this result?

16.3.1 *Parallelizing requests using a parallel Stream*

After reading chapter 7, the first and quickest improvement that should occur to you would be to avoid this sequential computation by using a parallel `Stream` instead of a sequential, as shown in the next listing.

Listing 16.10   Parallelizing the `findPrices` method

```
public List<String> findPrices(String product) {
    return shops.parallelStream()
        .map(shop -> String.format("%s price is %.2f",
                            shop.getName(), shop.getPrice(product)))
        .collect(toList());
}
```

Use a parallel Stream to retrieve the prices from the different shops in parallel.

Find out whether this new version of `findPrices` is any better by again running the code in listing 16.9:

```
[BestPrice price is 123.26, LetsSaveBig price is 169.47, MyFavoriteShop price
    is 214.13, BuyItAll price is 184.74]
Done in 1180 msecs
```

Well done! It looks like this idea is simple but effective. Now the four shops are queried in parallel, so the code takes a bit more than a second to complete.

Can you do even better? Try to turn all the synchronous invocations to the shops in the `findPrices` method into asynchronous invocations, using what you've learned so far about `CompletableFutures`.

16.3.2 *Making asynchronous requests with CompletableFutures*

You saw earlier that you can use the factory method `supplyAsync` to create `CompletableFuture` objects. Now use it:

```
List<CompletableFuture<String>> priceFutures =
        shops.stream()
        .map(shop -> CompletableFuture.supplyAsync(
            () -> String.format("%s price is %.2f",
            shop.getName(), shop.getPrice(product))))
        .collect(toList());
```

With this approach, you obtain a `List<CompletableFuture<String>>`, where each `CompletableFuture` in the `List` contains the `String` name of a shop when its computation is complete. But because the `findPrices` method you're trying to reimplement with `CompletableFutures` has to return a `List<String>`, you'll have to wait for the completion of all these futures and extract the values they contain before returning the `List`.

To achieve this result, you can apply a second `map` operation to the original `List<CompletableFuture<String>>`, invoking a `join` on all the futures in the `List` and then waiting for their completion one by one. Note that the `join` method of the `CompletableFuture` class has the same meaning as the `get` method also declared in the `Future` interface, the only difference being that `join` doesn't throw any checked exception. By using `join`, you don't have to bloat the lambda expression passed to this second `map` with a `try/catch` block. Putting everything together, you can rewrite the `findPrices` method as shown in the listing that follows.

> **Listing 16.11   Implementing the `findPrices` method with `CompletableFutures`**

```
public List<String> findPrices(String product) {            Calculate each price
    List<CompletableFuture<String>> priceFutures =          asynchronously with
            shops.stream()                                  a CompletableFuture.
            .map(shop -> CompletableFuture.supplyAsync(   <──┘
                    () -> shop.getName() + " price is " +
                            shop.getPrice(product)))
            .collect(Collectors.toList());
    return priceFutures.stream()                            Wait for the completion
            .map(CompletableFuture::join)              <──┤ of all asynchronous
            .collect(toList());                             operations.
}
```

Note that you use two separate stream pipelines instead of putting the two `map` operations one after the other in the same stream-processing pipeline—and for a good reason. Given the lazy nature of intermediate stream operations, if you'd processed the stream in a single pipeline, you'd have succeeded only in executing all the requests to different shops synchronously and sequentially. The creation of each `Completable-Future` to interrogate a given shop would start only when the computation of the previous one completed, letting the `join` method return the result of that computation. Figure 16.2 clarifies this important detail.

The top half of figure 16.2 shows that processing the stream with a single pipeline implies that the evaluation order (identified by the dotted line) is sequential. In fact, a new `CompletableFuture` is created only after the former one is completely evaluated. Conversely, the bottom half of the figure demonstrates how first gathering the `CompletableFutures` in a list (represented by the oval) allows all of them to start before waiting for their completion.

Running the code in listing 16.11 to check the performance of this third version of the `findPrices` method, you could obtain output along these lines:

```
[BestPrice price is 123.26, LetsSaveBig price is 169.47, MyFavoriteShop price
    is 214.13, BuyItAll price is 184.74]
Done in 2005 msecs
```

This result is quite disappointing, isn't it? With a runtime of more than 2 seconds, this implementation with `CompletableFutures` is faster than the original naïve sequential

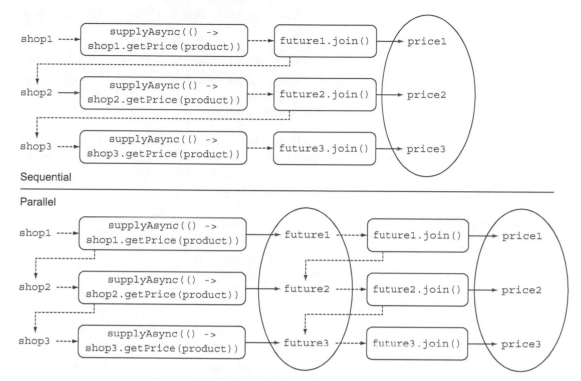

Figure 16.2 Why `Stream`'s laziness causes a sequential computation and how to avoid it

and blocking implementation from listing 16.8. But it's also almost twice as slow as the previous implementation using a parallel stream. It's even more disappointing considering the fact that you obtained the parallel stream version with a trivial change to the sequential version.

The newer version with `CompletableFutures` required quite a bit of work. But is using `CompletableFutures` in this scenario a waste of time? Or are you overlooking something important? Take a few minutes before going forward, particularly recalling that you're testing the code samples on a machine that's capable of running four threads in parallel.[1]

16.3.3 *Looking for the solution that scales better*

The parallel stream version performs so well only because it can run four tasks in parallel, so it's able to allocate exactly one thread for each shop. What happens if you decide to add a fifth shop to the list of shops crawled by your best-price-finder application? Not

---

[1] If you're using a machine that's capable of running more threads in parallel (say, eight), you need more shops and processes in parallel to reproduce the behavior shown in these pages.

surprisingly, the sequential version requires a bit more than 5 seconds to run, as shown in the following output:

```
[BestPrice price is 123.26, LetsSaveBig price is 169.47, MyFavoriteShop price
    is 214.13, BuyItAll price is 184.74, ShopEasy price is 166.08]
Done in 5025 msecs      ◁
```

The output of the program using a sequential stream

Unfortunately, the parallel stream version also requires a whole second more than before, because all four threads that it can run in parallel (available in the common thread pool) are now busy with the first four shops. The fifth query has to wait for the completion of one of the former operations to free a thread, as follows:

```
[BestPrice price is 123.26, LetsSaveBig price is 169.47, MyFavoriteShop price
    is 214.13, BuyItAll price is 184.74, ShopEasy price is 166.08]
Done in 2167 msecs      ◁
```

The output of the program using a parallel stream

What about the `CompletableFuture` version? Give it a try with the fifth shop:

```
[BestPrice price is 123.26, LetsSaveBig price is 169.47, MyFavoriteShop price
    is 214.13, BuyItAll price is 184.74, ShopEasy price is 166.08]
Done in 2006 msecs      ◁
```

The output of the program using CompletableFutures

The `CompletableFuture` version seems to be a bit faster than the one using parallel stream, but this version isn't satisfying either. If you try to run your code with nine shops, the parallel stream version takes 3143 milliseconds, whereas the `Completable-Future` cersion requires 3009 milliseconds. The versions look equivalent for a good reason: both internally use the same common pool that by default has a fixed number of threads equal to the one returned by `Runtime.getRuntime().available-Processors()`. Nevertheless, the `CompletableFutures` version has an advantage: by contrast with the parallel `Streams` API, it allows you to specify a different `Executor` to submit tasks to. You can configure this `Executor`, and size its thread pool, in a way that better fits the requirements of your application. In the next section, you translate this better level of configurability into practical performance gain for your application.

16.3.4 *Using a custom Executor*

In this case, a sensible choice seems to be to create an `Executor` with a number of threads in its pool that takes into account the actual workload you could expect in your application. How do you size this `Executor` correctly?

Sizing thread pools

In the great book *Java Concurrency in Practice* (Addison-Wesley, 2006; http://jcip.net), Brian Goetz and his co-authors give some advice on finding the optimal size for a thread pool. This advice is important because if the number of threads in the pool is too big, the threads end up competing for scarce CPU and memory resources, wasting their time performing context switching. Conversely, if this number is too small (as it likely is in your application), some of the cores of the CPU will remain underused. Goetz suggests that you can calculate the right pool size to approximate a desired CPU use rate with the following formula:

$$N^{threads} = N^{CPU} * U^{CPU} * (1 + W/C)$$

In this formula, NCPU is the number of cores, available through `Runtime.get-Runtime().availableProcessors()`

- U^{CPU} is the target CPU use (between 0 and 1).
- W/C is the ratio of wait time to compute time.

The application is spending about 99 percent of its time waiting for the shops' responses, so you could estimate a W/C ratio of 100. If your target is 100 percent CPU use, you should have a pool with 400 threads. In practice, it's wasteful to have more threads than shops, because you'll have threads in your pool that are never used. For this reason, you need to set up an `Executor` with a fixed number of threads equal to the number of shops you have to query, so that you have one thread for each shop. Also set an upper limit of 100 threads to avoid a server crash for a larger number of shops, as shown in the following listing.

Listing 16.12 A custom `Executor` fitting the best-price-finder application

```
private final Executor executor =
        Executors.newFixedThreadPool(Math.min(shops.size(), 100),
                                     (Runnable r) -> {
            Thread t = new Thread(r);
            t.setDaemon(true);
            return t;
        }
);
```

Use daemon threads, which don't prevent the termination of the program.

Create a thread pool with a number of threads equal to the minimum of 100 and the number of shops.

Note that you're creating a pool made of daemon threads. A Java program can't terminate or exit while a normal thread is executing, so a leftover thread waiting for a never-satisfiable event causes problems. By contrast, marking a thread as a daemon means that it can be killed on program termination. There's no performance difference. Now you can pass the new `Executor` as the second argument of the `supplyAsync` factory method. In addition, now create the `CompletableFuture` that retrieves the price of the requested product from a given shop as follows:

```
CompletableFuture.supplyAsync(() -> shop.getName() + " price is " +
                              shop.getPrice(product), executor);
```

After this improvement, the `CompletableFutures` solution takes 1021 milliseconds to process five shops and 1022 milliseconds to process nine shops. This trend carries on until the number of shops reaches the threshold of 400 that you calculated earlier. This example demonstrates the fact that it's a good idea to create an `Executor` that fits the characteristics of your application and to use `CompletableFutures` to submit tasks to it. This strategy is almost always effective and something to consider when you make intensive use of asynchronous operations.

Parallelism: via Streams or CompletableFutures?

You've seen two ways to do parallel computing on a collection: convert the collection to a parallel stream and use operations such as `map` on it, or iterate over the collection and spawn operations within a `CompletableFuture`. The latter technique provides more control by resizing thread pools, which ensures that your overall computation doesn't block because all your (fixed number of) threads are waiting for I/O.

Our advice for using these APIs is as follows:

- If you're doing computation-heavy operations with no I/O, the `Stream` interface provides the simplest implementation and the one that's likely to be most efficient. (If all threads are compute-bound, there's no point in having more threads than processor cores.)
- If your parallel units of work involve waiting for I/O (including network connections), the `CompletableFutures` solution provides more flexibility and allows you to match the number of threads to the wait/computer (W/C) ratio, as discussed previously. Another reason to avoid using parallel streams when I/O waits are involved in the stream-processing pipeline is that the laziness of streams can make it harder to reason about when the waits happen.

You've learned how to take advantage of `CompletableFutures` to provide an asynchronous API to your clients and to function as the client of a synchronous but slow server, but you performed only a single time-consuming operation in each `Future`. In the next section, you use `CompletableFutures` to pipeline multiple asynchronous operations in a declarative style similar to what you learned by using the Streams API.

16.4   *Pipelining asynchronous tasks*

Suppose that all the shops have agreed to use a centralized discount service. This service uses five discount codes, each of which has a different discount percentage. You represent this idea by defining a `Discount.Code` enumeration, as shown in the next listing.

Listing 16.13 An enumeration defining the discount codes

```java
public class Discount {
    public enum Code {
        NONE(0), SILVER(5), GOLD(10), PLATINUM(15), DIAMOND(20);
        private final int percentage;
        Code(int percentage) {
            this.percentage = percentage;
        }
    }
    // Discount class implementation omitted, see Listing 16.14
}
```

Also suppose that the shops have agreed to change the format of the result of the get-Price method, which now returns a String in the format ShopName:price:Discount-Code. Your sample implementation returns a random Discount.Code together with the random price already calculated, as follows:

```java
public String getPrice(String product) {
    double price = calculatePrice(product);
    Discount.Code code = Discount.Code.values()[
                        random.nextInt(Discount.Code.values().length)];
    return String.format("%s:%.2f:%s", name, price, code);
}
private double calculatePrice(String product) {
    delay();
    return random.nextDouble() * product.charAt(0) + product.charAt(1);
}
```

Invoking getPrice might then return a String such as

```
BestPrice:123.26:GOLD
```

16.4.1 Implementing a discount service

Your best-price-finder application should now obtain the prices from the shops; parse the resulting Strings; and, for each String, query the discount server's needs. This process determines the final discounted price of the requested product. (The actual discount percentage associated with each discount code could change, which is why you query the server each time.) The parsing of the Strings produced by the shop is encapsulated in the following Quote class:

```java
public class Quote {
    private final String shopName;
    private final double price;
    private final Discount.Code discountCode;
    public Quote(String shopName, double price, Discount.Code code) {
        this.shopName = shopName;
        this.price = price;
        this.discountCode = code;
    }
```

```
    public static Quote parse(String s) {
        String[] split = s.split(":");
        String shopName = split[0];
        double price = Double.parseDouble(split[1]);
        Discount.Code discountCode = Discount.Code.valueOf(split[2]);
        return new Quote(shopName, price, discountCode);
    }
    public String getShopName() { return shopName; }
    public double getPrice() { return price; }
    public Discount.Code getDiscountCode() { return discountCode; }
}
```

You can obtain an instance of the Quote class—which contains the name of the shop, the nondiscounted price, and the discount code—by passing the String produced by a shop to the static parse factory method.

The Discount service also has an applyDiscount method that accepts a Quote object and returns a String stating the discounted price for the shop that produced that quote, as shown in the following listing.

> **Listing 16.14 Listing 16.14 The Discount service**

```
public class Discount {
    public enum Code {
        // source omitted ...
    }
    public static String applyDiscount(Quote quote) {      ⟵ Apply the
        return quote.getShopName() + " price is " +           discount code to
                Discount.apply(quote.getPrice(),              the original price.
                            quote.getDiscountCode());
    }
    private static double apply(double price, Code code) {  ⟵ Simulate a delay
        delay();                                               in the Discount
        return format(price * (100 - code.percentage) / 100); service response.
    }
}
```

16.4.2 Using the Discount service

Because the Discount service is a remote service, you again add a simulated delay of 1 second to it, as shown in the next listing. As you did in section 16.3, first try to reimplement the findPrices method to fit these new requirements in the most obvious (but, sadly, sequential and synchronous) way.

> **Listing 16.15 Simplest findPrices implementation that uses the Discount service**

```
public List<String> findPrices(String product) {
    return shops.stream()                                    Retrieve the nondiscounted
            .map(shop -> shop.getPrice(product))     ⟵       price from each shop.
            .map(Quote::parse)
            .map(Discount::applyDiscount)            ⟵ Contact the Discount service to
            .collect(toList());                        apply the discount on each Quote.
}
```

Transform the Strings returned by the shops in Quote objects.

You obtain the desired result by pipelining three `map` operations on the stream of shops:

- The first operation transforms each shop into a `String` that encodes the price and discount code of the requested product for that shop.
- The second operation parses those `Strings`, converting each of them in a `Quote` object.
- The third operation contacts the remote `Discount` service, which calculates the final discounted price and returns another `String` containing the name of the shop with that price.

As you might imagine, the performance of this implementation is far from optimal. But try to measure it as usual by running your benchmark:

```
[BestPrice price is 110.93, LetsSaveBig price is 135.58, MyFavoriteShop price
    is 192.72, BuyItAll price is 184.74, ShopEasy price is 167.28]
Done in 10028 msecs
```

As expected, this code takes 10 seconds to run, because the 5 seconds required to query the five shops sequentially is added to the 5 seconds consumed by the discount service in applying the discount code to the prices returned by the five shops. You already know that you can improve this result by converting the stream to a parallel one. But you also know (from section 16.3) that this solution doesn't scale well when you increase the number of shops to be queried, due to the fixed common thread pool on which streams rely. Conversely, you learned that you can better use your CPU by defining a custom `Executor` that schedules the tasks performed by the `CompletableFutures`.

16.4.3 *Composing synchronous and asynchronous operations*

In this section, you try to reimplement the `findPrices` method asynchronously, again using the features provided by `CompletableFuture`. This next listing shows the code. Don't worry if something looks unfamiliar; we explain the code in this section.

> **Listing 16.16 Implementing the `findPrices` method with `CompletableFutures`**

Transform the String returned by a shop into a Quote object when it becomes available.

Asynchronously retrieve the nondiscounted price from each shop.

```
public List<String> findPrices(String product) {
    List<CompletableFuture<String>> priceFutures =
        shops.stream()
            .map(shop -> CompletableFuture.supplyAsync(
                              () -> shop.getPrice(product), executor))
            .map(future -> future.thenApply(Quote::parse))
            .map(future -> future.thenCompose(quote ->
                    CompletableFuture.supplyAsync(
                        () -> Discount.applyDiscount(quote), executor)))
                .collect(toList());
    return priceFutures.stream()
```

Compose the resulting Future with another asynchronous task, applying the discount code.

```
                .map(CompletableFuture::join)
                .collect(toList());
}
```

> Wait for all the Futures in the stream to be completed and extract their respective results.

Things look a bit more complex this time, so try to understand what's going on step-by-step. Figure 16.3 depicts the sequence of these three transformations.

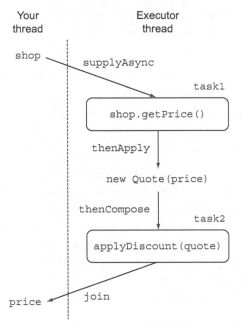

Figure 16.3   Composing synchronous operations and asynchronous tasks

You're performing the same three map operations that you did in the synchronous solution of listing 16.15, but you make those operations asynchronous when necessary, using the feature provided by the CompletableFuture class.

GETTING THE PRICES

You've seen the first of these three operations in various examples in this chapter; you query the shop asynchronously by passing a lambda expression to the supplyAsync factory method. The result of this first transformation is a Stream<Completable-Future<String>>, where each CompletableFuture contains, when complete, the String returned by the corresponding shop. Note that you configure the CompletableFutures with the custom Executor developed in listing 16.12.

PARSING THE QUOTES

Now you have to convert those Strings to Quotes with a second transformation. But because this parsing operation isn't invoking any remote service or doing any I/O in general, it can be performed almost instantaneously and can be done synchronously without introducing any delay. For this reason, you implement this second transformation by invoking the `thenApply` method on the `CompletableFutures` produced by the first step and passing to it a `Function` converting a `String` to an instance of `Quote`.

Note that using the `thenApply` method doesn't block your code until the `CompletableFuture` on which you're invoking it is complete. When the `Completable-Future` finally completes, you want to transform the value that it contains by using the lambda expression passed to the `then-Apply` method, thus transforming each `CompletableFuture<String>` in the stream into a corresponding `CompletableFuture<Quote>`. You can see this process as building a recipe that specifies what to do with the result of the `CompletableFuture`, as when you worked with a stream pipeline.

COMPOSING THE FUTURES FOR CALCULATING THE DISCOUNTED PRICE

The third `map` operation involves contacting the remote `Discount` service to apply the appropriate discount percentage to the nondiscounted prices received from the shops. This transformation is different from the previous one because it has to be executed remotely (or, in this case, has to simulate the remote invocation with a delay), and for this reason, you also want to perform it asynchronously.

To achieve this goal, as you did with the first invocation of `supplyAsync` with `get-Price`, you pass this operation as a lambda expression to the `supplyAsync` factory method, which returns another `CompletableFuture`. At this point you have two asynchronous operations, modeled with two distinct `CompletableFutures`, that you want to perform in a cascade:

- Retrieve the price from a shop and then transform it into a `Quote`.
- Take this `Quote` and pass it to the `Discount` service to obtain the final discounted price.

The Java 8 `CompletableFuture` API provides the `thenCompose` method specifically for this purpose, allowing you to pipeline two asynchronous operations, passing the result of the first operation to the second operation when it becomes available. In other words, you can compose two `CompletableFutures` by invoking the `thenCompose` method on the first `CompletableFuture` and passing to it a `Function`. This `Function` has as an argument the value returned by that first `CompletableFuture` when it completes, and it returns a second `CompletableFuture` that uses the result of the first as input for its computation. Note that with this approach, while the `Futures` are retrieving the quotes from the shops, the main thread can perform other useful operations, such as responding to UI events.

Collecting the elements of the `Stream` resulting from these three `map` operations into a `List`, you obtain a `List<CompletableFuture<String>>`. Finally, you can wait for the completion of those `CompletableFutures` and extract their values by using `join`, exactly as you did in listing 16.11. This new version of the `findPrices` method implemented in listing 16.8 might produce output like this:

```
[BestPrice price is 110.93, LetsSaveBig price is 135.58, MyFavoriteShop price
    is 192.72, BuyItAll price is 184.74, ShopEasy price is 167.28]
Done in 2035 msecs
```

The thenCompose method you used in listing 16.16, like other methods of the CompletableFuture class, has a variant with an Async suffix, thenComposeAsync. In general, a method without the Async suffix in its name executes its task in the same thread as the previous task, whereas a method terminating with Async always submits the succeeding task to the thread pool, so each of the tasks can be handled by a different thread. In this case, the result of the second CompletableFuture depends on the first, so it makes no difference to the final result or to its broad-brush timing whether you compose the two CompletableFutures with one or the other variant of this method. You chose to use the one with thenCompose only because it's slightly more efficient due to less thread-switching overhead. Note, however, that it may not always be clear which thread is being used, especially if you run an application that manages its own thread pool (such as Spring).

16.4.4 Combining two CompletableFutures: dependent and independent

In listing 16.16, you invoked the thenCompose method on one CompletableFuture and passed to it a second CompletableFuture, which needed as input the value resulting from the execution of the first. In another common case, you need to combine the results of the operations performed by two independent CompletableFutures, and you don't want to wait for the first to complete before starting the second.

In situations like this one, use the thenCombine method. This method takes as a second argument a BiFunction, which defines how the results of the two CompletableFutures are to be combined when both become available. Like thenCompose, the thenCombine method comes with an Async variant. In this case, using the thenCombineAsync method causes the combination operation defined by the BiFunction to be submitted to the thread pool and then executed asynchronously in a separate task.

Turning to this chapter's running example, you may know that one of the shops provides prices in € (EUR), but you always want to communicate them to your customers in $(USD). You can asynchronously ask the shop the price of a given product *and separately* retrieve, from a remote exchange-rate service, the current exchange rate between € and $. After both requests have completed, you can combine the results by multiplying the price by the exchange rate. With this approach, you obtain a third CompletableFuture that completes when the results of the two CompletableFutures are both available and have been combined by means of the BiFunction, as shown in the following listing.

Listing 16.17   Combining two independent CompletableFutures

Create a first task querying the shop
to obtain the price of a product.

```
Future<Double> futurePriceInUSD =
    CompletableFuture.supplyAsync(() -> shop.getPrice(product))     ⟵
    .thenCombine(
        CompletableFuture.supplyAsync(
            () -> exchangeService.getRate(Money.EUR, Money.USD)),   ⟵
        (price, rate) -> price * rate
    ));
```

Combine the price and exchange rate by multiplying them.

Create a second independent task to retrieve
the conversion rate between USD and EUR.

Here, because the combination operation is a simple multiplication, performing it in a separate task would have been a waste of resources, so you need to use the then-Combine method instead of its asynchronous thenCombineAsync counterpart. Figure 16.4 shows how the tasks created in listing 16.17 are executed on the different threads of the pool and how their results are combined.

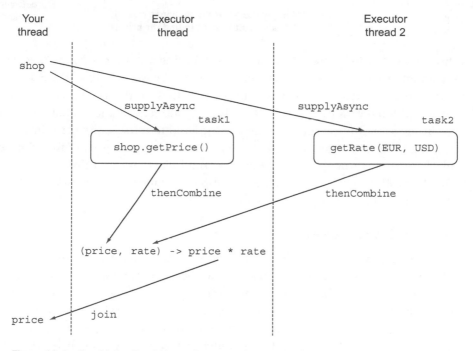

Figure 16.4   Combining two independent asynchronous tasks

16.4.5 *Reflecting on Future vs. CompletableFuture*

The last two examples in listings 16.16 and 16.17 clearly show one of the biggest advantages of CompletableFutures over the other pre-Java 8 Future implementations. CompletableFutures use lambda expressions to provide a declarative API. This API allows you to easily combine and compose various synchronous and asynchronous tasks to perform a complex operation in the most effective way. To get a more tangible idea of the code-readability benefits of CompletableFuture, try to obtain the result of listing 16.17 purely in Java 7. The next listing shows you how.

Listing 16.18   Combining two Futures in Java 7

Create an ExecutorService allowing you
to submit tasks to a thread pool.

```
ExecutorService executor = Executors.newCachedThreadPool();     ⟵
final Future<Double> futureRate = executor.submit(new Callable<Double>() {
        public Double call() {
```

```
                        return exchangeService.getRate(Money.EUR, Money.USD);    ◁────────────┐
                  }});                                                                         │
         Future<Double> futurePriceInUSD = executor.submit(new Callable<Double>() {           │
                  public Double call() {                                          Create a Future
                     double priceInEUR = shop.getPrice(product);                  retrieving the
                     return priceInEUR * futureRate.get();    ◁────────────┐      exchange rate
                  }});                                                     │      between EUR
                            Multiply the price and exchange rate in        │      and USD.
                            the same Future used to find the price.
```

Find the price of the requested product for a given shop in a second Future.

In listing 16.18, you create a first `Future`, submitting a `Callable` to an `Executor` querying an external service to find the exchange rate between EUR and USD. Then you create a second `Future`, retrieving the price in EUR of the requested product for a given shop. Finally, as you did in listing 16.17, you multiply the exchange rate by the price in the same future that also queried the shop to retrieve the price in EUR. Note that using `thenCombineAsync` instead of `thenCombine` in listing 16.17 would have been equivalent to performing the price by rate multiplication in a third `Future` in listing 16.18. The difference between these two implementations may seem to be small only because you're combining two `Futures`.

16.4.6 *Using timeouts effectively*

As mentioned in section 16.2.2, it's always a good idea to specify a timeout when trying to read the value calculated by a `Future` to avoid being blocked indefinitely while waiting for the computation of that value. Java 9 introduced a couple of convenient methods that enrich the timeout capabilities provided by the `CompletableFutures`. The `orTimeout` method uses a `ScheduledThreadExecutor` to complete the `CompletableFuture` with a `TimeoutException` after the specified timeout has elapsed, and it returns another `CompletableFuture`. By using this method, you can further chain your computation pipeline and deal with the `TimeoutException` by providing a friendly message back. You can add a timeout to the `Future` in listing 16.17 and make it throw a `TimeoutException` if not completed after 3 seconds by adding this method at the end of the methods chain, as shown in the next listing. The timeout duration should match your business requirements, of course.

Listing 16.19   Adding a timeout to `CompletableFuture`

```
Future<Double> futurePriceInUSD =
        CompletableFuture.supplyAsync(() -> shop.getPrice(product))
        .thenCombine(
            CompletableFuture.supplyAsync(
                () -> exchangeService.getRate(Money.EUR, Money.USD)),
            (price, rate) -> price * rate
        ))
        .orTimeout(3, TimeUnit.SECONDS);    ◁──  Make the Future throw a Timeout-
                                                 Exception if not completed after
                                                 3 seconds. Asynchronous timeout
                                                 management was added in Java 9.
```

Sometimes, it's also acceptable to use a default value in case a service is momentarily unable to respond in a timely manner. You might decide that in listing 16.19, you want to wait for the exchange service to provide the current EUR-to-USD exchange rate for no more than 1 second, but if the request takes longer to complete, you don't want to abort the whole the computation with an `Exception`. Instead, you can fall back by using a predefined exchange rate. You can easily add this second kind of timeout by using the `completeOnTimeout` method, also introduced in Java 9 (the following listing).

> **Listing 16.20 Completing a `CompletableFuture` with a default value after a timeout**

```
Future<Double> futurePriceInUSD =
        CompletableFuture.supplyAsync(() -> shop.getPrice(product))
        .thenCombine(
            CompletableFuture.supplyAsync(
                () -> exchangeService.getRate(Money.EUR, Money.USD))
              .completeOnTimeout(DEFAULT_RATE, 1, TimeUnit.SECONDS),   <─┐
            (price, rate) -> price * rate
        ))                                          Use a default exchange rate if
        .orTimeout(3, TimeUnit.SECONDS);            the exchange service doesn't
                                                    provide a result in 1 second.
```

Like the `orTimeout` method, the `completeOnTimeOut` method returns a `Completable-Future`, so you can chain it with other `CompletableFuture` methods. To recap, you've configured two kinds of timeouts: one that makes the whole computation fail if it takes more than 3 seconds, and one that expires in 1 second but completes the `Future` with a predetermined value instead of causing a failure.

You're almost finished with your best-price-finder application, but one ingredient is still missing. You'd like to show your users the prices provided by the shops as soon as they become available (as car insurance and flight-comparison websites typically do), instead of waiting for all the price requests to complete, as you've done up to now. In the next section, you discover how to achieve this goal by reacting to the completion of a `CompletableFuture` instead of invoking `get` or `join` on it and thereby remaining blocked until the `CompletableFuture` itself completes.

16.5 *Reacting to a CompletableFuture completion*

In all the code examples you've seen in this chapter, you've simulated methods that do remote invocations with a 1-second delay in their response. In a real-world scenario, the remote services you need to contact from your application are likely to have unpredictable delays caused by everything from server load to network delays, and perhaps by how valuable the server regards your application's business to be compared with that of applications that pay more per query.

For these reasons, it's likely the prices of the products you want to buy will be available for some shops far earlier than for others. In the next listing, you simulate this scenario by introducing a random delay of 0.5 to 2.5 seconds, using the random-Delay method instead of the delay method that waits 1 second.

Listing 16.21   A method to simulate a random delay between 0.5 and 2.5 seconds

```
private static final Random random = new Random();
public static void randomDelay() {
    int delay = 500 + random.nextInt(2000);
    try {
        Thread.sleep(delay);
    } catch (InterruptedException e) {
        throw new RuntimeException(e);
    }
}
```

Up to now, you've implemented the findPrices method so that it shows the prices provided by the shops only when all of them are available. Now you want to have the best-price-finder application display the price for a given shop as soon as it becomes available without waiting for the slowest one (which may even time out). How can you achieve this further improvement?

16.5.1 *Refactoring the best-price-finder application*

The first thing to avoid is waiting for the creation of a List that already contains all the prices. You need to work directly with the stream of CompletableFutures, in which each CompletableFuture is executing the sequence of operations necessary for a given shop. In the next listing, you refactor the first part of the implementation from listing 16.16 into a findPricesStream method to produce this stream of CompletableFutures.

Listing 16.22   Refactoring the findPrices method to return a stream of Futures

```
public Stream<CompletableFuture<String>> findPricesStream(String product) {
    return shops.stream()
            .map(shop -> CompletableFuture.supplyAsync(
                                () -> shop.getPrice(product), executor))
            .map(future -> future.thenApply(Quote::parse))
            .map(future -> future.thenCompose(quote ->
                    CompletableFuture.supplyAsync(
                        () -> Discount.applyDiscount(quote), executor)));
}
```

At this point, you add a fourth map operation on the Stream returned by the find-PricesStream method to the three already performed inside that method. This new operation registers an action on each CompletableFuture; this action consumes the value of the CompletableFuture as soon as it completes. The Java 8 Completable-Future API provides this feature via the thenAccept method, which takes as an argument a Consumer of the value with which it completes. In this case, this value is the

String returned by the discount services and containing the name of a shop together with the discounted price of the requested product for that shop. The only action that you want to perform to consume this value is to print it:

```
findPricesStream("myPhone").map(f -> f.thenAccept(System.out::println));
```

As you've seen for the thenCompose and thenCombine methods, the thenAccept method has an Async variant named thenAcceptAsync. The Async variant schedules the execution of the Consumer passed to it on a new thread from the thread pool instead of performing it directly, using the same thread that completed the Completable-Future. Because you want to avoid an unnecessary context switch, and because (more important) you want to react to the completion of the CompletableFuture as soon as possible instead waiting for a new thread to be available, you don't use this variant here.

Because the thenAccept method already specifies how to consume the result produced by the CompletableFuture when it becomes available, it returns a Completable-Future<Void>. As a result, the map operation returns a Stream<CompletableFuture <Void>>. You can't do much with a CompletableFuture<Void> except wait for its completion, but this is exactly what you need. You also want to give the slowest shop a chance to provide its response and print its returned price. To do so, you can put all the CompletableFuture<Void>s of the stream into an array and then wait for all of them to complete, as shown in this next listing.

Listing 16.23 Reacting to CompletableFuture completion

```
CompletableFuture[] futures = findPricesStream("myPhone")
        .map(f -> f.thenAccept(System.out::println))
        .toArray(size -> new CompletableFuture[size]);
CompletableFuture.allOf(futures).join();
```

The allOf factory method takes as input an array of CompletableFutures and returns a CompletableFuture<Void> that's completed only when all the CompletableFutures passed have completed. Invoking join on the CompletableFuture returned by the allOf method provides an easy way to wait for the completion of all the Completable-Futures in the original stream. This technique is useful for the best-price-finder application because it can display a message such as All shops returned results or timed out so that a user doesn't keep wondering whether more prices might become available.

In other applications, you may want to wait for the completion of only one of the CompletableFutures in an array, perhaps if you're consulting two currency-exchange servers and are happy to take the result of the first to respond. In this case, you can use the anyOf factory method. As a matter of detail, this method takes as input an array of CompletableFutures and returns a CompletableFuture<Object> that completes with the same value as the first-to-complete CompletableFuture.

16.5.2   *Putting it all together*

As discussed at the beginning of section 16.5, now suppose that all the methods simulating a remote invocation use the `randomDelay` method of listing 16.21, introducing a random delay distributed between 0.5 and 2.5 seconds instead of a delay of 1 second. Running the code in listing 16.23 with this change, you see that the prices provided by the shops don't appear all at the same time, as happened before, but are printed incrementally as soon as the discounted price for a given shop is available. To make the result of this change more obvious, the code is slightly modified to report a timestamp showing the time taken for each price to be calculated:

```
long start = System.nanoTime();
CompletableFuture[] futures = findPricesStream("myPhone27S")
        .map(f -> f.thenAccept(
            s -> System.out.println(s + " (done in " +
                ((System.nanoTime() - start) / 1_000_000) + " msecs)")))
        .toArray(size -> new CompletableFuture[size]);
CompletableFuture.allOf(futures).join();
System.out.println("All shops have now responded in "
                + ((System.nanoTime() - start) / 1_000_000) + " msecs");
```

Running this code produces output similar to the following:

```
BuyItAll price is 184.74 (done in 2005 msecs)
MyFavoriteShop price is 192.72 (done in 2157 msecs)
LetsSaveBig price is 135.58 (done in 3301 msecs)
ShopEasy price is 167.28 (done in 3869 msecs)
BestPrice price is 110.93 (done in 4188 msecs)
All shops have now responded in 4188 msecs
```

You can see that, due to the effect of the random delays, the first price now prints more than twice as fast as the last!

16.6   *Road map*

Chapter 17 explores the Java 9 Flow API, which generalizes the idea of Computable-Future (one-shot, either computing or terminated-with-a-value) by enabling computations to produce a series of values before optionally terminating.

Summary

- Executing relatively long-lasting operations by using asynchronous tasks can increase the performance and responsiveness of your application, especially if it relies on one or more remote external services.
- You should consider providing an asynchronous API to your clients. You can easily implement one by using `CompletableFutures` features.
- A `CompletableFuture` allows you to propagate and manage errors generated within an asynchronous task.
- You can asynchronously consume from a synchronous API by wrapping its invocation in a `CompletableFuture`.

- You can compose or combine multiple asynchronous tasks when they're independent and when the result of one of them is used as the input to another.
- You can register a callback on a `CompletableFuture` to reactively execute some code when the `Future` completes and its result becomes available.
- You can determine when all values in a list of `CompletableFutures` have completed, or you can wait for only the first to complete.
- Java 9 added support for asynchronous timeouts on `CompletableFuture` via the `orTimeout` and `completeOnTimeout` methods.

Reactive programming 17

This chapter covers

- Defining reactive programming and discussing the principles of the Reactive Manifesto
- Reactive programming at the application and system levels
- Showing example code using reactive streams and the Java 9 Flow API
- Introducing RxJava, a widely used reactive library
- Exploring the RxJava operations to transform and combine multiple reactive streams
- Presenting marble diagrams that visually document operations on reactive streams

Before we dig into what reactive programming is and how it works, it's helpful to clarify why this new paradigm is of growing importance. A few years ago, the largest applications had tens of servers and gigabytes of data; response times of several seconds and offline-maintenance times measured in hours were considered to be acceptable. Nowadays, this situation is changing rapidly for at least three reasons:

- *Big Data*—Big Data usually is measured in petabytes and increasing daily.
- *Heterogeneous environments*—Applications are deployed in diverse environments ranging from mobile devices to cloud-based clusters running thousands of multicore processors.
- *Use patterns*—Users expect millisecond response times and 100 percent uptime.

These changes imply that today's demands aren't being met by yesterday's software architectures. This situation has become evident especially now that mobile devices are the biggest source of internet traffic, and things can only worsen in the near future when such traffic is overtaken by the Internet of Things (IoT).

Reactive programming addresses these issues by allowing you to process and combine streams of data items coming from different systems and sources in an asynchronous way. In fact, applications written following this paradigm react to data items as they occur, which allows them to be more responsive in their interactions with users. Moreover, the reactive approach can be applied not only to building a single component or application, but also to coordinating many components into a whole reactive system. Systems engineered in this way can exchange and route messages in varying network conditions and provide availability under heavy load while taking into consideration failures and outages. (Note that although developers traditionally see their systems or applications as being built from components, in this new mashup, loosely coupled style of building systems, these components are often whole applications themselves. Hence, *components* and *applications* are near synonyms.)

The features and advantages that characterize reactive applications and systems are crystallized in the Reactive Manifesto, which we discuss in the next section.

17.1 The Reactive Manifesto

The Reactive Manifesto (https://www.reactivemanifesto.org)—developed in 2013 and 2014 by Jonas Bonér, Dave Farley, Roland Kuhn, and Martin Thompson—formalized a set of core principles for developing reactive applications and systems. The Manifesto identified four characteristic features:

- *Responsive*—A reactive system has a fast and, even more important, consistent, predictable response time. As a result, the user knows what to expect. This fact in turn increases user confidence, which is without a doubt the key aspect of a usable application.
- *Resilient*—A system has to remain responsive despite failures. The Reactive Manifesto suggests different techniques to achieve resiliency, including replicating the execution of components, decoupling these components in time (sender and receiver have independent life cycles) and space (sender and receiver run in different processes), and letting each component asynchronously delegate tasks to other components.
- *Elastic*—Another issue that harms the responsiveness of applications is the fact that they can be subject to different workloads during their life cycles. Reactive

systems are designed to react automatically to a heavier workload by increasing the number of resources allocated to the affected components.

- *Message-driven*—Resilience and elasticity require the boundaries of the components that form the system to be clearly defined to ensure loose coupling, isolation, and location transparency. Communication across these boundaries is performed through asynchronous message passing. This choice enables both resiliency (by delegating failures as messages) and elasticity (by monitoring the number of exchanged messages and then scaling the number of the resources intended to manage them accordingly).

Figure 17.1 shows how these four features are related and dependent on one another. These principles are valid at different scales, from structuring the internals of a small application to determining how these applications have to be coordinated to build a large system. Specific points concerning the level of granularity where these ideas are applied, however, deserve to be discussed in further detail.

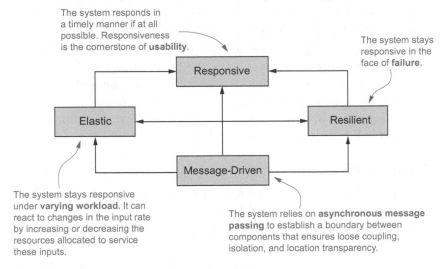

Figure 17.1   The key features of a reactive system

17.1.1 *Reactive at application level*

The main feature of reactive programming for application-level components allows tasks to be executed asynchronously. As we discuss in the rest of this chapter, processing streams of events in an asynchronous and nonblocking way is essential for maximizing the use rate of modern multicore CPUs and, more precisely, of the threads competing for their use. To achieve this goal, the reactive frameworks and libraries share threads (relatively expensive and scarce resources) among lighter constructs such as futures; actors; and (more commonly) event loops dispatching a sequence of callbacks intended to aggregate, transform, and manage the events to be processed.

Background knowledge check

If you're puzzled by terms such as *event*, *message*, *signal*, and *event loop* (or *publish-subscribe*, *listener*, and *backpressure*, which are used later in this chapter), please read the gentler introduction in chapter 15. If not, read on.

These techniques not only have the benefit of being cheaper than threads, but also have a major advantage from developers' point of view: they raise the level of abstraction of implementing concurrent and asynchronous applications, allowing developers to concentrate on the business requirements instead of dealing with typical problems of low-level multithreading issues such as synchronization, race conditions, and deadlocks.

The most important thing to pay attention to when using these thread-multiplexing strategies is to never perform blocking operations inside the main event loop. It's helpful to include as blocking operations all I/O-bound operations such as accessing a database or the file system or calling a remote service that may take a long or unpredictable time to complete. It's easy and interesting to explain why you should avoid blocking operations by providing a practical example.

Imagine a simplified yet typical multiplexing scenario with a pool of two threads processing three streams of events. Only two streams can be processed at the same time and the streams have to compete to share those two threads as fairly and efficiently as possible. Now suppose that processing one stream's event triggers a potentially slow I/O operation, such as writing into the file system or retrieving data from a database by using a blocking API. As figure 17.2 shows, in this situation Thread 2 is wastefully blocked waiting for the I/O operation to complete, so although the Thread 1 can process the first stream, the third stream can't be processed before the blocking operation finishes.

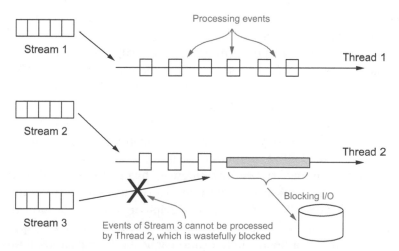

Figure 17.2 A blocking operation wastefully keeps a thread busy preventing it from performing other computations.

To overcome this problem, most reactive frameworks (such as RxJava and Akka) allow blocking operations to be executed by means of a separate dedicated thread pool. All the threads in the main pool are free to run uninterruptedly, keeping all the cores of the CPU at the highest possible use rate. Keeping separate thread pools for CPU-bound and I/O-bound operations has the further benefit of allowing you to size and configure the pools with a finer granularity and to monitor the performance of these two kinds of tasks more precisely.

Developing applications by following the reactive principles is only one aspect of reactive programming and often not even the hardest one. Having a set of beautifully designed reactive applications performing efficiently in isolation is at least as important as making them cooperate in a well-coordinated reactive system.

17.1.2 *Reactive at system level*

A *reactive system* is a software architecture that allows multiple applications to work as a single coherent, resilient platform and also allows these applications to be sufficiently decoupled so when one of them fails, it doesn't bring down the whole system. The main difference between reactive applications and systems is that the former type usually perform computations based on ephemeral streams of data and are called event-driven. The latter type are intended to compose the applications and facilitate communication. Systems with this property are often referred to as being message-driven.

The other important distinction between messages and events is the fact that messages are directed toward a defined single destination, whereas events are facts that will be received by the components that are registered to observe them. In reactive systems, it's also essential for these messages to be asynchronous to keep the sending and the receiving operations decoupled from the sender and receiver, respectively. This decoupling is a requirement for full isolation between components and is fundamental for keeping the system *responsive* under both failures (*resilience*) and heavy load (*elasticity*).

More precisely, resilience is achieved in reactive architectures by isolating failures in the components where they happen to prevent the malfunctions from being propagated to adjacent components and from there in a catastrophic cascade to the rest of the system. Resilience in this reactive sense is more than fault-tolerance. The system doesn't gracefully degrade but fully recovers from failures by isolating them and bringing the system back to a healthy state. This "magic" is obtained by containing the errors and reifying them as messages that are sent to other components acting as supervisors. In this way, the management of the problem can be performed from a safe context external to the failing component itself.

As isolation and decoupling are key for resilience, the main enabler for elasticity is *location transparency*, which allows any component of a reactive system to communicate with any other service, regardless of where the recipient resides. Location transparency in turn allows the system to replicate and (automatically) scale any application depending on the current workload. Such location-agnostic scaling shows another difference between reactive applications (asynchronous and concurrent and decoupled in time) and reactive systems (which can become decoupled in space through location transparency).

In the rest of this chapter, you put some of these ideas into practice with a few examples of reactive programming, and in particular, you explore Java 9's Flow API.

17.2 Reactive streams and the Flow API

Reactive programming is programming that uses reactive streams. Reactive streams are a standardized technique (based on the publish-subscribe, or pub-sub, protocol explained in chapter 15) to process potentially unbounded streams of data asynchronously, in sequence and with mandatory nonblocking backpressure. Backpressure is a flow-control mechanism used in publish-subscribe to prevent a slow consumer of the events in the stream from being overwhelmed by one or more faster producers. When this situation occurs, it's unacceptable for the component under stress to fail catastrophically or to drop events in an uncontrolled fashion. The component needs a way to ask the upstream producers to slow down or to tell them how many events it can accept and process at a given time before receiving more data.

It's worth noting that the requirement for built-in backpressure is justified by the asynchronous nature of the stream processing. In fact, when synchronous invocations are being performed, the system is implicitly backpressured by the blocking APIs. Unfortunately, this situation prevents you from executing any other useful task until the blocking operation is complete, so you end up wasting a lot of resources by waiting. Conversely, with asynchronous APIs you can maximize the use rate of your hardware, but run the risk of overwhelming some other slower downstream component. Backpressure or flow-control mechanisms come into play in this situation; they establish a protocol that prevents data recipients from being overwhelmed without having to block any threads.

These requirements and the behavior that they imply were condensed in the Reactive Streams[1] project (www.reactive-streams.org), which involved engineers from Netflix, Red Hat, Twitter, Lightbend, and other companies, and produced the definition of four interrelated interfaces representing the minimal set of features that any Reactive Streams implementation has to provide. These interfaces are now part of Java 9, nested within the new `java.util.concurrent.Flow` class, and implemented by many third-party libraries, including Akka Streams (Lightbend), Reactor (Pivotal), RxJava (Netflix), and Vert.x (Red Hat). In the next section, we examine in detail the methods declared by these interfaces and clarify how they're expected to be used to express reactive components.

17.2.1 Introducing the Flow class

Java 9 adds one new class for reactive programming: `java.util.concurrent.Flow`. This class contains only static components and can't be instantiated. The `Flow` class

---

[1] We capitalize for the Reactive Streams project, but use reactive streams for the concept.

contains four nested interfaces to express the publish-subscribe model of reactive programming as standardized by the Reactive Streams project:

- Publisher
- Subscriber
- Subscription
- Processor

The `Flow` class allows interrelated interfaces and static methods to establish flow-controlled components, in which `Publishers` produce items consumed by one or more `Subscribers`, each managed by a `Subscription`. The `Publisher` is a provider of a potentially unbounded number of sequenced events, but it's constrained by the backpressure mechanism to produce them according to the demand received from its `Subscriber`(s). The `Publisher` is a Java functional interface (declares only one single abstract method) that allows a `Subscriber` to register itself as a listener of the events issued by the `Publisher`; flow control, including backpressure, between `Publishers` and `Subscribers` is managed by a `Subscription`. These three interfaces, along with the `Processor` interface, are captured in listings 17.1, 17.2, 17.3, and 17.4.

Listing 17.1   The `Flow.Publisher` interface

```
@FunctionalInterface
public interface Publisher<T> {
    void subscribe(Subscriber<? super T> s);
}
```

On the other side, the `Subscriber` interface has four callback methods that are invoked by the `Publisher` when it produces the corresponding events.

Listing 17.2   The `Flow.Subscriber` interface

```
public interface Subscriber<T> {
    void onSubscribe(Subscription s);
    void onNext(T t);
    void onError(Throwable t);
    void onComplete();
}
```

Those events have to be published (and the corresponding methods invoked) strictly following the sequence defined by this protocol:

```
onSubscribe onNext* (onError | onComplete)?
```

This notation means that onSubscribe is always invoked as the first event, followed by an arbitrary number of onNext signals. The stream of events can go on forever, or it can be terminated by an onComplete callback to signify that no more elements will be produced or by an onError if the `Publisher` experiences a failure. (Compare reading from a terminal when you get a string or an indication of an end-of-file or I/O error.)

When a `Subscriber` registers itself on a `Publisher`, the `Publisher`'s first action is to invoke the `onSubscribe` method to pass back a `Subscription` object. The `Subscription` interface declares two methods. The `Subscriber` can use the first method to notify the `Publisher` that it's ready to process a given number of events; the second method allows it to cancel the `Subscription`, thereby telling the `Publisher` that it's no longer interested in receiving its events.

Listing 17.3 The `Flow.Subscription` interface

```
public interface Subscription {
    void request(long n);
    void cancel();
}
```

The Java 9 Flow specification defines a set of rules through which the implementations of these interfaces should cooperate. These rules can be summarized as follows:

- The `Publisher` must send the `Subscriber` a number of elements no greater than that specified by the `Subscription`'s request method. A `Publisher`, however, may send fewer `onNext` than requested and terminate the `Subscription` by calling `onComplete` if the operation terminated successfully or `onError` if it failed. In these cases, when a terminal state has been reached (`onComplete` or `onError`), the `Publisher` can't send any other signal to its `Subscribers`, and the `Subscription` has to be considered to be canceled.

- The `Subscriber` must notify the `Publisher` that it's ready to receive and process n elements. In this way, the `Subscriber` exercises backpressure on the `Publisher` preventing the `Subscriber` from being overwhelmed by too many events to manage. Moreover, when processing the `onComplete` or `onError` signals, the `Subscriber` isn't allowed to call any method on the `Publisher` or `Subscription` and must consider the `Subscription` to be canceled. Finally, the `Subscriber` must be prepared to receive these terminal signals even without any preceding call of the `Subscription.request()` method and to receive one or more `onNext` even after having called `Subscription.cancel()`.

- The `Subscription` is shared by exactly one `Publisher` and `Subscriber` and represents the unique relationship between them. For this reason, it must allow the `Subscriber` to call its request method synchronously from both the `onSubscribe` and `onNext` methods. The standard specifies that the implementation of the `Subscription.cancel()` method has to be idempotent (calling it repeatedly has the same effect as calling it once) and thread-safe so that, after the first time it has been called, any other additional invocation on the `Subscription` has no effect. Invoking this method asks the `Publisher` to eventually drop any references to the corresponding `Subscriber`. Resubscribing with the same `Subscriber` object is discouraged, but the specification doesn't mandate an exception being raised in this situation because all previously canceled subscriptions would have to be stored indefinitely.

Figure 17.3 shows the typical life cycle of an application implementing the interfaces defined by the Flow API.

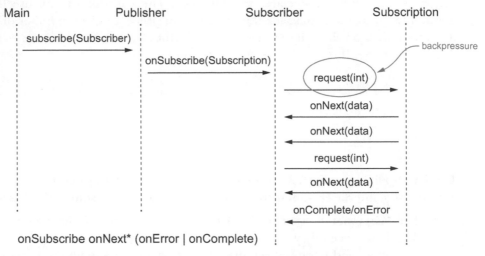

Figure 17.3   **The life cycle of a reactive application using the Flow API**

The fourth and final member of the `Flow` class is the `Processor` interface, which extends both `Publisher` and `Subscriber` without requiring any additional method.

Listing 17.4   The `Flow.Processor` interface

```
public interface Processor<T, R> extends Subscriber<T>, Publisher<R> { }
```

In fact, this interface represents a transformation stage of the events processed through the reactive stream. When receiving an error, the `Processor` can choose to recover from it (and then consider the `Subscription` to be canceled) or immediately propagate the `onError` signal to its `Subscriber`(s). The `Processor` should also cancel its upstream `Subscription` when its last `Subscriber` cancels its `Subscription` to propagate the cancellation signal (even though this cancellation isn't strictly required by the specification).

The Java 9 `Flow` API/Reactive Streams API mandates that any implementation of all the methods of the `Subscriber` interface should never block the `Publisher`, but it doesn't specify whether these methods should process the events synchronously or asynchronously. Note, however, that all methods defined by these interfaces return `void` so that they can be implemented in a completely asynchronous way.

In this next section, you try to put to work what you've learned so far through a simple, practical example.

17.2.2   Creating your first reactive application

The interfaces defined in the `Flow` class are, in most cases, not intended to be implemented directly. Unusually, the Java 9 library doesn't provide classes that implement them either! These interfaces are implemented by the reactive libraries that we've already mentioned (Akka, RxJava, and so on). The Java 9 specification of `java.util` `.concurrency.Flow` works both as a contract to which all those libraries must adhere and a lingua franca allowing reactive applications developed on top of different reactive libraries to cooperate and talk to one another. Moreover, those reactive libraries typically offer many more features (classes and methods that transform and merge reactive streams beyond the minimal subset specified by the `java.util.concurrency` `.Flow` interface).

That being said, it makes sense for you to develop a first reactive application directly on top of the Java 9 `Flow` API to get a feeling for how the four interfaces discussed in the preceding sections work together. To this end, you'll write a simple temperature-reporting program using reactive principles. This program has two components:

- `TempInfo`, which mimics a remote thermometer (constantly reporting randomly chosen temperatures between 0 and 99 degrees Fahrenheit, which is appropriate for U.S. cities most of the time)
- `TempSubscriber`, which listens to these reports and prints the stream of temperatures reported by a sensor installed in a given city

The first step is defining a simple class that conveys the currently reported temperature, as shown in the following listing.

Listing 17.5 A Java bean conveying the currently reported temperature

```java
import java.util.Random;

public class TempInfo {

    public static final Random random = new Random();

    private final String town;
    private final int temp;

    public TempInfo(String town, int temp) {
        this.town = town;
        this.temp = temp;
    }

    public static TempInfo fetch(String town) {
        if (random.nextInt(10) == 0)
            throw new RuntimeException("Error!");
        return new TempInfo(town, random.nextInt(100));
    }

    @Override
    public String toString() {
        return town + " : " + temp;
    }
}
```

TempInfo instance for a given town is created via a static factory method.

Fetching the current temperature may randomly fail one time out of ten.

Returns a random temperature in the range 0 to 99 degrees Fahrenheit

```
        public int getTemp() {
            return temp;
        }

        public String getTown() {
            return town;
        }
    }
```

After defining this simple domain model, you can implement a Subscription for the temperatures of a given town that sends a temperature report whenever this report is requested by its Subscriber as shown in the following listing.

Listing 17.6   A Subscription sending a stream of TempInfo to its Subscriber

```
import java.util.concurrent.Flow.*;

public class TempSubscription implements Subscription {

    private final Subscriber<? super TempInfo> subscriber;
    private final String town;

    public TempSubscription( Subscriber<? super TempInfo> subscriber,
                             String town ) {
        this.subscriber = subscriber;
        this.town = town;
    }

    @Override
    public void request( long n ) {
        for (long i = 0L; i < n; i++) {
            try {
                subscriber.onNext( TempInfo.fetch( town ) );
            } catch (Exception e) {
                subscriber.onError( e );
                break;
            }
        }
    }

    @Override
    public void cancel() {
        subscriber.onComplete();
    }
}
```

Loops once per request made by the Subscriber

Sends the current temperature to the Subscriber

In case of a failure while fetching the temperature propagates the error to the Subscriber

If the subscription is canceled, send a completion (onComplete) signal to the Subscriber.

The next step is creating a Subscriber that, every time it gets a new element, prints the temperatures received from the Subscription and asks for a new report as shown in the next listing.

Listing 17.7   A `Subscriber` printing the received temperatures

```
import java.util.concurrent.Flow.*;

public class TempSubscriber implements Subscriber<TempInfo> {

    private Subscription subscription;

    @Override
    public void onSubscribe( Subscription subscription ) {
        this.subscription = subscription;
        subscription.request( 1 );
    }

    @Override
    public void onNext( TempInfo tempInfo ) {
        System.out.println( tempInfo );
        subscription.request( 1 );
    }

    @Override
    public void onError( Throwable t ) {
        System.err.println(t.getMessage());
    }

    @Override
    public void onComplete() {
        System.out.println("Done!");
    }
}
```

Stores the subscription and sends a first request

Prints the received temperature and requests a further one

Prints the error message in case of an error

The next listing puts your reactive application to work with a `Main` class that creates a `Publisher` and then subscribes to it by using `TempSubscriber`.

Listing 17.8   A `main` class: creating a `Publisher` and subscribing `TempSubscriber` to it

```
import java.util.concurrent.Flow.*;

public class Main {
    public static void main( String[] args ) {
        getTemperatures( "New York" ).subscribe( new TempSubscriber() );
    }

    private static Publisher<TempInfo> getTemperatures( String town ) {
        return subscriber -> subscriber.onSubscribe(
                              new TempSubscription( subscriber, town ) );
    }
}
```

Creates a new Publisher of temperatures in New York and subscribes the TempSubscriber to it

Returns a Publisher that sends a TempSubscription to the Subscriber that subscribes to it

Here, the `getTemperatures` method returns a lambda expression that takes a `Subscriber` as an argument and invokes its `onSubscribe` method, passing to it a new

TempSubscription instance. Because the signature of this lambda is identical to the only abstract method of the Publisher functional interface, the Java compiler can automatically convert the lambda to a Publisher (as you learned in chapter 3). The main method creates a Publisher for the temperatures in New York and then subscribes a new instance of the TempSubscriber class to it. Running main produces output something like this:

```
New York : 44
New York : 68
New York : 95
New York : 30
Error!
```

In the preceding run, TempSubscription successfully fetched the temperature in New York four times but failed on the fifth reading. It seems that you correctly implemented the problem by using three of the four interfaces of the Flow API. But are you sure that there aren't any mistakes in the code? Give this question some thought by completing the following quiz.

Quiz 17.1:

The example developed so far has a subtle problem. This problem, however, is hidden by the fact that at some point, the stream of temperatures will be interrupted by the error randomly generated inside the TempInfo factory method. Can you guess what will happen if you comment out the statement generating the random error and let your main run long enough?

Answer:

The problem with what you've done so far is that every time the TempSubscriber receives a new element into its onNext method, it sends a new request to the Temp-Subscription, and then the request method sends another element to the Temp-Subscriber itself. These recursive invocations are pushed onto the stack one after the other until the stack overflows, generating StackOverflowError like the following:

```
Exception in thread "main" java.lang.StackOverflowError
    at java.base/java.io.PrintStream.print(PrintStream.java:666)
    at java.base/java.io.PrintStream.println(PrintStream.java:820)
    at flow.TempSubscriber.onNext(TempSubscriber.java:36)
    at flow.TempSubscriber.onNext(TempSubscriber.java:24)
    at flow.TempSubscription.request(TempSubscription.java:60)
    at flow.TempSubscriber.onNext(TempSubscriber.java:37)
    at flow.TempSubscriber.onNext(TempSubscriber.java:24)
    at flow.TempSubscription.request(TempSubscription.java:60)

...
```

What can you do to fix this problem and avoid overflowing the stack? One possible solution is to add an Executor to the TempSubscription and then use it to send new elements to the TempSubscriber from a different thread. To achieve this goal, you can modify the `TempSubscription` as shown in the next listing. (The class is incomplete; the full definition uses the remaining definitions from listing 17.6.)

Listing 17.9 Adding an `Executor` to the `TempSubscription`

```
import java.util.concurrent.ExecutorService;          Unmodified
import java.util.concurrent.Executors;                code of original
                                                      TempSubscription
public class TempSubscription implements Subscription {   ◁─┘  has been omitted.

    private static final ExecutorService executor =
                                    Executors.newSingleThreadExecutor();

    @Override
    public void request( long n ) {                   Sends the next elements
        executor.submit( () -> {           ◁───       to the subscriber from a
            for (long i = 0L; i < n; i++) {           different thread
                try {
                    subscriber.onNext( TempInfo.fetch( town ) );
                } catch (Exception e) {
                    subscriber.onError( e );
                    break;
                }
            }
        });
    }
}
```

So far, you've used only three of the four interfaces defined by the Flow API. What about the `Processor` interface? A good example of how to use that interface is to create a `Publisher` that reports the temperatures in Celsius instead of Fahrenheit (for subscribers outside the United States).

17.2.3 *Transforming data with a Processor*

As described in section 17.2.1, a `Processor` is both a `Subscriber` and a `Publisher`. In fact, it's intended to subscribe to a `Publisher` and republish the data that it receives after transforming that data. As a practical example, implement a `Processor` that subscribes to a `Publisher` that emits temperatures in Fahrenheit and republishes them after converting them to Celsius, as shown in this next listing.

Listing 17.10 A `Processor` transforming temperatures from Fahrenheit to Celsius

```
import java.util.concurrent.Flow.*;              A processor transforming a
                                                 TempInfo into another TempInfo
public class TempProcessor implements Processor<TempInfo, TempInfo> {   ◁─┘

    private Subscriber<? super TempInfo> subscriber;

    @Override
    public void subscribe( Subscriber<? super TempInfo> subscriber ) {
```

```
        this.subscriber = subscriber;
    }
```
Republishes the TempInfo
after converting the
temperature to Celsius
```
    @Override
    public void onNext( TempInfo temp ) {
        subscriber.onNext( new TempInfo( temp.getTown(),
                               (temp.getTemp() - 32) * 5 / 9) );    ◄─
    }

    @Override
    public void onSubscribe( Subscription subscription ) {
        subscriber.onSubscribe( subscription );    ◄─┐
    }
```
All other signals
are delegated
unchanged to
the upstream
subscriber.
```
    @Override
    public void onError( Throwable throwable ) {
        subscriber.onError( throwable );    ◄─
    }

    @Override
    public void onComplete() {
        subscriber.onComplete();    ◄─
    }
}
}
```

Note that the only method of the `TempProcessor` that contains some business logic is
`onNext`, which republishes temperatures after converting them from Fahrenheit to
Celsius. All other methods that implement the `Subscriber` interface merely pass on
unchanged (delegate) all received signals to the upstream `Subscriber`, and the
`Publisher`'s subscribe method registers the upstream `Subscriber` into the `Processor`.

The next listing puts the `TempProcessor` to work by using it in your `Main` class.

Listing 17.11   Main **class: create a** Publisher **and subscribe** TempSubscriber **to it**

```
import java.util.concurrent.Flow.*;

public class Main {
    public static void main( String[] args ) {
        getCelsiusTemperatures( "New York" )        ◄─
            .subscribe( new TempSubscriber() );     ◄─
    }

    public static Publisher<TempInfo> getCelsiusTemperatures(String town) {
        return subscriber -> {
            TempProcessor processor = new TempProcessor();    ◄─
            processor.subscribe( subscriber );
            processor.onSubscribe( new TempSubscription(processor, town) );
        };
    }
}
```

Creates a new Publisher
of Celsius temperatures
for New York

Subscribes the
TempSubscriber
to the Publisher

Creates a TempProcessor and puts it between
the Subscriber and returned Publisher

This time, running `Main` produces the following output, with temperatures that are typical of the Celsius scale:

```
New York : 10
New York : -12
New York : 23
Error!
```

In this section, you directly implemented the interfaces defined in the Flow API, and in doing so, you became familiar with asynchronous stream processing via the publish-subscribe protocol that forms the core idea of the Flow API. But there was something slightly unusual about this example, which we turn to in the next section.

17.2.4 Why doesn't Java provide an implementation of the Flow API?

The Flow API in Java 9 is rather odd. The Java library generally provides interfaces and implementations for them, but here, you've implemented the Flow API yourself. Let's make a comparison with the List API. As you know, Java provides the `List<T>` interface that's implemented by many classes, including `ArrayList<T>`. More precisely (and rather invisibly to the user) the class `ArrayList<T>` extends the abstract class `AbstractList<T>`, which implements the interface `List<T>`. By contrast, Java 9 declares the interface `Publisher<T>` and provides no implementation, which is why you had to define your own (apart from the learning benefit you got from implementing it). Let's face it—an interface on its own may help you structure your programming thoughts, but it doesn't help you write programs any faster!

What's going on? The answer is historic: there were multiple Java code libraries of reactive streams (such as Akka and RxJava). Originally, these libraries were developed separately, and although they implemented reactive programming via publish-subscribe ideas, they used different nomenclature and APIs. During the standardization process of Java 9, these libraries evolved so that their classes formally implemented the interfaces in `java.util.concurrent.Flow`, as opposed to merely implementing the reactive concepts. This standard enables more collaboration among different libraries.

Note that building a reactive-streams implementation is complex, so most users will merely use an existing one. Like many classes that implement an interface, they typically provide richer functionality than is required for a minimal implementation.

In the next section, you use one of the most widely used libraries: the RxJava (reactive extensions to Java) library developed by Netflix, specifically the current RxJava 2.0 version, which implements the Java 9 Flow interfaces.

17.3 Using the reactive library RxJava

RxJava was among one the first libraries to develop reactive applications in Java. It was born at Netflix as a port of the Reactive Extensions (Rx) project, originally developed by Microsoft in the. Net environment. RxJava version 2.0 was adjusted to adhere to the Reactive Streams API explained earlier in this chapter and adopted by Java 9 as `java.util.concurrent.Flow`.

When you use an external library in Java, this fact is apparent from the imports. You import the Java Flow interfaces, for example, including `Publisher` with a line such as this:

```
import java.lang.concurrent.Flow.*;
```

But you also need to import the appropriate implementing classes with a line such as

```
import io.reactivex.Observable;
```

if you want to use the `Observable` implementation of `Publisher`, as you'll choose to do later in this chapter.

We must emphasize one architectural issue: good systems-architectural style avoids making visible throughout the system any fine-details concepts that are used in only one part of the system. Accordingly, it's good practice to use an `Observable` only where the additional structure of an `Observable` is required and otherwise use its interface of `Publisher`. Note that you observe this guideline with the `List` interface without thinking. Even though a method may have been passed a value that you know to be an `ArrayList`, you declare the parameter for this value to be of type `List`, so you avoid exposing and constraining the implementation details. Indeed, you allow a later change of implementation from `ArrayList` to `LinkedList` not to require ubiquitous changes.

In the rest of this section, you define a temperature-reporting system by using RxJava's implementation of reactive streams. The first issue you come across is that RxJava provides two classes, both of which implement `Flow.Publisher`.

On reading the RxJava documentation, you find that one class is the `io.reactivex` `.Flowable` class, which includes the reactive pull-based backpressure feature of Java 9 `Flow` (using `request`) exemplified in listings 17.7 and 17.9. Backpressure prevents a `Subscriber` from being overrun by data being produced by a fast `Publisher`. The other class is the original RxJava `io.reactivex.Observable` version of `Publisher`, which didn't support backpressure. This class is both simpler to program and more appropriate for user-interface events (such as mouse movements); these events are streams that can't be reasonably backpressured. (You can't ask the user to slow down or stop moving the mouse!) For this reason, RxJava provides these two implementing classes for the common idea stream of events.

The RxJava advice is to use the nonbackpressured `Observable` when you have a stream of no more than a thousand elements or when you're are dealing with GUI events such as mouse moves or touch events, which are impossible to backpressure and aren't frequent anyway.

Because we analyzed the backpressure scenario while discussing the Flow API in the preceding section, we won't discuss `Flowable` anymore; instead, we'll demonstrate the `Observable` interface at work in a use case without backpressure. It's worth noting that any subscriber can effectively turn off backpressuring by invoking `request(Long` `.MAX_VALUE)` on the subscription, even if this practice isn't advisable unless you're sure that the Subscriber will always be able to process all the received events in a timely manner.

17.3.1 Creating and using an Observable

The Observable and Flowable classes come with many convenient factory methods that allow you to create many types of reactive streams. (Both Observable and Flowable implement Publisher, so these factory methods publish reactive streams.)

The simplest Observable that you may want to create is made of a fixed number of predetermined elements, as follows:

```
Observable<String> strings = Observable.just( "first", "second" );
```

Here, the just() factory method[2] converts one or more elements to an Observable that emits those elements. A subscriber to this Observable receives onNext("first"), onNext("second"), and onComplete() messages, in that order.

Another Observable factory method that's quite common, especially when your application interacts with a user in real time, emits events at a fixed time rate:

```
Observable<Long> onePerSec = Observable.interval(1, TimeUnit.SECONDS);
```

The interval factory method returns an Observable, named onePerSec, that emits an infinite sequence of ascending values of type long, starting at zero, at a fixed time interval of your choosing (1 second in this example). Now plan to use onePerSec as the basis of another Observable that emits the temperature reported for a given town each second.

As an intermediate step toward this goal, you can print those temperatures each second. To do so, you need to subscribe to onePerSec to be notified by it every time a second has passed and then fetch and print the temperatures of the town of interest. In RxJava, the Observable[3] plays the role of the Publisher in the Flow API, so the Observer similarly corresponds to Flow's Subscriber interface. The RxJava Observer interface declares the same methods as the Java 9 Subscriber given in listing 17.2, with the difference that the onSubscribe method has a Disposable argument rather than a Subscription. As we mentioned earlier, Observable doesn't support backpressure, so it doesn't have a request method that forms part of a Subscription. The full Observer interface is

```
public interface Observer<T> {
    void onSubscribe(Disposable d);
    void onNext(T t);
    void onError(Throwable t);
    void onComplete();
}
```

---

[2] This naming convention is slightly unfortunate, because Java 8 started using of() for similar factory methods as popularized by the Stream and Optional APIs.

[3] Note that the Observer interface and the Observable class have been deprecated since Java 9. New code should use the Flow API. It remains to be seen how RxJava will evolve.

Note, however, that RxJava's API are more flexible (have more overloaded variants) than the native Java 9 `Flow` API. You can subscribe to an `Observable`, for example, by passing a lambda expression with the signature of the `onNext` method and omitting the other three methods. In other words, you can subscribe to an `Observable` with an `Observer` that implements only the `onNext` method with a `Consumer` of the received event, leaving the other methods defaulting to a no-op for completion and error handling. By using this feature, you can subscribe to the `Observable onePerSec` and use it to print the temperatures in New York once a second, all in a single line of code:

```
onePerSec.subscribe(i -> System.out.println(TempInfo.fetch( "New York" )));
```

In this statement, the `onePerSec` `Observable` emits one event per second. and on receipt of this message, the `Subscriber` fetches the temperature in New York and prints it. If you put this statement in a `main` method and try to execute it, however, you see nothing because the `Observable` publishing one event per second is executed in a thread that belongs to RxJava's computation thread pool, which is made up of daemon threads.[4] But your `main` program terminates immediately and, in doing so, kills the daemon thread before it can produce any output.

As a bit of a hack, you can prevent this immediate termination by putting a thread sleep after the preceding statement. Better, you could use the `blockingSubscribe` method that calls the callbacks on the current thread (in this case, the main thread). For the purposes of a running demonstration, `blockingSubscribe` is perfectly suitable. In a production context, however, you normally use the `subscribe` method, as follows:

```
onePerSec.blockingSubscribe(
    i -> System.out.println(TempInfo.fetch( "New York" ))
);
```

You may obtain output such as the following:

```
New York : 87
New York : 18
New York : 75
java.lang.RuntimeException: Error!
at flow.common.TempInfo.fetch(TempInfo.java:18)
at flow.Main.lambda$main$0(Main.java:12)
at io.reactivex.internal.observers.LambdaObserver
          .onNext(LambdaObserver.java:59)
at io.reactivex.internal.operators.observable
          .ObservableInterval$IntervalObserver.run(ObservableInterval.java:74)
```

Unfortunately, the temperature fetching may, by design, fail randomly (and indeed does after three readings). Because your `Observer` implements only the happy path

---

[4] This fact doesn't seem to be clear from the documentation, although you can find statements to this effect in the stackoverflow.com online developer community.

and doesn't have any sort of error management, such as onError, this failure blows up in the user's face as an uncaught exception.

It's time to raise the bar and start complicating this example a bit. You don't want to add only error management. You also have to generalize what you have. You don't want to print the temperatures immediately but provide users a factory method that returns an Observable emitting those temperatures once a second for (say) at most five times before completing. You can achieve this goal easily by using a factory method named create that creates an Observable from a lambda, taking as an argument another Observer and returning void, as shown in the following listing.

Listing 17.12 Creating an `Observable` **emitting temperature once a second**

Creates an Observable from a function consuming an Observer

An Observable emitting an infinite sequence of ascending longs, one per second

```
public static Observable<TempInfo> getTemperature(String town) {
    return Observable.create(emitter ->
            Observable.interval(1, TimeUnit.SECONDS)
                .subscribe(i -> {
                    if (!emitter.isDisposed()) {
                        if ( i >= 5 ) {
                            emitter.onComplete();
                        } else {
                            try {
                                emitter.onNext(TempInfo.fetch(town));
                            } catch (Exception e) {
                                emitter.onError(e);
                            }
                        }
                    }})));
}
```

If the temperature has been already emitted five times, completes the observer terminating the stream

In case of error, notifies the Observer

Do something only if the consumed observer hasn't been disposed yet (for a former error).

Otherwise, sends a temperature report to the Observer

Here, you're creating the returned Observable from a function that consumes an ObservableEmitter, sending the desired events to it. The RxJava ObservableEmitter interface extends the basic RxJava Emitter, which you can think of as being an Observer without the onSubscribe method,

```
public interface Emitter<T> {
    void onNext(T t);
    void onError(Throwable t);
    void onComplete();
}
```

with a few more methods to set a new Disposable on the Emitter and check whether the sequence has been already disposed downstream.

Internally, you subscribe to an Observable such as onePerSec that publishes an infinite sequence of ascending longs, one per second. Inside the subscribing function (passed as an argument to the subscribe method), you first check whether the consumed Observer has been already disposed by the isDisposed method provided by the `ObservableEmitter` interface. (This situation could happen if an error occurred in an earlier iteration.) If the temperature has been already emitted five times, the code completes the `Observer`, terminating the stream; otherwise, it sends the most recent temperature report for the requested town to the `Observer` in a try/catch block. If an error occurs during the temperature fetching, it propagates the error to the `Observer`.

Now it's easy to implement a complete `Observer` that will later be used to subscribe to the `Observable` returned by the `getTemperature` method and that prints the temperatures it publishes as shown in the next listing.

Listing 17.13   An `Observer` printing the received temperatures

```java
import io.reactivex.Observer;
import io.reactivex.disposables.Disposable;

public class TempObserver implements Observer<TempInfo> {
    @Override
    public void onComplete() {
        System.out.println( "Done!" );
    }

    @Override
    public void onError( Throwable throwable ) {
        System.out.println( "Got problem: " + throwable.getMessage() );
    }

    @Override
    public void onSubscribe( Disposable disposable ) {
    }

    @Override
    public void onNext( TempInfo tempInfo ) {
        System.out.println( tempInfo );
    }
}
```

This `Observer` is similar to the `TempSubscriber` class from listing 17.7 (which implements Java 9's `Flow.Subscriber`), but you have a further simplification. Because RxJava's `Observable` doesn't support backpressure, you don't need to `request()` further elements after processing the published ones.

In the next listing, you create a main program in which you subscribe this `Observer` to the `Observable` returned by the `getTemperature` method from listing 17.12.

Listing 17.14   A `main` class printing the temperatures in New York

```java
public class Main {

    public static void main(String[] args) {
        Observable<TempInfo> observable = getTemperature( "New York" );
```

Creates an Observable emitting the temperatures reported in New York once a second

```
observable.blockingSubscribe( new TempObserver() );
```

**Subscribes to that Observable
with a simple Observer that
prints the temperatures**

```
    }
}
```

Supposing that this time, no error occurs while the temperatures are being fetched, `main` prints a line per second five times, and then the `Observable` emits the `onComplete` signal, so you might obtain output like the following:

```
New York : 69
New York : 26
New York : 85
New York : 94
New York : 29
Done!
```

It's time to enrich your RxJava example a bit further and in particular to see how this library allows you to manipulate one or more reactive streams.

17.3.2 Transforming and combining Observables

One of the main advantages of RxJava and other reactive libraries in working with reactive streams, compared with what's offered by the native Java 9 `Flow` API, is that they provide a rich toolbox of functions to combine, create, and filter any of those streams. As we demonstrated in the preceding sections, a stream can be used as an input to another one. Also, you've learned about the Java 9 `Flow.Processor` used in section 17.2.3 to transform temperatures in Fahrenheit to Celsius. But you can also filter a stream to get another one that has only the elements you're interested in, transform those elements with a given mapping function (both these things can be achieved with `Flow.Processor`), or even merge or combine two streams in many ways (which can't be achieved with `Flow.Processor`).

These transforming and combining functions can be quite sophisticated, to the point that explaining their behavior in plain words may result in awkward, convoluted sentences. To get an idea, see how RxJava documents its `mergeDelayError` function:

> *Flattens an Observable that emits Observables into one Observable, in a way that allows an Observer to receive all successfully emitted items from all of the source Observables without being interrupted by an error notification from one of them, while limiting the number of concurrent subscriptions to these Observables.*

You must admit that what this function does isn't immediately evident. To alleviate this problem, the reactive-streams community decided to document the behaviors of these functions in a visual way, using so-called marble diagrams. A *marble diagram*, such as that shown in figure 17.4, represents the temporally ordered sequence of elements in a reactive stream as geometric shapes on a horizontal line; special symbols represent error and completion signals. Boxes indicate how named operators transform those elements or combine multiple streams.

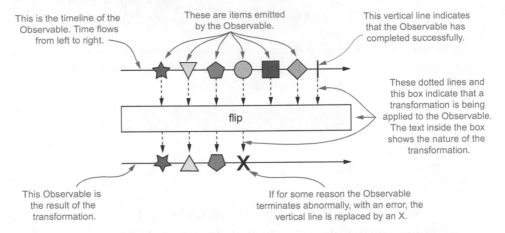

Figure 17.4   Legend of a marble diagram documenting an operator provided by a typical reactive library

Using this notation, it's easy to provide a visual representation of the features of all the RxJava library's functions as shown in figure 17.5, which exemplifies map (which transforms the elements published by an Observable) and merge (which combines the events emitted by two or more Observables into one).

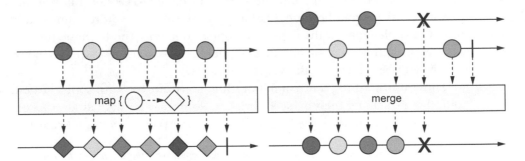

Figure 17.5   The marble diagrams for the map and merge functions

You may wonder how you can use map and merge to improve and add features to the RxJava example that you developed in the preceding section. Using map is a more concise way to achieve the transformation from Fahrenheit to Celsius that you implemented by using the Flow API's Processor, as shown in the following listing.

Listing 17.15 Using `map` on `Observable` to transform Fahrenheit into Celsius

```
public static Observable<TempInfo> getCelsiusTemperature(String town) {
    return getTemperature( town )
                .map( temp -> new TempInfo( temp.getTown(),
                                    (temp.getTemp() - 32) * 5 / 9) );
}
```

This simple method takes the `Observable` returned by the `getTemperature` method of listing 17.12 and returns another `Observable` that re-emits the temperatures published (once a second) by the first one after transforming them from Fahrenheit to Celsius.

To reinforce your understanding of how you can manipulate the elements emitted by an `Observable`, try to use another transforming function in the following quiz.

Quiz 17.2: Filtering only negative temperatures

The `filter` method of the `Observable` class takes a `Predicate` as an argument and produces a second `Observable` that emits only the elements that pass the test defined by that `Predicate`. Suppose that you've been asked to develop a warning system that alerts the user when there's risk of ice. How can you use this operator to create an `Observable` that emits the temperature in Celsius registered in a town only in case the temperature is below zero? (The Celsius scale conveniently uses zero for the freezing point of water.)

Answer:

It's enough to take the `Observable` returned by the method in listing 17.15 and apply to it the `filter` operator with a `Predicate` that accepts only negative temperature as follows:

```
public static Observable<TempInfo> getNegativeTemperature(String town) {
    return getCelsiusTemperature( town )
                .filter( temp -> temp.getTemp() < 0 );
}
```

Now also imagine that you've been asked to generalize this last method and allow your users to have an `Observable` that emits the temperatures not only for a single town, but also for a set of towns. Listing 17.16 satisfies the last requirement by invoking the method in listing 17.15 once for each town and combining all the `Observables` obtained from these invocations into a single one through the `merge` function.

Listing 17.16 Merging the temperatures reported for one or more towns

```
public static Observable<TempInfo> getCelsiusTemperatures(String... towns) {
    return Observable.merge(Arrays.stream(towns)
                        .map(TempObservable::getCelsiusTemperature)
                        .collect(toList()));
}
```

This method takes a varargs argument containing the set of towns for which you want temperatures. This varargs is converted to a stream of `String`; then each `String` is passed to the `getCelsiusTemperature` method of listing 17.11 (improved in listing 17.15). This way, each town is transformed into an `Observable` emitting the temperature of that town each second. Finally, the stream of `Observables` is collected into a list, and the list is passed to the merge static factory method provided by the `Observable` class itself. This method takes an `Iterable` of `Observables` and combines their output so that they act like a single `Observable`. In other words, the resulting `Observable` emits all the events published by all the `Observables` contained in the passed `Iterable`, preserving their temporal order.

To test this method, use it in one final `main` class as shown in the following listing.

Listing 17.17 A `main` class printing the temperatures in three towns

```java
public class Main {

    public static void main(String[] args) {
        Observable<TempInfo> observable = getCelsiusTemperatures(
                            "New York", "Chicago", "San Francisco" );
        observable.blockingSubscribe( new TempObserver() );
    }
}
```

This `main` class is identical to the one in listing 17.14 except that you're now subscribing to the `Observable` returned by the `getCelsiusTemperatures` method in listing 17.16 and printing the temperatures registered for three towns. Running this main produces output such as this:

```
New York : 21
Chicago : 6
San Francisco : -15
New York : -3
Chicago : 12
San Francisco : 5
Got problem: Error!
```

Each second, `main` prints the temperature of each requested town until one of the temperature-fetching operations raises an error that's propagated to the `Observer`, interrupting the stream of data.

The purpose of this chapter wasn't to provide a complete overview of RxJava (or any other reactive library), for which a complete book would be necessary, but to give you a feeling for how this kind of toolkit works and to introduce you to the principles of reactive programming. We've merely scratched the surface of this programming style, but we hope that we've demonstrated some of its advantages and stimulated your curiosity about it.

Summary

- The fundamental ideas behind reactive programming are 20 to 30 years old, but have become popular recently because of the high demands of modern applications in terms of amount of processed data and users' expectations.

- These ideas have been formalized by the Reactive Manifesto, which states that reactive software must be characterized by four interrelated features: responsiveness, resiliency, elasticity, and that quality of being message-driven.

- The principles of reactive programming can be applied, with some differences, in implementing a single application and in designing a reactive system that integrates multiple applications.

- A reactive application is based on asynchronous processing of one or more flows of events conveyed by reactive streams. Because the role of reactive streams is so central in development of reactive applications, a consortium of companies including Netflix, Pivotal, Lightbend, and Red Hat standardized the concepts to maximize the interoperability of different implementations.

- Because reactive streams are processed asynchronously, they've been designed with a built-in backpressure mechanism. This prevents a slow consumer from being overwhelmed by faster producers.

- The result of this design and standardization process has been incorporated into Java. The Java 9 `Flow` API defines four core interfaces: `Publisher`, `Subscriber`, `Subscription`, and `Processor`.

- These interfaces aren't intended, in most cases, to be implemented directly by developers, but to act as a lingua franca for the various libraries that implement the reactive paradigm.

- One of the most commonly used of these toolkits is RxJava, which (in addition to the basic features defined by the Java 9 `Flow` API) provides many useful, powerful operators. Examples include operators that conveniently transform and filter the elements published by a single reactive stream and operators that combine and aggregate multiple streams.

Part 6

Functional programming and future Java evolution

In the final part of this book, we draw back a little with a tutorial introduction to writing effective functional-style programs in Java, along with a comparison of Java 8 features with those of Scala.

Chapter 18 gives a full tutorial on functional programming, introduces some of its terminology, and explains how to write functional-style programs in Java.

Chapter 19 covers more advanced functional programming techniques including higher-order functions, currying, persistent data structures, lazy lists, and pattern matching. You can view this chapter as a mix of practical techniques to apply in your codebase as well as academic information that will make you a more knowledgeable programmer.

Chapter 20 follows by discussing how Java 8 features compare to features in the Scala language—a language that, like Java, is implemented on top of the JVM and that has evolved quickly to threaten some aspects of Java's niche in the programming language ecosystem.

Finally, chapter 21 reviews the journey of learning about Java 8 and the gentle push toward functional-style programming. In addition, we speculate on what future enhancements and great new features may be in Java's pipeline beyond Java 8 and Java 9.

Thinking functionally

This chapter covers

- Why functional programming?
- What defines functional programming?
- Declarative programming and referential transparency
- Guidelines for writing functional-style Java
- Iteration versus recursion

You've seen the term *functional* quite frequently throughout this book. By now, you may have some ideas about what being functional entails. Is it about lambdas and first-class functions or about restricting your right to mutate objects? What do you achieve from adopting a functional style?

In this chapter, we shed light on the answers to these questions. We explain what functional programming is and introduce some of its terminology. First, we examine the concepts behind functional programming—such as side effects, immutability, declarative programming, and referential transparency—and then we relate these concepts to Java 8. In chapter 19, we look more closely at functional programming techniques such as higher-order functions, currying, persistent data structures, lazy lists, pattern matching, and combinators.

18.1   Implementing and maintaining systems

To start, imagine that you've been asked to manage an upgrade of a large software system that you haven't seen. Should you accept the job of maintaining such a software system? A seasoned Java contractor's only slightly tongue-in-cheek maxim for deciding is "Start by searching for the keyword synchronized; if you find it, just say no (reflecting the difficulty of fixing concurrency bugs). Otherwise, consider the structure of the system in more detail." We provide more detail in the following paragraphs. First, however, we'll note that as you've seen in previous chapters, Java 8's addition of streams allows you to exploit parallelism without worrying about locking, provided that you embrace stateless behaviors. (That is, functions in your stream-processing pipeline don't interact, with one function reading from or writing to a variable that's written by another.)

What else might you want the program to look like so that it's easy to work with? You'd want it to be well structured, with an understandable class hierarchy reflecting the structure of the system. You have ways to estimate such a structure by using the software engineering metrics *coupling* (how interdependent parts of the system are) and *cohesion* (how related the various parts of the system are).

But for many programmers, the key day-to-day concern is debugging during maintenance: some code crashed because it observed an unexpected value. But which parts of the program were involved in creating and modifying this value? Think of how many of your maintenance concerns fall into this category![1] It turns out that the concepts of *no side effects* and *immutability*, which functional programming promotes, can help. We examine these concepts in more detail in the following sections.

18.1.1   Shared mutable data

Ultimately, the reason for the unexpected-variable-value problem discussed in the preceding section is that shared mutable data structures are read and updated by more than one of the methods on which your maintenance centers. Suppose that several classes keep a reference to a list. As a maintainer, you need to establish answers to the following questions:

- Who owns this list?
- What happens if one class modifies the list?
- Do other classes expect this change?
- How do those classes learn about this change?
- Do the classes need to be notified of this change to satisfy all assumptions in this list, or should they make defensive copies for themselves?

In other words, shared mutable data structures make it harder to track changes in different parts of your program. Figure 18.1 illustrates this idea.

---

[1] We recommend reading *Working Effectively with Legacy Code*, by Michael Feathers (Prentice Hall, 2004), for further information on this topic.

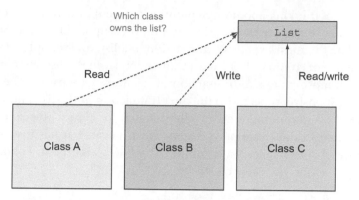

Figure 18.1 A mutable shared across multiple classes. It's difficult to understand what owns the list.

Consider a system that doesn't mutate any data structures. This system would be a dream to maintain because you wouldn't have any bad surprises about some object somewhere that unexpectedly modifies a data structure. A method that modifies neither the state of its enclosing class nor the state of any other objects and returns its entire results by using return is called *pure* or *side-effect-free*.

What constitutes a side effect? In a nutshell, a *side effect* is an action that's not totally enclosed within the function itself. Here are some examples:

- Modifying a data structure in place, including assigning to any field, apart from initialization inside a constructor (such as setter methods)
- Throwing an exception
- Performing I/O operations such as writing to a file

Another way to look at the idea of no side effects is to consider immutable objects. An *immutable object* is an object that can't change its state after it's instantiated, so it can't be affected by the actions of a function. When immutable objects are instantiated, they can never go into an unexpected state. You can share them without having to copy them, and they're thread-safe because they can't be modified.

The idea of no side effects may appear to be a severe restriction, and you may doubt whether real systems can be built this way. We hope to persuade you that they can be built by the end of the chapter. The good news is that components of systems that embrace this idea can use multicore parallelism without using locking, because the methods can no longer interfere with one another. In addition, this concept is great for immediately understanding which parts of the program are independent.

These ideas come from functional programming, to which we turn in the next section.

18.1.2 Declarative programming

First, we explore the idea of declarative programming, on which functional programming is based.

There are two ways of thinking about implementing a system by writing a program. One way centers on how things are done. (First do this, then update that, and so on.) If you want to calculate the most expensive transaction in a list, for example, you typically execute a sequence of commands. (Take a transaction from the list and compare it with the provisional most expensive transaction; if it's more expensive, it becomes the provisional most expensive; repeat with the next transaction in the list, and so on.)

This "how" style of programming is an excellent match for classic object-oriented programming (sometimes called *imperative programming*), because it has instructions that mimic the low-level vocabulary of a computer (such as assignment, conditional branching, and loops), as shown in this code:

```
Transaction mostExpensive = transactions.get(0);
if(mostExpensive == null)
    throw new IllegalArgumentException("Empty list of transactions");
for(Transaction t: transactions.subList(1, transactions.size())){
    if(t.getValue() > mostExpensive.getValue()){
        mostExpensive = t;
    }
}
```

The other way centers on what's to be done. You saw in chapters 4 and 5 that by using the Streams API, you could specify this query as follows:

```
Optional<Transaction> mostExpensive =
    transactions.stream()
               .max(comparing(Transaction::getValue));
```

The fine detail of how this query is implemented is left to the library. We refer to this idea as *internal iteration*. The great advantage is that your query reads like the problem statement, and for that reason, it's immediately clear, compared with trying to understand what a sequence of commands does.

This "what" style is often called *declarative programming*. You provide rules saying what you want, and you expect the system to decide how to achieve that goal. This type of programming is great because it reads closer to the problem statement.

18.1.3   *Why functional programming?*

Functional programming exemplifies this idea of declarative programming (say what you want using expressions that don't interact, and for which the system can choose the implementation) and side-effect-free computation, explained earlier in this chapter. These two ideas can help you implement and maintain systems more easily.

Note that certain language features, such as composing operations and passing behaviors (which we presented in chapter 3 by using lambda expressions), are required to read and write code in a natural way with a declarative style. Using streams, you can chain several operations to express a complicated query. These features characterize functional programming languages. We look at these features more carefully under the guise of combinators in chapter 19.

To make the discussion tangible and connect it with the new features in Java 8, in the next section we concretely define the idea of functional programming and its representation in Java. We'd like to impart the fact that by using functional-programming style, you can write serious programs without relying on side effects.

18.2 What's functional programming?

The oversimplistic answer to "What is functional programming?" is "Programming with functions." What's a function?

It's easy to imagine a method taking an int and a double as arguments and producing a double—and also having the side effect of counting the number of times it has been called by updating a mutable variable, as illustrated in figure 18.2.

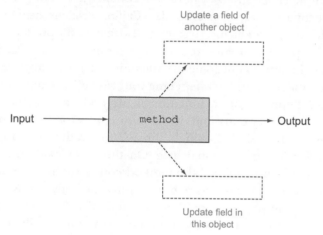

Figure 18.2 A function with side effects

In the context of functional programming, however, a *function* corresponds to a mathematical function: it takes zero or more arguments, returns one or more results, and has no side effects. You can see a function as being a black box that takes some inputs and produces some outputs, as illustrated in figure 18.3.

Figure 18.3 A function with no side effects

The distinction between this sort of function and the methods you see in programming languages such as Java is central. (The idea that mathematical functions such as log or sin might have such side effects in unthinkable.) In particular, mathematical functions always return the same results when they're called repeatedly with the same arguments. This characterization rules out methods such as Random.nextInt, and we further discuss this concept of referential transparency in section 18.2.2.

When we say *functional*, we mean like mathematics, with no side effects. Now a programming subtlety appears. Do we mean either: Is every function built only with functions and mathematical ideas such as if-then-else? Or might a function do nonfunctional things internally as long as it doesn't expose any of these side effects to the rest of the system? In other words, if programmers perform a side effect that can't be observed by callers, does that side effect exist? The callers don't need to know or care, because it can't affect them.

To emphasize the difference, we refer to the former as pure functional programming and the latter as functional-style programming.

18.2.1 *Functional-style Java*

In practice, you can't completely program in pure functional style in Java. Java's I/O model consists of side-effecting methods, for example. (Calling Scanner.nextLine has the side effect of consuming a line from a file, so calling it twice typically produces different results.) Nonetheless, it's possible to write core components of your system as though they were purely functional. In Java, you're going to write functional-style programs.

First, there's a further subtlety about no one seeing your side effects and, hence, in the meaning of *functional*. Suppose that a function or method has no side effects except for incrementing a field after entry and decrementing it before exit. From the point of view of a program that consists of a single thread, this method has no visible side effects and can be regarded as functional style. On the other hand, if another thread could inspect the field—or could call the method concurrently—the method wouldn't be functional. You could hide this issue by wrapping the body of this method with a lock, which would enable you to argue that the method is functional. But in doing so, you'd lose the ability to execute two calls to the method in parallel by using two cores on your multicore processor. Your side effect may not be visible to a program, but it's visible to the programmer in terms of slower execution.

Our guideline is that to be regarded as functional style, a function or method can mutate only local variables. In addition, the objects that it references should be immutable—that is, all fields are final, and all fields of reference type refer transitively to other immutable objects. Later, you may permit updates to fields of objects that are freshly created in the method, so they aren't visible from elsewhere and aren't saved to affect the result of a subsequent call.

Our guideline is incomplete, however. There's an additional requirement to being functional, that a function or method *shouldn't throw any exceptions*. A justification is that throwing an exception would mean that a result is being signaled other than via the function returning a value; see the black-box model of figure 18.2. There's scope for debate here, with some authors arguing that uncaught exceptions representing fatal errors are okay and that it's the act of catching an exception that represents nonfunctional control flow. Such use of exceptions still breaks the simple "pass arguments, return result" metaphor pictured in the black-box model, however, leading to a third arrow representing an exception, as illustrated in figure 18.4.

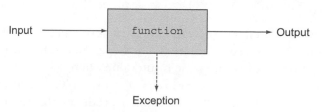

Figure 18.4 **A function throwing an exception**

Functions and partial functions

In mathematics, a function is required to give exactly one result for each possible argument value. But many common mathematical operations are what should properly be called partial functions. That is, for some or most input values, they give exactly one result, but for other input values, they're undefined and don't give a result at all. An example is division when the second operand is zero or sqrt when its argument is negative. We often model these situations in Java by throwing an exception.

How might you express functions such as division without using exceptions? Use types like Optional<T>. Instead of having the signature "double sqrt(double) but may raise an exception," sqrt would have the signature Optional<Double> sqrt(double). Either it returns a value that represents success, or it indicates in its return value that it couldn't perform the requested operation. And yes, doing so does mean that the caller needs to check whether each method call may result in an empty Optional. This may sound like a huge deal, but pragmatically, given our guidance on functional-style programming versus pure functional programming, you may choose to use exceptions locally but not expose them via large-scale interfaces, thereby gaining the advantages of functional style without the risk of code bloat.

To be regarded as functional, your function or method should call only those side-effecting library functions for which you can hide nonfunctional behavior (that is, ensuring that any mutations they make in data structures are hidden from your caller, perhaps by copying first and by catching any exceptions). In section 18.2.4, you hide the use of a side-effecting library function List.add inside a method insertAll by copying the list.

You can often mark these prescriptions by using comments or declaring a method with a marker annotation—and match the restrictions you placed on functions passed to parallel stream-processing operations such as Stream.map in chapters 4–7.

Finally, for pragmatic reasons, you may find it convenient for functional-style code to be able to output debugging information to some form of log file. This code can't be strictly described as functional, but in practice, you retain most of the benefits of functional-style programming.

18.2.2 *Referential transparency*

The restrictions on no visible side effects (no mutating structure visible to callers, no I/O, no exceptions) encode the concept of referential transparency. A function is referentially transparent if it always returns the same result value when it's called with the same argument value. The method `String.replace`, for example, is referentially transparent because `"raoul".replace('r', 'R')` always produces the same result (`replace` returns a new `String` with all lowercase rs replaced with uppercase Rs) rather than updating its `this` object, so it can be considered to be a function.

Put another way, a function consistently produces the same result given the same input, no matter where and when it's invoked. It also explains why `Random.nextInt` isn't regarded as being functional. In Java, using a `Scanner` object to get the input from a user's keyboard violates referential transparency because calling the method `nextLine` may produce a different result at each call. But adding two `final int` variables always produces the same result because the content of the variables can never change.

Referential transparency is a great property for program understanding. It also encompasses save-instead-of-recompute optimization for expensive or long-lived operations, a process that goes by the name *memoization* or *caching*. Although important, this topic is a slight tangent here, so we discuss it in chapter 19.

Java has one slight complication with regard referential transparency. Suppose that you make two calls to a method that returns a `List`. The two calls may return references to distinct lists in memory but containing the same elements. If these lists are to be seen as mutable object-oriented values (and therefore nonidentical), the method isn't referentially transparent. If you plan to use these lists as pure (immutable) values, it makes sense to see the values as being equal, so the function is referentially transparent. In general, in functional-style code, you choose to regard such functions as being referentially transparent.

In the next section, we explore whether to mutate from a wider perspective.

18.2.3 *Object-oriented vs. functional-style programming*

We start by contrasting functional-style programming with (extreme) classical object-oriented programming before observing that Java 8 sees these styles as being mere extremes on the object-oriented spectrum. As a Java programmer, without consciously thinking about it, you almost certainly use some aspects of functional-style programming and some aspects of what we'll call extreme object-oriented programming. As we remarked in chapter 1, changes in hardware (such as multicore) and programmer expectation (such as database-like queries to manipulate data) are pushing Java software-engineering styles more to the functional end of this spectrum, and one of the aims of this book is to help you adapt to the changing climate.

At one end of the spectrum is the extreme object-oriented view: everything is an object, and programs operate by updating fields and calling methods that update their associated object. At the other end of the spectrum lies the referentially transparent functional-programming style of no (visible) mutation. In practice, Java programmers have always mixed these styles. You might traverse a data structure by using an `Iterator` containing mutable internal state but use it to calculate, say, the sum of values in the data structure in a functional-style manner. (In Java, as discussed earlier, this process can include mutating local variables.) One of the aims of this chapter and chapter 19 is to discuss programming techniques and introduce features from functional programming to enable you to write programs that are more modular and more suitable for multicore processors. Think of these ideas as being additional weapons in your programming armory.

18.2.4 *Functional style in practice*

To start, solve a programming exercise given to beginning students that exemplifies functional style: given a `List<Integer>` value, such as {1, 4, 9}, construct a `List<List<Integer>>` value whose members are all the subsets of {1, 4, 9}, in any order. The subsets of {1, 4, 9} are {1, 4, 9}, {1, 4}, {1, 9}, {4, 9}, {1}, {4}, {9}, and {}.

There are eight subsets, including the empty subset, written {}. Each subset is represented as type `List<Integer>`, which means that the answer is of type `List<List<Integer>>`.

Students often have problems thinking how to start and need prompting[2] with the remark "The subsets of {1, 4, 9} either contain 1 or do not." The ones that don't are subsets of {4, 9}, and the ones that do can be obtained by taking the subsets of {4, 9} and inserting 1 into each of them. There's one subtlety though: we must remember that the empty set has exactly one subset—itself. This understanding gives you an easy, natural, top-down, functional-programming-style encoding in Java as follows:[3]

```
static List<List<Integer>> subsets(List<Integer> list) {
    if (list.isEmpty()) {
        List<List<Integer>> ans = new ArrayList<>();
        ans.add(Collections.emptyList());
        return ans;
    }
    Integer fst = list.get(0);
    List<Integer> rest = list.subList(1,list.size());
    List<List<Integer>> subAns = subsets(rest);
    List<List<Integer>> subAns2 = insertAll(fst, subAns);
    return concat(subAns, subAns2);
}
```

If the input list is empty, it has one subset: the empty list itself.

Otherwise take out one element, fst, and find all subsets of the rest to give subAns; subAns forms half the answer.

Then concatenate the two subanswers.

The other half of the answer, subAns2, consists of all the lists in subAns but adjusted by prefixing each of these element lists with fst.

---

[2] Troublesome (bright!) students occasionally point out a neat coding trick involving binary representation of numbers. (The Java solution code corresponds to 000,001,010,011,100,101,110,111.) We tell such students to calculate instead the list of all permutations of a list; for the example {1, 4, 9}, there are six.

[3] For concreteness, the code we give here uses `List<Integer>`, but you can replace it in the method definitions with generic `List<T>`; then you could apply the updated `subsets` method to `List<String>` as well as `List<Integer>`.

The solution program produces {{}, {9}, {4}, {4, 9}, {1}, {1, 9}, {1, 4}, {1, 4, 9}} when given {1, 4, 9} as input. Do try it when you've defined the two missing methods.

To review, you've assumed that the missing methods insertAll and concat are themselves functional and deduced that your function subsets is also functional, because no operation in it mutates any existing structure. (If you're familiar with mathematics, you'll recognize this argument as being by induction.)

Now look at defining insertAll. Here's the first danger point. Suppose that you defined insertAll so that it mutated its arguments, perhaps by updating all the elements of subAns to contain fst. Then the program would incorrectly cause subAns to be modified in the same way as subAns2, resulting in an answer that mysteriously contained eight copies of {1,4,9}. Instead, define insertAll functionally as follows:

```
static List<List<Integer>> insertAll(Integer fst,
                                      List<List<Integer>> lists) {
    List<List<Integer>> result = new ArrayList<>();
    for (List<Integer> list : lists) {
        List<Integer> copyList = new ArrayList<>();   ◄───
        copyList.add(fst);
        copyList.addAll(list);
        result.add(copyList);
    }
    return result;
}
```

> Copy the list so you can add to it. You wouldn't copy the lower-level structure even if it were mutable. (Integers aren't mutable.)

Note that you're creating a new List that contains all the elements of subAns. You take advantage of the fact that an Integer object is immutable; otherwise, you'd have to clone each element too. The focus caused by thinking of methods like insertAll as being functional gives you a natural place to put all this carefully copied code: inside insertAll rather in its callers.

Finally, you need to define the concat method. In this case, the solution is simple, but we beg you not to use it; we show it only so that you can compare the different styles:

```
static List<List<Integer>> concat(List<List<Integer>> a,
                                  List<List<Integer>> b) {
    a.addAll(b);
    return a;
}
```

Instead, we suggest that you write this code:

```
static List<List<Integer>> concat(List<List<Integer>> a,
                                  List<List<Integer>> b) {
    List<List<Integer>> r = new ArrayList<>(a);
    r.addAll(b);
    return r;
}
```

Why? The second version of concat is a pure function. The function may be using mutation (adding elements to the list r) internally, but it returns a result based on its arguments and modifies neither of them. By contrast, the first version relies on the fact that after the call `concat(subAns, subAns2)`, no one refers to the value of `subAns` again. For our definition of `subsets`, this situation is the case, so surely using the cheaper version of `concat` is better. The answer depends on how you value your time. Compare the time you'd spend later searching for obscure bugs compared with the additional cost of making a copy.

No matter how well you comment that the impure `concat` is "to be used only when the first argument can be arbitrarily overwritten, and intended to be used only in the `subsets` method, and any change to `subsets` must be reviewed in the light of this comment," somebody sometime will find it useful in some piece of code where it apparently seems to work. Your future nightmare debugging problem has been born. We revisit this issue in chapter 19.

Takeaway point: thinking of programming problems in terms of function-style methods that are characterized only by their input arguments and output results (what to do) is often more productive than thinking about how to do it and what to mutate too early in the design cycle.

In the next section, we discuss recursion in detail.

18.3 Recursion vs. iteration

Recursion is a technique promoted in functional programming to let you think in terms of what-to-do style. Pure functional programming languages typically don't include iterative constructs such as `while` and `for` loops. Such constructs are often hidden invitations to use mutation. The condition in a `while` loop needs to be updated, for example; otherwise, the loop would execute zero times or an infinite number of times. In many cases, however, loops are fine. We've argued that for functional style, you're allowed mutation if no one can see you doing it, so it's acceptable to mutate local variables. When you use the `for-each` loop in Java, `for(Apple apple : apples) { }`, it decodes into this `Iterator`:

```
Iterator<Apple> it = apples.iterator();
while (it.hasNext()) {
    Apple apple = it.next();
    // ...
}
```

This translation isn't a problem because the mutations (changing the state of the `Iterator` with the next method and assigning to the `apple` variable inside the `while` body) aren't visible to the caller of the method where the mutations happen. But when you use a `for-each` loop, such as a search algorithm, for example, what follows is problematic because the loop body is updating a data structure that's shared with the caller:

```
public void searchForGold(List<String> l, Stats stats){
    for(String s: l){
        if("gold".equals(s)){
```

```
                stats.incrementFor("gold");
        }
    }
}
```

Indeed, the body of the loop has a side effect that can't be dismissed as functional style: it mutates the state of the stats object, which is shared with other parts of the program.

For this reason, pure functional programming languages such as Haskell omit such side-effecting operations. How are you to write programs? The theoretical answer is that every program can be rewritten to prevent iteration by using recursion instead, which doesn't require mutability. Using recursion lets you get rid of iteration variables that are updated step by step. A classic school problem is calculating the factorial function (for positive arguments) in an iterative way and in a recursive way (assume that the input is > 0), as shown in the following two listings.

Listing 18.1   Iterative factorial

```
static long factorialIterative(long n) {
    long r = 1;
    for (int i = 1; i <= n; i++) {
        r *= i;
    }
    return r;
}
```

Listing 18.2   Recursive factorial

```
static long factorialRecursive(long n) {
    return n == 1 ? 1 : n * factorialRecursive(n-1);
}
```

The first listing demonstrates a standard loop-based form: the variables r and i are updated at each iteration. The second listing shows a recursive definition (the function calls itself) in a more mathematically familiar form. In Java, recursive forms typically are less efficient, as we discuss immediately after the next example.

If you've read the earlier chapters of this book, however, you know that Java 8 streams provide an even simpler declarative way of defining factorial, as shown in the following listing.

Listing 18.3   Stream factorial

```
static long factorialStreams(long n){
    return LongStream.rangeClosed(1, n)
                     .reduce(1, (long a, long b) -> a * b);
}
```

Now we'll turn to efficiency. As Java users, beware of functional-programming zealots who tell you that you should always use recursion instead of iteration. In general, making a recursive function call is much more expensive than issuing the single machine-level branch instruction needed to iterate. Every time the `factorial-Recursive` function is called, a new stack frame is created on the call stack to hold the state of each function call (the multiplication it needs to do) until the recursion is done. Your recursive definition of factorial takes memory proportional to its input. For this reason, if you run `factorialRecursive` with a large input, you're likely to receive a `StackOverflowError`:

```
Exception in thread "main" java.lang.StackOverflowError
```

Is recursion useless? Of course not! Functional languages provide an answer to this problem: *tail-call optimization.* The basic idea is that you can write a recursive definition of factorial in which the recursive call is the last thing that happens in the function (or the call is in a tail position). This different form of recursion style can be optimized to run fast. The next listing provides a tail-recursive definition of factorial.

Listing 18.4 Tail-recursive factorial

```
static long factorialTailRecursive(long n) {
    return factorialHelper(1, n);
}
static long factorialHelper(long acc, long n) {
    return n == 1 ? acc : factorialHelper(acc * n, n-1);
}
```

The function `factorialHelper` is tail-recursive because the recursive call is the last thing that happens in the function. By contrast, in the earlier definition of `factorial-Recursive`, the last thing was a multiplication of n and the result of a recursive call.

This form of recursion is useful because instead of storing each intermediate result of the recursion in separate stack frames, the compiler can decide to reuse a single stack frame. Indeed, in the definition of `factorialHelper`, the intermediate results (the partial results of the factorial) are passed directly as arguments to the function. There's no need to keep track of the intermediate result of each recursive call on a separate stack frame; it's accessible directly as the first argument of `factorialHelper`. Figures 18.5 and 18.6 illustrate the difference between the recursive and tail-recursive definitions of factorial.

The bad news is that Java doesn't support this kind of optimization. But adopting tail recursion may be a better practice than classic recursion because it opens the way to eventual compiler optimization. Many modern JVM languages such as Scala, Groovy, and Kotlin can optimize those uses of recursion, which are equivalent to iteration (and execute at the same speed). As a result, pure-functional adherents can have their purity cake and eat it efficiently too.

The guidance in writing Java 8 is that you can often replace iteration with streams to avoid mutation. In addition, you can replace iteration with recursion when recursion allows you write an algorithm in a more concise, side-effect-free way. Indeed,

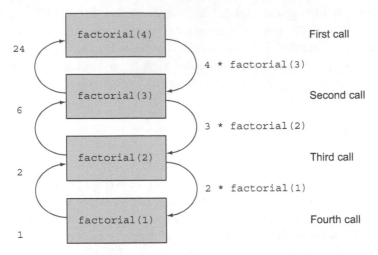

Figure 18.5   **Recursive definition of factorial, which requires several stack frames**

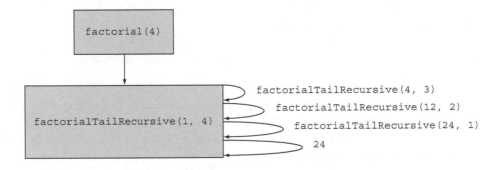

Figure 18.6   **Tail-recursive definition of factorial, which can reuse a single stack frame**

recursion can make examples easier to read, write, and understand (as in the subsets example shown earlier in this chapter), and programmer efficiency is often more important than small differences in execution time.

In this section, we discussed functional-style programming with the idea of a method being functional; everything we said would have applied to the first version of Java. In chapter 19, we look at the amazing and powerful possibilities offered by the introduction of first-class functions in Java 8.

Summary

- Reducing shared mutable data structures can help you maintain and debug your programs in the long term.
- Functional-style programming promotes side-effect-free methods and declarative programming.
- Function-style methods are characterized only by their input arguments and their output result.
- A function is referentially transparent if it always returns the same result value when called with the same argument value. Iterative constructs such as `while` loops can be replaced by recursion.
- Tail recursion may be a better practice than classic recursion in Java because it opens the way to potential compiler optimization.

Functional
programming techniques

19

This chapter covers

- First-class citizens, higher-order functions, currying, and partial application
- Persistent data structures
- Lazy evaluation and lazy lists as generalizing Java streams
- Pattern matching and how to simulate it in Java
- Referential transparency and caching

In chapter 18, you saw how to think functionally; thinking in terms of side-effect-free methods can help you write more maintainable code. In this chapter, we introduce more advanced functional programming techniques. You can view this chapter as being a mix of practical techniques to apply in your code base, as well as academic information that will make you a more knowledgeable programmer. We discuss higher-order functions, currying, persistent data structures, lazy lists, pattern matching, caching with referential transparency, and combinators.

19.1 Functions everywhere

In chapter 18 we used the phrase *functional-style programming* to mean that the behavior of functions and methods should be like that of mathematical-style functions, with no side effects. Functional-language programmers often use the phrase with more generality to mean that functions may be used like other values: passed as arguments, returned as results, and stored in data structures. Functions that may be used like other values are referred to as *first-class functions*. First-class functions are what Java 8 added over previous versions of Java: you may use any method as a function value, using the : : operator to create a method reference, and lambda expressions (such as (int x) -> x + 1) to express function values directly. In Java 8 it's perfectly valid[1] to store the method Integer.parseInt in a variable by using a method reference as follows:

```
Function<String, Integer> strToInt = Integer::parseInt;
```

19.1.1 Higher-order functions

So far, you've mainly used the fact that function values are first-class only to pass them to Java 8 stream-processing operations (as in chapters 4–7) and to achieve the similar effect of behavior parameterization when you passed Apple::isGreen-Apple as a function value to filterApples in chapters 1 and 2. Another interesting example was using the static method Comparator.comparing, which takes a function as a parameter and returns another function (a Comparator), as illustrated in the following code and figure 19.1:

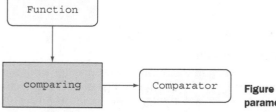

Figure 19.1 comparing **takes a function as parameter and returns another function.**

```
Comparator<Apple> c = comparing(Apple::getWeight);
```

You did something similar when you composed functions in chapter 3 to create a pipeline of operations:

```
Function<String, String> transformationPipeline
    = addHeader.andThen(Letter::checkSpelling)
             .andThen(Letter::addFooter);
```

---

[1] If Integer::parseInt is the only method you plan to store in variable strToInt, you might want to make strToInt have type ToIntFunction<String> to save boxing. You don't do so here because using such Java primitive applications can get in the way of seeing what's happening, even if those applications improve efficiency for primitive types.

Functions (such as `Comparator.comparing`) that can do at least one of the following are called *higher-order functions* within the functional programming community:

- Take one or more functions as a parameter
- Return a function as a result

This characterization directly relates to Java 8 functions because they can not only be passed as arguments, but also returned as results, assigned to local variables, or even inserted into structures. A pocket-calculator program might have a `Map<String, Function<Double, Double>>` that maps the `String "sin"` to `Function<Double, Double>` to hold the method reference `Math::sin`. You did something similar when you learned about the factory design pattern in chapter 8.

Readers who liked the calculus example at the end of chapter 3 can regard the type of differentiation as being

```
Function<Function<Double,Double>, Function<Double,Double>>
```

because it takes a function as an argument (such as `(Double x) -> x * x`) and returns a function as a result (in this example, `(Double x) -> 2 * x`). We've written this code as a function type (the leftmost `Function`) to explicitly affirm the fact that you could pass this differentiating function to another function. But it's good to recall that the type for differentiating and the signature

```
Function<Double,Double> differentiate(Function<Double,Double> func)
```

say the same thing.

> ### Side effects and higher-order functions
> We noted in chapter 7 that functions passed to stream operations generally are side-effect-free, and we noted the problems that arise otherwise (such as incorrect results and even unpredictable results due to race conditions you hadn't thought of). This principle also applies in general when you use higher-order functions. When you're writing a higher-order function or method, you don't know in advance what arguments will be passed to it and, if the arguments have side effects, what these side effects might do. It becomes far too complicated to reason about what your code does if it uses functions passed as arguments that make unpredictable changes in the state of your program; such functions might even interfere with your code in some hard-to-debug way. It's a good design principle to document what side effects you're willing to accept from functions passed as parameters. None is best of all!

In the next section, we turn to currying: a technique that can help you modularize functions and reuse code.

19.1.2 *Currying*

Before we give you the theoretical definition of currying, we'll present an example. Applications almost always need to be internationalized, so converting from one set of units to another set is a problem that comes up repeatedly.

Unit conversion always involves a conversion factor and, from time to time, a baseline adjustment factor. The formula to convert Celsius to Fahrenheit, for example, is `CtoF(x) = x*9/5 + 32`. The basic pattern of all unit conversion is as follows:

1 Multiply by the conversion factor.
2 Adjust the baseline if relevant.

You can express this pattern with the following general method:

```
static double converter(double x, double f, double b) {
    return x * f + b;
}
```

Here, `x` is the quantity you want to convert, `f` is the conversion factor, and `b` is the baseline. But this method is a bit too general. Typically, you require a lot of conversions between the same pair of units, such as kilometers to miles. You could call the `converter` method with three arguments on each occasion, but supplying the factor and baseline each time would be tedious, and you might accidentally mistype them.

You could write a new method for each application, but doing so would miss the reuse of the underlying logic.

Here's an easy way to benefit from the existing logic while tailoring the converter for particular applications. You can define a factory that manufactures one-argument conversion functions to exemplify the idea of currying:

```
static DoubleUnaryOperator curriedConverter(double f, double b){
    return (double x) -> x * f + b;
}
```

Now all you have to do is pass `curriedConverter` the conversion factor and baseline (`f` and `b`), and it obligingly returns a function (of `x`) to do what you asked for. Then you can use the factory to produce any converter you require, as follows:

```
DoubleUnaryOperator convertCtoF = curriedConverter(9.0/5, 32);
DoubleUnaryOperator convertUSDtoGBP = curriedConverter(0.6, 0);
DoubleUnaryOperator convertKmtoMi = curriedConverter(0.6214, 0);
```

Because `DoubleUnaryOperator` defines a method `applyAsDouble`, you can use your converters as follows:

```
double gbp = convertUSDtoGBP.applyAsDouble(1000);
```

As a result, your code is more flexible, and it reuses the existing conversion logic!

Reflect on what you're doing here. Instead of passing all the arguments `x`, `f`, and `b` all at once to the `converter` method, you ask only for the arguments `f` and `b` and return another function—which, when given an argument x, returns x * f + b. This two-stage process enables you to reuse the conversion logic and create different functions with different conversion factors.

Formal definition of currying

Currying[a] is a technique in which a function f of two arguments (such as x and y) is instead viewed as a function g of one argument that returns a function also of one argument. The value returned by the latter function is the same as the value of the original function—that is, f(x,y) = (g(x))(y).

This definition generalizes, of course. You can curry a six-argument function to first take arguments numbered 2, 4, and 6, which returns a function taking argument 5, which returns a function taking the remaining arguments, 1 and 3.

When some arguments (but fewer than the full complement of arguments) have been passed, the function is *partially applied*.

[a] The word *currying* is unconnected to Indian food; the term is named after the logician Haskell Brooks Curry, who popularized the technique. He attributed it to Moses Ilyich Schönfinkel, however. Should we refer to currying as *schönfinkeling* instead?

In the next section, we turn to another aspect of functional-style programming: data structures. Is it possible to program with data structures if you're forbidden to modify them?

19.2   *Persistent data structures*

Data structures used in functional-style programs have various names, such as functional data structures and immutable data structures, but perhaps the most common is persistent data structures. (Unfortunately, this terminology clashes with the notion of *persistent* in databases, meaning "outliving one run of the program.")

The first thing to notice is that a functional-style method isn't allowed to update any global data structure or any structure passed as a parameter. Why? Because calling it twice is likely to produce different answers, violating referential transparency and the ability to understand the method as a simple mapping from arguments to results.

19.2.1 *Destructive updates vs. functional*

Consider the problems that can arise. Suppose that you represent train journeys from A to B as a mutable `TrainJourney` class (a simple implementation of a singly linked list), with an `int` field modeling some detail of the journey, such as the price of the current leg of the journey. Journeys that require changing trains have several linked `TrainJourney` objects via the `onward` field; a direct train or the final leg of a journey has `onward` being `null`:

```
class TrainJourney {
    public int price;
    public TrainJourney onward;
```

```
public TrainJourney(int p, TrainJourney t) {
    price = p;
    onward = t;
}
}
```

Now suppose that you have separate `TrainJourney` objects representing a journey from X to Y and from Y to Z. You may want to create one journey that links the two `TrainJourney` objects (that is, X to Y to Z).

Here is a simple traditional imperative method to `link` these train journeys:

```
static TrainJourney link(TrainJourney a, TrainJourney b){
    if (a==null) return b;
    TrainJourney t = a;
    while(t.onward != null){
        t = t.onward;
    }
    t.onward = b;
    return a;
}
```

This method works by finding the last leg in the `TrainJourney` for a and replacing the `null` marking the end of a's list with list b. (You need a special case if a has no elements.)

Here's the problem: suppose that a variable `firstJourney` contains the route from X to Y and that a variable `secondJourney` contains the route from Y to Z. If you call `link(firstJourney, secondJourney)`, this code destructively updates `first-Journey` to also contain `secondJourney`, so in addition to the single user who requests a trip from X to Z seeing the combined journey as intended, the journey from X to Y has been updated destructively. Indeed, the `firstJourney` variable is no longer a route from X to Y, but one from X to Z, which breaks code that depends on `firstJourney`'s not being modified! Suppose that `firstJourney` represented the early-morning London-to-Brussels train, which all subsequent users trying to get to Brussels will be surprised to see requires an onward leg, perhaps to Cologne. We've all fought battles with such bugs concerning how visible a change in a data structure should be.

The functional-style approach to this problem is to ban such side-effecting methods. If you need a data structure to represent the result of a computation, you should make a new one, not mutate an existing data structure, as you've done previously. Doing so is often a best practice in standard object-oriented programming, too. A common objection to the functional approach is that it causes excess copying, and the programmer says, "I'll remember" or "I'll document" the side effects. But such optimism is a trap for maintenance programmers who have to deal with your code later. Thus, the functional-style solution is as follows:

```
static TrainJourney append(TrainJourney a, TrainJourney b){
    return a==null ? b : new TrainJourney(a.price, append(a.onward, b));
}
```

This code is clearly functional-style (uses no mutation, even locally) and doesn't modify any existing data structures. Note, however, that the code doesn't create a new `TrainJourney`. If a is a sequence of n elements and b is a sequence of m elements, the code returns a sequence of $n+m$ elements, in which the first n elements are new nodes and the final m elements share with `TrainJourney` b. Note that users are required not to mutate the result of append because by doing so, they may corrupt the trains passed as sequence b. Figures 19.2 and 19.3 illustrate the difference between the destructive append and the functional-style append.

Destructive append

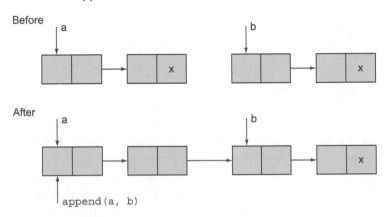

Figure 19.2   The data structure is destructively updated.

Functional-style append

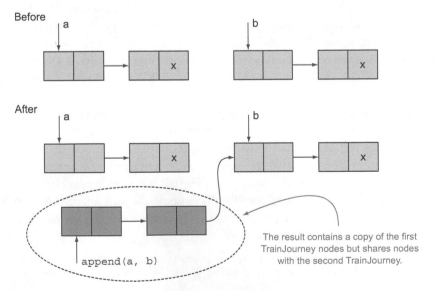

The result contains a copy of the first TrainJourney nodes but shares nodes with the second TrainJourney.

Figure 19.3   Functional style with no modifications to the data structure

19.2.2 *Another example with Trees*

Before leaving this topic, consider another data structure: a binary search tree that might be used to implement a similar interface to a HashMap. The idea is that a Tree contains a String representing a key and an int representing its value, perhaps names and ages:

```
class Tree {
   private String key;
   private int val;
   private Tree left, right;
   public Tree(String k, int v, Tree l, Tree r) {
     key = k; val = v; left = l; right = r;
   }
}
class TreeProcessor {
   public static int lookup(String k, int defaultval, Tree t) {
       if (t == null) return defaultval;
       if (k.equals(t.key)) return t.val;
       return lookup(k, defaultval,
                        k.compareTo(t.key) < 0 ? t.left : t.right);
   }
   // other methods processing a Tree
}
```

You want to use the binary search tree to look up String values to produce an int. Now consider how you might update the value associated with a given key (assuming for simplicity that the key is already present in the tree):

```
public static void update(String k, int newval, Tree t) {
   if (t == null) { /* should add a new node */ }
   else if (k.equals(t.key)) t.val = newval;
   else update(k, newval, k.compareTo(t.key) < 0 ? t.left : t.right);
}
```

Adding a new node is trickier. The easiest way is to make the method update return the Tree that has been traversed (unchanged unless you had to add a node). Now this code is slightly clumsier because the user needs to remember that update tries to update the tree in place, returning the same tree as passed. But if the original tree were empty, a new node is returned as a result:

```
public static Tree update(String k, int newval, Tree t) {
   if (t == null)
       t = new Tree(k, newval, null, null);
   else if (k.equals(t.key))
       t.val = newval;
   else if (k.compareTo(t.key) < 0)
       t.left = update(k, newval, t.left);
   else
       t.right = update(k, newval, t.right);
   return t;
}
```

Note that both versions of update mutate the existing Tree, meaning that all users of the map stored in the tree see the mutation.

19.2.3 *Using a functional approach*

How might you program such tree updates functionally? You need to create a new node for the new key-value pair. You also need to create new nodes on the path from the root of the tree to the new node, as follows:

```
public static Tree fupdate(String k, int newval, Tree t) {
    return (t == null) ?
        new Tree(k, newval, null, null) :
         k.equals(t.key) ?
            new Tree(k, newval, t.left, t.right) :
       k.compareTo(t.key) < 0 ?
            new Tree(t.key, t.val, fupdate(k,newval, t.left), t.right) :
            new Tree(t.key, t.val, t.left, fupdate(k,newval, t.right));
}
```

In general, this code isn't expensive. If the tree is of depth d and reasonably well balanced, it can have around 2^d entries, so you re-create a small fraction of it.

We've written this code as a single conditional expression instead of using if-then-else to emphasize the idea that the body is a single expression with no side effects. But you may prefer to write an equivalent if-then-else chain, each containing a return.

What's the difference between update and fupdate? We noted previously that the method update assumes that every user wants to share the data structure and see updates caused by any part of the program. Therefore, it's vital (but often overlooked) in nonfunctional code that whenever you add some form of structured value to a tree, you copy it, because someone may assume later that he can update it. By contrast, fupdate is purely functional; it creates a new Tree as a result but shares as much as it can with its argument. Figure 19.4 illustrates this idea. You have a tree consisting

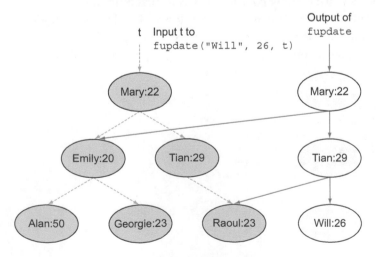

Figure 19.4 No existing data structure was harmed during the making of this update to Tree.

of nodes that store a name and an age of a person. Calling `fupdate` doesn't modify the existing tree; it creates new nodes "living at the side of" the tree without harming the existing data structure.

Such functional data structures are often called *persistent*—their values persist and are isolated from changes happening elsewhere—so as a programmer, you're sure that `fupdate` won't mutate the data structures passed as its arguments. There's one proviso: the other side of the treaty requires all users of persistent data structures to follow the do-not-mutate requirement. If not, a programmer who disregards this proviso might mutate the result of `fupdate` (by changing Emily's 20, for example). Then this mutation would be visible as an (almost certainly unwanted) unexpected and delayed change to the data structure passed as argument to `fupdate`!

Viewed in these terms, `fupdate` can be more efficient. The "no mutation of existing structure" rule allows structures that differ only slightly (such as the `Tree` seen by user A and the modified version seen by user B) to share storage for common parts of their structure. You can get the compiler to help enforce this rule by declaring fields `key`, `val`, `left`, and `right` of class `Tree` to be `final`. But remember that `final` protects only a field, not the object pointed to, which may need its own fields to be `final` to protect it, and so on.

You might say, "I *want* updates to the tree to be seen by some users (but admittedly not by some others)." You have two choices. One choice is the classical Java solution: be careful when updating something to check whether you need to copy it first. The other choice is the functional-style solution: you logically make a new data structure whenever you do an update (so that nothing is ever mutated) and arrange to pass the correct version of the data structure to users as appropriate. This idea could be enforced through an API. If certain clients of the data structure need to have updates visible, they should go through an API that returns the latest version. Clients who don't want updates visible (such as for long-running statistical analysis) use whatever copy they retrieve, knowing that it can't be mutated from under them.

This technique is like updating a file on a CD-R, which allows a file to be written only once by burning with a laser. Multiple versions of the file are stored on the CD (smart CD-authoring software might even share common parts of multiple versions), and you pass the appropriate block address of the start of the file (or a filename encoding the version within its name) to select which version you want to use. In Java, things are rather better than on a CD, in that old versions of the data structure that can no longer be used are garbage-collected.

19.3 *Lazy evaluation with streams*

You saw in previous chapters that streams are great ways to process a collection of data. But for various reasons, including efficient implementation, the Java 8 designers added streams to Java in a rather specific way. One limitation is that you can't define a stream recursively because a stream can be consumed only once. In the following sections, we show you how this situation can be problematic.

19.3.1 *Self-defining stream*

Revisit the example from chapter 6 of generating prime numbers to understand this idea of a recursive stream. In that chapter, you saw that (perhaps as part of a MyMath-Utils class), you can compute a stream of prime numbers as follows:

```
public static Stream<Integer> primes(int n) {
    return Stream.iterate(2, i -> i + 1)
                 .filter(MyMathUtils::isPrime)
                 .limit(n);
}
public static boolean isPrime(int candidate) {
    int candidateRoot = (int) Math.sqrt((double) candidate);
    return IntStream.rangeClosed(2, candidateRoot)
                 .noneMatch(i -> candidate % i == 0);
}
```

But this solution is somewhat awkward. You have to iterate through every number every time to see whether it can be divided by a candidate number. (In fact, you need only test numbers that have been already classified as prime.)

Ideally, the stream should filter out numbers that are divisible by the prime that the stream is producing on the go. Here's how this process might work:

1 You need a stream of numbers from which you'll select prime numbers.
2 From that stream, take the first number (the head of the stream), which will be a prime number. (In the initial step, this number is 2.)
3 Filter all the numbers that are divisible by that number from the tail of the stream.
4 The resulting tail is the new stream of numbers that you can use to find prime numbers. Essentially, you go back to step 1, so this algorithm is recursive.

Note that this algorithm is poor for a few reasons,[2] but it's simple to reason about algorithms for the purpose of working with streams. In the following sections, you try to write this algorithm by using the Streams API.

STEP 1: GET A STREAM OF NUMBERS

You can get an infinite stream of numbers starting from 2 by using the method Int-Stream.iterate (which we described in chapter 5) as follows:

```
static Intstream numbers(){
    return IntStream.iterate(2, n -> n + 1);
}
```

---

[2] You can find more information about why the algorithm is poor at www.cs.hmc.edu/~oneill/papers/Sieve-JFP.pdf.

STEP 2: TAKE THE HEAD

An `IntStream` comes with the method `findFirst`, which you can use to return the first element:

```
static int head(IntStream numbers){
    return numbers.findFirst().getAsInt();
}
```

STEP 3: FILTER THE TAIL

Define a method to get the tail of a stream:

```
static IntStream tail(IntStream numbers){
    return numbers.skip(1);
}
```

Given the head of the stream, you can filter the numbers as follows:

```
IntStream numbers = numbers();
int head = head(numbers);
IntStream filtered = tail(numbers).filter(n -> n % head != 0);
```

STEP 4: RECURSIVELY CREATE A STREAM OF PRIMES

Here comes the tricky part. You may be tempted to try passing back the resulting filtered stream so that you can take its head and filter more numbers, like this:

```
static IntStream primes(IntStream numbers) {
    int head = head(numbers);
    return IntStream.concat(
            IntStream.of(head),
            primes(tail(numbers).filter(n -> n % head != 0))
        );
}
```

BAD NEWS

Unfortunately, if you run the code in step 4, you get the following error: `java.lang.IllegalStateException: stream has already been operated upon or closed`. Indeed, you're using two terminal operations to split the stream into its head and tail: `findFirst` and `skip`. Remember from chapter 4 that after you call a terminal operation on a stream, it's consumed forever!

LAZY EVALUATION

There's an additional, more important problem: the static method `IntStream.concat` expects two instances of a stream, but its second argument is a direct recursive call to `primes`, resulting in an infinite recursion! For many Java purposes, restrictions on Java 8 streams such as no recursive definitions are unproblematic and give your database-like queries expressivity and the ability to parallelize. Thus, the Java 8 designers chose a sweet spot. Nonetheless, the more general features and models of streams from functional languages such as Scala and Haskell can be useful additions to your programming toolbox. What you need is a way to lazily evaluate the call to the method primes in the second argument of concat. (In a more technical programming vocabulary, we refer to this concept as *lazy evaluation, nonstrict evaluation* or even *call by name.*) Only when you need to process the prime numbers (such as with the limit method) should the stream be evaluated. Scala (which we explore in chapter 20) provides support for this idea. In Scala, you can write the preceding algorithm as follows, where the operator #:: does lazy concatenation (arguments being evaluated only when you need to consume the stream):

```
def numbers(n: Int): Stream[Int] = n #:: numbers(n+1)
def primes(numbers: Stream[Int]): Stream[Int] = {
  numbers.head #:: primes(numbers.tail filter (n => n % numbers.head != 0))
}
```

Don't worry about this code. Its only purpose is to show you an area of difference between Java and other functional programming languages. It's good to reflect for a moment about how the arguments are evaluated. In Java, when you call a method, all its arguments are fully evaluated immediately. But when you use #:: in Scala, the concatenation returns immediately, and the elements are evaluated only when needed.

In the next section, we turn to implementing this idea of lazy lists directly in Java.

19.3.2 *Your own lazy list*

Java 8 streams are often described as being lazy. They're lazy in one particular aspect: a stream behaves like a black box that can generate values on request. When you apply a sequence of operations to a stream, these operations are merely saved up. Only when you apply a terminal operation to a stream is anything computed. This delaying has a great advantage when you apply several operations (perhaps a filter and a map followed by a terminal operation reduce) to a stream: the stream has to be traversed only once instead of for each operation.

In this section, you consider the notion of lazy lists, which are forms of a more general stream. (Lazy lists form a concept similar to stream.) Lazy lists also provide an excellent way of thinking about higher-order functions. You place a function value in a data structure so that most of the time, it can sit there unused, but when it's called (on demand), it can create more of the data structure. Figure 19.5 illustrates this idea.

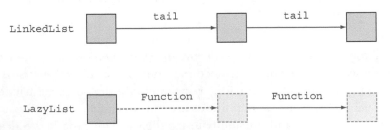

Figure 19.5 Elements of a LinkedList exist (are spread out) in memory. But elements of a LazyList are created on demand by a Function; you can see them as being spread out in time.

Next, you see how this concept works. You want to generate an infinite list of prime numbers by using the algorithm we described earlier.

CREATING A BASIC LINKED LIST

Recall that you can define a simple linked-list-style class called `MyLinkedList` in Java by writing it as follows (with a minimal `MyList` interface):

```java
interface MyList<T> {
    T head();
    MyList<T> tail();
    default boolean isEmpty() {
        return true;
    }
}
class MyLinkedList<T> implements MyList<T> {
    private final T head;
    private final MyList<T> tail;
    public MyLinkedList(T head, MyList<T> tail) {
        this.head = head;
        this.tail = tail;
    }
    public T head() {
        return head;
    }
    public MyList<T> tail() {
        return tail;
    }
    public boolean isEmpty() {
        return false;
    }
}
class Empty<T> implements MyList<T> {
    public T head() {
        throw new UnsupportedOperationException();
    }
    public MyList<T> tail() {
        throw new UnsupportedOperationException();
    }
}
```

Now you can construct a sample `MyLinkedList` value as follows:

```java
MyList<Integer> l =
    new MyLinkedList<>(5, new MyLinkedList<>(10, new Empty<>()));
```

CREATING A BASIC LAZY LIST

An easy way to adapt this class to the concept of a lazy list is to cause the tail not to be present in memory all at once, but to have the `Supplier<T>` that you saw in chapter 3 (you can also see it as being a factory with a function descriptor `void -> T`) produce the next node of the list. This design leads to the following code:

```
import java.util.function.Supplier;
class LazyList<T> implements MyList<T>{
    final T head;
    final Supplier<MyList<T>> tail;
    public LazyList(T head, Supplier<MyList<T>> tail) {
        this.head = head;
        this.tail = tail;
    }
    public T head() {
        return head;
    }
    public MyList<T> tail() {
        return tail.get();
    }
    public boolean isEmpty() {
        return false;
    }
}
```

Note that tail using a Supplier encodes laziness, compared with method head.

Calling the method get from the Supplier causes the creation of a node of the Lazy-List (as a factory would create a new object).

Now you can create the infinite lazy list of numbers starting at n as follows. Pass a Supplier as the tail argument of the LazyList constructor, which creates the next element in the series of numbers:

```
public static LazyList<Integer> from(int n) {
    return new LazyList<Integer>(n, () -> from(n+1));
}
```

If you try the following code, you see that it prints 2 3 4. Indeed, the numbers are generated on demand. To check, insert System.out.println appropriately or note that from(2) would run forever if it tried to calculate all the numbers starting from 2:

```
LazyList<Integer> numbers = from(2);
int two = numbers.head();
int three = numbers.tail().head();
int four = numbers.tail().tail().head();
System.out.println(two + " " + three + " " + four);
```

GENERATING PRIMES AGAIN

See whether you can use what you've done so far to generate a self-defining lazy list of prime numbers (something that you were unable to do with the Streams API). If you were to translate the code that was using the Streams API earlier, using the new LazyList, the code would look like something like this:

```
public static MyList<Integer> primes(MyList<Integer> numbers) {
    return new LazyList<>(
                numbers.head(),
                () -> primes(
                        numbers.tail()
```

```
                                      .filter(n -> n % numbers.head() != 0)
                        )
            );
}
```

IMPLEMENTING A LAZY FILTER

Unfortunately, a LazyList (more accurately, the List interface) doesn't define a filter method, so the preceding code won't compile! To fix this problem, declare a filter method, as follows:

```
public MyList<T> filter(Predicate<T> p) {          You could return new
    return isEmpty() ?                             Empty<>(), but using 'this'
            this :                            ◁─┘  is as good and empty.
            p.test(head()) ?
                new LazyList<>(head(), () -> tail().filter(p)) :
                tail().filter(p);
}
```

Your code compiles and is ready for use! You can calculate the first three prime numbers by chaining calls to tail and head, as follows:

```
LazyList<Integer> numbers = from(2);
int two = primes(numbers).head();
int three = primes(numbers).tail().head();
int five = primes(numbers).tail().tail().head();
System.out.println(two + " " + three + " " + five);
```

This code prints 2 3 5, which are the first three prime numbers. Now you can have some fun. You could print all the prime numbers, for example. (The program will run infinitely by writing a printAll method, which iteratively prints the head and tail of a list.)

```
static <T> void printAll(MyList<T> list){
    while (!list.isEmpty()){
        System.out.println(list.head());
        list = list.tail();
    }
}
printAll(primes(from(2)));
```

This chapter being a functional programming chapter, we should explain that this code can be neatly written recursively:

```
static <T> void printAll(MyList<T> list){
    if (list.isEmpty())
        return;
    System.out.println(list.head());
    printAll(list.tail());
}
```

This program wouldn't run infinitely, though. Sadly, it would eventually fail due to stack overflow because Java doesn't support tail call elimination, as discussed in chapter 18.

REVIEW

You've built a whole lot of technology with lazy lists and functions, using them only to define a data structure containing all the primes. What's the practical use? Well, you've seen how to place functions inside data structures (because Java 8 allows you to), and you can use these functions to create parts of the data structure on demand instead of when the structure is created. This capability may be useful if you're writing a game-playing program, perhaps for chess; you can have a data structure that notionally represents the whole tree of possible moves (far too big to calculate eagerly) but that can be created on demand. This data structure would be a lazy tree, as opposed to a lazy list. We've concentrated on lazy lists in this chapter because they provide a link to another Java 8 feature, streams, which enabled us to discuss the pros and cons of streams compared with lazy lists.

There remains the question of performance. It's easy to assume that doing things lazily is better than doing things eagerly. Surely, it's better to calculate only the values and data structures needed by a program on demand than to create all those values (and perhaps more), as done in traditional execution. Unfortunately, the real world isn't so simple. The overhead of doing things lazily (such as the additional Suppliers between items in your LazyList) outweighs the notional benefit unless you explore, say, less than 10 % of the data structure. Finally, there's a subtle way in which your LazyList values aren't truly lazy. If you traverse a LazyList value such as from(2), perhaps up to the 10th item, it also creates all the nodes twice, creating 20 nodes rather than 10. This result is hardly lazy. The issue is that the Supplier in tail is repeatedly called on each on-demand exploration of the LazyList. You can fix this problem by arranging for the Supplier in tail to be called only on the first on-demand exploration, with the resulting value being cached, in effect solidifying the list at that point. To achieve this goal, add a `private Optional<LazyList<T>> alreadyComputed` field to your definition of LazyList and arrange for the tail method to consult and update it appropriately. The pure functional language Haskell arranges that all its data structures are properly lazy in the latter sense. Read one of the many articles on Haskell if you're interested.

Our guideline is to remember that lazy data structures can be useful weapons in your programming armory. Use these structures when they make an application easier to program; rewrite them in more traditional style if they cause unacceptable inefficiency.

The next section deals with another feature of almost all functional programming languages except Java: pattern matching.

19.4 *Pattern matching*

There's one other important aspect to what's generally regarded as functional programming: (structural) *pattern matching*, which isn't to be confused with pattern matching and regex. Chapter 1 ended by observing that mathematics can write definitions such as

```
f(0) = 1
f(n) = n*f(n-1) otherwise
```

whereas in Java, you have to write an `if-then-else` or a `switch` statement. As data types become more complex, the amount of code (and clutter) needed to process them increases. Using pattern matching can reduce this clutter.

To illustrate, take a tree structure that you'd like to traverse. Consider a simple arithmetic language consisting of numbers and binary operations:

```
class Expr { ... }
class Number extends Expr { int val; ... }
class BinOp extends Expr { String opname; Expr left, right; ... }
```

Suppose that you're asked to write a method to simplify some expressions. 5 + 0 can be simplified to 5, for example. Using our `Expr` class, `new BinOp("+", new Number(5), new Number(0))` could be simplified to `Number(5)`. You might traverse an `Expr` structure as follows:

```
Expr simplifyExpression(Expr expr) {
    if (expr instanceof BinOp
            && ((BinOp)expr).opname.equals("+")
            && ((BinOp)expr).right instanceof Number
            && ... // it's all getting very clumsy
            && ... ) {
        return (Binop)expr.left;
    }
    ...
}
```

You can see that this code rapidly gets ugly!

19.4.1 *Visitor design pattern*

Another way to unwrap the data type in Java is to use the visitor design pattern. In essence, you create a separate class that encapsulates an algorithm to visit a specific data type.

The visitor class works by taking as input a specific instance of the data type; then it can access all its members. Here's an example. First, add the method `accept` to `BinOp`, which takes `SimplifyExprVisitor` as argument and passes itself to it (and add a similar method for `Number`):

```
class BinOp extends Expr{
    ...
    public Expr accept(SimplifyExprVisitor v){
        return v.visit(this);
    }
}
```

Now the `SimplifyExprVisitor` can access a `BinOp` object and unwrap it:

```
public class SimplifyExprVisitor {
    ...
    public Expr visit(BinOp e){
        if("+".equals(e.opname) && e.right instanceof Number && …){
            return e.left;
        }
```

```
        return e;
    }
}
```

19.4.2 *Pattern matching to the rescue*

A simpler solution uses a feature called pattern matching. That feature isn't available in Java, so we're going to use small examples from the Scala programming language to illustrate pattern matching. The examples give you an idea of what could be possible in Java if pattern matching were supported.

   Given data type `Expr` representing arithmetic expressions, in the Scala programming language (which we use because its syntax is closest to Java), you can write the following code to decompose an expression:

```
def simplifyExpression(expr: Expr): Expr = expr match {
    case BinOp("+", e, Number(0)) => e   // Adding zero
    case BinOp("*", e, Number(1)) => e   // Multiplying by one
    case BinOp("/", e, Number(1)) => e   // Dividing by one
    case _ => expr                       // Can't simplify expr
}
```

This use of pattern matching gives you an extremely concise and expressive way to manipulate many treelike data structures. Typically, this technique is useful for building compilers or engines for processing business rules. Note that the Scala syntax

```
Expression match { case Pattern => Expression ... }
```

is similar to the Java syntax

```
switch (Expression) { case Constant : Statement ... }
```

with Scala's wildcard pattern _ making the final `case _` play the role of `default:` in Java. The main visible syntactic difference is that Scala is expression-oriented, whereas Java is more statement-oriented. But for the programmer, the main expressiveness difference is the fact that Java patterns in `case` labels are restricted to a couple of primitive types, enumerations, a few special classes that wrap certain primitive types, and `Strings`. One of the biggest practical advantages of using languages with pattern matching is that you can avoid using big chains of `switch` or `if-then-else` statements interleaved with field-selection operations.

   It's clear that Scala's pattern matching wins on ease of expressiveness over Java, and you can look forward to a future Java allowing more-expressive `switch` statements. (We make a concrete proposal for this feature in chapter 21.)

   In the meantime, we show you how Java 8 lambdas can provide an alternative way of achieving pattern-matching-like code in Java. We describe this technique purely to show you another interesting application of lambdas.

FAKING PATTERN MATCHING IN JAVA

First, consider how rich Scala's pattern-matching `match` expression form is. The case

```
def simplifyExpression(expr: Expr): Expr = expr match {
    case BinOp("+", e, Number(0)) => e
    ...
```

means "Check that `expr` is a `BinOp`, extract its three components (`opname`, `left`, `right`), and then pattern-match these components—the first against the `String +`, the second against the variable `e` (which always matches), and the third against the pattern `Number(0)`." In other words, pattern matching in Scala (and many other functional languages) is multilevel. Your simulation of pattern matching with Java 8's lambdas produces only single-level pattern matching. In the preceding example, your simulation would express cases such as `BinOp(op, l, r)` or `Number(n)` but not `BinOp("+", e, Number(0))`.

First, we make a slightly surprising observation: now that you have lambdas, you could in principle never use `if-then-else` in your code. You could replace code such as `condition ? e1 : e2` with a method call, as follows:

```
myIf(condition, () -> e1, () -> e2);
```

Somewhere, perhaps in a library, you'd have a definition (generic in type `T`):

```
static <T> T myIf(boolean b, Supplier<T> truecase, Supplier<T> falsecase) {
    return b ? truecase.get() : falsecase.get();
}
```

The type `T` plays the role of the result type of the conditional expression. In principle, you can perform similar tricks with other control-flow constructs such as `switch` and `while`.

In normal code, this encoding would make your code more obscure because `if-then-else` captures this idiom perfectly. But we've noted that Java's `switch` and `if-then-else` don't capture the idiom of pattern matching, and it turns out that lambdas can encode (single-level) pattern matching—rather more neatly than the chains of `if-then-else`.

Returning to pattern-matching values of class `Expr` (which has two subclasses, `BinOp` and `Number`), you can define a method `patternMatchExpr` (again generic in `T`, the result type of the pattern match):

```
interface TriFunction<S, T, U, R>{
    R apply(S s, T t, U u);
}
static <T> T patternMatchExpr(
                    Expr e,
                    TriFunction<String, Expr, Expr, T> binopcase,
                    Function<Integer, T> numcase,
                    Supplier<T> defaultcase) {
    return
        (e instanceof BinOp) ?
            binopcase.apply(((BinOp)e).opname, ((BinOp)e).left,
                                               ((BinOp)e).right) :
```

```
    (e instanceof Number) ?
        numcase.apply(((Number)e).val) :
        defaultcase.get();
}
```

The result is that the method call

```
patternMatchExpr(e, (op, l, r) -> {return binopcode;},
                    (n) -> {return numcode;},
                    () -> {return defaultcode;});
```

determines whether e is a BinOp (and if so, runs binopcode, which has access to the fields of the BinOp via identifiers op, l, r) or a Number (and if so, runs numcode, which has access to the value n). The method even makes provision for defaultcode, which would be executed if someone later created a tree node that was neither a BinOp nor a Number.

The following listing shows you how to start using patternMatchExpr by simplifying addition and multiplication expressions.

Listing 19.1 Implementing pattern matching to simplify an expression

```
public static Expr simplify(Expr e) {                           Deals with a
    TriFunction<String, Expr, Expr, Expr> binopcase =           BinOp expression
        (opname, left, right) -> {
            if ("+".equals(opname)) {                    Deals with the
                if (left instanceof Number && ((Number) left).val == 0) {    addition case
                    return right;
                }
                if (right instanceof Number && ((Number) right).val == 0) {
                    return left;
                }
            }                                            Deals with the
            if ("*".equals(opname)) {                    multiplication
                if (left instanceof Number && ((Number) left).val == 1) {    case
                    return right;
                }
                if (right instanceof Number && ((Number) right).val == 1) {
                    return left;
                }
            }
            return new BinOp(opname, left, right);                   Deals with
        };                                                          a Number
    Function<Integer, Expr> numcase = val -> new Number(val);
    Supplier<Expr> defaultcase = () -> new Number(0);
    return patternMatchExpr(e, binopcase, numcase, defaultcase);    Applies
}                                                                   pattern
                                                                    matching
```

A default case if the user provides an Expr that's not recognized

Now you can call the simplify method as follows:

```
Expr e = new BinOp("+", new Number(5), new Number(0));
Expr match = simplify(e);
System.out.println(match);        <——— Prints 5
```

You've seen a lot of information so far: higher-order functions, currying, persistent data structures, lazy lists, and pattern matching. The next section looks at certain subtleties that we've deferred to the end to avoid overcomplicating the text.

19.5 *Miscellany*

In this section, we explore two subtleties of being functional and of having referential transparency: one about efficiency and the other about returning the same result. These issues are interesting, but we place them here because the subtleties concern side effects and aren't conceptually central. We also explore the idea of *combinators*—methods or functions that take two or more functions and return another function. This idea has inspired many of the additions to the Java 8 API and more recently the Java 9 Flow API.

19.5.1 *Caching or memoization*

Suppose that you have a side-effect-free method computeNumberOfNodes(Range) that calculates the number of nodes inside a given range in a network with a treelike topology. Assume that the network never changes (that is, the structure is immutable), but that calling the method computeNumberOfNodes is expensive to calculate because the structure needs to be traversed recursively. You may want to calculate the results over and over. If you have referential transparency, you have a clever way to avoid this additional overhead. One standard solution is *memoization*—adding a cache (such as a HashMap) to the method as a wrapper. First, the wrapper consults the cache to see whether the (argument, result) pair is already in the cache. If so, it can return the stored result immediately. Otherwise, you call computeNumberOfNodes, but before returning from the wrapper, you store the new (argument, result) pair in the cache. Strictly speaking, this solution isn't purely functional because it mutates a data structure shared by multiple callers, but the wrapped version of the code is referentially transparent.

In practice, this code works as follows:

```
final Map<Range,Integer> numberOfNodes = new HashMap<>();
Integer computeNumberOfNodesUsingCache(Range range) {
    Integer result = numberOfNodes.get(range);
    if (result != null){
        return result;
    }
    result = computeNumberOfNodes(range);
    numberOfNodes.put(range, result);
    return result;
}
```

NOTE Java 8 enhances the Map interface (see appendix B) with a computeIf-Absent method for such use cases. You could use computeIfAbsent to write clearer code:

```
Integer computeNumberOfNodesUsingCache(Range range) {
    return numberOfNodes.computeIfAbsent(range,
                                    this::computeNumberOfNodes);
}
```

It's clear that the method `computeNumberOfNodesUsingCache` is referentially transparent (assuming that the method `computeNumberOfNodes` is also referentially transparent). But the fact that `numberOfNodes` has mutable shared state and that `HashMap` isn't synchronized[3] means that this code isn't thread-safe. Even using (lock-protected) `Hashtable` or (concurrent-without-locking) `ConcurrentHashMap` instead of `HashMap` may not produce the expected performance if parallel calls are made to `numberOf-Nodes` from multiple cores. There's a race condition between your finding that `range` isn't in the `map` and inserting the (argument, result) pair back into the `map`, which means that multiple processes might compute the same value to add to the `map`.

Perhaps the best thing to take away from this struggle is the fact that mixing mutable state with concurrency is trickier than you'd imagine. Functional-style programming avoids this practice except for low-level performance hacks such as caching. A second takeaway is that apart from implementing tricks such as caching, if you code in functional style, you never need to care whether another functional-style method that you call is synchronized, because you *know* that it has no shared mutable state.

19.5.2 *What does "Return the same object" mean?*

Consider again the binary tree example from section 19.2.3. In figure 19.4, variable `t` points to an existing `Tree`, and the figure shows the effect of calling `fupdate("Will",` `26, t)` to produce a new `Tree`, which presumably is assigned to variable `t2`. The figure makes clear that `t` and all the data structures reachable from it aren't mutated. Now suppose that you perform a textually identical call in the additional assignment:

```
t3 = fupdate("Will", 26, t);
```

Now `t3` points to three more newly created nodes containing the same data as those in `t2`. The question is whether `fupdate` is referentially transparent. *Referentially transparent* means "equal arguments (the case here) imply equal results." The problem is that `t2` and `t3` are different references, and therefore (`t2 == t3`) is `false`, so it looks as though you'll have to conclude that `fupdate` isn't referentially transparent. But when you're using persistent data structures that aren't to be modified, no logical difference exists between `t2` and `t3`.

We can debate this point at length, but the simplest adage is that functional-style programming generally uses `equals` to compare structured values rather than `==` (reference equality) because data isn't modified, and under this model, `fupdate` *is* referentially transparent.

---

[3] This place is one where bugs breed. It's so easy to use `HashMap` and to forget the fact that the Java manual notes that it's not thread-safe (or not to care because *your* program is currently single-threaded).

19.5.3 *Combinators*

In functional programming, it's common and natural to write a higher-order function (perhaps written as a method) that accepts, say, two functions and produces another function that somehow combines these functions. The term *combinator* generally is used for this idea. Much of the new Java 8 API is inspired by this idea, such as then-Combine in the CompletableFuture class. You can give this method two Completable-Futures and a BiFunction to produce another CompletableFuture.

Although a detailed discussion of combinators in functional programming is beyond the scope of this book, it's worth looking at a couple of special cases to give you the flavor of how operations that take and return functions are a common and natural functional programming construct. The following method encodes the idea of function composition:

```
static <A,B,C> Function<A,C> compose(Function<B,C> g, Function<A,B> f) {
    return x -> g.apply(f.apply(x));
}
```

This method takes functions f and g as arguments and returns a function whose effect is to do f first and then g. Then you can define an operation that captures internal iteration as a combinator. Suppose that you want to take data and apply function f to it repeatedly, *n* times, as in a loop. Your operation (call it repeat) takes a function, f, saying what happens in one iteration and returning a function that says what happens in *n* iterations. A call such as

```
repeat(3, (Integer x) -> 2*x);
```

returns x ->(2*(2*(2*x)) or equivalently x -> 8*x.

You can test this code by writing

```
System.out.println(repeat(3, (Integer x) -> 2*x).apply(10));
```

which prints 80.

You can code the repeat method as follows (noting the special case of a zero-trip loop):

```
static <A> Function<A,A> repeat(int n, Function<A,A> f) {
    return n==0 ? x -> x                          ◄─── Return the
                                                       do-nothing
                : compose(f, repeat(n-1, f));  ◄──┐   identity
}                                                 │   function if
      Otherwise do f, repeated n-1 times, followed by doing it once more.  n is zero.
```

Variants of this idea can model richer notions of iteration, including having a functional model of mutable state passed between iterations. But it's time to move on. This chapter's role was to give you a summary of functional programming as the basis for Java 8. Many excellent books explore functional programming in greater depth.

Summary

- First-class functions are functions that can be passed as arguments, returned as results, and stored in data structures.

- A higher-order function takes one or more functions as input or returns another function. Typical higher-order functions in Java include `comparing`, `andThen`, and `compose`.

- Currying is a technique that lets you modularize functions and reuse code.

- A persistent data structure preserves the previous version of itself when it's modified. As a result, it can prevent unnecessary defensive copying.

- Streams in Java can't be self-defined.

- A lazy list is a more-expressive version of a Java stream. A lazy list lets you produce elements of the list on demand by using a supplier that can create more of the data structure.

- Pattern matching is a functional feature that lets you unwrap data types. You can view data matching as generalizing Java's `switch` statement.

- Referential transparency allows computations to be cached.

- Combinators are functional ideas that combine two or more functions or other data structures.

Blending OOP and FP: Comparing Java and Scala

This chapter covers

- An introduction to Scala
- How Java relates to Scala and vice versa
- How functions in Scala compare to Java
- Classes and traits

Scala is a programming language that mixes object-oriented and functional programming. It's often seen as an alternative language to Java for programmers who want functional features in a statically typed programming language that runs on the JVM while keeping a Java feel. Scala introduces many more features than Java: a more-sophisticated type system, type inference, pattern matching (as presented in chapter 19), constructs that define domain-specific languages simply, and so on. In addition, you can access all Java libraries within Scala code.

You may wonder why we have a chapter about Scala in a Java book. This book has largely centered on adopting functional-style programming in Java. Scala, like Java, supports the concepts of functional-style processing of collections (that is, streamlike operations), first-class functions, and default methods. But Scala pushes these ideas further, providing a larger set of features that support these ideas compared with Java. We believe that you may find it interesting to compare Scala with the approach taken by Java and see Java's limitations. This chapter aims to shed light on this matter to appease your curiosity. We don't necessarily encourage the adoption of Scala over Java. Other interesting new programming languages on the JVM, such as Kotlin, are also worth looking at. The purpose of this chapter is to open your horizons to what's available beyond Java. We believe that it's important for a well-rounded software engineer to be knowledgeable about the wider programming-languages ecosystem.

Also keep in mind that the purpose of this chapter isn't to teach you how to write idiomatic Scala code or to tell you everything about Scala. Scala supports many features (such as pattern matching, for-comprehensions, and implicits) that aren't available in Java, and we won't discuss those features. Rather, we focus on comparing the Java and Scala features to give you an idea of the bigger picture. You'll find that you can write more concise and readable code in Scala compared with Java, for example.

This chapter starts with an introduction to Scala: writing simple programs and working with collections. Next, we discuss functions in Scala: first-class functions, closures, and currying. Finally, we look at classes in Scala and at a feature called traits, which is Scala's take on interfaces and default methods.

20.1   *Introduction to Scala*

This section briefly introduces basic Scala features to give you a feel for simple Scala programs. We start with a slightly modified "Hello world" example written in an imperative style and a functional style. Then we look at some data structures that Scala supports—List, Set, Map, Stream, Tuple, and Option—and compare them with Java. Finally, we present *traits*, Scala's replacement for Java's interfaces, which also support inheritance of methods at object-instantiation time.

20.1.1 *Hello beer*

To change a bit from the classic "Hello world" example, bring in some beer. You want to print the following output on the screen:

```
Hello 2 bottles of beer
Hello 3 bottles of beer
Hello 4 bottles of beer
Hello 5 bottles of beer
Hello 6 bottles of beer
```

IMPERATIVE-STYLE SCALA

Here's how the code to print this output looks in Scala when you use an imperative style:

```
object Beer {
  def main(args: Array[String]){
    var n : Int = 2
    while( n <= 6){
      println(s"Hello ${n} bottles of beer")      ◁——┐ String
      n += 1                                          │ interpolation
    }
  }
}
```

You can find information about how to run this code on the official Scala website (see https://docs.scala-lang.org/getting-started.html). This program looks similar to what you'd write in Java, and its structure is similar to that of Java programs, consisting of one method called `main`, which takes an array of strings as argument. (Type annotations follow the syntax `s : String` instead of `Strings`, as in Java.) The `main` method doesn't return a value, so it's not necessary to declare a return type in Scala as you'd have to do in Java when you use `void`.

> **NOTE** In general, nonrecursive method declarations in Scala don't need an explicit return type, because Scala can infer the type for you.

Before we look at the body of the `main` method, we need to discuss the `object` declaration. After all, in Java you have to declare the method `main` within a class. The declaration `object` introduces a singleton object, declaring a class `Beer` and instantiating it at the same time. Only one instance is created. This example is the first example of a classical design pattern (the singleton design pattern) implemented as a language feature, and it's free to use out of the box. In addition, you can view methods within an `object` declaration as being declared as static, which is why the signature of the `main` method isn't explicitly declared as `static`.

Now look at the body of `main`. This method also looks similar to a Java method, but statements don't need to end with a semicolon (which is optional). The body consists of a `while` loop, which increments a mutable variable, `n`. For each new value of `n`, you print a string on the screen, using the predefined `println` method. The `println` line showcases another feature of Scala: *string interpolation*, which allows you to embed variables and expressions directly in string literals. In the preceding code, you can use the variable n directly in the string literal `s"Hello ${n} bottles of beer"`. Prepending the string with the interpolator `s` provides that magic. Normally in Java, you have to do an explicit concatenation such as `"Hello " + n + " bottles of beer"`.

FUNCTIONAL-STYLE SCALA

But what can Scala offer after all our talk about functional-style programming throughout this book? The preceding code can be written in a more functional-style form in Java as follows:

```
public class Foo {
    public static void main(String[] args) {
        IntStream.rangeClosed(2, 6)
                .forEach(n -> System.out.println("Hello " + n +
                                                " bottles of beer"));
    }
}
```

Here's how that code looks in Scala:

```
object Beer {
  def main(args: Array[String]){
    2 to 6 foreach { n => println(s"Hello ${n} bottles of beer") }
```

```
    }
}
```

The Scala code is similar to the Java code but less verbose. First, you can create a range by using the expression 2 to 6. Here's something cool: 2 is an object of type `Int`. In Scala, *everything* is an object; there's no concept of primitive types, as in Java, which makes Scala a complete object-oriented language. An `Int` object in Scala supports a method named `to`, which takes as an argument another `Int` and returns a range. You could have written `2.to(6)` instead. But methods that take one argument can be written in an infix form. Next, `foreach` (with a lowercase e) is similar to `forEach` in Java (with an uppercase E). This method is available on a range (you use the infix notation again), and it takes a lambda expression as an argument to apply on each element. The lambda-expression syntax is similar to that in Java, but the arrow is `=>` instead of `->`.[1] The preceding code is functional; you're not mutating a variable as you did in the earlier example using a `while` loop.

20.1.2 *Basic data structures: List, Set, Map, Tuple, Stream, Option*

Are you feeling good after having a couple of beers to quench your thirst? Most real programs need to manipulate and store data, so in this section, you manipulate collections in Scala and see how that process compares with Java.

CREATING COLLECTIONS

Creating collections in Scala is simple, thanks to Scala's emphasis on conciseness. To exemplify, here's how to create a `Map`:

```
val authorsToAge = Map("Raoul" -> 23, "Mario" -> 40, "Alan" -> 53)
```

Several things are new in this line of code. First, it's awesome that you can create a `Map` and associate a key with a value directly, using the syntax `->`. There's no need to add elements manually, as in Java:

```
Map<String, Integer> authorsToAge = new HashMap<>();
authorsToAge.put("Raoul", 23);
authorsToAge.put("Mario", 40);
authorsToAge.put("Alan", 53);
```

You learned in chapter 8, however, that Java 9 has a couple of factory methods, inspired by Scala, that can help you tidy this type of code:

```
Map<String, Integer> authorsToAge
    = Map.ofEntries(entry("Raoul", 23),
                    entry("Mario", 40),
                    entry("Alan", 53));
```

---

[1] Note that the Scala terms *anonymous functions* and *closures* (interchangeable) refer to what Java calls lambda expressions.

The second new thing is that you can choose not to annotate the type of the variable authorsToAge. You could have explicitly written val authorsToAge : Map[String, Int], but Scala can infer the type of the variable for you. (Note that the code is still checked statically. All variables have a given type at compile time.) We come back to this feature in chapter 21. Third, you use the val keyword instead of var. What's the difference? The keyword val means that the variable is read-only and can't be reassigned to (like final in Java). The var keyword means that the variable is read-write.

What about other collections? You can create a List (a singly linked list) or a Set (no duplicates) easily, as follows:

```
val authors = List("Raoul", "Mario", "Alan")
val numbers = Set(1, 1, 2, 3, 5, 8)
```

The authors variable has three elements, and the numbers variable has five elements.

IMMUTABLE VS. MUTABLE

One important fact to keep in mind is that the collections you created previously are immutable by default, which means that they can't be changed after they're created. Immutability is useful because you know that accessing the collection at any point in your program always yields a collection with the same elements.

How can you update an immutable collection in Scala? To come back to the terminology used in chapter 19, such collections in Scala are said to be *persistent*. Updating a collection produces a new collection that shares as much as possible with the previous version, which persists without being affected by changes (as we show in figures 19.3 and 19.4). As a consequence of this property, your code has fewer implicit data dependencies: there's less confusion about which location in your code updates a collection (or any other shared data structure) and at what point in time.

The following example demonstrates this idea. Add an element to a Set:

```
val numbers = Set(2, 5, 3);
val newNumbers = numbers + 8
println(newNumbers)
println(numbers)
```

Here, + is a method that adds 8 to the Set, creating a new Set object as a result.

(2, 5, 3, 8)

(2, 5, 3)

In this example, the set of numbers isn't modified. Instead, a new Set is created with an additional element.

Note that Scala doesn't force you to use immutable collections—only makes it easy to adopt immutability in your code. Also, mutable versions are available in the package scala.collection.mutable.

Unmodifiable vs. immutable

Java provides several ways to create unmodifiable collections. In the following code, the variable `newNumbers` is a read-only view of the set `numbers`:

```
Set<Integer> numbers = new HashSet<>();
Set<Integer> newNumbers = Collections.unmodifiableSet(numbers);
```

This code means that you won't be able to add new elements through the `new-Numbers` variable. But an unmodifiable collection is a wrapper over a modifiable collection, so you could still add elements by accessing the `numbers` variable.

By contrast, immutable collections guarantee that nothing can change the collection, regardless of how many variables are pointing to it.

We explained in chapter 19 how you could create a persistent data structure: an immutable data structure that preserves the previous version of itself when modified. Any modifications always produce a new updated structure.

WORKING WITH COLLECTIONS

Now that you've seen how to create collections, you need to know what you can do with them. Collections in Scala support operations similar to those in the Java `Stream` API. You may recognize `filter` and `map` in the following example and as illustrated in figure 20.1:

```
val fileLines = Source.fromFile("data.txt").getLines.toList()
val linesLongUpper
  = fileLines.filter(l => l.length() > 10)
          .map(l => l.toUpperCase())
```

Figure 20.1 Streamlike operations with Scala's `List`

Don't worry about the first line, which transforms a file into a list of strings consisting of the lines in the file (similar to what `Files.readAllLines` provides in Java). The second line creates a pipeline of two operations:

- A `filter` operation that selects only the lines that have a length greater than 10
- A `map` operation that transforms these long lines to uppercase

This code can be also written as follows:

```
val linesLongUpper
  = fileLines filter (_.length() > 10) map(_.toUpperCase())
```

You use the infix notation as well as the underscore (_) character, which is a place-holder that's positionally matched with any arguments. In this case, you can read `_.length()` as `l => l.length()`. In the functions passed to `filter` and `map`, the underscore is bound to the line parameter that is to be processed.

Many more useful operations are available in Scala's collection API. We recommend taking a look at the Scala documentation to get an idea (https://docs.scala-lang.org/ overviews/collections/introduction.html). Note that this API is slightly richer than the Streams API (including support for zipping operations, which let you combine elements of two lists), so you'll definitely gain a few programming idioms by checking it out. These idioms may also make it into the Streams API in future versions of Java.

Finally, remember that in Java, you can ask for a pipeline to be executed in parallel by calling `parallel` on a `Stream`. Scala has a similar trick. You need only use the `par` method:

```
val linesLongUpper
  = fileLines.par filter (_.length() > 10) map(_.toUpperCase())
```

TUPLES

This section looks at another feature that's often painfully verbose in Java: tuples. You may want to use tuples to group people by name and phone number (here, simple pairs) without declaring an ad hoc new class and instantiating an object for it: `("Raoul", "+44 7700 700042")`, `("Alan", "+44 7700 700314")`, and so on.

Unfortunately, Java doesn't provide support for tuples, so you have to create your own data structure. Here's a simple `Pair` class:

```
public class Pair<X, Y> {
    public final X x;
    public final Y y;
    public Pair(X x, Y y){
        this.x = x;
        this.y = y;
    }
}
```

Also, of course you need to instantiate pairs explicitly:

```
Pair<String, String> raoul = new Pair<>("Raoul", "+44 7700 700042");
Pair<String, String> alan = new Pair<>("Alan", "+44 7700 700314");
```

Okay, but how about triplets and arbitrary-size tuples? Defining a new class for every tuple size is tedious and ultimately affects the readability and maintainability of your programs.

Scala provides *tuple literals*, which allow you to create tuples through simple syntactic sugar with the normal mathematical notation, as follows:

```
val raoul = ("Raoul", "+44 7700 700042")
val alan = ("Alan", "+44 7700 700314")
```

Scala supports arbitrary-size[2] tuples, so the following are possible:

```
val book = (2018 "Modern Java in Action", "Manning")
val numbers = (42, 1337, 0, 3, 14)
```

A tuple of type (Int, String, String)

A tuple of type (Int, Int, Int, Int, Int)

You can access the elements of the tuples by their positions by using the accessors _1, _2 (starting at 1), as in this example:

```
println(book._1)        ⟵——   Prints 2018
println(numbers._4)     ⟵——   Prints 3
```

Isn't that example much nicer than what you'd have to write in Java? The good news is that there are discussions about introducing tuple literals in future versions of Java. (See chapter 21 for more discussion of possible new features in Java.)

STREAM

The collections that we've described so far—List, Set, Map, and Tuple—are all evaluated eagerly (that is, immediately). By now, you know that streams in Java are evaluated on demand (that is, lazily). You saw in chapter 5 that because of this property, streams can represent an infinite sequence without overflowing memory.

Scala also provides a corresponding lazily evaluated data structure called Stream. But Streams in Scala provide more features than those in Java. Streams in Scala remember values that were computed so that previous elements can be accessed. In addition, Streams are indexed so that elements can be accessed by an index, like a list. Note that the trade-off for these additional properties is the fact that Streams are less memory-efficient compared with Java's Streams, because being able to refer to previous elements means that the elements need to be remembered (cached).

OPTION

Another data structure that you'll be familiar with is Option—Scala's version of Java's Optional, which we discussed in chapter 11. We argued that you should use Optional when possible to design better APIs, in which by reading the signature of a method, users can tell whether they can expect an optional value. You should use this data structure instead of null whenever possible to prevent null-pointer exceptions.

You saw in chapter 11 that you can use Optional to return the name of a person's insurance if the person's age is greater than some minimum age, as follows:

```
public String getCarInsuranceName(Optional<Person> person, int minAge) {
    return person.filter(p -> p.getAge() >= minAge)
                 .flatMap(Person::getCar)
                 .flatMap(Car::getInsurance)
                 .map(Insurance::getName)
                 .orElse("Unknown");
}
```

---

[2] Tuples have a limit of 22 elements.

In Scala, you can use `Option` in a way similar to `Optional`:

```
def getCarInsuranceName(person: Option[Person], minAge: Int) =
  person.filter(_.age >= minAge)
        .flatMap(_.car)
        .flatMap(_.insurance)
        .map(_.name)
        .getOrElse("Unknown")
```

You can recognize the same structure and method names apart from `getOrElse`, which is the equivalent of `orElse` in Java. You see, throughout this book, you've learned new concepts that you can apply directly to other programming languages! Unfortunately, `null` also exists in Scala for Java compatibility reasons, but its use is highly discouraged.

20.2 Functions

Scala functions can be viewed as being sequences of instructions that are grouped to perform a task. These functions are useful for abstracting behavior and are the cornerstone of functional programming.

In Java, you're familiar with *methods*: functions associated with a class. You've also seen lambda expressions, which can be considered to be anonymous functions. Scala offers a richer set of features to support functions than Java does, and we look at those features in this section. Scala provides the following:

- *Function types*—syntactic sugar that represents the idea of Java function descriptors (that is, notations that represent the signature of the abstract method declared in a functional interface), which we described in chapter 3
- Anonymous functions that don't have the no-writing restriction on nonlocal variables that Java's lambda expressions have
- Support for *currying*, which means breaking a function that takes multiple arguments into a series of functions, each of which takes some of the arguments

20.2.1 First-class functions in Scala

Functions in Scala are *first-class values*, which means that they can be passed around as parameters, returned as a result, and stored in variables, like values such as `Integer` and `String`. As we've shown you in earlier chapters, method references and lambda expressions in Java can also be seen as first-class functions.

Here's an example of how first-class functions work in Scala. Suppose that you have a list of strings representing tweets you've received. You'd like to filter this list with different criteria, such as tweets that mention the word *Java* or tweets of a certain short length. You can represent these two criteria as *predicates* (functions that return a `Boolean`):

```
def isJavaMentioned(tweet: String) : Boolean = tweet.contains("Java")
def isShortTweet(tweet: String) : Boolean = tweet.length() < 20
```

In Scala, you can pass these methods directly to the built-in `filter` as follows (as you can pass them by using method references in Java):

```
val tweets = List(
    "I love the new features in Java",
    "How's it going?",
    "An SQL query walks into a bar, sees two tables and says 'Can I join
     you?'"
)
tweets.filter(isJavaMentioned).foreach(println)
tweets.filter(isShortTweet).foreach(println)
```

Now inspect the signature of the built-in method `filter`:

```
def filter[T](p: (T) => Boolean): List[T]
```

You may wonder what the type of the parameter p means (here, `(T) => Boolean`), because in Java, you'd expect a functional interface. This Scala syntax isn't (yet) available in Java, but it describes a *function type*. Here, the type represents a function that takes an object of type `T` and returns a `Boolean`. In Java, this type is expressed as a `Predicate<T>` or `Function<T, Boolean>`, which has the same signature as the `isJava-Mentioned` and `isShortTweet` methods, so you can pass them as arguments to `filter`. The designers of the Java language decided not to introduce similar syntax for function types to keep the language consistent with previous versions. (Introducing too much new syntax in a new version of the language is viewed as adding too much cognitive overhead.)

20.2.2 *Anonymous functions and closures*

Scala also supports anonymous functions, which have syntax similar to that of lambda expressions. In the following example, you can assign to a variable named `isLong-Tweet` an anonymous function that checks whether a given tweet is long:

```
val isLongTweet : String => Boolean          ⟵──┐  A variable of function
    = (tweet : String) => tweet.length() > 60         type String to Boolean
                                             ⟵──┐  An anonymous function
```

In Java, a lambda expression lets you create an instance of a functional interface. Scala has a similar mechanism. The preceding code is syntactic sugar for declaring an anonymous class of type `scala.Function1` (a function of one parameter), which provides the implementation of the method `apply`:

```
val isLongTweet : String => Boolean
    = new Function1[String, Boolean] {
        def apply(tweet: String): Boolean = tweet.length() > 60
      }
```

Because the variable `isLongTweet` holds an object of type `Function1`, you can call the method `apply`, which can be seen as calling the function:

```
isLongTweet.apply("A very short tweet")          ◁— Returns false
```

In Java, you could do the following:

```
Function<String, Boolean> isLongTweet = (String s) -> s.length() > 60;
boolean long = islongTweet.apply("A very short tweet");
```

To allow you to use lambda expressions, Java provides several built-in functional interfaces such as `Predicate`, `Function`, and `Consumer`. Scala provides traits (you can think of traits as being interfaces for now) to achieve the same thing: `Function0` (a function with 0 parameters and a return result) up to `Function22` (a function with 22 parameters), all of which define the method `apply`.

Another cool trick in Scala allows you to implicitly call the `apply` method by using syntactic sugar that looks more like a function call:

```
isLongTweet("A very short tweet")          ◁— Returns false
```

The compiler automatically converts a call `f(a)` to `f.apply(a)` and, more generally, a call `f(a1, ..., an)` to `f.apply(a1, ..., an)`, if `f` is an object that supports the `apply` method. (Note that `apply` can have any number of arguments.)

CLOSURES

In chapter 3, we commented on whether lambda expressions in Java constitute closures. A *closure* is an instance of a function that can reference nonlocal variables of that function with no restrictions. But lambda expressions in Java have a restriction: they can't modify the content of local variables of a method in which the lambda is defined. Those variables have to be implicitly `final`. It helps to think that lambdas close over values, rather than variables.

By contrast, anonymous functions in Scala can capture variables themselves, not the *values* to which the variables currently refer. The following is possible in Scala:

```
def main(args: Array[String]) {
    var count = 0
    val inc = () => count+=1       ◁—┐ A closure capturing and
    inc()                             incrementing count
    println(count)          ◁— Prints 1
    inc()
    println(count)          ◁— Prints 2
}
```

But in Java, the following results in a compiler error because `count` is implicitly forced to be `final`:

```
public static void main(String[] args) {
    int count = 0;
    Runnable inc = () -> count+=1;   ◁—┐ Error: Count must be
                                        final or effectively final.
```

```
    inc.run();
    System.out.println(count);
    inc.run();
}
```

We argued in chapters 7, 18, and 19 that you should avoid mutation whenever possible to make your programs easier to maintain and parallelizable, so use this feature only when strictly necessary.

20.2.3 *Currying*

In chapter 19, we described a technique called *currying*, in which a function f of two arguments (x and y, say) is seen instead as a function g of one argument, which returns a function also of one argument. This definition can be generalized to functions with multiple arguments, producing multiple functions of one argument. In other words, you can break down a function that takes multiple arguments into a series of functions, each of which takes a subset of the arguments. Scala provides a construct that makes it easy to curry an existing function.

To understand what Scala brings to the table, first revisit an example in Java. You can define a simple method to multiply two integers:

```
static int multiply(int x, int y) {
  return x * y;
}
int r = multiply(2, 10);
```

But this definition requires all the arguments to be passed to it. You can break down the multiply method manually by making it return another function:

```
static Function<Integer, Integer> multiplyCurry(int x) {
    return (Integer y) -> x * y;
}
```

The function returned by multiplyCurry captures the value of x and multiplies it by its argument y, returning an Integer. As a result, you can use multiplyCurry as follows in a map to multiply each element by 2:

```
Stream.of(1, 3, 5, 7)
    .map(multiplyCurry(2))
    .forEach(System.out::println);
```

This code produces the result 2, 6, 10, 14. This code works because map expects a Function as argument and multiplyCurry returns a Function.

It's a bit tedious in Java to split up a function manually to create a curried form, especially if the function has multiple arguments. Scala has a special syntax that performs this automatically. You can define the normal multiply method as follows:

```
def multiply(x : Int, y: Int) = x * y
val r = multiply(2, 10)
```

And here is the curried form:

```
def multiplyCurry(x :Int)(y : Int) = x * y
val r = multiplyCurry(2)(10)
```

Defining a curried function

Invoking a curried function

When you use the `(x: Int)(y: Int)` syntax, the `multiplyCurry` method takes *two* argument lists of one `Int` parameter. By contrast, `multiply` takes *one list* of two `Int` parameters. What happens when you call `multiplyCurry`? The first invocation of `multiplyCurry` with a single `Int` (the parameter x), `multiplyCurry(2)`, returns another function that takes a parameter y and multiplies it by the captured value of x (here, the value 2). We say that this function is *partially applied* as explained in chapter 19, because not all arguments are provided. The second invocation multiplies x and y. You can store the first invocation to `multiplyCurry` inside a variable and reuse it, as follows:

```
val multiplyByTwo : Int => Int = multiplyCurry(2)
val r = multiplyByTwo(10)
```

20

By comparison with Java, in Scala you don't need to provide the curried form of a function manually, as in the preceding example. Scala provides a convenient function-definition syntax to indicate that a function has multiple curried argument lists.

20.3 Classes and traits

In this section, we look at how classes and interfaces in Java compare with those in Scala. These two constructs are paramount to design applications. You'll see that Scala's classes and interfaces can provide more flexibility than those in Java.

20.3.1 Less verbosity with Scala classes

Because Scala is a full object-oriented language, you can create classes and instantiate them to produce objects. In its most basic form, the syntax to declare and instantiate classes is similar to that of Java. Here's how to declare a `Hello` class:

```
class Hello {
  def sayThankYou(){
    println("Thanks for reading our book")
  }
}
val h = new Hello()
h.sayThankYou()
```

GETTERS AND SETTERS

Scala becomes more interesting when you have a class with fields. Have you ever come across a Java class that purely defines a list of fields and had to declare a long list of getters, setters, and an appropriate constructor? What a pain! In addition, you often see tests for the implementation of each method. A large amount of code typically is devoted to such classes in Enterprise Java applications. Consider this simple `Student` class:

```java
public class Student {
    private String name;
    private int id;
    public Student(String name) {
        this.name = name;
    }
    public String getName() {
        return name;
    }
    public void setName(String name) {
        this.name = name;
    }
    public int getId() {
        return id;
    }
    public void setId(int id) {
        this.id = id;
    }
}
```

You have to manually define the constructor that initializes all fields, two getters, and two setters. A simple class now has more than 20 lines of code. Several IDEs (integrated development environments) and tools can help you generate this code, but your code base still has to deal with a large amount of additional code that's not too useful compared with real business logic.

In Scala, constructors, getters, and setters can be generated implicitly, which results in code with less verbosity:

```scala
class Student(var name: String, var id: Int)
val s = new Student("Raoul", 1)
println(s.name)
s.id = 1337
println(s.id)
```

Initialize a Student object.

Get the name and print Raoul.

Set the id.

Print 1337.

In Java, you could get similar behavior by defining public fields, but you'd still have to define the constructor explicitly. Scala classes save you boilerplate code.

20.3.2 *Scala traits vs. Java interfaces*

Scala has another useful feature for abstraction, called traits, which are Scala's replacement for Java's interfaces. A trait can define both abstract methods and methods with a default implementation. Traits can also be multiply inherited like interfaces in Java, so you can see them as being similar to Java interfaces that support default methods. Traits can also contain fields such as abstract classes, which Java interfaces don't support. Are traits like abstract classes? No, because unlike abstract classes, traits can be multiply inherited. Java has always had multiple inheritance of types because a class can implement multiple interfaces. Java 8, through default methods, introduced multiple inheritance of behaviors but still doesn't allow multiple inheritance of state—something permitted by Scala traits.

To see what a trait looks like in Scala, define a trait called `Sized` that contains one mutable field called `size` and one method called `isEmpty` with a default implementation:

```
trait Sized {
  var size : Int = 0          ⟵───┐   A field called size
  def isEmpty() = size == 0        ⟵───   A method called isEmpty with
}                                           a default implementation
```

You can compose this code at declaration time with a class, such as an `Empty` class that always has size 0:

```
                                              A class inheriting from
                                              the trait Sized
class Empty extends Sized       ⟵──┘
println(new Empty().isEmpty())  ⟵────── Prints true
```

Interestingly, compared with Java interfaces, traits can be composed at object instantiation time (but this operation is still a compile-time operation). You can create a `Box` class and decide that one specific instance should support the operations defined by the trait `Sized`, as follows:

```
                                          Composing the trait at
                                          object instantiation time
class Box
val b1 = new Box() with Sized   ⟵──┘
println(b1.isEmpty())           ⟵────── Prints true
val b2 = new Box()
b2.isEmpty()              ⟵──┐  Compile error: The Box class declaration
                              doesn't inherit from Sized.
```

What happens if multiple traits are inherited, declaring methods with the same signatures or fields with the same names? Scala provides restriction rules similar to those that apply to default methods (chapter 13).

Summary

- Java and Scala combine object-oriented and functional-programming features into one programming language; both run on the JVM and to a large extent can interoperate.
- Scala supports collection abstractions similar to those in Java—`List`, `Set`, `Map`, `Stream`, `Option`—but also supports tuples.
- Scala provides richer features that support more functions than Java does. These features include function types, closures that have no restrictions on accessing local variables, and built-in currying forms.
- Classes in Scala can provide implicit constructors, getters, and setters.
- Scala supports traits, which are interfaces that can include fields and default methods.

Conclusions and
where next for Java

This chapter covers

- The new Java 8 features and their evolutionary effect on programming style
- The new Java 9 module system
- The new six-monthly Java incremental-release life cycle
- The first incremental release forming Java 10
- A few ideas that you'll likely see implemented in some future version of Java

We've covered a lot of material in this book, and we hope that you feel that you're ready to start using the new Java 8 and 9 features in your own code, perhaps building on our examples and quizzes. In this chapter, we review the journey of learning about Java 8 and the gentle push toward functional-style programming, as well as the advantages of the new modularization capability and other minor improvements introduced with Java 9. You also learn about what is included in Java 10. In addition, we speculate on what future enhancements and great new features may be in Java's pipeline beyond Java 9, 10, 11, and 12.

21.1 Review of Java 8 features

A good way to help you understand Java 8 as a practical, useful language is to revisit the features in turn. Instead of simply listing them, we'd like to present them as being interlinked to help you understand them not only as a set of features, but also as a high-level overview of the coherent language design that is Java 8. Our other aim in this review chapter is to emphasize how most of the new features in Java 8 are facilitating functional-style programming in Java. Remember, supporting function programming wasn't a capricious design choice but a conscious design strategy centered on two trends, which we regard as climate change in the model from chapter 1:

- The increasing need to exploit the power of multicore processors now that, for silicon technology reasons, the additional transistors annually provided by Moore's law no longer translate into higher clock speeds of individual CPU cores. Put simply, making your code run faster requires parallel code.
- The increasing tendency to concisely manipulate collections of data with a declarative style for processing data, such as taking some data source, extracting all data that matches a given criterion, and applying some operation to the result (summarizing it or making a collection of the result for further processing later). This style is associated with the use of immutable objects and collections, which are then processed to produce further immutable values.

Neither motivation is effectively supported by the traditional, object-oriented, imperative approach, which centers on mutating fields and applying iterators. Mutating data on one core and reading it from another is surprisingly expensive, not to mention that it introduces the need for error-prone locking. Similarly, when you're focused on iterating over and mutating existing objects, the stream-like programming idiom can feel alien. But these two trends are supported by ideas from functional programming, which explains why the Java 8 center of gravity has moved a bit from what you've come to expect from Java.

This chapter reviews, in a big-picture unifying view, what you've learned from this book and shows you how everything fits together in the new climate.

21.1.1 Behavior parameterization (lambdas and method references)

To write a reusable method such as `filter`, you need to specify as its argument a description of the filtering criterion. Although Java experts could achieve this task in earlier versions of Java by wrapping the filtering criterion as a method inside a class and passing an instance of that class, this solution was unsuitable for general use because it was too cumbersome to write and maintain.

As you discovered in chapters 2 and 3, Java 8 provides a way, borrowed from functional programming, to pass a piece of code to a method. Java conveniently provides two variants:

- Passing a lambda (a one-off piece of code) such as

```
apple -> apple.getWeight() > 150
```

- Passing a *method reference* to an existing method, such as `Apple::isHeavy`

These values have types such as `Function<T, R>`, `Predicate<T>`, and `BiFunction<T, U, R>`, and the recipient can execute them by using the methods `apply`, `test`, and so on. These types are called functional interfaces and have a single abstract method, as you learned in chapter 3. Of themselves, lambdas can seem to be rather a niche concept, but the way that Java 8 uses them in much of the new Streams API propels them to the center of Java.

21.1.2 Streams

The collection classes in Java, along with iterators and the for-each construct, have served programmers honorably for a long time. It would have been easy for the Java 8 designers to add methods such as `filter` and `map` to collections, exploiting lambdas to express database-like queries. Instead, the designers they added a new Streams API, which is the subject of chapters 4–7, and it's worth pausing to consider why.

What's wrong with `Collections` that requires them to be replaced or augmented by a similar notion of `Streams`? We'll summarize this way: if you have a large collection and apply three operations to it (perhaps mapping the objects in the collection to sum two of their fields, filtering the sums that satisfy some criterion, and sorting the result), you make three separate traversals of the collection. Instead, the Streams API lazily forms these operations into a pipeline and does a single stream traversal performing all the operations together. This process is much more efficient for large datasets, and for reasons such as memory caches, the larger the dataset, the more important it is to minimize the number of traversals.

The other, no less important, reason concerns processing elements in parallel, which is vital to the efficient exploitation of multicore CPUs. Streams, and in particular the `parallel` method, allow a stream to be marked as suitable for parallel processing. Recall that parallelism and mutable state fit badly together, so core functional concepts (side-effect-free operations and methods parameterized with lambdas and method references that permit internal iteration instead of external iteration, as discussed in chapter 4) are central to exploiting streams in parallel by using `map`, `filter`, and the like.

In the following section, we look at how these ideas, which we introduced in terms of streams, have a direct analog in the design of `CompletableFuture`.

21.1.3 CompletableFuture

Java has provided the `Future` interface since Java 5. `Future`s are useful for exploiting multicore because they allow a task to be spawned onto another thread or core and allow the spawning task to continue executing along with the spawned task. When the spawning task needs the result, it can use the get method to wait for the Future to complete (produce its value).

Chapter 16 explains the Java 8 CompletableFuture implementation of Future, which again exploits lambdas. A useful, if slightly imprecise, motto is "Completable-Future is to Future as Stream is to Collection." To compare:

- Stream lets you pipeline operations and provides behavior parameterization with map, filter, and the like, eliminating the boilerplate code that you typically have to write when you use iterators.
- CompletableFuture provides operations such as thenCompose, thenCombine, and allOf, which provide functional-programming-style concise encodings of common design patterns involving Futures and let you avoid similar imperative-style boilerplate code.

This style of operations, albeit in a simpler scenario, also applies to the Java 8 operations on Optional, which we revisit in the next section.

21.1.4 *Optional*

The Java 8 library provides the class Optional<T>, which allows your code to specify that a value is a proper value of type T or a missing value returned by the static method Optional.empty. This feature is great for program comprehension and documentation. It provides a data type with an explicit missing value instead of the previous error-prone use of the null pointer to indicate missing values, which programmers could never be sure was a planned missing value or an accidental null resulting from an earlier erroneous computation.

As discussed in chapter 11, if Optional<T> is used consistently, programs should never produce NullPointerExceptions. Again, you could see this situation as a one-off, unrelated to the rest of Java 8, and ask, "How does changing from one form of missing value to another help me write programs?" Closer inspection shows that the Optional<T> class provides map, filter, and ifPresent. These methods have behavior similar to that of corresponding methods in the Streams class and can be used to chain computations, again in functional style, with the tests for missing value done by the library instead of user code. The choice of internal versus external testing in Optional<T> is directly analogous to how the Streams library does internal versus external iteration in user code. Java 9 added various new methods to the Optional API, including stream(), or(), and ifPresentOrElse().

21.1.5 *Flow API*

Java 9 standardized reactive streams and the reactive-pull-based backpressure protocol, a mechanism designed to prevent a slow consumer from being overwhelmed by one or more faster producers. The Flow API includes four core interfaces that library implementations can support to provide wider compatibility: Publisher, Subscriber, Subscription, and Processor.

Our final topic in this section concerns not functional-style programming, but Java 8 support for upward-compatible library extensions driven by software-engineering desires.

21.1.6 *Default methods*

Java 8 has other additions, none of which particularly affects the expressiveness of any program. But one thing that's helpful to library designers allows default methods to be added to an interface. Before Java 8, interfaces defined method signatures; now they can also provide default implementations for methods that the interface designer suspects not all clients will want to provide explicitly.

This tool is a great new tool for library designers because it gives them the ability to augment an interface with a new operation without having to require all clients (classes implementing this interface) to add code to define this method. Therefore, default methods are also relevant to users of libraries because they shield the users from future interface changes (see chapter 13).

21.2 *The Java 9 module system*

Java 8 added a lot, both in terms of new features (lambdas and default methods on interfaces, for example) and new useful classes in the native API, such as `Stream` and `CompletableFuture`. Java 9 didn't introduce any new language features but mostly polished the work started in Java 8, completing the classes introduced there with some useful methods such as `takeWhile` and `dropWhile` on a `Stream` and `completeOn-Timeout` on a `CompletableFuture`. In fact, the main focus of Java 9 was the introduction of the new module system. This new system doesn't affect the language except for the new `module-info.java` file, but nevertheless improves the way in which you design and write applications from an architectural point of view, clearly marking the boundaries of subparts and defining how they interact.

Java 9, unfortunately, harmed the backward compatibility of Java more than any other release (try compiling a large Java 8 code base with Java 9). But this cost is worth paying for the benefits of proper modularization. One reason is to ensure better and stronger encapsulation across packages. In fact, Java visibility modifiers are designed to define encapsulation among methods and classes, but across packages, only one visibility is possible: `public`. This lack makes it hard to modularize a system properly, in particular to specify which parts of a module are designed for public use and which parts are implementation details that should be hidden from other modules and applications.

The second reason, which is an immediate consequence of the weak encapsulation across packages, is that without a proper module system, it's impossible to avoid exposing functionalities that are relevant for security of all the code running in the same environment. Malicious code may access critical parts of your module, thus bypassing all security measures encoded in them.

Finally, the new Java module system enables the Java runtime to be split into smaller parts, so you can use only the parts that are necessary for your application. It would be surprising if CORBA was a requirement for your new Java project, for example, but it's likely to be included in all your Java applications. Although this act may be of limited relevance for traditional-size computing devices, it's important for embedded appliances and for the increasingly frequent situation in which your Java applications run in a containerized environment. In other words, the Java module system is an enabler that allows the use of the Java runtime in Internet of Things (IoT) applications and in the cloud.

As discussed in chapter 14, the Java module system solves these problems by introducing a language-level mechanism to modularize your large systems and the Java runtime itself. The advantages of the Java module system include the following:

- *Reliable configuration*—Explicitly declaring module requirements allows early detection of errors at build time rather than at runtime in the case of missing, conflicting, or circular dependencies.
- *Strong encapsulation*—The Java Module System enables modules to export only specific packages and then separate the public and accessible boundaries of each module with internal implementation.
- *Improved security*—Not allowing users to invoke specific parts of your module makes it much harder for an attacker to evade the security controls implemented in them.
- *Better performance*—Many optimization techniques can be more effective when a class can refer to few components rather than to any other classes loaded by the runtime.
- *Scalability*—The Java module system allows the Java SE platform to be decomposed into smaller parts containing only the features required by the running application.

In general, modularization is a hard topic, and it's unlikely to be a driver for quick adoption of Java 9 as lambdas were for Java 8. We believe, however, that in the long run, the effort you invest in modularizing your application will be repaid in terms of easier maintainability.

So far, we've summarized the concepts of Java 8 and 9 covered in this book. In the next section, we turn to the thornier subject of future enhancements and great features that may be in Java's pipeline beyond Java 9.

21.3 *Java 10 local variable type inference*

Originally in Java, whenever you introduced a variable or method, you gave its type at the same time. The example

```
double convertUSDToGBP(double money) { ExchangeRate e = ...; }
```

contains three types, which give the result the type of convertUSDToGBP, the type of its argument money, and the type of its local variable e. Over time, this requirement has been relaxed in two ways. First, you may omit type parameters of generics in an expression when the context determines them. This example

```
Map<String, List<String>> myMap = new HashMap<String, List<String>>();
```

can be abbreviated to the following since Java 7:

```
Map<String, List<String>> myMap = new HashMap<>();
```

Second, to use the same idea of propagating the type determined by context into an expression, a lambda expression such as

```
Function<Integer, Boolean> p = (Integer x) -> booleanExpression;
```

can be shortened to

```
Function<Integer, Boolean> p = x -> booleanExpression;
```

by omitting types. In both cases, the compiler infers the omitted types.

Type inference has a few advantages when a type consists of a single identifier, the main one being reduced editing work when replacing one type with another. But as types grow in size, generics parameterized by further generic types, type inference can aid readability.[1] The Scala and C# languages permit a type in a local-variable-initialized declaration to be replaced by the (restricted) keyword var; the compiler fills in the appropriate type from the right side. The declaration of myMap shown earlier in Java syntax could be rendered like this:

```
var myMap = new HashMap<String, List<String>>();
```

This idea is called *local variable type inference* and is included in Java 10.

There's some small cause for concern, however. Given a class Car that subclasses a class Vehicle, does the declaration

```
var x = new Car();
```

implicitly declare x to have type Car or Vehicle (or even Object)? In this case, a simple explanation that the missing type is the type of the initializer (here, Car) is perfectly clear. Java 10 formalizes this fact, also stating that var can't be used when there's no initializer.

---

[1] It's important that type inference be done sensibly, of course. Type inference works best when you have only one way, or one easily documentable way, to re-create the type that the user omitted. Problems occur if the system infers a different type from the one that the user was thinking of. So a good design of type inference produces a fault when two incomparable types could be inferred; heuristics can give the appearance of picking the wrong one seemingly at random.

21.4 What's ahead for Java?

Some of the points we cover in this section are discussed in more detail on the JDK Enhancement Proposal website at http://openjdk.java.net/jeps/0. Here, we take care to explain why seemingly sensible ideas have subtle difficulties or interactions with existing features that inhibit their direct incorporation into Java.

21.4.1 Declaration-site variance

Java supports wildcards as flexible mechanisms that allow subtyping for generics (generally referred to as *use-site variance*). This support makes the following assignment valid:

```
List<? extends Number> numbers = new ArrayList<Integer>();
```

But the following assignment, omitting the "? extends", produces a compile-time error:

```
List<Number> numbers = new ArrayList<Integer>();      ◁─┤ Incompatible
                                                          types
```

Many programming languages, such as C# and Scala, support a different variance mechanism called *declaration-site variance*. These languages allow programmers to specify variance when defining a generic class. This feature is useful for classes that are inherently variant. `Iterator`, for example, is inherently covariant, and `Comparator` is inherently contravariant, and you shouldn't need to think in terms of `? extends` or `? super` when you use them. Adding declaration-site variance to Java would be useful, because these specifications appear instead at the declaration of classes. As a result, this addition would reduce some cognitive overhead for programmers. Note that at the writing (2018), a JDK enhancement proposal would allow default declaration-site variance in upcoming versions of Java (http://openjdk.java.net/jeps/300).

21.4.2 Pattern matching

As we discussed in chapter 19, functional-style languages typically provide some form of pattern matching—an enhanced form of `switch`—in which you can ask, "Is this value an instance of a given class?" and (optionally) recursively ask whether its fields have certain values. In Java a simple case test looks like this:

```
if (op instanceof BinOp){
    Expr e = ((BinOp) op).getLeft();
}
```

Note that you have to repeat the type `BinOp` within the cast expression, even though it's clear that the object referenced by `op` is of that type.

You may have a complicated hierarchy of expressions to process, of course, and the approach of chaining multiple `if` conditions will make your code more verbose. It's worth reminding you that traditional object-oriented design discourages the use of `switch` and encourages patterns such as the visitor pattern, in which data-type-dependent control flow is done by method dispatch instead of by `switch`. At the other end of the programming language spectrum, in functional-style programming, pattern matching over values of data types is often the most convenient way to design a program.

Adding Scala-style pattern matching in full generality to Java seems to be a big job, but following the recent generalization to switch to allow Strings, you can imagine a more modest syntax extension that allows switch to operate on objects by using the instanceof syntax. In fact, a JDK enhanced proposal explores pattern matching as a language feature for Java (http://openjdk.java.net/jeps/305). The following example revisits our example from chapter 19 and assumes a class Expr, which is subclassed into BinOp and Number:

```
switch (someExpr) {
    case (op instanceof BinOp):
        doSomething(op.getOpName(), op.getLeft(), op.getRight());
    case (n instanceof Number):
        dealWithLeafNode(n.getValue());
    default:
        defaultAction(someExpr);
}
```

Notice a couple of things. First, this code steals from pattern matching the idea that in case (op instanceof BinOp):, op is a new local variable (of type BinOp), which becomes bound to the same value as someExpr. Similarly, in the Number case, n becomes a variable of type Number. In the default case, no variable is bound. This proposal eliminates much boilerplate code compared with using chains of if-then-else and casting to subtype. A traditional object-oriented designer probably would argue that such data-type dispatch code would better be expressed with visitor-style methods overridden in subtypes, but to functional-programming eyes, this solution results in related code being scattered over several class definitions. This classical design dichotomy is discussed in the literature as the expression problem.[2]

21.4.3 *Richer forms of generics*

This section discusses two limitations of Java generics and looks at a possible evolution to mitigate them.

REIFIED GENERICS

When generics were introduced in Java 5, they had to be backward-compatible with the existing JVM. To this end, the runtime representations of ArrayList<String> and ArrayList<Integer> are identical. This model is called the *erasure model of generic polymorphism.* Certain small runtime costs are associated with this choice, but the most significant effect for programmers is that parameters of generic types can be only objects and not primitive types. Suppose that Java allowed, say, ArrayList<int>. Then you could allocate an ArrayList object on the heap containing a primitive value such as int 42, but the

---

[2] For a more complete explanation, see http://en.wikipedia.org/wiki/Expression_problem.

ArrayList container wouldn't contain any indicator of whether it contained an Object value such as a String or a primitive int value such as 42.

At some level, this situation seems to be harmless. If you get a primitive 42 from an ArrayList<int> and a String object "abc" from an ArrayList<String>, why should you worry that the ArrayList containers are indistinguishable? Unfortunately, the answer is garbage collection, because the absence of runtime type information about the contents of the ArrayList would leave the JVM unable to determine whether element 13 of your ArrayList was a String reference (to be followed and marked as in use by garbage collection) or an int primitive value (most definitely not to be followed).

In the C# language, the runtime representations of ArrayList<String>, Array-List<Integer>, and ArrayList<int> are in principle different. But even if these representations were the same, sufficient type information is kept at runtime to allow, for example, garbage collection to determine whether a field is a reference or a primitive. This model is called the *reified model of generic polymorphism* or, more simply, *reified generics.* The word *reification* means "making explicit something that otherwise would be implicit."

Reified generics are clearly desirable because they enable a more full unification of primitive types and their corresponding object types—something that you'll see as problematic in the following sections. The main difficulty for Java is backward compatibility, both in the JVM and in existing programs that use reflection and expect generics to be erased.

ADDITIONAL SYNTACTIC FLEXIBILITY IN GENERICS FOR FUNCTION TYPES

Generics proved to be a wonderful feature when they were added to Java 5. They're also fine for expressing the type of many Java 8 lambdas and method references. You can express a one-argument function this way:

```
Function<Integer, Integer> square = x -> x * x;
```

If you have a two-argument function, you use the type BiFunction<T, U, R>, where T is the type of the first parameter, U the second, and R the result. But there's no Tri-Function unless you declare it yourself.

Similarly, you can't use Function<T, R> for references to methods that take zero arguments and return result type R; you have to use Supplier<R> instead.

In essence, Java 8 lambdas have enriched what you can write, but the type system hasn't kept up with the flexibility of the code. In many functional languages, you can write, for example, the type (Integer, Double) => String, to represent what Java 8 calls BiFunction<Integer, Double, String>, along with Integer => String to represent Function<Integer, String>, and even () => String to represent Supplier<String>. You can understand => as an infix version of Function, BiFunction, Supplier, and the like. A simple extension to Java syntax for types to allow infix => would result in more readable types analogous to what Scala provides, as discussed in chapter 20.

PRIMITIVE SPECIALIZATIONS AND GENERICS

In Java, all primitive types (int, for example) have a corresponding object type (here, java.lang.Integer). Often, programmers refer to these types as unboxed and boxed. Although this distinction has the laudable aim of increasing runtime efficiency, the types can become confusing. Why, for example, do you write Predicate<Apple> instead of Function<Apple, Boolean> in Java 8? An object of type Predicate<Apple>, when called by the test method, returns a primitive boolean.

By contrast, like all Java generics, a Function can be parameterized only by object types. In the case of Function<Apple, Boolean>, this is the object type Boolean, not the primitive type boolean. Predicate<Apple> is more efficient because it avoids boxing the boolean to make a Boolean. This issue has led to the creation of multiple similar interfaces such as LongToIntFunction and BooleanSupplier, which add further conceptual overload.

Another example concerns the differences between void, which can qualify only method return types and has no values, and the object type Void, which has null as its only value (a question that regularly appears in forums). The special cases of Function such as Supplier<T>, which could be written () => T in the new notation proposed in the previous section, further attest to the ramifications caused by the distinction between primitive and object types. We discussed earlier how reified generics could address many of these issues.

21.4.4 *Deeper support for immutability*

Some expert readers may have been a little upset when we said that Java 8 has three forms of values:

- Primitive values
- (References to) objects
- (References to) functions

At one level, we're going to stick to our guns and say, "But these are the values that a method may now take as arguments and return as results." But we also want to concede that this explanation is a little problematic. To what extent do you return a (mathematical) value when you return a reference to a mutable array? A String or an immutable array clearly is a value, but the case is far less clear-cut for a mutable object or array. Your method may return an array with its elements in ascending order, but some other code may change one of its elements later.

If you're interested in functional-style programming in Java, you need linguistic support for saying "immutable value." As noted in chapter 18, the keyword final doesn't achieve this purpose; it only stops the field that it qualifies from being updated. Consider this example:

```
final int[] arr = {1, 2, 3};
final List<T> list = new ArrayList<>();
```

The first line forbids another assignment `arr = ...` but doesn't forbid `arr[1] = 2`; the second line forbids assignments to `list` but doesn't forbid other methods from changing the number of elements in `list`. The keyword `final` works well for primitive values, but for references to objects, it often produces a false sense of security.

What we're leading up to is this: given that functional-style programming puts strong emphasis on not mutating existing structure, a strong argument exists for a keyword such as `transitively_final`, which can qualify fields of reference type and ensure that no modification can take place in the field or any object directly or indirectly accessible via that field.

Such types represent one intuition about values: values are immutable, and only variables (which contain values) may be mutated to contain a different immutable value. As we remarked at the beginning of this section, Java authors (including us) sometimes inconsistently talk about the possibility of a Java value's being a mutable array. In the next section, we return to proper intuition and discuss the idea of value types, which can contain only immutable values even if variables of value types can still be updated unless they're qualified with `final`.

21.4.5 *Value types*

In this section, we discuss the difference between primitive types and object types, following up on the discussion of the desire for value types, which help you write programs functionally, as object types are necessary for object-oriented programming. Many of the issues we discuss are related, so there's no easy way to explain one problem in isolation. Instead, we identify the problem by its various facets.

Can't the compiler treat Integer and int identically?

Given all the implicit boxing and unboxing that Java has slowly acquired since Java 1.1, you might ask whether it's time for Java to treat, for example, `Integer` and `int` identically and to rely on the Java compiler to optimize into the best form for the JVM.

This idea is wonderful in principle, but consider the problems surrounding adding the type `Complex` to Java to see why boxing is problematic. The type `Complex`, which models so-called complex numbers with real and imaginary parts, is naturally introduced as follows:

```
class Complex {
    public final double re;
    public final double im;
    public Complex(double re, double im) {
        this.re = re;
        this.im = im;
    }
    public static Complex add(Complex a, Complex b) {
        return new Complex(a.re+b.re, a.im+b.im);
    }
}
```

But values of type `Complex` are reference types, and every operation on `Complex` needs to do an object allocation, dwarfing the cost of the two additions in `add`. Programmers need a primitive-type analog of `Complex`, perhaps called `complex`.

The issue is that programmers want an unboxed object, for which neither Java nor the JVM offers any real support. You can return to the lament "Oh, but surely the compiler can optimize this." Sadly, this process is much harder than it appears; although a compiler optimization based on so-called escape analysis can sometimes determine that unboxing is okay, its applicability is limited by Java's assumptions of `Objects`, which have been present since Java 1.1. Consider the following puzzler:

```
double d1 = 3.14;
double d2 = d1;
Double o1 = d1;
Double o2 = d2;
Double ox = o1;
System.out.println(d1 == d2 ? "yes" : "no");
System.out.println(o1 == o2 ? "yes" : "no");
System.out.println(o1 == ox ? "yes" : "no");
```

The result is "yes", "no", "yes." An expert Java programmer probably would say, "What silly code. Everyone knows you should use `equals` on the last two lines instead of `==`." But we'll persist. Even though all these primitives and objects contain the immutable value 3.14 and should be indistinguishable, the definitions of o1 and o2 create new objects, and the `==` operator (identity comparison) can tell them apart. Note that on primitives, the identity comparison does bitwise comparison, but on objects, it does reference equality. Often, you accidentally create a new distinct `Double` object, which the compiler needs to respect because the semantics of `Object`, from which `Double` inherits, require this. You've seen this discussion before, both in the discussion of value types in this chapter and in chapter 19, where we discussed referential transparency of methods that functionally update persistent data structures.

VALUE TYPES: NOT EVERYTHING IS A PRIMITIVE OR AN OBJECT

We suggest that the resolution of this problem is to rework the Java assumptions that (1) everything that isn't a primitive is an object and hence inherits `Object` and (2) all references are references to objects.

The development starts this way. Values take two forms:

- `Object` types that have mutable fields unless forbidden with `final` and that also have identity, which may be tested with `==`.
- Value types, which are immutable and don't have reference identity. Primitive types are a subset of this wider notion.

You could allow user-defined value types (perhaps starting with a lowercase letter to emphasize their similarity to primitive types such as `int` and `boolean`). On value types, `==` would, by default, perform an element-by-element comparison in the same way that hardware comparison on `int` performs a bit-by-bit comparison. We need to be careful for floating-point members as comparison is a somewhat more sophisticated operation. The type Complex would be a perfect example of a nonprimitive value type; such types resemble C# structs.

In addition, value types can reduce storage requirements because they don't have reference identity. Figure 21.1 illustrates an array of size three, whose elements 0, 1, and 2 are light gray, white, and dark gray, respectively. The left diagram shows a typical storage requirement when Pair and Complex are Objects, and the right

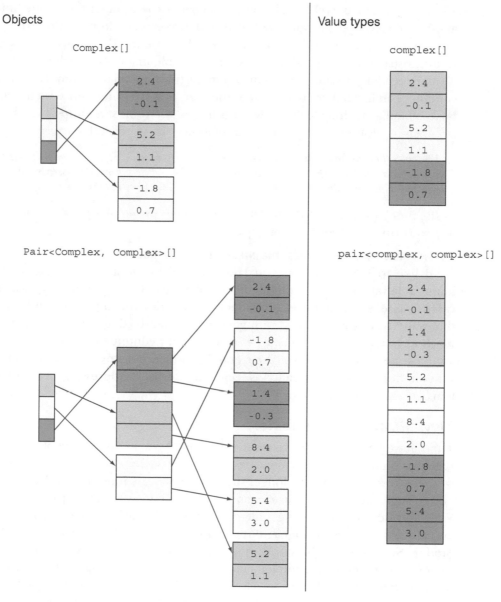

Figure 21.1 Objects versus value types

diagram shows the better layout when Pair and Complex are value types. Note that we call them pair and complex in lowercase in the diagram to emphasize their similarity to primitive types. Note also that value types are likely to produce better performance, not only for data access (multiple levels of pointer indirection replaced by a single indexed-addressing instruction), but also for hardware cache use (due to data contiguity).

Note that because value types don't have reference identity, the compiler can box and unbox them at its choice. If you pass a complex as argument from one function to another, the compiler can naturally pass it as two separate doubles. (Returning it without boxing is trickier in the JVM, of course, because the JVM provides only method-return instructions for passing values representable in a 64-bit machine register.) But if you pass a larger value type as an argument (perhaps a large immutable array), the compiler can instead, transparently to the user, pass it as a reference when it has been boxed. Similar technology already exists in C#. Microsoft says (https://docs.microsoft .com/en-us/dotnet/csharp/language-reference/keywords/value-types):

> *Variables that are based on value types directly contain values. Assigning one value type variable to another copies the contained value. This differs from the assignment of reference type variables, which copies a reference to the object but not the object itself.*

At the time of writing (2018), a JDK enhancement proposal is pending for value types in Java (http://openjdk.java.net/jeps/169).

BOXING, GENERICS, VALUE TYPES: THE INTERDEPENDENCY PROBLEM

We'd like to have value types in Java because functional-style programs deal with immutable values that don't have identity. We'd like to see primitive types as a special case of value types, but the erasure model of generics, which Java currently has, means that value types can't be used with generics without boxing. Object (boxed) versions (such as Integer) of primitive types (such as int) continue to be vital for collections and Java generics because of their erasure model, but now their inheriting Object (and, hence, reference equality) is seen as a drawback. Addressing any of these problems means addressing them all.

21.5   *Moving Java forward faster*

There have been ten major releases of Java in 22 years—an average of more than two years between releases. In some cases, the wait was five years. The Java architects realized that this situation is no longer sustainable because it doesn't evolve the language fast enough and is the main reason why emerging languages on the JVM (such as Scala and Kotlin) are creating a huge feature gap for Java. Such a long release cycle is arguably reasonable for huge and revolutionary features such as lambdas and the Java Module System, but it also implies that minor improvements have to wait, for no valid reason, for the complete implementation of one of those big changes before being incorporated into the language. The collection factory methods discussed in chapter 8, for example, were ready to ship long before the Java 9 module system was finalized.

For these reasons, it has been decided that from now on, Java will have a six-month development cycle. In other words, a new major version of Java and the JVM will appear every six months, with Java 10 released in March 2018 and Java 11 due in September 2018. The Java architects also realized that although this faster development cycle is beneficial for the language itself, and also for agile companies and developers who are used to constantly experimenting with new technologies, it could be problematic for more conservative organizations, which generally update their software at a slower pace. For that reason, the Java architects also decided that every three years, there'll be a long-term support (LTS) release that will be supported for the subsequent three years. Java 9 isn't an LTS release, so it's considered to be at the end of its life now Java 10 is out. The same thing will happen with Java 10. Java 11, by contrast, will be an LTS version, with release planned for September 2018 and supported until September 2021. Figure 21.2 shows the life cycle of the Java versions that are planned for released in the next few years.

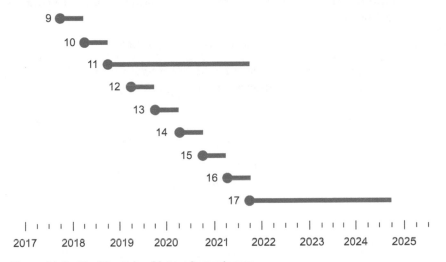

Figure 21.2   The life cycle of future Java releases

We strongly empathize with the decision to give Java a shorter development cycle, especially nowadays, when all software systems and languages are meant to improve as quickly as possible. A shorter development cycle enables Java to evolve at the right speed and allows the language to remain relevant and appropriate in the coming years.

21.6   The final word

This book explored the main new features added by Java 8 and 9. Java 8 represents perhaps the biggest evolution step ever taken by Java. The only comparably large evolution step was the introduction, a decade previously (in 2005), of generics in Java 5. The most characteristic feature of Java 9 is the introduction of the long-awaited module system, which is likely to be more interesting for software architects than to developers. Java 9 also embraced reactive streams by standardizing its protocol through the Flow API. Java 10 introduces local-variable type inference, which is a popular feature in other programming languages to help productivity. Java 11 allows the var syntax of local-variable type inference to be used in the list of parameters of an implicitly typed lambda expression. Perhaps more importantly, Java 11 embraces the concurrency and reactive programming ideas discussed in this book and brings a new asynchronous HTTP client library that fully adopts CompletableFutures. Finally, at the time of writing, Java 12 was announced to support an enhanced switch construct that can be used as an expression instead of just a statement—a key feature of functional programming languages. In fact, switch expressions pave the way for the introduction of pattern matching in Java, which we discussed in section 21.4.2. All these language updates show that functional programming ideas and influence will continue to make their way into Java in the future!

In this chapter, we looked at pressures for further Java evolution. In conclusion, we propose the following statement:

Java 8, 9, 10, and 11 are excellent places to pause but not to stop!

We hope that you've enjoyed this learning adventure with us and that we've sparked your interest in exploring the further evolution of Java.

appendix A
Miscellaneous language updates

In this appendix, we discuss three other language updates in Java 8: repeated annotations, type annotations, and generalized target-type inference. Appendix B discusses library updates in Java 8. We don't discuss JDK 8 updates such as Nashorn and Compact Profiles because they're new JVM features. This book focuses on *library* and *language* updates. We invite you to read the following links if you're interested in Nashorn and Compact Profiles: http://openjdk.java.net/projects/nashorn/ and http://openjdk.java.net/jeps/161.

A.1   Annotations

The annotation mechanism in Java 8 has been enhanced in two ways:

- You can repeat annotations.
- You can annotate any type uses.

Before we explain these updates, it's worth quickly refreshing what you can do with annotations before Java 8.

Annotations in Java are a mechanism that lets you decorate program elements with additional information (note that prior to Java 8 only declarations can be annotated). In other words, it's a form of *syntactic metadata*. For example, annotations are popular with the JUnit framework. In the following code, the method setUp is annotated with the annotation @Before, and the method testAlgorithm is annotated with @Test:

```
@Before
public void setUp(){
    this.list = new ArrayList<>();
}
```

```
@Test
public void testAlgorithm(){
    ...
    assertEquals(5, list.size());
}
```

Annotations are suitable for several use cases:

- In the context of JUnit, annotations can differentiate methods that should be run as a unit test and methods that are used for setup work.

- Annotations can be used for documentation. For instance, the @Deprecated annotation is used to indicate that a method should no longer be used.

- The Java compiler can also process annotations in order to detect errors, suppress warnings, or generate code.

- Annotations are popular in Java EE, where they're used to configure enterprise applications.

A.1.1 Repeated annotations

Previous versions of Java forbid more than one annotation of a given annotation type to be specified on a declaration. For this reason, the following code is invalid:

```
@interface Author { String name(); }
@Author(name="Raoul") @Author(name="Mario")   @Author(name="Alan")  ⟵   Error:
class Book{ }                                                             duplicate
                                                                         annotation
```

Java EE programmers often make use of an idiom to circumvent this restriction. You declare a new annotation, which contains an array of the annotation you want to repeat. It looks like this:

```
@interface Author { String name(); }
@interface Authors {
    Author[] value();
}
@Authors(
  { @Author(name="Raoul"), @Author(name="Mario") , @Author(name="Alan")}
)
class Book{}
```

The nested annotation on the Book class is pretty ugly. This is why Java 8 essentially removes this restriction, which tidies things a bit. You're now allowed to specify multiple annotations of the same annotation type on a declaration, provided they stipulate that the annotation is repeatable. It's not the default behavior; you have to explicitly ask for an annotation to be repeatable.

MAKING AN ANNOTATION REPEATABLE

If an annotation has been designed to be repeatable, you can just use it. But if you're providing annotations for your users, then setup is required to specify that an annotation can be repeated. There are two steps:

1 Mark the annotation as @Repeatable.
2 Provide a container annotation.

Here's how you can make the `@Author` annotation repeatable:

```
@Repeatable(Authors.class)
@interface Author { String name(); }
@interface Authors {
    Author[] value();
}
```

As a result, the `Book` class can be annotated with multiple `@Author` annotations:

```
@Author(name="Raoul") @Author(name="Mario")   @Author(name="Alan")
class Book{ }
```

At compile time `Book` is considered to be annotated by `@Authors({ @Author(name=`
`"Raoul"), @Author(name="Mario"), @Author(name="Alan") })`, so you can view this
new mechanism as syntactic sugar around the previous idiom used by Java programmers. Annotations are still wrapped in a container to ensure behavioral compatibility
with legacy reflection methods. The method `getAnnotation(Class<T> annotation-`
`Class)` in the Java API returns the annotation of type `T` for an annotated element.
Which annotation should this method return if there are several annotations of type `T`?

Without diving into too much detail, the class `Class` supports a new `get-`
`AnnotationsByType` method that facilitates working with repeatable annotations.
For example, you can use it as follows to print all the `Author` annotations on the
`Book` class:

> Retrieve an array consisting of the
> repeatable Author annotations

```
public static void main(String[] args) {
    Author[] authors = Book.class.getAnnotationsByType(Author.class);   ⟵
    Arrays.asList(authors).forEach(a -> { System.out.println(a.name()); });
}
```

For this to work, both the repeatable annotation and its container must have a `RUNTIME`
retention policy. More information about compatibility with legacy reflection methods can be found here: http://cr.openjdk.java.net/~abuckley/8misc.pdf.

A.1.2 Type annotations

As of Java 8, annotations can be also applied to any type uses. This includes the `new`
operator, type casts, `instanceof` checks, generic type arguments, and `implements` and
`throws` clauses. Here we indicate that the variable `name` of type `String` can't be `null`
using a `@NonNull` annotation:

```
@NonNull String name = person.getName();
```

Similarly, you can annotate the type of the elements in a list:

```
List<@NonNull Car> cars = new ArrayList<>();
```

Why is this interesting? Annotations on types can be useful to perform program analysis. In these two examples, a tool could ensure that `getName` doesn't return `null` and
that the elements of the list of cars are always non-`null`. This can help reduce unexpected errors in your code.

Java 8 doesn't provide official annotations or a tool to use them out of the box. It provides only the ability to use annotations on types. Luckily, a tool called the Checker framework exists, which defines several type annotations and lets you enhance type checking using them. If you're curious, we invite you to take a look at its tutorial: http://www.checkerframework.org. More information about where you can use annotations in your code can be found here: http://docs.oracle.com/javase/specs/jls/se8/html/jls-9.html#jls-9.7.4.

A.2   *Generalized target-type inference*

Java 8 enhances the inference of generic arguments. You're already familiar with type inference using context information before Java 8. For example, the method `empty-List` in Java is defined as follows:

```
static <T> List<T> emptyList();
```

The method `emptyList` is parameterized with the type parameter `T`. You can call it as follows to provide an explicit type to the type parameter:

```
List<Car> cars = Collections.<Car>emptyList();
```

But Java is capable of inferring the generic argument. The following is equivalent:

```
List<Car> cars = Collections.emptyList();
```

Before Java 8, this inference mechanism based on the context (that is, target typing) was limited. For example, the following wasn't possible:

```
static void cleanCars(List<Car> cars) {

}
cleanCars(Collections.emptyList());
```

You'd get the following error:

```
cleanCars (java.util.List<Car>)cannot be applied to
    (java.util.List<java.lang.Object>)
```

To fix it you'd have to provide an explicit type argument like the one we showed previously.

In Java 8 the target type includes arguments to a method, so you don't need to provide an explicit generic argument:

```
List<Car> cleanCars = dirtyCars.stream()
                               .filter(Car::isClean)
                               .collect(Collectors.toList());
```

In this code, it's exactly this enhancement that lets you write `Collectors.toList()` instead of `Collectors.<Car>toList()`.

appendix B
Miscellaneous
library updates

This appendix reviews the main additions to the Java 8 library.

B.1   Collections

The biggest update to the Collections API is the introduction of streams, which we discussed in chapters 4, 5, and 6. There are also other updates discussed in Chapter 9 and additional minor additions summarized in this appendix.

B.1.1   Additional methods

The Java API designers made the most out of default methods and added several new methods to collection interfaces and classes. The new methods are listed in table B.1.

Table B.1   New methods added to collection classes and interfaces

Class/interface	New methods
Map	getOrDefault, forEach, compute, computeIfAbsent, computeIfPresent, merge, putIfAbsent, remove(key, value), replace, replaceAll, of, ofEntries
Iterable	forEach, spliterator
Iterator	forEachRemaining
Collection	removeIf, stream, parallelStream
List	replaceAll, sort, of
BitSet	stream
Set	of

MAP

The Map interface is the most updated interface, with support for several new convenient methods. For example, the method getOrDefault can be used to replace an existing idiom that checks whether a Map contains a mapping for a given key. If not, you can provide a default value to return instead. Previously you would do this:

```
Map<String, Integer> carInventory = new HashMap<>();
Integer count = 0;
if(map.containsKey("Aston Martin")){
  count = map.get("Aston Martin");
}
```

You can now more simply do the following:

```
Integer count = map.getOrDefault("Aston Martin", 0);
```

Note that this works only if there's no mapping. For example, if the key is explicitly mapped to the value null, then no default value will be returned.

Another particularly useful method is computeIfAbsent, which we briefly mentioned in chapter 19 when explaining memoization. It lets you conveniently use the caching pattern. Let's say that you need to fetch and process data from a different website. In such a scenario, it's useful to cache the data, so you don't have to execute the (expensive) fetching operation multiple times:

```
public String getData(String url){
    String data = cache.get(url);           Check if the data is
    if(data == null){                        already cached.
        data = getData(url);
        cache.put(url, data);               If not, fetch the data and
    }                                        then cache it in the Map
    return data;                             for future use.
}
```

You can now write this code more concisely by using computeIfAbsent as follows:

```
public String getData(String url){
    return cache.computeIfAbsent(url, this::getData);
}
```

A description of all other methods can be found in the official Java API documentation (http://docs.oracle.com/javase/8/docs/api/java/util/Map.html). Note that ConcurrentHashMap was also updated with additional methods. We discuss them in section B.2.

COLLECTION

The removeIf method can be used to remove all elements in a collection that match a predicate. Note that this is different than the filter method included in the Streams API. The filter method in the Streams API produces a new stream; it doesn't mutate the current stream or source.

LIST

The replaceAll method replaces each element in a List with the result of applying a given operator to it. It's similar to the map method in a stream, but it mutates the elements of the List. In contrast, the map method produces new elements.

For example, the following code will print [2, 4, 6, 8, 10] because the List is modified in place:

```
List<Integer> numbers = Arrays.asList(1, 2, 3, 4, 5);
numbers.replaceAll(x -> x * 2);
System.out.println(numbers);
```
Prints
[2, 4, 6, 8, 10]

B.1.2 *The Collections class*

The Collections class has been around for a long time to operate on or return collections. It now includes additional methods to return unmodifiable, synchronized, checked, and empty NavigableMap and NavigableSet. In addition, it includes the method checkedQueue, which returns a view of Queue that's extended with dynamic type checking.

B.1.3 *Comparator*

The Comparator interface now includes default and static methods. You used the Comparator.comparing static method in chapter 3 to return a Comparator object given a function that extracts the sorting key.

New instance methods include the following:

- reversed—Returns a Comparator with the reverse ordering of the current Comparator.
- thenComparing—Returns a Comparator that uses another Comparator when two objects are equal.
- thenComparingInt, thenComparingDouble, thenComparingLong—Work like the thenComparing method, but take a function specialized for primitive types (respectively, ToIntFunction, ToDoubleFunction, and ToLongFunction).

New static methods include these:

- comparingInt, comparingDouble, comparingLong—Work like the comparing method, but take a function specialized for primitive types (respectively ToIntFunction, ToDoubleFunction, and ToLongFunction).
- naturalOrder—Returns a Comparator object that imposes a natural order on Comparable objects.
- nullsFirst, nullsLast—Return a Comparator object that considers null to be less than non-null or greater than non-null.
- reverseOrder–Equivalent to naturalOrder().reverse().

B.2   Concurrency

Java 8 brings several updates related to concurrency. The first is, of course, the introduction of parallel streams, which we explore in chapter 7. There's also the introduction of the CompletableFuture class, which you can learn about in chapter 16.

There are other noticeable updates. For example, the Arrays class now supports parallel operations. We discuss these operations in section B.3.

In this section, we look at updates in the java.util.concurrent.atomic package, which deals with atomic variables. In addition, we discuss updates to the Concurrent-HashMap class, which supports several new methods.

B.2.1   Atomic

The java.util.concurrent.atomic package offers several numeric classes, such as AtomicInteger and AtomicLong that support atomic operation on single variables. They were updated to support new methods:

- getAndUpdate—Atomically updates the current value with the results of applying the given function, returning the previous value.
- updateAndGet—Atomically updates the current value with the results of applying the given function, returning the updated value.
- getAndAccumulate—Atomically updates the current value with the results of applying the given function to the current and given values, returning the previous value.
- accumulateAndGet—Atomically updates the current value with the results of applying the given function to the current and given values, returning the updated value.

Here's how to atomically set the minimum between an observed value of 10 and an existing atomic integer:

```
int min = atomicInteger.accumulateAndGet(10, Integer::min);
```

ADDERS AND ACCUMULATORS

The Java API recommends using the new classes LongAdder, LongAccumulator, Double-Adder, and DoubleAccumulator instead of the Atomic classes equivalent when multiple threads update frequently but read less frequently (for example, in the context of statistics). These classes are designed to grow dynamically to reduce thread contention.

The classes LongAdder and DoubleAdder support operations for additions, whereas LongAccumulator and DoubleAccumulator are given a function to combine values. For example, to calculate the sum of several values, you can use a LongAdder as follows.

Listing B.1   LongAdder to calculate the sum of values

```
LongAdder adder = new LongAdder();
adder.add(10);
// …
long sum = adder.sum();
```

Get the sum at some point.

Do some addition in several different threads.

The initial sum value is set to 0 with the default constructor.

Or you can use a LongAccumulator as follows.

```
LongAccumulator acc = new LongAccumulator(Long::sum, 0);
acc.accumulate(10);                                          ◄─┤  Accumulate values in
// ...                                                          several different threads.
long result = acc.get();        ◄─┤  Get the result
                                     at some point.
```

B.2.2 ConcurrentHashMap

The ConcurrentHashMap class was introduced to provide a more modern HashMap, which is concurrent friendly. ConcurrentHashMap allows concurrent add and updates that lock only certain parts of the internal data structure. Thus, read and write operations have improved performance compared to the synchronized Hashtable alternative.

PERFORMANCE

ConcurrentHashMap's internal structure was updated to improve performance. Entries of a map are typically stored in buckets accessed by the generated hashcode of the key. But if many keys return the same hashcode, performance will deteriorate because buckets are implemented as Lists with $O(n)$ retrieval. In Java 8, when the buckets become too big, they're dynamically replaced with sorted trees, which have $O(\log(n))$ retrieval. Note that this is possible only when the keys are Comparable (for example, String or Number classes).

STREAM-LIKE OPERATIONS

ConcurrentHashMap supports three new kinds of operations reminiscent of what you saw with streams:

- forEach—Performs a given action for each (key, value)
- reduce—Combines all (key, value) given a reduction function into a result
- search—Applies a function on each (key, value) until the function produces a non-null result

Each kind of operation supports four forms, accepting functions with keys, values, Map.Entry, and (key, value) arguments:

- Operates with keys and values (forEach, reduce, search)
- Operates with keys (forEachKey, reduceKey, searchKey)
- Operates with values (forEachValue, reduceValue, searchValues)
- Operates with Map.Entry objects (forEachEntry, reduceEntries, searchEntries)

Note that these operations don't lock the state of the ConcurrentHashMap. They operate on the elements as they go along. The functions supplied to these operations shouldn't depend on any ordering or on any other objects or values that may change while computation is in progress.

In addition, you need to specify a parallelism threshold for all these operations. The operations will execute sequentially if the current map size is estimated to be less than the given threshold. Using a value of 1 enables maximal parallelism using the common thread pool. Using a value of Long.MAX_VALUE runs the operation on a single thread.

In this example we use the method reduceValues to find the maximum value in the map:

```
ConcurrentHashMap<String, Integer> map = new ConcurrentHashMap<>();
Optional<Integer> maxValue =
    Optional.of(map.reduceValues(1, Integer::max));
```

Note that there are primitive specializations for int, long, and double for each reduce operation (for example, reduceValuesToInt, reduceKeysToLong, and so on).

COUNTING

The ConcurrentHashMap class provides a new method called mappingCount, which returns the number of mappings in the map as a long. It should be used instead of the method size, which returns an int. This is because the number of mappings may not fit in an int.

SET VIEWS

The ConcurrentHashMap class provides a new method called keySet that returns a view of the ConcurrentHashMap as a Set (changes to the map are reflected in the Set and vice versa). You can also create a Set backed by a ConcurrentHashMap using the new static method newKeySet.

B.3   Arrays

The Arrays class provides various static methods to manipulate arrays. It now includes four new methods (which have primitive specialized overloaded variants).

B.3.1   Using parallelSort

The parallelSort method sorts the specified array in parallel, using a natural order, or using an extra Comparator for an array of objects.

B.3.2   Using setAll and parallelSetAll

The setAll and parallelSetAll methods set all elements of the specified array, respectively sequentially or in parallel, using the provided function to compute each element. The function receives the element index and returns a value for that index. Because parallelSetAll is executed in parallel, the function must be side-effect free, as explained in chapters 7 and 18.

As an example, you can use the method setAll to produce an array with the values 0, 2, 4, 6, …:

```
int[] evenNumbers = new int[10];
Arrays.setAll(evenNumbers, i -> i * 2);
```

B.3.3 Using parallelPrefix

The `parallelPrefix` method cumulates, in parallel, each element of the given array, using the supplied binary operator. In the next listing you produce the values 1, 2, 3, 4, 5, 6, 7, ...

> **Listing B.3** `parallelPrefix` **cumulates in parallel elements of an array**

```
int[] ones = new int[10];
Arrays.fill(ones, 1);
Arrays.parallelPrefix(ones, (a, b) -> a + b);
```
ones is now
[1, 2, 3, 4, 5, 6, 7, 8, 9, 10]

B.4 Number and Math

The Java 8 API enhances the `Number` and `Math` classes with new methods.

B.4.1 Number

The new methods of the `Number` class are as follows:

- The `Short`, `Integer`, `Long`, `Float`, and `Double` classes include the `sum`, `min`, and `max` static methods. You saw these methods in conjunction with the `reduce` operation in chapter 5.
- The `Integer` and `Long` classes include the methods `compareUnsigned`, `divide-Unsigned`, `remainderUnsigned`, and `toUnsignedString` to work with unsigned values.
- The `Integer` and `Long` classes also respectively include the static methods `parseUnsignedInt` and `parseUnsignedLong`, to parse strings as an unsigned `int` or `long`.
- The `Byte` and `Short` classes include the methods `toUnsignedInt` and `toUnsigned-Long`, to convert the argument to an `int` or `long` by an unsigned conversion. Similarly, the `Integer` class now includes the static method `toUnsignedLong`.
- The `Double` and `Float` classes include the static method `isFinite`, to check whether the argument is a finite floating-point value.
- The `Boolean` class now includes the static methods `logicalAnd`, `logicalOr`, and `logicalXor`, to apply the and, or, and xor operations between two booleans.
- The `BigInteger` class includes the methods `byteValueExact`, `shortValueExact`, `intValueExact`, and `longValueExact`, to convert this `BigInteger` to the respective primitive type. But it throws an arithmetic exception if there's a loss of information during the conversion.

B.4.2 Math

The `Math` class includes new methods that throw an arithmetic exception if the result of the operation overflows. These methods consist of `addExact`, `subtractExact`, `multiplyExact`, `incrementExact`, `decrementExact`, and `negateExact` with `int` and `long` arguments. In addition, there's a static `toIntExact` method to convert a `long` value to an `int`. Other additions include the static methods `floorMod`, `floorDiv`, and `nextDown`.

B.5   *Files*

Noticeable additions to the `Files` class let you produce a stream from files. We mention the new static method `Files.lines` in chapter 5; it lets you read a file lazily as a stream. Other useful static methods that return a stream include the following:

- `Files.list`—Produces a `Stream<Path>` consisting of entries in a given directory. The listing isn't recursive. Because the stream is consumed lazily, it's a useful method for processing potentially very large directories.
- `Files.walk`—Just like `Files.list`, it produces a `Stream<Path>` consisting of entries in a given directory. But the listing is recursive and the depth level can be configured. Note that the traversal is performed depth-first.
- `Files.find`—Produces a `Stream<Path>` from recursively traversing a directory to find entries that match a given predicate.

B.6   *Reflection*

We discussed several changes to the annotation mechanism in Java 8 in appendix A. The Reflection API was updated to support these changes.

Another addition to the Reflection API is that information about parameters of methods such as names and modifiers can now be accessed with the help of the new `java.lang.reflect.Parameter` class, which is referenced in the new `java.lang.reflect.Executable` class that serves as a shared superclass for the common functionality of `Method` and `Constructor`.

B.7   *String*

The `String` class now includes a convenient static method called `join` to—as you may guess—join strings with a delimiter! You can use it as follows:

```
String authors = String.join(", ", "Raoul", "Mario", "Alan");    Raoul, Mario,
System.out.println(authors);                                     Alan
```

appendix C
Performing multiple operations in parallel on a stream

One of the biggest limitations of a Java 8 stream is that you can operate on it only once and get only one result while processing it. Indeed, if you try to traverse a stream for a second time, the only thing you can achieve is an exception like this:

```
java.lang.IllegalStateException: stream has already been operated upon or closed
```

Despite this, there are situations where you'd like to get several results when processing a single stream. For instance, you may want to parse a log file in a stream, as we did in section 5.7.3, but gather multiple statistics in a single step. Or, keeping with the menu data model used to explain Stream's features in chapters 4, 5, and 6, you may want to retrieve different information while traversing the stream of dishes.

In other words, you'd like to push a stream through more than one lambda on a single pass, and to do this you need a type of fork method and to apply different functions to each forked stream. Even better, it would be great if you could perform those operations in parallel, using different threads to calculate the different required results.

Unfortunately, these features aren't currently available on the stream implementation provided in Java 8, but in this appendix we'll show you a way to use a Spliterator and in particular its late-binding capacity, together with BlockingQueues and Futures, to implement this useful feature and make it available with a convenient API.[1]

---

[1] The implementation presented in the rest of this appendix is based on the solution posted by Paul Sandoz in the email he sent to the lambda-dev mailing list: http://mail.openjdk.java.net/pipermail/lambda-dev/2013-November/011516.html.

C.1   *Forking a stream*

The first thing necessary to execute multiple operations in parallel on a stream is to create a `StreamForker` that wraps the original stream, on which you can define the different operations you want to perform. Take a look at the following listing.

Listing C.1   Defining a `StreamForker` to execute multiple operations on a stream

```java
public class StreamForker<T> {

    private final Stream<T> stream;
    private final Map<Object, Function<Stream<T>, ?>> forks =
                                                new HashMap<>();

    public StreamForker(Stream<T> stream) {
        this.stream = stream;
    }

    public StreamForker<T> fork(Object key, Function<Stream<T>, ?> f) {
        forks.put(key, f);
        return this;
    }

    public Results getResults() {
        // To be implemented
    }
}
```

> Return this to fluently invoke the fork method multiple times.

> Index the function to be applied on the stream with a key.

Here the fork method accepts two arguments:

- A `Function`, which transforms the stream into a result of any type representing one of these operations
- A key, which will allow you to retrieve the result of that operation and accumulates these key/function pairs in an internal `Map`

The `fork` method returns the `StreamForker` itself; therefore, you can build a pipeline by forking several operations. Figure C.1 shows the main ideas behind the `StreamForker`.

Here the user defines three operations to be performed on a stream indexed by three keys. The `StreamForker` then traverses the original stream and forks it into three other streams. At this point the three operations can be applied in parallel on the forked streams, and the results of these function applications, indexed with their corresponding keys, are used to populate the resulting `Map`.

The execution of all the operations added through the `fork` method is triggered by the invocation of the method `getResults`, which returns an implementation of the `Results` interface defined as follows:

```java
public static interface Results {
    public <R> R get(Object key);
}
```

This interface has only one method to which you can pass one of the key `Object`s used in one of the `fork` methods, and that method returns the result of the operation corresponding to that key.

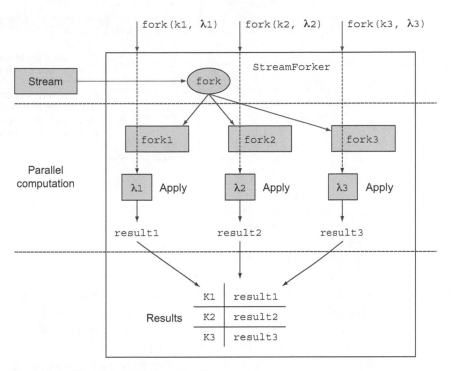

Figure C.1 The `StreamForker` in action

C.1.1 *Implementing the Results interface with the ForkingStreamConsumer*

The getResults method can be implemented as follows:

```
public Results getResults() {
    ForkingStreamConsumer<T> consumer = build();
    try {
        stream.sequential().forEach(consumer);
    } finally {
        consumer.finish();
    }
    return consumer;
}
```

The ForkingStreamConsumer implements both the Results interface defined previously and the Consumer interface. As you'll see when we analyze its implementation in more detail, its main task is to consume all the elements in the stream and multiplex them to a number of BlockingQueues equal to the number of operations submitted via the fork method. Note that it is ensured that the stream is sequential, because if the method forEach were performed on a parallel stream, its elements could be pushed to the queues out of order. The finish method adds special elements to those queues to signal that there are no more items to be processed. The build method used to create the ForkingStreamConsumer is shown in the next listing.

Listing C.2   The `build` method used to create `ForkingStreamConsumer`

```
private ForkingStreamConsumer<T> build() {
    List<BlockingQueue<T>> queues = new ArrayList<>();

    Map<Object, Future<?>> actions =
            forks.entrySet().stream().reduce(
                    new HashMap<Object, Future<?>>(),
                    (map, e) -> {
                        map.put(e.getKey(),
                                getOperationResult(queues, e.getValue()));
                        return map;
                    },
                    (m1, m2) -> {
                        m1.putAll(m2);
                        return m1;
                    });

    return new ForkingStreamConsumer<>(queues, actions);
}
```

Create a list of queues, with a queue for each operation.

Map the Futures that will contain the results of the operations with the keys used to identify those operations.

In listing C.2, you first create the List of BlockingQueues mentioned previously. Then you create a Map, having as keys the same keys used to identify the different operations to be executed on the stream, and having as values the Futures that will contain the corresponding results of these operations. The List of BlockingQueues and the Map of Futures are then passed to the constructor of the ForkingStreamConsumer. Each Future is created with this getOperationResult method, as shown in the next listing.

Listing C.3   `Futures` created with the `getOperationResult` method

```
private Future<?> getOperationResult(List<BlockingQueue<T>> queues,
                                     Function<Stream<T>, ?> f) {
    BlockingQueue<T> queue = new LinkedBlockingQueue<>();
    queues.add(queue);
    Spliterator<T> spliterator = new BlockingQueueSpliterator<>(queue);
    Stream<T> source = StreamSupport.stream(spliterator, false);
    return CompletableFuture.supplyAsync( () -> f.apply(source) );
}
```

Create a Spliterator traversing the elements in that queue.

Create a queue and add it to the list of queues.

Create a stream having that Spliterator as source.

Create a Future calculating asynchronously the application of the given function on that stream.

The method getOperationResult creates a new BlockingQueue and adds it to the List of queues. This queue is passed to a new BlockingQueueSpliterator, which is a late-binding Spliterator, reading the item to be traversed from the queue; we'll examine how it's made shortly.

You then create a sequential stream traversing this Spliterator, and finally you create a Future to calculate the result of applying the function representing one of the operations you want to perform on this stream. This Future is created using a static factory method of the CompletableFuture class that implements the Future interface. This is another new class introduced in Java 8, and we investigated it in detail in chapter 16.

C.1.2 Developing the ForkingStreamConsumer and the BlockingQueueSpliterator

The last two outstanding parts you need to develop are the ForkingStreamConsumer and BlockingQueueSpliterator classes we introduced previously. The first one can be implemented as follows.

> **Listing C.4 A `ForkingStreamConsumer` to add stream elements to multiple queues**

```
static class ForkingStreamConsumer<T> implements Consumer<T>, Results {
    static final Object END_OF_STREAM = new Object();

    private final List<BlockingQueue<T>> queues;
    private final Map<Object, Future<?>> actions;

    ForkingStreamConsumer(List<BlockingQueue<T>> queues,
                          Map<Object, Future<?>> actions) {
        this.queues = queues;
        this.actions = actions;
    }

    @Override
    public void accept(T t) {
        queues.forEach(q -> q.add(t));
    }

    void finish() {
        accept((T) END_OF_STREAM);
    }

    @Override
    public <R> R get(Object key) {
        try {
            return ((Future<R>) actions.get(key)).get();
        } catch (Exception e) {
            throw new RuntimeException(e);
        }
    }
}
```

Propagates the traversed element of the stream to all the queues

Adds one last element to the queue to signal that the stream is finished

Returns the result of the operation indexed by the given key and waits for the completion of the Future calculating it

This class implements both the Consumer and Results interfaces and holds a reference to the List of BlockingQueues and to the Map of Futures executing the different operations on the stream.

The Consumer interface requires an implementation for the method accept. Here, every time ForkingStreamConsumer accepts an element of the stream, it adds that element to all the BlockingQueues. Also, after all the elements of the original stream have been added to all queues, the finish method causes one last item to be added to all of them. This item, when met by BlockingQueueSpliterators, will make the queues understand that there are no more elements to be processed.

The Results interface requires an implementation for the get method. Here, it retrieves the Future that's indexed in the Map with the argument key and unwraps its result or waits until a result is available.

Finally, there will be a `BlockingQueueSpliterator` for each operation to be performed on the stream. Each `BlockingQueueSpliterator` will have a reference to one of the `BlockingQueues` populated by the `ForkingStreamConsumer`, and it can be implemented as shown in the following listing.

Listing C.5 A `Spliterator` reading the elements it traverses from a `BlockingQueue`

```java
class BlockingQueueSpliterator<T> implements Spliterator<T> {
    private final BlockingQueue<T> q;

    BlockingQueueSpliterator(BlockingQueue<T> q) {
        this.q = q;
    }

    @Override
    public boolean tryAdvance(Consumer<? super T> action) {
        T t;
        while (true) {
            try {
                t = q.take();
                break;
            } catch (InterruptedException e) { }
        }

        if (t != ForkingStreamConsumer.END_OF_STREAM) {
            action.accept(t);
            return true;
        }

        return false;
    }

    @Override
    public Spliterator<T> trySplit() {
        return null;
    }

    @Override
    public long estimateSize() {
        return 0;
    }

    @Override
    public int characteristics() {
        return 0;
    }
}
```

In this listing a `Spliterator` is implemented, not to define the policy of how to split a stream but only to use its late-binding capability. For this reason the `trySplit` method is unimplemented.

Also, it's impossible to return any meaningful value from the `estimatedSize` method because you can't foresee how many elements can be still taken from the queue. Further, because you're not attempting any split, this estimation will be useless.

This implementation doesn't have any of the Spliterator characteristics we listed in table 7.2, so the characteristic method returns 0.

The only method implemented here is tryAdvance, which waits to take from its BlockingQueue the elements of the original stream added to it by the ForkingStream-Consumer. It sends those elements to a Consumer that (based on how this Spliterator was created in the getOperationResult method) is the source of a further stream (on which the corresponding function, passed to one of the fork method invocations, has to be applied). The tryAdvance method returns true, to notify its invoker that there are other elements to be consumed, until it finds on the queue the special Object added by ForkingStreamConsumer to signal that there are no more elements to be taken from the queue. Figure C.2 shows an overview of the StreamForker and its building blocks.

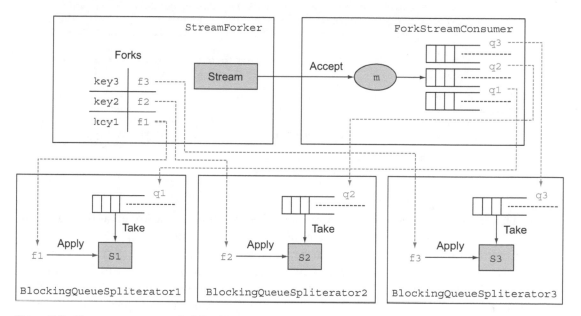

Figure C.2   The StreamForker building blocks

In the figure, the StreamForker in the upper left has a Map, where each operation to be performed on the stream, defined by a function, is indexed by a key. The Forking-StreamConsumer on the right holds a queue for each of these operations and consumes all the elements in the original stream, multiplexing them to all the queues.

At the bottom of the figure, each queue has a BlockingQueueSpliterator pulling its items and acting as a source for a different stream. Finally, each of these streams, forked by the original one, is passed as argument to one of the functions, thus executing one of the operations to be performed. You now have all the components of your StreamForker, so it's ready to use.

C.1.3 *Putting the StreamForker to work*

Let's put the `StreamForker` to work on the menu data model that we defined in chapter 4, by forking the original stream of dishes to perform four different operations in parallel on it, as shown in the next listing. In particular, you want to generate a comma-separated list of the names of all available dishes, calculate the total calories of the menu, find the dish with the most calories, and group all dishes by their type.

Listing C.6 Putting the `StreamForker` to work

```
Stream<Dish> menuStream = menu.stream();

StreamForker.Results results = new StreamForker<Dish>(menuStream)
        .fork("shortMenu", s -> s.map(Dish::getName)
                                 .collect(joining(", ")))
        .fork("totalCalories", s -> s.mapToInt(Dish::getCalories).sum())
        .fork("mostCaloricDish", s -> s.collect(reducing(
                (d1, d2) -> d1.getCalories() > d2.getCalories() ? d1 : d2))
                .get())
        .fork("dishesByType", s -> s.collect(groupingBy(Dish::getType)))
        .getResults();

String shortMenu = results.get("shortMenu");
int totalCalories = results.get("totalCalories");
Dish mostCaloricDish = results.get("mostCaloricDish");
Map<Dish.Type, List<Dish>> dishesByType = results.get("dishesByType");

System.out.println("Short menu: " + shortMenu);
System.out.println("Total calories: " + totalCalories);
System.out.println("Most caloric dish: " + mostCaloricDish);
System.out.println("Dishes by type: " + dishesByType);
```

The `StreamForker` provides a convenient, fluent API to fork a stream and assign a different operation to each forked stream. These operations are expressed in terms of functions applied on the stream and can be identified by any arbitrary object; in this case we've chosen to use `Strings`. When you have no more forks to add, you can invoke `getResults` on the `StreamForker` to trigger the execution of all the defined operations and obtain `StreamForker.Results`. Because these operations are internally performed asynchronously, the `getResults` method returns immediately, without waiting for all the results to be available.

You can obtain the result of a specific operation by passing the key used to identify it to the `StreamForker.Results` interface. If in the meantime the computation of that operation completes, the `get` method will return the corresponding result; otherwise, it will block until such a result isn't available.

As expected, this piece of code generates the following output:

```
Short menu: pork, beef, chicken, french fries, rice, season fruit, pizza,
    prawns, salmon
Total calories: 4300
Most caloric dish: pork
Dishes by type: {OTHER=[french fries, rice, season fruit, pizza], MEAT=[pork,
    beef, chicken], FISH=[prawns, salmon]}
```

C.2 *Performance considerations*

For performance reasons you shouldn't take for granted that this approach is more efficient than traversing the stream several times. The overhead caused by the use of the blocking queues can easily outweigh the advantages of executing the different operations in parallel when the stream is made of data that's all in memory.

Conversely, accessing the stream only once could be a winning choice when this involves some expensive I/O operations, such as when the source of the stream is a huge file; so (as usual) the only meaningful rule when optimizing the performance of your application is to "Just measure it!"

This example demonstrates how it can be possible to execute multiple operations on the same stream in one shot. More importantly, we believe this proves that even when a specific feature isn't provided by the native Java API, the flexibility of lambda expressions and a bit of creativity in reusing and combining what's already available can let you implement the missing feature on your own.

appendix D
Lambdas and
JVM bytecode

You may wonder how the Java compiler implements lambda expressions and how the Java virtual machine (JVM) deals with it. If you think lambda expressions can simply be translated to anonymous classes, you should read on. This appendix briefly discusses how lambda expressions are compiled, by examining the generated class files.

D.1 *Anonymous classes*

We showed in chapter 2 that anonymous classes can be used to declare and instantiate a class at the same time. As a result, just like lambda expressions, they can be used to provide the implementation for a functional interface.

Because a lambda expression provides the implementation for the abstract method of a functional interface, it would seem straightforward to ask the Java compiler to translate a lambda expression into an anonymous class during the compilation process. But anonymous classes have some undesirable characteristics that impact the performance of applications:

- *The compiler generates a new class file for each anonymous class.* The filename usually looks like `ClassName$1`, where `ClassName` is the name of the class in which the anonymous class appears, followed by a dollar sign and a number. The generation of many class files is undesirable, because each class file needs to be loaded and verified before being used, which impacts the startup performance of the application. If lambdas were translated to anonymous classes, you'd have one new class file for each lambda.

- *Each new anonymous class introduces a new subtype for a class or interface.* If you had a hundred different lambdas for expressing a `Comparator`, that would mean a hundred different subtypes of `Comparator`. In certain situations, this can make it harder to improve runtime performance by the JVM.

D.2 Bytecode generation

A Java source file is compiled to Java bytecode by the Java compiler. The JVM can then execute the generated bytecode and run the application. Anonymous classes and lambda expressions use different bytecode instructions when they're compiled. You can inspect the bytecode and constant pool of any class file using the command

```
javap -c -v ClassName
```

Let's try to implement an instance of the `Function` interface using the old Java 7 syntax, as an anonymous inner class, as shown in the following listing.

Listing D.1 A `Function` implemented as an anonymous inner class

```
import java.util.function.Function;
public class InnerClass {
    Function<Object, String> f = new Function<Object, String>() {
        @Override
        public String apply(Object obj) {
            return obj.toString();
        }
    };
}
```

Doing this, the corresponding generated bytecode for the `Function` created as an anonymous inner class will be something along the lines of this:

```
 0: aload_0
 1: invokespecial #1        // Method java/lang/Object."<init>":()V
 4: aload_0
 5: new           #2        // class InnerClass$1
 8: dup
 9: aload_0
10: invokespecial #3        // Method InnerClass$1."<init>":(LInnerClass;)V
13: putfield      #4        // Field f:Ljava/util/function/Function;
16: return
```

This code shows the following:

- An object of type `InnerClass$1` is instantiated using the byte code operation `new`. A reference to the newly created object is pushed on the stack at the same time.
- The operation `dup` duplicates that reference on the stack.
- This value then gets consumed by the instruction `invokespecial`, which initializes the object.
- The top of the stack now still contains a reference to the object, which is stored in the `f1` field of the `LambdaBytecode` class using the `putfield` instruction.

InnerClass$1 is the name generated by the compiler for the anonymous class. If you want to reassure yourself, you can inspect the InnerClass$1 class file as well, and you'll find the code for the implementation of the Function interface:

```
class InnerClass$1 implements
          java.util.function.Function<java.lang.Object, java.lang.String> {
  final InnerClass this$0;
  public java.lang.String apply(java.lang.Object);
    Code:
      0: aload_1
      1: invokevirtual #3 //Method
                          java/lang/Object.toString:()Ljava/lang/String;
      4: areturn
}
```

D.3   *Invokedynamic to the rescue*

Now let's try to do the same using the new Java 8 syntax as a lambda expression. Inspect the generated class file of the code in the following listing.

Listing D.2   A Function implemented with a lambda expression

```
import java.util.function.Function;
public class Lambda {
    Function<Object, String> f = obj -> obj.toString();
}
```

You'll find the following bytecode instructions:

```
 0: aload_0
 1: invokespecial #1      // Method java/lang/Object."<init>":()V
 4: aload_0
 5: invokedynamic #2,  0 // InvokeDynamic
                          #0:apply:()Ljava/util/function/Function;
10: putfield       #3     // Field f:Ljava/util/function/Function;
13: return
```

We explained the drawbacks in translating a lambda expression in an anonymous inner class, and indeed you can see that the result is very different. The creation of an extra class has been replaced with an invokedynamic instruction.

The invokedynamic instruction

The bytecode instruction invokedynamic was introduced in JDK7 to support dynamically typed languages on the JVM. invokedynamic adds a further level of indirection when invoking a method, to let some logic dependent on the specific dynamic language determine the call target. The typical use for this instruction is something like the following:

```
def add(a, b) { a + b }
```

Here the types of a and b aren't known at compile time and can change from time to time. For this reason, when the JVM executes an invokedynamic for the first time, it consults a bootstrap method, implementing the language-dependent logic that determines the actual method to be called. The bootstrap method returns a linked call site. There's a good chance that if the add method is called with two ints, the subsequent call will also be with two ints. As a result, it's not necessary to redis- cover the method to be called at each invocation. The call site itself can contain the logic defining under which conditions it needs to be relinked.

In listing D.2, the features of the invokedynamic instruction have been used for a slightly different purpose than the one for which they were originally introduced. In fact, here it used to delay the strategy used to translate lambda expressions in byte- code until runtime. In other words, using invokedynamic in this way allows deferring code generation for implementing the lambda expression until runtime. This design choice has positive consequences:

- The strategy used to translate the lambda expression body to bytecode becomes a pure implementation detail. It could also be changed dynamically, or opti- mized and modified in future JVM implementations, preserving the bytecode's backward compatibility.
- There's no overhead, such as additional fields or static initializer, if the lambda is never used.
- For stateless (noncapturing) lambdas it's possible to create one instance of the lambda object, cache it, and always return the same. This is a common use case, and people were used to doing this explicitly before Java 8; for example, declar- ing a specific Comparator instance in a static final variable.
- There's no additional performance cost because this translation has to be per- formed, and its result linked, only when the lambda is invoked for the first time. All subsequent invocations can skip this slow path and call the formerly linked implementation.

D.4   *Code-generation strategies*

A lambda expression is translated into bytecode by putting its body into one of a static method created at runtime. A stateless lambda, one that captures no state from its enclosing scope, like the one we defined in listing D.2, is the simplest type of lambda to be translated. In this case the compiler can generate a method having the same sig- nature of the lambda expression, so the result of this translation process can be logi- cally seen as follows:

```
public class Lambda {
    Function<Object, String> f = [dynamic invocation of lambda$1]

    static String lambda$1(Object obj) {
        return obj.toString();
    }
}
```

The case of a lambda expression capturing final (or effectively final) local variables or fields, as in the following example, is a bit more complex:

```
public class Lambda {
    String header = "This is a ";
    Function<Object, String> f = obj -> header + obj.toString();
}
```

In this case the signature of the generated method can't be the same as the lambda expression, because it's necessary to add extra arguments to carry the additional state of the enclosed context. The simplest solution to achieve this is to prepend the arguments of the lambda expression with an additional argument for each of the captured variables, so the method generated to implement the former lambda expression will be something like this:

```
public class Lambda {
    String header = "This is a ";
    Function<Object, String> f = [dynamic invocation of lambda$1]

    static String lambda$1(String header, Object obj) {
        return obj -> header + obj.toString();
    }
}
```

More information about the translation process for lambda expressions can be found here: http://cr.openjdk.java.net/~briangoetz/lambda/lambda-translation.html.

index

RELATED MANNING TITLES

The Java Module System
by Nicolai Parlog

    ISBN: 9781617294280
    400 pages, $44.99
    February 2019

Spring Microservices in Action
by John Carnell

    ISBN: 9781617293986
    384 pages, $49.99
    June 2017

Kotlin in Action
by Dmitry Jemerov and Svetlana Isakova

    ISBN: 9781617293290
    360 pages, $44.99
    February 2017

Functional Programming in Java
How functional techniques improve your Java programs
by Pierre-Yves Saumont

    ISBN: 9781617292736
    472 pages, $49.99
    January 2017